THE POLITICAL WRITINGS OF William Penn

WILLIAM PENN

The Political Writings *of* William Penn

INTRODUCTION & ANNOTATIONS

BY ANDREW R. MURPHY

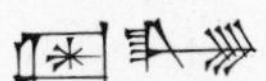

LIBERTY FUND

INDIANAPOLIS

This book is published by Liberty Fund, Inc.,
a foundation established to encourage study of the
ideal of a society of free and responsible individuals.

The cuneiform inscription that serves as our logo
and as the design motif for our endpapers is the earliest-known
written appearance of the word "freedom" (*amagi*), or "liberty."
It is taken from a clay document written about 2300 B.C.
in the Sumerian city-state of Lagash.

Printed in the United States of America
Frontispiece courtesy Bettman/CORBIS
06 05 04 03 02 C 5 4 3 2 1
06 05 04 03 02 P 5 4 3 2 1

Library of Congress Cataloging-in-Publication Data
Penn, William, 1644–1718.
The political writings of William Penn / introduction and
annotations by Andrew R. Murphy.
p. cm.
Includes bibliographical references and index.
ISBN 0-86597-317-2 (hc)—ISBN 0-86597-318-0 (pb)
1. Freedom of religion—Early works to 1800. 2. Freedom of
religion—Great Britain—Early works to 1800.
I. Murphy, Andrew R., 1967– II. Title.
BV741 .P45 2002
323.44′2—dc21
2001023401

LIBERTY FUND, INC.
8335 Allison Pointe Trail, Suite 300, Indianapolis, Indiana
46250-1684

To

BERNARD YACK, BOOTH FOWLER,

and PATRICK RILEY—

scholars, mentors, colleagues, and friends

CONTENTS

ACKNOWLEDGMENTS

In preparing this edition of Penn's political writings, I have relied heavily on the expertise and advice of an array of colleagues. Chief among these are a number of friends in the Core Humanities Program at Villanova University, where I began work on this volume: I was fortunate to have close by a gifted group of interdisciplinary scholars who exemplified all the virtues of collegiality. Let me especially thank Kevin Hughes, Maura Lafferty, Kim Paffenroth, and Sheryl Forste-Grupp: from a variety of disciplinary perspectives, these four aided me in tracking down a number of Penn's often-elusive references. The project was completed under the auspices of a senior fellowship at the Martin Marty Center of the University of Chicago Divinity School; I thank former Dean Clark Gilpin and current Dean Rick Rosengarten for facilitating my work at the Center. Johann Sommerville of the University of Wisconsin-Madison and Cary Nederman of Texas A & M University also generously shared their considerable expertise. Beth Angell helped with the introduction and assisted in too many ways to mention. Peter and Sam were themselves, a gift easy to acknowledge but impossible to repay.

INTRODUCTION

William Penn: His Life, His Times, and His Work

William Penn was born in London on 14 October 1644, and died in Buckinghamshire on 30 July 1718. His life spanned the two great political and religious upheavals in seventeenth-century England: the Civil Wars of the 1640s and the 1688 Revolution. Son of an admiral who served the parliamentarian cause during the Civil Wars and Commonwealth but who made his peace with the restored monarchy after 1660, Penn found himself involved in the turmoil of the 1680s because of his friendship with King James II and his relentless pursuit of religious liberty.

Expelled in 1662 from Christ Church College, Oxford, for religious nonconformity, Penn traveled to France and studied for a time at the Protestant Academy at Saumur. He later returned to England and studied law at Lincoln's Inn, then converted to Quakerism in 1667 while in Ireland on business for his father. His conversion marked the beginning of a lifelong career as religious controversialist, preacher, writer, and spokesman for the Society of Friends (or, as they were commonly known, Quakers).[1] During the course of a public career that spanned over four decades, Penn worked tirelessly to promote religious liberty as a general principle as well as to advance the specific interests of Friends and his colonizing endeavor in America. This volume reprints Penn's primary political writings from the 1670s and 1680s, writings that illustrate his approach to toleration as an English, a European, a Christian, and indeed a human value, and which provide a background against which to view Penn's efforts to achieve a level of religious liberty in America that was not possible in his homeland.

The Society of Friends had emerged from the religious and political ferment of the English Civil Wars, and their denial of the Trinity, their doctrine of inner light, and their refusal to swear oaths and show social deference instantly attracted charges of anarchism, atheism, and disloyalty. William Penn

1. The best account of Penn's religion is Melvin B. Endy, Jr., *William Penn and Early Quakerism* (Princeton, 1973). An invaluable new source on the Friends is Rosemary Moore, *The Light in Their Consciences: The Early Quakers in Britain 1646–1666* (University Park, Pa., 2000). The most important primary sources are George Fox's *Journal* (London, 1694); and Penn, *A brief account of the rise and progress of the people, called Quakers* (London, 1694).

had ample opportunity to respond to these accusations: Not only was he a man of means, but he also put his several imprisonments to good use, writing many tracts defending his particular religion and advocating liberty of conscience as a principle. Penn spent the decade following his conversion writing and traveling throughout England, Europe, and America on behalf of Quaker causes. He was also increasingly interested in the possibility of founding a colony based on principles of religious freedom.

In 1681, calling on an old friendship and debts owed his father by the Crown, Penn received his colonial charter from Charles II. The next year he crossed the Atlantic, and, in the following spring, the first Pennsylvania General Assembly adopted the *Frame of Government* by which the colony would be ruled for the next ten years. Although business and legal matters, including a protracted border dispute with Lord Baltimore and activities on behalf of toleration in England, would keep Penn away from Pennsylvania for most of his remaining days, he always considered his colony an attempt to instantiate the principles of political and religious liberty he articulated in his writings. Penn's close association with James—and his support for the king's extralegal efforts to implement toleration—landed him under house arrest after the 1688 Revolution. Financial woes were almost continuous for Penn as well, and he spent time in debtor's prison in 1708. A series of strokes incapacitated him in 1712, and he died six years later.

As the reader of this volume will soon discover, William Penn's political writings present an impassioned and richly articulated—though not always highly systematic—vision of the political, philosophical, theological, and pragmatic foundations of liberty of conscience. For Penn, religious liberty was part and parcel of English liberty more generally, a fundamental right and a necessary element of legitimate government. Penn's arguments for liberty of conscience followed all of the conventional routes rehearsed in English political rhetoric over the course of the seventeenth century. None of his justifications for liberty of conscience was entirely original. But in his synthetic corpus, Penn provides a coherent encapsulation of the many and varied routes to toleration sought by early modern English thinkers and actors. Insofar as Penn attempted to put his principles into practice in his colonial ventures, the texts reprinted in this volume possess a continuing relevance to scholars not only of English political and religious history but also of American political development, colonial history, and the constitutional foundations of American religious liberty.

Penn's Times

Though Penn was a young child during the Civil Wars and strife of the 1640s and 1650s, the events of those decades cast a long shadow over English public life for the rest of the century. The political instability following the death, in 1658, of Oliver Cromwell—who had commanded parliamentary forces during the Civil Wars, overseen the execution of Charles I in 1649, militarily subdued Scotland and Ireland, and ruled as Lord Protector since 1653—had paved the way for the restoration of Charles II and the Stuart monarchy in 1660. Restoration parliaments were hostile to religious dissent, associating it with the unrest of the Commonwealth period and Cromwell's Protectorate and becoming increasingly concerned about the possibility of toleration serving as a cover for introducing Catholicism into England. Formally reestablishing the Anglican supremacy, Parliament passed the Clarendon Code, a series of measures aimed at suppressing religious dissent, between 1661 and 1665. These acts restricted the rights of independent congregations to assemble, reinstated the Book of Common Prayer, and required assent to its liturgy by all clergy.[2] With the revival of the Conventicles Act in 1670—and the passage of the Test Act, which required abjuration of Catholic doctrine and papal supremacy of all public officeholders, three years later—Parliament sought to construct a solid edifice against religious dissent.

Stuart kings after the Restoration, on the other hand, were decidedly more receptive to the idea of religious toleration. (The fact that Charles II, who reigned from 1660 to 1685, was a discreet Catholic, and James II, who reigned from 1685 to 1688, was an openly practicing one, played no small part in this position.) Charles II had signaled a willingness to "indulge tender consciences" in his Declaration of Breda, issued just prior to the Restoration, and in declarations issued in 1662 and 1672. He was blocked, however, by parliamentary resistance. Parliamentary opponents asserted that such royal actions ignored *their* role in governing the commonwealth under the traditional understanding of the English ancient constitution, in which monarch and Parliament shared responsibility for governance. Such procedural dis-

2. The best overviews of Restoration religio-political debate are Paul Seaward, *The Cavalier Parliament and the Reconstruction of the Old Regime, 1661–1667* (New York, 1988), 162–95; *The Politics of Religion in Restoration England,* ed. Tim Harris, Paul Seaward, and Mark Goldie (Cambridge, Mass., 1990); and John Spurr, *The Restoration Church of England, 1646–1689* (New Haven, 1991).

putes between king and Parliament had figured prominently in the troubles of the 1640s as well, and would eventually contribute to James II's ouster in 1688.

Ubiquitous anti-Catholicism and anti-French sentiment, as well as parliamentary suspicion of royal motives, received additional force in the early 1670s, when Charles entered into an alliance with Louis XIV (and, at the same time, war with England's sometime Protestant ally, the Dutch). Charles's 1672 Declaration of Indulgence appeared in the context of hostilities with the Dutch and plans for a French alliance and standing army. Many influential English political figures saw signs of a growing conspiracy to assert divine right theory, achieve absolute monarchy, and overthrow Parliament. Though it seems unlikely that such a plot was ever seriously planned, rumors of a "popish plot" during the later 1670s (with tales of a conspiracy to bring Catholicism into England under the cover of religious toleration) fueled the Whig effort to keep James off the throne. In this Exclusion Crisis (1679–81), the emerging Whig party raised concerns about the safety of English liberties, both political and religious, under a Catholic monarch. As one contemporary put it, "As soon as ever the papal authority is admitted among us, all the Protestants in these nations are dead men in law. . . . Our estates, lives, and souls are in extreme hazard."[3] Their Tory opponents, however, skillfully raised the specter of political and religious radicalism, linking Whigs and "excluders" to the radicalism of the 1640s and 1650s. The lessons of history, for Tories, were clear: To allow dissidents and dissenters to challenge royal power, especially given human nature, the likelihood of human error, and recent English history, would result in chaos, civil war, and irreligion. In other words, they claimed, Whigs were using fears of a Catholic monarch to mask the same aim that they shared with their parliamentary predecessors of 1642: political rebellion. After Charles's dissolution of Parliament in 1681, the Exclusion Crisis was effectively over and a Tory reaction set in at the local level, supplanting Whigs from many of their positions in local governments.

The short reign of James II confirmed the worst Whig fears about a Catholic king, his propensity for extralegal political activities and the perceived Stuart attempt to achieve absolute government. James maintained a standing army. He received papal emissaries, instituted a policy of exempting Roman

3. *The case of protestants in England under a popish prince* (London, 1681), in *Somers Tracts: A collection of scarce and valuable tracts, but chiefly such as relate to the history and constitution of these kingdoms,* 2d ed. (13 vols., London, 1809–15), VIII:153, 164.

Catholics from the requirements of the Test Act, and reinstituted celebration of the Mass in the royal household. None of those events, of course, took place in a vacuum: in 1685 Louis XIV revoked the Edict of Nantes, which had guaranteed toleration to French Protestants, and Huguenot exiles who reached England with tales of persecution fueled fears of Catholic absolutism and its threat to English liberties. In April 1687, James issued a Declaration of Indulgence, granting liberty of worship to Roman Catholics and Protestant Dissenters. Legally speaking, the declaration was based upon the king's suspending power, but James went one step further and claimed authority to halt enforcement of ecclesiastical laws, such as the Test Act, for entire classes of people (namely, English Catholics). James hoped to receive parliamentary approval for his declaration and began an unsuccessful campaign to pack the next Parliament with members willing to codify it into law. These actions progressively alienated his staunchest allies, Anglican royalists opposed to the toleration of religious dissent (whether Catholic or Protestant), who had supported James's cause during the Exclusion Crisis and had trusted his promises to maintain the Church of England in its privileged social position.

Shrewdly, James reissued his Declaration of Indulgence in the spring of 1688, commanding that it be read from all Anglican pulpits. He was clearly attempting to drive apart Anglicans and Dissenters, the nation's two major Protestant groups. James's reasoning was clear: If, on the one hand, Anglicans refused to read the declaration, Dissenters would (continue to) view them as persecutors hostile to religious liberty. If, on the other hand, Anglicans complied and read the declaration, James's tolerationist policy would receive the Church's imprimatur, in appearance if not in reality. James's demands met with surprising resistance from Anglican bishops and other clergy. Anglican bishops refused to read the declaration, yet managed to convince most Dissenters—with the notable exception of Penn—not to endorse the King's toleration as offered. (Penn, as the reader will note, sought religious liberty by whichever route it could be had and was not willing to forfeit the opportunity presented by James's declaration.) These events culminated in the acquittal of seven bishops who had refused to read the declaration, a united front of Anglicans and Dissenters opposing the royal declaration. With opposition to James at new heights, William of Orange invaded and James fled.[4]

4. Ironically, then, one of the chief reasons for James's overthrow lay in the almost unanimous *opposition* among the English political nation to his dogged pursuit of toleration. We might also note that the Toleration Act of 1689, so often viewed as a watershed

Questions of toleration during the Restoration period, then, were always twofold: Did one support or oppose toleration, and for which groups; and did one support or oppose the ways in which Charles II (and later James II) sought to achieve such toleration? Both Charles and James, in choosing to issue Declarations of Indulgence, attempted to institute toleration without prior parliamentary assent. Even many who favored liberty of conscience were deeply disturbed by the precedent they saw in this extralegal pursuit of toleration by royal decree, involving as it did the contested legal and political claim to an extensive royal prerogative. To parliamentary advocates, such claims of authority struck at the heart of their idea of England as a law-governed society, in which the monarch and Parliament *shared* in the task of legislation.

Penn's Political Thought: A Brief Overview[5]

Penn's early political writings (Part I of this volume) illuminate his Whig understanding of legitimate English politics as grounded in the ancient constitution. The values of liberty, property, and consent provide the basis for Penn's advocacy of liberty of conscience in Restoration England. Penn's views on consent as the foundation of political legitimacy, and the ways in which these concerns intersect with religious liberty, are notably particularist: He refers almost exclusively to English practice and precedent.

> We, the Commons of England, are a great part of the fundamental government of it; and three rights are so peculiar and inherent to us, that if we will not throw them away . . . they cannot be altered or abrogated. . . . The first of these fundamentals is property, that is, right and title to your own lives, liberties and estates.
>
> The second . . . is legislation, or the power of making laws; No law

---

in the history of religious liberty, *rejected* James's broad toleration proposals. Despite the fact that the act represented a huge advance for dissenting Protestants and discreet Catholics, the religious liberty granted by the Toleration Act was far less extensive than Cromwell's Protectorate, not to mention James's Declarations of Indulgence, had guaranteed. The Test Act remained in effect into the nineteenth century, barring Catholics and non-Trinitarian Protestants from serving in public office. I develop these claims more fully in my *Conscience and Community: Revisiting Toleration and Religious Dissent in Early Modern England and America* (University Park, Pa., 2001), ch. 4.

5. I explore Penn's political thought and its relationship with his colonizing endeavor in Pennsylvania more thoroughly in chapter 5 of *Conscience and Community.*

can be made or abrogated in England without you. . . . No law can be made, no money levied, nor a penny legally demanded (even to defray the charges of the government) without your own consent: Than which, tell me, what can be freer, or what more secure to any people?

[The third is] . . . your share in the judicatory power, in the execution and application of those laws, that you agree to be made.[6]

Penn makes no reference to Old Testament exegesis, as did Puritan convenantal theorists, nor does he theorize about how individuals might behave in a natural state, as did his more famous contemporaries Thomas Hobbes and John Locke. Rather, Penn asks how English subjects—who, he argues, do not hold their property by virtue of church membership but rather by established custom and usage—can be deprived of such property (in the form of forfeitures and fines) for religious nonconformity.

[W]e are English men . . . a title full of liberty and property, the foundation of the government of this kingdom to claim which, is not only our interest but our duty. . . . We have a right to our lives, liberties, and estates, and that none of these are to be taken from us but by the judgment of twelve of our peers . . . this has for ages been the common and fundamental law. . . . We take further leave to remind you that the civil society or government of this country is antecedent either to protestancy or popery.[7]

The ancient constitution was a lifelong political commitment for Penn. In 1687, he based his case for repeal of penal laws and the Test Act on "native rights, the Great Charter, what we all of us call, our birthright."[8]

6. *England's Great Interest, in the Choice of this New Parliament,* this volume, pp. 385–86.

7. "Petition to Parliament," ca. November 1680, in *The Papers of William Penn,* ed. Mary Maples Dunn et al. (Philadelphia, 1981–86), II:52. (Hereafter I refer to the *Papers* as *PWP,* volume: page.) See also "To J. H. and his companions, Justices in Middlesex," 31 March 1674, *PWP,* I:277–82; *England's Present Interest Considered,* this volume, pp. 48–53; and "Narrative of the sufferings of Quakers in the isle of Ely," ca. November 1671, *PWP,* I:223–24. Penn also asserted this claim that penal laws violated the ancient constitution in his proposed toleration bill of 1678, *PWP,* I:537.

8. [Penn], *A Letter from a Gentleman in the Country . . . upon the Penal Laws and Tests,* this volume, p. 394. See also *Good Advice to the Church of England,* this volume, p. 372: "You claim the character of Englishmen. Now, to be an Englishman, in the sense

Part II of this volume presents Penn's argument for religious liberty, born out of the experience of persecution and Penn's own broad reading and thought on the nature of human belief and the requirements of Christian conduct; Part III presents several shorter texts relating those general principles of liberty to particular events in English politics. Perhaps the most fundamental objection to compulsion in religious affairs, according to Penn, was an epistemological one: *It does not work.* Belief, he argued, was a function of the understanding and not of the will: Force can make hypocrites, but "never did it convert or preserve one soul to God."[9] Persecution was a category mistake, since "the understanding can never be convinced by other arguments than what are adequate to her nature."[10] Even if an individual's religious beliefs were demonstrably erroneous, coercion remained unjustified, "for though their consciences be blind, yet they are not to be forced; such compulsion giveth no sight, neither do corporal punishments produce conviction."[11]

While attempting to remove religious belief from the sphere of coercive civil power, Penn consistently sought to enlarge liberty of conscience to include religiously inspired *conduct.* In this regard, he rejected standard anti-tolerationist arguments that postulated a belief-action dichotomy, in which the civil magistrate was justified in restricting the latter though not the former.[12] "Liberty of conscience . . . is this; namely, the free and uninterrupted exercise of our consciences, in that way of worship, we are most clearly persuaded, God requires us to serve him in . . . which being [a] matter of faith, we sin if we omit . . ."; elsewhere, Penn defined liberty of conscience as the "free and open profession and exercise of [man's] duty to God."[13]

---

of the government, is to be a freeman, whether Lord or Commoner, to hold his liberty and possessions by laws of his own consenting unto."

9. "To the council and senate of the city of Embden" (1674), in *A Collection of the Works of William Penn* (London, 1726; reprinted New York, 1972), I:610. (Hereafter I refer to *Works,* volume: page.)

10. "To Lord Arlington" (1669), in *Works,* I:153; and *PWP,* I:89–97. See also "Narrative of the sufferings of Quakers in the Isle of Ely," *PWP,* I:225.

11. *A Brief Examination and State of Liberty Spiritual,* this volume, p. 283. See also Penn's letter to William, Prince of Orange, 26 February 1680, *PWP,* II:27.

12. See, most famously, Hobbes, *Leviathan,* ed. Edwin Curley (Indianapolis, 1994), ch. 37, p. 300; and Hobbes, *Elements of Law* (1650), ed. Ferdinand Tonnies, 2d ed. (New York, 1969), p. 114.

13. *The Great Case of Liberty of Conscience,* this volume, p. 82; *A Perswasive to Moderation to Church-Dissenters,* this volume, p. 292.

Not only was the use of force inappropriate from a psychological or epistemological point of view, and not only did belief imply action, but the fallibility of human knowledge argued against persecution. This argument contained both epistemological and ecclesiastical connotations, since the assumption of infallibility (be it papal or conciliar) was seen by many Protestants as the great error of the Roman Catholic Church. "We must never reproach the papists with persecuting Protestants, if Protestants themselves will persecute Protestants because of some different apprehensions about religion," Penn wrote to the Prince of Orange.[14] Epistemologically, Penn stressed the inherent partiality of understandings of truth and the humility called for by such an admission.[15] In one of his earliest battles with the English legal system, Penn accused the judge of forgetting his English Protestant

> forefathers for liberty of conscience. . . . Twas then plea good enough, my conscience won't let me go to Mass, and my conscience wills that I should have an English testament. But that simple plea, for separation then reasonable is now by you that pretend to succeed them, ajudged unreasonable and factious. I say, since the only just cause of the first revolt from Rome was a dissatisfaction in point of conscience, you cannot reasonably persecute others, who have right to the same plea.[16]

For Penn, however, saying that one must be convinced in one's own mind regarding the truth of religion was not an invitation to anarchy and license. Since the sects that had emerged from the English Civil War were often accused of just such anarchic tendencies, Penn hastened throughout his writings to clarify the magistrate's role in suppressing vice and enforcing moral behavior. Penn affirmed the duty and right of civil magistrates to punish evildoers in *The Great Case* and in petitions to Parliament in April 1671.[17] Although he opposed the use of force to impose religious practice on individuals, Penn did assert that certain moral and ethical transgressions simply could not be held

14. "To William, Prince of Orange," 26 February 1680, *PWP,* II:26.

15. *Great Case,* this volume, p. 87; *An Address to Protestants of All Perswasions,* this volume, pt. II, sec. 5, pp. 196–234.

16. "Injustice detected," February 1671, *PWP,* I:200. See also "Narrative of sufferings," *PWP,* I:222–30, sec. 5.

17. *Great Case,* this volume, pp. 86, 96–97; "Petition to Parliament," April 1671, *PWP,* I:205–8.

conscientiously, since they violated fundamental dictates of nature or widely accepted standards of behavior. "There can be no pretense of conscience to be drunk, to whore, to be voluptuous, to game, swear, curse, blaspheme, and profane. . . . These are sins against nature; and against government, as well as against the written laws of God. They lay the ax to the root of human society."[18] Penn later wrote that "I always premise this conscience to keep within the bounds of morality, and that it be neither frantic nor mischievous, but a good subject, a good child, a good servant, in all the affairs of life."[19]

Certainly the magistrate could and should punish those who violated standards of civil behavior. Penn separated moral and ecclesiastical functions of civil magistracy and affirmed the right, even the *duty,* of political leaders to uphold the former. The distinction, for Penn, echoed his clarification that Christian liberty was not to be equated with license. In early Pennsylvania, as the founder envisioned it, civil magistrates were to be empowered to enforce observance of the Sabbath, to regulate, if not outlaw, taverns, and to restrain vice more generally. Penn did not view public enforcement of the Sabbath as equivalent to the imposition of a religious worship on his colony: In his words, refraining from labor on the Sabbath "may the better dispose [citizens] to worship God according to their own understandings."[20] The first draft of the *Fundamental Constitutions* declared that "there shall be no taverns, nor alehouses, endured in the [province], nor any playhouses, nor morris dances, nor games as dice, cards, board tables, lotteries, bowling greens, horse races, bear baitings, bull baitings, and such like sports, which tend only to idleness and looseness."[21] Since "the wildness and looseness of the people provoke[s] the indignation of God against a country," Penn restated these prohibitions in his final version of the *Frame of Government and Laws Agreed Upon in England.*[22] When Penn did draw up a tavern law, he included a number of very detailed

18. *An Address to Protestants,* this volume, p. 138.

19. *A Perswasive to Moderation,* this volume, p. 292.

20. *Frame of Government and Laws Agreed Upon in England, PWP,* II:225.

21. "Fundamental Constitutions of Pennsylvania," ibid., p. 151. In Penn's draft of the *Laws Agreed Upon in England* (ca. April 1682), he restates his opposition to "all prizes, plays, may games, gamesters, masques, revels, bullbaitings, cockfightings, bear baitings, and the like, which excite the people to rudeness, looseness, and irreligion," accounting them petty treason (ibid., p. 209).

22. Ibid., p. 225.

regulations regarding the rates that innkeepers could charge and the personal conduct that was to be permitted by the guests at such establishments.[23]

The psychological or epistemological arguments concerning belief, action, judgment, will, and understanding were always firmly and fundamentally anchored in Penn's Christianity. His restriction of the magistrate's role in religion was, for Penn, largely derived from the example of Jesus and the early history of the Christian Church. He often attributed persecution to mistaken notions about the nature of Jesus' ministry and kingdom. Coercion is unchristian, says Penn, because Jesus "defined to us the nature of his religion in this one great saying of his, My kingdom is not of this world."[24] He attributed the rise of persecution in the Christian Church to earthly designs of power-seeking clergy, giving voice once again to the long tradition of English anticlericalism stretching back at least to the fourteenth-century Lollard movement. Penn unified the arguments from reason and those from Scripture in his letter to the Prince Elector of Heidelberg: Religious toleration is both "natural, because it preserves nature from being made a sacrifice to the savage fury of fallible, yet proud opinions . . . [and] Christian, since the contrary expressly contradicteth both the precept and example of Christ."[25] In Penn's words, the failure to understand Christ's "unworldly way of speaking" of his kingdom lay at the root of all persecuting policies: "This gross apprehension of the nature of Christ's kingdom may well be an occasion of their mistake about the means of promoting it, else it were not credible, that men should think, clubs, prisons, and banishments the proper mediums of enlightening the understanding."[26]

The summation toward which all of Penn's arguments for liberty of conscience point is the notion of England as a civil commonwealth, characterized

23. "Tavern Regulations," ca. 23 March 1683, *PWP,* II:367–68.

24. *Great Case,* this volume, p. 88; see also "To the King of Poland," 4 August 1677, *PWP,* I:437; and *Good Advice,* this volume, pp. 331–33.

25. "To the Prince Elector Palatinate of Heidelberg," 25 June 1677, *Works,* I:75 (also in *PWP,* I:451–54).

26. "To William, Prince of Orange," 26 February 1680, *PWP,* II:27; see also "Petition to Parliament," ca. November 1680, *PWP,* II:54; and "To the Earl of Arran," 9 January 1684, in which Penn calls on the earl not to "vex men for their beliefs and modest practice of that faith with respect to the other world, into which providence and sovereignty, temporal power reaches not, from its very nature and end" (*PWP,* II:511).

by a reverence for traditional standards of political legitimacy (the ancient constitution) and united in a general Protestantism and basic Christian moral code. This commitment to civil unity, for Penn, contained within it the standard dichotomization proposed by many tolerationists, most notably Roger Williams and (later) John Locke, between the carnal and spiritual realms.[27] The idea of *civil interest* as the cement of civil society runs throughout Penn's works. "Certainly there is such a thing as civil uniformity, where a religious one may be inobtainable, and methinks there can be nothing more irrational, than to sacrifice the serenity of the one, to an adventurous (if not impossible) procurement of the other," he wrote in 1673.[28] "Civil interest is the foundation and end of civil government," Penn argued, and elsewhere he maintained that, "as Englishmen, we are . . . mutually interested in the inviolable conservation of each other's civil rights."[29] Assuming that English subjects lived peaceably with their neighbors, Penn wondered "whether going to parish churches, hearing of common prayer, and receiving confirmation by the hands of a bishop are such absolute and necessary qualifications to being good shipwrights, clothiers, masons, husbandmen, etc."[30]

Such civil-interest arguments implicitly or explicitly cast doubts on the political allegiance of English Catholics, and Penn did not hesitate to raise the same questions about their political loyalty that John Locke later did, noting the "fundamental inconsistency they carry with them to the security of the English government and constitution unto which they belong, by acknowledging a foreign jurisdiction in these kingdoms."[31] The difference between Catholic and Protestant in England, Penn stressed repeatedly, was a *political* one at root. Still, although Penn's society was shot through with anti-Catholic prejudice, he never suggested persecuting Catholics and concluded a letter to an imprisoned Roman Catholic by saying that, although he disagreed on many points of theology, "I am, by my principle, to write as well for toleration for the Romanists."[32] Penn would not persecute law-abiding Catholics who affirmed civil allegiance. "For though I give the true liberty of soul and

27. See Roger Williams, *The bloudy tenent of persecution* (London, 1644); and John Locke, *A Letter Concerning Toleration* (London, 1689).

28. "To Justice Fleming," 1673, *Works,* I:157; also in *PWP,* I:268–69.

29. *Good Advice* (1687), this volume, p. 373.

30. "Petition to Parliament," ca. November 1680, *PWP,* II:53.

31. *One Project for the Good of England* (1679), this volume, p. 129.

32. "To Richard Langhorne," 1671, *Works,* I:43; also in *PWP,* I:209–11.

conscience to those only that are set free by the power of Christ . . . yet do I not intend, that any person or persons should be in the least harmed for the external exercise of their dissenting consciences in worship to God, though erroneous."[33]

Finally, Penn did not neglect the more practical concerns of prudence and prosperity. On a purely prudential level, Penn counseled the Church of England to consider the consequences of a future non-Anglican magistrate's adopting persecuting principles: Anglicans would suffer, as had Protestants in the days of Queen Mary.[34] Similarly, in the context of James II's attempts to extend toleration during the late 1680s, Penn noted to Anglicans that persecution threatened to drive dissenting Protestants into a political alliance with English Catholics.[35] But if invocations of prudence were not enough, Penn asserted that prosperity would follow a relaxation of the enforcement of penal laws. "The kingdom is under a great decay both of people and trade," he wrote in 1680, "does not [persecution] lessen the imperial crown and dignity of this realm, if it ruins trade, lessens and impoverishes the people, and increases beggery?"[36] He concluded *One Project* with an appeal to the prosperity of the kingdom.

> I ask, if more custom comes not to the king, and more trade to the kingdom, by encouraging the labour and traffic of an Episcopalian, Presbyterian, Independent, Quaker, and Anabaptist, than by an Episcopalian only? . . . What schism or heresy is there in the labour and commerce of the Anabaptist, Quaker, Independent, and Presbyterian, more than in the labour and traffic of the Episcopalian?[37]

Although religious dissent had been associated for many years with Cromwell's republicanism and antimonarchical politics, Penn argued that this need not be the case. Not only does toleration not threaten monarchy, but "experience tells us, where [toleration] is in any degree admitted, the King's affairs prosper most; people, wealth, and strength being sure to follow such indulgence."[38]

33. *A Brief Examination,* this volume, p. 283.
34. *England's Present Interest Considered,* this volume, pp. 58–59, 61–62.
35. *Good Advice,* this volume, p. 364.
36. "Petition to Parliament," ca. November 1680, *PWP,* II:51–52.
37. *One Project for the Good of England,* this volume, p. 126.
38. *A Perswasive to Moderation* (1686), this volume, p. 303.

Part IV concludes the volume with Penn's most far-reaching work, *An Essay towards the Present and Future Peace of Europe* (1693). Penn opens the essay with an appeal to his audience's humanity and compassion for sufferers, a theme that appears throughout his writings in favor of toleration. "He must not be a man, but a statue of brass or stone, whose bowels do not melt when he beholds the bloody tragedies of this war, in Hungary, Germany, Flanders, Ireland, and at sea."[39] Religious liberty was Penn's lifelong commitment, and he saw that liberty as part of the broader English fundamentals of life, liberty, and property. Since religious intolerance had fired bloodshed and conflict across Europe since the Reformation, the *Essay towards the Present and Future Peace* represents Penn's attempt to provide Europeans the chance to live and flourish without the threat of constant war. Although his plan for a diet, or parliament of European states, might seem naive to an age that has witnessed many failed attempts at marshaling moral force to eliminate war, Penn's proposal deserves a careful reading as an extrapolation of the principles outlined earlier in his writings. At the same time, the essay illustrates once more, at a continental level, Penn's abiding devotion to the principles of political and religious liberty and his willingness to enter the public realm to help heal the "incomparable miseries" of his time.[40] In those qualities, I suggest, far more than in the specifics of the system he proposes, we shall find William Penn's true legacy.

Andrew R. Murphy
Martin Marty Center
University of Chicago Divinity School
July 2001

39. *An Essay towards the Present and Future Peace of Europe* (1693), this volume, p. 402.

40. Ibid., p. 419.

NOTES ON TEXTS AND ANNOTATIONS

William Penn's political writings can pose challenges to the modern reader. Like many of his contemporaries, Penn refers to Scripture, classical sources, church fathers, Reformation and post-Reformation history, and other sources prodigiously, unsystematically, and often obliquely. Many references presented as direct quotes turn out, upon visiting the primary sources, to be Penn's paraphrases. Italicization and capitalization follow no discernible pattern. Such procedures were the norm, not the exception, in early modern political writing, especially for a writer like Penn who often wrote in the heat of political debate.

The purpose of my annotations is not to provide an exhaustive clarification of each of Penn's many citations—such an endeavor would be unhelpful and distracting—but rather to guide the reader in appreciating the many building blocks upon which Penn built his theory of religious liberty. Thus, the antiquated spelling, punctuation, and syntax have not been altered; however, typographical errors have been silently corrected. For general references to individuals and groups, I have not, as a rule, included an annotation: Penn simply makes too many, too scattered references for a volume of this sort to address each one individually. I would refer readers interested in pursuing such references to the *Dictionary of National Biography* or to the *Oxford Encyclopedia of the Reformation.*

Where individuals or groups are mentioned in connection with specific texts, I have generally provided a note. I have also annotated Penn's many scriptural references, and all quotations of my own are taken from the King James version of the Bible. Where Penn provides the reference in his text, I have not provided any additional annotations. Otherwise, I have included some general information on the author or text to guide those readers who wish to explore Penn's sources more deeply. (For sources that have gone through multiple printings, I have cited by chapter rather than page number.) Similarly, on Latin quotations, I have not translated where Penn himself includes a translation in the text, and I have not annotated single-word Latin phrases or ones whose meaning seems clear in context.

None of the editorial annotations can be considered a substitute for reading Penn's works alongside good histories of England, of the Reformation, of the Christian Church more generally, and of the rise of religious toleration in early modern Europe; below I suggest a few. Regardless of whether the reader is fully conversant with the wide range of historical, philosophical, scriptural, and political references that fill Penn's political works, however, I hope that this edition will renew interest in Penn as a political thinker and in Penn's works as an important element of the Anglo-American heritage. All texts in this volume are reproduced from *A Collection of the Works of William Penn,* 2 volumes (London, 1726).

EARLY CHRISTIANITY AND THE REFORMATION

Chadwick, Owen. *The Reformation* (Penguin History of the Church, vol. 3). Harmondsworth: Penguin, 1964.

Dickens, A. G. *The English Reformation.* New York: Schocken, 1964.

The Encyclopedia of Early Christianity. 2d ed. Edited by Everett Ferguson (Garland Reference Library of the Humanities, vol. 1839). New York and London: Garland Publishing, 1997.

The Oxford Encyclopedia of the Reformation. Edited by Hans J. Hillerbrand. 4 vols. Oxford: Oxford University Press, 1996.

ENGLISH HISTORY

The Dictionary of National Biography. 22 vols. Edited by Sir Leslie Stephen and Sir Sidney Lee. London: Oxford University Press, 1921–22.

Kishlansky, Mark. *A Monarchy Transformed: Britain 1603–1714.* London: Penguin, 1996.

The statutes of the realm . . . From original records and authentic manuscripts . . . 10 vols. London: G. Eyre and A. Strahan, 1810–28.

RELIGIOUS TOLERATION

Jordan, W. K. *The Development of Religious Toleration in England and America.* 4 vols. Cambridge, Mass.: Harvard University Press, 1932–40.

Lecler, Joseph. *Toleration and the Reformation.* 2 vols. Translated by T. L. Westow. New York: Association Press, 1960.

CHRONOLOGY OF PENN'S LIFE AND TIMES

1642	Outbreak of English Civil War between parliamentary and royalist forces.
1644	14 October, Penn born in London.
1648	Peace of Westphalia ends Thirty Years' War in Europe.
1649	Execution of King Charles I in England. Proclamation of English Commonwealth.
1653	Oliver Cromwell inaugurates Protectorate.
1658	Cromwell dies.
1660	Restoration of Stuart monarchy in England (accession of Charles II). Penn enters Christ Church College, Oxford.
1662	Penn expelled from Oxford for religious nonconformity.
1663	Penn studies at the Protestant Academy in Saumur, France.
1665	Penn enters Lincoln's Inn, London, to study law.
1667	Penn converts to Quakerism in Ireland; is arrested for the first time.
1670	September: Penn-Mead trial, commemorated in Penn's *People's Ancient and Just Liberties Asserted.* Death of Penn's father, Admiral Sir William Penn.
1672	Penn marries Gulielma Springett. Charles II issues Declaration of Indulgence tolerating religious nonconformists. Forced to withdraw Declaration after parliamentary objections.
1673	Parliament enacts Test Act, requiring English officeholders to swear oaths of allegiance and to abjure papal supremacy and Catholic doctrine.
1675	Penn's first involvement in colonization. Arbitrates dispute between Quakers in West Jersey. Becomes trustee of West New Jersey.
1677	Travels to Holland and Germany defending Quakers and promoting liberty of conscience.
1679–81	Popish Plot in England, with turmoil over rumors to bring Catholicism to England under guise of toleration.
1681	March: Penn receives charter for Pennsylvania.

1682	Death of Penn's mother, Lady Margaret Penn. August: Penn arrives in Pennsylvania.
1684	Returns to England to pursue boundary disputes with Lord Baltimore.
1685	Charles II dies. James II, a Catholic, crowned King of England. Louis XIV revokes the Edict of Nantes, basis for toleration of French Protestants.
1687	James II issues Declaration of Indulgence, tolerating religious nonconformists. Penn supports James's cause.
1688	Glorious Revolution: William of Orange invades England. James ejected from the throne. William and Mary crowned King and Queen of England.
1689	Toleration Act passed. Penn arrested, accused of treason.
1691–93	Penn in hiding.
1694	Gulielma Springett Penn dies.
1696	Penn marries Hannah Callowhill.
1699	December: Penn arrives in Pennsylvania.
1701	Returns to England.
1702	William III dies. Queen Anne crowned.
1708	Legal troubles, Penn in debtor's prison for a time.
1712	Penn suffers strokes, is incapacitated for rest of life.
1714	Death of Queen Anne. George I of Hanover crowned King of England.
1715	Death of Louis XIV.
1718	30 July, Penn dies.

{ PART I }

Foundations

The Ancient Constitution and English Liberties

The People's Ancient and Just LIBERTIES Asserted, in the Trial of *William Penn* and *William Mead,* at the Sessions held at the *Old-Baily* in *London,* the First, Third, Fourth and Fifth of *September,* 1670, against the most Arbitrary Procedure of that COURT (1670)

To the English READER.

I*F EVER it were Time to Speak, or Write, 'tis now, so many strange Occurrences requiring both.*

How much thou art concerned in this ensuing Trial where (not only the Prisoners, but) the Fundamental Laws of England *have been most Arbitrarily Arraigned, Read, and thou may'st plainly Judge.*

Liberty of Conscience, *is counted a Pretence for* Rebellion, *and* Religious Assemblies, Routs *and* Riots; *and the* Defenders *of both, are by them reputed* Factious, *and* Dis-affected.

Magna Charta, *is* Magna Far—*with the* Recorder *of* London; *and to demand* Right, *an* Affront to the Court.

Will *and* Power *are their* Great Charter, *but to call for* England's, *is a Crime; incurring the Penalty of their* Bale Dock *and* Nasty Hole; *nay, the Menace of a* Gag, *and* Iron Shackles *too.*

The Jury (*though proper* Judges of Law and Fact) *they would have over-ruled in both, as if their* Verdict *signified no more, than to Echo back the illegal Charge of the Bench; and because their Courage and Honesty, did more than hold Pace with the Threat and Abuse of those who sate as Judges (after two Days and two Nights Restraint for a Verdict) in the End were Fined and Imprisoned for giving it.*

Oh! What monstrous and illegal Proceedings are these? Who reasonably can call his Coat his own? When Property is made subservient to the Will and Interest of his Judges; *or, Who can truly esteem himself a Free Man?* When all Pleas for Liberty are esteemed Sedition, and the Laws that give, and maintain them, so many insignificant Pieces of Formality.

And what do they less than plainly tell us so, who at Will and Pleasure, break open our Locks, rob our Houses, raze our Foundations, imprison our Persons, and finally, deny us Justice to our Relief; *as if they then acted most like* Christian Men, *when they were most* Barbarous, *in Ruining such as are really so; and that* no Sacrifice *could be so acceptable to* GOD, *as the* Destruction of those that most Fear him.

In short, That the Conscientious should only be Obnoxious, and the just Demand of our Religious Liberty, the Reason why we should be denied our Civil Freedom *(as if to be a* Christian *and an* Englishman *were inconsistent) and that so much* Solicitude *and* deep Contrivance, *should be imployed only to* Ensnare *and* Ruin so many Ten Thousand Conscientious Families *(so* Eminently Industrious, Serviceable *and* Exemplary; *whilst* Murders *can so easily* obtain Pardon, Rapes *be* remitted, Publick Uncleanness *pass unpunished, and all manner of* Levity, Prodigality, Excess, Prophaneness *and* Atheism, *universally* connived at, *if not in some Respect manifestly* encouraged) *cannot but be detestably abhorrent to every Serious and Honest Mind.*

Yet that this Lamentable State is true, and the present Project *in Hand, let* London's Recorder, *and* Canterbury's Chaplain *be heard.*

The first in his publick Panegyrick upon the Spanish Inquisition, highly admiring the Prudence of the Romish Church, in the Erection of it, as an excellent Way to prevent Schism, *which unhappy Expression at once passeth Sentence; both against our* Fundamental Laws, *and* Protestant Reformation.

The second in his Printed Mercenary Discourse against Toleration, *asserting for a main Principle,* That it would be less injurious to the Government, to dispence with Prophane and Loose Persons, than to allow a Toleration to Religious Dissenters: *It were to over-do the Business, to say any more, where there is so much said already.*

And therefore to conclude, We cannot chuse but Admonish all, as well Persecutors, *to Relinquish their Heady, Partial, and Inhumane Persecutions (as what will certainly issue in Disgrace here, and inevitable condign Punishment hereafter) as those who yet dare express their Moderation (however out of Fashion, or made the Brand of Fanaticism) not to be Huff'd, or Menaced out of that excellent Temper, to make their Parts and Persons subservient to the base Humors, and sinister Designs of the biggest Mortal upon Earth; but Reverence and Obey the Eternal Just GOD,* before whose Great Tribunal all must render their Accounts, and where he will Recompence to every Person according to his Works.

The TRIAL, *&c.*

AS THERE can be no Observation, where there is no Action; so its impossible there shall be a Judicious Intelligence without due Observation.

And since there can be nothing more Reasonable than a Right Information, especially of *Publick Acts;* and well knowing, how industrious some will be, to misrepresent this Trial, to the Disadvantage of the Cause and Prisoners, it was thought requisite, in Defence of both, and for the Satisfaction of the People, to make it more publick; nor can there be any Business wherein the People of *England* are more concerned, than in that which relates to their Civil and Religious Liberties, questioned in the Persons before named at the *Old-Baily,* the First, Third, Fourth and Fifth of *Sept.* 1670.

There being present on the Bench, as Justices,

Sam. Starling, Mayor,	*John Robinson,* Alderm.	
John Howel, Recorder,	*Joseph Shelden,* Alderm.	
Tho. Bludworth, Alderm.	*Richard Brown,*	Sheriffs.
William Peak, Alderm.	*John Smith,*	
Richard Ford, Alderm.	*James Edwards,*	

The Citizens of *London* that were summoned for Jurors, appearing, were Impanelled, *viz.*

Cle. Call over the Jury.

Cry. O yes, *Thomas Veer, Ed. Bushel, John Hammond, Charles Milson, Gregory Walklet, John Brightman, Wil. Plumstead, Henry Henley, James Damask, Henry Michel, Wil. Lever, John Baily.*

The Form of the Oath.

You shall well and truly Try, and True Deliverance make betwixt our Sovereign Lord the King, and the Prisoners at the Bar, according to your Evidence: So help you God.

The Indictment.

That *William Penn,* Gent. and *William Mead,* late of *London,* Linnen-Draper, with divers other Persons, to the Jurors unknown, to the Number of Three

Hundred, the 15th Day of *August*, in the 22th Year of the King,[1] about Eleven of the Clock in the Forenoon the same Day, with Force and Arms, *&c.* in the Parish of St. *Bennet Grace-Church*, in *Bridge-Ward, London*, in the Street called *Grace-Church-Street*, Unlawfully and Tumultuously did Assemble and Congregate themselves together, to the Disturbance of the Peace of the said Lord the King: And the aforesaid *William Penn* and *William Mead*, together with other Persons, to the Jurors aforesaid unknown, then and there so Assembled and Congregated together; the aforesaid *William Penn*, by Agreement between him and *William Mead*, before made, and by Abetment of the aforesaid *William Mead*, then and there in the open Street, did take upon himself to Preach and Speak, and then, and there, did Preach and Speak, unto the aforesaid *William Mead*, and other Persons there, in the Street aforesaid, being Assembled and Congregated together, by Reason whereof a great Concourse and Tumult of People in the Street aforesaid, then and there, a long Time did remain and continue, in Contempt of the said Lord the King, and of his Law; to the great Disturbance of his Peace, to the great Terror and Disturbance of many of his Liege People and Subjects, to the ill Example of all others in the like Case Offenders, and against the Peace of the said Lord the King, his Crown and Dignity.

What say you *William Penn*, and *William Mead*, are you Guilty, as you stand Indicted, in Manner and Form as aforesaid, or Not Guilty?

Penn. It is impossible that we should be able to remember the Indictment *Verbatim*, and therefore we desire a Copy of it, as is Customary on the like Occasions.

Rec. *You must first plead to the Indictment, before you can have a Copy of it.*

Penn. I am unacquainted with the Formality of the Law, and therefore before I shall answer directly, I request Two Things of the Court. *First*, That no Advantage may be taken against me, nor I deprived of any Benefit, which I might otherwise have received. *Secondly*, That you will promise me a fair Hearing, and Liberty of making my Defence.

Court. No Advantage shall be taken against you: You shall have Liberty; you shall be heard.

Penn. Then I plead not Guilty in Manner and Form.

1. 1670. Charles II always dated his reign, not from his restoration in 1660, but from his father's execution in 1649.

Cle. What say'st thou, William Mead: *Art thou Guilty in Manner and Form, as thou stand'st Indicted, or Not Guilty?*

Mead. I shall desire the same Liberty as is promised to *William Penn.*

Court. You shall have it.

Mead. Then I plead not Guilty in Manner and Form.

The Court adjourned until the Afternoon.

Cry. O Yes, *&c.*

Cle. Bring William Penn *and* William Mead *to the Bar.*

Obser. The said Prisoners were brought, but were set aside, and other Business prosecuted: Where we cannot choose but observe, that it was the constant and unkind Practice of the Court to the Prisoners, to make them wait upon the Tryals of Felons and Murderers, thereby designing in all Probability, *both to affront and tire them.*

After Five Hours Attendance, the Court broke up, and adjourned to the Third Instant.

The Third of *September,* 1670, the Court Sat.

Cry. O Yes, *&c.*

Mayor. Sirrah, Who bid you put off their Hats? Put on their Hats again.

Obser. Whereupon one of the Officers putting the Prisoners Hats upon their Heads (pursuant to the Order of the Court) brought them to the Bar.

Record. Do you know where you are?

Penn. Yes.

Rec. Do you know it is the King's Court?

Penn. I know it to be a Court, and I suppose it to be the King's Court.

Rec. Do you know there is Respect due to the Court?

Penn. Yes.

Rec. Why do you not pay it then?

Penn. I do so.

Rec. Why do you not put off your Hat then?

Penn. Because I do not believe that to be any Respect.

Rec. Well, the Court sets Forty Marks a-piece upon your Heads, as a Fine, for your Contempt of the Court.

Penn. I desire it may be observed, that we came into the Court with our Hats off, (that is, taken off) and if they have been put on since, it was by Order from the Bench; and therefore not we, but the Bench should be Fined.[2]

Mead. I have a Question to ask the Recorder: Am I Fined also?

Rec. Yes.

Mead. I desire the Jury, and all People to take Notice of this Injustice of the Recorder, who spake not to me to pull off my Hat, and yet hath he put a Fine upon my Head. O fear the Lord, and dread his Power, and yield to the Guidance of His Holy Spirit; for He is not far from every one of you.

The Jury Sworn again.

Obser. J. Robinson, Lieutenant of the *Tower,* disingenuously objected against *Edw. Bushel,* as if he had not kist the Book, and therefore would have him Sworn again; though indeed it was on Purpose, to have made Use of his Tenderness of Conscience, in avoiding reiterated Oaths, to have put him by his being a Juryman, apprehending him to be a Person not fit to answer their Arbitrary Ends.

The Clerk read the Indictment, as aforesaid.

Cle. Cryer, Call *James Cook* into the Court, give him his Oath.

Cle. James Cook, lay your Hand upon the Book, "The Evidence you shall give to the Court, betwixt our Sovereign the King, and the Prisoners at the Bar, shall be the Truth, and the whole Truth, and nothing but the Truth: So help you God, *&c.*"

Cook. *I was sent for from the* Exchange, *to go and disperse a Meeting in* Gracious-Street, *where I saw Mr.* Penn *speaking to the People, but I could not hear what he said, because of the Noise; I endeavoured to make Way to take him, but I could not get to him for the Crowd of People; upon which Captain* Mead *came to me, about the Kennel of the Street, and desired me to let him go on; for when he had done, he would bring Mr.* Penn *to me.*

Court. What Number do you think might be there?

Cook. *About three or four Hundred People.*

Court. Call *Richard Read,* give him his Oath.

Read being Sworn, was ask'd, *What do you know concerning the Prisoners at the Bar?*

Read. *My Lord, I went to* Gracious-Street, *where I found a great Crowd of*

2. The refusal to give people "hat-honor" was one of the ways in which Friends' religious principles violated traditional social hierarchies.

People, and I heard Mr. Penn *Preach to them, and I saw Captain* Mead *speaking to Lieutenant* Cook, *but what he said I could not tell.*

Mead. What did *William Penn* say?

Read. *There was such a great Noise, that I could not tell what he said.*

Mead. Jury, Observe this Evidence, he saith, He heard him Preach, and yet saith, He doth not know what he said.

Jury, Take Notice, he Swears now a clean contrary Thing, to what he Swore before the *Mayor,* when we were committed: For now he Swears that he saw me in *Gracious-Street,* and yet Swore before the Mayor, when I was committed, that he did not see me there. I appeal to the *Mayor* himself if this be not true; but no Answer was given.

Court. What Number do you think might be there?

Read. *About four or five Hundred.*

Penn. I desire to know of him what Day it was?

Read. *The 14th Day of* August.

Penn. Did he speak to me, or let me know he was there; for I am very sure I never saw him.

Cle. Cryer, Call —— into the Court.

Court. Give him his Oath.

—— *My Lord,* I *saw a great Number of People, and Mr.* Penn *I suppose was Speaking; I saw him make a Motion with his Hands, and heard some Noise, but could not understand what he said; but for Captain* Mead, *I did not see him there.*

Rec. What say you Mr. *Mead?* Were you there?

Mead. It is a Maxim in your own Law, *Nemo tenetur accusare seipsum,* which if it be not True Latin, I am sure that it is true English, *That no Man is bound to accuse himself:* And why dost thou offer to ensnare me with such a Question? Doth not this shew thy Malice? Is this like unto a Judge, that ought to be Council for the Prisoner at the Bar?

Rec. Sir, hold your Tongue, I did not go about to ensnare you.

Penn. I desire we may come more close to the Point, and that Silence be commanded in the Court.

Cry. O Yes, All manner of Persons keep Silence upon Pain of Imprisonment. —— Silence in the Court.

Penn. We confess our selves to be so far from recanting, or declining to vindicate the Assembling of our selves, to Preach, Pray, or Worship the Eternal, Holy, Just God, that we declare to all the World, that we do believe it to be our indispensable Duty, to meet incessantly upon so Good an Account; nor shall

all the Powers upon Earth be able to divert us from Reverencing and Adoring our God, who made us.

Brown. *You are not here for Worshipping God, but for breaking the Law: You do your selves a great deal of Wrong in going on in that Discourse.*

Penn. I affirm I have broken no Law, nor am I guilty of the Indictment that is laid to my Charge: And to the End, the Bench, the Jury, and my self, with those that hear us, may have a more direct Understanding of this Procedure, I desire you would let me know by what Law it is you Prosecute me, and upon what Law you ground my Indictment.

Rec. *Upon the Common-Law.*

Penn. Where is that Common-Law?

Rec. *You must not think that I am able to run up so many Years, and over so many adjudged Cases, which we call Common-Law, to answer your Curiosity.*

Penn. This Answer I am sure is very short of my Question; for if it be Common, it should not be so hard to produce.

Rec. *Sir, Will you plead to your Indictment?*

Penn. Shall I plead to an Indictment that hath no Foundation in Law? If it contain that Law you say I have broken, why should you decline to produce that Law, since it will be impossible for the *Jury* to determine, or agree to bring in their Verdict, who have not the Law produced, by which they should measure the Truth of this Indictment, and the Guilt, or contrary of my Fact.

Rec. *You are a sawcy Fellow; speak to the Indictment.*

Penn. I say, it is my Place to speak to Matter of Law; I am arraigned a Prisoner; my Liberty, which is next to Life itself, is now concerned; you are many Mouths and Ears against me, and if I must not be allowed to make the Best of my Case, it is hard: I say again, unless you shew me, and the People, the Law you ground your Indictment upon, I shall take it for granted, your Proceedings are meerly Arbitrary.

Obser. [At this Time several upon the Bench urged hard upon the Prisoner to bear him down.]

Rec. *The Question is, Whether you are Guilty of this Indictment?*

Penn. The Question is not whether I am Guilty of this Indictment, but whether this Indictment be Legal: It is too general and imperfect an Answer, to say it is the Common-Law, unless we knew both where, and what it is; For where there is no Law, there is no Transgression; and that Law which is not in being, is so far from being Common, that it is no Law at all.

Rec. *You are an impertinent Fellow; Will you teach the Court what Law is?*

It's Lex non scripta,[3] *that which many have studied thirty or forty Years to know, and would you have me tell you in a Moment?*

Penn. Certainly, if the Common-Law be so hard to be understood, it's far from being very Common; but if the Lord *Cook* in his *Institutes,* be of any Consideration, he tells us, *That Common-Law is Common-Right; and that Common-Right is the Great Charter Priviledges, confirmed* 9 Hen. 3. 29. 25 Edw. 1. 1. 2 Edw. 3. 8. Cook Inst. 2. p. 56.[4]

Rec. *Sir, you are a troublesome Fellow, and it is not for the Honour of the Court to suffer you to go on.*

Penn. I have asked but one Question, and you have not answered me; though the Rights and Priviledges of every *Englishman* be concerned in it.

Rec. *If I should suffer you to ask Questions till to Morrow-Morning, you would be never the wiser.*

Penn. That's according as the Answers are.

Rec. *Sir, we must not stand to hear you talk all Night.*

Penn. I design no Affront to the Court, but to be heard in my just Plea; and I must plainly tell you, that if you will deny me the *Oyer* of that Law, which you suggest I have broken, you do at once deny me an acknowledged Right, and evidence to the whole World your Resolution to sacrifice the Priviledges of *Englishmen,* to your Sinister and Arbitrary Designs.

Rec. *Take him away: My Lord, if you take not some Course with this pestilent Fellow, to stop his Mouth, we shall not be able to do any thing to Night.*

Mayor. *Take him away, take him away; turn him into the* Bale-Dock.

Penn. These are but so many vain Exclamations: Is this Justice, or True Judgment? Must I therefore be taken away because I plead for the Fundamental Laws of *England?* However, this I leave upon your Consciences, who are of the Jury, (and my sole Judges) that if these Ancient Fundamental Laws, which relate to *Liberty and Property,* (and are not limited to particular Perswasions in Matters of Religion) must not be indispensably maintained and observed, *Who can say he hath Right to the Coat upon his Back?* Certainly our Liberties are openly to be invaded; our Wives to be Ravished; our Children Slaved; our Families Ruined; and our Estates led away in Triumph, by every Sturdy Beg-

3. Unwritten law.

4. Sir Edward Coke (or Cook [1552–1634]), English jurist and chief justice from 1606 to 1616. Coke's *Institutes* elaborate and comment upon the English common law: Penn here refers to Coke's *Second part of the Institutes* (London, 1642), ch. 29.

gar, and Malicious Informer, as their Trophies, but our (pretended) Forfeits for *Conscience-Sake:* The Lord of Heaven and Earth will be Judge between us in this Matter.

Rec. *Be Silent there.*

Penn. I am not to be Silent in a Case wherein I am so much concerned; and not only myself, but many Ten Thousand Families besides.

Obser. They having rudely haled him into the Bale Dock, *William Mead* they left in Court, who spake as followeth.

Mead. You Men of the *Jury,* here I do now stand to answer to an Indictment against me, which is a Bundle of Stuff full of Lyes, and Falshoods; for therein I am accused that I met *Vi & Armis, Illicitè & Tumultuose:*[5] Time was, when I had Freedom to use a Carnal Weapon, and then I thought I feared no Man; but now I fear the Living GOD, and dare not make Use thereof, nor hurt any Man; nor do I know I demeaned myself as a Tumultuous Person. I say, I am a Peaceable Man, therefore it is a very proper Question what *William Penn* demanded in this Case, *An OYER of the Law,* on which our Indictment is grounded.

Rec. I *have made Answer to that already.*

Mead. Turning his Face to the *Jury,* said, You Men of the Jury, who are my Judges, if the Recorder will not tell you what makes a Riot, a Rout, or an Unlawful Assembly, *Cook,* he that once they called the *Lord Cook,* tells us what makes a Riot, a Rout, and an Unlawful Assembly,—A Riot is when Three, or more, are met together to beat a Man, or to enter forcibly into another Man's Land, to cut down his Grass, his Wood, or break down his Pales.[6]

Obser. Here the *Recorder* interrupted him, and said, I *thank you Sir, that you will tell me what the Law is,* scornfully pulling off his Hat.

Mead. Thou mayst put on thy Hat, I have never a Fee for thee now.

Brown. *He talks at Random, one While an* Independent, *another While some other Religion, and now a* Quaker, *and next a* Papist.

Mead. Turpe est doctori cum culpa redarguit ipsum.[7]

Mayor. *You deserve to have your Tongue Cut out.*

Rec. *If you discourse on this Manner, I shall take Occasion against you.*

5. With force and arms, illegally and riotously.

6. Sir Edward Coke, *Third part of the Institutes* (London, 1644), ch. 79.

7. It is disgusting for the teacher whose own faults accuse him.

Mead. Thou didst promise me, I should have fair Liberty to be heard. Why may I not have the Priviledge of an Englishman? I am an Englishman, and you might be ashamed of this Dealing.

Rec. *I look upon you to be an Enemy to the Laws of* England, *which ought to be observed and kept, nor are you worthy of such Priviledges as others have.*

Mead. The Lord is Judge between me and thee in this Matter.

Obser. Upon which they took him away into the Bale-Dock, and the *Recorder* proceeded to give the *Jury* their Charge, as followeth.

Rec. *You have heard what the Indictment is; it is for Preaching to the People, and drawing a Tumultuous Company after them; and Mr.* Penn *was Speaking: If they should not be disturbed, you see they will go on; there are three or four Witnesses that have proved this, that he did Preach there, that Mr.* Mead *did allow of it; after this, you have heard by Substantial Witnesses what is said against them: Now we are upon the Matter of Fact, which you are to keep to and observe, as what hath been fully Sworn, at your Peril.*

Obser. The Prisoners were put out of the Court, into the Bale-Dock, and the Charge given to the Jury in their Absence, at which *W. P.* with a very raised Voice, it being a considerable Distance from the Bench, spake.

Penn. I appeal to the Jury, who are my Judges, and this great Assembly, whether the Proceedings of the Court are not most Arbitrary, and void of all Law, in offering to give the Jury their Charge in the Absence of the Prisoners: I say, it is directly opposite to, and destructive of the undoubted Right of every *English* Prisoner, as *Cook* in the 2 *Inst.* 29. on the Chapter of *Magna Charta* speaks.

Obser. The *Recorder* being thus unexpectedly lasht for his extra-judicial Procedure, said, with an inraged Smile,

Rec. *Why ye are present, you do hear: Do you not?*

Penn. No Thanks to the Court, that commanded me into the Bale-Dock; and you of the Jury take Notice, that I have not been heard, neither can you Legally depart the Court, before I have been fully heard, having at least Ten or Twelve Material Points to offer, in Order to invalidate their Indictment.

Rec. *Pull that Fellow down; pull him down.*

Mead. Are these according to the Rights and Priviledges of *Englishmen,* that we should not be heard, but turned into the Bale-Dock, for making our Defence, and the Jury to have their Charge given them in our Absence? I say, these are barbarous and unjust Proceedings.

Rec. *Take them away into the Hole; to hear them talk all Night, as they would, that I think doth not become the Honour of the Court; and I think you* (i.e. the Jury) *your selves would be Tired out, and not have Patience to hear them.*

Obser. The Jury were commanded up to agree upon their Verdict, the Prisoners remaining in the stinking Hole; after an Hour and Half's Time, Eight came down agreed, but Four remained above; the Court sent an Officer for them, and they accordingly came down: The Bench used many unworthy Threats to the Four that dissented; and the Recorder addressing himself to *Bushel,* said, *Sir, You are the Cause of this Disturbance, and manifestly shew yourself an Abettor of Faction; I shall set a Mark upon you, Sir.*

J. Robinson. Mr. Bushel, *I have known you near this fourteen Years; you have thrust your self upon this Jury, because you think there is some Service for you; I tell you, You deserve to be Indicted more than any Man that hath been brought to the Bar this Day.*

Bushel. No, Sir *John,* there were Threescore before me, and I would willingly have got off, but could not.

Bludw. I said when I saw Mr. *Bushel,* what I see is come to pass; for I knew he would never yield. Mr. *Bushel,* we know what you are.

Mayor. *Sirrah, You are an impudent Fellow, I will put a Mark upon you.*

Obser. They used much menacing Language, and behaved themselves very imperiously to the Jury, as Persons not more void of Justice, than Sober Education. After this barbarous Usage, they sent them to consider of bringing in their Verdict, and after some considerable Time they returned to the Court. Silence was called for, and the Jury called by their Names.

Cle. Are you agreed upon your Verdict?

Jury. Yes.

Cle. Who shall speak for you?

Jury. Our Foreman.

Cle. Look upon the Prisoners at the Bar: How say you? Is *William Penn* Guilty of the Matter whereof he stands Indicted in Manner and Form, or Not Guilty?

Foreman. Guilty of Speaking in *Gracious-Street.*

Court. Is that All?

Foreman. That is All I have in Commission.

Rec. You had as good say Nothing.

Mayor. *Was it not an Unlawful Assembly? You mean he was Speaking to a Tumult of People there?*

Foreman. My Lord, This was All I had in Commission.

Obser. Here some of the Jury seemed to buckle to the Questions of the Court, upon which *Bushel, Hammond,* and some others, opposed themselves, and said, *They allowed of no such Word, as an Unlawful Assembly, in their Verdict;* at which the *Recorder, Mayor, Robinson,* and *Bludworth,* took great Occasion to vilify them with most opprobrious Language; and this Verdict not serving their Turns, the Recorder expressed himself thus:

Rec. *The Law of* England *will not allow you to depart, till you have given in your Verdict.*

Jury. We have given in our Verdict, and we can give in no other.

Rec. *Gentlemen, you have not given in your Verdict, and you had as good say Nothing; therefore go and consider it once more, that we may make an End of this troublesom Business.*

Jury. We desire we may have Pen, Ink, and Paper.

Obser. The Court adjourns for Half an Hour; which being expired, the Court returns, and the Jury not long after.

The Prisoners were brought to the Bar, and the Jurors Names called over.

Cle. Are you agreed of your Verdict?

Jury. Yes.

Cle. Who shall speak for you?

Jury. Our Foreman.

Cle. What say you? Look upon the Prisoners: Is *William Penn* Guilty in Manner and Form, as he stands Indicted, or not Guilty?

Foreman. Here is our Verdict; holding forth a Piece of Paper to the Clerk of the Peace, which follows:

WE the Jurors, hereafter Named, do find *William Penn* to be Guilty of Speaking or Preaching to an Assembly, met together in *Gracious-Street,* the 14th of *August* last, 1670, and that *William Mead* is not Guilty of the said Indictment.

Foreman, *Thomas Veer,*	*Henry Michel,*	*John Baily,*
Edward Bushel,	*John Brightman,*	*William Lever,*
John Hammond,	*Charles Milson,*	*James Damask,*
Henry Henly,	*Gregory Walklet,*	*William Plumstead.*

Obser. This both *Mayor* and *Recorder* resented at so high a Rate, that they exceeded the Bounds of all Reason and Civility.

Mayor. *What will you be led by such a silly Fellow as* Bushel; *an impudent canting Fellow? I warrant you, You shall come no more upon Juries in Hast; you are a Foreman indeed,* (addressing himself to the Foreman) *I thought you had understood your Place better.*

Rec. *Gentlemen, you shall not be dismist, till we have a Verdict that the Court will accept; and you shall be lock'd up, without Meat, Drink, Fire, and Tobacco: You shall not think thus to abuse the Court; we will have a Verdict by the Help of God, or you shall starve for it.*

Penn. My Jury, who are my Judges, ought not to be thus menaced; their Verdict should be Free, and not Compelled; the Bench ought to wait upon them, but not Forestal them: I do desire that Justice may be done me, and that the Arbitrary Resolves of the Bench may not be made the Measure of my Juries Verdict.

Rec. *Stop that prating Fellow's Mouth, or put him out of the Court.*

Mayor. *You have heard that he Preach'd; that he gathered a Company of Tumultuous People; and that they do not only disobey the Martial Power, but the Civil also.*

Penn. It is a great Mistake; we did not make the Tumult, but they that interrupted us. The Jury cannot be so ignorant, as to think that we met there with a Design to disturb the Civil Peace, since (1*st*) we were by Force of Arms kept out of our Lawful House, and met as near it in the Street, as the Soldiers would give us Leave: And (2*d*) because it was no New Thing, (nor with the Circumstances exprest in the Indictment, but what was usual and customary with us;) 'tis very well known that we are a Peaceable People, and cannot offer Violence to any Man.

Obser. The Court being ready to break up, and willing to huddle the Prisoners to their Jail, and the Jury to their Chamber, *Penn* spake as follows:

Penn. The Agreement of Twelve Men is a Verdict in Law, and such a one being given by the Jury, *I require the Clerk of the Peace to record it, as he will answer it at his Peril:* And if the Jury bring in another Verdict contrary to this, I affirm they are perjured Men in Law. (And looking upon the Jury, said) *You are* Englishmen, *mind your Priviledge, give not away your Right.*

Bushel, &c. *Nor will we ever do it.*

Obser. One of the Jury-Men pleaded Indisposition of Body, and therefore desired to be dismist.

Mayor. *You are as strong as any of them; Starve then, and hold your Principles.*

Rec. *Gentlemen, you must be content with your hard Fate; let your Patience overcome it; for the Court is resolved to have a Verdict, and that before you can be dismist.*

Jury. We are agreed, we are agreed, we are agreed.

Obser. The Court Swore several Persons, to keep the Jury all Night, without Meat, Drink, Fire, or any other Accommodation; they had not so much as a Chamber-Pot, though desired.

Cry. O Yes, *&c.*

Obser. The Court adjourn'd till Seven of the Clock next Morning, (being the Fourth Instant, vulgarly called *Sunday*) at which Time the Prisoners were brought to the Bar, the Court sat, and the Jury called in, to bring in their Verdict.

Cry. O Yes, *&c.*—Silence in the Court upon Pain of Imprisonment.

The Juries Names called over.

Cle. Are you agreed upon your Verdict?

Jury. Yes.

Cle. Who shall speak for you.

Jury. Our Foreman.

Cle. What say you? Look upon the Prisoners at the Bar: Is *William Penn* Guilty of the Matter whereof he stands Indicted, in Manner and Form as aforesaid, or Not Guilty?

Foreman. William Penn is Guilty of Speaking in *Gracious-Street.*

Mayor. *To an Unlawful Assembly.*

Bushel. No, my Lord, we give no other Verdict, than what we gave last Night; we have no other Verdict to give.

Mayor. *You are a factious Fellow; I'll take a Course with you.*

Bludw. *I knew Mr.* Bushel would not yield.

Bushel. Sir *Thomas,* I have done according to my Conscience.

Mayor. *That Conscience of yours would Cut my Throat.*

Bushel. No, my Lord, it never shall.

Mayor. *But I will cut yours so soon as I can.*

Rec. *He has inspired the Jury; he has the Spirit of Divination; methinks I feel him; I will have a positive Verdict, or you shall Starve for it.*

Penn. I desire to ask the Recorder one Question: Do you allow of the Verdict given of *William Mead?*

Rec. *It cannot be a Verdict, because you are Indicted for a Conspiracy; and one being found not Guilty, and not the other, it could not be a Verdict.*

Penn. If not Guilty be not a Verdict, then you make of the *Jury,* and *Magna Charta,* but a meer Nose of Wax.

Mead. How! Is Not Guilty no Verdict?

Rec. *No, 'tis no Verdict.*

Penn. I affirm, That the Consent of a Jury is a Verdict in Law; and if *William Mead* be not Guilty, it consequently follows, that I am clear, since you have Indicted us of a Conspiracy, and I could not possibly Conspire alone.

Obser. There were many Passages that could not be taken, which past between the Jury and the Court. The Jury went up again, having received a fresh Charge from the Bench, if possible to extort an unjust Verdict.

Cry. O Yes, *&c.*—Silence in the Court.

Court. Call over the Jury —— Which was done.

Cle. What say you? Is *William Penn* Guilty of the Matter whereof he stands Indicted, in Manner and Form aforesaid, or Not Guilty?

Foreman. Guilty of Speaking in *Gracious-Street.*

Rec. *What is this to the Purpose? I say I will have a Verdict. And speaking to* E. Bushel, *said, You are a Factious Fellow; I will set a Mark upon you; and whilst I have any Thing to do in the City, I will have an Eye upon you.*

Mayor. *Have you no more Wit than to be led by such a pitiful Fellow? I will Cut his Nose.*

Penn. It is intolerable that my Jury should be thus menaced; is this according to the Fundamental Law? Are not they my proper Judges by the *Great Charter of England?*[8] What Hope is there of ever having Justice done, when Juries are threatned, and their Verdicts rejected? I am concerned to speak, and grieved to see such Arbitrary Proceedings. *Did not the Lieutenant of the* Tower *render one of them worse than a Felon?* And do you not plainly seem to condemn such for Factious Fellows, who answer not your Ends? Unhappy are those Juries, who are threatned to be Fined, and Starved, and Ruined, if they give not in their Verdicts contrary to their Consciences.

Rec. *My Lord, you must take a Course with that same Fellow.*

Mayor. *Stop his Mouth; Jailer, bring Fetters, and Stake him to the Ground.*

Penn. Do your Pleasure, I matter not your Fetters.

Rec. *Till now I never understood the Reason of the Policy and Prudence of the* Spaniards, *in suffering the Inquisition among them: And certainly it will never be well with us, till something like the* Spanish *Inquisition be in* England.

8. See Magna Charta, ch. 39.

Obser. The Jury being required to go together, to find another Verdict, and stedfastly refusing it (saying they could give no other Verdict than what was already given) the Recorder in great Passion was running off the Bench, with these Words in his Mouth, *I protest I will sit here no longer to hear these Things.* At which the Mayor calling, Stay, Stay, he returned, and directed himself unto the Jury, and spake as followeth.

Rec. *Gentlemen, we shall not be at this pass always with you; you will find the next Sessions of Parliament, there will be a Law made, that those that will not conform, shall not have the Protection of the Law. Mr.* Lee, *draw up another Verdict, that they may bring it in special.*

Lee. I cannot tell how to do it.

Jury. We ought not to be returned, having all agreed, and set our Hands to the Verdict.

Rec. *Your Verdict is nothing, you play upon the Court; I say, you shall go together, and bring in another Verdict, or you shall Starve; and I will have you carted about the City, as in* Edward *the Third's Time.*

Foreman. We have given in our Verdict, and all agreed to it, and if we give in another, it will be a Force upon us to save our Lives.

Mayor. Take them up.

Officer. My Lord they will not go up.

Obser. The Mayor spoke to the Sheriff, and he came off his Seat, and said:

Sher. *Come Gentlemen, you must go up; you see I am commanded to make you go.*

Obser. Upon which the Jury went up; and several sworn to keep them without any Accomodation, as aforesaid, till they brought in their Verdict.

Cry. O Yes, *&c.* The Court adjourns till to Morrow-morning at Seven of the Clock.

Obser. The Prisoners were remanded to *Newgate,* where they remained till next Morning, and then were brought into the Court, which being sat, they proceeded as followeth.

Cry. O yes, *&c.*—Silence in the Court upon Pain of Imprisonment.

Clerk. Set *William Penn* and *William Mead* to the Bar. Gentlemen of the Jury, answer to your Names, *Thomas Veer, Edward Bushel, John Hammond, Henry Henley, Henry Michel, John Brightman, Charles Milson, Gregory Walklet, John Bailey, William Lever, James Damask, William Plumstead,* are you all agreed of your Verdict?

Jury. Yes.

Clerk. Who shall speak for you?

Jury. Our Foreman.

Clerk. Look upon the Prisoners. What say you; is *William Penn* guilty of the Matter whereof he stands indicted, in Manner and Form, *&c.* or not guilty?

Foreman. You have there read in Writing already our Verdict, and our Hands subscribed.

Obser. The Clerk had the Paper, but was stop'd by the Recorder from Reading of it; and he commanded to ask for a positive Verdict.

Foreman. If you will not accept of it; I desire to have it back again.

Court. That Paper was no Verdict, and there shall be no Advantage taken against you by it.

Clerk. How say you? Is *William Penn* Guilty, *&c.* or not Guilty?

Foreman. Not Guilty.

Clerk. How say you? Is *William Mead* Guilty, *&c.* or not Guilty?

Foreman. Not Guilty.

Clerk. Then hearken to your Verdict, you say, that *William Penn* is not Guilty in Manner and Form, as he stands indicted; you say, that *William Mead* is not Guilty in Manner and Form, as he stands indicted, and so you say all.

Jury. Yes, we do so.

Obser. The Bench being unsatisfied with the Verdict, commanded that every Person should distinctly answer to their Names, and give in their Verdict, which they unanimously did, in saying, *Not Guilty,* to the great Satisfaction of the Assembly.

Record. I am sorry, Gentlemen, you have followed your own Judgments and Opinions, rather than the good and wholesom Advice, which was given you; God keep my Life out of your Hands; but for this the Court fines you Forty Marks a Man, and Imprisonment till paid: At which *Penn* stept up towards the Bench, and said,

Penn. I demand my Liberty, being freed by the Jury.

Mayor. No, you are in for your Fines.

Penn. Fines, for what?

Mayor. For Contempt of the Court.

Penn. I ask if it be according to the Fundamental Laws of *England,* that any Englishman should be fined, or amerced, but by the Judgment of his Peers, or Jury? Since it expresly contradicts the Fourteenth and Twenty Ninth Chapter of the *Great Charter of* England, which says, No Freeman ought to be amerced, but by the Oath of good and lawful Men of the Vicinage.

Rec. *Take him away, take him away, take him out of the Court.*

Penn. I can never urge the Fundamental Laws of *England,* but you cry, Take him away, take him away; but 'tis no Wonder, *since the* Spanish *Inquisition hath so great a Place in the Recorder's Heart;* God Almighty who is Just, will judge you all for these Things.

Obser. They haled the Prisoners to the *Bale-dock,* and from thence sent them to *Newgate,* for Non-payment of their Fines; and so were their Jury.

England's Present Interest Considered,

WITH

Honour to the Prince, *and Safety to the* People

(1675)

In Answer to this one Question,

What is most Fit, Easy and Safe at this Juncture of Affairs to be done, for quieting of Differences, allaying the Heat of contrary Interests, and making them subservient to the Interest of the Government, and consistent with the Prosperity of the Kingdom?

Submitted to the Consideration of our Superiors.

Lex est Ratio sine Appetitu.[1]

The Introduction.

THERE is no Law under Heaven, which hath its Rise from Nature or Grace, that forbids Men to deal Honestly and Plainly, with the Greatest, in Matters of Importance to their present and future Good: On the contrary, the Dictates of both enjoyn every Man that Office to his Neighbour; and from Charity among Private Persons, it becomes a Duty indispensible to the Publick. Nor do *Worthy Minds* think ever the less kindly of Honest and Humble Monitors; and God knows, that oft-times *Princes* are deceived, and *Kingdoms* languish for Want of them. How far the Posture of our Affairs will justify this Address, I shall submit to the Judgment, and Observation of every *Intelligent Reader.*

Certain it is, that there are few Kingdoms in the World more divided within themselves, and whose Religious Interests lye more seemingly cross to all Accommodation, than that we Live in; which renders the *Magistrate's Task hard,* and giveth him a Difficulty next to invincible.

Your Endeavours for an *Uniformity* have been many; Your Acts not a few to enforce it; but the *Consequence,* whether you intended it or no, through

1. Law is reason without passion.

the Barbarous Practices of those that have had their Execution, hath been the spoiling of several Thousands of the Free Born People of this Kingdom, of their Unforfeited Rights. *Persons have been flung into Goals,*[2] *Gates and Trunks broke open, Goods distrained, till a Stool hath not been left to sit down on: Flocks of Cattle driven, whole Barns full of Corn seized, Thresh'd, and carried away: Parents left without their Children, Children without their Parents, both without Subsistence.*

But that which aggravates the Cruelty, is, *The Widow's Mite* hath not escaped their Hands; they have made her *Cow the Forfeiture of her Conscience;* not leaving her a Bed to lye on, nor a Blanket to cover her.[3] And which is yet more Barbarous, and helps to make up this Tragedy, the *Poor Helpless Orphan's Milk, Boiling over the Fire, has been flung to the Dogs, and the Skillet made Part of their Prize:* That, had not Nature in Neighbours been stronger than Cruelty in such Informers and Officers, to open her Bowels for their Relief and Subsistence, they must have utterly perish'd.

Nor can these inhuman Instruments plead Conscience or Duty to those Laws, who have abundantly transcended the severest Clause in them; for to see the imprison'd, has been Suspicion enough for a Goal; and to Visit the Sick, to make a Conventicle: Fining and Straining for Preaching, and being at a Meeting, where there hath been neither; and *Forty Pound for Twenty,* at Pick and Choose too, is a moderate Advance with some of them.

Others thinking this a Way too dull and troublesome, alter the Question, and turn, *Have you met?* Which the Act intends; to, *Will you Swear?* Which it intendeth not: So that in some Places it hath been sufficient to a *Premunire,* that Men have had Estates to lose; I mean such Men, who, through Tenderness, refuse the Oath; but by Principle like the Allegiance, not less than their Adversaries.[4]

Finding then by sad Experience, and a long Tract of Time, that the very Remedies applied to cure Dissension, increase it; and that the more Vigorously an *Uniformity* is Coercively Prosecuted, the wider Breaches grow, the more inflamed Persons are, and fix'd in their Resolutions to stand by their Principles, it should, methinks, put an End to the Attempt: For besides all

2. Here and hereafter, read "jails" for "goals."

3. See Mark 12:42; and Luke 21:2.

4. On the Quaker attitude toward oaths, see Penn's *A Treatise of Oaths* (London, 1675).

other Inconveniences to those that give them Trouble, their very Sufferings beget that Compassion in the Multitude, which rarely misses of making many Friends, and proves often a *Preparation for not a few Proselytes.* So much more Reverend is Suffering, than making Men suffer for Religion, even of those that cannot suffer for their Religion, if yet they have any Religion to suffer for. Histories are full of Examples: *The Persecution of the Christian Religion* made it more illustrious than it's Doctrine. Perhaps it will be denied to *English Dissenters,* that they rely upon so good a Cause, and therefore a Vanity in them to expect that Success. But *Arrianism* it self, once reputed the foulest *Heresie* by the Church, was by no Artifice of its Party so disseminated, as the severe Opposition of the *Homoousians.*[5]

Contests naturally draw Company, and the Vulgar are justified in their Curiosity, if not Pity, when they see so many Wiser Men busie themselves to suppress a People, by whom they see no other Ill, than that for *Non-Conformity,* in Matters of Religion, they bear Injuries and Indignities Patiently.

To be short; If all the *Interruptions, Informations, Fines, Plunders, Imprisonments, Exiles and Blood,* which the great Enemy of Nature, as well as Grace, hath excited Man to, in all Ages, about Matters of Faith and Worship, from *Cain* and *Abel*'s Time to ours, could furnish us with sufficient Presidents,[6] that the Design proposed by the Inflictors of so much Severity, *was ever Answered;* that they have smother'd Opinions, and not inflamed, but extinguish'd Contest; it might perhaps, at least prudentially, give Check to our Expectations, and allay my just Confidence in this Address: But since such Attempts have ever been found Improsperous, as well as that they are too costly, and have always procured the *Judgments of God, and the Hatred of Men: To the Sufferers, Misery; to their Countries, Decay of People and Trade; and to their own Consciences an extream Guilt;* I fall to the *Question,* and then the *Solution* of it: In which, as I declare, I intend nothing that should in the least abate of that

5. The Arian controversy focused on the nature of Christ's divinity. Arians emphasized Christ's created nature, whereas their opponents stressed his eternal coexistence with the Father. The Council of Nicaea (325), in a setback for Arians, established a creed referring to Christ as "of one essence" (homoousian) with the Father. Constantine later planned to reinstate Arius (and exiled his opponent Athanasius), but Arius died before this could be carried out. Penn refers to the Arian disputes repeatedly throughout this volume.

6. Here and hereafter, read "precedents."

Love, Honour and Service that are due to you, so I beseech you, do me the Justice as to make the Fairest Interpretation of my Expressions: For the whole of my Plain and Honest Design is, *To offer my Mite for the Increase of your True Honour, and my Dear Country's Felicity.*

The QUESTION.

W*HAT is most Fit, Easie and Safe, at this Juncture of Affairs, to be done, for Composing, at least Quieting Differences; for allaying the Heat of contrary Interests, and making them Subservient to the Interest of the Government, and Consistent with the Prosperity of the Kingdom?*

The ANSWER.

I. AN INVIOLABLE and Impartial Maintenance of *English* Rights.

II. Our *Superiors* Governing themselves upon a *Ballance,* as near as may be, towards the several *Religious Interests.*

III. A Sincere Promotion of *General and Practical Religion.*

I shall briefly discourse upon these Three Things, and endeavour to prove them a *Sufficient,* if not the *Only Best Answer,* that can be given to the Question propounded.

CHAP. I.
Of ENGLISH RIGHTS.

I. *Of* English *Rights, in the* British, Saxon *and* Norman *Times. Particularly of* Liberty *and* Property. *Of* Legislation. *Of* Juries. *That they are* Fundamental *to the Government, and but* Repeated *and* Confirmed *by the* Great Charter. The Reverence *paid them by* Kings and Parliaments, and their Care to preserve them. *The* Curse *and* Punishment *that attended the* Violators. *More General Considerations of Property,* &c. *The* Uncertainty *and* Ruin of Interests, *where is it not maintain'd: Divers Presidents:* That *it is the Prince's Interest to preserve it inviolably:* That *it is not justly* Forfeitable for Ecclesiastical Non-

Conformity; *and that where the* Property *is Sacrificed for it, the* Government *is chang'd from* Civil *to* Ecclesiastical, *from the* Parliament-House *to the* Vestry.

THERE is no Government in the World, but it must either stand upon *Will and Power,* or *Condition and Contract:* The one Rules by Men, the other by Laws. And above all Kingdoms under Heaven, it is *England*'s Felicity to have her Constitution so impartially Just and Free, as there cannot well be any Thing more remote from Arbitrariness, and Zealous of preserving the Laws, by which it's Rights are maintained.

These Laws are either *Fundamental,* and so Immutable; or more Superficial and Temporary, and consequently alterable.

By *Superficial Laws,* we understand such Acts, Laws or Statutes, as are suited to present Occurrences, and Emergencies of State; and which may as well be abrogated, as they were first made, for the Good of the Kingdom: For Instance, those Statutes that relate to Victuals, Cloaths, Times, and Places of Trade, *&c.* which have ever stood, whilst the Reason of them was in Force; but when that Benefit, which did once redound, fell by fresh Accidents, they ended, according to that Old Maxim, *Cessante ratione legis, cessat lex.*[7]

By *Fundamental Laws* I do not only understand such as immediately spring from *Synteresis* (that Eternal Principle of Truth and Sapience)[8] more or less disseminated through Mankind, which are as the Corner-Stones of Humane Structure, the Basis of Reasonable Societies, without which all would run into Heaps and Confusion; to wit, *Honestè vivere, Alterum non laedere, jus suum cuique tribuere,* that is, To live honestly, not to hurt another, and to give every one their Right, (Excellent Principles, and common to all Nations) though that it self were sufficient to our present Purpose: But those Rights and Priviledges, which I call *English,* and which are the proper *Birth-Right* of *Englishmen,* and may be reduced to these Three.

I. *An Ownership, and Undisturbed Possession: That what they have, is Rightly theirs, and no Body's else.*

7. When the reason for a law ceases, the law ceases.

8. Synderesis (or synteresis) refers to the inherent moral knowledge possessed by all individuals (see Thomas Aquinas, *Summa Theologica,* pt. 1, qu. 79, a. 12); for the three principles of Roman law, see the opening passages to Justinian's *Institutes.*

II. *A Voting of every Law that is made, whereby that Ownership or Propriety may be maintained.*

III. *An Influence upon, and a Real Share in that Judicatory Power that must apply every such Law, which is the Ancient Necessary and Laudable Use of Juries: If not found among the* Britains, *to be sure Practised by the* Saxons, *and continued through the* Normans *to this very Day.*

That these have been the Ancient and Undoubted Rights of *Englishmen,* as Three great Roots, under whose Spacious Branches the *English People* have been wont to shelter themselves against the Storms of Arbitrary Government, I shall endeavour to prove.

I. *An Ownership and Undisturbed Possession.*

This relates both to Title and Security of *Estate,* and Liberty of *Person,* from the Violence of Arbitrary Power.

'Tis true, the Foot-Steps of the *British Government* are very much overgrown by Time. There is scarcely any Thing remarkable left us, but what we are beholden to Strangers for: Either their own Unskilfulness in Letters, or their Depopulations and Conquests by Invaders, have deprived the World of a particular Story of their Laws and Customs, in Peace or War. However, *Caesar, Tacitus,* and especially *Dion,* say enough to prove their Nature and their Government to be as far from Slavish, as their Breeding and Manners were remote from the Education and greater Skill of the *Romans.*[9] *Beda* and *M. Westminster* say as much.[10]

The Law of *Property* they observed, and made those Laws that concern'd the Preservation of it.

9. Caesar, *Commentaries on the Gallic War,* bk. 4; Tacitus, *Life of Agricola,* chs. 10–13; and Dio, *Roman History,* bk. 39, chs. 51–53.

10. These two references appear to refer to Penn's more specific comments about the relation between British and Roman manners and education. See Bede's *Ecclesiastical History,* bk. I, ch. 17; and the historical collection *Flowers of History* (fourteenth century; formerly attributed to Matthew Westminster, currently attributed to Roger of Wendover or Matthew Paris), entry for the year 416. *Flowers of History* has recently been republished as *Roger of Wendover's Flowers of History: Formerly Attributed to Matthew of Paris,* trans. J. A. Giles (Felinfach, 1994).

The *Saxons* brought no Alteration to these Two Fundamentals of our *English* Government; for they were a *Free People,* govern'd by Laws, of which they themselves were the Makers: That is, there was no Law made without the Consent of the People, *de majoribus omnes,* as *Tacitus* observeth of the *Germans* in general.[11] They lost nothing by Transporting of themselves hither; and doubtless found a greater Consistency between their Laws, than their Ambition. For the Learned Collector of the *British Councils* tells us, That *Ethelston,* the *Saxon* King, pleading with the People, told them, *Seeing I, according to your Law, allow what is yours, do ye so with me.*[12] Whence Three Things are observable. *First,* That something was *Theirs,* that no Body else could dispose of. *Secondly,* That they had *Property* by their own Law, therefore they had a *Share* in making their own Laws. *Thirdly,* That the Law was *Umpire* between King and People; neither of them ought to infringe: This, *Ina,* the Great *Saxon* King, confirms. *There is no Great Man,* saith he, *nor any other in the whole Kingdom, that may abolish Written Laws.* It was also a great Part of the *Saxon* Oath, administred to the Kings, at their Entrance upon the Government, *To Maintain and Rule according to the Laws of the Nation.*

Their Parliament they called *Micklemote,* or *Wittangemote.* It consisted of *King, Lords,* and *People,* before the *Clergy* interwove themselves with the *Civil Government.* And *Andrew Horn,* in his *Mirror of Justice,* tells us, *That the Grand Assembly of the Kingdom in the* Saxon *Time, was to confer of the Government of God's People, how they might be kept from* Sin, *in* Quiet, *and have* Right done them, *according to the Customs and Laws.*[13]

Nor did this Law end with the *Saxon* Race: *William* the *Conqueror,* as he is usually called, quitting all *Claim* by *Conquest,* gladly stooped to the Laws observed by the *Saxon* Kings, and so became a King by Leave; valuing a Title by *Election,* before that which is founded in *Power* only. He therefore, at his *Coronation,* made a *Solemn Covenant, to maintain the Good, Approved, and Ancient Laws of this Kingdom, and to Inhibit all Spoil and Unjust Judgment.*

And this, *Henry* the First, his Third Son, among other his Titles, mentioned in his Charter, to make *Ely* a Bishoprick, calls himself, *Son of* William

11. Tacitus, *Germany and Its Tribes,* ch. 11.

12. Sir Henry Spelman, *Concilia, decreta, leges, constitutiones, in re ecclesiarum orbis Brittanici* (London, 1639), p. 397.

13. Andrew Horn (d. 1328), *Mirror of Justices,* bk. 1, ch. 2. Horn was a London fishmonger, city chamberlain, and legal archivist. His *Mirror of Justices* appears as volume 7 of the *Publications of the Selden Society,* ed. William Joseph Whittaker (London, 1893).

the Great, who by Hereditary Right, (not *Conquest*) succeeded King *Edward* (called *the Confessor*) in this Kingdom.

An Ancient Chronicle of *Litchfield,* speaks of a Council of Lords that advised *William* of *Normandy, To call together all the Nobles and Wise Men throughout their Counties of* England, *that they might set down their own Laws and Customs;* which was about the Fourth Year of his Reign: Which implies that they had Fundamental Laws, and that he intended their Confirmation.

And one of the first Laws made by this King, which, as a Notable Author saith, *may be called the First Magna Charta in the* Norman *Times* (by which he reserved to himself nothing of the Freemen of this Kingdom, but their Free-Service) in the Conclusion of it, saith, *That the Lands of the Inhabitants of this Kingdom were granted to them in Inheritance of the King, and by the Common Council of the whole Kingdom;* which Law doth also provide, *That they shall hold their Lands and Tenements well or quietly, and in Peace, from all unjust Tax and Tillage:* Which is farther expounded in the Laws of *Henry* the First, Chap. 4. *That no Tribute or Tax should be taken, but what was due in* Edward *the Confessor's Time.* So that the *Norman* Kings claim no other Right in the Lands and Possessions of any of their Subjects, than according to *English* Law and Right.

And so tender were they of *Property* in those Times, that when *Justice* it self became Importunate in a Case, no Distress could issue without publick Warrant obtained: Nor that neither, but upon Three Complaints first made. Nay, when *Rape* and *Plunder* were Rife, and Men seem'd to have no more Right to their own, than they had Power to maintain, even then was this Law a sufficient Sanctuary to the Oppressed, by being publickly pleaded at the Bar against all *Usurpation;* though it were under the Pretence of their Conqueror's Right it self; as by the Case of *Edwin* of *Sharnbourn* in *Camden*'s *Britannia,* plainly appears.[14]

The like Obligation to maintain this Fundamental Law of *Property,* with the appendent Rights of the People, was taken by *William Rufus, Henry* the First, *Stephen, Henry* the Second, *Richard* the First, *John,* and *Henry* the Third: Which brings me to that Famous Law, called, *Magna Charta,* or *The Great Charter of* England, of which more anon; it being my Design to shew, That nothing of the *Essential Rights of Englishmen* was thereby, *De Novo,* granted,

14. William Camden, *Britannia: Britain, or, A chorographicall description of the most flourishing kingdoms* (London, 1637), p. 480.

as in Civility to King *Henry* the Third it is termed; but that they were therein only Repeated and Confirmed. Wherefore I shall return to Antecedent Times, to fetch down the remaining Rights.

The second Part of this first Fundamental is, *Liberty of Person.* The *Saxons* were so tender in the Point of Imprisonment, that there was little or no use made of it: Nor would they so Punish their Bond-men, *vinculis coercere rarum est.*

In case of Debt or Damage, the Recovery thereof was either by a Delivery of the just Value in Goods, or, upon the Sheriffs Sale of the Goods, in Money; and if that satisfied not, the Land was extended: And when all was gone, they were accustomed to make their last Siezure upon the Party's Arms, and then he was reputed an Undone Man, and cast upon the Charity of his Friends for Subsistence: But his Person was never Imprison'd for the Debt: No, not in the King's Case. And to the Honour of King *Alfred* be it spoken, *He imprison'd one of his Judges for Imprisoning a Man in that Case.*

We find among his Laws this Passage, *Qui immerentem Paganum vinculis constrinxerit, decem solidis noxam sarcito:* "That if a Man should Imprison his Vassal or Bondman Unjustly, his Purgation of that Offence should not be less than the Payment of Ten Shillings"; A Sum very considerable in those Days, more than Ten Pounds now.

Nor did the Revolution from *Saxon* to *Norman* drop this Priviledge: For besides the general Confirmation of former Rights by *William,* sirnamed the *Conqueror,* his Son *Henry* the First, particularly took such Care of continuing *This Part of Property,* inviolable, that, in his Time, no Person was to be Imprison'd for committing of Mortal Crime it self, unless he were first attainted by the Verdict of Twelve Men; that is, a Jury, which was to be of the Neighbourhood.

Thus much for the first of my Three Fundamentals, *Right of Estate,* and *Liberty of Person:* That is to say, I am no Man's Bond-man, and what I Possess *is Absolutely Mine Own.*

II. *A Voting of every Law that is made, whereby that Ownership or Property may be maintained.*

This second Fundamental of our *English* Government, was no Incroachment upon the Kings of more modern Ages, but extant long before the *Great Char-*

ter made in the Reign of *Hen.* III. Even as early as the *Britain*'s themselves; and that it continued to the Time of *Hen.* 3. is evident from several Instances.

Caesar, in his Commentaries, tells us, That it was the Custom of the *British* Cities to elect their General, or Commander in Chief, in Case of War. *Dion* assures us, in the Life of *Severus* the Emperor, That in *Britain* the People held a Share in Power and Government; which is the modestest Construction his Words will bear. And *Tacitus* in the Life of *Agrippa,* says, They had a Common Council, and that one great Reason of their Overthrow by the *Romans,* was, their not *Consulting with, and Relying upon their Common Council.*[15] Again, Both *Beda* and *Mat. Westminster* tell us, That the *Britain*'s summoned a Synod, chose their Moderator, and expell'd the *Pelagian* Creed. All which supposes Popular Assemblies, with Power to order National Affairs.[16]

And indeed, the Learned Author of the *British* Councils gives some Hints to this Purpose, That they had a Common Council, and call'd it *Kyfr-y-then.*

The *Saxons* were not inferiour to the *Britain*'s in this Point, and Story furnisheth us with more and plainer Proofs. They brought this Liberty along with them, and it was not likely they should lose it, by transporting themselves into a Country where they also found it. *Tacitus* reports it to have been generally the *German*-Liberty; like unto the *Concio* of the *Athenians* and *Lacedaemonians.*[17]

They called their Free-men *Frilingi,* and These had Votes in the Making and Executing the General Laws of the Kingdom.

In *Ethelbert*'s Time, after the Monk *Austin*'s Insinuations had made his Followers a Part of the Government, the *Commune Concilium* was *tam Cleri quam Populi, as well Clergy as People.* In *Ina*'s Time, *Suasu & instituto Episcoporum, omnium Senatorum & natu majorum Sapientum populi;* Bishops, Lords, and Wise Men of the People. *Alfred* after him reform'd the former Laws, *Consulto sapientum,* by the Advice of the Sages of the Kingdom. Likewise Matters of Publick and General Charge, in Case of War, *&c.* we have granted in the Assembly, *Rege, Baronibus & Populo.* By the King, Barons and People.

15. Caesar, *Commentaries,* bk. 1, ch. 16; bk. 7, ch. 63; Dio, *Roman History,* bk. 77, ch. 12; and Tacitus, *Agricola,* ch. 12.

16. Bede, *Ecclesiastical History,* bk. I, ch. 17; and *Flowers of History* (entry for 404) notes the rise of Pelagianism, but Penn's specific reference to popular assemblies is unclear.

17. Tacitus, *Germany and Its Tribes,* chs. 28–45, esp. 28, 37.

And though the *Saxon* Word properly imports the Meeting of Wise Men, yet *All* that would come might be present, and interpose their Like or Dislike of the present Proposition: As that of *Ina, in magnâ servorum Dei frequentiâ.* Again, *Commune Concilium seniorum & populorum totius regni;* "The Common Council of the Elders, or Nobles, and People of the whole Kingdom.' The Council of *Winton,* Ann. 855. is said to be in the Presence of the Great Men, *aliorumque fidelium infinitâ multitudine;* "And an Infinite Multitude of other Faithful People"; which was nigh Four Hundred Years before the *Great Charter* was made.

My last Instance of the *Saxon* Ages shall be out of the *Glossary* of the learned *English* Knight, *H. Spelman: The* Saxon Witangemote *or Parliament* (saith he) *is a Convention of the* Princes, *as well* Bishops *as* Magistrates, *and the* Free People *of the Kingdom:* And that the said *Wittangemote* consulted of the common *Safety in Peace and War,* and for the Promotion of the common Good.[18]

William of *Normandy* chose rather *to rely upon the People's Consent, than his own Power to obtain the Kingdom.* He Swore to them to maintain their *old Laws and Priviledges;* they to him *Obedience* for his so Governing of them: For, as a certain Author hath it, *He bound himself to be Just, that he might be Great; and the People to submit to Justice, that they might be Free.* In his Laws, C. 55. "*We* by the *Common Council* of the whole Kingdom, *have granted the People's Lands to them in Inheritance, according to their Ancient Laws.*"

Matters of general Expence upon the whole Body of the People, were settled by this Great Council, especially in the *Charge of Arms* imposed upon the Subject. The Law saith it to have been done by the *Commune Concilium of the Kingdom.*

So *W. Rufus* and *Henry* the First, were received *by the common Consent of the People.* And *Stephen*'s Words were *Ego* Stephanus, *Dei gratia, Assensu Cleri & Populi in Regno Angliae* Electus, &c. "I *Stephen,* by the Grace of God, and Consent of the Clergy and People, Chosen *King of England,* &c." So King *John* was chosen, *Tam Cleri quan Populi unanimi consensu & favore,* "By the Favour and Unanimous *Consent* of the Clergy and People": And his Queen is said to have been crown'd *de communi consensu & concordi voluntate Archiepiscoporum, Comitum, Baronum, Cleri & Populi totius Regni,* i.e. "by the common Assent and unanimous Good-will of the *Arch-Bishops, Bishops, Counts, Bar-*

18. Sir Henry Spelman, *Glossarium archaiologicum* (London, 1664), p. 261.

ons, Clergy and People of the whole Kingdom." King *Edw.* I. also desired Money of the *commune Concilium* or Parliament, "as you have given in my Time, and that of my Progenitors, Kings, *&c.*"

All which shows, that it was Antecedent to the *Great Charter,* not the Rights therein repeated and confirmed, but the Act it self.

And King *John*'s Resignation of the Crown to the Pope, being question'd upon some Occasion in *Edward* III. Time, it was agreed upon, that he had *no Power to do it, without the Consent of the Dukes, Prelates, Barons, and Commons:*

And as Paradoxal as any may please to think it, 'tis the great Interest of a Prince, that the People should have a *Share* in the making of their own Laws; where 'tis otherwise, they are no Kings of Free-men, but Slaves, and those their Enemies for making them so. *Leges nullâ aliâ causâ nos tenent, quam quod judicio populi receptae sunt;* "The Laws (saith *Ulpian*) do therefore oblige the People, because they are allowed of by their Judgment."[19] And *Gratian,* in Dec. distinct. 4. *Tum demum humanae leges habent vim suam, cum fuerint non modo institutae, sed etiam firmatae Approbatione Communitatis:* "It is then (*saith he*) that Humane Laws have their due Force, when they shall not only be devised, but confirm'd by the Approbation of the People."[20]

I. It makes Men Diligent, and increaseth *Trade,* which advances the Revenue: For where Men are not Free, they will never seek to improve, because they are not sure of what they have, and less of what they get.

II. It frees the Prince from the *Jealousie* and Hate of his People; and consequently, the Troubles and Danger that follow; and makes his *Province* easie and safe.

III. If any Inconvenience attends the Execution of any Law, the Prince is not to be blam'd: It is their own Fault that made it.

I shall now proceed to the *Third Fundamental,* and by plain Evidence prove it to have been a Material Part of the Government, before the *Great Charter* was Enacted.

19. Ulpian, Roman jurist (d. 228).
20. Gratian, *Decretum Gratiani* (ca. 1140).

III. *The People have an Influence upon, and a Great Share in the Judicatory Power,* &c.

That it was a *Brittish* Custom, I will not affirm, but have some Reason to suppose: For if the *Saxons* had brought it with them, they would also have left it behind them, and in all Likelihood there would have been some Footsteps in *Saxony* of such a Law or Custom, which we find not. I will not enter the Lists with any about this: This shall suffice me, that we find it early among the *Saxons* in this Country, and if they, a Free People in their own Country, settling themselves here as a New Planted Colony, did supply what was defective in their own Government, or add some New Freedom to themselves, as all Planters are wont to do; which are as those First and Corner Stones, their Posterity, with all Care and Skill, are to build upon, *That,* it self, will serve my Turn to prove it a *Fundamental:* That is, such a *First Principle* in our *English* Government, by the Agreement of the People, as ought not to be Violated. I would not be understood of the Number, but of the Way of Tryal: I mean, *That Men were not to be Condemned but by the Votes of the Freemen.*

N. Bacon thinks that in ruder Times the Multitude tryed all among themselves; and fancies it came from the *Grecians,* who determin'd Controversies by the Suffrage of 34, or the major Part of them.[21]

Be it as it will, *Juries* the *Saxons* had; for in the Laws of King *Etheldred,* about Three Hundred Years before the Entrance of the *Norman* Duke, we find Enacted, *in singulis Centuriis,* &c. thus English'd, *In every Hundred let there be a Court, and let Twelve Ancient* Freemen, *together with the Lord of the Hundred, be Sworn, that they will not Condemn the Innocent, or Acquit the Guilty.* And so strict were they of those Ages, in observing this Fundamental Way of Judicature, that *Alfred* put one of his Judges to *Death,* for passing Sentence upon a Verdict (corruptly obtain'd) upon the Votes of the Jurors, *Three of Twelve* being in the Negative. *If the Number was so Sacred, What was the Constitution it self?*

The very same King *Executed* another of his *Judges,* for passing Sentence of *Death upon an Ignoramus* return'd by the Jury; and a third, for Condemning a Man upon an Inquest taken *ex officio,* when as the Delinquent had not put himself upon their Trial. More of his Justice might be mention'd even in this very Case.

21. Nathaniel Bacon, *An historicall discourse on the unity of the government of England: The first part* (London, 1647), ch. 4.

There was also a Law made in the Time of *Ætheldred,* when the *Brittains* and *Saxons* began to grow tame to each other, and intercommon amicably, that faith, *Let there be Twelve Men of Understanding,* &c. *Six* English, *and Six* Welsh, *and let them deal Justice, both to* English *and* Welsh.

Also in those simple Times, if a Crime extended but to some *Shameful Punishment, as Pillory or Whipping* (the last whereof, as usual as it has been with us, was inflicted only upon their Bondmen) the Penance might be reduc'd to a *Ransom,* according to the Nature of the Fault; but it must be Assest in the Presence of the Judge, and by the *Twelve,* that is, the Jury of *Frilingi,* or Freemen.

Hitherto Stories tell us of *Trials by Juries,* and those to have consisted, in General Terms, of *Freemen:* But *Per Pares,* or by *Equals,* came after, occasion'd by the considerable *Saxons,* neglecting that Service, and leaving it to the inferiour People, who lost the Bench, *Their Ancient Right,* because they were not thought Company for a Judge or Sheriff: And also from the *Growing Pride of the Danes,* who slighted such a *Rural Judicature,* and despised the Fellowship of the mean *Saxon Freemen* in publick Service. The Wise *Saxon* King perceiving this, and the dangerous Consequence of submitting the *Lives* and *Liberties* of the *Inferiour* (but not less useful People) *to the Dictates of any such Haughty Humour;* and on the other Hand, of subjecting the *Nobler Sort to the Suffrage of the Inferiour Rank,* did, with the Advice of his *Wittangemote,* or *Parliament,* provide a third Way, more Equal and Grateful, and by Agreement with *Gunthurn* the *Dane,* settled the *Law of Peers,* or *Equals;* which is the *Envy of Nations,* but the *Famous Priviledge of our English People:* One of those *Three Pillars* the Fabrick of this Ancient and *Free Government* stands upon.

This *Benefit* gets Strength by Time, and is receiv'd by the *Norman-Duke* and his Successors; and not only confirm'd in the Lump of other Priviledges, but in one Notable Case, for all, which might be brought to prove, that the *Fundamental Priviledges,* mentioned in the *Great Charter,* 9 of *Hen.* 3. were *Before it.* The Story is more at large deliver'd by our Learned *Selden:*[22] But thus, *William* having given his Half Brother *Odo,* a large Territory in *Kent,* with the Earldom, and he taking Advantage at the *King's being displeased with the Archbishop of* Canterbury, to possess himself of some of the Lands of that See, *Landfrank,* that succeeded the Archbishop, inform'd hereof, petition'd the King for Justice, *secundum legem terrae,* according to the Law of the Land: Upon which the

22. John Selden (1584–1654), English jurist and scholar.

King summon'd a *County-Court,* where the Debate lasted three Days, before the *Freemen of Kent,* in the Presence of *Lords and Bishops,* and others Skilful in the Law, and the Judgment passed for the Archbishop, *Upon the Votes of the Freemen.*

By all which it is (I hope) sufficiently and inoffensively manifested, that these three Principles, *viz.*

1. *That* English *Men have the alone Right of Possession and Disposition of what is theirs.*

2. *That they are Parties to the Laws of their Country, for the Maintenance thereof.*

3. *That they have an Influence upon, and a real Share in the Judicatory Power, that applys those Laws,* have been the *Ancient Rights* of the Kingdom, and common *Basis* of the Government: That which Kings, under all Revolutions have sworn to maintain, and History affords us so many Presidents to confirm. So that the *Great Charter* made in the 9th of *Henry* the IIId. was not the *Nativity,* but *Restoration* of Ancient *Priviledges* from Abuses. No Grant of *New Rights,* but a *New* Grant, or *Confirmation* rather, of *Ancient Laws and Liberties,* violated by King *John,* and restored by his Successor, at the Expence of a long and bloody War; which shewed them as resolute to keep, as their Ancestors had been careful to make those excellent Laws.

And so I am come to the *Great Charter,* which is comprehensive of what I have already been discoursing, and which I shall briefly touch upon, with those successive *Statutes* that have been made in Honour and Preservation of it.

I shall rehearse so much of it as falls within the Consideration of the foregoing Matter (which is a great deal in a little) with something of the Formality of *Grant* and *Curse;* that this Age may see, with what *Reverence* and *Circumspection* our *Ancestors* governed themselves in confirming and preserving of it.

"*Henry by the Grace of God King of* England, &c. *To all* Archbishops, Earls, Barons, Sheriffs, Provosts, Officers, *unto all* Bailiffs, *and our faithful* Subjects, *who shall see this present* Charter, *Greeting,* Know ye, that we, unto the *Honour* of Almighty God, and for the *Salvation* of the Souls of our Progenitors, and our Successors, Kings of *England,* to the Advancement of Holy Church, and Amendment of our Realm, of our *meer and free Will* have given and granted to all Archbishops, *&c.* and to all *Freemen* of this our Realm, these Liberties underwritten, to be holden and kept in this our Realm of *England* for evermore."

Tho' in Honour to the King, it is said to be out of his *meer and free Will,* as if it were his meer Favour, yet the Qualification of the Persons, he is said to grant the ensuing Liberties to, shews, that they are Terms of Formality, *viz. To all Freemen of this Realm.* Which supposes there were *Freemen* before this Grant; and that Character also implies they must have had *Laws* and *Liberties:* Consequently, this was not an Infranchising of them, but a *confirming* to Freemen their just Privileges they had before. The Words of the Charter are these:

> A *Freeman* shall not be *Amerced* for a small Fault, but *after the Quantity of the Fault,* and for a great Fault, after the Manner thereof, saving to him his *Contenements or Freehold:* And a *Merchant* likewise shall be amerced, saving to him his Merchandize; and none of the said Amercements shall be assessed, but by the Oath of good and honest Men of the Vicinage.
>
> No *Freeman* shall be taken or *imprison'd, nor be disseized of his Freehold or Liberties,* or free Customs, or be outlaw'd or exil'd, or any other Ways destroy'd; nor we shall not pass upon him, nor condemn him, but by *lawful Judgment of his* Peers, *or by the Law of the Land.* We shall sell to no Man, we shall deny or defer to no Man. either Justice or Right.[23]

I stand amazed, how any Man can have the Confidence to say, *These Privileges were extorted by the Barons Wars,* when the King declares, that what he did herein, was done *freely:* Or that they were new Privileges, when the very Tenour of the Word proves the contrary: For *Freehold, Liberties,* or *Free Customs,* are by the Charter it self supposed to be in the Possession of the Freemen at the making and publishing thereof. For observe, *No Freeman shall be taken or imprison'd:* Then he was free: This Liberty is his Right. Again, *No Freeman shall be disseised of his Freehold, Liberties, or free Customs.* Then certainly he was in Possession of them: And that great Doctor in the Laws of *England,* Chief Justice *Cook,* in his Proem to the 2d Part of his *Institutes,* tells us, that

23. 9 Henry III c. 14, 29. This is the standard format for notation of English legislation. For a comprehensive, chronological outline of English legislation, see *The statutes of the realm . . . From original records and authentic manuscripts* in "Notes on Texts and Annotations," above.

these Laws and Liberties were gathered and observed, amongst others, in an intire Volume, by King Edward *the Confessor;* confirmed by *William,* sirnamed the *Conqueror;* which were afterwards ratify'd by *Henry the First;* enlarged by *Henry the Second,* in his Constitutions at *Clarendon;* and after much Contest, and Blood spilt, between King *John* and the *Barons* concerning them, were solemnly established at *Running-Mead* by *Stanes:* And lastly, brought to their former Station, and publish'd by this King *Henry the Third,* in the 9th Year of his Reign.

And though evil Counsellors would have provok'd him to void his Father's Act and his own, as if the first had been the Effect of *Force,* the other of *Non-Age;* yet it so pleased Almighty God, who hath ever been propitious to this ungrateful Island, that in the 20th Year of his Reign, he did confirm and compleat this *Charter,* for a perpetual Establishment of Liberty to all *Free-born Englishmen,* and their Heirs for ever: Ordaining, *Quod contravenientes per dominum Regem, cum convicti fuerint, graviter puniantur, i.e.* "That whosoever should act any thing contrary to these Laws, upon Conviction, should be grievously punished" by our Lord the King. And in the 22d Year of his Reign, it was confirmed by the Statute of *Marleb,* Chap. 5. And so venerable an Esteem have our Ancestors had for this *Great Charter,* and so indispensibly necessary have they thought it to their own and Posterities Felicity, that it hath been above Thirty Times ratified and commanded, under great Penalties, to be put in Execution.

Here are the three Fundamentals comprehended and express'd, to have been the Rights and Privileges of *Englishmen.*

I. Ownership, *consisting of Liberty and Property. In that it supposes* Englishmen *to be* free, *there's* Liberty: *Next, that they have* Freeholds, *there's* Property.

II. *That they have the* Voting of their own Laws: *For that was an ancient free Custom, as I have already prov'd, and all such Customs are expresly confirmed by this* Great Charter: *Besides, the People help'd to make it.*

III. *An Influence upon, and a real* Share in the Judicatory Power, *in the Execution and Application thereof.*

This is a substantial Part, thrice provided for in those sixteen Lines of the Great Charter before rehears'd: 1. *That no Amercement shall be assessed, but by Oath of* Good and Honest Men of the Vicinage. 2. *Nor we shall not pass upon him, nor condemn him, but by* lawful Judgment of his Peers. 3. *Or by the* Law of the Land: Which is *Synonymous,* or a Saying of equal Signification with lawful

Judgment of Peers: For *Law of the Land,* and *lawful Judgment of Peers,* are the *Proprium quarto modo,* or Essential Qualities of these Chapters of our *Great Charter;* being communicable *Omni, soli & semper,* to all and every Clause thereof alike.

Chief Justice *Cook* well observes, in his Second Institutes, that *per Legem Terrae;* or by the Law of the Land, imports no more than a *Tryal by Process, and Writ originally at Common Law;* which cannot be without the lawful Judgment of *Equals,* or a *Common Jury:* Therefore *per Legale Judicium Parium, by* the lawful Judgment of Peers, and *per Legem Terrae,* by the Law of the Land, plainly signify the same Privilege to the People. So that it is the Judgment of the *Freemen* of *England,* which gives the *Cast,* and turns the *Scale* in English Justice.[24]

These being so evidently prov'd by long Use, and several Laws, to have been the *First Principles* or *Fundamentals* of the *English* Free Government, I take Leave to propose this Question: *May the Free People of* England *be justly disseised of all, or any of these Fundamentals without their Consent Collectively?*

Answ. With Submission, I conceive, *Not;* for which I shall produce, first my *Reasons,* then *Authorities.*

I. Through the *British, Saxon,* and *Norman* Times, the People of this Island have been reputed and call'd *Freemen* by *Kings, Parliaments, Records* and *Histories:* And as a *Son* supposes a *Father,* so *Freemen* suppose *Freedom.* This Qualification imports an Absolute Right: Such a Right as none has Right to Disseise or Dispossess an Englishman of: Therefore an Unalterable Fundamental Part of the Government.

II. It can never be thought, that they intrusted any *Representatives* with these Capital Privileges, farther than to use their best Skill to secure and maintain them. They never so delegated or impower'd any Men, that *de jure,* they could deprive them of that Qualification? And *a Facto ad Jus non valet Argumentum:*[25] For the Question is not, *What* May *be done?* but *what* Ought *to be done?* Overseers and Stewards are impower'd, not to *Alienate,* but preserve and improve other Men's Inheritances. *No Owners* deliver their Ship and Goods into any Man's Hands to give them away, or run upon a Rock; neither do they consign their Affairs to Agents or Factors without Limitation.

24. Coke, *Second part of the Institutes,* ch. 29.

25. An argument moving from the deed to the law is not valid.

All *Trusts* suppose such a Fundamental Right in them that give them, and for whom the Trusts are, as is altogether indissolvable by the Trustees. The Trust is the Liberty and Property of the People; the Limitation is, that it should not be invaded, but inviolably preserved, according to the Law of the Land.

III. If *Salus Populi* be *Suprema Lex,* the Safety of the People the highest Law, as say several of our Ancient Famous Lawyers and Law-Books; then since the aforesaid Rights are as the *Sinews* that hold together this *Free Body Politick,* it follows, they are at least a Part of the Supreme Law; and therefore ought to be a Rule and Limit to all subsequent Legislation.

IV. The Estate goes before the Steward, the Foundation before the House, People before their Representatives, and the Creator before the Creature. The Steward lives by preserving the Estate; the House stands by Reason of it's Foundation; the Representative depends upon the People, as the Creature subsists by the Power of it's Creator.

Every *Representative* may be call'd, the *Creature of the People,* because the People make them, and to them they owe their Being. Here is no Transessentiating or Transubstantiating of Being, from People to Representative, no more than there is an absolute Transferring of a Title in a *Letter of Attorney.*

The very Term *Representative* is enough to the contrary; Wherefore as the House cannot stand without its Foundation, nor the Creature subsist without it's Creator; so can there be *no Representative without a People,* nor that People *Free,* which all along is intended (as inherent to, and inseparable from the *English* People) *without Freedom;* nor can there be any *Freedom* without something be *Fundamental.*

In short, I would fain know of any Man how the Branches can cut up the Root of the Tree that bears them? How any Representative, that has not only a meer *Trust to preserve Fundamentals,* the People's Inheritance; but that is a Representative that makes Laws, by Virtue of this Fundamental Law, *viz. that the People have a Power in Legislation* (the 2d Principle prov'd by me) can have a Right to remove or destroy that Fundamental? The Fundamental makes the People Free, this Free People makes a Representative; Can this Creature unqualify it's Creator? What Spring ever rose higher than it's Head? The Representative is at best but a true Copy, an Exemplification; the Free People are the Original, not cancellable by a Transcript: And if that Fundamental which gives to the People a Power of *Legislation,* be not nullable by that Representative, because it makes them what they are; much less can that Representative disseise Men of their Liberty and Property, the first Great Fundamental, that is, *Parent* of this Other; and which intitles to a Share in making Laws for the preserving of the first Inviolable.

Nor is the Third Fundamental other than the necessary Production of the two First, to intercept *Arbitrary Designs,* and make *Power Legal:* For where the People have not a *Share in Judgment,* that is, in the Application, as well as making of the Law, the other two are imperfect; open to daily Invasion, should it be our Infelicity ever to have a violent Prince. For as Property is every Day expos'd, where those that have it are destitute of Power to hedge it about by *Law-making;* so those that have both, if they have not a Share in the Application of the Law, how easily is that Hedge broken down?

And indeed, as it is a most just and necessary, as well as ancient and honourable Custom, so it is the *Prince*'s Interest: For still the People are concerned in the Inconveniences with him, and he is freed from the Temptation of doing arbitrary Things, and their Importunities, that might else have some Pretence for such Addresses, as well as from the Mischiefs that might ensue such Actions. It might be enough to say, that there are above *Fifty Statutes* now in Print, besides it's venerable Antiquity, that warrant and confirm this *Legale Judicium Parium suorum,* or the Tryal of *English Men* by their Equals.

But I shall hint at a few Instances: The first is, The *Earl of Lancaster,* in the 14th of *Edw.* II. adjudged to dye without lawful Tryal of his Peers: And afterwards *Henry,* Earl of *Lancaster* his Brother, was restored. The Reasons given were two: 1. Because the said *Thomas* was *not Arraign'd and put to Answer.* 2. That he was *put to Death without Answer,* or *Lawful Judgment of his Peers.* The like Proceedings were in the Case of *John* of *Gaunt,* p. 39. *Coram Rege* And in the *Earl* of *Arundels* Case. *Rot. Parl.* 4. *Edw.* 3. N 13. Also in Sir *John Alee's* Case 4. *Edw.* III. N. 2. Such was the Destruction committed on the Lord *Hastings* in the Tower of *London,* by *Richard* the III. But above all, the Attainder of *Thomas Cromwel, Earl* of *Essex,* who was attainted of high Treason, as appears, *Rot. Parl.* 32. *Hen.* 8. of which, saith Chief Justice *Cook,* as I remember, *Let Oblivion take away the Memory of so foul a Fact, if it can; if not, however, let Silence cover it.*

'Tis true, there was a Statute obtained in the 11th of *Henry* the 7th, in Defiance of the *Great Charter,* which authorized several Exactions, contrary to the free Customs of this Realm: Particularly in the Case of *Juries,* both *Assessing* and *Punishing,* by *Justices* of *Assize,* and of the Peace, without the Fining and Presentment of *Twelve Free-Men. Empson* and *Dudley* were the great Actors of those Oppressions; but they were *Hang'd* for their Pains, and that illegal Statute repealed in the first of *Henry* the 8*th* Ch. 6.

The Consequence is plain; that Fundamentals give Rule to *Acts of Parliament,* else why was the Statute of the 8*th Edw.* 4. Ch. 2. Of *Liveries* and *Information,* by the Discretion of the Judges, to stand as an *Original,* and this of the 11*th* of *Henry* the 7*th,* repealed as *Illegal?* For, therefore any Thing is unlawful, because it transgresseth a Law. But what Law can an *Act of Parliament* transgress, but that which is Fundamental? Therefore *Tryal* by *Juries,* or lawful Judgment of *Equals,* is by *Acts of Parliament* confest to be a *Fundamental* Part of our Government. And because *Chief Justice Cook* is so generally esteem'd an *Oracle of the Law,* I shall in it's proper Place present you with his Judgment upon the whole Matter.

V. These Fundamentals are *unalterable* by a *Representative,* which were the Result and Agreement of *English Free-Men,* collectively, the Ancienter Times not being acquainted with Representatives: For then the *Free-Men* met in their own Persons. In all the *Saxon* Story we find no Mention of any such Thing; for it was the *King, Lords and Free-Men: The Elders* and *People.* And at the Council of *Winton,* in 855, is reported to have been present, *The great Men of the Kingdom, and an* Infinite Multitude *of other faithful People.* Also *that,* of King *Ina, the Common Council of the Elders and People of the whole Kingdom:* That is, the most or generality of the Free-Men of the Kingdom; for all might come that pleased. It is not to be doubted but this continued after the *Norman* Times, and that at *Running-Mead,* by *Stanes,* the *Free-Men* of *England* were Personally present at the *Confirmation* of that *great Charter,* in the Reign of *King John.* But as the Ages grew more Humane, and free with Respect to *Villains* and *Retainers,* and that the *Number of Free-Men* encreased, there was a *Necessity* for a *Representative;* especially, since Fundamentals were long ago agreed upon, and those *Capital Privileges* put out of the Reach and Power of a little Number of Men to endanger. And so careful were the *Representatives* of the People, in the Time of *Edward the Third,* of suffering their *Liberties* and *Free Customs* to be infring'd, that *in Matters of extraordinary Weight, they would not determine, till they had first returned to, and conferred with their several Counties or Boroughs that delegated them. Thus the* Parl. Rolls of his Time.

Several Authorities *in Confirmation of the* Reasons *before mentioned.*

So indubitably are these *Fundamentals,* the *People's Right,* and so necessary to be preserved, that *Kings have* successively known no other *Safe* or *Legal Passage to their Crown and Dignity, than their Solemn Obligation inviolably to maintain them.* "So *Sacred* were they reputed in the Days of *Henry* the III. That not to continue or confirm them, was to affront God, *and to damn the* Souls *of his Progenitors and Successors; and to depress the Church, and deprave the Realm:* That *the great Charter comprehensive of them, should be allowed as the* Common Law of the Land, *by all Officers of Justice, that is, the* Lawful Inheritance *of all Commoners:* That *all Statute-Laws or Judgments whatsoever, made in Opposition thereunto, should be null and void:* That *all the Ministers of State, and Officers of the Realm, should constantly be sworn to the Observation thereof.*" And so deeply did after Parliaments reverence it, and so careful were they to preserve it, that they both confirm'd it by *Thirty two several Acts,* and enacted *Copies* to be taken and lodged in each Cathedral of the Realm, to be read four Times a Year publickly before the People: As if they would have them more obliged to their *Ancestors,* for Redeeming and Transmitting those Privileges, than for *begetting* them. And that *twice every Year,* the Bishops *apparelled in their* Pontificials, *with Tapers burning,* and other Solemnities, *should pronounce the greater Excommunication against the Infringers of the* Great Charter, *though it were but in Word or Counsel;* for so saith the Statute. I shall, for farther Satisfaction, repeat the *Excommunication* or *Curse,* pronounced both in the Days of *Henry the Third* and *Edward the First.*

The Sentence of the Curse given by the Bishops, with the King's Consent against the Breakers of the Great Charter.

"In the Year of our Lord 1253, the third Day of *May,* in the great Hall of the King at *Westminster,* in the Presence, and by the Consent of the Lord *Henry,* by the Grace of God King of *England,* and the Lord *Richard,* Earl of *Cornwall,* his Brother; *Roger Bigot,* Earl of *Norfolk,* Marshal of *England; Humphrey,* Earl of *Oxford; John,* Earl *Warren;* and other Estates of the Realm of *England;* We *Boniface,* by the Mercy of God, Arch-Bishop of *Canterbury,* Primate of *England, F.* of *London, H.* of *Ely, S.* of *Worcester, E.* of *Lincoln, W.* of *Norwich, P.* of *Hereford, W.* of *Salisbury, W.* of *Durham, R.* of *Excester, M.* of *Carlile, W.*

of *Bath, A.* of *Rochester, T.* of St. *Davids,* Bishops, apparelled in Pontificials, with Tapers burning, against the Breakers of the Churches Liberties, and of the Liberties and other Customs of this Realm of *England,* and namely these which are contained in the Charter of the common Liberties of *England,* and Charter of the *Forest,* have denounced Sentence of Excommunication in this Form: By the Authority of Almighty God, the Father, the Son, and the Holy Ghost, *&c.* of the blessed Apostles *Peter* and *Paul,* and of all Apostles, and of all Martyrs, of blessed *Edward* King of *England,* and of all the Saints of Heaven; We excommunicate and accurse, and from the Benefit of our Holy Mother, the Church, we sequester, all those that hereafter willingly and maliciously deprive or spoil the Church of her Right; and all those that by any Craft or Willingness, do violate, break, diminish, or change the Churches Liberties, and Free-Customs contained in the Charters of the common Liberties, and of the *Forest,* granted by our Lord the King, to Arch-Bishops, Bishops, and other Prelates of *England,* and likewise to the Earls, Knights, and other Free-Holders of the Realm; and all that secretly and openly, by Deed, Word, or Counsel do make Statutes, or observe them being made, and that bring in Customs, to keep them, when they be brought in, against the said Liberties, or any of them, and all those that shall presume to judge against them; and all and every such Person before mentioned, that wittingly shall commit any Thing of the Premises, let them well know, that they incurr the aforesaid Sentence, *ipso Facto.*"

The Sentence of the CLERGY, against the Breakers of the ARTICLES before-mentioned.

IN THE *Name of the Father, the Son, and the Holy Ghost,* Amen. *Whereas our Soveraign Lord the King, to the Honour of God, and of Holy Church, and for the common Profit of the Realm, hath granted for him, and his Heirs for ever, these Articles above-written,* Robert, *Archbishop of* Canterbury, *Primate of all* England, *Admonished all his Province once, twice and thrice, because that Shortness will not suffer so much Delay, as to give Knowledge to all the People of* England, *of these Presents in Writing: We therefore enjoyn all Persons, of what Estate soever they be, that they, and every of them, as much as in them is, shall uphold and maintain these Articles granted by our Soveraign Lord the King, in all Points: And all those that in any Point do resist or break, or in any Manner hereafter Procure, Counsel, or in any wise Assent to Resist or Break those Ordinances, or go about it, by Word or Deed, openly or privily, by any Manner of Pretence or Colour; We, the aforesaid Archbishops, by our Authority in this Writing expressed, do Excommunicate and Accurse, and from the Body of our Lord Jesus Christ, and from all the Company of Heaven, and from all the Sacraments of Holy Church do sequester and exclude.*

We may here see, that in the obscurest Times of *Popery,* they were not left without a Sense of Justice, and a Care of Freedom; and that even *Papists,* whom many think no Friends to Liberty and Property, under dreadful Penalties, enjoyn an inviolable Observance of this *Great Charter,* by which they are confirmed. And though I am no *Roman Catholick,* and as little value their other *Curses* pronounc'd upon *Religious Dissenters,* yet I declare ingeniously, I would not, for the World, incur this *Curse,* as every Man *deservedly doth,* that offers Violence to the Fundamental Freedoms thereby repeated and confirmed. And that any *Church,* or *Church Officers* in our Age, should have so little Reverence to *Law, Excommunication or Curse,* as to be the Men that either Vote or countenance such Severities, as bid Defiance to the *Curse,* and tear this *Memorable Charter* in Pieces, by Disseizing *Freemen* of *England* of their *Freeholds, Liberties and Properties,* without *Juries,* or meerly for the inoffensive Exercise of their Conscience to God in Matters of Religion, *is a Civil Sort of Sacrilege.*

I know it is usually objected, *That a great Part of the Charter is spent on the Behalf of the* Roman Church, *and other Things, now abolish'd; and if one Part of the Great Charter may be repeal'd, or invalidated, why not the other?*

But to this I answer, That the True Fundamentals in the *Charter,* are not the less firm or forceable, or inviolable for that; because they do not stand upon that *Act,* though it was in Honour of them, but the *Ancient and Primitive Institution of the Kingdom.* If the *Petition of Right* were repeal'd, the *Great Charter* were nevertheless in Force, it not being the Original Establishment, but a Declaration and Confirmation of that Establishment.[26] But those Things that are abrogable, or abrogated in the *Great Charter,* were never a Part of the Funda-

26. The Petition of Right was addressed by Parliament to Charles II in 1628. See J. P. Kenyon, *Stuart Constitution: Documents and Commentary,* 2d ed. (Cambridge, 1986), doc. 24, pp. 68–71.

mentals, but hedg'd in by the *Clergy,* and allowed by the *Barons* upon present Emergency. Besides, that which I have hitherto maintained to be the Common and Fundamental Law of the Land, is so reputed, and farther ratified, by the *Petition of Right,* 3 *Car.* 1. which was long since the *Church of Rome* lost her Share in the *Great Charter.* Nor did it relate to Matters of Faith and Worship, but Temporalities only; the Civil Interest or Propriety of the Church. But with what Pretence to Mercy or Justice, can the *Protestant Church* retain the *English Part* of the Charter, without conforming to *Rome,* and yet now cancel the *English Part* it self to every *Free-born Englishman* that will not conform to her? But no more of this at this Time; only give me Leave to remind a Sort of Active Men in our Times, that the cruel Infringers of the People's Liberties, and Violaters of these Noble Laws, did not escape with bare *Excommunications* and *Curses;* for such was the Venerable Esteem our Ancestors had for these Great Privileges, and deep Sollicitude to preserve them from the Defacings of Time, or Usurpation of Power, that King *Alfred* executed *Forty Judges* for warping from the Ancient Laws of the Realm. *Hubert de Burgo,* Chief Justice of *England,* in the Time of *Edw.* 1. was sentenced by his Peers in open Parliament, for advising the King *against the Great Charter.* Thus the *Speneers,* both Father and Son, for their *Arbitrary Rule* and *Evil Counsel* to *Edw.* 2. were exiled the Realm. No better Success had the Actions of *Tresilian* and *Belknap:* And as for *Empson* and *Dudley,* though Persons of Quality, in the Time of King *Henry* the Seventh, the most ignominious Death of our Country, such as belongs to *Theft* and *Murder,* was hardly Satisfaction enough to the Kingdom, for their *Uncharterall* Proceeding. I shall chuse to deliver it in the Words of Chief Justice *Cook,* a Man, whose Learning in Law hath, not without Reason, obtained him a Venerable Character of our *English* Nation.

There was (saith he) *an Act of Parliament made in the 11th Year of King* Henry *the Seventh, which had a Fair Flattering Preamble, pretending to avoid divers Mischiefs, which were* First, *To the high Displeasure of Almighty God.* Secondly, *The Great Let of the Common Law.* And, Thirdly, *The Great Let of the Wealth of this Land. And the Purven of that Act tended, in the Execution, contrary,* Ex Diametro, *viz. To the high Displeasure of Almighty God, and the Great Let, nay, the utter Subversion of the Common Law, and the Great Let of the Wealth of this Land,* as hereafter shall appear; the Substance of which Act follows in these Words.

THAT from henceforth, as well Justices of Assize, as Justices of the Peace, in every County, upon Information for the King, before them made, without any Finding or Presenting by Twelve Men, shall have full Power and Authority, by their Discretion, to hear and determine all Offences, as Riots, unlawful Assemblies, &c. *committed and done against Act or Statute made, and not repeal'd,* &c.

By Pretext of this Law, Empson *and* Dudley *did commit upon the Subject insufferable Pressure and Oppressions; and therefore this Statute was justly, soon after the Decease of* Hen. 7. *repealed at the next Parliament, by the Statute of* 1 Hen. 8. chap. 6.

A good Caveat, says he, *to Parliaments, to leave all Causes to be measur'd by the Golden and Strait Metwand of the Law, and not to the uncertain and crooked Cord of Discretion.* He goes on,

It is almost incredible to foresee, when any Maxim, or Fundamental Law of this Realm is altered (as elsewhere hath been observed) what dangerous Inconveniences do follow: Which most expresly appears by this Most Unjust and Strange Act *of the* 11*th of* Hen. 7. *For hereby not only* Empson *and* Dudley *themselves, but such Justices of Peace (Corrupt Men) as they caused to be authorized, committed most Grievous and Heavy Oppressions and Exactions: Grinding the Faces of the Poor Subjects by Penal Laws (be they never so obsolete or unfit for the Time) by Information only, without any Presentment or Trial by Jury,* Being the Ancient Birthright of the Subject; *but to hear and determine the same by their Discretions; inflicting such Penalty as the Statutes, not repealed, imposed. These, and other like Oppressions and Exactions, by the Means of* Empson *and* Dudley, *and their Instruments, brought infinite Treasure to the King's Coffers, whereof the King himself, at the End,* with Great Grief and Compunction Repented, *as in another Place we have observed.*

This Statute of the 11*th of* Hen. 7. *we have recited, and shewed the just Inconveniences thereof; to the End that the like should* Never *hereafter be attempted in any Court of Parliament; and that others might avoid the Fearful End of those two Time-Servers,* Empson *and* Dudley, Qui eorum vestigiis insistant, exitus perhorrescant. *Thus much Chief Justice* Cook.[27]

27. Sir Edward Coke, *Fourth part of the Institutes* (London, 1644), ch. 1. Edmund Dudley and Richard Empson served Henry VII and were executed by Henry VIII.

I am sure, there is nothing I have offer'd in Defence of *English* Law-Doctrine, that riseth higher than the Judgment and Language of this Great Man, the Preservation and Publication of whose Labours, became the Care of a Great Parliament. And it is said of no *inconsiderable Lawyer,* that he should thus express himself in our Occasion, *viz. The Laws of* England *were never the Dictates of any Conqueror's Sword, or the Placita of any King of this Nation; or,* (saith he) *to speak impartially and freely, the Results of any Parliament that ever sat in this Land.*

Thus much for the Nature of *English Rights,* and the Reason and Justice for their inviolable Maintenance. I shall now offer some more General Considerations for the Preservation of Property, and therein hint at some of those Mischiefs that follow spoiling it, for Conscience sake, both to Prince and People.

I. The Reason of the Alteration of the Law, ought to be the Discommodity of continuing it; but there can never be so much as the least Inconveniency in continuing *That of Liberty and Property;* therefore there can be no just Ground for infringing, much less abrogating the Laws that secure them.

II. No Man in *England* is born Slave to another; neither hath One Right to inherit the Sweat of the Others Brow, or Reap the Benefit of his Labour, but by Consent; therefore no Man should be deprived of his Property, unless he injure another Man's, and then by Legal Judgment.

III. But certainly nothing is more unreasonable, than to sacrifice the Liberty and Property of any Man (being his Natural and Civil Rights) for *Religion,* where he is not found breaking any Law relating to Natural and Civil Things. *Religion,* under any Modification, is no Part of the Old *English* Government. *Honestè vivere, Alterum non laedere, jus suum cuique tribuere,* are enough to entitle every Native to *English* Privileges.[28] A Man may be a very good *Englishman,* and yet a very indifferent *Churchman.* Nigh Three Hundred Years before *Austin* set his Foot on *English* Ground, had the Inhabitants of this Island a *Free Government.*[29] It is want of distinguishing between it and the Modes of Religion, which fills every clamorous Mouth with such impertinent Cries as this, *Why do not you submit to the Government?* As if the *English* Civil Government came in with *Luther,* or were to go out with *Calvin.* What Prejudice is it for a

28. See note 8.

29. Augustine of Canterbury (d. ca. 605), Italian missionary and first archbishop of Canterbury.

Popish Landlord, to have a *Protestant Tenant;* or a *Presbyterian Tenant,* to have an *Episcopalian Landlord?* Certainly, the *Civil Affairs* of all Governments in the World, may be peaceably transacted under the different *Liveries,* or *Trims of Religion,* where Civil Rights are inviolably observ'd.

Nor is there any Interest so inconsistent with Peace and Unity, as *That* which dare not solely rely upon the Power of Perswasion, but affects Superiority, and seeks after an Earthly Crown. This is not to act the Christian, but the *Caesar;* not to promote Property, but Party, and make a Nation Drudges to a Sect.

Be it known to such narrow Spirits, we are a Free People by the Creation of God, the Redemption of Christ, and careful Provision of our (never to be forgotten) Honourable Ancestors: So that our Claim to these *English* Privileges rising higher than the Date of Protestancy, can never justly be invalidated for Non-conformity to any Form of it. This were to Lose by the Reformation, which God forbid: I am sure 'twas to enjoy Property, with Conscience, that promoted it. Nor is there a much better Definition of Protestancy, than *Protesting against Spoiling Property for Conscience.* I must therefore take Leave to say, that I know not how to Reconcile what a great Man lately deliver'd in his Eloquent Speech to the *House of Lords:* His Words are these:

> For when we consider Religion in Parliament, we are supposed to consider it as a Parliament should do, and as Parliaments in all Ages have done; that is, as it is a Part of our Laws, a Part and a necessary Part of our Government: For as it works upon the Conscience, as it is an *Inward Principle* of the *Divine Life,* by which good Men do Govern all their Actions, *the State hath nothing to do with it:* It is a Thing which belongs to another Kind of Commission, than that by which we sit here.

I Acquiesce in, and Honour the latter Part of this Distinction, taking it to be a Venerable Truth; and would to God Mankind would believe it, and Live it: But how to agree it with the former, I profess Ignorance: For if the Government had nothing to do with the Principle it self, what more can She pretend over the Actions of those Men, who Live that *Good Life?* Certainly, if Religion be an Inward Principle of *Divine Life,* exerting it self by Holy Living, and that, as such, it belongs not to the Commission of our Superiors, I do with Submission conceive, that there is very little else of Religion left for them to have to do with: The rest merits not the Name of Religion, and less doth such a

Formality deserve Persecution. I hope such Circumstances are no necessary Part of *English* Government, that cannot reasonably be reputed a necessary Part of Religion; And, I believe he is too great a Divine and Lawyer, upon second Thoughts, to Repute that *a Part of our Laws, a Part and a necessary Part of our Government,* that is such a Part of Religion, as is neither the *Divine Principle,* nor yet the *Actions immediately flowing from it;* since the Government was most Compleat and Prosperous many Ages without it, and hath never known more perplex'd Contests and Troublesome Interruptions, than since it hath been receiv'd and valu'd as a Part of the *English* Government: And God, I hope, will forbid it, in the Hearts of our Superiors, that *English* Men should be deprived of their *Civil Inheritance* for their *Non-Conformity* to Church Formality: For no Property out of the Church (the plain *English* of publick Severity for *Non-conformity*) is a Maxim that belongs not to the Holy Law of God, or Common Law of the Land.

IV. If Liberty and Property must be the Forfeit of Conscience for *Non-conformity* to the Prince's Religion, the Prince and his Religion shall only be Lov'd as the next best Accession to other Men's Estates, and the Prince perpetually provok'd to expose many of his inoffensive People to *Beggary,* for what is no Fault at Common Law.

V. It is our Superiors Interest, that Property be preserved, because it is their own Case: None have more Property than Themselves. But if Property be exposed for Religion, the Civil Magistrate exposes both his Conscience and Property to the Church, and disarms himself of all Defence upon any Alteration of Judgment. This is plainly for the *Prince* to hold under the *Prelate,* and the *State* to suffer it self to be Rid by the *Church.*

VI. It obstructs all *Improvement* of Land and Trade; for who will Labour that hath no Property, or hath it exposed to an Unreasonable Sort of Men, for the bare Exercise of his Conscience to God? And a poor Country can never make a Rich and Powerful Prince. Heaven is therefore Heaven, to Good and Wise Men, because they are to have an *Eternal Propriety* therein.

VII. This Sort of Procedure, hitherto opposed, on the Behalf of Property, puts the whole Nation upon miserable Uncertainties, that are follow'd with great Disquiets and Distractions; which certainly it is the Interest of all Government to prevent: The Reigns of *Henry* 8. *Edward* 6. Q. *Mary* and Q. *Eliz.* both with Relation to the Marriages of the first, and the *Religious Revolutions* of the rest, are a plain Proof in the Case.

King *Henry* voids the Pope's Supremacy, and assumes it himself. Comes

Edw. 6. and Enacts Protestancy with an Oath to maintain it. 1 Q. *Mary,* Ch. 1. This is abrogated: *Popery* Solemnly Restored; and an Oath inforc'd to Defend it: And this Queen Repeals also all Laws Her Father made against the *Pope,* since the 12th of *Hen.* 8. Next, follows Q. *Elizabeth,* and Repeals Her Laws, calls back *Protestancy,* ordains a new Oath, to un-Oath Queen Mary's *Oath;* and all this under the Penalty of losing *Estate, Liberty,* and sometimes Life it self; which, Thousands, to avoid, Lamentably Perjur'd themselves, *four or five Times over,* within the Space of Twenty Years. In which Sin, the Clergy Transcended: *Not an Hundred for every Thousand,* but left their Principles for their Parishes. Thus hath Conscience been Debauch'd by Force, and Property toss'd up and down by the Impetuous Blasts of Ignorant Zeal, or Sinister Design.

VIII. Where Liberty and Property are Violated; there must always be a State of Force: And though I pray God that we never need those Cruel Remedies, whose Calamitous Effects we have too lately felt, yet certainly, Self-Preservation is of all Things dearest to Men; insomuch that being not Conscious to themselves of having done an ill Thing, They, to defend their Unforfeited Priviledges, chearfully Hazard all they have in this World. So very strangely Vindictive are the Sons of Men, in Maintenance of their Rights. And such are the Cares, Fears, Doubts and Insecurities of that Administration, as render Empire a Slavery, and Dominion the worst sort of Bondage to the Possessor. On the contrary, nothing can give greater Chearfulness, Confidence, Security and Honour to any *Prince,* than Ruling by Law; for it is a Conjunction of *Title* with *Power,* and Attracts *Love* as well as it Requires *Duty.*

Give me Leave, without Offence (for I have God's Evidence in my own Conscience, I intend nothing but a Respectful Caution to my Superiours) to Confirm this Reason, with the Judgment and Example of other Times. The Governours of the *Eleans* held a strict Hand over the People; who, Despairing of Relief at home, called in the *Spartans,* and by their Help Freed all their Cities from the sharp Bondage of their Natural Lords.

The State of *Sparta* was grown Powerful, and Opprest the *Thebans;* They, though but a weak People, whetted by Despair, and the Prospect of greater Miseries, did, by the *Athenians,* deliver themselves from the Spartan Yoak.

Nor is there any other considerable Reason given for the Ruin of the *Carthaginian* State, than Avarice and Severity. More of this is to be found in *Rawleigh*'s History of the World, l. 3. who hath this Witty Expression in the same Story, l. 5. of a Severe Conduct. *When a forced Government,* saith he, *shall decay in Strength, It will suffer, as did the old* Lyon, *for the Oppression done in his*

Youth; being Pinch'd by the Wolf, Goar'd by the Bull, and kick'd *also by the* Ass: The Senseless Mobb.[30]

This lost *Caesar Borgia,* his new and great Conquests in *Italy.* No better Success attended the Severe Hand held over the People of *Naples,* by *Alphonso* and *Ferdinand.* 'Twas the undue Severity of the *Sicilian* Governours, that made the *Syracusians, Leontines* and *Messenians* so Easie a Conquest to the *Romans.* An harsh Answer to a Petitioning People lost *Rehoboam* Ten Tribes. On the contrary, in *Livy,* Dec. 1. l. 3. We find, that *Petilia,* a City of the *Brutians* in *Italy,* chose rather to endure all Extremity of War from *Hannibal,* than upon any Condition to Desert the *Romans,* who had Govern'd them moderately, and by that gentle Conduct procur'd their *Love;* even then, when the *Romans* sent them Word, *The were not able to relieve them, and wish'd them to provide for their own Safety.*[31]

N. Machiavel in his Discourses upon *Livy,* p. 542. tells us, that one Act of *Humanity* was of more Force with the Conquer'd *Falisci,* than many Violent Acts of *Hostility:* Which makes good that Saying of *Seneca, Mitius imperanti melius paretur,* They are best obeyed, that Govern most mildly.[32]

IX. If these Ancient *Fundamental Laws,* so Agreeable with Nature, so suited to the Dispositions of our Nation, so often defended with *Blood and Treasure,* so Carefully and Frequently Ratified by our Ancestors, shall not be, to our great Pilots, as *Stars* or *Compass* for them to Steer the Vessel of this Kingdom by, or *Limits* to their Legislature; no Man can tell how long he shall be secure of his Coat, Enjoy his House, have Bread to give his Children, Liberty to Work for Bread, and Life to eat it. Truly, this is to justifie what we condemn in *Roman Catholicks.* It is one of our main *Objections,* that *their Church assumes a Power of Imposing Religion,* thereby denying Men the Liberty of walking by the Rules of their own *Reason* and *Conscience, and Precepts of Holy Writ:* To whom, we oppose both. We say, the *Church* is tyed to act nothing contrary to Reason; and that *Holy Writ* is the declar'd Law of Heaven, which to maintain, Power is given to the *True Church.* Now let us apply this Argument to our Civil Af-

30. Sir Walter Raleigh, *History of the World* (London, 1652).

31. Livy, *History of Rome,* bk. 23, ch. 20.

32. Niccolò Machiavelli, *Discourses on the First Ten Books of Livy,* bk. 3, ch. 20; and Seneca (ca. 60 B.C.E.–37 C.E.), Stoic philosopher. Bouvier's law dictionary (John Bouvier, *A Law dictionary Adapted to the constitution and laws of the United States of America and of the several states of the American union* [6th ed., Philadelphia, 1856]) traces this quotation to Coke's *Third part of the Institutes,* ch. 2, which is likely Penn's source.

fairs, and it will certainly end in a reasonable *Limitation of our Legislators,* that they should not impose that upon our Understandings, which is inconsistent with them to Embrace; nor offer any the least Violation to Common Right. Do the Romanists say, *Believe as the Church Believes?* Do not the *Protestants,* and which is harder, *Legislators* say so too? Do we say to the *Romanists,* at this rate, *Your Obedience is Blind,* and *your Ignorance is the Mother of Devotion?* Is it not also true of our selves? Do we object to them, *This makes your Religion uncertain, one Thing to Day, and another to Morrow?* Doth not our own Case submit us to the like Variation in Civils? Have we not long told them, that *under Pretence of obeying the Church, and not controuling her Power, she hath raised a Superstructure inconsistent with that Foundation she pretends to build upon.* And are not we the Men in Civils, that make our Privileges rather to depend upon Men, than Laws, as she doth upon Councils, not Scripture? If this be not *Popery* in Temporals, what is?

It is humbly beseech'd of Superiors, that it would please them to consider what Reflection such Severity justly brings upon Their Proceedings; and remember, that in their ancient Delegations, it was not to Define, Resolve, and Impose Matters of Religion, and sacrifice Civil Privileges for it; but, to Maintain the People's Properties, according to the ancient Fundamental Laws of the Land, and to add such Statutes only, as were Consistent with, and Preservative of those Fundamental Laws.

Lastly, To conclude this Head; My plain and honest Drift has been, to show that *Church Government* is no Essential Part of the old *English Government,* and to disintangle Property from Opinion, the untoward Knot, the Clergy, for several Ages have tyed, which is not only the People's Right, but our Superiors Interest to Undo; for it gauls both People and Prince. For, where Property is subjected to Opinion, the Church interposes, and makes something else requisite to enjoy Property, than belongs to the Nature of Property; and the Reason of our Possession is not our *Right* by, and Obedience to, the Common Law, but *Conformity* to Church Law, or Laws for Church Conformity. A Thing dangerous to Civil Government, since 'tis an Alteration of old *English Tenure,* a suffering the Church to Trip up and supplant the State; and a making People to owe their Protection not to the *Civil,* but *Ecclesiastical* Authority. For let the Church be my Friend, and all is well; make her my Foe, and I am made her Prey, let *Magna Charta* say what she will for me: My Horses, Cows, Sheep, Corn, Goods, go first, my Person to Goal next, for all That: Behold, some *Church Trophies* made at the Conquest of a peaceable Dissenter!

This is that anxious Thing; May our Superiors please to weigh it in the Equal Scale of *Doing as they would be done by;* Let those *Common Laws* that Fix and Preserve Property, be the *Rule* and Standard of their Legislation and Administration. Make *Englishmen's Rights* as Inviolable, as *English Church Rights,* Disintangle and Distinguish them: And let no Man sustain *Civil Punishments* for *Ecclesiastical Faults,* but for Sins against the ancient, establish'd *Civil Government* only; that the Natures of Acts and Rewards may not be *confounded.* So shall the *Civil* Magistrate preserve Law, secure his Civil Dignity and Empire, and make himself belov'd of *Englishmen;* whose Cry is, and the Cry of whose Laws hath ever been, *Property rather than Opinion, Civil Rights not concern'd with Ecclesiastical Discipline, nor forfeitable for Religious Non-conformity.*

But tho' an inviolable Preservation of *English Rights,* of all Things, best secureth to our Superiors, the Love and Allegiance of the People; yet there is something farther, that, with Submission, I offer to their serious Consideration, which in the second Place concerns their Interest, and the People's Felicity; and that is their *Disagreement* about *Religion,* notwithstanding their unanimous Cry for *Property;* a prudent Management of which, may turn to the great Quiet, Honour and Profit of the King and Kingdom.

CHAP. II.

Of our Superiors governing themselves upon a *Ballance,* as near as may be, towards the several Religious Interests.

II. *Of a Ballance, respecting Religious Differences. Eight Prudential Reasons why the Civil Magistrate should embrace it. Three Objections Answer'd. A Comprehension consider'd, but a Toleration Preferr'd, upon Reason and Example.*

TO PERFORM my Part, in this Point, being the second Branch of my Answer to the Question; I shall not, at this Time, make it my Business to manifest the *Inconsistency* that there is between the *Christian Religion,* and a *forced Uniformity,* not only because it hath been so often and excellently done by Men of Wit, Learning and Conscience, and that I have else-where largely deliver'd my Sense about it; but because every free and impartial Temper, hath, of a long Time, observ'd, that such *Barbarous Attempts* were so far from being indulg'd, that they were most severely Prohibited by Christ himself; who instructed his Disciples, *to Love their Enemies,* and not to persecute their Friends for every Difference in Opinion: That the Tares should grow with the Wheat: That *his Kingdom is not of this World:* That *Faith is the Gift of God:* That the *Will* and *Understanding* of Men are Faculties not to be work'd upon by any *Corporal Penalties:* That TRUTH *is All-sufficient to her own Relief:* That ERROR *and* ANGER go together: That *Base Coyn* only stands in need of *Imposition* to make it current, but that *True Metal* passeth for its own *Intrinsick Value;* with a great deal more of that Nature.[33] I shall therefore chuse to oppose my self, at this Time, to any such Severity, upon meer Prudence; that such as have *No Religion* (and certainly they that Persecute for *Religion,* have as little as need to be) may be induced to Tolerate Them that have.

First, However Advisable it may be, in the Judgment of some Worldly Wise Men, to prevent, even by Force, the arising of any *New Opinion,* where a Kingdom is Universally of another Mind; especially if it be Odious to the People, and inconsistent with the Safety of the Government; it cannot be so, where a Kingdom is of *Many Minds,* unless some One Party hath all the *Wisdom, Wealth, Number, Sober Life, Industry* and *Resolution* of it's side; which I am sure is not to be found in *England.* So that the Wind hath plainly shifted it's Corner, and consequently obliges to another Course: I mean, *England*'s Circumstances are greatly changed, and they require *new Expedients* and another Sort of *Application.*

Physicians vary their Medicines according to the Revolution and the Mixture of Distempers. They that seek to tye the Government to absolute and inadequate Methods (supposing them once apt, which Cruelty in this Case never was) are not Friends to it's Interest, whatever they may be to their own. If our *Superiors* should make it their Business so to prefer *one Party,* as to depress or deprive the rest, they insecure themselves, by making their Friends their Enemies, who before were one another's. To be sure it createth *Hatred* between the Party advanced, and those deprest. *Jacob*'s preferring *Joseph* put his Brethren upon that Conspiracy against him.[34]

33. See the following: on loving enemies, Matthew 5:44, Luke 6:27, 35; on the tares and wheat, Matthew 13:24–30; on Christ's kingdom not of this world, John 18:36; on faith, Ephesians 2:8; on the truth, John 8:22, 16:13; and on anger, Matthew 5:21–22.

34. Genesis 37.

I will allow that they may have a more particular Favour for the Church Party, than for any other Perswasion, but not more than for all other Parties in *England:* That certainly would break the *Ballance;* the keeping up of which, will make every Party to owe its Tranquility to their Prudence and Goodness, which will never fail of Returns of Love and Loyalty. For since we see each Interest looks jealously upon the other, 'tis reasonable to believe, they had rather the Dominion should lodge where it is, while impartial in their Judgment, than to trust it with any one Sort of themselves.

Many inquisitive Men into Humane Affairs have thought, that the Concord of Discords hath not been the infirmest Basis Government can rise or stand upon: It hath been observed, that less Sedition and Disturbance attended *Hannibal*'s Army, that consisted of many Nations, than the *Roman* Legions, that were of one People. It is marvellous how the Wisdom of that General secured them to his Designs: *Livy* saith, *That his Army for Thirteen Years, that had roved up and down the* Roman *Empire, made up of many Countries, divers Languages, Laws, Customs, Religions; under all their Successes of War and Peace,* never mutined. Malvetzy, *as well as* Livy, ascribes it to that Variety, well managed by the General.[35]

By the like Prudence *Jovianus* and *Theodosius Magnus* brought Tranquility to their Empire, after much Rage and Blood for Religion.

In Nature we also see, all Heat consumes, all Cold kills; that three Degrees of Cold to two of Heat, allay the Heat, but introduce the contrary Quality, and over-cool by a Degree; but two Degrees of Cold, to two of Heat, make a *Poyze* in Elements, and a *Ballance* in Nature.

The like in Families: It is not probable that a Master should have his Work so well done, at least with that Love and Respect, who continually *Smiles* upon one Servant, and severely *Frowns* upon all the rest; on the contrary, 'tis apt to raise Feuds amongst Servants, and turn Duty into Revenge at least Contempt. *In Fine,* it is to make our *Superior*'s Dominion less than God made it, and to blind their Eyes, stop their Ears, and shut up their Breasts, from beholding the Miseries, hearing the Cries, and redressing the Grievances of a vast Number of People, under their Charge, vexed in this World, for their *Belief* and inoffensive Practice about the next.

Secondly, *It is the Interest of Governours, to be put upon no thankless Offices;*

35. Livy, *History of Rome,* bk. 28, ch. 12; and Virgilio Malvezzi, *Discourses upon Cornelius Tacitus,* trans. Sir Richard Baker (London, 1642), discourse 49, pp. 475–77.

that is, to blow no Coals in their own Country, especially when it is to consume their People, and, it may be, themselves too: Not to be the Cat's Foot, *nor to make Work for themselves, or fill their own Hands with Trouble, or the Kingdom with Complaints. It is to forbid them the Use of* Clemency, *wherein they ought most of all to imitate God Almighty,* whose Mercy is above all his Works; *and renders them a sort of* Extortioners *to the People, the most remote from the End and Goodness of their Office. In short, it is the best Receipt that their Enemies can give, to make them uneasie to the Country.*

Thirdly, It not only makes them Enemies, but there is no such Excitement to revenge, as a *Rap'd* Conscience. He that hath been forced to break his Peace, to gratifie the Humour of another, must have a great Share of Mercy and self-denial, to forgive that Injury, and forbid himself the Pleasure of Retribution upon the Authors of it: For Revenge, in other Cases condemnable of all, is here look'd upon by too many, to be the next way to Expiation. To be sure, whether the Grounds of their Dissent be rational in themselves, such Severity is unjustifiable with them; for this is a Maxim with Sufferers, whoever is in the Wrong, *the Persecutor cannot be in the right.* Men, not conscious to themselves of Evil, and harshly treated, not only resent it unkindly, but are bold to shew it.

Fourthly, *Suppose the Prince, by his Severity, conquers any into a Compliance, he can upon no prudent Ground assure himself of their Fidelity, whom he hath taught to be treacherous to their own Convictions. Wise Men rarely confide in those whom they have debauch'd from Trust to serve themselves: At best it resembleth but forced Marriages, that seldom prove happy to the Parties. In short, Force makes* Hypocrites, *'tis* Perswasion *only that makes Converts.*

Fifthly, This Partiality, of sacrificing the Liberty and Property of all Dissenters, to the Promotion of a single Party, be they good or ill Men, as it is the lively Representation of *J. Calvin's Horrendum Decretum;*[36] so the Consequences of the one belong unto the other; it being but that ill-natured Principle put into *Practice.* Men are put upon the same desperate Courses, either to have no Conscience at all, or to be hanged for having a Conscience not fashionable: For, let them be *Virtuous,* let them be *Vicious,* if they fall not in with that *Mode* of Religion, they must be *reprobated* to all Civil and Ecclesias-

36. "Dreaded decree"; a reference to John Calvin's theory of predestination and election. Calvin (1509–64) takes the election of the saints as part of God's providential ordering of the world. See Calvin's *Institutes of the Christian Religion, passim,* esp. bk. 3.

tical Intents and Purposes. Strange! that Men must either deny their Faith and Reason, or be destroyed for acting according to them, be they otherwise never so peaceable. What Power is this, or rather what Principle? But that Men are to be protected upon Favour, not right or merit; and that no Merit out of the publick Church Dress should find Acceptance, is severe. We justly blame that Father, that narrows his Paternal Love to some one of his Children, though the rest be not one Jot less Virtuous than the Favourite: Such Injustice can never flow from a Soul acted by Reason, but a Mind govern'd by Fancy, and enslaved to Passions.

Sixthly, *Consider* Peace, Plenty, *and* Safety, *the three great Inducements to any Country to* Honour *the Prince, and* Love *the Government, as well as the best Allurements to* Foreigners *to trade with it and transport themselves to it, are utterly lost by such Partialities: for instead of Peace, Love and good Neighbourhood, behold* Animosity *and* Contest! *One Neighbour watches another, and makes him an Offender for his Conscience; this divides them, their Families and Acquaintance: perhaps, with them the Towns and Villages where they live: And most commonly, the* Sufferer *hath the* Pity, *and the* Persecutor *the* Odium *of the Multitude. And truly when People see Cruelty practised upon their inoffensive Neighbours, by a troublesom sort of Men, and those countenanced by a Law, it breedeth ill Blood against the Government.* Certainly, *Haling People to Goals, breaking open their Houses, siezing of their Estates,* and that without all Proportion; leaving Wives without their Husbands, and Children without their Parents, and their Families, Relations, Friends and Neighbours, under Amaze and Trouble, is almost as far from the Peace of a well-govern'd Kingdom, as it is from the Meekness of *Christianity.*

Plenty will be hereby exchanged for *Poverty,* by the Destruction of many thousand Families within this Realm, who are greatly instrumental for the carrying on of the most *substantial Commerce* therein: Men of *Virtue, good Contrivance, Great Industry;* whose Labours, not only keep the Parishes from the Trouble and Charge of maintaining them and theirs, but help to maintain the *Poor,* and are great *Contributors* to the *King's Revenue* by their Traffick. This very Severity will make more *Bankrupts* in the Kingdom of *England* in seven Years, than have been in it upon all other Accounts in Seven Ages: which Consequence, how far it may consist with the Credit and Interest of the Government, I leave to better judgments.

This Sort of great Severity that hath been lately, and still is used amongst us, is like to prove a great Check to that Readiness, which otherwise we find in

Foreigners to Trade with the Inhabitants of this Kingdom; for if Men cannot call any Thing their *Own,* under a different Exercise of Conscience from the National Way of Religion, their Correspondents may justly and prudently say, *We will not further concern our selves with Men that stand upon such ticklish Terms: What know we but such Persons are ruin'd in their Estates, by Reason of their* Non-Conformity, *before such Time as we shall be reimburst for Money paid, or Goods deliver'd: Nay, we know not how soon those who are* Conformists, *may be* Non-Conformists, *or what Revolutions of Councils may happen, since the Fundamental Laws, so jealous of the People's Property, are so little valued by some of their own Magistrates; for though we are told of very worthy and excellent Laws in* England, *for the Security of the People's Rights, yet we are also told, that they all hang at the Church's Girdle, insomuch as no* Church-Conformity *no* Property; *which is,* No Churchman, No Englishman. *So that in Effect the Rights of their Country depend upon the Rights of their Church; and those Churches have taken their Turns so often, that a Body knows not how to manage one's self securely to one's own Affairs, in a Correspondence with any of them. For in King* Henry *the Eighth's Days, Popery was the only Orthodox Religion, and* Zuinglius, Luther, Melancthon, Oecolampadius, &c. *were great Hereticks. In* Edward *the Sixth's Time, they were Saints, and* Popery was Idolatry. *A few Years after, Queen* Mary *makes the* Papists *Holy Church, and* Protestancy *Heresie. About Six Years compleats her Time, and Queen* Elizabeth *enters her Reign, in which* Protestants *are* Good Christians, *and the Church of* Rome *the* Whore of Babylon. *In Her Reign, and that of King* James, *and King* Charles *the First, sprung the* Puritans, *who divided themselves into* Presbyterians, *and* Independents. *The Bishops exclaimed against them for* Schismaticks, *and they against the Bishops for* Papistical *and* Antichristian. *In the* Long Parliament's *Time, the* Presbyterian *drives out the* Bishop; O. Cromwel *defeating them, and sending the* Presbyterian *to keep Company with the Bishop, confers it mostly upon the* Independent *and* Anabaptist, *who kept it through the other Fractions of Government, till the* Presbyter and Bishop got it from them: *And the* Bishop *now from the* Presbyter; *But how long it will rest there, who knows?* Thus a Foreigner may justly argue.

Nor is my Supposition idle or improbable, unless Moderation take Place of Severity, and *Property* the Room of Punishment for Opinion; for that must be the Lasting Security, as well as that it is the Fundamental Right of *English People.*

There is also a farther Consideration, and that is, the rendring just and very good Debts desperate, both at Home and Abroad, by giving Opportunity to the Debtors of Dissenters to detain their Dues. Indeed it seems a Natural Consequence with all, but Men of Mercy and Integrity: *What should we pay them for,* may they say, *that are not in a Capacity to demand or receive it, at least to compel us?* Nay, they may plead a sort of Kindness to their Creditors, and say, *We had as good keep it, for if we pay it them, they will soon lose it; 'tis better to remain with us, than that they should be pillag'd of it by Informers;* though Want should in the mean Time overtake the Right Owners and their Families.

Nor is it unworthy of the most deliberate Thoughts of our Superiors, that *the Land already swarms with Beggars,* and that there is hardly so ready a Course to increase their Number, as the severe Prosecution of Dissenters, both by making them such, and those that their Employs have kept from *Begging* all this While: So that though they immediately suffer, the Kingdom, in the End, must be the Loser. For besides a Decay of Trade, *&c.* this driving away of *Flocks of Sheep, and Herds of Cattel, seizing of Barns full of Corn, breaking open of Doors and Chests, taking away the best Goods that those Instruments of Cruelty can find, sometimes* All, *even to a Bed, a Blanket, Wearing Apparel, and the very Tools of Trade, by which People honestly labour to get their Bread, till they leave Men, Women and Children, destitute of Subsistence, will necessitate an extream Advance of the Poor's Rate in every Parish of* England, *or they must be Starv'd.* O, that it would please them that are in Authority, to put a Stop to this inhumane Usage, lest the Vengeance of the Just GOD, break forth farther against this poor Land!

Safety, another Requisite to an Happy Government, must needs be at an End, where the Course oppugn'd is followed, by tempting People to irregular Methods to be easy, or to Quit the Land. And truly it is but some prudent Prince's proclaiming Liberty of Conscience within his Territories, and a Door is opened for a Million of People to pass out of their Native Soil, which is not so extreamly improved, that it should not want Two or Three Hundred Thousand Families more than it hath, to advance it; especially at this Time of Day, when our Foreign Islands Yearly take off so many Inhabitants from us, who, from Necessity, are made unable to stay at Home: And as of Contraries there is the same Reason, so let the Government of *England* but give that Prudent Invitation to Foreigners, and She maketh Her self Mistress of the Arts and Manufactures of *Europe.* Nothing else hath preserv'd *Holland* from Truckling under the *Spanish* Yoak, and being Ruin'd above Threescore Years ago, and given her that Rise to Wealth and Glory.

Seventhly, Nor is this Severity only injurious to the Affairs of *England,* but the whole Protestant World: For besides that it calls the Sincerity of their Proceedings against the *Papists* into Question, it furnisheth them with this Sort of unanswerable Interrogatory: *The Protestants exclaim against us for Persecutors, and are they now the* Very Men themselves? *Was Severity an Instance of Weakness in our Religion, and is it become a Valid Argument in theirs? Are not our Actions* (once void of all Excuse with them) *now defended by their own Practice? But if Men must be restrained upon Prudential Considerations from the Exercise of their Consciences in* England, *Why not the same in* France *and* Germany, *where Matters of State may equally be pleaded?* Certainly whatever Shifts Protestants may use to palliate these Proceedings, they are thus far Condemnable upon the Foot of Prudence.

Eighthly, Such Procedure is a great Reflection upon the Justice of the Government, in that it Enacts Penalties inadequate to the Fault committed, *viz.* That I should lose my Liberty and Property, Fundamental Civil Privileges, for some Error in Judgment about Matters of Religion: *As if I must not be a Man,* because I am not such a Sort of Religious Man as the Government would have me; but must lose my Claim to all Natural Benefits, though I agree with them in Civil Affairs, because I fall not in with the Judgment of the Government in some Points of a Supernatural Import, tho' no real Part of the Ancient Government. Perhaps instead of going to the Left Hand, I go to the Right: And whereas I am commanded to hear *A. B.* I rather chuse to hear *C. D.* my Reason for it, *being the more Religious Influence the latter hath over me, than the former; and that I find by Experience, I am better affected, and more Religiously edified to Good Living.* What *Blemish* is this to the Government? What *Insecurity* to the *Civil Magistrate?* Why may not this Man Sell, Buy, Plow, Pay his Rents, be as good a Subject, and as True an *Englishman,* as any *Conformist* in the Kingdom? Howbeit, Fines and Goals are very ill Arguments to convince Sober Men's Understandings, and disswade them from the Continuance of so harmless a Practice.

Lastly, But there is yet another Inconvenience that will attend this Sort of Severity, that so naturally follows upon our Superiors making *Conformity* to the Doctrine and Worship of the Church of *England,* the *Sine Quâ Non,* or Inlet to all Property, and Ground of Claim to all *English Civil Privileges,* to wit, *That they make a Rod, for ought they know, to Whip their own Posterity with;* since it is impossible for them to secure their *Children to the English Church:* And if it happen that any of them are never so *Conscientiously* of another Perswasion, they are liable to all the Miseries that may attend the Execution of those Laws. Such a *King* must not be *King,* such *Lords* and *Commons* must not Sit in Parliament: Nay, they must not administer any Office, be it never so inferior within the Realm, and they never so Virtuous and capable to do it: Their very *Patrimony* becomes a Prey to a Pack of *Lewd Informers,* and their Persons exposed to the Abuse of Men, Poor or Malicious.

But there are *Three Objections* that some make against what I have urged, not unfit to be consider'd. The First is this: *If the Liberty desired be granted, what know we but* Dissenters *may employ their Meetings to insinuate against the Government, inflame People into a Dislike of their Superiors, and thereby prepare them for Mischief?*

Answ. This *Objection* may have some Force, so long as our Superiors continue Severity; because it doth not only sharpen and excite Dissenters, but it runs many of them into such Holes and Corners, that if they were disposed to any such *Conspiracies,* they have the securest Places and Opportunities to effect their Design. But what *Dissenter* can be so destitute of Reason, and of Love to common Safety, as to expose himself and Family, by *Plotting against a Government that is Kind to them, and gives him the Liberty he desires, and that he could only be supposed, in common Sense, to Plot for.*

To be sure, Liberty to worship God, according to their several Professions, will be, *as the People's Satisfaction, so the Government's greatest Security:* For if Men enjoy their Property, and their Conscience, which is the Noblest Part of it, without Molestation, what should they object against, or Plot for? Mad Men only Burn their own Houses, Kill their own Children, and Murder themselves. Doth Kindness or Cruelty most take with Men that are themselves? *H. Grotius,* with *Campanella,* well observ'd, *That a fierce and rugged Hand was very improper for Northern Countries.* Englishmen *are gain'd with Mildness, but inflamed by Severity.*[37] And many that do not suffer, are as apt to compassionate them that do. And if it will please our *Superiors* to make Trial of such an *Indulgence,* doubtless they will find Peace and Plenty to ensue. The Practice of other Nations, and the Trade, Tranquility, Power and Opulency that have attended it, is a Demonstration in the Case, and ought not to be slighted by them that aim at as High and Honourable Things for their Country. And if we had no other *Instance* than our own *Intervals of Connivance,* they were enough to satisfie *Reasonable Men,* how much more *Moderation* contributes to pub-

37. Hugo Grotius, *Politick maxims and observations* (London, 1654), pp. 43–45.

lick Good, than the Prosecution of People for their *Religious Dissent; since the One hath ever produced Trade and Tranquility, the Other, Greater Poverty and Dissension.*

The *Second Objection,* and by far the more Weighty, runs thus:

Object. *The King and Parliament are Sworn to Maintain and Protect the* Church of England, *as Establish'd,* &c. *therefore to Tolerate other Opinions is against their Oath.*

Answ. Were the Consequence True, as it is not, it were highly unreasonable to expect *Impossibilities* at their Hands. Kings and Parliaments can no more make *Brick without Straw than Captives:*[38] They have not Sworn to do Things beyond their Ability; if they have, their Oaths are void. Had it been in His and their Time and Choice, when the Church of *England* had been first disturbed with *Dissenting Opinions,* it might have reflected more colourably a Kind of Neglect upon them: But since the Church of *England* was no sooner a Church, then She found some *Sort of Dissenters,* and that the utmost Policy and Severity of Queen *Elizabeth,* King *James,* and King *Charles* the First, were not *Successful* towards an *Absolute Uniformity,* Why should it reflect upon them, that the Church of *England* hath not yet rid Herself of *Dissenting Parties?* Besides, it is Notorious, that the late Wars gave that Opportunity to *Differing Perswasions to spread,* that it was utterly impossible for them to hinder, much less during the several Years of the King's Exile; at what Time the present Parliament was no Parliament, nor the Generality of the Members of it scarce of any Authority.

Let it be considered, that 'twas the Study of the Age to make People *Anti-Papistical* and *Anti-Episcopal,* and that Power and Preferment went on that Side. Their Circumstances therefore, and their Ancestors, are not the same; they found the Kingdom divided into several Interests, and it seems a Difficulty insuperable to reduce them to any one Perswasion; wherefore to render themselves Masters of their Affections, they must necessarily Govern themselves towards them on a *Ballance,* as is before exprest; otherwise, they are put upon the greatest Hazards, and extreamest Difficulties to themselves and the Kingdom, and all to perform the Uncharitable Office of suppressing many Thousands of inoffensive Inhabitants, for the different Exercise of their Consciences to God: *It is not to make them resemble Almighty God, the Goodness of whose Nature extends it self Universally, thus to narrow their Bowels, and con-*

38. Exodus 5:18.

fine their Clemency to one Single Party: It ought to be remembred, that Optimus *went before* Maximus *of Old, and that Power without Goodness, is a Frightful Sort of a Thing.*

But *Secondly,* I deny the Consequence, viz. *That the King is therefore obliged to persecute Dissenters, because He or the Parliament hath taken an Oath to Maintain the* Church of England: For it cannot be supposed or intended, that by maintaining Her, they are to destroy the Rest of the Inhabitants. *Is it impossible to Protect Her without knocking all the rest on the Head? Do they allow any to supplant Her Clergy, Invade Her Livings, Possess Her Emoluments, Exercise Her Authority? What would She have? Is She not Church of* England *still, Invested with the same Power, Bearing the same Character? What Grandeur or Interest hath She lost by them? Are they not manifestly Her Protector? Is She not National Church still?* And can any of Her Children be so insensible, as either to challenge her Superiors with Want of Integrity, because they had not performed Impossibilities? Or to excite them to that Harshness, which is not only Destructive of many Thousands of Inhabitants, but altogether injurious to their own Interest, and dishonourable to a *Protestant Church?* Suppose Dissenters not to be of the Visible Church, are they therefore unfit to live? Did the *Jews* treat Strangers so severely, that had so much more to say than Her self? *Is not the King Lord of Wasts and Commons as well as Inclosures? Suppose God hath Elected some to Salvation, doth it therefore follow he hath Reprobated all the rest? And because he was God of the* Jews, *was He not therefore God of the* Gentiles? *Or were not the* Gentiles *his People, because the* Jews *were his peculiar People?*

To be brief, they have answered their Obligation, and consented to *Severe Laws,* and commanded their Execution, and have not only preferr'd her above every Interest in *England,* but against them, to render her more Powerful and Universal; till they have good Reason to be *Tired* with the Lamentable Consequences of those Endeavours, and conclude, that the *Uniformity* thereby intended, is a Thing impracticable, as well as Mischievous.

And I wonder that these Men should so easily forget that *Great Saying of King* Charles *the First,* (whom they pretend so often, and with so much Honour to remember) in his Advice to the present King, where he saith,

> *Beware of exasperating any Factions, by the Crossness and Asperity of some Men's Passions, Humors, or Private Opinions, imployed by you, grounded only upon their Differences in Lesser Matters, which are but*

> *the Skirts and Suburbs of Religion, wherein a* Charitable Connivance, *and* Christian Toleration *often dissipates their Strength, whom rougher Opposition fortifieth, and puts the Despised and Oppressed Party into such Combinations, as may most enable them to get a full Revenge upon those they count their Persecutors; who are commonly assisted with that Vulgar Commiseration, which attends all that are said to suffer under the Common Notion of Religion.*[39]

So that we have not only the King's Circumstances, but his Father's Counsel, upon Experience, who yet saw not the End of One Half of them, defending a Charitable Connivance, and Christian Toleration of *Dissenters.*

Obj. 3. But it may be further alledged, *This makes Way for* Popery *or* Presbytery, *to undermine the Church of* England, *and mount the Chair of Preferment, which is more than a Prudential Indulgence of different Opinions.*

And yet there is not any so probable an Expedient to vanish those Fears, and prevent any such Design, as keeping all Interests upon the Ballance; *for so the* Protestant *makes at least Six Parties against* Popery, *and the Church of* England *at least Five against Presbytery:* And how either of them should be able to turn the Scale against Five or Six, as Free and Thriving Interests, as either of them can pretend to be, I confess I cannot understand. But if One only Interest must be Tolerated, which implies a Resolution to suppress the Rest, plain it is, that the *Church of England* ventures Her Single Party against Six Growing Interests, and thereby gives *Presbytery* and *Popery* by far an easier Access to Supremacy; especially the latter, for that it is the Religion of those Parts of *Europe,* which neither want Inclination, nor Ability to prosper it. So that besides the Consistency of such an Indulgence with the Nature of a Christian Church, there can be nothing more in Prudence advisable for the *Church of England,* than to allow of the Ballance propounded: In the *first,* no Person of any real Worth, will ever the sooner decline her; on the contrary, it will give her a greater Reputation in a Country so hating Severity: And next, it gives her Opportunity to turn the Scale against any one Party that may aspire to her Pulpits and Endowments: And she never need to fear the Agreement of all of them to any such Design; *Episcopacy* being not more intolerable than *Presbytery* in Power, even to an Independency it self; and yet between them, lies the narrowest Difference that is among the Dissenting Interests in this Kingdom.

39. Charles I, *Eikon Basilike, The portraiture of His Sacred Majestie in his solitude and sufferings* (London, 1649), ch. 27.

But this seems too large, and yielding, and therefore to find a *Medium,* something that may compass the Happy End of Good Correspondence and Tranquility, at least so to fortifie the *Church of England,* as that she may securely give Law to all other Religious Interests, I hear a *Comprehension* is pitch'd upon, and diligently pursued by both *Episcopalians* and *Presbyterians,* at least, some of each Party.

But if it becomes Wise Men to Look before they Leap; it will not be unadvisable for them to weigh the *Consequences* of such an Endeavour.

For, in the first Place, there is no People I know in *England,* that stands at a greater Distance from Her Doctrine, as it is maintain'd by her present Sons, then the *Presbyterians,* particularly about *Absolute Reprobation, the Person of Christ, Satisfaction and Justification:* And he must be a Stranger in the Religious Contests of our Times, that knows not this.

II. In the next Place, none have govern'd themselves with a plainer Denial, and more peremptory Contempt of *Episcopacy,* and the whole Discipline and Worship of the *Church of England,* than the *Presbyterians* have ever done: Let them put me to prove it if they please, even of their *Most Reverend Fathers.*

III. Who knows not that their Reciprocal Heats about these very Things, went a great Way towards our late Lamentable Civil Wars? Now if the same Principles remain with each Party, and that they are so far from repenting of their Tenaciousness, that on the contrary they justifie their Dissent from one another in these Matters, how can either Party have Faith enough to rely upon each other's Kindness, or so much as attempt a Comprehension? What must become of the Labours of Bishop *Whitgift, R. Hooker,* Bishop *Bancroft,* Bishop *Laud,* &c. in Rebuke of the *Presbyterian Separation,* and the Names of those Leading Dissenters, as *Cartwright, Dod, Bradshaw, Rutterford, Galaspee,* &c. so Famous among the present *Presbyterians,* and that for their Opposition to the Church? This consider'd, what Reason can any render, why the *Episcopalians* should so singularly provide for, and confide in an Interest that hath already been so destructive to theirs? On the other Hand, With what Prudence may the *Presbyterians* embrace the other's *Offer,* that to be sure, intend it not in stark Kindness to them, and who, they must needs think, cannot but owe Revenge, and retain deep Grudges for old Stories? But

IV. The very Reason given for a *Comprehension,* is the greatest that can be urged against it, namely, *The Suppression of other Dissenting Persuasions.* I will suppose a *Comprehension,* and the Consequences of it, to be an *Eradication of all other Interests,* the Thing desired: But if the Two remaining Parties shall fall out, as it is not likely that they will long agree, what can the *Presbyterian* have to Ballance himself against the Ruling Power of *Episcopacy?* Or the *Episcopalian* to secure himself against the Aspirings of *Presbytery?* They must either *All* become *Episcopalians,* or *Presbyterians,* else they will mix like *Iron and Clay,* which made ill Legs for the Image in *Daniel:*[40] Nor is it to be thought, that their *Legs* should stand any better upon a *Comprehension.*

But some are ready to say, *That their Difference is very Minute:* Grant it; Are they ever the more deserving for that? Certainly, *Forbearance* should carry some Proportion with the Greatness of the Difference, by how much it is easier to comply in Small than Great Matters. He that dissents *Fundamentally,* is more excusable than those that *Sacrifice the Peace and Concord of a Society about Little Circumstances;* for there cannot be the same Inducement to suspect Men of *Obstinacy* in an *Essential,* as Circumstantial Non-Conformity.

Besides, How far can this Accommodation extend with Security to the *Church of England?* Or, on what better Terms will the *Presbyterians* Conform to Her Discipline and Formal Acts of Devotion, than those upon which *Peter du Moulin* offer'd to Preach the Gospel at *Rome?* viz. *That if the* Pope *would give him Leave to Preach at* Rome, *he would be contented to Preach in a Fool's Coat.* I question if the *Presbyterian* can go so far, I am sure he could not; and as sure, that *Peter du Moulin* hop'd, by preaching there in a *Fool's Coat,* to inculcate that Doctrine which should *Un-Mitre* the Pope, and alter his Church; the very Thing the *Church of England* Fears and Fences against. For *Peter du Moulin* intended to preach in a *Fool's Coat* no longer, than till he had preach'd the People Wise enough to throw it off again. So the *Presbyterians,* they may Conform to certain Ceremonies (once as Sinful to them, as a *Fool's Coat* could be Ridiculous to *Peter du Moulin*) that they may the better introduce their Alterations both in Doctrine and Discipline.

But that which ought to go a great Way with our Superiors, in their Judgment of this Matter, is not only the Benefit of a *Ballance* against the Presumption of any One Party, and the Probability, if not Certainty of their never being overdriven by any One Persuasion, whilst they have others that will more than Poize against the Growing Power of it: But the Conceit it self, if not altogether impracticable, is at least very difficult to the Promoters, and an Office as Thankless from the Parties concern'd.

This appears in the Endeavours used for a *Comprehension of Arrians and*

40. Daniel 2:31–35.

Homoousians under One Orthodoxy, related not only in our common *Ecclesiastical History,* but more amply in the Writings of *Hilary,* an Enemy to the *Arrians,* and *Mariana's Spanish History.*[41] Their publick Tests, or comprehensive Creeds were many, *Nice, Ariminum, Sirmium,* &c. in order to reconcile both Parties, that neither might stigmatize the other with the odious Crime of *Heresie:* But the Consequence of all this Convocation and Prolix Debate was, that neither Party could be satisfied, each continuing their former Sentiments, and so grew up into stronger Factions, to the Division, Distraction, and almost Destruction of the whole Empire: Recover'd a little by the prudent Moderation of *Jovianus,* and much improved, not by a *Comprehension,* but Restauration of a *Seasonable Liberty of Conscience,* by *Theodosius Magnus.*

Also in *Germany,* about the Time of the Reformation, nothing seemed more Sincere than the Design of Union between the *Lutherans* and *Zuinglians:* For *Luther* and *Zuinglius* themselves, by the Earnest Endeavours of the *Landgrave* of *Hessen,* came together; but the Success was so small, notwithstanding the *Grave*'s Mediation, that they parted scarcely Civil: To be sure, as far from Unity as Controversie is.

Luther and Cardinal *Cajetan* met for a Composure of the Breach betwixt the *Protestants* and the *Pope,* but it was too wide for those Conferences to reconcile: No *Comprehension* could be practicable. A second Essay to the same Purpose, was by *Melancthon; Cassander* and others; the Consequence of it was, that the Parties were displeased, and the Heads suspected, if not hated of their Followers. Nor had *Bucer*'s Meeting with *Julius Pflugg* any better Success.

And how fruitless their Endeavours have been, that with greatest Art and Industry, have, of a long Time, endeavoured a Reconciliation of *Lutherans* and *Calvinists,* is well known to those that are acquainted with the Affairs of *Germany:* And such as are not, may furnish themselves from the publick Relations given by those that are employed about that Accommodation: Where, besides a dull and heavy Progress, the *Reader* may be a Witness of their Complaint; not only that both Parties are too Tenacious, but that the Mediators suffer Detraction for their good Endeavours; each Side grudging every Tittle they yield; and murmuring as if they were to lose their Religion. And if Persons so disinterested, and worthy in their Attempts, have had no better Issue,

41. Bede, *Ecclesiastical History,* bk. 1, ch. 8; bk. 4, ch. 17; Hilary of Poitiers (ca. 301–68), *Contra Auxentium Arrianum;* and Juan Mariana, *General history of Spain* (1592), bk. 4, ch. 6.

I cannot see how those, who seem compell'd by Worldly Interest more than Conscience, to seek and propagate a *Comprehension,* especially, when it determines in the Persecution of the rejected Perswasions, can, with any Reason, expect from God, or Good Men, any better Success.

Lastly, There is nothing any Man, touched with Justice and Mercy, can alledge for a *Comprehension,* that may not much better be urged for a *Toleration,* For the Church is less in Danger, when she knows the worst, than where the Danger is hid. Five Enemies without Doors being not so mischievous as one within. But they are also Men, and *Englishmen* as well as those of other Perswasions: Their Faith is as *Christian,* they believe as sincerely, live as conscientiously, are as useful in the Kingdom, and manage their Dissent with as much Modesty and Prudence, the Church of *England* her self being in great Measure Judge, as those on whose Account a *Comprehension* may be desired: To be sure they are *Englishmen,* and have an Equal Claim to the Civil Rights of their Native Country, with any that live in it, whom to persecute, whilst others, and those no better Men in themselves are more than tolerated, is, as I have already said, *The unreasonable and unmerciful Doctrine of Absolute Reprobation put in Practice in Civils:* From which the Lord deliver us.

CHAP. III.
A sincere Promotion of General and Practical Religion.

III. *Of* General *and* Practical Religion, *That the Promotion of it, is the only* Way *to* take in, *and stop the Mouth of all Perswasions, being the Center to which all Parties* verbally *tend, and therefore the Station for a prudent* Magistrate, *to meet every Interest in: The Neglect of it pernicious: Instances: That it is the* unum Necessarium[42] *to Felicity here and hereafter.*

I AM NOW come to the last, which, to be sure, is not the least Part of my Answer to the Question propounded, viz. *The sincere Promotion of general and practical Religion;* by which I mean the *Ten Commandments, or moral Law, and Christ's Sermon upon the Mount,* with other Heavenly Sayings, excellently improved, and earnestly recommended by several Passages in the

42. One necessary thing.

Writings of his Disciples, which forbid *Evil,* not only in *Deed* but *Thought;* and enjoyn *Purity and Holiness,* as *without which no Man,* be his Pretences what they will, *shall ever see God.* In short, General, True and Requisite *Religion,* in the Apostle *James*'s Definition is, *To visit the Widow and Fatherless, and to keep our selves,* through the Universal Grace, *unspotted of the World.*[43] This is the most easie and probable way, to fetch in all Men professing God and Religion: Since every Perswasion acknowledges this in Words, be their Lives never so disagreeable to their Confession. And this being the *Unum Necessarium,* that one Thing needful, to make Men happy here and hereafter, why, alas, should Men sacrifice their Accord in this great Point, for an Unity in minute or circumstantial Things, that perhaps is inobtainable, and if it were not, would signifie little or nothing, either to the Good of humane Society, or the particular Comfort of any, in the World which is to come?

No one Thing is more unaccountable and condemnable among Men, than their Uncharitable Contests about Religion, indeed about Words and Phrases; whilst they all verbally meet in the most, if not only necessary Part of *Christian Religion:* For nothing is more certain, than if Men would but live up to one half of what they know in their own Consciences they ought to practice, their Edge would be taken off, their Blood would be sweetned by Mercy and Truth, and this unnatural Sharpness qualified: They would quickly find Work enough at Home, each Man's Hands would be full by the Unruliness of his own Passions, and in subjecting of his own Will, and instead of devouring one another's *good Name, Liberty,* or *Estate, Compassion* would rise, and mutual Desires to be Assistant to each Other, in a *better* Sort of Living. O how decent, and how delightful would it be, to see Mankind (the Creation of one God, that hath upheld them to this Day) of One Accord, at least in the Weighty Things of God's *Holy Law!*

'Tis Want of *Practice,* and too much *Prate,* that hath made Way for all the *Incharity* and *ill Living* that is in the World. No Matter what Men say, if the Devil keep the House. Let the *Grace of God, the Principle of divine Life* (as a great Man lately called it in his Speech) but be *Heartily* and *Reverently* entertained of Men, that *teaches us to deny all Ungodliness, and converse soberly, righteously and godly, in this present evil World,* and it is not to be doubted but *Tranquility,* at least a very *Amicable Correspondence* will follow.

Men are not to be reputed *Good* by their Opinions or Professions of Reli-

43. James 1:27.

gion: Nor is it that which ought to engage the Government, but Practice; 'tis this that must *save* or *damn.* Christ in his Representation of the great Day, doth not tell us, that it shall be said to Men, *Well said* or *Well talked,* but *Well done, Good and Faithful Servant:* Neither is the *Depart from me,* directed to any, but the *Workers* of *Iniquity;*[44] *Error* is now translated from the Signification of an *evil Life,* to an *unsound Proposition,* as *Philosophy* is from the *Mortification,* and Well living, to an *Unintelligible Way of Wrangling.* And a Man is more bitterly harrass'd for a *mistaken Notion,* though the Party holding thinks it not so, and the Party charging it denies an Infallible Judgment (so that it may as well be true as false for all them) than for the *most dissolute* or *immoral Life.* And truly it is high Time, that Men should give better Testimony of their *Christianity:* For *Cruelty* hath no Share in Christ's Religion, and *Coercion* upon Conscience, is utterly inconsistent with the very Nature of his Kingdom. He rebuked that Zeal which would *have Fire come down from Heaven, to devour Dissenters,* tho' it came from his own Disciples; and forbad them to pluck up the *Tares,* though none had a more gentle or infallible Hand to do it with.[45]

He preferred *Mercy* before *Sacrifice,*[46] and therefore we may well believe, that the unmerciful Sacrifices some Men now offer, I mean *Imprisoning Persons, Spoiling of Goods, and leaving whole Families destitute of Subsistence,* as well as disinheriting them of all civil Privileges in the Government, are far from being grateful to him, who therefore came into the World, and preach'd that Heavenly Doctrine of *Forbearing,* and *Loving of Enemies,* and laid down his most *innocent* Life for us, whilst we were Rebels, that by such peaceable Precepts, and so patient an Example, the World might be prevailed upon to leave those barbarous Courses. And doubtless, very lamentable will their Condition be, who at the Coming of the great Lord, shall be found *Beaters of their Fellow-Servants.*[47]

In vain do Men *go to Church, pray, preach, and stile themselves Believers, Christians, Children of God,* &c. Whilst such Acts of Severity are cherished among them; and any Disposition to molest harmless Neighbours for their Conscience, so much as *countenanc'd* by them. A Course quite repugnant to

44. Matthew 25:21–23; Luke 19:17; Matthew 7:23; and Luke 13:27.

45. Luke 9:51–56; Matthew 13:24–30.

46. Matthew 9:13, 12:7; see also Hosea 6:6.

47. Matthew 18:21–35.

Christ's Example and Command. In short, the *Promoting* of this *General Religion,* by a severe *Reprehension and Punishment of Vice,* and *Encouragement of Virtue,* is the *Interest of our Superiors,* several Ways.

1. In that it meets with, and takes in all the Religious Perswasions of the Kingdom, for all pretend to make this their *Corner Stone.* Let them be equally encouraged to square their Building by it. *Penal Laws for Religion, is a Church* with a *Sting in her Tail;* take that out, and there is no Fear of the People's Love and Duty: And what better Obligation or Security can the civil Magistrate desire? Every Man owns the Text; 'tis the *Comment* that's disputed. Let it but please him to make the *Text only Sacred and Necessary,* and leave Men to keep Company with their own Meanings or Consequences, and he does not only prudently take in all, but suppresseth nice Searches, Fixes Unity upon Materials, Quiets present Differences about Things of lesser Moment, retrieves Humanity, and *Christian* Clemency, and fills the Kingdom with Love and Respect to their Superiors.

2. *Next,* A Promotion of General Religion, which, being in it self practical; brings back ancient *Virtue.* Good Living will thrive in this Soil: Men will grow *Honest, Trusty,* and *Temperate;* we may expect Good Neighbourhood and cordial Friendship: One may then depend more upon a *Word,* than now upon an *Oath.* How lamentable is it to see People afraid of one another; Men made and provided for of one God, and that must be judged by that one Eternal God, yet full of Diffidence in what each other says, and most commonly interpret, as people read *Hebrew,* all Things *backward.*

3. The *Third* Benefit is, that Men will be more industrious; more diligent in their lawful *Callings,* which will encrease our Manufacture, set the Idle and Poor to work for their Lively-Hood, and enable the several Countries, with more Ease and Decency to maintain the Aged and impotent among them. Nor will this only help to make the *Lazy* conscientiously industrious, but the Industrious and Conscientious Man *chearful* at his Labour, when he is assured to keep what he works for, and that the Sweat of his Brows shall not be made a Forfeit for his Conscience.

4. It will render the Magistrates Province more facil, and Government a Safe as well as Easy Thing. For, as *Tacitus* says of *Agricola*'s instructing the *Britains* in Arts and Sciences, and using them with more Humanity than other Governors had done, that it made them fitter for Government;[48] So if Practi-

48. Tacitus, *Agricola,* chs. 19–22.

cal Religion, and the Laws made to maintain it, were duly regarded, the very Natures of Men, now wild and froward, by a Prejudiced Education and Cross and Jealous Interests, would learn Moderation, and see it to be their greatest Interest to pursue a Sober and Amicable Conversation; which would Ease the Magistrate of much of his present Trouble, and increase the Number of Men fit to govern; of which the Parliament-Times are an undeniable Instance. And the Truth is, 'tis a Piece of Slavery to have the Regiment of Ignorants and Ruffians; but there is true Glory in having the Government of Men, instructed in the Justice and Prudence of their own Laws and Country.

Lastly, It is out of this Nursery of Virtue, Men should be drawn to be planted in the Government, not what is their Opinion, but what is their Manners and Capacity? Here the Field is large, and the Magistrate has Room to choose good Officers for the Publick Good. Heaven will prosper so natural, so noble, and so Christian an *Essay;* which ought not to be the least Consideration with a good Magistrate; and the rather, because the Neglect of this Practical Religion, hath been the Ruin of Kingdoms and Commonwealths, among *Heathens, Jews* and *Christians.* This laid *Tarquin* low, and his Race never rose more.[49] How puissant were *Lacedaemon* and *Athens* of *Greece,* 'till Luxury had eaten out their Severity, and a Pompous Living, contrary to their Excellent Laws, render'd their Execution intolerable? And was not *Hanibal*'s Army a Prey to their own Idleness and Pleasure, which by effeminating their Natures, conquer'd them, when the whole Power of *Rome* could not do it? What else betray'd *Rome* to *Caesar*'s Ambition, and made Way for the After-rents and Divisions of the Empire, the Merit as well as Conquest and Inheritance of a well govern'd People for several Ages, as long as their Manners lasted? The *Jews* likewise were prosperous, while they *kept the Judgments and Statutes of their God;* but when they became Rebellious and Dissolute, the Almighty either visited them from Heaven, or exposed them to the Fury of their Neighbours. Nothing else sent *Zedekiah* to *Babylon,* and gave him and the People a Victim to *Nebuchadnezzar* and his Army.[50]

Neglect of Laws and Dissolute Living, Andrew Horn (that lived in the Time of *Edward the First,* as before cited) tells us, was the *Cause of the Miserable*

49. According to Roman legend, Lucius Tarquinius Priscus gained the throne in Rome ca. 600 B.C.E. His son murdered his own father-in-law to get the throne, and his grandson, Sextus Tarquinius, raped Brutus's wife Lucretia, precipitating the founding of the Republic ca. 500 B.C.E.

50. 2 Kings 24–25; and Jeremiah 21.

Thraldom and Desolation the Britains *sustained by Invaders and Conquerors.*[51] And pray, what else hath been the English of our *Sweeping Pestilence, Dreadful Fires,* and *Outragious Factions* of late Years? Hundreds of Examples might be brought in this Case; but their Frequency shall excuse me.

Thus have I honestly and plainly clear'd my Conscience for my *Country,* and answer'd, I hope, modestly, and tho' briefly, yet fully, the Import of the *Question* propounded, with *Honour* to the Magistrate and Safety to the People, by an happy Conjunction of their Interests. I shall conclude,

That as Greater Honour and Wisdom cannot well be attributed to any Sort of Men, than for our Superiors, under their Circumstances, to be sought to by all Perswasions, *confided in by all* Perswasions, *and obey'd by all* Perswasions; *and to make those* Perswasions *know, that it is their Interest so to do, as well as that it is the Interest of our Superiors, they should, and to which the Expedients proposed naturally tend; So, for a farther Inducement to embrace it, let them be constantly remembred, that the Interest of our English Governors is like to stand longer upon the Legs of the* English People, *than of the* English Church: *Since the one takes in the Strength of all Interests, and the other leaves out all but her own: And it may happen that the* English Church *may fail, or go travel again, but it is not probable that the* English People *should do either; especially while* Property *is preserv'd, a Ballance kept, General Religion propagated, and the World continues.*

May all this prevail with our Superiors to make the best Use of their little Time; Remembring, in the midst of all their Power *and* Grandeur, *that they carry Mortality about them, and are equally liable to the Scrutiny and Judgment of the* Last Day, *with the poorest* Peasant; *and that they have a great* Stewardship *to account for: So that* Moderation *and* Virtue *being their Course, they, for the future, shall steer; after having faithfully discharged that great Trust reposed in them, by God and this Free People, they may, with Comfort to their* Souls, *and Honour to their* Names *and* Actions, *safely anchor in the Haven of Eternal Blessedness: So prays, with much Sincerity,*

An *English-Christian-Man,*
And Their True Friend,
WILLIAM PENN.

51. Horn, *Mirror of Justices,* bk. 1, ch. 2.

A COROLLARY.

THAT the *People* are under a great *Dissatisfaction*. That the Way to *Quiet Differences,* and render contrary *Interests Subservient* to the Interest of the Government, is,

First, *To maintain inviolably the Rights of it,* viz. Liberty *and* Property, Legislation *and* Juries, *without Neglect. That, Slighting and Infringing them hath been the* Injury of Prince and People, *and early or late the* Ruin *of the Contrivers of so ill Designs; and when all has been done, the only Expedient has been, to come back again to* English Law. *This takes in all, pleases all, because it secures and profits all. Sacrificing Privileges for the Sake of Conformity, makes a Breach upon the Civil Government, alienates the People's Affections from their Prince, lodges Property in the Church, so as none can come at it, but through Obedience to her Rites, for she at this Rate has the Keeping of it; a Thing unknown, as well as unsafe to the Ancient* English Government.

2dly. *That the Prince govern himself upon a Ballance towards all Religious Interests: That this best poizes Parties to his Security, renders him Master of an Universal Affection, and makes him truly and safely Prince of all his Country: But the contrary Course narrows his Justice and Mercy, makes the Government to shine but upon one Part of the Kingdom; to be just but to one Party, and disinherit the rest from their Birth-right: That this Course ends in great Disadvantage to the Peace, Plenty, and Safety of Prince and People.*

3dly. *And Lastly, Instead of being Uncharitable, Severe and Cruel for Modifications, let the Debate about them Sleep, and General and Practical Religion be promoted, that which receives an* Amen *in every Man's Conscience, from the* Principle of Divine Life *(as the Lord Keeper well called it) in every Breast, That all agree in the most weighty Doctrines; and that nothing will sooner sweeten Men's Blood, and mollify their Natures, than employing that Time and Pains they bestow on fruitless Contests, in* living up to what they both know, believe and accord in: *That this leaves Men to keep Company with their own Comments, and makes the Text only Sacred, and Holy Living Necessary, not only to Heavenly, but Earthly Places, I mean Preferments: Whence* Virtue *becomes the Door to* Favour, and Conscience *(now smother'd in the Crowd of Sinister Interests) the* Noble Rule of Living.

God Almighty, if it please him, beget Noble Resolutions in the Hearts of our Superiors to use these Plain and Safe Expedients, that Charity may supplant

Cruelty, Contest yield to Good Life, and present Distances meet in a just and kind Neighbourhood.

Great and Honourable is that Prince, and Free and Happy that People, where these Things take Place.

William Penn.

{ PART II }

Penn's Argument for Religious Liberty

THE
Great CASE of Liberty of Conscience
Once more briefly Debated and Defended, by the Authority of REASON, SCRIPTURE, and ANTIQUITY: Which may serve the Place of a General Reply to such late Discourses; as have Oppos'd a *Toleration* (1670)
The Author *W. P.*

Whatsoever ye would that Men should do to you, do ye even so to them: *Mat. 7. 12.*

Render unto Caesar, the Things that are Caesar's; and to God, the Things that are God's. Mark 12. 17.

To the Supream Authority of *England.*

TOLERATION (for these Ten Years past) has not been more the Cry of some, than PERSECUTION has been the Practice of others, though not on *Grounds equally Rational.*

The present Cause of this Address, is to solicite a Conversion of that Power to our Relief, which hitherto has been imploy'd to our Depression; that after this large Experience of our Innocency, and long since expir'd *Apprenticeship of Cruel Sufferings,* you will be pleas'd to cancel all our Bonds, and give us a Possession of those Freedoms, to which we are entituled by *English* Birthright.

This has been often promised to us, and we as earnestly have expected the Performance; but to this Time we labour under the unspeakable Pressure of Nasty Prisons, and daily Confiscation of our Goods, to the apparent Ruin of intire Families.

We would not attribute the whole of this Severity to Malice, since not a little share may justly be ascribed to Mis-intelligence.

For 'tis the Infelicity of Governours to see and hear by the Eyes and Ears of other Men; which is equally unhappy for the People.

And we are bold to say, that Suppositions and meer Conjectures, have been the best Measures, that most have taken of Us, and of our Principles; for whilst there have been none more inoffensive, we have been mark't for Capital Offenders.

'Tis hard that we should always lie under this undeserved Imputation; and which is worse, be Persecuted as such, without the Liberty of a just Defence.

In short, if you are apprehensive, that our Principles are inconsistent with the Civil Government, grant us a free Conference about the Points in Question, and let us know, what are those Laws, essential to Preservation, that our Opinions carry an Opposition to? And if upon a due enquiry we are found so Heterodox, as represented, it will be then but time enough to inflict these heavy Penalties upon us.

And as this Medium seems the fairest, and most reasonable; so can you never do your selves greater Justice, either in the Vindication of your Proceedings against us, if we be Criminal; or if Innocent, in dis-ingaging your Service of such, as have been Authors of so much Mis-information.

But could we once obtain the Favour of such Debate we doubt not to evince a clear Consistency of our Life and Doctrine with the *English* Government; and that an indulging of Dissenters in the Sense defended, is not only most Christian and Rational, but Prudent also. And the Contrary (how plausibly soever insinuated) the most injurious to the Peace, and destructive of that discreet Ballance, which the Best and Wisest States, have ever carefully Observ'd.

But if this fair and equal Offer, find not a Place with you, *on which to rest it's Foot;* much less that it should bring us back the *Olive Branch of TOLERATION;* we heartily embrace and bless the Providence of God; and in his Strength resolve, by Patience, to outweary *Persecution,* and by our constant Sufferings, seek to obtain a Victory, more Glorious, than any our Adversaries can atchieve by all their Cruelties.

Vincit qui patitur.[1]

From a Prisoner for Conscience-Sake,

Newgate, the 7th of the 12th
Month, call'd *February,* 1670.

W. P.

1. He conquers who endures.

The PREFACE.

WERE some as Christian, as they boast themselves to be, 'twould save us all the Labour we bestow in rendring *Persecution* so Unchristian, as it most truly is: Nay were they those Men of Reason they Character themselves, and what the *Civil Law* stiles good Citizens, it had been needless for us to tell them, that neither can any external Coercive Power convince the Understanding of the poorest Idiot, nor Fines and Prisons be judg'd fit and adequate Penalties for Faults purely intellectual; as well as that they are destructive of all Civil Government.

But we need not run so far as beyond the Seas, to fetch the Sense of the *Codes, Institutes,* and *Digests,* out of the *Corpus Civile,* to adjudge such Practices incongruous with the good of Civil Society; since our own good, old, admirable Laws of *England,* have made such excellent Provision for it's Inhabitants, that if they were but thought as fit to be executed by this present Age, as they were rightly judg'd necessary to be made by our careful Ancestors: We know how great a Stroak they would give such as venture to lead away our Property in *Triumph* (as our just Forfeiture) for only Worshipping our God in a differing Way, from that which is more generally Profest and Establisht.

And indeed it is most truly lamentable, That above others (who have been found in so Un-natural and Antichristian an Imployment) those, that by their own frequent Practices and Voluminous Apologies, have defended a Separation (from the *Papacy*) should now become such earnest Persecutors for it, not considering, that the Enaction of such Laws, as restrain Persons from the free Exercise of their Consciences, in Matters of Religion, is but a knotting Whip-cord to lash their own Posterity; whom they can never promise to be conformed to a *National Religion.* Nay, since Mankind is subject to such Mutability, they can't ensure themselves, from being taken by some Perswasions, that are esteem'd Heterodox, and consequently catch themselves in Snares of their own providing. And for Men thus liable to change, (and no ways certain of their own Belief to be the most infallible,) as by their multiply'd Concessions may appear, to enact any Religion, or prohibit Persons from the free Exercise of theirs, sounds harsh in the Ears of all modest and unbya'st Men. We are bold to say *our Protestant Ancestors* thought of nothing less, than to be succeeded by *Persons Vain glorious of their Reformation,* and yet *Adversaries to Liberty of Conscience; for to People in their Wits, it seems a Paradox.*

Not that we are so ignorant, as to think it is within the Reach of Humane Power to fetter Conscience, or to restrain it's Liberty *strictly taken:* But that plain *English, of Liberty of Conscience,* we would be *understood* to mean, is this; namely, *The Free and Uninterrupted Exercise of our Consciences, in that Way of Worship, we are most clearly perswaded, God requires us to serve Him in (without endangering our undoubted Birthright of* English *Freedoms) which being Matter of FAITH; we Sin if we omit, and they can't do less, that shall endeavour it.*

To tell us, we are Obstinate and *Enemies to Government,* are but those Groundless Phrases, the first Reformers were not a little pestered with; but as they said, so say we, The being call'd *this,* or *that,* does not conclude us so; and hitherto we have not been detected of that Fact, which only justifies such Criminations.

But however free we can approve our selves of Actions prejudicial to the *Civil Government;* 'tis most certain we have not suffered a little, as Criminals, and therefore have been far from being free from Sufferings; indeed, in some respect, Horrid Plunders: *Widows* have lost their *Cows, Orphans their Beds, and Labourers their Tools.* A Tragedy so sad, that methinks it should oblige them to do in *England,* as they did at *Athens;* when they had sacrificed their Divine *Socrates* to the sottish Fury of their lewd and Comical Multitude, they so regretted their hasty Murder, that not only the Memorial of *Socrates* was most venerable with them, but his Enemies they esteemed so much theirs, that none would Trade or hold the least Commerce with them; for which some turned their own Executioners, and without any other Warrant than their own Guilt, hang'd themselves. How near a-kin the wretched mercenary Informers of our Age are to those, the great Resemblance that is betwixt their Actions manifestly shews.

And we are bold to say, the grand Fomenters of Persecution, are no better Friends to the *English* State, than were *Anytus* and *Aristophanes* of old to that of *Athens,* the Case being so nearly the same, as that they did not more bitterly envy the Reputation of *Socrates* amongst the *Athenians* for his grave and Religious Lectures (thereby giving the Youth a Diversion from frequenting their Plays) than some now emulate the true Dissenter, for his Pious Life, and great Industry.[2]

2. Anytus is one of Socrates' prosecutors in Plato's *Apology;* Aristophanes satirized Socrates in his play *The Clouds.*

And as that famous Common-wealth was noted to decline, and the most observing Persons of it dated its decay from that illegal and ingrateful Carriage towards *Socrates* (witness their dreadful Plagues, with other multiply'd Disasters). So it is not less worthy Observation, that Heaven hath not been wholly wanting to scourge this Land, for, as well their Cruelty to the Conscientious, as their other multiply'd Provocations.

And when we seriously consider the dreadful Judgments that now impend the Nation (by Reason of the Robbery, Violence, unwonted Oppression, that almost every where, have not only been committed, upon the Poor, the Widow, and the Fatherless; but most tenaciously justified, and the Actors manifestly encourag'd) in meer Pity, and Concern, for the Everlasting Welfare of such as have not quite sinn'd away their Visitation (for some have) we once more bring to publick View, our Reasons against Persecution, backt with the plainest Instances, both of Scripture and Antiquity. If but one may be perswaded, to desist from making any farther Progress in such an Anti-protestant, and truly Anti-christian Path, as that of persecuting Honest and Virtuous Englishmen, for only worshipping the God that made them, in the Way they judge most acceptable with him.

But if those, who ought to think themselves oblig'd to weigh these Affairs with the greatest Deliberation, *will obstinately close their Eyes, to these last Remonstrances;* and slightly over-look the *pinching Case of so many thousand Families,* that are by these Severities expos'd for Prey, to the unsatiable Appetites of a *Villanous Crew of broken Informers* (daubing themselves with that deluding Apprehension of pleasing God, or at least of profiting the Country; whilst they greatly displease the one, and evidently ruin the other as certain as ever the *Lord God Almighty* destroyed *Sodom,* and lay'd waste *Gomorrah,* by the consuming Flames of His just Indignations); will he hasten to make desolate this wanton Land, and not leave an Hiding Place for the Oppressor.[3]

Let no man therefore think himself too big to be admonish'd, nor put too slight a Value upon the *Lives, Liberties,* and *Properties,* of so many Thousand Free-born *English* Families, Embark't in that one Concern of *Liberty of Conscience.* It will become him better to reflect upon his own Mortality, and not forget his Breath is in his Nostrils, and that every Action of his Life the Everlasting God will bring to Judgment, and him for them.

3. Genesis 19.

CHAP. I.

That Imposition, Restraint, and Persecution for Conscience-Sake, highly Invade the Divine Prerogative, and Divest the Almighty of a Right, due to none beside Himself, and that in five eminent Particulars.

THE great Case of *Liberty of Conscience* so often Debated and Defended (however dissatisfactorily to such *as have so little Conscience as to Persecute for it)* is once more brought to publick View, by a late Act against Dissenters, and Bill, or an additional one, that we all hop'd the Wisdom of our Rulers had long since laid aside, as what was fitter to be passed into an Act of perpetual Oblivion.[4] The Kingdoms are alarm'd at this Procedure, and Thousands greatly at a Stand, wondring what should be the Meaning of such hasty Resolutions, that seem as fatal as they were unexpected: *Some ask what Wrong they have done; others, what Peace they have broken; and all, what Plots they have form'd, to prejudice the present Government, or occasions given, to hatch new Jealousies of them and their Proceedings,* being not conscious to themselves of Guilt in any such Respect.

For mine own Part, I publickly confess my self to be a *very hearty Dissenter from the establish't Worship of these Nations,* as believing *Protestants* to have much degenerated from their first Principles, and as owning the *poor despised Quakers,* in Life and Doctrine, to have espoused the Cause of God, and to be the undoubted Followers of Jesus Christ, in his most Holy, Straight and Narrow Way that leads to the Eternal Rest. In all which I know no Treason, nor any Principle that would urge me to a Thought injurious to the Civil Peace. If any be defective in this particular, 'tis equal, both Individuals and whole Societies should answer for their own Defaults, but we are clear.

However, all conclude that Union very Ominous, and Unhappy, which

4. The Conventicles Act (22 Car. II, cap. 1), originally passed in 1664 and reinstated in 1670. It forbade religious gatherings of more than five people not of the same household. The act is reprinted in J. P. Kenyon, *The Stuart Constitution: Documents and Commentary,* 2d ed. (Cambridge, 1986), doc. 106, pp. 356–59.

makes the first Discovery of it self, *by a* John Baptist's *Head in a Charger,*[5] They mean that Feast some are design'd to make upon the Liberties and Properties of Free-born *Englishmen, since to have the Intail of those undoubted hereditary Rights cut off (for Matters purely relative of another World) is a severe beheading in the Law;* which must be obvious to all, but such as measure the Justice of Things only by that Proportion they bear with their own Interest.

A Sort of Men that seek themselves, though at the apparent Loss of whole Societies, *like to that barbarous Fancy of old, which had rather that* Rome *should burn, than it be without the Satisfaction of a Bon-fire:* And sad it is, when Men have so far stupified their Understandings with the *strong doses of their private Interest,* as to become insensible of the Publick's. Certainly such an Over-fondness for self, or that strong Inclination, to raise themselves in the Ruin of what does not so much oppose them, as that they will believe so, because they would be persecuting, is a malignant Enemy to that Tranquillity, *which, all Dissenting Parties seem to believe, would be the Consequence of a Toleration.*

In short we say, there can be but two Ends in *Persecution,* the one to satisfie (which none can ever do) the *insatiable Appetites of a decimating Clergy (whose best Arguments are Fines and Imprisonments)* and the other, as thinking therein *they do God good Service;* but 'tis so hateful a Thing upon any Account, that we shall make it appear by this ensuing Discourse, to be a declared Enemy to *God, Religion,* and the *Good of humane Society.*

The whole will be small, since it is but an *Epitome* of no larger a Tract than fourteen Sheets; yet divides it self into the same Particulars, every of which we shall defend against *Imposition, Restraint,* and *Persecution,* though not with that Scope of *Reason* (nor consequently *Pleasure* to the Readers) being by other contingent Disappointments, limited to a narrow Stint.

The Terms explained, and the Question stated.

First, By *Liberty of Conscience,* we understand not only a meer *Liberty of the Mind,* in believing or disbelieving this or that Principle or Doctrine, *but the Exercise of our selves in a visible Way of Worship, upon our believing it to be indispensibly required at our Hands, that if we neglect it for Fear or Favour of any*

5. Matthew 14:1–12; and Mark 6:14–29.

Mortal Man, we Sin, and incur Divine Wrath: Yet we would be so understood to extend and justifie the Lawfulness of our so meeting to worship God, as not to contrive, or abet any Contrivance destructive of the Government and Laws of the Land, tending to Matters of an external Nature, directly, or indirectly; but so far only, as it may refer to religious Matters, and a Life to come, and consequently wholly independent of the secular Affairs of this, wherein we are suppos'd to Trangress.

Secondly, By Imposition, Restraint, and Persecution, we don't only mean, the strict Requiring of us to believe this to be true, or that to be false; and upon Refusal, to incur the Penalties enacted in such Cases; but by those Terms we mean thus much, any coercive Lett or Hindrance to us, from meeting together to perform those Religious Exercises which are according to our Faith and Perswasion.

The Question stated.

For Proof of the aforesaid Terms thus given, we singly state the Question thus,

Whether *Imposition, Restraint,* and *Persecution,* upon Persons for Exercising such a Liberty of Conscience, as is before expressed, and so circumstantiated, be not to impeach the Honour of God, the Meekness of the Christian Religion, the Authority of Scripture, the Priviledge of Nature, the Principles of common Reason, the Well-being of Government, and Apprehensions of the greatest Personages of former and latter Ages.

First, Then we say that *Imposition, Restraint,* and *Persecution,* for Matters relating to Conscience, *directly invade the Divine Prerogative, and Divest the Almighty of a Due, proper to none besides himself.* And this we prove by these five Particulars.

1. *First,* If we do allow the Honour of our Creation, due to God only, and that no other besides himself has endow'd us with those excellent Gifts of *Understanding, Reason, Judgment,* and *Faith,* and consequently that he only is the Object as well as Author, both of our *Faith, Worship,* and *Service,* then whosoever shall interpose their Authority to enact *Faith* and *Worship,* in a Way that seems not to us congruous with what he has discover'd to us to be *Faith* and *Worship* (whose alone Property it is to do it) or to restrain us from what we are perswaded is our *indispensible Duty,* they evidently usurp this Authority and invade his incommunicable Right of Government over Con-

science: *For the Inspiration of the Almighty gives Understanding: And Faith is the Gift of God,* says the *Divine Writ.*[6]

Secondly. *Such magisterial Determinations carry an evident Claim to that Infallibility,* which *Protestants* have been hitherto so jealous of owning, that to avoid the *Papists,* they have denied it to all, but God himself.

Either they have forsook their old Plea, or if not, we desire to know when, and where, they were invested with that divine Excellency, and whether *Imposition, Restraint,* and *Persecution,* were deem'd by God ever the Fruits of his Spirit: However, that it self was not sufficient; for unless it appear as well to us, that they have it, as to them who have it, we cannot believe it upon any convincing Evidence, but by Tradition only; an *Anti-Protestant Way of Believing.*

Thirdly, *It enthrones Man as King over Conscience, the alone just Claim and Priviledge of his Creator, whose Thoughts are not as Men's Thoughts* but has reserv'd to himself, *that Empire* from all the *Caesars* on Earth; for if Men in Reference to Souls, and Bodies, things appertaining to this and t'other World, shall be subject to their Fellow-Creatures, what follows? but that *Caesar* (however he got it) has all, God's Share, and his own too; and being Lord of both, Both are *Caesar's* and not *God's.*[7]

Fourthly, *It defeats God's Work of Grace, and the invisible Operation of his Eternal Spirit, which can alone beget Faith, and is only to be obey'd, in and about Religion and Worship, and attributes* Men's Conformity *to outward Force and Corporal Punishments.* A Faith subject to as many Revolutions as the Powers that enact it.

Fifthly and Lastly, *Such* Persons *assume the Judgment of the great Tribunal unto* themselves; for to whomsoever Men are imposedly or restrictively subject and accountable in Matters of Faith, Worship and Conscience; in them alone must the Power of Judgment reside; but it is equally true that God shall judge all by Jesus Christ, and that no Man is so accountable to his fellow Creatures, as to be imposed upon, restrain'd, or persecuted for any Matter of Conscience whatever.

Thus and in many more particulars are Men accustomed to intrench upon *Divine Property,* to gratifie particular Interests in the World (and at best)

6. Job 32:8; and Ephesians 2:8.

7. On God's and men's thoughts, see Isaiah 55:8–9; on rendering to Caesar and God, see Matthew 22:15–22; Mark 12:13–17; and Luke 20:20–26.

through a Misguided Apprehension to imagine *they do God good Service,* that where they cannot give Faith, *They will use Force,* which kind of Sacrifice is nothing less unreasonable *than the other is abominable:* God will not give his Honour to another, and to him only that searches the Heart and tries the Reins, it is our Duty to ascribe the Gifts of Understanding and Faith, without which none can please God.

CHAP. II.

They overturn the Christian Religion; 1. *In the* Nature *of it, which is* Meekness; 2. *In the* Practice *of it, which is* Suffering; 3. *In the* Promotion *of it, since all further Discoveries are prohibited;* 4. *In the* Rewards *of it, which are* Eternal.

THE next great Evil which attends External Force in Matters of *Faith* and *Worship,* is no less than the Overthrow of the whole Christian Religion, and this we will briefly evidence in these four particulars 1. *That there can be nothing more remote from the Nature.* 2. *The Practice.* 3. *The Promotion.* 4. *The* Rewards *of it.*

1. First, it is the Priviledge of the Christian Faith above the dark Suggestions of ancient and modern Superstitious Traditions, to carry with it a most Self-evidencing Verity, which ever was sufficient to proselyte Believers, *without the weak Auxiliaries of external Power;* The Son of God, *and great Example of the World,*[8] was so far from calling his Father's Omnipotency in Legions of Angels to his Defence, that he at once repeal'd all Acts of Force, and defin'd to us the Nature of his Religion in this one great Saying of his, *MY KINGDOM IS NOT OF THIS WORLD.*[9] It was spiritual, not carnal, accompanied with Weapons, as heavenly as it's own Nature, and design'd for the Good and Salvation of the Soul, and not the Injury and Destruction of the Body: No Goals,

8. John 13:15; and 1 Peter 2:21.

9. For Jesus' renunciation of force, see Matthew 26:52–54, John 18:11; and for his otherworldly kingdom, see John 18:36.

Fines, Exiles, &c. but *sound Reason, clear Truth* and a *strict Life.* In short, the Christian Religion intreats all, but compels none.

Secondly, *That Restraint and Persecution overturn the Practice of it; I* need go no farther than the allowed *Martyrologies* of several Ages, of which the Scriptures claim a Share; begin with *Abel,* go down to *Moses,* so to the *Prophets,* and then to the Meek Example of *Jesus Christ* himself; How patiently devoted was he, to undergo the Contradictions of Men? and so far from persecuting any, that he would not so much as revile his Persecutors, but prayed for them;[10] thus lived his *Apostles* and the true Christians, of the first three Hundred Years: Nor are the famous Stories of our first Reformers silent in the Matter; witness the Christian Practices of the *Waldenses, Lollards, Hussites, Lutherans,* and our noble *Martyrs,* who as became the true Followers of Jesus Christ, enacted and confirm'd their Religion, with their own Blood, and not with the Blood of their Opposers.

Thirdly, *Restraint and Persecution obstruct the Promotion of the Christian Religion,* for if such as restrain, confess themselves, *miserable Sinners, and altogether imperfect,* it either follows, that they never desire to be better, or that they should encourage such as may be capable of farther informing and reforming them; they condemn the Papists for encoffening the Scriptures and their Worship, in an unknown Tongue, and yet are guilty themselves of the same kind of Fact.

Fourthly; *They prevent many of eternal Rewards,* for where any are Religious for Fear, and that of Men, 'tis slavish, and the Recompence of such Religion is Condemnation, not Peace: besides 'tis Man that is served, who having no *Power* but what is *Temporary,* his Reward must needs be so too; he that imposes a Duty, or restrains from one, must reward; but because no Man can Reward for such Duties, no Man can or ought to impose them, or restrain from them, so that we conclude *Imposition, Restraint* and *Persecution,* are destructive of the Christian Religion, in the Nature, Practice, Promotion and Rewards of it, which are Eternal.

10. Matthew 5:44.

CHAP. III.

They oppose the plainest Testimonies of Divine Writ that can be, which condemn all Force *upon* Conscience.

WE FARTHER say, that *Imposition, Restraint* and *Persecution* are repugnant to the plain Testimonies and Precepts of the Scriptures.

1. *The Inspiration of the Almighty gives Understanding,* Job 32. 8.

If no Man can believe before he understands, and no Man can understand before he is inspir'd of God, then are the Impositions of Men excluded as unreasonable, and their Persecutions for non-Obedience as inhuman.

2. *Wo unto them that take Counsel, but not of me,* Isa. 30. 1.

3. *Wo unto them that make a Man an* Offender *for a Word, and lay a Snare for him that reproves in the Gate, and turn aside the Just for a Thing of Nought,* Isa. 29. 15. 21.

4. *Let the Wheat and the Tares* grow together, *until the Time of the Harvest, or End of the World.* Matt. 13. 27, 28, 29.

5. *And Jesus called them unto him, and said ye know that the Princes of the* Gentiles, *exercise Dominion over them, and they that are great exercise Authority upon them,* but it shall not be so amongst you. Matt. 20. 25, 26.

6. *And* Jesus said unto them, *Render unto Caesar the Things that are Caesar's, and unto God the Things that are God's.* Luke 20. 25.

7. *When his Disciples* saw this (that there were Non-conformists then as well as now) *they said, wilt thou that we command Fire to come down from Heaven and consume them, as* Elias *did; but he turned, and* rebuked them, *and said, Ye know not what Spirit ye are of;* for the Son of Man is not come to destroy Men's Lives but to save them, *Luke* 9. 54, 55, 56.

8. *Howbeit, when the Spirit of Truth is come,* he shall lead you into all Truth, *John* 16. 8. 13.

9. *But now the Anointing which ye have received of him, abides in you, and you need not that any Man teach you, (much less* impose upon any, or restrain them from what any are perswaded it leads to) *but as the same Anointing teaches you of all Things, and is Truth and is no Lye,* 1 John 2. 27.

10. *Dearly Beloved, avenge not your selves, but rather give Place unto Wrath* (much less should any be Wrathful that are called Christians, where no Occa-

sion is given) *therefore if thine Enemy Hunger feed him, and if he Thirst, give him Drink; Recompence no Man Evil for Evil,* Rom. 12. 19, 20, 21.

11. *For though we walk in the Flesh* (that is in the Body or visible World) *we do not war after the Flesh, for the Weapons of our Warfare are not Carnal.* 2 Cor. 10. 3. (but Fines and Imprisonments are, and such use not the Apostle's Weapons that employ those) for a *Bishop,* 1 Tim. 3. 3. (saith Paul) *must be of good Behaviour, apt to teach,* no Striker, but be gentle unto all Men, *Patient, in Meekness instructing (not Persecuting) those that oppose themselves, if God peradventure will give them Repentance to the Acknowledging of the Truth,* 2 Tim. 2. 24, 25.

12. Lastly, We shall subjoyn one Passage more, and then no more of this particular; *Whatsoever ye would that Men should do you, do ye even so to them.* Mat. 7. 12. Luke 6. 31.

Now upon the whole we seriously ask, *Whether any should be imposed upon, or restrain'd, in Matters of* Faith *and* Worship? *Whether such Practices become the Gospel, or* are suitable to Christ's meek Precepts and suffering Doctrine? And lastly, *Whether those, who are herein guilty, do to us,* as they would be done unto by others.

What if any were once severe to you; many are unconcerned in that, who are yet liable to the Lash, as if they were not. But if you once thought *the Imposition of a Directory Unreasonable, and a Restraint from your Way of Worship, Unchristian,* can you believe that *Liberty of Conscience* is changed, because the *Parties,* in Point of Power, are?[11] or that the same Reasons do not yet remain in Vindication of an Indulgence for others, that were once employed by you, for your selves? Surely such Conjectures would argue gross Weakness.

To conclude, whether *Persecutors* at any Time read the *Scriptures,* we know not; but certain we are, *such Practice, as little of them as may be,* who with so much Delight reject them, and think it no small Accession to the Discovery of their Loyalty, *to lead us and our Properties in Triumph after them.*

11. Penn here refers to the *Directory for the Publique Worship of God Throughout the Three Kingdomes* (London, 1646), which Parliament approved after it banned use of the Book of Common Prayer in 1645. A selection from the directory is reprinted in *Religion and Society in Early Modern England: A Sourcebook,* ed. David Cressy and Lori Anne Ferrell (London, 1996), pp. 186–92.

CHAP. IV.

They are Enemies to the Priviledge of Nature; 1. as rendring some more, and Others less than Men; 2. As subverting the Universal Good that is God's Gift to Men; 3. As destroying all natural Affection. Next, they are Enemies to the noble Principle of Reason, as appears in eight great Instances.

WE FARTHER say, That *Imposition, Restraint,* and *Persecution, are also destructive of the great* Priviledge of Nature *and* Principle of Reason: *Of Nature in three Instances:*

1. First, If God Almighty has made of one *Blood all Nations,* as himself has declar'd,[12] and that he has given them both Senses *Corporal* and *Intellectual,* to discern Things and their Differences, so as to assert or deny from Evidences and Reasons proper to each; then Where any Enacts the Belief or Disbelief of any Thing upon the rest, or restrains any from the Exercise of their Faith *to them indispensible,* such *exalts himself* beyond his *Bounds; Enslaves his Fellow Creatures, invades their Right of Liberty, and so perverts the whole Order of Nature.*

Secondly, *Mankind* is hereby robbed of the Use and benefit of that *Instinct* of a *Deity,* which is so natural to him, that he can be no more without it, and be, than he can be without the most essential Part of himself; For to what serves that *Divine Principle* in the *Universality of* Mankind, if Men be restricted by the Prescriptions of some Individuals? But if the excellent Nature of it *inclines Men to God,* not Man; *if the Power of Accusing and Excusing be committed to it; if the troubled Thoughts and sad Reflections of Forlorn and Dying Men make their Tendency that Way only,* (as being hopeless of all other Relief and Succour from any *external Power* or *Command*) What shall we say, but that such as *invalidate* the Authority of this *Heavenly* Instinct, (*as Imposition and Restraint evidently do*) *destroy Nature,* or *that Priviledge which Men are born with, and to.*

Thirdly, *All natural Affection is destroy'd;* for those who have so little tender-

12. Acts 17:26.

ness, as to persecute Men, that cannot for Conscience sake yield them Compliance, manifestly act injuriously to their Fellow Creatures, and consequently are Enemies to Nature; For Nature being one in all, *such as ruin those who are equally intituled with themselves to Nature, ruin it in them,* as in Liberty, Property, *&c. And so bring the State of Nature to the State of War, the great* Leviathan *of the Times, as ignorantly, as Boldly, does assert.*[13]

But *Secondly,* we also prove them destructive of the noble Principle of Reason, and that in these eight *Particulars.*

1. *In that those who impose, or restrain, are uncertain of the Truth, and Justifiableness of their Actions in either* of these, their own Discourses and Confessions are *pregnant Instances,* where they tell us, that *they do not pretend to be infallible, only they humbly conceive 'tis thus, or it is not.* Since then they are uncertain and fallible, how can they impose upon, or restrain others whom they are so far from assuring, as they are not able to do so much for themselves? *what is this, but to impose an uncertain Faith, upon certain Penalties?*

3. As he that acts doubtfully is damned, so Faith in all Acts of Religion is necessary: Now in Order to *believe,* we must first *Will;* to *Will,* we must *Judge;* to *Judge* any Thing, we must first *Understand;* if then we cannot be said to *understand* any Thing against our *Understanding;* no more can we *Judge, Will,* or *Believe* against our *Understanding:* and if the Doubter be damned, what must he be that conforms directly against his *Judgment and Belief,* and they likewise that require it from him? In short, that Man cannot be said to have any Religion, that takes it by another Man's Choice, not his own.

4. Where Men are limited in Matters of Religion, there the Rewards which are entail'd on the free Acts of Men, are quite overthrown; and such as supersede that *Grand Charter* of Liberty of Conscience, frustrate all Hopes of Recompence, *by rendring the Actions of Men unavoidable:* But those think perhaps, *they do not destroy all Freedom, because they use so much of their own.*

5. *Fifthly;* They subvert all *True Religion;* for where Men believe not because it is *True,* but because they are required to do so, there they will unbelieve, not because 'tis *False,* but so commanded by their *Superiors,* whose Authority their Interest and Security oblige them rather to obey, than dispute.

6. *Sixthly,* They delude, or rather compel People out of their Eternal Rewards; for where Men are commanded to act in reference to Religion, and can neither be secur'd of their Religion, nor yet sav'd Harmless from Punishment,

13. Thomas Hobbes, *Leviathan* (London, 1652), ch. 13.

that so acting and believing, dispriviledges them for ever of that Recompence which is provided for the Faithful.

7. *Seventhly,* Men have their Liberty and Choice in External Matters; they are not compelled to *Marry this Person, to Converse with that, to Buy here, to Eat there, nor to Sleep yonder;* yet if Men had Power to impose or restrain in any Thing, one would think it should be in such exteriour Matters; but that this Liberty should be unquestion'd, and that of the Mind destroy'd, issues here. *That it does not Unbrute us; but Unman us; for, take away Understanding, Reason, Judgment, and Faith, and like* Nebuchadnezzar, *let us go Graze with the Beasts of the Field.*[14]

8. *Eighthly and Lastly,* That *which most of all blackens the Business, is PERSECUTION;* for though it is very unreasonable to require *Faith,* where Men cannot chuse but doubt, yet after all, to punish them for Disobedience, is Cruelty in the Abstract, for we demand, *Shall Men Suffer for not doing what they cannot do?* Must they be Persecuted here if they do not go against their Consciences, and punished hereafter if they do? But neither is this all; for that Part that is yet most unreasonable, and that gives the clearest Sight of Persecution, is still behind, namely, *The Monstrous Arguments they have to Convince an Heretick with:* Not those of Old, as Spiritual as the Christian Religion, *which were to admonish, warn, and finally to reject;*[15] but such as were imploy'd by the persecuting *Jews* and Heathens against the great Example of the World, and such as follow'd him, and by the inhuman *Papists* against our first *Reformers, as Clubs, Staves, Stocks, Pillories, Prisons, Dungeons, Exiles,* &c. In a Word, *Ruin to whole Families, as if it were not so much their Design to Convince the Soul, as to Destroy the Body.*

To conclude: There ought to be an Adequation and Resemblance betwixt all Ends, and the Means to them, but in this Case there can be none imaginable: *The End is the Conformity of our Judgments and Understandings to the Acts of such as require it, the Means are Fines and Imprisonments (and Bloody Knocks to boot.)*

Now, what Proportion or Assimulation these bear, let the Sober judge: The Understanding can never be convinc'd, nor properly submit, but by such Arguments, *as are Rational, Perswasive, and suitable to its own Nature;* something that can *resolve it's Doubts, answer it's Objections, enervate it's Propo-*

14. Daniel 4:33.
15. Titus 3:10.

sitions, but to imagine *those barbarous* Newgate *Instruments of* Clubs, Fines, Prisons, *&c. with that whole Troop of external and dumb Materials of Force, should be fit Arguments to convince the Understanding, scatter it's Scruples, and finally, convert it to their Religion,* is altogether irrational, cruel, and impossible. Force may make an Hypocrite; *'tis Faith grounded upon Knowledge, and Consent that makes a Christian.* And to conclude, as we can never betray the Honour of our Conformity (only due to Truth) by a base and timorous Hypocrisie to any external Violence under Heaven, so must we needs say, *Unreasonable are those* Imposers, *who secure not the* Imposed *or* Restrained *from what may occur to them, upon their Account; and most inhuman are those* Persecutors *that punish Men for not obeying them, though to their utter Ruin.*

CHAP. V.

They carry a Contradiction to Government: 1. *In the* Nature *of it, which is* Justice. 2. *In the* Execution *of it, which is* Prudence. 3. *In the* End *of it, which is* Fidelity. *Seven Common, but Grand Objections, fairly stated, and briefly answered.*

WE NEXT urge, *That Force in Matters relating to Conscience, carries a plain Contradiction to* Government *in the Nature, Execution, and End of it.*

By Government we understand, *An External Order of Justice, or the right and prudent Disciplining of any Society, by Just Laws, either in the Relaxation, or Execution of them.*

First, It carries a Contradiction to Government in the Nature of it, which is *Justice,* and that in three Respects.

1. It is the First Lesson, that *Great Synteresis,*[16] so much renowned by *Philosophers* and *Civilians,* learns Mankind, *To do as they would be done to;* since he that gives what he would not take, or takes what he would not give, only shews Care for himself, but neither Kindness nor Justice for another.

16. See ch. 2, p. 26, n. 8.

2. *The Just Nature of Government lies in a fair and equal Retribution;* but what can be more unequal, *than that Men should be rated more than their Proportion,* to answer the Necessities of Government, and yet that they should not only receive *No Protection from it, but by it be disseiz'd of their dear Liberty and Properties;* we say to be compell'd to pay that Power, that exerts it self to ruin those that pay it, or that any should be requir'd to enrich those, that ruin them, is hard, and unequal, and therefore contrary to the Just Nature of Government. *If we must be Contributaries to the Maintenance of it, we are entituled to a Protection from it.*

3. *It is the Justice of Government to proportion Penalties to the Crime committed.* Now granting our Dissent to be a Fault, yet the Infliction of a Corporal or External Punishment, for a meer Mental Error (and that not voluntary) is Unreasonable and Inadequate, as well as against particular Directions of the *Scriptures, Tit.* iii. 9, 10, 11. For as Corporal Penalties cannot convince the *Understanding;* so neither can they be commensurate Punishments for Faults purely *Intellectual:* And for the *Government* of this World to intermeddle with what belongs to the *Government of another,* and which can have no ill Aspect or Influence upon it, *shews more of Invasion than Right and Justice.*

Secondly, *It carries a Contradiction to Government in the Execution of it, which is Prudence, and that in these Instances.*

1. The State of the Case is this, That there is no *Republick* so great, no *Empire* so vast, but the Laws of them are Resolvable into these Two Series or Heads, *Of Laws Fundamental, which are Indispensible and Immutable: And Laws Superficial, which are Temporary and Alterable:* And as it is Justice and Prudence to be punctual in the Execution of the former, so by Circumstances it may be neither, to Execute the latter, *they being suited to the present Conveniency and Emergency of State;* as the Prohibiting of Cattle out of *Ireland,* was judg'd of Advantage to the Farmers of *England,* yet a Murrain would make it the Good of the Whole, that the Law should be broke, or at least the Execution of it suspended. That the Law of *Restraint in Point of Conscience is of this Number,* we may farther manifest, *and the Imprudence of thinking otherwise:* For, first, if the Saying were as True as 'tis False, *No Bishop, no King,* (which admits of Various Readings; *As no Decimating Clergy, or no Persecution, no King,*) we should be as silent, as some would have us; but the Confidence of their Assertion, and the Impolicy of such as believe it, makes us to say, *That a greater Injury cannot be done to the present Government.* For if such Laws and Establishments are Fundamental, they are as immutable as Mankind it self; but that

they are as alterable, as the Conjectures and Opinions of Governours have been, is evident; *Since the same Fundamental Indispensible Laws and Policy of these Kingdoms have still remain'd, through all Variety of opposite Ruling Opinions and Judgments,* and disjoyn'd from them all. Therefore to admit such a Fixation to Temporary Laws, must needs be highly imprudent, and Destructive of the Essential Parts of the Government of these Countries.

2. That since there has been a Time of Connivance, and that with no ill Success to Publick Affairs, it cannot be Prudence to discontinue it, unless it was Imprudence before to give it, *and such little deserve it that think so.*

3. *Dissenters* not being Conscious to themselves of any Just Forfeiture of that Favour, are as well griev'd in their Resentments of this Alteration, as the contrary did oblige them to very Grateful Acknowledgments.

4. This must be done to gratifie all, or the greatest Part, or but some few only; it is a Demonstration all are not pleased with it; that the greatest Number is not, *the empty publick Auditories will speak:* In short, how should either be, when Six Parties are sacrificed to the Seventh; that this cannot be Prudence, *Common Maxims and Observations prove.*

5. It strikes fatally at *Protestant Sincerity;* for will the *Papists* say, *Did Protestants exclaim against us for Persecutors, and are they now the Men themselves? Was it an Instance of Weakness in our Religion, and is't become a Demonstration of Strength in theirs? Have they transmuted it from Anti-christian in us, to Christian in themselves? Let Persecutors answer.*

6. *It is not only an Example, but an Incentive to the* Romanists, *to Persecute the Reformed Religion abroad;* for when they see their Actions *(once void of all Excuse)* now defended by the Example of *Protestants,* that once accus'd them, (but now themselves) doubtless they will revive their Cruelty.

7. *It overturns the very Ground of the* Protestants *Retreat from* Rome; for if Men must be Restrain'd upon pretended Prudential Considerations, from the Exercise of their Conscience in *England;* why not the same in *France, Holland, Germany, Constantinople,* &c. where Matters of State may equally be pleaded? This makes Religion, State-Policy; and Faith and Worship, subservient to the Humours and Interests of Superiors: Such Doctrine would have prevented our Ancestor's Retreat; and we wish it be not the Beginning of a Back-march; for some think it shrewdly to be suspected, *where Religion is suited to the Government, and Conscience to it's Conveniency.*

8. *Vice is encourag'd;* for if *Licentious Persons* see Men of Virtue molested for Assembling with a Religious Purpose to Reverence and Worship God, and

that are otherwise most serviceable to the Common-Wealth, they may and will inferr, it is better for them to be as they are, since not to be *Demure,* as they call it, is Half Way to that Kind of Accomplishment, which procures Preferment.

9. For such Persons as are so poor Spirited as to truckle under such Restraints; What Conquest is there over them? that before were Conscientious Men, and now Hypocrites; who so forward to be aveng'd of them, that brought this *Guilt* upon them, as they themselves? And how can the *Imposers* be secure of their Friendship, whom they have taught to change with the Times?

10. Such Laws are so far from benefitting the Country, that the Execution of them will be the assured Ruin of it, in the Revenues, and consequently in the Power of it; For where there is a Decay of Families, there will be of Trade; so of Wealth, and in the End of Strength and Power; and if both Kinds of Relief fail, *Men, the Prop of Republicks; Money, the Stay of Monarchies; this, as requiring Mercenaries; that, as needing* Freemen; *farewel the Interest of* England; *'Tis true, the Priests get (though that's but for a Time) but the King and People lose; as the Event will shew.*

11. It ever was the Prudence of Wise Magistrates to oblige their People; but what comes shorter of it than Persecution? What's dearer to them than the Liberty of their Conscience? What cannot they better spare than it? Their Peace consists in the Enjoyment of it: And he that by Compliance has lost it, carries his Penalty with him, and is his own Prison. Surely such Practices must render the Government uneasie, and beget a great Disrespect to the Governours, in the Hearts of the People.

12. But that which concludes our Prudential Part, shall be this, That after all their Pains and Good Will to stretch Men to their Measure, they never will be able to accomplish their End: And if he be an unwise Man, that provides Means where he designs no End, how near is he Kin to him that proposes an End inobtainable. Experience has told us, 1. How *Invective* it has made the *Impos'd on.* 2. What Distractions have insued such Attempts. 3. What Reproach has follow'd to the Christian Religion, when the Professors of it have us'd a Coercive Power upon Conscience. And lastly, That *Force* never yet made either a *Good Christian,* or a *Good Subject.*

Thirdly and Lastly, Since the Proceedings we argue against, are prov'd so Destructive to the Justice and Prudence of Government, we ought the less to wonder that they should hold the same Malignity against the End of it, which is *Felicity,* since the Wonder would be to find it otherwise; and this is evident from these three Considerations.

1. *Peace* (the End of War and Government, and it's great Happiness too) has been, is, and yet will be broken by the frequent Tumultuary Disturbances, that ensue the Disquieting our Meetings, and the Estreating Fines upon our Goods and Estates. And what these Things may issue in, concerneth the Civil Magistrate to consider.

2. *Plenty,* (another great End of Government) will be converted into Poverty by the Destruction of so many Thousand Families as refuse Compliance and Conformity, and that not only to the *Sufferers,* but influentially to all the *Rest;* a Demonstration of which we have in all those Places where the late Act has been any Thing considerably put in Execution. Besides, how great Provocation such Incharity and Cruel Usage, as stripping *Widows, Fatherless,* and *Poor of their very Necessaries for human Life, meerly upon an Account of Faith or Worship, must needs be to the Just and Righteous Lord of Heaven and Earth;* Scriptures, and Plenty of other Histories plainly shew us.

3. *Unity,* (not the least, but greatest End of Government) is lost for by seeking an Unity of Opinion (by the Ways intended) the Unity requisite to uphold us, as a *Civil Society,* will be quite destroy'd. And such as relinquish *that,* to get the *other* (besides that they are Unwise) *will infallibly lose both in the End.*

In short, We say, that 'tis unreasonable we should not be entertain'd as Men, because some think we are not as Good Christians as they pretend to wish us; or that we should be depriv'd of our Liberties and Properties, who never broke the Laws that gave them to us: What can be harder, than to take that from us by a Law, which the great Indulgence and Solicitude of our Ancestors took so much Pains to intail upon us by Law; An. 18 *Ed.* 3. Stat. 3. also Stat. 20 *Ed.* 3. Cap. 1. again *Petition of Right,* An. 3. *Car.* and more fully in *Magna Charta;* further peruse 37 *Ed.* 5. Cap. 8. 28. 42 *Ed.* 3. Cap. 3. 28 *Hen.* Cap. 7.

And we are perswaded, that no Temporary Subsequential Law whatever to our Fundamental Rights, (as this of Force on Conscience is) can invalid so essential a Part of the Government, as *English* Liberty and Property: Nor that it's in the Power of any on Earth, to deprive us of them, till we have first done it our selves, *by such Enormous Facts, as those very Laws prohibit,* and make our Forfeiture of that Benefit we should otherwise receive by them; for these being such *Cardinal* and *Fundamental Points of* English *Law-Doctrine,* individually, and by the collective Body of the People agreed to; and on which as the most solid Basis, our *Secondary Legislative Power,* as well as Executive is built; it seems most rational that the Superstructure cannot quarrel or invalidate it's own Foundation, without manifestly endangering it's own Security, the Effect is ever less noble than the Cause, the Gift than the Giver, and the Superstructure than the Foundation.

The single Question to be resolved in the Case, briefly will be this, *Whether any Visible Authority (being founded in its primitive Institution upon those Fundamental Laws, that inviolably preserve the People in all their just Rights and Priviledges) may invalidate all, or any of the said Laws, without an implicit shaking of it's own Foundation, and a clear Overthrow of it's own Constitution of Government, and so reduce them to their* Statu quo prius, *or first Principles: The Resolution is every Man's, at his own Pleasure. Read* Hen. 3. 9. 14. 29. 25 Ed. 3. Cook's Instit. 2. 19. 50, 51.

Those who intend us no Share or Interest in the Laws of *England,* as they relate to civil Matters, unless we correspond with them in Points of Faith and Worship, must do two Things: First, It will lie heavy on their Parts to prove, *That the Ancient Compact and Original of our Laws* carries that Proviso with it; else we are manifestly disseized of our Free-Customs.

Secondly, They are to prove the Reasonableness of such Proceedings to our Understandings, that we may not be concluded by a Law, we know not how to understand; for if I take the Matter rightly (as I think I do) we must not Buy, or Sell unless of this or that Perswasion in Religion; not considering Civil Society was in the World before the Protestant Profession; *Men,* as such, and in Affairs peculiarly relative of them, in an External and Civil Capacity, have subsisted many Ages, under great Variety of Religious Apprehensions, and therefore not so dependent on them as to receive any Variation or Revolution with them. What shall we say then? but that some will not that we should *Live, Breath, and Commerce as Men,* because we are not such model'd Christians as they coercively would have us; they might with as much Justice and Reputation to themselves forbid us to look or see unless our Eyes were *Grey, Black, Brown, Blue,* or some one Colour best suiting theirs: For not to be able to give us Faith, or save our Consciences harmless, and yet to persecute us for refusing Conformity, is intolerable hard Measure.

In short, That coercive Way of bringing all Men to their Height of Perswasion, must either arise *from Exorbitant Zeal and Superstition;* or from a Consciousness of Error and Defect, which is unwilling any Thing more sincere and reformed should take Place; being of that Cardinal's Mind, who therefore would not hearken to a Reformation, at the sitting of the Counsel of *Trent;* because he would not so far approve the Reformers Judgment *(for having once condescended to their Apprehensions, he thought 'twould forever inslave them to their Sense)* though otherwise he saw as much as any Man, the Grand Necessity of a Reformation, both of the *Roman* Doctrine and Conversation.[17]

Some Grand Objections in the Way must be Considered.

Objection 1. *But you are a People that meet with Designs to Disaffect the People, and to ruin the Government.*

Answer. A Surmise is no Certainty, neither is A may-be, or Conjecture, any Proof: That from the first we have behaved our selves inoffensively is a Demonstration; that our Meetings are open, where all may hear our Matter, and have Liberty to object or discuss any Point, is notorious. *Ignorant Calumnies are Sandy Foundations to build so high a Charge upon.* Let us fairly be heard in a publick Conference, how far we can justifie our Principles from being deservedly suspected of Sedition or Disloyalty, and not over run us with meer Suppositions. We declare our Readiness to obey the Ordinance of Man, which is only relative of Human or Civil Matters, and not Points of Faith, or Practice in Worship: But if Accusations must stand for *Proofs,* we shall take it for granted, that we must stand for Criminals; but our Satisfaction will be, that we shall not deserve it otherwise than as Prejudice seeks to traduce us.

Object. 2. *But you strike at the Doctrine, at least the Discipline of the Church, and consequently are Hereticks.*

Answ. This Story is as old as the Reformation; If we must be objected against out of pure Reputation, let it be in some other Matter than what the *Papists* objected against the first Protestants; otherwise you do but hit your selves in aiming at us? *To say you were in the Right, but we are in the Wrong,* is but a meer begging of the Question; for doubtless the *Papists* said the same to you, and all that you can say to us: Your best Plea was, Conscience upon Principles, the most evident and rational to you: Do not we the like? What if you think our Reasons thick, and our Ground of Separation mistaken? Did not the *Papists* harbour the same Thoughts of you? You perswaded as few of

17. The Council of Trent (19th Ecumenical Council of the Roman Catholic Church) met intermittently from 1545 to 1563, instituting church reforms and responding to Protestant criticisms of Catholic doctrine and practice.

them, as we of you: Were you therefore in the Wrong? No more are we: It was not what they thought of you, or enacted against you, that concluded you: And why should your Apprehensions conclude us? If you have the Way of giving Faith beyond what they had, and have the Faculty of Perswasion, evidence as much; but if you are as destitute of both, as they were to you; why should *Fines and Prisons,* once us'd by them against you, *and by you exclaimed against, as Unchristian Ways of reclaiming Hereticks* (supposing your selves to be such) be employ'd by you as Rational, Christian, and Convincing upon us? To say we deserve them more, is to suppose your selves in the Right, and us in the Wrong, which proves nothing. Besides, the Question is not barely this, whether *Hereticks* or no *Hereticks;* but whether an *Heretick should be Persecuted into a disclaiming of his Error;* your old Arguments run thus, as I well remember.

1. *Error is a Mistake in the Understanding.*

2. *This is for Want of a better Illumination.*

3. *This Error can never be dislodged, but by Reason and Perswasion, as what are most suitable to the Intellect of Man.*

4. *Fines, Goals, Exiles, Gibbets, &c. are no convincing Arguments to the most erring Understanding in the World, being slavish and brutish.*

5. *This Way of Force makes, instead of an honest Dissenter, but an Hypocritical Conformist; than whom nothing is more detestable to God and Man.*

This being the *Protestants* Plea, we are not to be disliked by *Protestants,* for following their own avow'd Maxims and *Axioms of Conscience in Defence of it's own Liberty.*

In short, either allow Separation upon the single Principle of, *My Conscience owns this, or disowns that;* or never dwell in that Building, which knew no better Foundation, (indeed good enough) *but, accusing your Forefathers of Schism, and Heresie, return to the Romish Church.* What short of this can any say to an *Anti-liberty-of-Conscience-Protestant.*

Object. 3. *But at this Rate ye may pretend to Cut our Throats, and do all Manner of savage Acts.*

Ans. Though the Objection be frequent, yet it is as foully ridiculous. We are pleading only for such a *Liberty of Conscience,* as preserves the Nation in Peace, Trade, and Commerce; and would not exempt any Man, or Party of

Men, from not keeping those excellent Laws, that tend to Sober, Just, and Industrious Living. *It is a Jesuitical Moral, To Kill a Man before he is Born:* First, to suspect him of an Evil Design, and then kill him to prevent it.

Object. 4. *But do not you see what has been the End of this Separation? Wars, and Revolutions, and Danger to Government; witness our late Troubles.*

Ans. We see none of all this, but are able to make it appear, that the true Cause of all that *perplext Disturbance,* which was amongst the *Homoousians* and *Arrians* of old, and among us of latter Years (as well as what has modernly attended our Neighbouring Countries) took its first rise from a Narrowness of Spirit, *in not Tolerating others to live the Freemen God made them, in External Matters upon the Earth,* meerly upon some Difference in Religion.

And were there once but an Hearty Toleration establisht, 'twould be a Demonstration of the Truth of this Assertion. On this Ground, *Empire* stands safe; on the other, it seems more uncertain.

But these are only the popular Devices of some to traduce honest Men, and their Principles; whose *lazy Life, and intolerable Advice* become question'd, by a Toleration of People better inclin'd.

Object. 5. *But what need you take this Pains to prove Liberty of Conscience Reasonable and Necessary, when none questions it; all that is required is, That you meet but four more than your own Families; and can you not be contented with that? Your Disobedience to a Law, so favourable, brings suffering upon you.*

Ans. Here is no Need of answering the former Part of the Objection; 'Tis too apparent throughout the Land, that *Liberty of Conscience,* as we have stated it, has been severely prosecuted, and therefore not so frankly injoyned: The latter Part, I answer thus, If the Words *Lawful* or *Unlawful,* may bear their Signification from the Nature of the Things they stand for, then we conceive *that a Meeting of Four Thousand is no more Unlawful,* than a Meeting of Four; for *Number singly consider'd criminates no Assembly:* But the Reason of their assembling; the Posture in which; and the Matter transacted, with the Consequences thereof.

Now if those Things are taken for granted, to be Things dispensible *(as appears by the Allowance of Four besides every Family)* certainly the Number can never render it Unlawful; so that the Question will be this, *Whether if Four met to worship God, be an Allowable Meeting, Four thousand met with the same Design be not an allowable Meeting?*

It is so plain a Case, that the Matter in Question resolves it.

Object. 6. *But the Law forbids it.*

Answ. If the enacting *any Thing* can make it lawful, we have done; but if an Act so made by the *Papists* against *Protestants,* was never esteem'd so by a true *Protestant;* and if the Nature of the Matter will not bear it; and lastly, that we are as much commanded by God to meet Four Thousand, as Four; we must desire to be excused, if we forbear not the assembling of our selves together, as the Manner of some is.

Object. 7. *But the Reason of the Prohibition of the Number is* (for you see they allow all that can be said to Four Thousand to be said to the Family and Four) *that Tumults may arise, and Plots may be made, and the like Inconveniencies happen to the Government.*

Ans. Great Assemblies are so far from being injurious, that they are the most inoffensive; for, First, They are open, exposed to the View of all, which of all Things *Plotters are the shyest of;* but how fair an Opportunity 'twere, for Men so principled, to do it in those allowed Meetings of but Four besides the Family, is easie to guess, when we consider, *that few make the best and closest Council; and next, that such an Assembly is the most private and clandestine, and so fitted for Mischief and Surprize.*

Secondly, Such Assemblies, are not only publick and large, but they are frequented, as well by those that are not of their Way, as by their own; from whence it follows, that we have the greatest Reason to be cautious and wise in our Behaviour, *since the more there be at our Meetings, the more Witnesses are against us, if we should say or act any Thing that may be prejudicial to the Government.*

Lastly, For these several Years none could ever observe such an ill use made of that Freedom, or such wicked Designs to follow such Assemblies; and therefore it is high Incharity to proceed so severely upon meer Suppositions.

To this we shall add several Authorities and Testimonies for farther Confirmation of our Sense of the Matter, and to let Imposers see, that we are not the only Persons, who have impleaded Persecution, and justified *Liberty of Conscience,* as Christian and Rational.

CHAP. VI.

They reflect upon the Sense and Practice of the Wisest, Greatest, and best States, and Persons of Ancient and Modern Times; as of the Jews, Romans, AEgyptians, Germans, French, Hollanders, *nay* Turks *and* Persians *too. And* Cato, Livy, Tacitus, Justin Martyr, Tertullian, Jovianus, Chaucer, Dominicus Soto, Malvetzey, Grotius, Rawleigh, Doctor and Student, French *and* Dutch Protestants *in* England, *Dr.* Hammond, *Dr.* Taylor, *A nameless but great Person,* Lactantius, Hilary, Jerom, Chrysostom, Polish *and* Bohemian *Kings, King* James, *and King* Charles *the First.*

A BRIEF Collection of the Sense and Practice of the *Greatest, Wisest,* and *Learned'st Common-Wealths, Kingdoms, and particular Persons* of their Times, concerning *Force upon Conscience.*

First, Though the *Jews* above all People had the most to say for Imposition and Restraint within their own Dominions, having their Religion instituted by so many signal Proofs of Divine Original, it being deliver'd to them by the Hand of God himself, yet such was their Indulgence to Dissenters, that if they held the common receiv'd *Noachical* Principles tending to the Acknowledgment of *One God,* and a Just Life, they had the Free Exercise of their distinct Modes or Ways of Worship, which were numerous. Of this their own Rabbies are Witnesses, and *Grotius* out of them.[18]

2. The *Romans* themselves, as strict as they were, not only had Thirty Thousand *Gods* (if *Varro* may be credited) but almost every Family of any note, had its distinct *Sacra,* or peculiar Way of Worship.[19]

18. Moses Maimonides (1135–1204); Hugo Grotius (1583–1645), Dutch jurist and humanist.

19. Marcus Terentius Varro (116–27 B.C.E.). All but a few of Varro's seventy-odd works

3. It was the Sense of that grave, exemplary Common Wealth's-Man, *Cato,* in *Salust,* that among other Things which ruin any Government, *Want of Freedom of Speech,* or Men's being obliged to humour Times, *is a great one;* which we find made good by the *Florentine Republick,* as *Guiccardine* relates.[20]

4. *Livy* tells us, It was a Wonder that *Hannibal*'s Army, consisting of *divers Nations, divers Humours, differing Habits, contrary Religions, various Languages, should live Thirteen Years from their own Country under his Command without so much as once mutining, either against their General, or among themselves.*[21] But what *Livy* relates for a Wonder, *that ingenious Marquess, Virgilio Malvetzy* gives the Reason of, namely, *that the Difference of their Opinion, Tongues, and Customs, was the Reason of their Preservation and Conquest;* For, said he, 'Twas impossible so many contrary Spirits should Combine, and if any should have done it, 'twas in the General's Power to make the greater Party by his equal Hand; they owing him more of Reverence, than they did of Affection to one another: This, says he, some impute to *Hannibal,* but how great soever he was, I give it to the Variety of Humours in the Army. For (adds he) Rome's *Army was ever less given to Mutining when joyned with the Provincial Auxiliaries, than when intirely Roman;* thus much and more, in his publick Discourses upon *Cornelius Tacitus.*[22]

5. The same, best Statist of his Time, *C. Tacitus,* tells us in the Case of *Cremtius,* That it had been the Interest of *Tiberius* not to have punished him, in as much as Curiosity is begotten by Restriction of Liberty to Write or Speak, which never mist of Proselytes.[23]

6. *Just. Martyr.* I will forbear to quote, in less than this, two whole Apologies, dedicated to *Adrian* and *Antoninus Pius,* as I take it.[24]

7. *Tertullian ad Scapulam,* that Learned and Judicious Apologist, plainly tells us, *That 'tis not the Property of Religion to Compel or Persecute for Religion,* she should be accepted for her Self, not for Force; that being a poor

---

have been lost, though he receives an extended treatment in books 6 and 7 of Augustine's *City of God.* His *Antiquities* elaborates the Roman system of gods.

20. Sallust, *Conspiracy of Catiline,* ch. 52, though Penn's direct reference is unclear, as Cato's speech advocates harsh punishment for the conspirators (as opposed to Caesar's pleas for leniency). Francesco Guicciardini, *History of Florence* (ca. 1508–9).

21. Livy, *History of Rome,* bk. 28, ch. 12.

22. Malvezzi, *Discourses on Tacitus,* discourse 49, pp. 475–77.

23. Tacitus, *Annals,* bk. 4, chs. 34–35.

24. Justin Martyr (ca. 114–65), *First Apology;* and *Second Apology.*

and beggarly one, that has no better Arguments to Convince; and a manifest Evidence of her Superstition and Falshood.[25]

8. Of this we take the nine Month's Reign of the Emperor *Jovianus* to be an excellent Demonstration, whose great Wisdom, and admirable Prudence in granting Toleration (expresly saying, *He would have none molested for the Exercise of their Religion*) Calm'd the impetuous Storms of Dissention betwixt the *Homoousians* and *Arrians;* and reduc'd the whole Empire, before agitated with all Kind of Commotions during the Reigns of *Constantine, Constantius,* and *Julian,* to a wonderful Serenity and Peace, as *Socrates Scholasticus* affirms.[26]

9. That little Kingdom of *AEgypt* had no less than Forty Thousand Persons retir'd to their private and separate Ways of Worship, as *Eusebius* out of *Philo Judeus,* and *Josephus* relates.[27]

10. And here let me bring in honest *Chaucer,* whose Matter (and not his Poetry) heartily affects me: 'Twas in a Time when Priests were as rich, and lofty, as they are now, and Causes of Evil alike.[28]

(a) *THE Time was once, and may return again,*
(for oft may happen that hath been beforn)
when Shepherds had none Inheritance,
ne of Land, nor Fee in Sufferance,
But what might arise of the bare Sheep,
(were it more or less) which they did keep,
Well ywis was it with Shepherds tho':
nought having, nought fear'd they to forgo,
For PAN (God) himself was their Inheritance,
and little them serv'd for their Maintenance,
The Shepherd's God so well them guided,
that of nought were they unprovided;

(*a*) The Primitive State of Things observed by a Poet, more than 300 Years old; by which the Clergy may read their own Apostacy and Character.

25. Tertullian (ca. 160–220), *Ad Scapulam,* ch. 2.

26. Socrates Scholasticus (ca. 379–450), *Ecclesiastical History,* bk. 3, ch. 25.

27. Eusebius Pamphilius, Bishop of Caesarea (ca. 260–341), *Ecclesiastical History,* bk. 2, ch. 17, sec. 6–10 (with marginal references to Philo Judaeus [ca. 25 B.C.E.–41 C.E.]); and Flavius Josephus (37–101), *Against Apion,* bk. 1, sec. 224–26.

28. This poem is likely not, in fact, from Chaucer; though it was perhaps erroneously attributed to him at the time of Penn's writing.

(b) *Butter enough, Honey, Milk, and Whay,*
and their Flock Fleeces them to array.
But Tract of Time and long Prosperity,
(that Nurse of Vice, this of Insolency)
Lulled the Shepherds in such Security,
that not content with Loyal Obeysance,
Some gan to gap for greedy Governance,
and match themselves with mighty Potentates.

(c) Lovers of Lordships and Troublers of States;
then gan Shepherds Swains to look aloft,
And leave to live hard, and learn to lig soft,
though under colour of Shepherds same while
There crept in Wolves *full of Fraud and Guile,*
that often devour'd their own Sheep,
And often the Shepherd that did them keep,

(d) *This was the first Source of the Shepherds Sorrow.*
that nor will be quit, with bale, nor borrow.

11. Who knows not that our first Reformers were great Champions for *Liberty of Conscience,* as *Wickliff* in his Remonstrance to the Parliament. The *Albigenses* to *Lewis* the 11th and 12th of *France. Luther* to the several Diets under *Frederick* and *Charles* the Fifth; *Calvin* to *Francis* the First, and many of our *English* Martyrs, as the poor *Plowman's Famous Complaint,* in *Fox's Martyrology,* &c.[29]

(*b*) Time and Prosperity corrupted them, and then they grew States-Men.

(*c*) 'Twas now they began to persecute; they hated any that were more devout than themselves: Devotion was counted Disaffection; Religious Assemblies, Conventicles; primitive-Spirited Christians, Upstart Hereticks; thus the Tragedy began, *Cain* slaying *Abel* about Religion.

(*d*) He truly maketh their Avarice the Cause of their Degeneration; for 'tis the Root of all Evil.

29. John Wyclif, here spelled Wickliff (1324–84), English reformer; Albigenses were a neo-Manichean sect in southern France during the twelfth and thirteenth centuries, suppressed by Pope Innocent III; of Luther's responses to the councils and diets he faced, the most famous must be "Luther at the Diet of Worms," reprinted in *Career of the Reformer,* vol. 32 of *Luther's Works,* ed. Helmut L. Lehmann (Philadelphia, 1958); the "Prefatory Address" to Calvin's *Institutes of the Christian Religion* is addressed to King Francis I of

12. The present *Affairs* of *Germany,* plainly tell us, that Toleration is the Preservation of their States; the contrary having formerly, almost quite wasted them.

13. The same in *France:* who can be so ignorant of their Story, as not to know that the timely *Indulgence* of *Henry* the fourth; and the discreet *Toleration* of *Richlieu* and *Mazarin,* saved that Kingdom from being ruin'd both by the *Spaniards; and one another.*

14. *Holland,* than which, what Place is there so improved in Wealth, Trade and Power, *chiefly owes it to her Indulgence, in Matters of Faith and Worship.*

15. Among the very *Mahumetans* of *Turky,* and *Persia,* what Variety of *Opinions,* yet what *Unity* and *Concord* is there? We mean in Matters of a Civil Importance.

16. It Was the Opinion of that great Master of the *Sentences, Dominicus a Soto, that every Man had a natural Right, to instruct others in Things that are good: And he may teach the Gospel-Truths also, but cannot compel any to believe them, he may explain them, and to this,* (says he) *every Man has a Right,* as in his 4 Sent. Dist. 5. Art. 10. Pag. 115. 7.[30]

17. *Strifes about Religion,* said *Judicious* and learned *Grotius, are the most pernicious and destructive, where Provision is not made for* Dissenters: *the contrary most happy;* As in *Muscovy;* he farther says upon the Occasion of *Campanella, that not a rigid but easy Government suits best with the Northern People;* he often pleads the Relaxation of temporary Laws, to be reasonable and necessary. As in the Case of the *Curatij* and *Horatij,* and *Fabius Vitulanus;* and others stinted to *Time* and *Place,* as the *Jewish Laws,* &c. Polit. Maxims, P. 12, 18. 78, 98.[31]

18. The famous *Rawleigh* tell us, that the Way for Magistrates to govern well, and Gain the Esteem of their People, *is to govern by Piety, Justice, Wisdom, and a Gentle and Moderate Carriage towards them;* And that Disturbance attends those States, *where Men are raised, or depress'd by Parties.* See his Observations and Maxims of State.[32]

19. If I mistake not, the *French* and *Dutch Protestants* enjoy their separate

---

France; and "The Poor Plowman's Complaint" appears in John Foxe's (1515–87) *Actes and Monuments* (commonly referred to as the *Book of Martyrs*), vol. 2, bk. 5.

30. Dominic (or Dominicus) Soto, *Commentariorum fratris Dominici Soto . . . in Quartum Sententiarum* (Salamanca, 1562).

31. Grotius, *Politick maxims and observations* (London, 1654).

32. Sir Walter Raleigh, *Maxims of State* (London, 1651).

Ways of Worship in *London,* if not in other Parts of these Lands, without Molestation; we do the like in remote Countreys, *but not in our own.*

20. This must needs be the Meaning of the learned Doctor, to his Inquisitive *Student,* in their judicious Dialogue, about the Fundamental Laws of the Kingdoms, when he says, *That such Laws as have not their Foundation in Nature, Justice and Reason, are void* ipso facto. And whether *Persecution* or *Restraint* upon Conscience, be congruous with either, Let the impartial Judge. *lib.* 1. *chap.* 6.[33]

21. *Doctor Hammond* himself, and the *grand Patron of the English Church,* was so far from urging the Legality of Restriction, in Matters relating to Conscience, that he Writ, Argued, and left upon his Dying-Bed, his Sense to the Contrary: As the *Author* of his Life might have been pleased to observe, but that Interest stood in the Way, *The Doctor exhorting his Party, not to seek to displace those, then in the University; or to Persecute them for any Matter of Religious Difference.*[34]

22. That a Person, of no less Ability, in the *Irish* Protestant Church did the same. I mean *D. Jer. Taylor,* his whole Discourse *of Liberty of Prophecy,* is a most pregnant Demonstration.[35]

23. It was the Saying of a Person once, too great to be named now, *That Liberty of Conscience is every Man's natural Right, and he who is deprived of it, is a Slave in the midst of the greatest Liberty: And since every Man should do as he would be done to, such only don't deserve to have it, that won't give it.*

24. *Lactantius* reflects upon Persecutors thus, *If you will with Blood, with Evil, and with Torments defend your Worship, it shall not thereby be defended, but polluted,* lib. 5. cap. 20.[36]

25. *Hilary* against *Auxentius,* saith, *The Christian Church does not persecute, but is persecuted.*[37]

33. Christopher St. Germain (ca. 1460–1540), *The dialogue in English between a doctor of divinity and a student in the laws of England* (London, 1660).

34. John Fell, *The life of the most learned, reverend, and pious Dr. H. Hammond* (London, 1661).

35. Jeremy Taylor, *Theologike eklektike; or A discourse on the liberty of prophesying* (London, 1647).

36. Lactantius (260–330), *Divine Institutes,* bk. 5, ch. 20.

37. Hilary of Poitiers, *Contra Auxentium Arrianum;* Hilary debated Auxentius, the Arian bishop of Milan, in 364.

26. *Jerom,* thus, *Heresie must be cut off, with the Sword of the Spirit;* Proaem. Lib. 4.[38]

27. *Chrysostom* saith, *That it is not the Manner of the Children of God, to persecute about their Religion, but an evident Token of Antichrist,*—Relig. Uris. Pag. 192.[39]

28. *Stephen* King *of Poland,* declared his Mind in the Point controverted, thus, *I am King of Men, not of Conscience; a Commander of Bodies, not of Souls.*

29. The King of *Bohemia,* was of Opinion, *That Men's Consciences ought in no Sort, to be violated, urged, or constrained.*

30. And lastly, let me add (as what is, or should be now of more Force) the Sense of *King James,* and *Charles the first,* Men fam'd for their great natural Abilities, and acquired Learning; *that no Man ought to be punished for his Religion, nor disturb'd for his Conscience; In that it is the Duty of every Man to give what he would receive.* "It is a sure Rule in Divinity, *said King James,* that God never loves to plant his Church by Violence, and Bloodshed.[40] *And in his Exposition on* Revel. 20. *he saith, T*hat PERSECUTION is the Note of a false Church.[41] And in the last King's Advice to the present King, he says. Take Heed of abetting any Factions; your partial Adhering to *ANY ONE SIDE,* gains you not so great Advantages in some Men's Hearts, (*who are prone to be of their King's Religion*) as it loseth you in others, who think themselves, and their Profession, first despised, then persecuted by you."

Again, "*Beware of exasperating any Factions, by the Crossness, and Asperity of some Men's Passions, Humors, or private Opinions imployed by you* grounded only upon their Difference, in lesser Matters, which are but the Skirts, and Suburbs of Religion. *Wherein a Charitable Connivence, and Christian Toleration, often dissipates their Strength,* whom rougher Opposition fortifies; *and puts the* despised *and* Oppressed Party, *into such Combinations; as may most enable them to get a full Revenge, on those they count their Persecutors,* who are commonly assisted *by that vulgar Commiseration, which attends all that are said to suffer under the Notion of Religion.*

38. Jerome (ca. 341–420), Christian ascetic and saint.

39. John Chrysostom (347–407), preacher and doctor of the church.

40. James I, king of England 1603–25 (and, as James VI, of Scotland 1567–1625), "Speech to Parliament, 21 March 1609/1610," in *King James VI and I: Political Writings,* ed. Johann P. Sommerville (Cambridge, 1994), p. 199.

41. James I, *Ane fruitfull meditatioun* (Edinburgh, 1588).

"Always keep up *SOLID PIETY,* and those Fundamental Truths (which mend both Hearts and Lives of Men) with *Impartial Favour and Justice.* Your Prerogative is best shown and exercised in *Remitting,* rather than *Exacting* the Rigour of Laws; there being nothing worse than *Legal Tyranny.*"[42]

Now upon the whole, we ask, what can be more *equal, what more reasonable than Liberty of Conscience;* so correspondent with the *Reverence* due to *God,* and *Respect* to the *Nature, Practice, Promotion,* and *Rewards* of the *Christian Religion;* the *Sense* of divine *Writ;* the great *Priviledge* of *Nature,* and *noble Principle* of *Reason;* the *Justice, Prudence,* and *Felicity* of *Government;* And lastly, to the *Judgment* and *Authority* of a whole Cloud of *Famous Witnesses,* whose *Harmony* in Opinion, as much detects the Unreasonableness, and Incharity of *Persecutors,* as their Savage Cruelties imply an high Contempt of so solid Determinations; of which Number I cannot forbear the Mention of two, whose Actions are so near of Kin to one another, and both to Inhumanity, as the same Thing can be to it self.

The first is a *great Lord of Buckinghamshire,* but so hearty a *Persecutor* of the poor *Quakers,* that rather than they should peaceably enjoy the Liberty of Worshipping God, (and to supply the County-Defect of *Informers*) he has encouraged a pair of such *Wretches,* that it had been a *Disgrace* for the meanest Farmer to converse with; one having been Prisoner in *Ailsbury,* for *Theft,* & said to have been *burnt* in the *Hand;* and the other of a *Complexion* not much less Scandalous and Immoral.

To give an undeniable Testimony of their *Merit,* once for all, I shall briefly relate a most notorious Piece of *Perjury.* They suspecting a Religious Assembly, to be at a certain Place in the same *County,* came; and finding one in reality, repaired to one they call, Sir *Tho Clayton,* and a Justice, where they depos'd, *That not only a Meeting was at such an House, but one* Tho. Zachery and his Wife *were there,* who at the same Time, as at the Tryal upon Indictment for *Perjury* at *Ailsbury,* was proved by sufficient Witnesses from *London,* were then at that City, yet fined not only for being there, but for the Speaker also, though none spoke that Day.

Upon the Prosecution of these Men, as *perjured Men,* and by the Law *dispriviledged of all Employ,* and never to be credited more in Evidence; several Delays were made, much Time spent, and not a little Pains bestowed, all in

42. Charles I, *Eikon Basilike* (London, 1649), ch. 27.

Hopes of an *Exemplary Success,* which proved so, but the wrong Way, for the very last *Sessions,* when the Matter should have received an absolute *Decision, and the Attendants have been dismist* (especially on the Score of the Witnesses, that came from *London* the second Time, upon no other Account) a Letter was reported to have been writ from the aforesaid *Lord,* in Favour of these Informers, to this Purpose, *That since Sir* Tho. Clayton *was not present, the Business could not well be determined, but if the Court would undertake the Ending of it, he besought them to be favourable to those* HONEST MEN, if this be true as said, 'tis a most aggravated Shame to *Nobility:* what! to protect them from the Lash of the Law, who went about to destroy Truth the Life of it: 'Tis a *Dishonour to the Government, a Scandal to the County, and a manifest Injury to an inoffensive and useful Inhabitant.*

'Tother is as well known by his *Cruelty,* as by his *Name,* and he scarce deserves another; However, he is understood by that of the *Reading Knight Arrant,* and always in *Armour* for the Devil; a Man whose Life seems to be whole BONNER *revived:* Hogestrant, *the Popish Inquisitor,* could not hate *Martin Luther* more, than he does a poor Dissenter; and wants but as much Power, as he has Will, to hang more than he has imprisoned. The Laws made against *Papists,* he inflicts upon the *Quakers; and makes it Crime enough for a Premunire, to have an Estate to lose.*

The single Question is not, *were you at such a Meeting?* which the Act intends, *But will you swear,* which it intends not, *and Women escape him as little for this, as those of his own Tribe do for* SOME THINGS ELSE: but what of all Things, most aggravates the Man's Impiety, is the making a devilish Snare of a Christian Duty; since such as have come to visit the Imprisoned, have been imprisoned themselves for their Charity; so that with him it seems a Current Maxim, that those must not come to see Prisoners, and not be such themselves, who will not take the Oath of Allegiance to do it.

To relate the whole *Tragedy,* would render him as *Bad,* as the Discourse *Big;* and the latter not less *voluminous,* than the former *Odious.* But three Things I shall observe.

First, That he has crouded 72 Persons (of those called *Quakers*) Men and Women, immodestly into Jail, not suffering them to enjoy common Conveniences. And for his Diversion, and the Punishment of little Children, he pours cold Water down their Necks.

Secondly, His Imprisonments are almost perpetual. First, *he premunires them,* without any just Cause of Suspicion, *then imprisons them;* and lastly

Plunders them, and that by a Law enacted against *Romanists;* which, if all be true, that is said, *is more his Concern than theirs,* If without offence, it may be supposed he has any Religion at all.

Thirdly, Some have been there about eight Years, and should be eighteen more, were he as sure to live (being more than 70) and enjoy his Power, as doubtless he hopes to die before those good Laws over-take him, that would make an Example of such an Oppressor; in short, Wives, Widows, Poor and Fatherless, are all Fish for his Net; and whether over or under Age; he casts none away, but seems to make it his Priviledge to correct Law, by out-doing it. When we have said all we can (and we can never say too much, if enough) he is still his own best *Character.*

Such are the *Passions, Follies,* and *Prejudices,* Men devoted to a Spirit of *Imposition,* and *Persecution,* are attended with.

Non enim possumus quae vidimus, & audivimus non loqui.[43]

In short, What Religious, what wise, what prudent, what good natured Person would be a Persecutor; *certainly it's an Office only fit for those who being void of all Reason, to evidence the Verity of their own Religion, fancy it to be true, from that strong Propensity and greedy Inclination they find in themselves to persecute the contrary;* A Weakness of so ill a Consequence to all civil Societies, that the Admission of it ever was, and ever will prove their utter Ruin, as well as their great Infelicity who pursue it.

And though we could not more effectually express our Revenge, *than by leaving such Persons to the Scope of their own Humours;* Yet being taught *to love and pray for our Persecutors,* we heartily wish their better Information, that (if it be possible) they may act more *suitably* to the good Pleasure of the eternal just God, and *beneficially* to these Nations.

To conclude, *Liberty of Conscience* (as thus stated and defended) *we ask as our undoubted Right by the Law of God, of Nature, and of our own Country: it has been often promised, we have long waited for it, we have writ much, and suffered in it's Defence,* and have made many true Complaints, but found little or no Redress.

However, we take the righteous Holy God to record, against all Objections, that are ignorantly or designedly rais'd against us. That.

43. We are not able to say the things we have heard and seen.

1st. *We hold no* Principle *destructive of the English Government.*

2d. *That we plead for no such Dissenter (if such an one there be.)*

3d. *That we desire the Temporal and Eternal Happiness of all* Persons (in Submission to the divine Will of God) *heartily forgiving our cruel* Persecutors:

4thly, and lastly, *We shall engage, by God's Assistance, to lead peaceable, just and industrious Lives, amongst Men, to the Good and Example of all.* But if after all we have said, this short Discourse should not be credited, nor answered in any of it's sober Reasons, and Requests; but Sufferings should be the present Lot of our Inheritance from this Generation, be it known to them all *THAT MEET WE MUST, and MEET we cannot but encourage all to do (whatever Hardship we sustain) in God's Name and Authority, who is Lord of Hosts and King of Kings; at the Revelation of whose Righteous Judgments, and glorious Tribunal, Mortal Men shall render an Account of the Deeds done in the Body;* and whatever the Apprehensions of such may be, concerning this Discourse, 'twas writ in Love and from a true Sense of the present State of Things: and *TIME,* and the *EVENT* will vindicate it from Untruth. In the mean while, 'tis Matter of great Satisfaction to the Author, that he has so plainly cleared his Conscience, *in pleading for the Liberty of other Men's,* and publickly born his honest Testimony for God, *not out of Season to his POOR COUNTRY.*

POSTSCRIPT.

A few brief Observations upon the late Act, and the usual Terms of Acts of this Nature.

That which we have to say, relates, either to the Terms of the *Act,* or the Application of them to us.

As to the Terms of the Act, they are these, *Seditious Conventicles, Seditious Sectaries,* and *Meetings under Colour or Pretence of Religion,* P. 1,

1. SEDITIOUS, from *Sedition,* imports as much as *Turbulent, Contentious, Factious, which sows Strife, and Debate, and hazards the Civil Peace of the Government.*

2. Conventicle, *is a diminutive private Assembly, designing and contriving*

Evil to particular Persons, or the Government in general, See Lamb. p. 173.[44] In *Tertullian*'s Sense, It is *an Assembly of immodest and unclean Persons;* at least it was so taken in those Days, and objected against the Christians as their Practice, whom he defends. *Ter. Apol.*[45]

3. Sectaries, *must be such as disjoin or dis-member themselves from the Body of Truth, and confess to a strange and untrue Opinion. If any Subject of this Realm being Sixteen Years of Age, or upwards, shall be present at any Assembly, or Conventicle, on pretence of Religion,* &c. which can signify no more than thus much, *That true it is some may meet and assemble to Worship God, and upon a religious Account, that are Dissenters,* such we censure not, but those *who under Colour or Pretence of any Exercise of Religion* conspire, *&c.* they are to be suspected and prosecuted. This being the true Explanation of the Terms of the Act, we proceed to shew how unreasonably they are applied to us.

1. Words are but so many intelligible Marks, and Characters set and employ'd to inform us of each other's Conceptions, and therein of the Nature of those Things they stand for: Now because we take the Act to mean what it speaks, and that the Law concludes no Man guilty upon Conjectures, but from the Detection of some Fault; we affirm our selves altogether unconcern'd in that Word *Seditious,* because it was never our Practice in Words or Actions to disturb the Government; *or suggest Principles that might hatch Conspiracies, or feed the Vulgar with Disaffection to their Rulers;* but before the King's Coming in, at his Coming in, and ever since, notwithstanding our frequent Suffering, *we have made it our Business to heal Animosities, preach Forgiveness and Charity amongst Men,* and that they would by an hearty Repentance turn to God, rather than hunt after Revenge upon one another; therefore we assert we have not done one thing that may be prov'd *Seditious* in the Sense above mention'd.

2. That we are Strangers to *Conventicles* is most evident, for where the Parts that render it such, are wanting, there can be no *Conventicle;* but that they are in our Assemblies, appears;

First, *Because our Meetings are not Small. 2. Neither are they Private or Clandestine; but in the View of all People.* Nor are they riotous, licentious, or otherwise immodest, or immoral; but on purpose to dissuade Persons from such

44. Possibly a reference to Thomas Lamb (d. 1686), but Penn's specific referent is unclear.

45. Tertullian, *Apology,* ch. 39.

Impieties; so that we are clear in the Interpretation of the Law, 13 *H.* 5. *cap.* 8. 19. and 19 *H.* 7. *cap.* 13. and in the Sense of the famous Father *Tertullian.*

3. *Sectaries,* is a Word, that whosoever has but Confidence enough to conceit himself in the Right, by Consequence wants none to suppose the contrary in the wrong, and so to call him a *Sectary;* but this is but a meer begging of the Question; For to say those are *Sectaries* does not conclude them such, nor does the Act speak so plainly of *Dissenters:* But granting it did, yet they must be *Seditious Ones,* or else all will be in vain; where we may observe, that purely to be a *Sectary* is not what the Act strikes at, but to be a *Seditious One:* For a Man may differ in Judgment about Matters of Faith, from the National Religion, and yet correspond with the Government in Matters Civil; so that ACT upon the whole aims not at *Sectaries* simply, but they must be such as are Enemies to the Civil Constitution to be rendred *Seditious Ones,* from which we have sufficiently clear'd ourselves.

4. *That we meet under Colour and Pretence, and not really to worship God;* we deny, and none can prove. 'Twere high Incharity to affirm positively, *This, or that People meet only under a Colour of Religion;* yet unless the Act had so express'd it self, we conceive their Authority lame and imperfect that Persecute us by it. It will help but little to say, *The King, Lords and Commons, by the following Words, in other Manner than according to the Liturgy of the Church of* England, *meant, that such meet under a Pretence that did not conform to that Worship;* since the precedent Words say, *under Colour or Pretence of any Exercise of Religion in other Manner, &c.* So that they are only struck at, who are not sincere Dissenters, but that are such, with Design to carry on another End.

Obj. But may some say, *'Tis granted, you have very evidently evaded the Force of the Act, so far as relates to these recited Expressions; but what if a Bill be ready, for an Explanatory and Supplementary Act to the former, wherein this Scope for Argument will not be found, because your Meetings will be absolutely adjudged Seditious, Riotous, and Unlawful.*

To which we Answer, That as the granting of the first, which none reasonably can deny, is a manifest Impeachment of such as have violently prosecuted People for being present at Religious Assemblies (almost to their utter Undoing) so shall we as easily answer the second, which amounts to the Force of an Objection, and briefly thus.

First, It is not more impossible for *Mankind* to preserve their *Society* without *Speech,* than it is absolutely requisite that the *Speech be regular and certain.* For, if what we call a *Man,* a *Lion,* a *Whale* to Day, we should call a *Woman,* a

Dog, a *Sprat* to Morrow; there would be such Uncertainty and Confusion, as it would be altogether impossible to preserve Speech or Language intelligible.

Secondly, It is not in the Power of all the Men in the *World to reconcile an absolute Contradiction, to convert the Nature of Light into that of Darkness, nor to enact a Thing to be that which it is not;* but that Those endeavour to do, who think of making our Religious Meetings *Routs* and *Riots;* for first they offer Violence to our common Propriety of Language, it being the first time that ever a Religious and Peaceable Assembly would be enacted a Rout or Riot: *Nature, Reason, the Law of the Land, and common Practice, and Observation,* give a clear contrary Definition of a *Rout* and *Riot.*

Secondly, They endeavour to reconcile Contradictions; *for they would have a Thing that, which by Nature it cannot be;* for that which is *Peaceable* cannot be *Riotous,* and what is *Religious* can never be *Seditious.* For any to say, our *Meetings are not Religious,* is not only a poor *Evasion,* but great *Incharity; for that is properly a Religious Assembly where Persons are congregated with a real Purpose of worshipping God, by Prayer, or otherwise, let the Persons met be esteem'd Doctrinally Orthodox, or not.* Can any be so Ignorant, or so Malicious, as to believe we do not Assemble to Worship God, to the best of our Understanding? If they think otherwise, they must, and do assume unto themselves a Power beyond the Arrogancy of the *POPE* himself, that never yet adventur'd to tell Man his Thoughts, nor the Purposes and Intents of his Heart, which he, or they must do, that definitively judge our Assemblies, *void of Sword or Staff, Drum or Musket, Tumult or Violence, and circumstantiated with all the Tokens of Christian Devotion,* a Rout or a Riot. And truly, *If Protestants deny the Legality of those Acts or Edicts, which were contriv'd and executed in order to their Suppression, by the respective Kings and Parliaments that own'd the* Romish *Faith and Authority, where they either did or do live, let them not think it strange, if we on the same Terms* (namely, Scruple of Conscience) *refuse Compliance with their Laws of Restraint.* And as the first Reformers were no whit daunted at the Black Characters the *Romanists* fastened on them, neither thought their *Assemblies* in a way of profest Separation, the more unlawful, for their representing them such; no more are we surpriz'd or scar'd at the ugly *Phrases,* daily cast upon us by a Sort of Men, that either do not know us, *or would not that others should:* For we are not so easily to be Brav'd, Menac'd, or Persecuted out of our *Sense, Reason,* and *Priviledge.*

They say, *LOSERS have leave to Speak,* at least, we take it; none being greater *Losers,* than such as for Dissenting from National Institutions in Point of Faith or Worship, are depriv'd of their Common *Rights* and *Freedoms,* and hindred as much as may be, from reverencing the God that made them, in that Way which to them seems most acceptable to him.

To Conclude, we say, and by it let our Intentions in our whole Discourse be measur'd, that we have not defended any *Dissenters,* whose *Quarrel* or *Dissent* is rather *Civil* and *Political,* than *Religious* and *Conscientious;* for both we really think such unworthy of Protection from the *English* Government, who seek the Ruin of it; and that such as are Contributors to the Preservation of it, (though Dissenters in Point of Faith or Worship) are unquestionably intituled to a Protection from IT.

ONE

Project for the Good of *England*

THAT IS,

Our Civil Union is our Civil Safety

Humbly Dedicated to the Great Council,

The Parliament of ENGLAND (1679)

RELIGION, as it is the noblest End of Man's Life, so it were the best Bond of *Human Society,* provided Men did not err in the Meaning of that excellent Word. Scripture interprets it to be *Loving God above all, and our Neighbours as our selves;*[1] but Practice teacheth us, that too many meerly resolve it into *Opinion* and *Form;* in which, not the *Text,* but the *Comment* too often prevails; whence it comes to pass, that those Bodies of Men, who have but one *Common Civil Interest,* are miserably distracted in Favour of their *adopted Notions,* upon which they are impatient to bestow an Earthly Crown. And this is the Reason of that Mischief and Uncertainty that attend Government. No sooner one Opinion prevails upon another, (though all hold the *Text* to be sacred) but *Human Society* is *shaken,* and the *Civil Government* must receive and suffer a *Revolution;* insomuch, that when we consider the Fury and Unnaturalness of some People for Religion, (which shews they have none that's True, Religion making Men most Natural as well as Divine) we have Reason to bewail the *Mis-understanding* as well as *Mis-living* of that venerable Word.

But since 'tis so hard to disabuse Men of their wrong Apprehensions of Religion, and the true Nature and Life of it, and consequently as yet too early in the Day to fix such a Religion upon which Mankind will readily agree as a common *Basis* for Civil Society, we must recur to some lower but true, Principle for the Present, and I think there will be no Difficulty of Succeeding.

'Tis this, *That Civil Interest is the Foundation and End of Civil Government,* and *where it is not maintained entire, the Government must needs decline.* The Word INTEREST has a good and bad Acceptation; when it is taken in an ill Sense, it signifies *a Pursuit of Advantage without Regard to Truth or Justice;*

1. Matthew 22:38–39; Mark 12:30–31; and Luke 10:27.

which I mean not: The good Signification of the Word, and which I mean, *is a Legal Endeavour to keep Rights, or augment honest Profits,* whether it be in a private Person or a Society. By GOVERNMENT, I understand a *Just and Equal Constitution,* where *Might* is not *Right,* but *Laws* rule, and not the *Wills* or *Power* of Men; for that were plain *Tyranny.*

This Government must have a Supreme Authority in it self to Determine, and not be superseded or controuled by any other Power, for then it would not be a Government, but a Subjection, which is a plain Contradiction.

Having thus explained the Terms of the *Principle* I have laid down, I repeat it, *viz. That Civil Interest is the Foundation and End of Civil Government,* and prove it thus: The *Good* of the Whole is the *Rise* and *End* of Government; but the *Good* of the *Whole* must needs be the *Interest* of the *Whole,* and consequently the *Interest* of the *Whole,* is the Reason and End of Government. None can stumble at the Word *Good,* for every Man may easily and safely interpret that to himself, since he must needs believe, 'tis *Good for him to be preserv'd in an undisturb'd Possession of his Civil Rights,* according to the *Free* and *Just Laws of the Land,* and the Construction he makes for himself will serve his Neighbour, and so the whole Society.

But as the *Good* of the People is properly the *Civil Interest* of the People, and *that,* the Reason and End of Government; so is the Maintenance of that *Civil Interest entire,* the Preservation of Government. For where People are sure of their *Own,* and are protected from Violence or Injury, they cheerfully yield their Obedience, and pay their Contribution to the Support of that Government. But on the contrary, where Men are insecure of their Civil Rights, nay, where they are daily violated, and themselves in Danger of Ruin, and that for no Sin committed against the Nature of Civil Interest, (to preserve which, Government was instituted) we ought to suppose their Affections will flag, that they will grow dead-hearted, and that what they pay or do, may go against the Grain: And to say true, such Unkindness is ready to tempt them to believe they should not of Right contribute to the Maintenance of such Governments as yield them no Security or Civil Protection. Which unhappy *Flaw* in the Civil Interest, proves an untoward *Crack* in the Government; Men not being cordially devoted to the Prosperity of that Government that is exercised in their Destruction; and how far that Fraction upon the Common Interest of the People may affect the Government I cannot tell, but to be sure it is insecure to any Government, to have the People (it's Strength) divided, as they will be, where their Interest is so disjointed by the Government; One

Protected, the Other *Expos'd.* Wherefore, Wise Governments have ever taken Care to preserve their People, as knowing they do thereby *preserve* their own *Interest,* and that how *Numerous* their People, so *large* their Interest. For not only *Solomon* has told us, *That the Honour of a Prince is in the Multitude of his People,*[2] but Experience teaches, that *Plenty* of People is the Riches and Strength of a Wise and Good Government; as that is, where Vice is corrected and Virtue encouraged, and *All* taken in and secured in Civils, that have the same Civil Interest with the Government.

But as the *Good* and *Interest* of the *Whole* is the Rise and End of Government, so must it suppose, that the *Whole* (which takes in all Parties) concurs in seeking the *Good* of the Government; for the Reason of the Government will not suffer it to protect those that are Enemies to it's Constitution and Safety; for so it would admit of something dangerous to the Society, for the Security of which, *Government* was at first *Instituted.*

It will follow, that those that own another Temporal Power superior to the Government they properly belong to, make themselves Subjects not of the Government they are born under, but to that Authority which they avow to be superior to the Government of their own Country, and consequently Men of another Interest, because 'tis their Interest to pursue the Advantages of that Power they acknowledge to be sovereign; But those that own, embrace and obey the Government of their own Country as their temporal supreme Authority, and whose Interest is one and the same with that of their own proper Government, ought to be valued and protected by that Government.

The *Principle* thus far lies *General,* I will now bring it to our own Case.

ENGLAND is a Country *Populous* and *Protestant,* and though under some *Dissents* within it self, yet the *Civil Interest* is the *same,* and in some Sense the *Religious too.* For, *first,* all *English Protestants,* whether *Conformists* or *Nonconformists* agree in this, *that they only owe Allegiance and Subjection unto the Civil Government of* England, and offer any Security in their Power to give of their Truth in this Matter. And in the next Place, they do not only consequentially disclaim the *Pope's Supremacy,* and all Adhesion to *Foreign Authority* under any Pretence, but therewith deny and oppose the *Romish Religion,* as it stands degenerated from *Scripture,* and the *first* and *purest Ages* of the *Church;* which makes up a great *Negative Union.*

2. Proverbs 14:28.

And it cannot be unknown to Men read in the Reasons of the *Reformation,* that a *Protestation* made by the *German Reformers* against the *Imperial Edicts of* Charles the Fifth, *imposing Romish Traditions,* gave Beginning to the Word *Protestant.*[3]

In short, It is the *Interest* of the *Ruling,* or *Church-Protestants of England,* that the *Pope* should have no Claim or Power in *England.* It is also the *Interest* of the *Dissenting Protestants,* that the Pope should have no Claim or Power here in *England,* because they are subject to the same Mischiefs and Sufferings in their Civil and Religious Rights that the Church-Protestants are liable to; if then both are like to lose by *Pope* and *Foreign Authority,* their *Interest* must needs be *one* against *Pope* and *Foreign Authority;* and if they have but *one Interest,* it will follow, that the *Church-Protestant* cannot prejudice the *Dissenting-Protestant,* but he must *weaken and destroy his own Interest.*

The *Civil Interest* of English Protestants being thus the same, and their Religious Interest too, so far as concerns a *Negative to the Usurpation and Error of* Rome; I do humbly ask, if it be the Interest of the Government, to expose those to Misery that have *no other Civil Interest than THAT of the Government?* Or if it be just or equal that the *Weaker* should be prosecuted by the *more powerful* Protestants, whose Interest is *positively the same in Civils, and in Religion Negatively?* One would think 'twere reasonable that they should not suffer by *Protestants,* who if *Popery* have a Day, are likely to suffer with them, and that upon the same Principles. Experience tells us, That the wisest Architects lay their Foundations broad and strong, and raise their Squares and Structure by the most exact Rules of Art, that the Fabrick may be secure against the Violence of Storms; but if People must be destroy'd by those of the same Interest, truly that *Interest* will stand but Totteringly, and every Breath of Opposition will be ready to shake it.

'Twas the Inconfutable Answer *Christ* made to the *Blasphemers* of that Power by which he wrought Miracles; *A Kingdom divided against it self cannot stand:* what he said then, let me on another Occasion say now, an *Interest divided against it self must fall.*[4]

3. The Diet of the Holy Roman Empire at Speyer (1529) resolved that communities in which the new religion was firmly established should introduce no further innovations in religion. A number of princes protested that they did not intend to tolerate Catholicism within their borders. On that account they were called Protestants; prior to this time they had referred to themselves as "Evangelicals."

4. Matthew 12:25; Mark 3:24–25; and Luke 11:17.

I know some Men will take *Fire* at this, and by crying The CHURCH, The CHURCH, hope to silence all Arguments of this Nature; But they must excuse me, if I pay no Manner of Regard to their Zeal, and hold their Devotion both Ignorant and Dangerous at this Time. It is not the Way to fill the Church, to destroy the People. A Church without People is a Contradiction, especially when the Scripture tells us, that 'tis the People that makes the Church.

And 'tis not without an Appearance of Reason that some good and wise Men are apprehensive, that the greatest *Sticklers* for persecuting *Protestant Dissenters* in Favour of the *Church of* England, are Men addicted and devoted to the *Church of Rome,* or at least animated by such as are; who, despairing of doing any great Feats, if known, hide themselves under these Pretences; but the Meaning of it is to debilitate the *Protestant* Cause in general, by exciting the Church of *England,* to destroy all other *Protestant* Interests in these Kingdoms, that so nothing may remain for *Popery* to conflict with but the few Zealous *Abettors* of that Church.

And that this may not look disingenuous, or like a *Trick* of mine, I will enforce it by a Demonstration. It is plain Fact, that the *Church of Rome* hath ever since the Reformation practised the Restoration of her Religion and Power in these Kingdoms. It is as evident that *Religion* is with her a Word for *Civil Interest,* that is, that she may have the *Rule over Men both Body and Soul. For 'tis Government she aims at, to have the Reins of Power in her Hand, to give Law and wield the Scepter.*

To do this she must either have a greater Interest than the *Protestants* that are now in Possession, or else divide their Interest, and so weaken them by themselves, and make them Instruments to her Ends. That her own Force is Inconsiderable is clear: She has nothing within Doors to give her Hope but the *Discord* of *Protestants.* It follows then that she must of Necessity bestir her self, and use her Arts to enflame the Reckoning among *Protestants,* and carry their Dissents about *Religious* Matters to a *Division* in the *Civil Interest.* And it is the more to be fear'd, because whatever she has been to others, she has been ever true to her self.

If this then be the only Domestick Expedient left her, we are sure she will use it: and if so, it must needs be of great Importance with all *Protestants* to let fall their private Animosities, and take all possible Care that their *Dissents* about Faith or Worship, (which regard the other World) *divide* not their Affection and Judgment about the Common and Civil Interest of their Country: because if that be kept entire, it *equally frustrates* the Designs of *Rome,* as if you were of *one* Religion. For since, as I said before, *Religion,* with the great Men of that Church, is nothing else but a softer Word for *Civil Empire,* preserve you but your Civil Interest from Fraction, and you are in that Sense of *one Religion* too; and that such an one, as you need not fear the Temptation of *Smithfield,* if you will but be true to it.[5]

This being the Case, I would take Leave to ask the *Zealous Gentlemen* of the *English* Church, *If Conformity to the Fashion of their Worship be dearer to them than* England's *Interest and the Cause of Protestancy?* If their Love to Church-Government be greater than to the Church and her Religion, and to their Country and her Laws? Or, lastly, Whether in Case they are sincere in their Allegations for the *Church,* (which, I confess ingenuously, I am apt to suspect) it is to be supposed that the present *Church-men* (Conformists I mean) are better able of themselves to secure *Protestancy* and our *Civil Interest* against the Attempts of *Rome,* than in *Conjunction with the Civil Interest of all Protestant Dissenters?* If they say, yes, I would have them at the same Time, for the same Reason, to give it under their Hands, that 'tis a standing Rule in *Arithmetick,* that ONE is more than SIX, and that hitherto we have been all mistaken in the Art of Numbers.

Being brought to this Pinch, I conceive they must say, that they had rather deliver up their *Church* to the *Power* and *Designs* of *Popery,* than suffer *Dissenters* to live freely among them, though *Protestants, of one Negative Religion, and of the same Civil Interest;* or else hasten to break those Bonds that are laid upon Dissenters of truly tender (and by Experience) of peaceable Consciences; and by Law establish the free Exercise of their Worship to Almighty God, that the *Fears, Jealousies, Disaffection* and *Distraction,* that now affect the one common Interest of *Protestants,* may be removed; for it seems impossible to preserve a distinct Interest from both. But to which of these they may incline, I must not determine; and yet I hope, they will not be of the Mind of a late Monk of *Cullen,* that in his publick Exercise exhorted the *Civil Magistrates* to chuse to have their City *Poor* and *Catholick,* that is *Popish,* rather than *Great* and *Opulent* by the Admission of *trading Hereticks;* but if they should, may our *Magistrates* have at least their Prudence; for the *Culleners* gave him the Hearing, but were as true to their Interest, as the *Monk* to his *Superstition.*

Under Favour, the *Civil Government* is greatly concern'd to discountenance such *Biggotry;* for it *Thins* the People, *Lessens* Trade, *Creates* Jealousies, and

5. A number of Protestant martyrs under Queen Mary were burned at Smithfield.

Endangers the Peace and Wealth of the Whole. And, with Submission, of what should the *Civil Magistrate* be more tender, than of suffering the *Civil Interest* of a Great People to be disturb'd and narrow'd for the *Humour* of any one *Party* of them? for since the *Civil Interest* lies as large, as the People of that Interest, *the People must be preserv'd in order to preserve that Common Interest.* Other Notions ever did divide and weaken *Empire,* and in the End they have rarely miss'd to pull the Old House about their Ears, that have govern'd themselves by such disproportionable Measures: By all Means, interest the Affections of the People in the Prosperity of the Government, by making the Government a SECURITY to their particular Rights and Properties.

I ask, if more Custom comes not to the King, and more Trade to the Kingdom, by encouraging the Labour and Traffick of an *Episcopalian, Presbyterian, Independent, Quaker* and *Anabaptist,* than by an *Episcopalian* only? If this be true, why should the rest be render'd uncapable of Trade, yea, of Living? What *Schism* or *Heresy* is there in the Labour and Commerce of the *Anabaptist, Quaker, Independent* and *Presbyterian,* more than in the Labour and Traffick of the *Episcopalian?*

I beseech you give me Leave, Is there ever a *Church-man* in *England,* that in Distress would refuse the Courtesy of one of these *Dissenters?* If one of them should happen to fall into a Pond or Ditch, would he deny to be helped out by a *Dissenter*'s Hand? Is it to be supposed, he would in such a Pickle be Stomachful, and chuse to lie there, and be Smother'd or Drown'd, rather than owe Aid to the Good-will of a poor *Phanatick?* Or if his House were on Fire, may we think that he would have it rather burnt to the Ground than acknowledge it's Preservation to a *Non-conformist?* Would not the *Act* be *Orthodox,* whatever were the Man? So in Case of being *Sick, Imprison'd, Beset, Benighted, out of the Way, far from Kindred* or *Acquaintance,* with an hundred other Cases that may happen daily, can we think, that such Men would ask Questions for Conscience Sake, or charge *Schism* upon the *Relief* given them? No, no; *Self* will always be true to it's *Interest,* let Superstition mutter what it will.

But since the *Industry, Rents* and *Taxes* of the *Dissenters* are as currant as their Neighbours, who loses by such narrowness more than *England,* than the Government and the Magistracy? For till it be the *Interest of the Farmer* to *destroy* his *Flock, to Starve the Horse he rides, and the Cow that gives him Milk,* it cannot be the *Interest* of *England* to let a great Part of her Sober and Useful Inhabitants be destroy'd about Things that concern another World. And 'tis to be hoped, that the Wisdom and Charity of our *Governors* will better guide them both to their own real Interest and their People's Preservation, which are inseparable; that so they may not *Starve them for Religion, that are as willing, as able, to work for the Good of King and Country.*

I beseech you, let *Nature* speak, who is so much a better Friend to Human Society, than False or Froward *Opinion,* that she often rectifies the Mistakes of a Prejudiced Education, that we may say, how *Kind,* how *Gentle,* how *Helpful* does she teach us to be to each other, till that *Make-bate OPINION* (falsly called *Religion*) begins the Jangle, and Foments to Hatred.

All the Productions of Nature are by *Love, and shall Religion propagate by Force?* If we consider the poor *Hen,* she will teach us Humanity. Nature does not only learn her to hatch, but to be tender over her Feeble Chickens, that they may not be a Prey to the *Kite.* All the *Seeds* and *Plants* that grow for the Use and Nourishment of Man, are produced by the kind and warm Influences of the *Sun.* Nothing but *Kindness* keeps up *Human Race:* Men and Women don't get Children in *Spite,* but *Affection.* 'Tis wonderful to think by what friendly and gentle Ways Nature produces, and Matures the Creatures of the World; and that Religion should teach us to be *Froward* and *Cruel,* is Lamentable: This were to make her the *Enemy* instead of the *Restorer* of Nature. But I think, we may without Offence say, That since *True Religion* gives Men *Greater Mildness* and *Goodness* than they had before, that *Religion* which teaches them *less,* must needs be *False.* What shall we say then, but that even *Nature* is a truer Guide to Peace, and *better informs us to preserve Civil Interest, than False Religion,* and consequently, that we ought to be true to the Natural and Just Principles of Society, and not suffer one of them to be violated for *Humour* or *Opinion.*

Let us go together as *far as our Way lies,* and preserve our Unity in those Principles, which maintain our Civil Society. This is our Common and our Just Interest, all *Protestant Dissenters* agree in this, and it is both Wise and Righteous to admit no Fraction upon this Pact, no Violence upon this Concord. For the Consequence of permitting any Thing to break in upon the Principles of Human Society, that is *Foreign* to the Nature of it, will distract and weaken that Society.

We know, that in all *Plantations* the Wisdom of *Planters* is well aware of this: and let us but consider, that the *same* Ways that plant Countries, *must be kept to for preserving the Plantation,* else 'twill quickly be *Depopulated.*

That Country which is false to it's first Principles of Government, and mistakes or divides it's *Common* and *Popular Interest,* must unavoidably decay.

And let me say, That had there been this Freedom granted Eighteen Years ago,[6] *Protestancy* had been too potent for the Enemies of it; nor had there been those Divisions for *Popery* to make it's Advantage by; at least, not in the *Civil Interest* of the Nation. And where that has been preserv'd entire, it has been never able to prevail: Witness the careful Government of *Holland,* where the Preservation of their Civil Interest from Fraction hath secured them against the Growth of *Popery,* though it be almost tolerated by them: So powerful are the Effects of an *United Civil Interest* in Government. Now because the *Civil Interest* of this Nation is the *Preservation of the Free and Legal Government of it from all Subjection to Foreign Claim,* and that the several Sorts of *Protestants* are united, as in the *Common Protestancy,* that is, a *General Renunciation of* Rome, so in the Maintenance of this *Civil Government* as a Common Security, (for it strikes at both their Rights, Civil and Sacred; their Conscience, Religion and Law, to admit any Foreign Jurisdiction here) it must follow, that had these several, as well *English* as *Protestant* Parties, been timely encouraged to this United Civil Interest, they had secured the Government from this Danger by rendring it too formidable for the Attempt.

But there is a two fold Mistake that I think fit to remove. *First,* That the Difference betwixt *Protestants* and their *Dissenters* is generally manag'd, as if it were Civil. *Secondly,* The Difference betwixt *Papist* and *Protestant* is carried on, as if it were chiefly Religious.

To the First, I say, 'Tis plausible, but false; it is an Artifice of ill Men to enflame the Government against good People, to make base Ends by other Mens Ruin; whereas they that dissent, are at a *Ne plus ultra* on the Behalf of the English Government, as well as themselves. They neither acknowledge nor submit to any other Authority. They *hold the one common Civil Head,* and not only acquiesce in the Distribution of Justice by Law; but embrace it as the best Part of their *Patrimony.* So that the Difference between *Protestants* and their Dissenters is purely Religious, and mostly about *Church-Government,* and some Forms of Worship, apprehended to be not so pure and Apostolical as could be desired; and here it is, that Tenderness should be exercis'd, if in any Case in the World, or St. *Paul* is Mistaken.[7]

But as to the *Second,* under Correction, the Case is alter'd, for though it be mostly manag'd on the Side of *Religion,* The great Point is meerly *Civil,* and

6. I.e., at or just following the restoration of Charles II.

7. Romans 15:1–2; 2 Timothy 2:24–26; 1 Corinthians 1:10; and Ephesians 4:1–3.

should never be otherwise admitted or understood. For want of this Caution *Protestants* suffer themselves to be drawn into tedious Controversies about Religion, and give occasion to the *Professors* and *Favourers* of that Way to exclaim against them, as *Persecutors* for Religion, who had reprobated such Severity in the *Papists* to their Ancestors (a most plausible and very often a successful *Plea*) when in reality the Difference is not so much *Religious* as *Civil.* Not but that there is a vast *Contrariety* in Doctrine and Worship too; but this barely should not be the Cause of our so great Distance, and that Provision the Laws make against them; but rather that *Fundamental inconsistency* they carry with them to the Security of the *English Government* and *Constitution* unto which they belong, by acknowledging a Foreign Jurisdiction in these Kingdoms. So that drawing into Question and Danger the Constitution and Government, to which Scripture, and Nature, and *Civil Pact,* oblige their Fidelity and Obedience, there seems a Discharge upon the *Civil Government* from any farther Care of their Protection, that make it a *Piece of Conscience to seek it's Ruin* and which is worse, a *Principle, not to be informed of better Things,* for even here not Reason or Law, but the Pope must be Judge.

This being the Brief and modest State of the Case, I must return to my first great Principle, *That Civil Interest is the Foundation and End of Civil Government:* and that how much Men desert the Interest of a Kingdom, so much they *Wound* and *Subvert* the Government of it. I appeal to all Wise and Considerate Men of the Truth of this by the present Posture of Affairs and their proper Cause.

To come then to our Point, Shall English Men by *English Men,* and Protestants by *Protestants,* be Free or Opprest? This is, *Whether shall we receive as* English-men *and* Protestants, *those that have no other Civil Interest than that which is purely* English, *and who sincerely profess and embrace the same Protestation, for which the Ancient Reformers were stiled* Protestants, *or for the Sake of Humour or Base Ends disown them and expose them and their Families to utter Misery?*

I would hope better of our great Church-Men's Charity and Prudence; but if they should be so unhappy as to keep to their old Measures, and still play the Gawdy, but empty, Name of *Church* against the *Civil Interest and Religion of the Nation,* they will shew themselves deserted of God, and then how long it will be, before they will be seen and left of all sober Men, let them Judge. For to speak freely, after all this *Light* that is now in the World, no *Ignorance* can excuse such *Zeal,* nor will wise Men believe it to be either, but a Trick to weaken *Protestancy,* that her declared Enemy may with less hazard gain the Chair. And there is not so much reason to fear Profest *Roman Catholicks,* as those *Gentlemen,* who valuing themselves by their respects to the *Church* and Tenderness of it's *Independent* Honour, *have the Opportunity with less Suspicion of letting in* Popery *at the Back door.* These are Men that pay off the *Phanatick* in the Name of the Church, but for the good of the Pope, to whose Account those Endeavours must be placed.

But it will go a great Way to our Deliverance, if we are not Careless to observe the Secret Workings of those that have vow'd our Misery, and of them, such as are in *Masquerade,* and wear the Guise of Friends, are most Dangerous: But some Men are *Pur-blind,* they can see Danger as near as their Nose, but in a Difficulty, that is not a Foot from them, they are Presumptive, Rusty and not to be govern'd. Could some *Church-men* but see the Irreparable Mischiefs that will attend them (if sincere to their present Profession) unless prevented by a *Modest and Christian condescension to* Dissenting Protestant Christians, they would never suffer themselves to be Mis-guided by Stiff and Rigid Principles at this Time of Day.

If *Christianity,* that most Meek and Self-denying Religion, cannot prevail upon them, methinks the Power of Interest, and that *Self-interest* too, should have some Success, for in those Cases they use not to be obstinate.

But I expect it should be told me, *That this is the Way to Ruin the Church, and let in an Anarchy in Religion: Cujus contrarium verum.*[8] I am glad to obviate this, before I leave you, seeing the Contrary is most true; for it leaves the Church and Church-men as they are, with this Distinction, that whereas now Conformity is Coercive, which is *Popish,* it will be then Perswasive, which is Christian. And there may be some hopes, when the *Parsons,* destitute of the Magistrates Sword, shall of necessity enforce their Religion by good Doctrine and Holy Living; nor ought they to murmur, for that which satisfied Christ and his Apostles should satisfy them: *His Kingdom is not of this World,*[9] therefore they should not Fight for him, if they would be his Servants and the *Children* of his *Kingdom,* Christ, and not Civil Force, is the Rock his Church is built upon. Nor indeed has any Thing so Tarnisht the Cause of *Protestancy,* as the Professors of it betaking themselves to Worldly Arms to propagate their Reli-

8. Which is contrary to truth.
9. John 18:36.

gion. *David* could not wear *Saul*'s Armour,[10] and true *Protestants* cannot use *Popish* Weapons, *Imposition* and *Persecution.* In short; 'Tis the very Interest of the Church of *England,* to preserve the civil Interest entire, or else *Popery* will endanger all; but that cannot be unless all of that Civil Interest be preserved; therefore *Protestant Dissenters* should be indulg'd.

But some will say, *There is a Difference even among Dissenters; Some will give a Security to the Civil Government by taking the Oaths, others will not, and be it through Tenderness, how do we know, but Papists will shrow'd themselves under the Wings of such Dissenters, and so in Tolerating Protestant Dissenters to fortify Protestancy, in reality Popery will be hereby shelter'd* incognito.

I answer, *First,* That such Oaths are little or no Security to any Government, and though they may give some Allay to the Jealousy of Governours, they never had the Effect desired. For neither in private Cases, nor yet in Publick Transactions have Men adher'd to their Oaths, but their Interest. He that is a Knave, was never made Honest by an Oath: Nor is it an Oath, but Honesty, that keeps Honest Men such. Read Story and consult our Modern Times, tell me what Government stood the firmer or longer for them? Men may take them for their own Advantage, or to avoid Loss and Punishment: But the Question is, What real Benefit, or Security comes thereby to the Government? It is certain they have often *ensnared a Good Man,* but never *caught one Knave yet:* We ought not to put so great a Value upon Oaths, as to render the Security of our Government so low and hazardous.

God's Providence and the Wisdom of our Ancestors have found out a better Test for us to rest upon, and that is, our *Common Interest, and the Laws of the Land* DULY *executed:* These are the Security of our Government.

For Example, a Man Swears he will not Plot, yet Plots; pray what Security is this Oath to the Government? But though 'tis evident, that this be no Security; that Law which Hangs him for Plotting, is an *unquestionable one.* So that 'tis not for wise Governours, by Swearing Men to the Government to think to secure it; but all having agreed to the Laws, by which they are to be governed, *let any Man break them at his Peril.* Wherefore good Laws, and a Just Execution of them, and not Oaths, are the *Natural and Real Security of a Government.*

But next, though some may scruple the Oaths, 'tis not for the Sake of the

10. 1 Samuel 17:38–39.

Matter so much as Form, which you know is not the Case of *Roman Catholicks,* (pray distinguish) and those very Persons, whoever they be of *Protestant Dissenters,* I dare say, they will very cheerfully promise their Allegiance on the same Penalties, *and subscribe any Renunciation of Pope and Foreign Authority, which the Art of Man can Pen;* nor should it be hard for you to believe they should subscribe what they have always liv'd.

To that Part of the Objection, which mentions *the danger of* Papists *concealing themselves under the Character of* Protestant Dissenters; under Favour I say, it is most reasonable to believe, that those who will deny their Faith upon Record, as those that subscribe your Declaration do, will swallow the Oaths too; for the Declaration flatly denies the Religion, but the Oaths only the *Pope's Supremacy,* which even some of themselves pretend to reject.[11] Therefore those that can sincerely subscribe the Declaration cannot be *Papists.*

If it be yet objected, that *Papists* may have Dispensations to subscribe the Test, or a Pardon, when they have done it; I answer, they may as well have *Dispensations* to take the Oaths, or Pardons when they have taken them, and these last six Months prove as much. There is no Fence against this Flail. At this rate they may as well be *Protestants,* as *Protestant-Dissenters; Ministers* or *Bishops* in *Churches,* as Speakers or Preachers in Meeting-houses: This Objection only shows the Weakness of both Oaths and Declaration for the Purpose intended, and not, that they can hide themselves more under one People than another. For they that can have a Dispensation or Pardon for one Act, can have it for another; especially when the Matter of the Declaration is of a more general weight to them, than that of the Oath; all which confirms my former Judgment of the Insecurity of such Oaths to any Government.

Give me leave then upon this to ask you, if you will bring a certain Ruin upon any Protestant *Dissenters* for the Sake of such an uncertain Security to your selves? for this is the Question; I beseech you to weigh it as becomes wise and good Men: shall they be Reprobated for tenderly refusing, what being perform'd, cannot save or secure you?

Consider, you have no Reason to believe, but those that are allow'd to subscribe the Declaration, or that will be pardon'd when they have done it, may be allow'd to take the Oaths, or will be *pardon'd* or *absolv'd,* when they have taken them: but you are certain on the other Side, that the Imposing of the

11. Under the Test Act of 1673, officeholders were required to sign a declaration abjuring belief in transubstantiation, in addition to taking an oath denying papal supremacy.

Oaths will be a great *Snare* to many *Protestant-Dissenters,* that love the Government, and renounce both *Pope* and *Popery;* They will be ruin'd; which to me is of the Nature of an Argument for those People: For their not taking the Oaths, proves plainly, they have no Dispensations nor hopes of Absolution, and therefore no *Papists;* shall they then lie under the Severities intended against *Papists,* who have none of their Dispensations or Absolutions to deliver them from them? This is (with Submission but in plain Terms) to make the Case of the Kingdom worse; for it destroys those who are not Guilty, and whom, I believe, you would not destroy.

Having brought the Matter to this, I shall first offer you a new Test; Next, the Ways of taking it, with most Aggravation against the Party rejecting or breaking it; And lastly, how you may secure your selves from *Papists* disguising themselves among *Protestant-Dissenters;* that so nothing may remain a *Remora*[12] in the Way, that shall not be removed, to leave you a plain and even Path to Peace and Safety.

The New TEST.

I A. B. *do solemnly and in good Conscience, in the Sight of God and Men, acknowledge and declare, that* King *Charles* the second is Lawful King of this Realm, and all the Dominions thereunto belonging. *And that neither the* Pope *nor* See *of* Rome, *nor any else by their Authority have* Right *in any Case to Depose the King, or Dispose of his Kingdom, or upon any Score whatever to* absolve *his* Subjects *of their Obedience, or to give leave to any of them to* Plot *or* Conspire *the Hurt of the* King's Person, *his* State *or* People; *and that all such Pretences and Power are* False, Pernicious *and* Damnable.

And I do farther sincerely profess, and in good Conscience declare, that I do not believe, that the Pope is Christ's Vicar, *or* Peter's Lawful Successor, *or that He or the* See of Rome, *severally or joyntly, are the* Rule of Faith *or* Judge of Controversy, *or that they can* absolve *Sins: Nor do I believe, there is a* Purgatory *after Death; or that* Saints *should be* pray'd to, *or* Images *in any Sense be* worship'd. *Nor do I believe, that there is any* Transubstantiation *in the* Lord's Supper, *or* Elements *of* Bread *and* Wine, *at or after the Consecration thereof by any Person whatsoever. But I do firmly believe, that the Present Communion of*

12. Obstacle; impediment.

the Roman-Catholick Church *is both* Superstitious *and* Idolatrous. *And all this I do* acknowledge, intend, profess *and* declare *without any* Equivocation, *or* reserv'd, *or* other Sense, *than the* plain *and* usual Signification *of these Words, according to the* real Intention *of the* Law-makers, *and the* common Acceptation of all true Protestants.[13]

This is the *Test* I offer; large in Matter, because comprehensive of Oaths and Test too, yet brief in Words.

The next Thing is the Ways of taking it with most Aggravation upon the Refusers or Violaters of it.

1. That in all Cities and great Towns, Notice be given by the Magistrates thereof to the Inhabitants of every *Ward* or *Parish* to appear on such a Day, be it *New-Years-Day* or *Ash-Wednesday* rather (when the *Pope Curses all Protestants*) at their Publick Hall, or other Places of Commerce, where the *Magistrates* shall first openly *Read, Subscribe, and Seal the Test.* Then that it be read again by the proper Officer of the Place to the People, and that those that take it, *Do Audibly Pronounce* the Words after him that reads it; and when they have so done, that they Subscribe and Seal it. That such Subscriptions be *Register'd,* and Copies of each Parish's Subscription, transmitted to the *Parish,* and affixt upon some publick Place for all that will to see.

2. That in the Countries, the *Parishes of each Hundred or Rape,*[14] may be likewise Summon'd to appear upon the Day aforesaid, *at the Head Market-Town in the said Hundred or Rape,* and, *that the Justices of the Peace within that Part of the Country, shall first Read, Subscribe, and Seal the said Test, in View of the People, and then that the People Say, Subscribe, and Seal the Test, as is before exprest.* Which being done, let the said *Subscriptions* be collected into One Volumn, and kept in the County Court as a *Book of Record;* and that to each Parish, be transmitted a Copy of the said *Parish's Subscription,* to be affixt upon some Publick Place within *the said Parish, for all to see.*

Lastly, Let this be done Annually, that is, upon every *New-Years-Day,* or *Ash-Wednesday,* as a *Perpetual Testimony of the People's Affection to the King and Government, and their Abhorrence of the Practices of* Rome.

The Abuse of this *Discrimination* should be very Penal; *For 'tis a Great Lye*

13. Equivocation and mental reservation were two forms of casuistry by which, Protestants feared, Jesuits or other Catholics could evade the force of oaths.

14. An administrative district comprising several hundred people.

upon a Man's own Conscience, and a Cheat put upon the Government: Your Wisdom can best proportion and direct the Punishment; but it can scarcely be too severe, as our Business stands.

But as in Case of such Hypocrisie, a severe Penalty should be inflicted, so pray let Provision be made, that if any Person so subscribing, should be afterwards call'd by the *Name of Jesuit or Papist,* without very good Proof, it should be *deem'd* and *punish'd* in open Sessions, *for a Slander and Breach of Peace,* yet so, as that the Penalty may be remitted at the Request of the *Abused Party.*

I should think that this Business, carefully done, might render needless my Answer to the last Objection, viz. *Which Way shall we be able to prevent* Papists *from passing for* Protestant Dissenters, *that so the Security propounded to the Government, be not baffled by Disguise?* For no *Papist* can subscribe this, but he will Lye in the Face of the Government and Country, and that *Yearly,* and upon *Record* too; which is Ten Times more than a *Transient Oath,* mutter'd with *One Word spoken, and another dropt.* However, that we may carry it as far as Human Prudence can go,—

I yet offer Two Expedients:

First, That upon Jealousie of any Person's being a *Papist,* or *Popishly Inclined,* who is known to frequent the Assemblies of *Protestant Dissenters,* Four of that Party, of most Note and Integrity, unto which he pretends to adhere, should be Summoned to appear before those *Justices of the Peace,* unto whom the Complaint is made, to testifie their Knowledge of the Person suspected, his *Education, Principles,* and *Manner of Life;* which Way of Inspection, as it goes as far as Man can reach, so can it scarcely fail; for those Persons will not only discover their own *Hypocrisie* if they conceal him, but expose themselves and their Friends to Ruin. So that to say True, *The Government has the Interest and Security of an Entire Party, for the Discovery of every such suspected Person.*

But if this will not do, then

Secondly, Be you pleased to refer the Discrimination of suspected Persons, to the Good Old Way of the Government, that is, *The Enquiry and Judgment of Twelve Men of the Neighbourhood;* to wit, *A Jury,* provided always, that they be such as have taken, or will themselves take the *Test;* else, that they may be *Excepted against by the Party suspected.*

Indeed a Good Expedient may be made out of both, for the *First* may be the *Evidence to the Last,* and I think you will hardly fail of your Ends.

I shall conclude with this Request, First, *to Almighty God, that He would please to make us truly and deeply sensible of His present Mercies to us, and to Reform our Hearts and Lives to improve them thankfully.* And, Secondly, *to you, that we may be Loving, Humble and Diligent, one to, and for another; for as from such Amendments we may dare promise great and sudden Felicity to* England, *so if Loosness in Life, and Bitterness in Religion be not speedily Reprehended and Reform'd, and the Common Civil Interest maintained entire, God will, I justly fear, Repent He has begun to do us Good, Adjourn the Day of our Deliverance to that of our Repentance and Moderation, and Overcast these Happy Dawnings of His Favour, by a thick and dismal Cloud of Confusion and Misery:* Which GOD Avert!

These Things that I have written, are no Wild Guesses, or May-Be's, but the Disease and Cure, the Danger and Safety of *England;* in treating of which, that God that made the World knows, I have not gratified any private Spleen or Interest (for I am sorry at the Occasion) but singly and conscientiously intended His Honour, and the Lasting Good of *England,* to which all Personal and Party Considerations ought ever to submit.

Amicus Plato, Amicus Aristoteles, sed magis Amica Veritas. i.e. *Anglia:*[15]

Your own Faithful and Most Affectionate

PHILANGLUS.

15. A friend of Plato, a friend of Aristotle, but most of all a friend of truth, i.e., England.

AN
Address to *Protestants* of All Perswasions
More Especially the
Magistracy and Clergy,
FOR THE
Promotion of Virtue *and* Charity (1679)
In Two Parts. By *W. P.* a *Protestant.*

2 Pet. 1. 5, 6, 7, 8, 9. *Giving all Diligence, add to your Faith,* Virtue; *and to* Virtue, Knowledge; *and to* Knowledge, Temperance; *and to* Temperance, Patience; *and to* Patience, Godliness; *and to* Godliness, Brotherly Kindness; *and to* Brotherly Kindness, Charity. *For if these Things be in you, and abound, they make you that ye shall neither be barren nor unfruitful in the Knowledge of our Lord Jesus Christ. But he that lacketh these Things, is blind, and cannot see far off, and hath forgotten that he was purged from his old Sins.*

THE FIRST PART.

Sect. 8. *An Address to the* Civil Magistrate *for Redress.*

HAVING thus ended my *Reflections upon the Five Great Crying Sins* of the Kingdom,[1] and my Reproof of the *Actors and Promoters* of them; give me Leave to make my *Humble* and *Christian Address* to you that are in *Authority.* And in the *First* Place, I beseech you to remember, that tho' ye are as Gods on Earth, yet ye shall dye like Men: That ye are encompass'd with like Passions, and are subject to Sin. Such therefore of you, as may be concerned in any of these *Enormities* (to what ever Degree of Guilt it be) I beg you in the Name of God to *search your selves,* and to be just to your own Souls. O! let

1. The five great crying sins of the kingdom, elaborated by Penn in Part I of this *Address,* are drunkenness, fornication, luxury, gambling, and oaths (which Penn considered a form of blasphemy).

the Mercies and Providences of God constrain you to *Unfeigned Repentance!* Turn to the Lord, Love Righteousness, Hate Oppression, and he will turn to you, and love you and bless you.

In the next Place, be pleased to consider your Commission, and examine the Extent of your Authority, you will find that God and the Government have impower'd you to punish these Impieties: And it is so far from being a Crime, that it is your Duty. This is not troubling Men for Faith, nor perplexing People for Tenderness of Conscience; for there can be no Pretence of Conscience to be *Drunk,* to *Whore,* to be *Voluptuous,* to *Game, Swear, Curse, Blaspheme* and *Profane;* no such Matter. These are Sins against Nature; and against *Government,* as well as against the *Written Laws* of God. They lay the Ax to the Root of *Human Society,* and are the *Common Enemies* of Mankind. 'Twas to prevent these *Enormities,* that *Government* was instituted; and shall *Government* indulge that which it is instituted to Correct? This were to render *Magistracy* Useless, and the Bearing of the *Sword* Vain: There would be then no such Thing in *Government* as *A Terror to Evil-Doers;*[2] but every one would do that which he thought Right in his own Eyes. God Almighty defend us from this Sort of *Anarchy.*

There are three great *Reasons,* which enforce my *Supplication.* The First is, The *Preservation of the Government,* which by such *Improvidence and Debauchery,* is like to be greatly weakned, if not destroyed. The *Industry, Wealth, Health* and *Authority* of the Nation, are deeply concern'd in the Speedy and exemplary Punishment of these Extravagancies. This is the *Voice* of *Interest,* for the Common Good of the whole Society; *Rulers* and *Ruled.*

But there is an higher Voice, unto which *Christian Men* ought to have Regard, and that is the *Voice of God,* who requires us to fear him and obey his Righteous Commandments, at the Peril of making him our *Enemy,* whom we should make our common *Friend* and *Protector:* For upon his Goodness, depends our very Natural and Civil Comforts. So that it is our Interest to be good; and it is none of the least Arguments for Religion, that the Piety and Practice of it is the *Peace* and *Prosperity* of *Government;* and consequently, that *Vice* the Enemy of *Religion,* is, at the same Time, the Enemy of *Humane Society.* What then should be more concern'd for the Preservation of *Virtue,* than *Government;* that in it's abstract and true Sense is not only founded upon *Virtue,* but without the Preservation of *Virtue,* it is impossible to maintain the

2. 1 Peter 2:14.

best Constitution that can be made? And however some particular Men may *prosper,* that are *Wicked,* and several private *good Men miscarry* in the Things of this World, in which Sense Things may be said to happen alike to all, to the *Righteous* as to the *Wicked,* yet I dare boldly affirm, and challenge any Man to the Truth thereof, that in the many Volumes of the History of all the *Ages* and *Kingdoms* of the World, there is not one Instance to be found, where the Hand of God was against a Righteous Nation, or where the Hand of God was not against an Unrighteous Nation first or last? Nor where a just Government perish't, or an unjust Government long prospered? *Kingdoms* are rarely as short lived as Men, yet they also have a Time to die: But as *Temperance* giveth Health to Men, so *Virtue* gives Time to Kingdoms; and as *Vice* brings Men betimes to their Grave, so Nations to their Ruin.

'Tis the Reason given by God himself, for the Destruction of the old World. We have that Example before our Eyes; that a whole World has perisht for it's Sin, *it's Forgetfulness of God and their Duty to him; one Family only excepted.* Gen. 6. That is the Reason which God renders for casting out the People of those Countries, that he gave into the Hands of the Children of *Israel;* they were full of *Uncleanness, Adulteries, Fornication,* and other Impieties. And though he is *Soveraign Lord* of the World, and may dispose of the Kingdoms therein, as pleaseth him (for he that gives can take away; and he that builds, can cast down; and Mankind is but a Tenant at Will, to receive or surrender at his Lord's *Good Pleasure*) yet he useth not that *Prerogative* to justifie his Gift of those Countries to the *Jews;* but at the End of his Prohibition of Unlawful Marriages and Lusts, he charges them in these Words; *defile not your selves in any of these Things:* for in all these the Nations are defiled, which I cast out before you; *And the Land is defiled:* therefore do I visit the Iniquity thereof upon it; *and the Land it self, vomiteth out her Inhabitants. Ye shall therefore keep my Statutes and Judgments, and shall not commit any of these Abominations, neither any of your own Nation, nor any Stranger, that sojourneth among you; that the Land spue not you out also, when ye defile it, as it spued out the Nations that were before you.*[3]

So *Saul's* Disobedience was his Destruction, and his Sin made Way for *David's Title. Saul* died (saith the Sacred Story) *for his Transgression:* This made the *Philistines* Conquerors; his own Sin beat him and kill'd him.[4] *Saul*

3. Leviticus 18:24–26, 28.
4. 1 Chronicles 10:13.

died for his Transgression; then if he had not sinned, he had lived; he had beaten his Enemies and kept the Kingdom? yes, the Place implies it. *This* then should deter Men, but Kings especially, who have so much to lose here, and so much to answer for hereafter. But what was *Saul's Sin?* It was, First, *Not keeping but disobeying the Word of the Lord,* both as it came by the *Mouth* of *Samuel,* God's Prophet, and as it spoke the Mind of God to him in his own *Conscience* (for *Moses* had said before that the *Word* of *God* was *nigh, in the Heart,* and in God's Name commanded the Children of *Israel* to *obey* and do it.)[5] In short, he refused the *Counsel of God,* and God for his *Counsellor:* For in the next Place, he betakes himself to one that had a *Familiar Spirit* for *Advice,* saith the Story: *He enquired not of the Lord, therefore he slew him and turned the Kingdom unto* David.[6] There are too many People troubled with *Familiar Spirits;* it were well, if they were less *Familiar* with them: Had *Saul* trusted in God, he needed not to have been driven to that Strait. He that was made King by God's Appointment, and endued with a *Good Spirit,* so *basely* to degenerate, as to run to a *Witch* for Counsel, could not but miscarry. To this Darkness and Extremity *Iniquity* will bring Men: And truly, a *Wo* follows all such Persons; answerable to that Expression of God by the Prophet; *Wo unto them that take Counsel, and not of me.*[7] When *Saul* (saith the Place) was little in his own Eyes, *God honour'd him; he made him Head and King of the Tribes of* Israel:[8] But when *Saul* grew Proud, God *deserted* him, and for his Disobedience destroyed him. And what befel the Family of *Saul,* in some *After-Ages* befell both *Kings* and *People,* and worse: For their Land was invaded, first by the *AEgyptians,* then by the *Chaldeans* and *Babylonians:* Their Temple was rifled, their Treasure taken, and their *Kings, Princes, Nobles, Artificers,* and *Mighty* Men *of Valour,* yea all, save the poorest of the *People,* were *kill'd or carried away* Captive, by the King of *Babylon.* The Reason rendred is this: Because the Kings *did that which was* Evil *in the Sight of God, and stiffned their Necks, and hardned their Hearts from turning unto the Lord God of* Israel; and because the Chief of the *Priests* and of the *People* transgressed very much after the Abominations of the *Heathen.*[9] And when God sent his Messengers to reprove and warn them,

5. Deuteronomy 30:14.
6. 1 Chronicles 10:14.
7. Isaiah 30:1.
8. 1 Samuel 15:17.
9. 2 Kings 24:10–14; and 2 Chronicles 36:14.

and that out of his *Great Compassion,* they wickedly mocked his *Messengers,* despised his *Words,* and mis-used his *Prophets,* till his *Wrath* came upon them, and over-threw them.

I will here end my Instances out of *Sacred Story;* and let us now briefly consider, what the *Histories* of other *Places* will tell us; that we may observe some Proportion of *Agreement* in the *Providence* of God throughout the World.

The *first Empire* had *Nimrod's Strength,* and the Wisdom of the *Chaldeans* to establish it; and whilst their Prudence and Sobriety lasted, they prospered. No sooner came *Voluptuousness,* than the *Empire* decayed; and was at last by the *base Effeminacies* of *Sardanapalus,* in whom that Race ended, transfer'd to another Family.[10] It was the Policy of an *Assyrian* King, in Order to subdue the Strength of *Babylon,* then under good *Discipline,* not to invade it with *Force,* but to debauch it. Wherefore he sent in *Players, Musicians, Cooks, Harlots,* &c. and by those Means introducing *Corruption* of *Manners,* there was little more to do, than to take it. *Nebuchadnezzar* by his *Virtue* and *Industry,* seen in the Siege of *Tyre,* and in many *Enterprises,* recover'd and enlarg'd the Empire; and it seems his *Discipline* (those Times considered) was so excellent, that it was praised in Scripture. But when he grew *Proud* and *Foolish,* forgetting that *Providence* that had shown it self so kind to him, he became a *Beast,* and grased amongst *Beasts;* till God, whom he had forgotten, had restored him the *Heart* of a *Man* and his Throne together.[11]

He, dying left *Evil-Merodach* Heir to his Crown, not his Conduct, nor the Heart to consider what God had done by him: In his Time *Pride* and *Luxury* encreased, but came not to it's full Pitch, till the Reign of *Belshazzar,* who did not only as *Nebuchadnezzar, live,* but *dye a Beast.*[12] In him we have the exact Example of a Dissolute and Miserable Prince: He thought to fence himself against Heaven and Earth; dissolved in Pleasures, he worshipped no other God; his Story may make us well conclude, that *God and Man desert* those, *that* desert themselves, *and neglect the Means of their own* Preservation. The City was taken before he knew it, and the Sword almost in his Bowels, before he believed it: His Sensuality had wrapt him in such a Desperate Security. But he

10. For the strength of Nimrod, see Genesis 10:8–9; and for the Chaldeans, see Daniel 1:4, 2:2, 5:11. Sardanapalus was an Assyrian monarch who burned his entire court (and himself) to death. See the *Persica* of Ctesias (fl. 400 B.C.E.).

11. Daniel 4:33.

12. Daniel 5.

fell not by the Hand of one like himself; for *God* who had determined the End, prepared the Means. *Cyrus* and his *Persians* were the Men: The People were poor, inhabiting a barren Country; but hardy and of Sober Manners. *Cyrus* God had endued with *Excellent Natural Qualities,* cultivated (as Story tells us) by the Care of four of the most temperate, just and Wise Persons of those Times. This was he, whom God honour'd with the Name of his Shepherd, and who was the Executioner of his Vengeance upon the *Assyrians.* While he reigned, all was well; but after he and his virtuous Companions deceased, their Children fell into the Vices of the *Assyrians;* and though they reigned from the *Indus* to the *Hellespont,* they soon became the Conquest of the *Greeks.*

Never was there a greater Instance given of the Weakness of Pomp and Luxury, than in the Resistance made at *Thermopolae,* where Three Hundred *Virtuous Spartans* encounter'd the Vast Army of *Xerxes,* consisting of no less than *Seventeen Hundred Thousand Men.* In short, the Defeats of *Salamine* and *Platea,* the Expeditions of *Xenophon* with *Cyrus* the Younger, almost into *Babylon,* and the Wars of *Agesilaus* into *Asia,* made it evident, that *Greece* wanted only Union and an Head, to make her self Mistress of that Vast Empire.[13]

At last comes *Alexander of Macedon,* with the best Disciplin'd People that was then known: The Dispute was short, where Steel was against Gold, Sobriety against Luxury, and Men against Men that were turn'd Women. Thus, the *Persians* prepar'd by their own Vices, God deliver'd into the Hands of the *Greeks,* who as much excelled them in their Virtue, as they were short of their Dominion and Wealth. But this lasted not long; for *Alexander,* who died young, surviv'd his Virtue and Reputation, by falling into those Vices of the Nations, God had given him Power to trample under Foot; insomuch that he, who was before Generous, became Barbarous and Tyrannical. *Egypt, Asia,* and *Macedon,* held up their Heads a while; but not resisting the Torrent of Lewdness, that came upon them, suffer'd themselves to be over-whelm'd with Misery and Confusion.

Nor has this Calamity been peculiar to Monarchies; for several Republicks have fallen by the same Mischief. That of *Lacedaemon* or *Sparta,* so Severe in her Constitution, and so Remarkable for the Virtue of her People, and that

13. On Thermopylae, see Herodotus, *Histories,* bk. 7; Xenophon's *Anabasis* tells the story of the Greek expedition to aid Cyrus the Younger, 401–399 B.C.E.; Agesilaus II (ca. 444–360 B.C.E.) was king of Sparta.

for many Ages, at last growing slack in the Execution of her Laws, and suffering Corruption insensibly to creep into her Manners, she became no more Considerable, but Weak and Contemptible.

The same may be said of *Athens,* the *Great School of Learning,* and of all the Republicks of *Greece,* most Famous for her Virtue and Philosophy, when that Word was understood not of *Vain Disputing,* but of *Pious Living:* She no sooner fell into Luxury, but Confusion and Revolutions made her as Inconsiderable, as she had been Great.

Rome, as she was the Greatest Common-Wealth, so the greatest Example of *Gentiles* in Virtue and Vice, in Happiness and in Misery: Her Virtue and Greatness are Commemorated by *Austin* the Father, and the latter made the Effect of the former. *God* (saith he) *gave the* Romans *the Government of the World, as a Reward for their Virtue.*[14] Their Manners were so Good, and their Policy so Plain and Just, that nothing could stand before them. And truly, they seem'd to have been employ'd by God to punish the Impious, and to instruct the Barbarous Nations: And so very Jealous was she of the Education of her Youth, that she would not suffer them to converse with the *Luxurious Greeks.* But Carelessness, with Length of Time, over-coming the Remarkable Sobriety of her Manners, who before seemed invincible, she falls into equal, if not greater Miseries, than those that went before her, though she had not only Warning enough from their Example, but from *Hannibal*'s Army, and her great Enemy: For one Winter's Quarter of *Hannibal* and his Army, in the Luxurious City of *Capua,* prov'd a greater Overthrow to them, than all the *Roman* Consuls and Armies had given them. They that had been Victors in so many Battles, turn'd Slaves at last to *Dancers, Buffoons, Cooks and Harlots;* so as from that Time they never did any Thing suitable to the Reputation gain'd by their former Actions; but fell without much Difficulty into the *Roman Hands.*[15] Nay, not long before, *Rome* her self encountred one of the greatest Dangers, that ever had befallen her, by the Corruption of her own People, in the same Place, by the like Means: And though this Defection was recover'd by those that remain'd entire in their Manners, yet after the Overthrow of *Antiochus, Mithridates, Tigranes,* that the Riches and Vices of *Asia* came with a full Stream upon them, the very Heart of the City became infected; and the Lewd *Asiaticks* had this Revenge in their own Fall, that they ruin'd, by their Vices,

14. St. Augustine (354–430), *City of God,* bk. 5, ch. 13.
15. Livy, *History of Rome,* bk. 23, ch. 18.

those they were no Ways able to resist by their Force; like the Story of the *Dying Centaur.*[16] Thus Pride, Avarice and Luxury having prepared *Rome* for Destruction, it soon followed. Virtue now grew intolerable in *Rome,* where Vice dared not for Ages to show it's Face. The Worthiest Men were cut off by Proscriptions, Battels or Murders, as if she resolved *Ipsam Virtutem exscindere:*[17] She destroyed her own Citizens, and sent for Strangers to protect her, which ruin'd her. Which proves, that the Kingdom or State, that, under God, doth not subsist by it's own Strength, Prudence and Virtue, cannot stand: For the *Goths, Hunns,* and others, despised to serve those, whom they excelled in Power and Virtue, and instead of Guarding, took their Dominion from them. And truly, it might rather be called a Journey, than a Military Expedition, to go and pillage *Rome;* so weak had her Vices made her. Thus she that was feared by all Nations, became the Prey of all Nations about her. So ended that once Potent and Virtuous Common-Wealth.

The *Vandals* in *Africk* soon became *Effeminate* and Lewd, which brought upon themselves speedy Ruin. The *Goths* set up a Powerful Kingdom in *Spain* and Part of *France,* and by the Sobriety of their Manners, it flourished near Four Hundred Years; but it's End was not unlike the rest. Two corrupt Princes, *Vuitza,* and *Roderic,* by their dissolute Example, debauch'd the People, insomuch that Men ran an Hazard to be Virtuous: This made their Destruction easie to those whom God sent against them; which were the *Moors,* occasion'd by the last of these Kings dishonouring Count *Juliano*'s Daughter. In the Time of his Calamity, in vain did he expect the Aid of those that had been the Flatterers, and the Companions of his Vices: His Security (the Effect of his Luxury) was his Ruin. For whilst he thought he had no Body to subdue, but his own People, by abusing them, he Cut off his own Arms, and made himself an easie Prey to his Real Enemies: And so he perisht with his Posterity, that had been the Cause of the Mischief, which befel that Great Kingdom. However, so it came to pass, that the Remainder of the *Goths* mixing with the Ancient *Spaniards* (to that Day distinct) recovered the Liberty and Reputation of the Kingdom by an Entire Reformation of Manners, and a Virtue in

16. In the story of Hercules, the centaur Nessus attacks Deianeira. After being shot with one of Hercules' poison arrows, the dying centaur tells Deianeira that anyone wearing a garment smeared with his blood would love her forever. When Hercules later fell in love with Iole, Deianeira sent him such a garment. Nessus's blood turned out to be a poison, and Hercules died.

17. To extinguish virtue itself.

Conversation as Admirable, as the Vices, by which their Fathers had fallen, were Abominable. But the present impoverisht State of *Spain* can tell us, they have not continued that Virtuous Conduct of their Ancestors; the Increase of their Vices having decayed their Strength, and lessened their People and their Commerce.

But why should we overlook our own Country? that, whether we consider the Invasion of the *Romans, Saxons,* or *Normans,* it is certain the Neglect of Virtue and Good Discipline, and the present Inhabitants giving themselves up to Ease and Pleasure, was the Cause (if *Gildas* the *Brittain,* and *Andrew Horn* may be credited) of their Overthrow: For as the first bitterly inveighed against the Looseness of the *Brittains,* threatning them with all those Miseries that afterwards followed; so the *last* tells us, that the *Brittains* having forgotten God, and being overwhelm'd with Luxury and Vice, it pleased God to give the Land to a poor People of the Northern Parts of *Germany,* called *Saxons,* that were of plain and honest Manners.[18] God is unchangeable in the Course of his Providence, as to these Things: The like Causes produce the like Effects, as every Tree doth naturally produce it's own Fruits. 'Tis true, God is not careless of the World; *He feeds the young Ravens, clothes the Lillies, takes Care of Sparrows, and of us, so as not an Hair of our Heads falls to the Ground without his Providence;*[19] but if Men despise his Law, hate to be Reformed, spend their Time and Estate in Luxury, and persist to work Wickedness, he will visit them in his Wrath, and consume them in his sore Displeasure. To conclude, *Wars, Bloodshed, Fires, Plunders, Wastings, Ravishments, Slavery,* and *the like, are the Miseries that follow Immoralities, the Common Mischiefs of Irreligion, the Neglect of Good Discipline and Government.*

Nothing weakens Kingdoms like Vice; it does not only displease Heaven, but disable them. All we have said, proves it: But, above all, the Iniquity and Voluptuousness of the *Jews,* God's chosen, who from being the most Prudent, Pious and Victorious People, made themselves a Prey to all their Neighbours. Their Vice had prepared them to be the Conquest of the First Pretender; and thus from Freemen they became Slaves. Is God asleep, or does he change? Shall not the same Sins have the like Punishment? At least, shall they not be punisht? Can we believe there is a God, and not believe, that he is the Rewarder,

18. Gildas (ca. 504–70), *Concerning the Ruin of Britain,* chs. 22–24; and Andrew Horn, *Mirror of Justice,* bk. 1, ch. 2.

19. Luke 12:24; Matthew 6:26–31; Matthew 10:29–31; and Luke 12:6–7.

as of the Deeds of Private Men, so of the Works of Government? Ought we to think him Careful of the Lesser, and Careless of the Greater? This were to suppose he minded Sparrows more than Men, and that he took more Notice of private Persons than of States. But let not our Superiors deceive themselves, neither put the Evil Day afar off; they are greatly accountable to God for these Kingdoms. If every poor Soul must account for the Employment of the small Talent he has received from God, can we think, that those High Stewards of God, the Great Governors of the World, that so often account with all others, must never come to a Reckoning themselves? Yes, there is a Final Sessions, a General Assize, and a Great Term once for all, where he will Judge among the Judges, who is Righteous in all his Ways. There Private Men will answer only for themselves, but Rulers for the People, as well as for themselves. The Disparity that is here, will be observed there, and the Greatness of such Persons, as shall be then found Tardy, will be so far from extenuating their Guilt, that it will fling Weight in the Scale against them. Therefore give me Leave, I do beseech you, to be earnest in my humble Address to you; Why should ye not, when none are so much concern'd in the Good Intention of it? Thus much for the First Reason of my Supplication.

THE SECOND PART.

Sect. 1. *Five Capital Evils that relate to the Ecclesiastical State of these Kingdoms.*

HAVING finish'd the *First Part* of my *Address* relating to the Immoralities of the Times, and left it with the *Civil Magistrate,* as, in Conscience, I found my self oblig'd to do, whose peculiar Charge it is, and, I earnestly and humbly desire and pray, that it may be his great Care effectually to rebuke them, I shall betake my self to the *Second Part* of this *Address,* that more immediately concerns us as *Profess'd Christians* and *Protestants.* But before I begin, I desire to premise, and do with much Sincerity declare, that I intend not the Reproach of any Person or Party: I am weary with seeing *so much of it in the World:* It gains nothing, that is worth keeping; but often hardens, what 'tis our Duty to endeavour to soften and win. But if, without Offence, I may speak the Truth, that which, to the best of my Understanding, tends to the present Settlement and future Felicity of my poor Country, I shall, by God's Help, deliver my self with the Modesty, Plainness and Integrity, that becomes a Christian, a Protestant, and an Englishman.

Those Capital Sins and Errors that relate to the *Ecclesiastical State* or Church-Capacity of these Kingdoms, and which are so inconsistent with *Christian Religion* and Purest Protestancy, and that, above all, displease Almighty God, are,

First, *Making* Opinions Articles *of* Faith, *at least giving them the* Reputation of Faith, *and making them the* Bond *of* Christian Society.

Secondly, *Mistaking the* Nature *of* True Faith, *and taking that for* Faith *which is not* Gospel-Faith.

Thirdly, *Debasing the true* Value *of* Morality *under Pretence of* Higher Things, *mistaking much of the* End *of* Christ's Coming.

Fourthly, *Preferring* Human Authority *above* Reason *and Truth.*

Fifthly, *Propagating* Faith *by* Force, *and Imposing Religion by* Worldly Compulsion.

These I take to be the *Church-Evils,* that have too much and too long prevail'd even in these Parts of the *Reformed World:* And though the *Roman Church* hath chiefly transcended other *Societies* in these *Errors,* and may, in a Sense, be said to be the Mother of them, She, from whom they took *Birth,* by whom they were brought forth and have been propagated in *Christendom,* yet there hath not been that *Integrity* to the Nature of *Christianity,* and *First Reason* of *Reformation* from the Papacy in our own Country, as had been and is our Duty to conserve.

Sect. 2. *Of* Opinions *passing for* Faith.

FIRST, *That* Opinions *pass for* Faith, *and are made* Articles *of* Faith, *and are enjoyn'd to be embrac'd as the* Bond *of* Communion.

That this is so, let us take the most impartial View we can, and we shall find it to be true, both of the *National* and many other *Select Societies.* That I may be understood in the Signification of the Word *Opinions,* I explain it thus: "Opinions *are all those* Propositions *or* Conclusions *made by Men* Doctrines *of* Faith *and* Articles *of* Communion, *which either are not* Expresly *laid down in* Scripture, *or not so evidently* Deduceable *from* Scripture, *as to leave no Occasion of Doubt of the Truth of them in their Minds who sincerely and reverently believe the Text: Or, lastly, such as have no new or* Credible Revelation *to vouch them.*"

That this is our Case, let the several *Confessions* of *Faith* published by almost every Party in *England* be perused, and you will find such *Propositions* translated into Doctrines of Faith and Articles of Communion, as are, *first,* not only *not express'd in Scripture,* but, perhaps *not well deduceable from Scripture:* And if one Party may be but believ'd against another, we can want no Evidence to prove what we say. And, in the next Place, such as are, though not express'd, yet it may be, deduceable as to the Matter of them, are either carried so high, spun so fine, or so disguised by barbarous School-Terms, that they are rather a Bone of Contention, than a Bond of Concord to Religious Societies. Yet this has been the Unhappiness even of this Kingdom after all the Light of *Reformation,* which God hath graciously sent amongst us, *Men are to be received or rejected for denying or owning of such Propositions.* Wilt thou be a *Presbyterian?* Embrace and keep the Covenant, subscribe the *Westminster-Confession* and *Directory:* And so on to the End of every Society, that grounds Communion upon *Conformity* to such *Propositions* and *Articles* of Faith.

What a Stir have we had in *England* about the Word *Ἐπίσκοπος* He that says it signifies an *Higher Office* than *Πρεσβύτερος* shall have no Part or Fellowship with us: On t'other Hand, they that will debase *Episcopos* to *Presbuteros,*[20] and turn *Levellers* or *Degraders* of *Episcopal Dignity,* shall be excommunicated, silenc'd, punish't. Is not this plain *Fact?* can any deny it, that love Truth more than a *Party?* The Fire kindled by this *Contention,* hath warm'd the Hands of *Violence:* It had been well, if Men had entertained *Equal Zeal* against *Impiety,* and been but half as much *Enemies* to Sin, as they have been against one another on such Accounts.

If we look a little back, we shall find, that the Debate of *Free-Will* and *unconditional Reprobation* filled this Kingdom with *Uncharitableness* and *Division.* In the Arch-Episcopacy of *Abbot* (reputed in himself *a good Man*) whosoever held, that Christ so died for *all Men,* that *all Men might be saved,* (if

20. Respectively, bishop and presbyter. This debate was partly philological, regarding translation from the Greek, but such an issue also carried important ecclesiastical, social, and political ramifications. Debate about these two terms—and their respective models of church government, episcopal and presbyterian—divided Presbyterians and Anglicans in seventeenth-century England.

they would accept the Means) and that none were absolutely decreed to *Eternal Reprobation,* was reputed an *Heretick,* and *Excommunicated* as an Enemy to the *Free-Grace of* God, which, it seems, at that Time of Day, lay in *being narrow.*

In the Reign of Arch-Bishop *Laud* the *Tide turned:* And those that held an *absolute Election,* and *Reprobation,* without Regard had to the *Good* or *Evil Actions* of Men, and asserted, that *Christ only died* for the Elect, *and not for all,* must be discountenanced, displaced and pointed at as *Men* out of *Fashion,* though at the same Time *Conscientious, Sober* and (at worst) *mistaken;* and to be pitied rather than persecuted; and informed, not destroyed.

This Controversie begat the *Synod* of *Dort:* He that reads the *Epistles* of that Judicious Man *J. Hales* of *Eaton* Colledge, upon the Matter and Conduct of that *Assembly,* will find Cause of being sad at Heart; too many of them talking of *Religion* without the *Spirit* of it.[21] *Men,* perhaps, *learned* in Books, but few of the *Sticklers* gave any great Testimony of their Proficiency in that *Science,* which is first *pure,* then *peaceable, gentle,* and *easie to be entreated.*[22] This Flame kindled between *Arminius* and *Episcopius,* &c. for the *Remonstrants,* and *Gomarus, Sibrandus,* &c. for the *Predestinarians,* distracted *Holland* not a little, and had an ill Influence upon the *Affairs* of *England,* at least so far, as concerned the *Church.* But the mournfullest Part of that History is the ill Usage, *Martinius Crocius,* the Bishop of *Landaff,* and others had; who, though they were acknowledg'd to be sound in the *Faith* of those Things, which generally followed the Judgment of *Calvin,* as to the main Points controverted, yet if at any Time they appeared moderate in their Behaviour, gentle in their Words, and for Accomodation in some particulars, with the *Remonstrants* or *Free-Willers; Gomarus* and his Followers, not observing the Gravity due to the *Assembly,* the Rules of Debate, and least of all the Meekness of *Christian Communion,* fell foul of their Brethren, reproached their Tenderness, and began to fix Treachery upon their sober Endeavours of Accommodation; as if they intended to execute as well as maintain their Reprobation, and blow up their Friends rather than not destroy their Adversaries.

But if we will rise higher in our Enquiry, and view the Mischiefs of earlier

21. The synod of reformed churches at Dort (1618–19) met to address the growing influence of Arminianism and resulted in a victory for orthodox Calvinists. See the letters appended to John Hales, *Golden remains, or dealing with erring Christians* (London, 1673), to find his letter on the synod.

22. James 3:17.

Times, flowing from this Practice, the Fourth and Fifth *Centuries* after Christ will furnish us with *Instances* enough. We cannot possibly forget the heavy Life some Men made about the Observation of *Easter-Day,* as if their Eternal Happiness had been in Jeopardy: For so far were they degenerated from the Love and Meekness of Christianity, that about keeping of a Day, which perhaps was no Part, but to be sure, no *Essential Part* of the Christian Religion, they fell to Pieces; *reproach't, revil'd, hated,* and *Persecuted* one another. A Day was more to them than Christ, who was the Lord and End of Days; and Victory over Brethren, sweeter than the Peace and Concord of the Church, the great Command of Jesus, whom they called Lord.[23]

But the remarkable and tragical Story of *Alexander* Bishop of *Alexandria* and *Arius* his Priest, in their known Debate about the Nature and Existence of the Son of God, with the lamentable Consequence thereof, (as all Writers upon that Subject have related) witnesseth to the Truth of what I say. The Bishop's Curiosity, and the Strictness of *Arius;* the Presumption of the one to expound beyond the Evidence and Simplicity of the Text, and the captious Humour of the other, that would not bate the Bishop any Thing for his Age, or Rank he held in the Church, but Logically exacted the utmost Farthing of the Reckoning from his old Pastor, first began the Fray: Which as it became the Perplexity of *Church* and *State* some Ages, so it raged to Blood; and those that had been persecuted like Sheep by the *Heathen* not long before, turned Wolves against each other, and made Sport for the *Infidels,* doing their Work to their own Destruction. Nay, so much more Christian was *Themistius* the Philosopher, that he in his *Oration,* called *CONSUL,* commended the Emperour *Jovianus* for his Moderation, and advised him to give that *Liberty* of *Conscience,* which profest Christians, refused to allow each other; who seemed to think, they never did God better Service, than in Sacrificing one another for Religion, even as soon as ever they had escaped the *Heathen's* Shambles.[24]

Did we duly reflect upon the unnatural Heats, Divisions and Excommunications among them, the many Councils that were called, the strong and tedious *Debates* held, the Translations of *Sees,* the *Anathemas,* the *Banishments, Wars, Sackings, Fires* and *Blood-shed* that followed this unnatural Division, that sprang from so nice a Controversie, one would verily believe no less,

23. The controversy over the dating of Easter was resolved at the Synod of Whitby (664).

24. Themistius (4th century), Oration 5.

than that Religion it self had been in utmost Hazard; that *Judaism* or *Paganism* were over-running Christianity; and not, that all this Stir had been made about an *Iota.* For the whole Question was, whether *Homousia,* or *Homoiousia* should be received for Faith? In which the Difference is but the single Letter, I: Certainly, we must do Violence to our Understanding, if we can think that these Men were Followers of that *Jesus* that *loved his Enemies and gave his Blood for the World,* who hated their Brethren and *shed one another's Blood* for *Opinions:* The *Heathen Philosophers,* never were so barbarous to one another, but maintained a better Understanding and Behaviour in their Differences.

But how easily might all these Confusions have been prevented; if their *Faith* about Christ had been delivered in the Words of *Scripture;* since all Sides pretend to believe the *Text?* And why should any Man presume to be wiser, or plainer in Matters of Faith, than the Holy Ghost? 'Tis strange, that God and Christ should be wanting to express or discover their own Mind; or that the Words used by the *Holy Ghost,* should have that Shortness, Ambiguity or Obliquity in them, that our *frail Capacities* should be needed to make them more easie, proper and intelligible. But that we should scarcely deliver any one *Article* of *Faith* in *Scripture-Terms,* and yet make such *Acts* the *Rule* and *Bond* of *Christian Communion,* is, in my Judgment, an Offence hainous against *God* and *Holy Scripture,* and very injurious to *Christian Charity* and *Fellowship.* Who can express any Man's Mind so fully, as himself? And shall we allow that Liberty to our selves, and refuse it to God? *The Scriptures came not in old Time* (said the Apostle *Peter*) *by the Will of Man; but holy Men of God spake, as they were moved by the* Holy Ghost.[25] Who can speak better, or express the Mind of the *Holy Ghost* plainer, than the *Holy Ghost?* The Scripture is the great *Record* of *Truth,* That which all these *Parties* in *Controversie* agree to be the declared Mind and Will of *God,* and they unanimously say, it ought to be *believed,* and *profest* as *such.* If this be true, in what Language can we so safely and properly declare our Belief of those Truths, as in the very *Language* of the *Scripture?*

And I cannot see how those Persons can be excused in the Day of *Gods Judgment,* who make Men *Heterodox* or *Heretical,* for refusing to subscribe their *Articles* of *Faith* that are not in *Scripture-Terms,* who in the same Time offer to declare their Belief of *God, Christ, Spirit, Man's Lapse* or *Fall, Repentance, Sanctification, Justification, Salvation, Resurrection,* and *Eternal Recompence* in the *Language* of *Holy Scripture?* I must say, it is preposterous and a Contradic-

25. 2 Peter 1:21.

tion, that those who desire to deliver their *Faith* of *Truth,* in the *Language* of *Truth,* shall not be reputed *true Believers,* nor their *Faith* admitted. This were to say, that therefore their *Faith* is not to be received, because it is declared in the *Language* of that very *Truth,* which is the *Object* of that *Faith,* for which it ought to be received, and which is, on all Hands, concluded to be our *Duty to believe.* It seems then we must not express our Belief of God in his Words, but our own; nor is the *Scripture* a *Creed* plain or proper enough to declare a true Believer, or an Orthodox Christian, without our Glosses.

Are not Things come to a sad pass, that to refuse any other Terms than those the *Holy Ghost* has given us, and which are confest to be the Rule or Form of sound Words, is to expose a Man to the Censure of being *unsound* in the *Faith* and unfit for *Christian-Communion?* Will nothing do but *Man's Comment* instead of *God's Text?* His Consequences and Conclusions in the Room of *Sacred Revelation?* I cannot see how any Man can be obliged *to receive, or believe revealed Truths in any other Language, than that of the Revelation it self;* especially if those that vary the Expression, have not the same Spirit to lead them in doing so, or that it appears not to me that they have the *Guidance* of that Holy Spirit. If the *Holy Ghost* had left *Doubts* in Scripture, which is yet irreverent to believe, I see not how *Men* can resolve them; it is the *Work* of that *Spirit.* And since Men are so apt to err, *Doubts* are better left in Scripture, than made or left by us. But it is to cross that Order of *Prudence* and *Wisdom* among Men, who chuse to conform their *Expressions* to the Thing they believe. If an honest Man hath related a *Story* to me, of something he hath seen, and I am to declare my *Faith* about it, if I believe the *Fact,* I will chuse to deliver it in the *Terms* of the *Relator,* as being nearest to the Truth.

Suppose a Father dying, makes his *Last Will* and *Testament,* and, as he thinks, so plain, that there can be no Mistake made by the *Executors,* but what is wilful: If they, instead of proving this Will, and acting according to the Plainness of it, turn *Commentators,* make more Difficulties than they find, and perplex the whole *Matter,* to the Children and Legatees, and send them to the *Law* for *Right;* will we not esteem such *Executors ill Men,* and justifie those Persons concern'd in their *Refusal* of their *Paraphrase? God hath at sundry Times and in diverse Manners,* by his *Prophets,* his *Beloved Son and his Apostles,* delivered to the World a *Declaration* of his blessed *Will;*[26] but some have claim'd and taken to themselves the *Keeping, Explanation* and *Use* of it, so as those

26. Hebrews 1:1–2.

that chuse to be concluded by the *Letter* and *Text* of *Christ's Testament* in it's *most important Points,* expose themselves to great Prejudice for so doing; for they are Excommunicated from all other Share in it, than the *Punishment* of the *Breakers* of it, which is part of their *Anathema,* who, of all others, are most guilty of *adding* or *diminishing,* by undertaking to determine, for others as well as themselves, the *Mind* and *Intention* of the *holy Ghost* in it.

But if it be True, as True it is, that few have writ of the Divine Authority of Scripture, who do not affirm that the very Penmen of it were not only inspired by the Holy Ghost, but so extraordinarily acted by him, as that they were wholly asleep to their own Will, Desires or Affections, like People taken out of themselves, and purely Passive, *as Clay in the Hand of the Potter, to the Revelation, Will, and Motion of the Spirit;*[27] and for this End, that nothing deliver'd by them, might have the least Possibility of Mistake, Error, or Imperfection, but be a *Compleat Declaration of the Will of God to Men;* I cannot see which Way such Men can excuse themselves from Great Presumption, that will, notwithstanding, have the *Wording of Creeds of Communion,* and reject that Declaration of Faith as insufficient, which is deliver'd in the very Terms of the Holy Ghost; and deny those Persons to be Members of Christ's Church, that in Conscience refuse to subscribe any other Draught than that the Lord has given them.

Two Things oppose themselves to this Practice: *The Glory of God, and the Honour of the Scripture;* in that it naturally draws People from the Regard due to God and the Scripture, and begets too much Respect for Men and their Tradition. This was the Difficulty Christ met with, and complained of in his Time; they had set up so many *Rabbies* to learn them Religion, that the Lord of the True Religion could hardly find Place amongst them. And what did they do? *They taught for Doctrines the Traditions of Men:*[28] They gave their own and their Predecessors Apprehensions, Constructions, and Paraphrases upon Scripture, for the Mind and Will of God, the Rule of the People's Faith. They were near at this Pass in the Church of *Corinth,* when they cryed out, *I am for* Paul, *I am for* Apollos, *and I am for* Cephas, though they had not the same Temptation.[29]

And that which followed then, ever will follow in the like Case, and that

27. Job 10:8–9; Isaiah 64:8; and Romans 9:21.

28. Mark 7:8.

29. 1 Corinthians 1:12.

is *Distraction;* which is the contrary to the Second Thing that opposeth it self to this Practice, and that is the Concord of Christians. For the Sake of Peace consider it: *Lo here and Lo there always followed; one of this Mind, and another of that: As many Sects as Great Men to make and Head them.* This was the Case of the *Jews;* and yet I do not hear, that they devoured one another about their Opinions and Commentaries upon Scripture; but the Christians have done both; Divided and Persecuted too. *First,* they have divided, and that mostly upon the Score of Opinions about Religion. They have not been contented with the Expressions of the *Holy Ghost;* they liked their own better. And when they were set up in the Room of Scripture, and in the Name of Scripture, *Submission* was required upon Pain of Worldly Punishments. This dissatisfied Curiosity, this Unwarrantable, what shall I say? This Wanton Search has cost *Christendom* dear, and poor *England* dearest of any Part of it.

I design not to grate upon any, or to revive old Stories, or search old Wounds, or give the least Just Occasion of Displeasure to those that are in present Power; yet I must needs say, that Opinion on one Side or t'other, has been the Cause of much of that Discord, Animosity and Confusion that have troubled this Kingdom. And it seems to have been the great Stratagem of Satan, to prevent the spreading of the *Glorious Gospel of Salvation* in the World, by taking Men off from the Serious Pursuit of Piety and Charity, Humility, and Holy Living, Peace, and Concord: And, under Pretence of more raised Apprehensions, and sublime Knowledge of Religion, to put them upon introducing Curious and Doubtful Questions, that have given Occasion, first for Contention, and That, for Persecution. This was no more uncondemned, than unforeseen of the Apostle *Paul,* who exhorted his beloved Son *Timothy,* 1 Tim. 6. 3, 4, 5. *To avoid those that doted about Questions,* those Men that would be thought Skilful, Inquisitive Searchers after Truth, such as love to exercise their Faculties, and improve their Talents; but let us hear his Judgment, *Of which* (says he) *cometh Strife, Railing, Surmises, perverse Disputings of Men of Corrupt Minds.* And the Truth is, none else love such Disputings: *They, who seek a Daily Victory over the World, the Flesh and the Devil, and press fervently after Fellowship with God, and that Consolation that ensues such an Employment of their Time, have very little to lose upon Contention about Words.* I could wish I were able to say, that Vain Controversie were not our Case! But this is not all, the Apostle does expressly tell Timothy, *That if any Man consent not to Wholsom Words, even the Words of our Lord Jesus Christ, and the Doctrine that is according to Godliness, he is Proud, knowing nothing, but doting about Questions,* &c.[30] They were such as used *Philosophy, and Vain Deceit,* as he writes to the *Colossians,* Col. ii. 8. *Beware,* says he, *lest any Man spoil you through Philosophy and Vain Deceit,* that is, *drawn them away from the Simplicity of the Gospel, and the Wholsome Words of Christ, after the Traditions of Men, after the Rudiments of the World, and not after Christ.* He used no Humane Wisdom, yet he spake Wisdom, but it was in a Mystery, tho' to the humble Disciples of Jesus nothing was plainer; *but it was a Mystery to the Wise Men of this World.*[31] And truly, they that are not unacquainted with the more degenerate Ages of the *Greek* Philosophers, how *Philosophy,* once taken for the Love of Virtue and Self-Denial, which they esteem'd *Truest Wisdom,* and was begun by Men of ordinary Rank, but great Example of Life, became little else, *than an Art of Wrangling upon a Multitude of idle Questions, and so they entertain'd the Apostle* Paul *at* Athens,[32] may very well guess which Way Apostacy entred among *Christians;* especially, when we consider, that in the third and fourth *Centuries,* the Heathen-Philosophers had the *Education of Christian Youth,* and that no Man had any Reputation among the *Christian Doctors,* who were not well initiated in the *Philosophy, Rhetorick, and Poetry of the Gentiles.* Which made for Impurity of Language, and laid a Foundation for great Feuds in the Church: Christ and his Doctrine must be prov'd by *Aristotle* and his Philosophy. Yes, *Aristotle* must explain Scripture, and by Degrees methodize the loose Parts of it, and reduce them to Formal Propositions and Axioms; and by the Help of such Philosophers, the poor Fisher-Men were taught to speak *Metaphysically,* and grew Polite in the Sense of *Athens,* who, to say True, were neither Guilty of *using nor understanding it.* But as the first Rules of *Philosophy* were few and plain, and consisted in Virtuous Living, so the *Christian Religion* was deliver'd with much Brevity, yet much Plainness; suited to the Capacity of the Young, the Ignorant, and the Poor; to inform their Understandings, subdue their Affections, and convert their Souls to God, as well as Persons of more Age, Knowledge, and Ability.

And truly, when we consider the Smallness of the Writings of the Evangelists, the Shortness of Christ's Sermons, the Fewness of the Epistles writ by the Apostles, and the many and great Volumes of Commentators and Criticks since, we may justly say, *The Text is almost lost in the Comment, and Truth hid, rather than*

30. 1 Timothy 6:3–4.
31. 1 Corinthians 1:19–21.
32. Acts 17:15–34.

revealed in those Heaps of Fallible Apprehensions. Where by the Way, let me say, *That the Voluminousness of the Books is no small Token of the Unclearness of the Writers; for the more evident and better digested any Matter is, the more easie and short it will be in expressing.* But after the Christians had declin'd the Simplicity of their own Religion, and grew Curious and Wanton, loving God above All, *their Neighbours as themselves, and keeping the Plain Commandments of Christ, that relate to Good Life, became but Ordinary and Homely Things: Their Easiness rendred them Contemptible: They gave but little Pleasure to Speculative Minds; they had nothing in them above Ordinary Capacities; and it seemed hard, that Men of Inquisitive and Rais'd Spirits, should sit down with the* Lesson of Rusticks and Peasants: *Philosophers did not do so; and they would be like other Nations.* 'Twas not enough now to know *There was a GOD,* and that He was but One, Just and Good, the Observer of their Actions, and the Rewarder of their Deeds, and that therefore they should serve him; but they must be distinctly inform'd of his Nature, and all his Attributes, his Purposes and his Decrees, and the Suitableness of them all to the Line and Plummet of their Understanding: *So that God was to be, what their Conclusions would allow him to be; that yet knew not themselves.* Nor did it satisfie that there was a Christ, that this Christ was the Son of God, that God so loved Mankind, as beholding them in a Way of Destruction, he sent his Son to proclaim Pardon upon True Repentance, and offer'd a General Reconciliation to as many as received and embrac'd his Testimony; and that to that End He laid down his Life a Ransom, Rose and Ascended, and gave his Good Spirit to lead his Followers after his Example, in the Way of Truth and Holiness: *But they must search into the Secret of this Relation, how, and after what Manner he is the Son of God? His Nature, Power and Person must be discuss'd: They will be satisfied in this, before they can find in their Hearts to believe in him.* Next, *Whether he be the Cause, or the Effect of God's Love? What was that Price he paid, and Ransom he gave? And how he died for us? If Properly and Strictly, or Tropically and Elegantly, to satisfie the Justice of God? And whether God could, or could not have Saved Man another Way? If this Mercy were offer'd to all, or but some? And whether Acceptance and Repentance be with the Consent of the Creature, or by an irresistible Grace? What Body he Rose and Ascended with? And what Bodies we shall have in the Resurrection, in Nature, Stature, and Proportion?* Lastly, *What this Spirit is, that comes from Christ? If it comes from God also? Whether it be God, or an Inferior Minister? How it Exists? If a Person, in what Relation, Degree, or Dignity it stands to the Father and Son?* With Abundance more of this Unreasonable Strain, flowing from the Curious, Ungovern'd, and Restless Minds of Men. No Man would be used by his Servant as they treat God. He must wait our Leisure, before we will believe, receive, and obey him: His Message is obscure, we don't understand it; he must gratifie our Curiosity; we desire to be better satisfied with it before we believe or deliver it; it comes not presently up to Men's Understandings; 'tis too obscurely exprest; we will explain it, and deliver it with more Caution, Clearness and Success, than it is delivered to us. Thus God's Revelation hath been scan'd, and his Precepts examin'd, before Licens'd by his Creature: Man would be Wiser than God; more wary then the Holy Ghost. Our Lord, it should seem, understood not what Kind of Creature Man was; he wanted his Wisdom to admonish him of the Danger; or haply he thought not upon that Corruption, which should befall Mankind in these Latter Ages of the World, which might require the Abilities of Men to supply the Wants and Defects left by the Holy Ghost, in the Wording of the Scripture.—I wrong not this Practice; I render it not more Odious than it is: It is an inexcusable Piece of Presumption, that which debases the External Testimony of God, and draws Men off from that which is Eternal too. It introduces the Traditions of Men, in the Room of God's Records, and setteth up their Judgment and Results for the Rule of Christian Faith, and Canons of Christ's Church. This is one of those Things, that made *Rome* so hateful, and her Yoke intolerable to our Predecessors: Pretended Deductions from Scripture, put in the Room of Scripture, with a Superfedeas to all Dissent upon never so Just a Ground of Dissatisfaction.

I beseech you *Protestants,* by the Mercies of GOD, and Love of JESUS CHRIST, ratified to you in his Most Precious Blood, *Flee* Rome *at Home;* Look to the Enemies of your own House! Have a Care of this Presumption; carry it not too high; lay not Stress, where God has laid none, neither use His Royal Stamp to Authorize your Apprehensions in the Name of his Institutions.

I do not say, that Men are never to express their Minds upon any Place of Scripture to Edification: There is a *Christian Liberty* not to be denied; but never to lay down *Articles of Faith, which ever ought to be in the Very Language of Holy Writ, to avoid Temptation and Strife.* You see, how the contrary Method hath been the *Great Make-Bate* in all Ages, and the Imposition of such Opinion, the Privilege of Hypocrites, but the Snare of many Honest Minds; to be sure the sad Occasion of Feuds and miserable Divisions. It was plainly seen, that by the many Disputes that rose from hence, Men's Wits were confounded with their Matters, Truth was lost, and Brotherhood was destroyed.

Thus the Devil acted the Part both of Opponent and Defendant, and managed the Passions of both Parties to his End, which was Discord. And but too many were ready to perswade themselves, from the Miscarriages on both Sides, *That nothing Certain could be concluded about Religion;* for it so fell out, that whilst Men were perpetually wrangling and brawling about some one Opinion of Religion, the most important Points of Faith and Life were little regarded, Unity broken, Amity destroyed, and those Wounds made, that were never closed but with the Extinction of one Party: Not a *Good Samaritan* being to be found to heal and close them.[33] Now it was that a *Godly Man* was distinguish'd from an Ungodly by this, let his Life have been almost what it would, that he seem'd to maintain the Opinions in Vogue, *and to abhor the Doctrine, which, in some One or Two Points, might be reputed Heretical, or Schismatical.*

O that we could but see how many, and how *Great Defeats Satan hath given to the Work of God in the Hearts of Men!* What Desolations he hath made by this one Evil, Controversie; begot of Opinion, and used for it; *and how few have contended for the Faith, as it was once deliver'd to the Saints!*[34] He must be a Man of Brass, that could refrain from Weeping at these Calamities. And truly I must desire to take Leave sometimes to bewail this Broken Condition of *Christendom,* and to bestow my Tears in Secret upon these Common Ruins: And I beseech God Almighty, with a Soul sensibly touch't with the Mischiefs that naturally flow from this Practice, to awaken you to a most speedy and serious Consideration of your present Standing, and Amendment of your Miscarriage in this and all other Points that may concern your Good, and his Glory. Put away Wrath! Away with Clamours! Away with Arrogance and Impatience! Let that Holy Spirit of God, which we in common profess to be the *Christian's Guide,* have the ordering of our Understandings in Spiritual Things, lest Ignorance should mistake, Interest wrest, or Prejudice pervert the Sense of God's Book. For as too many are Ignorant of the Divine Truth through their own Concupiscence, and Vile Affections, that carry them away to the Desire of other Things, and therefore easily mistake about Nice or Obscure Matters; so there are not a few, who come to search the Scriptures with Pre-possess'd Minds, that are sorry to meet with a Contradiction to their own Judgment, instead of being glad to find the Truth, and who use their Wits to

33. Luke 10:30–37.

34. Jude 3.

rack out another Sense than that which is Genuine; which Sort of Men use the Scripture for it's Authority, and not it's Sense, or Truth.

All this While, the Head is set at Work, not the Heart, and that which Christ most insisted upon, is least concerned in this Sort of Faith and Christianity; and that is, *Keeping His Commandments.*[35] For 'tis Opinion, not Obedience; Notion, and not Regeneration, that such Men pursue. This Kind of Religion leaveth them as bad as it finds them, and worse; for they have something more to be proud of. Here is a *Creed* indeed, but of what? The *Conclusions of Men,* and what to do? To prove they believe in Christ, who, it seems, never made them. It had been happy for the World, that there had been no other *Creeds,* than what He and His Apostles gave and left. And it is not the least Argument against their being needful to *Christian Communion, that Christ and His Apostles did not think so, who were not wanting to declare the Whole Counsel of God to the Church.*

To conclude: If you desire Peace, love Truth, seek Piety, and hate Hypocrisie, lay by all those Things called *Articles of Faith, and Canons of the Church, that are not to be found in express Terms in Scripture, or so plainly Authorized by Scripture, as may, with Ease, be discerned by every Honest and Conscientious Person.* And in the Room of those numerous and disputed Opinions, made the Bond of External Communion, let some Plain, General and Necessary Truths be laid down in Scripture Terms, and let them be few; which leads me to the next Point, and that is FAITH, which is generally mistaken in the very Nature of it.

Sect. 3. *Of* FAITH, *and Mistakes about it.*

THE Second Mischief that is amongst us, is the *Misunderstanding of the Nature of* FAITH; whence it comes to pass, that Men take that for *Faith,* which is not; and sit down in a Security pernicious to their Eternal Happiness. I shall briefly say something of what is not Faith, before I speak of that, which appears to me to be Truly and Scripturally such.

The Faith of our Lord Jesus Christ is not only not believing Men's Opinions and Determinations from the Sacred Text, of which I have so freely de-

35. John 14:15.

liver'd my self, but it is not meerly the Belief even of the Things contain'd in Scripture, to be True: For this the Devils and Hypocrites do, and yet are very *Bad Believers:* They refuse not the Authority of Scripture: The Devil made Use of it to Christ himself; but he would have the explaining and applying of it:[36] And since he could not hinder the Divine Inspiration, if he may but be allow'd the Exposition, he hopes to secure his Kingdom. Since then the Verity and Authority of both History and Doctrine may be believ'd by the *Devil and Hypocrites,* that are false to their own Faith and Knowledge, we cannot without great Injustice to the *Faith of our Lord Jesus Christ,* which is the *Faith of all His Followers,* allow, That a meer Belief of the Verity and Authority of the History and Doctrine of Scripture, is that True and Precious Faith, which was the Saint's Victory over the World.

Faith then, in the Sense of the Holy Ghost, is by the Holy Ghost thus defined: viz. *The Evidence of Things not seen and the Substance of Things hoped for.*[37] This is General and runs through all Ages; being received of all Sorts of Christians as a true Definition of Faith: But with leave, I shall express it thus: *True Faith in God is entirely believing and trusting in God, confiding in his Goodness, resigning up to his Will, obeying his Commands, and relying upon his Conduct and Mercies, respecting this Life and that which is to come.* For a Man cannot be said to believe in God, that believes not what he says and requires: And no Man can be said to do that, who does not obey it, and conform to it; for that is believing in God, *to do as he says.* This is in Scripture called the *Gift of God;*[38] and well it may, for it is Supernatural: It crosses the Pride, Confidence and Lust of Man: It grows out of the Seed of Love, sown by God in the Heart, at least *it works by Love:*[39] And this distinguishes it from the Faith of Ill Men and Devils, that though they do believe, they don't *Love God above all,* but something else instead of God, and are full of *Pride, Anger, Cruelty* and all Manner of Wickedness. But this Faith that works by Love, that Divine Love which God plants in the Heart, it draws and inclines Man, and gives him Power to forsake all that displeaseth God: And every such Believer becomes an *Enoch,* Translated, that is, Changed from the Fashion of this World, the Earthly Image, the Corrupt Nature; and is renewed in the Likeness of the Son

36. Matthew 4:1–11; and Luke 4:1–13.
37. Hebrews 11:1.
38. Ephesians 2:8.
39. Galatians 5:6.

of God, and *walks with God.*[40] *The Just shall live by Faith:*[41] They have in all Ages liv'd by this Faith; that is, been *sustain'd, supported, preserved:* The Devil within nor the World without could never conquer them. They walked not by Sight, but by Faith, and had Regard to the Eternal Recompence: No Visible Things prevailed with them to depart from the Invisible God, to quench their Love, or slacken their Obedience to him; the great Testimony of their Faith in Him.

This *Holy Faith* excludes no Age of the World; the Just Men, the *Cornelius*'s in every Generation have had some Degree of it: It was more especially the Faith of the simpler Ages of the World, such as those in which the *Patriarchs* lived, who having not an outward Law, became a *Law to themselves, and did the Things contained in the Law;* for they believed in God, and, through Faith, *obtained a good Report.*[42] But because that it hath pleased God, in order to Man's Recovery from that grievous Lapse Disobedience hath cast him into, *at sundry Times and in divers Manners* to appear to the Sons of Men, first by his Prophets, and last of all by his Son;[43] and that these several Manifestations have had something peculiar to them, and very remarkable in them, so that they claim a Place in our Creed; It will not be amiss, that we briefly consider them.

The first was that of the Prophets, in which *Moses* preceded, by whom the Law came to the *Jews,* but *Grace* and *Truth* to mankind by Jesus Christ.[44] The first brought Condemnation, the last Salvation; the one Judgment, the other Mercy; which was glad Tidings indeed. The one did fore-run the other, as in Order of Time, so in Nature of Dispensation: The Law was the Gospel begun, the Gospel was the Law fulfilled or finisht: They cannot be parted.

The *Decalogue* or *Ten Commandments* were little more than what had been known and practised before; for it seem'd but an Epitome and Transcript of the *Law writ in Man's Heart* by the Finger of God: This is confest on all Hands and in all Ages since, as the Writings of ancient Gentiles as well as Jews and Christians tell us. This therefore must needs be a Part of our Creed; for it relates to that Righteousness which is Indispensible and Immutable: The other Part of their Constitution that was peculiar to their Politick, Typical and Mu-

40. Genesis 5:24; and Hebrews 11:5 (also Sirach 44:16, 49:14).

41. Hebrews 10:38.

42. Acts 10; Romans 2:14; and Hebrews 11:39.

43. Hebrews 1:1.

44. John 1:17.

table State, the Gospel is either unconcerned in it, or else ended it by the *bringing in of a better Hope and a more enduring Substance. But Grace and Truth came by Jesus Christ:*[45] *Grace* is opposed to the Condemnation of the Law, and Truth to Shadows. This is the most excellent Dispensation; it is ours, and it becomes us to weigh well our Interest in it. Take it in other Words of the Holy Ghost. *God, who at sundry Times and in divers Manners spake in Times past unto the Fathers by the Prophets, hath in these last Days spoken to us by his Son. God so loved the World, that* (after all the World's Provocations by *Omissions* and *Commissions*) *he gave his only begotten Son into the World, that the World through him might be saved.*[46]

And here Two Things present themselves to our Consideration: *First,* the Person, who he was? What his Authority? *Secondly,* his Message, his Doctrine, what he taught? Which though never so reasonable in it self, depended very much, in it's Entertainment among the People, upon the Truth of his Mission and Authority, that he was no Impostor, but came from God, and was the promised Messiah. This was done two Ways; by Revelation and by Miracles. By Revelation, to such as were as well prepared and inclined, as honest *Peter,* the Woman of *Samaria,* and those that were mov'd to believe him from the Authority in which he spake, so unlike that of the Formal *Scribes.*[47] By Miracles, to those that being blinded by Ignorance or Prejudice, needed to have their Senses struck with such Supernatural Evidences, from many of whom this Witness came, *that he was the Messiah, the Christ and Son of God.*

In fine, all was done within the Compass of that People, among whom he daily conversed, that was needful to prove he was from God, and had *God's Message* to declare to the World. In so much that when some of his Disciples were not so firm in their Belief of his Authority, as he deserved at their Hands, he calls his own Works to prove his Commission and convict them of Incredulity: *If ye will not believe, that the Father is in me, that he doth these Works by me; believe me for the very Works sake,* Thus he argueth with the *Jews: Say ye of him the Father hath sanctified and sent into the World, thou Blasphemest; because I said, I am the Son of God? If I do not the Works of my Father, believe me*

45. Hebrews 10:34.

46. Hebrews 1:1; and John 3:16–17.

47. Respectively: Honest Peter, Matthew 16:13–19, Mark 8:27–30, and Luke 9:18–22; the woman of Samaria, John 4:6–30; Jesus contrasted with the scribes, Matthew 7:28–29, and Mark 1:21–22.

not (this is reasonable; he that shall Judge the World, offers to be tryed himself; he goes on) *But if I do, though ye believe not me, believe the Works, that ye may know and believe, that the Father is in me.*[48] And he laid the Sin of the *Jews* upon this Foot, *viz.* That they rejected him, after he had *made Proof of his Divine Mission* by such extraordinary *Works, As no Men among them all could do:* which, to give them their Due, they do not deny, but shamefully pervert and foolishly abuse, by attributing them to the Power of the Devil. To which Malice and Slander he returned this inconfutable Answer; *A Kingdom divided against it self cannot stand:* What! *cast out Devils by the Prince of Devils?* 'Tis a Contradiction, and very Madness it self.[49]

I have nothing to do now with *Atheists,* or those that call themselves *Theists;* but such as own themselves Christians; and shall therefore keep to my Task, namely; *What of the* Christian Dispensation *is so Peculiar and Important, as to challenge of Right the Name of* Creed *or* Faith? I say then, *That the Belief of Jesus of* Nazareth *to be the Promised Messiah, the Son and Christ of God,* come and sent from God to restore and save Mankind, is the first and was then the *only requisite Article of Faith,* without any large Confessions, or an Heap of Principles or Opinions resolv'd upon after Curious and Tedious Debates by Councils and Synods: And this may be proved both by Example and Doctrine.

It is evident from *Example,* as in the Case of *Peter,* who for having believed in his Heart and confess'd with his Mouth, *That Jesus was the Christ and Son of God,* obtained that *Signal Blessing,* Mat. 16. This made *Nathaniel* a *Disciple; Rabbi,* said he, *Thou art the Son of God, thou art the King of* Israel. It was the like *Confession,* that made Amends for *Thomas*'s *Incredulity,* when he was sensibly assured of the *Resurrection of Jesus, My Lord and my God!* This was also the Substance of *Martha's Confession of Faith to Jesus,* when he said to her, *I am the Resurrection and the Life; he that believeth in me shall never die: believest thou this?* She answer'd, *Yea Lord, I believe, that thou art the Christ the Son of God, which should come into the World?* She answered him not as to that Particular of the *Resurrection,* but in General, *That he was the Christ, the Messiah, that was to come into the World,* and that sufficed. 'Twas a *Confession* not unlike to this, that the *Blind Man* made, to whom Christ gave *Sight,* when *Jesus* said to him, *Dost thou believe on the Son of God? Lord,* said he, *I do believe; and he worshipped him.* What shall we say of the Centurion, preferred

48. John 14:10–11; and John 10:36–38.

49. Matthew 12:25–26; Mark 3:24–26; and Luke 11:17.

by Christ himself before any in *Israel,* though a *Gentile?* Or of the Faith of the *Woman* and *Inhabitants* of *Samaria, that he was the Messiah?* Or of that *Importunate Woman* that cry'd to *Jesus, To cast a Devil out of her possest Daughter,* and would not be put off, to whom Christ said, *O Woman, great is thy Faith, be it unto thee even as thou wilt?* To which let me add the *Faith* of the People, that brought the *Man sick of the Palsy to* Christ, who *uncover'd the Roof to let him down to be toucht;* the *Faith* of *Jairus* the Ruler; and of that *Good Woman,* who *pressed through the Crowd to touch the* Hem of Christ's Garment, to whom *Jesus* said, *Be of good Comfort, Daughter, thy Faith has made thee whole:* Also the *Two Blind Men,* that followed him out of the *Ruler's House,* crying, *Thou Son of* David, *have Mercy on us;* who, when *Jesus* had said, *Believe ye that I am able to do this?* Answer'd, *Yea, Lord;* upon which he touch'd their Eyes and said, *According to your Faith be it unto you:* Also the *Blind Man* near *Jericho;* The *Leprous Samaritan* that Christ cleansed; and that notable Passage of the Woman that kissed his Feet and anointed his Head; to whom he pronounced this happy Sentence; *Thy Faith hath saved thee, go in Peace.*[50]

I will conclude this with that famous Instance of the *Thief* upon the *Cross,* who neither knew nor had Time to make a large Confession like the Creeds of these Days: but it seems he said enough; Lord, *remember me when thou comest into thy Kingdom.* And *Jesus* said unto him, *Verily, I say unto thee, to Day shalt thou be with me in Paradise.*[51] By which it is easy to learn that t'was the Heart, not the Mouth; the Sincerity, not the Words, that made the *Confession Valid.*

Nor was this only, in the Days of *Christ,* the Effect of his *Gracious Dispensation* or peculiar Indulgence, for after-times afford us the like Instances. This was the main Bent of *Peter's Sermon;* and when the *Three Thousand believed that he whom the Jews had crucified, was both Lord and Christ, and repented of their Sins, and gladly received his Word,* they are said to have been in a State of Salvation. Thus *Cornelius* and his Houshold and Kindred, so soon as *Peter* declared *Jesus to be the Messiah,* and that they had believed, the *Holy Ghost*

50. Citations, respectively: on Nathaniel, John 1:49; on Thomas, John 20:28; on Martha, John 11:24–27; on the blind man, John 9:35–38; on the centurion, Matthew 8:10; on the woman of Samaria, John 4:7–9; on the "importunate woman," Matthew 15:22–28; on the man sick of palsy, Mark 2:1–5; on Jairus and the woman who touched Jesus' garment, Mark 5:22–36; on the two blind men, Matthew 9:27–30; on the blind man near Jericho, Luke 18:35–43; on the leprous Samaritan, Luke 17:12–19; and on the woman who anointed Jesus' head, Luke 7:37–50.

51. Luke 23:42–43.

fell upon them; and they were received into the *Christian Communion.* But the Story of the *Eunuch* is very pat to our Purpose: As he rid in his Chariot, he was reading these Words out of the Prophet *Isaiah,* viz. *That he was led as a Sheep to the Slaughter, and like a Lamb dumb before the Shearers, so opened he not his Mouth. In his Humiliation his Judgment was taken away; and who shall declare his Generation? for his Life is taken from the Earth. Philip* join'd to him and ask'd him, *If he understood what he read?* He desir'd *Philip* to interpret the Mind of the Prophet, whether he spoke of himself or another? *Philip* upon the Place preached to him *Jesus:* The *Eunuch* was so well perswaded by the Apostle, that coming to a Water, he said, *What doth hinder me to be Baptized? Philip* answered him, *If thou believest with all thine Heart, thou may'st:* To this the *Eunuch* reply'd, I *believe that Jesus Christ is the Son of God.* Upon which he was baptized; and 'tis said, *He went away Rejoycing;* which indeed he might well do, that felt the Comfort of his Faith, the Remission of his Sin and the Joys of the Holy Ghost, which always follow true Faith in Christ.[52]

I will conclude these Examples with a Passage in the *Acts,* of *Paul* at *Thessalonica;* 'tis this: Paul, *as his Manner was, went in unto them, and three Sabbath-days reasoned with them out of the Scriptures; opening and alledging that Christ must needs have suffered and risen again from the Dead; and that this* Jesus (said he) *whom I preach unto you, is Christ. And some of them believed and consorted with* Paul *and* Silas, *and of the devout* Greeks *a great Multitude, and of the* Chief Women *not a few.*[53] Thus we may plainly see, that they were baptiz'd into the Faith of Jesus, and not into Numerous Opinions; and that this one Confession, from true Faith in the Heart, was the Ground and Principle of their *Church-Fellowship.* Then *God's Church* was at Peace; she thrive; there were then no Snares of Words made to catch Men of Conscience with. Then not many Words, but much Integrity; now much Talk, and little Truth: Many Articles, but *O ye of little Faith!*

Nor was this only the Judgment and Practice of that Time out of Condescension to Weakness, and Charity to Ignorance; for both Christ Jesus himself and his Apostles (those blessed *Messengers of Holy Truth*) have doctrinally laid it down, as the Great Test to Christians; that which should distinguish them from *Infidels,* and justly intitle them to his Discipleship, and Christian Com-

52. On the "Three Thousand," see Acts 2:41; on Cornelius, see Acts 10; and on Philip and the eunuch, see Acts 8:26–40.

53. Acts 17:2–4.

munion one with another. Let us read a little farther: *Then said they to Jesus, what shall we do, that we might work the Works of God? Jesus answered and said to them, This is the Work of God, that ye Believe on him, whom God hath sent. Verily, Verily, I say unto you, he that believeth on me, hath Everlasting Life.* And upon another Occasion, to the *Jews,* he said, *For if ye believe not, that I am he, ye shall die in your Sins.* It must follow then, that if they did believe him to be the Messiah, the Anointed of God to Salvation, *they should be saved.* Most plain is that Answer of the Apostle to the *Goaler,* when he came trembling to them and said, *Sirs, What must I do to be saved? Believe* (said they) *on the Lord Jesus Christ, and thou shalt be saved.* The Apostle *Paul* confirms this in his Epistle to the *Romans,* when he says, *If thou shalt confess with thy Mouth the Lord Jesus, and shalt believe in thine Heart, that God hath raised him from the Dead, thou shalt be saved. For with the Heart Man believeth unto Righteousness, and with the Mouth Confession is made unto Salvation:* For the Scripture saith, *Whosoever believeth on him, shall not be ashamed. For there is no Difference between the* Jew *and the* Greek; *for the same Lord over all is rich unto all, that call upon him. For whosoever shall call upon the Name of the Lord, shall be saved.*[54] This was the Word of Faith which they preached; and he testify'd, that it was *nigh in the Heart,* as *Moses* had done before him.[55] And, saith the Apostle *John,* on this Occasion, *Who is a Lyar, but he that denieth, that Jesus is the Christ?—Hereby know ye the Spirit of God; every Spirit that confesseth* (or every one that in Heart or Spirit confesseth) *that Jesus Christ is come in the Flesh, is of God.* Again, says he, *Whosoever shall confess, that Jesus is the Son of God, God dwelleth in him, and he in God:* Yet once more he affirms, *Whosoever believeth that Jesus is the Christ, is born of God.*[56] But this is more than an Historical Belief, a true Sound and hearty Perswasion: A Faith that influenceth the whole Man into a suitable Conformity to the Nature, Example and Doctrine of the object of that Faith.

I will conclude these Doctrinal Testimonies out of Scripture, with a conclusive Passage the *Apostle John* useth towards the End of his Evangelical History of Jesus Christ: *And many other Signs* truly *did Jesus in the Presence of his Dis-*

54. On everlasting life, see John 6:39–40; on dying in sins, see John 8:24; and on being saved, see Acts 16:29–31; and Romans 10:9–13.

55. Deuteronomy 30:14.

56. 1 John 2:22; 4:2, 15; 5:1.

ciples, which are not written in this Book; but these are written that ye might believe that Jesus is the Christ, the Son of God, and that believing ye might have Life in his Name.[57] In which Place two Things are remarkable; *First,* That whatever Things are written of Jesus, are written to this End, *that we might believe that Jesus is the Christ.* Secondly, *That those that sincerely believe, shall through him obtain Eternal Life.* Certainly then, if this be true, their *Incharity* and *Presumption* must be great who have taken other Measures, and set another *Rule* of *Christianity,* than Jesus and his Apostles gave. This *sincere Confession* contented Christ and his Apostles; but it will not satisfy those that yet pretend to believe them: It was enough then for a Miracle and Salvation too, but it goes for little or nothing now. A Man may sincerely believe this, and be stigmatiz'd for a *Schismatick,* an *Heretick,* an *Excommunicate:* but I may say, as Christ did to the Jews in another Case, *From the Beginning it was not so.*[58]

But here I expect to be assaulted with this Objection: *If this be all that is necessary to be believ'd to Salvation, Of what Use is the rest of* Scripture?

I Answer, Of Great Use, as the Apostle himself teaches us; *All* Scripture *is given by Inspiration of God, and is profitable for Doctrine, for Reproof, for Correction, for Instruction in Righteousness, that the Man of God may be perfect, throughly furnish'd unto all good Works.*[59] It concerns the whole Life and Conversation of a Man; but every Passage in it is not therefore fit to be such an Article of Faith, as upon which *Christian-Communion* ought or ought not to be maintained. For though it be all equally true, it is not all equally important: There is a great Difference between the Truth and Weight of a Thing. For Example: It is as true that Christ suffered under *Pontius Pilate,* as that he suffered; and that he was pierced, as that he died; and that he did eat after his Resurrection, as that he rose from the Dead at all; but no Person of common Understanding will conclude an equal Weight or Concernment in these Things, because they are equally true: The Death of Christ was of much greater Value than the Manner of it; his Resurrection, than any Circumstance of his Appearance after he was risen. The Question is not whether all the Truths contain'd in Scripture are not to be believ'd; but whether those Truths are equally Important? And whether the *Belief with the Heart and Confession with the*

57. John 20:30–31.
58. Matthew 19:8.
59. 2 Timothy 3:16–17.

Mouth that Jesus is the Christ and Son of God,[60] *be not as sufficient now to entitle a Man to Communion here and Salvation hereafter, as in those Times?* against which nothing can be, of Weight, objected.

If it be said, that this *Contradicts the Judgment and Practice of many great and good Men.*

I Answer, I can't help that. If they have been tempted, out of their own Curiosity or the Corruption of Times, to depart from the Ancient Paths, the Foot-steps of purest Antiquity and best Examples, let their Pretences have been what they will, it was Presumption: And it was Just with God, that Error and Confusion should be the Consequence of those Adventures; nor has it ever fail'd to follow them.

Lastly, if it be alledg'd, *That this will take in all Parties, yea, that* Schismaticks *and* Hereticks *will creep in under this General Confession, since few of them will refuse to make it.*

I do say, 'Twould be an Happy Day. What Man, loves God and Christ, seeks Peace and Concord, that would not rejoyce if all our Animosities and Vexations about Matters of Religion were buried in this one Confession of Jesus, the great Author and Lord of the *Christian Religion,* so often lost in pretending to contest for it? View the Parties on Foot in Christendom among those called Protestants, observe their Differences well, and how they are generally maintain'd, and you will tell me that they are rent and divided about their own Comments, Consequences and Conclusions: Not the Text, but the Meaning; and that too, which perhaps is not in it self essential to Salvation, as the Dispute betwixt the *Lutherans* and *Calvinists,* the *Arminians* and *Predestinarians,* and the like. Is it not lamentable to think that those who pretend to be Christians, and Reformed ones also, should divide with the Winds and fight, as *pro Aris & Focis,*[61] for such Things, as either are not expresly to be found in Scripture, or if there, yet never appointed or intended by Christ or his Apostles for Articles of Communion. Should they then erect their Communion on another Bottom, or break it for deviating from any other Doctrines than what they in so many Words have deliver'd to us for Necessary?

If we consider the Matter well, I fear it will be found that the Occasion of Disturbance in the Church of Christ hath in most Ages been found to lie on the Side of those who have had the greatest Sway in it. Very pertinent to our

60. Romans 10:9.

61. As if for their altars and their hearths.

present Purpose is that Passage of *J. Hales* of *Eaton* in his *Tract* concerning *Schism:*[62]

> It hath, saith he, been the Common Disease of Christians from the Beginning, not to content themselves with that Measure of Faith, which God and Scriptures have expresly afforded us; but out of a Vain Desire to know more than is Revealed, they have attempted to discuss Things, of which we can have no Light neither from Reason nor Revelation. Neither have they rested here, but upon Pretence of Church-Authority, which is NONE, or Tradition, which for the most Part is but FIGMENT, they have peremptorily concluded and confidently imposed upon others a Necessity of Entertaining Conclusions of that Nature; and to strengthen themselves have broken out into Divisions and Factions, opposing Man to Man, Synod to Synod, till the Peace of the Church vanished without all Possibility of Recall. Hence arose those Ancient and many Separations amongst *Christians, Arianism, Eutychianism, Nestorianism, Photinianism, Sabellianism;* and many more both Ancient and in our Time.

And as he hath told us one great Occasion of the Disease, so he offers what follows for the Cure:

> And were Liturgies (says he) and Publick Forms of Service so framed, as that they admitted not of particular and private Fancies, but contained only such Things, as in which all Christians do agree, Schisms on Opinion were utterly vanished: Whereas to load our Publick Forms with the Private Fancies upon which we differ, is the most soveraign Way to perpetuate Schism unto the World's End.—Remove from them, whatsoever is scandalous to any Party, and leave nothing, but what all agree on; and the Event shall be that the Publick Service and Honour of God shall no ways suffer. For to charge Churches and Liturgies with Things unnecessary, was the First Beginning of all Superstition—If the spiritual Guides and Fathers of the Church would be a little sparing of incumbring Churches with Superfluities, and not over-rigid, either in reviving obsolete Customs, or imposing *New, there were far less Danger of Schism or Superstition*—Mean while wheresoever false or suspected

62. John Hales (1584–1656), *A tract concerning schisme and schismaticks* (London, 1642), pp. 9, 10–11.

> Opinions are made a Piece of the Church *Liturgy, he that separates is not a Schismatick:* For it is alike Unlawful to make Profession of known or suspected Falshoods, as to put in Practice Unlawful or Suspected Actions.

He farther tells us in his Sermon of Dealing with Erring Christians, That it is the Unity of the Spirit in the Bond of Peace, and not the Identity (or Oneness) of Conceit, which the Holy Ghost requires at the Hands of Christians—

> A better Way my Conceit cannot reach unto, than that we should be willing to think, that these Things, which with some Shew of Probability we deduce from Scripture, are at the best but our Opinions. For this Peremptory Manner of setting down our Conclusions under this high Commanding Form of Necessary Truths, is generally one of the greatest Causes, which keeps the Churches this Day so far asunder; when as a Gracious Receiving of each other by mutual Forbearance, in this kind, might peradventure, in Time, bring them nearer together.[63]

Thus much of this Great Man concerning Schism, the Cause and Cure of it? And for the Notion of *Hereticks* he will help us altogether as well: For though they are generally taken for such who err in Judgment about Doctrines and Articles of Faith, yet if this Man may have any Credit, and perhaps none of his Profession has deserv'd more, he tells us, that "Heresie is an Act of the Will, not of Reason, and is indeed a Lye, not a Mistake: else (says he) how could that known Speech of *Austin* go for true, *Errare possum, Haereticus esse nolo:* I may err, but I am unwilling to be an Heretick." And indeed this is no other than what Holy Scripture teacheth; *A Man that is an Heretick, after the first and second Admonition, reject; knowing, that he that is such, is subverted and sinneth; being Condemned of Himself.*[64] Which is as much as to say, that no Body is an Heretick, but he that gives the Lye to his own Conscience and is Self-condemned: Which is not the Case of Men meerly mistaken, or who only err in Judgment. And therefore the Term of Hereticks is as Untruly as Uncharitably flung upon those that conscientiously dissent, either in Point of Discipline or Doctrine, from any Society of *Christians;* and it is not hard to observe that those who have most merited that Character, have most liberally bestow'd it.

63. Hales, *Golden remains,* pp. 49–50.
64. Titus 3:10–11.

But to show you that neither true *Schismatick*, who is *One that unnecessarily and unwarrantably separates from that Part of the Visible Church of which he was once a Member*, nor true *Heretick* who is a *Wilful Subverter of True or an Introducer of false Doctrines, a Self-condemned Person*, can ever shelter himself under this Common Confession of Christianity, sincerely made: Let us consider, that who-ever so declares Jesus to be the Messiah and Anointed Saviour of God to Men, must be supposed to believe *all that of him, with Respect to which he is so called.* Now that for which he is so denominated, is that which God sent him to do: The Reason and End of his coming he could best tell, who hath told us thus; *I am come, that ye may have Life, and that ye may have it more abundantly.*[65] The World was dead in Trespasses and Sins, the Guilt and Defilement of Transgression had kill'd the Soul as to Spiritual Life and Motion; and from under this powerful Death *he* came to redeem the Soul unto Life: In short, to restore Man from that fearful Degeneracy his Disobedience to God had reduced him unto.

The Way he took to accomplish this Blessed Work was First, To preach Repentance and the Approach of the Kingdom of God, which is his Rule and Authority in the Hearts of Men, and that brings to the Second Thing to be believed, namely.——

What he Taught?

First, His Doctrine led Men to *Repentance: Repent, for the Kingdom of God is at Hand.*[66] No Man could receive the Kingdom of God, whilst he lived under the Kingdom and Power of Satan: so that to Repent is not only to bring their Deeds to the Light, which Christ exhorteth Men to; but to forsake that upon Examination, which appears to be Evil. Wherefore I conclude, that such as have not been acquainted with this Holy Repentance, do not sincerely believe, neither can rightly confess Jesus to be the Christ the Son of God, the Saviour of the World. Therefore saith the Apostle, *Let him that nameth the Name of the Lord, depart from Iniquity;*[67] plainly implying that those do rather Prophane than Confess the Name of the Lord, who do not Depart from their Iniquities. And, saith the Apostle in another Place, *No Man can call Jesus Lord, but*

65. John 10:10.
66. Matthew 4:17; and Mark 1:14–15.
67. 2 Timothy 2:19.

by the Holy Ghost,[68] Which opens to us the Nature of the True Confession we ought to make, and which, being truly made in a Scripture Sense, makes us Christians in a right Christian Acception; to wit, *That the True Confession of Jesus to be both Lord and Christ, is from such a Belief in the Heart as is accompany'd with the embracing and practising of his Holy Doctrine: such a Faith is the Work of the Holy Ghost,* and those that do not so Confess him or call upon him, that is, by Virtue of the overshadowing of this Divine Spirit and Power, are not truly Christians, true Worshippers, or Believers and Disciples of our Lord Jesus.

Furthermore, they that receive Christ receive his Kingdom, his Power and Authority in their Souls; whereby the strong Man that kept the House becomes bound, and his Goods spoil'd by this stronger Man, the *Lord's Christ;* who is come from Heaven to dwell in us and be the Hope of our Glory; for so he was preached to the Gentiles. This Kingdom, the Apostle tells us, stands in Righteousness, Peace and Joy in the Holy Ghost; and Christ tells us, where it is to be set up? *The Kingdom of God is within you,* saith the King himself; and where should the King be, but in his own Kingdom?[69] They are blessed that feel him to Rule, and that live under the Swaying of his Righteous Scepter: for when this *Righteous One Rules the Earth, the Sons of Men rejoyce.*

So that no Man can truly Confess and rightly believe Jesus to be the Christ and Son of God, who does not receive him to be his King to rule his Heart and Affections. For can a Man be said to believe in one that he will not receive? but *To as many as received Christ of old, gave he Power to become the Sons of God; which were born, not of Blood, nor of the Will of the Flesh, nor of the Will of Man, but of God.*[70] What is this Will of God? *Paul* answers the Question: *The Will of God is your Sanctification;*[71] for this Christ came into the World. So that those that believe and receive Christ, he is made to them *Righteousness, Sanctification* and *Redemption;*[72] that is, he has saved them from their Sins, both Guilt and Defilement, and sanctified them from their Corruptions: They live now by the Grace of God, that teaches them to be of a *Sober, Righteous, Godlike Life. Ye shall know them by their Fruits,* saith Christ of the *Pharisees;*[73]

68. 1 Corinthians 12:3.
69. Romans 14:17; and Luke 17:21.
70. John 1:12–13.
71. 1 Thessalonians 4:3.
72. 1 Corinthians 1:30.
73. Matthew 7:16–20.

so shall Men know them, that sincerely believe and confess Christ, by their sanctified Manners and blameless *Conversations.* And Wo from the true and just God to them that make other Distinctions! for God has made no other; there will be but Goats and Sheep at the Last Day;[74] Holy and Unholy; Just and Unjust. Therefore let that be our Distinction, which ever was and will be God's Distinction; for all other Measures are the Effects of the Passions and Presumptions of Men. But because it may be expected, that I should fix upon some few General Heads of Christian Doctrine from the Mouth of Christ and his Apostles, as requisite to *Christian Communion,* I should proceed to mention what Christ eminently taught.

He that reads his Sermon upon the Mount will find in the Entrance, how many States and Conditions Christ Blessed; The *Poor in Spirit,* The *Mourners,* The *Meek,* They that *hunger after Righteousness;* The *Merciful,* The *Pure in Heart,* and the *Peace-makers;* which indeed comprehend the whole of Christianity.[75]

By *Mourners* we understand true Penitents, Men of Unfeigned Repentance; which leads them not only to confess but forsake their Sins. This *Godly Sorrow* Strips Men of all false Rests and Comforts, makes them *Poor in Spirit, Empty* of themselves, wanting the Comfort of the *Light, Life* and *Power of Jesus* to support and sustain them; yet as they stedfastly walk in that Measure they have, the *Atonement* of the Blood is felt, and it cleanseth them from all Unrighteousness, which makes them Pure in Heart. And in this Condition no Food will serve their Turn but Righteousness; after this they Hunger and Thirst more than for the Bread that perisheth. They are full of *Meekness* and *Mercy, Making Peace* and Promoting Concord where-ever they come: For being themselves reconciled to God, they endeavour to reconcile all Men unto God and one unto another: Submitting all Worldly Considerations to this incomparable Peace, that passeth all human Understanding.

In short, let us bring it Home to our Consciences, and deal faithfully with our selves. Do we know this *Holy Mourning?* This *Godly Sorrow?* Are we *Poor in Spirit indeed?* Not Self-conceited but *Humble, Meek* and *Lowly* in *Heart,* like him that bid us do so? *Do we Hunger after the Kingdom of God and Righteousness of it?* And are our *Hearts* purified by the Precious Faith of the Son of God that is a working, cleansing and conquering Faith? In fine, *Are we Merci-*

74. Matthew 25:31–46.
75. Matthew 5.

ful? Tender Hearted? Lovers of Peace more than Lovers of our selves? Persecuted, rather than Persecutors? Such as receive Stripes for Christ's Sake, and not those that beat our Fellow-Servants? No Man has True Faith in *Christ Jesus,* that is not acquainted with these Blessed Qualifications. This is Christ's Doctrine; and to believe in him, is to obey it, and be like him.

The great Intention of this Sermon,[76] is to press People to a more Excellent Righteousness than that of the *Scribes* and *Pharisees. For,* saith Jesus to the Multitude, *Except your Righteousness shall exceed the Righteousness of the* Scribes *and* Pharisees, *ye shall in no Case enter into the Kingdom of Heaven.*

(1.) He taught, not only that *Killing,* but *Anger* without a very Just Cause, is Unlawful to his Disciples, his Followers.

(2.) He prefers *Concord* above *Devotion; Mercy before Sacrifice:* He that will not use his utmost Endeavour to be reconciled to his Brother, shall find no Place for his Prayers with him that can only make them Effectual. *And every Man is this Brother.*

(3.) He not only forbids *Adultery,* which the Law forbids, but *Lust.* The *Ax of his Doctrine is laid to the Root of the Tree;* it reaches to the First Seeds of Things, to the innermost and most hidden Conceptions of the Mind because he has brought his Light near, and searches the innermost Parts of the Belly with his Divine Candle.

(4.) From keeping and performing Legal Vows, to *Not Swearing at all:* And indeed, what Use can there be of any Swearing, where Men's *Yea is Yea,* and their *Nay, Nay.* There their Speech, their Answers, on all Occasions, should be, at the most, but *Yea, Yea;* or *Nay, Nay.*

(5.) *He taught not to resist Evil, but to suffer Loss, rather than enter into Contention:* His Divine Wisdom did fore-see how much easier it would be to overcome the Violent Passions of Men by Patience, than Controversie. And he that justly considers the Unruliness of some Men's Dispositions, their Heats and Prejudices, will find, that it is not always a Real Injury, or Loss, *but some Passion, Revenge, or base Interest,* that puts them upon Clamours, and Suits of Law.

(6.) He taught us the highest Complacency and Charity: *If any Man compel thee to go a Mile, go with him Twain.* Be of an easie and ready Mind to *Do*

76. Points 1–14 immediately following refer to the Sermon on the Mount (Matthew 5 and 6).

Good; to all *Friendly Offices* be easily perswaded; and therein rather exceed, than fall short of any one's Entreaty, or Necessity.

(7.) He taught as *Great Liberality and Bounty, To give to him that asks, and from him that would borrow, not to turn away.* In short, to be Stewards of our *External Substance for the Good of Mankind,* according to our respective Abilities; not grudging, knowing whose it is, nor disbelieving, as knowing him who is both Able and Bountiful.

(8.) He advances the Doctrine of Loving Friends, to the Degree of Loving Enemies. *Ye have heard,* said Jesus, *that it hath been said, Thou shalt love thy Neighbour, and shalt hate thine Enemy; but I say unto you, Love your Enemies, bless them that Curse you, do Good to them that hate you, and pray for them that despitefully use you, and persecute you.* Surely then, where no Anger dwells, no Revenge can grow; and if we must *Love Enemies,* there is no Man left to be hated. This is the Doctrine of that JESUS that laid down his Life for all; and this is the End for which he preached it, *That* (says he) *ye may be the Children of your Father which is in Heaven; for he maketh his Sun to Rise on the Evil and the Good, and sendeth Rain on the Just and on the Unjust.* It is as much as if Christ had said, *No Man can be like God, who does not Love his Enemies, and cannot Do Good to All.* Consequently, *He that does Love Enemies, and is ready to Do Good unto All, he is like God the Father that is in Heaven, who is Love.*

(9.) Christ teaches us to avoid Ostentation in our Charity: *Take Heed that ye do not your Alms before Men, to be seen of them.*

(10.) He teaches us the Duty of Prayer, and what: *Not in the Corners of the Street, nor in the Synagogues to be seen of Men; but in the Closet, in the Secret of the Heart, betwixt God and the Soul.* O Heavenly Precepts! He knew our Natures, our Weakness, and how to meet with it, and mend it. *A Blessed Physician indeed!* Let us receive Him, for He is sure, and He is Free.

(11.) He forbids Hoarding, and Laying up of Money in Bank; but presses *Our Treasuring up Wealth in Heaven;* and the Reason is this, *That the One is Corruptible, and the other is Incorruptible.*

(12.) He teaches Dependence upon the Providence of God; calling the Distrustful, *O ye of Little Faith. Which of you* (says he) *by taking Thought, can add One Cubit to his Stature? Therefore take no Thought, saying, What shall we Eat, or what shall we Drink, or wherewith shall we be Clothed? For after all these Things the* Gentiles *seek; for your Heavenly Father knoweth, that you have Need of all these Things. But seek ye first the Kingdom of God and His Righteousness, and all these Things shall be added to you.*

(13.) He sets up a Discrimination or Distinction between False and True Prophets; those that are his Disciples, from Counterfeits. *Ye shall know them,* said Christ, *by their Fruits: Do Men gather Grapes of Thorns, or Figs of Thistles? Even so every Good Tree bringeth forth Good Fruit, but a Corrupt Tree bringeth forth Evil Fruit. A Good Tree cannot bring forth Evil Fruit, neither can a Corrupt Tree bring forth Good Fruit: Wherefore by their Fruits ye shall know them.* This was the Distinction given by Christ to His Followers; the Tree was not accounted a Good Tree by the Leaves, but the Fruits; not by a meer Opinion, but Holy Living. The Faith in that Day, was an Entire Resignation and Dependence upon God, and not a Subscription to Verbal Propositions and Articles, though never so True: That was the Work of After-times, more Corrupt and Superstitious Ages, that laid more Stress upon Consent, ay, the very Show of it, than Holiness, without which no Man shall ever see the Lord. But—

(14.) *Lastly,* Christ preaches the General Judgment. *Many will say to me in that Day,* [What Day? the Last Day, or Day of Account, and Final Reckoning with Mankind:] *Lord, Lord, have we not Prophesied in thy Name, and in thy Name Cast out Devils, and done many Wonderful Works? And then will I profess unto them, I never knew you, Depart from me, ye that work Iniquity. Not every one that saith, Lord, Lord, shall enter into the Kingdom of Heaven; but he that doth the Will of my Father which is in Heaven. Therefore whosoever heareth these Sayings of mine, and doth them, I will liken him unto a Wise Man, which built his House upon a Rock, and the Rain descended, and the Floods came, and the Winds blew, and beat upon that House, and it fell not, for it was builded upon a Rock. And every one that heareth these Sayings of mine, and doth them not, shall be likened unto a foolish Man, which built his House upon the Sand: And the Rain descended, and the Floods came, and the Winds blew, and beat upon that House, and it fell, and great was the Fall of it. And it came to pass, when Jesus had ended these Sayings, the People were astonished at his Doctrine; for he taught them as one having Authority, and not as the Scribes.*

By all which it is most plain, that as Christ is the Rock, on which True Christians build, so none can be said truly to build upon this Rock, but those that keep his Sayings, that do his Commandments, that obey his Doctrine. Wherefore that Faith of Jesus to be the Son and Christ of God, must be such a Faith, as does the Will of the Heavenly Father, and keepeth these Sayings of Christ.

There are Two Places, in which Christ seems to sum up his blessed Doctrine: One is this, *Therefore all Things, whatsoever ye would that Men should do to you, do ye even so to them; for this is the Law and the Prophets;* Which (by the Way) Christ came not to destroy, but to fulfil. But the other Passage seems to be more full, the first relating only to our Dealings with Men; this Second Passage comprehending our Duty both to God and Men, viz. *Thou shalt Love the Lord thy God with all thy Heart and with all thy Soul, and with all thy Mind; this is the first and great Commandment: and the second is like unto it, Thou shalt love thy Neighbour as thy self. On these two Commandments hang all the Law and the Prophets.*[77]

This is the Sum and Perfection of the Christian Religion, the *great Commandment* of Christ, and the certain Token of Discipleship, *A new Commandment* (said Christ) *I give unto you, that ye* Love one another; *as* I *have loved you, that ye also* love one another: *By this shall all Men know, that ye are my Disciples, if ye have* love one to another. Again Christ speaks to his Disciples; *If ye keep my Commandments, ye shall abide in my Love, even as I have kept my Father's Commandments, and abide in his Love: And this is my Commandment, that ye Love one another as I have loved you.* Yea, once more: *Ye are my Friends, if ye do, whatsoever I command you, that you Love one another. He that hath my Commandments and keepeth them, he it is that loveth me, and he that loveth me, shall be loved of my Father, and I will love him and will manifest my self to him: but he that loveth me not, keepeth not my Sayings.*[78] So that only those are Friends and Disciples of Christ Jesus that do his Sayings and keep his Commandments; and the Great Commandment of all is *Love;* for upon this one Commandment do all the rest depend.

And indeed the Reason is very obvious, since he that loves God above all, will leave all for God: Not one of his Commandments shall be slighted: And he that loves his Neighbour will much more love the *Houshold of Faith.*[79] Well may such be *True Christians,* when their Faith in Christ works by *Love,* by the Power of this *Divine Power:* He that dwells in this Love, dwells in God, (if *John* say True) for he is Love.[80] *And in this he recommended his Love unto us, that he sent his Only Begotten Son,—that whosoever believeth in him, should not perish, but have Everlasting Life. Also herein did Christ manifest his Love,*

77. Matthew 7:12, 22:37–39.

78. These three quotations, respectively: John 13:34–35; John 15:10, 12, 14, 17; and John 14:23–24.

79. Galatians 6:10.

80. 1 John 4:16.

in laying down his Life for us. This is my Commandment, said Christ, *that ye Love one another, as I have loved you; and greater Love hath no Man than this, that a Man lay down his Life for his Friends; ye are my Friends, if ye do whatsoever I command you.* Indeed he gave his Life for the World, and offered up *One Common Sacrifice* for Mankind: *And by this One Offering up of himself, once for all, he hath for ever perfected,* that is, *Quitted and discharged, and taken into Favour, them that are sanctified; who have received the Spirit of Grace and Sanctification in their Hearts; for such as resist it, receive not the Benefit of that Sacrifice, but Damnation to themselves.*[81]

This Holy Offering up of Himself by the Eternal Spirit, is a great Part of *His Messiahship;* for therein he hath both confirmed His Blessed Message of Remission of Sins, and Life Everlasting, to as many as truly believe in His Name, *and hath given Himself a Propitiation for all that have sinned, and thereby come short of the Glory of God:* Insomuch that God is said by the Apostle *Paul, to be Just, and the Justifier of him which believeth in Jesus, whom God hath set forth to be a Propitiation, through Faith in his Blood, to declare his Righteousness for the Remission of Sins that are past, through the Forbearance of God.*[82]

Unto which I shall join *His Mediatorship or Advocacy,* link'd together both by the Apostle of the *Gentiles,* and the Beloved Disciple *John:* The first in these Words; *For there is One God, and One Mediator between God and Men, the Man Christ Jesus, who gave himself a Ransom for all, to be Testified in due Time.* The Apostle *John* expresseth it thus: *My little Children, these Things write I unto you, that you Sin not; and if any Man sinneth, we have an Advocate with the Father, Jesus Christ the Righteous; he is the Propitiation for our Sins, and not for ours only, but also for the Sins of the whole World.*[83] So that to be brief, the *Christian Creed,* so far as it is Declaratory, lies eminently in a Confession of these Particulars: Of the Divine Authority of the New, as well of the Old Testament Writings, and particularly of these Great, General, and Obvious Truths therein expressed, to wit, *Of God, and Christ, his Miracles, Doctrine, Death, Resurrection, Advocateship* or *Mediation, the Gift of his Light, Spirit or Grace: Of Faith, and Repentance from Dead Works unto Remission of Sins, keeping his Commandments,* and lastly, *Of Eternal Recompence.*—Less, once, than all this, would have done; and it does not shew the Age more Christian, but more

81. John 15:12–14; and Hebrews 10:14.

82. Romans 3:25–26.

83. 1 Timothy 2:5–6; and 1 John 2:1–2.

Curious, indeed more *Infidel,* to be sure more Captious and Froward, *That there is this Stir made about External Creeds of Communion:* For Distrust of Brethren, and Incredulity among Christians, are no small Signs of their Decay of Faith towards God: *From the Beginning it was not so.*

But it may be here objected, *How shall we know that such a Declaration of Faith is Sincere?* I answer, *By recurring to that Evidence which God shall give us.*[84] They that can *Try Spirits* under the *Most Sheep-like-Clothing,* have the most immediate and certain Proof, and such an One there is by the Savour and Relish the Spirit of God gives, to them that have it, of the Spirits of Men: But let it suffice, that Christ hath told us, *By their Fruits ye shall know them. If any Man,* says Christ, *will come after me, let him take up his Cross and follow me:* And in another Place he tells us thus: *My Sheep hear my Voice, and I know them, and they follow me;* that is, they are led by my Spirit, they live my Life, they obey my Doctrine, they are of my own Nature. And the Apostle *Peter* assures us, *That True Faith purifies the Heart, and no Impurity can flow from a Pure Heart.*[85] You may know this *Faith* by that Way, by which *Abraham's Faith was known to be True,* to wit, *Obedience. He believed God,* that is, *He obeyed God;* he submitted to the Will of God, and relied upon his Goodness: As if he had said, and he said it doubtless to himself, *He that gave me my Son by a Miracle, can work another to save him: To God all Things are possible.*[86] It is called by the Apostle *Paul, The Spirit of Faith;* something more near and inward, than any External Articles and Declaration of Faith: That from whence all True Confessions and Good Works came; which made the Apostle *Paul* thus to say, *We give Thanks to God always for you all, making Mention of you in our Prayers, remembring without ceasing, your Work of Faith.*[87]

'Twas this true *Faith,* that brings forth *Works of Righteousness,* by which *Abel offered* to God, *Enoch* was *translated, Noah* was *saved.* It is said of him, that he became the *Heir* of the *Righteousness* which is by *Faith.* By this Faith *Abraham* left his own Country, and obeyed the Voice of God. By *Faith Moses* was preserved from his Childhood; and when he came to Years, refused to be called the *Son of Pharaoh's Daughter;* By *Faith* he forsook *AEgypt,* and passed the *Red Sea.* By *Faith* the Walls of *Jericho* fell down, and *Rahab* was saved. By *Faith*

84. 1 John 4:1.
85. Matthew 16:24; John 10:27; and Acts 15:9.
86. Romans 4.
87. 2 Corinthians 4:13; and 2 Thessalonians 1:3.

Gideon, Barak, Sampson, Jephtha, David, Samuel, and the Prophets, *subdued* Kingdoms, *wrought* Righteousness, *obtained* Promises, *stopped* the Mouths of Lyons, *quenched* the Violence of Fire, *escaped* the Edge of the Sword, with much more, too large to be utter'd here.[88]

This is that *Faith,* which the Apostle *James* magnifies against all false *Faiths: Faith* (says he) *if it has not* Works, *is dead.* A Man may say, *Thou hast* Faith, *and I have* Works; *shew me thy* Faith *without thy* Works, *and I will shew thee my Faith by my* Works. And as if he had fore-seen the Pother made by the Men of *Creeds* and *Articles,* he speaks on this wise; *Thou believest that there is one God, thou dost well; the* Devils also believe and tremble. *But wilt thou know, O vain Man, that* Faith *without* Works, *is dead? Was not* Abraham *our Father, justified by* Works, *when he had offered* Isaac *his Son upon the Altar? Seest thou how* Faith *wrought with his* Works? *and by* Works *was* Faith *made perfect.*—And he was called the *Friend* of *God.*[89] Very notable and informing is that Expression of his, *The Devils* also *believe and tremble;* and as if he had said, the Devil believes as well as you, and trembles too, which is more. This shows there is a Faith that is not the true Faith, and that not with Relation to the Matters believed, but the Spirit of the Mind in believing; For the *Devils* believe the Truth, literally, but their Faith works not by Love, no more than their Knowledge *by Obedience,* and therefore it does them no Good, and is not the true Faith. O that *Christendom* would lay this very one Thing to Heart! But I must proceed.

The Exhortation of the Apostle *Peter* is a farther and plain Discrimination of true Faith; *And besides this, giving all Diligence, add to your* Faith Virtue, *and to* Virtue Knowledge, *and to* Knowledge Temperance, *and to* Temperance Patience, *and to* Patience Godliness, *and to* Godliness Brotherly Kindness, *and to* Brotherly Kindness Charity. *For if these Things be in you and abound, they make you that ye shall neither be* barren *nor* unfruitful, *in the Knowledge of* our Lord Jesus Christ. *But he that lacketh these Things is* blind, *and cannot see far off, and hath forgotten that he was purged from his old Sins:*[90] As if he had said, they have forgot where they begun, that think they can be *Christians* without a Life of Holiness.

I will seal up these Scripture-Testimonies of *Faith,* with that *Account* which

88. Hebrews 11.
89. James 2:17–24.
90. 2 Peter 1:5–9.

is given us by the Apostle *John, For whatsoever is born of God,* overcometh *the World:* And this is the *Victory,* that overcometh the World, *even our Faith. Who is he that overcometh the World, but he that* believeth *that* Jesus *is the* Son of God?[91] So that the Belief in the *Son* of God, must have this Evidence to prove it a true Belief in God's Account, that by it Men are *born of God* and *overcome the World:* Wherefore their *Faith* is false whom the *World overcomes: I am not of this World,* saith Christ Jesus;[92] neither can that *Faith* be, that is rightly called the Faith of the *Son* of *God.*

There are *three Passages* left us upon Record by this Beloved Disciple of *Jesus* of great Weight and Importance to us: When he had discoursed of the *Propitiation* and *Advocateship* of Christ, he does immediately add; *And hereby do we know, that we know him, if we keep his Commandments.* He that saith, I know him, and keepeth not his Commandments, *is a* Lyar *and the Truth is not in him. But whoso keepeth his Word, in him verily is the* Love of God perfected: *Hereby know we, that we are in him.*[93] *He that saith, he abideth in him,* ought himself also so to walk, even as he walked.

The *Second Passage* very pertinent to this Matter, is in the next *Chapter; My little Children, let us not* love *in Word, neither in Tongue, but in* Deed *and in* Truth. *And hereby we know that we are of the Truth, and shall assure our Hearts before him: For if our Heart condemn us, God is greater than our Heart, and knoweth all Things. Beloved;* if our Heart condemn us not, then have we Confidence towards God: And whatsoever we ask, we receive of him, because we keep his Commandments, *and do those Things that are pleasing in his Sight. And this is his Commandment, that we should* believe *on the Name of his Son* Jesus Christ, *and* love one another, *as he gave us Commandment.*[94]

The *Third* and last Passage, which I shall mention on this Account, is in his fourth *Chapter* of the same *Epistle,* viz. *And we have seen and do testifie, that the* Father *sent the* Son, *to be the Saviour of the World. Whosoever shall confess that* Jesus *is the* Son *of* God, *God dwelleth in him, and he in God. And we have known and believed the* Love *God hath to us. God is* Love; *and he that dwelleth in Love,* dwelleth in God, and God in him. *Herein our* Love *is made perfect, that we may have* Boldness *in the Day of* Judgment, *because,* as he is, so are

91. 1 John 5:4–5.
92. John 14:17; and John 8:23.
93. 1 John 2:3–6.
94. 1 John 3:18–23.

we in this World.[95] So that keeping God's *Word,* and *Commandments,* and our *Consciences* from accusing us, and our being like to *Christ* in this World, is our *loving* of God as we ought to love him.

These are the *Holy Fruits* of all those that love *God,* and believe in *Christ,* that are the Family of the Faithful, regenerated and redeemed from the Earth: Where-ever two or three of them, are met together, *Christ* is in the Midst of them; they neither ask nor hope in Vain.[96] With this *Character* let us take a View of all Persons and Societies of Christians throughout the World, not forgetting our selves: *Let us hereby try their Faith and Religion, and our own; if it be of God the Father, it is Pure and Undefiled;* it leads them that have it, *to Visit the Fatherless and Widows in their Affliction, and to keep themselves Unspotted from the World.*[97] Is this our Case? O that it were so!

If it be objected, *Which Way shall we obtain this like Precious Faith?* I answer, *You must take diligent Heed to the Light and Grace that come by* Jesus; *that* Candle of the Lord *which he has set up in our Souls: We must bring our Deeds to this Light, and see if they be wrought in God or no?*[98] *For this gives us to discern betwixt the Precious and the Vile; the one gives Joy, the other brings a Load of Guilt upon the Soul.* Do we not know, *That we do the Things we ought not; and that we leave undone the Things we ought to do.* This, alas! will be our Judgment one Day, the Last, the Terrible Day: For therefore Men are Condemnable, because they know.

Those, therefore, that would obtain this *Precious Faith,* that overcomes the World, must embrace the *Grace of our Lord Jesus Christ,* by which this Faith is begotten; and they, who believe not in this Grace, nor receive it in the Love of it, nor give themselves up to be taught and led by it, can never be said truly to believe in him, from whom it comes, any more than the *Jews* may be said, *To believe in God, when they rejected Him that came from God, His Beloved Son.* He that denies the Measure, can never own or receive the *Fulness. John* bears Record, that he was *full of Grace and Truth, and that of his* Fulness *they received, and Grace for Grace: For the Law was given by* Moses, *but Grace and Truth came by Jesus Christ:*[99] So that 'tis utterly impossible for a Man, *to believe*

95. 1 John 4:14–17.
96. Matthew 18:20.
97. James 1:27.
98. John 3:20–21.
99. John 1:14, 16–17.

in Christ, and not to be taught and led by the *Grace* that comes from him, and by him.

'Tis a common Saying of People in these Days, *We are not under the Law, but under Grace;* who are in Truth under *Sin* and the *Law of Death,* and Subjects to the *Prince* of the Power of the Air; *who reigns in the Hearts of the Children of Disobedience;* and their Lives show it: No, those are under *Grace,* that live the holy Life of *Grace.* For the *Grace of God, that bringeth Salvation,* saith the Apostle *Paul, hath appeared unto all Men, teaching us, that denying Ungodliness and the Worldly Lusts, we should live* Soberly, Righteously, *and* Godly *in this present World:*[100] These are the People that believe in Christ, unto the Saving of the Soul. This is that blessed *Light* which shines in the Hearts of those that believe, and *gives the Knowledge of the Glory of God in the Face of* Jesus Christ. The Ancients walkt in it, and found Eternal Life by it. *I am the* Light of the *World,* said Christ, *he that follows me, shall not walk in Darkness, but have the* Light *of* Life.[101] The Saints armed themselves with it, against the *Fiery Darts* of *Satan,* and by the Virtue and Power that is in it, were enabled to overcome Temptation. And this will be the Condemnation of *Disobedient Men,* that they see, but shut their Eyes; they know the *Light,* but rebel against it. Christ, by his holy *Light* in the *Conscience,* shews Men their Danger, warns them of it, before it comes upon them: No Man on Earth can plead either *Ignorance* or *Surprise.*

'Tis true, the *Candle of the Wicked is often put out;*[102] But that implies, It is often lighted, and that Men Sin against Conviction, against Sight and Knowledge: It is wilful, and that's dangerous. No Faith in Disobedience will do; no Faith without Holy Fruits, Holy Works, will save. Men must be born again if ever they will enter into the Kingdom of God: there is no Fellowship between *Christ* and *Belial:* People must part with their *Vile Affections* and *Inordinate Desires,* or they are no Company for Christ;[103] they have no Share in him. What Part can Pride have in Humility, Wrath in Meekness, Lust in Self-denial, Revenge in Forgiveness? To pretend to believe in Christ, and not to be like him, is a Contradiction. *This is the Message* (said the Beloved Disciple) *which we have heard of him, and declare unto you, that God is* Light; *and in him is no*

100. Titus 2:11–12.
101. John 8:12.
102. Job 21:17.
103. John 3:3; and 2 Corinthians 6:14–15.

Darkness at all: If we say, that we have Fellowship with him, and walk in Darkness, we Lye *and do not the Truth.* The Truth is, all such *Faith* and Profession are a *Lye, and that in the Right Hand,* a Cheat upon a Man's self. *But,* says he, *if we walk in the* Light as God is in the Light, *we have Fellowship one with another, and the Blood of Jesus Christ his Son cleanseth us from all Sin. If we say, that we have no Sin,* [to be cleansed from] *we deceive our selves, and the Truth is not in us:* But *if we confess our Sins, he is Faithful and Just to forgive us our Sins, and to cleanse us from all Unrighteousness.*[104]

To conclude, Christ Jesus, the Son of God and Saviour of the World, is *Holy, Harmless,* and *Undefiled,* and so must his Followers be: He is no Head of a Corrupt Body, nor Master of Rebellious Servants: He that has not the *Wedding Garment,* must be cast out:[105] The Branch, that brings not forth Fruit, will be cut off. But those that truly believe in his Name, walk in his Light, and are taught by his Grace to renounce the *Lusts of the Eye, the Lusts of the Flesh, and Pride of Life;* the unjust Profits, Pleasures and Pomps of the World, and chuse to follow him in his own Holy Way of Resignation and Re-generation, the same is his Brother, his Sister and his Mother. And whatever Losses they may here sustain for his Name's Sake, they have the Promise of an *Hundred Fold* in this Life and the Inheritance of that which is Eternal.[106]

And I do fervently beseech Almighty God, the Giver of all Saving Faith, mercifully to vouchsafe, more and more, to beget a Serious Inquiry in us, What that Faith is which we have? Who is the Author of it? And what Fruits it hath brought forth? That so we may not profane the Name of God by a *Vain Profession* of it, nor abuse our selves unto *Eternal Perdition;* But that we may endeavour, by God's Assistance, to approve our selves such Believers as sincerely fear God, love Righteousness, and hate every Evil Way, as becomes the Redeemed of God by the Precious Blood of his Son. Since therefore we are not our own, but the Lord's, who hath bought us with that Great Price,[107] let us glorifie him in our Bodies, in our Souls, and in our Spirits, which are his: Then shall we be Children of *Abraham,* indeed, Heirs of the Promises, Partakers of that Resurrection and Life, that Immortality and Glory, which God the Righteous Judge will, one Day, plentifully distribute to them that abide in

104. 1 John 1:5–9.
105. Matthew 22:1–14.
106. Mark 3:32–35; Matthew 12:46–50; and Matthew 19:29.
107. 1 Corinthians 6:20; and 1 Corinthians 7:23.

this precious Faith unto the End. This naturally brings me to my third Head, and an Unhappiness we have long labour'd under.

Sect. 4. *Of Debasing the true Value of Morality under Pretence of* Higher Things; *and mistaking, in great Measure, the very* End *of* Christ's Coming.

BY *MORALITY* I understand Virtuous Living, Purity of Manners; that Justice, Temperance, Truth, Charity, and Blamelesness in Conversation, out of Conscience and Duty to God and Man, which may well Denominate the Man that lives that Life, a Man Just, Virtuous, and Pious: In short, one *that does unto all Men, as he would have all Men do unto him;*[108] this is my *Mortal Man.* It is notorious how small an Estimate two Sorts of People have put upon him, the Profane and the Professors, the *Publicans* and the *Pharisees:* The first despise him as too *Squeamish, Nice* and *Formal;* they deride his Regularity, and make a Jest of his Preciseness. And thinking *No Man can be good,* because they are Naught, and that all must needs fall by those Temptations they will not resist, they construe Sobriety to be a Trick to decoy Mankind, and put a Cheat upon the World. If they hear any one say, *Such a Man is a Sober and Just Person,* they have learned, by themselves, to call him *Knave;* that he has a Design upon some Body, by being *Just* in little Things, to cheat in Things of more Moment. This Man is very Unfashionable among Men of *Immoral Principles;* for his very Looks and Life carry a Reproof with them upon *Vicious Men;* who, as if Virtue were their *Common Enemy,* are in Combination against the Lovers and Entertainers of her: The Reason is, because such true *Virtuoso* will neither do the Ill Things they would have them, nor flatter them in the Ill they do; and therefore where Ill Men have the Power, Good Men are sure to be made the *Common Enemy.*

But the Reproaches that Men of Morality receive at the Hands of Lewd Men, are more their Honour than their Suffering: That which is most of all Anxious, is, that Morality is denied to be Christianity, that Virtue has any Claim to Grace, and that those who glory to be called Christians, can be so Partial and Cruel as to renounce a meer *Just Man* their Society, and send him packing among the *Heathen* for Damnation. And pray what's the Matter? *Why! though this Person be a* sober Liver, *yet he is but a* General Believer;

108. Matthew 7:12.

his Faith is at large. 'Tis true, he believes in God, but I hear little of his Faith in Christ. Very well: Does he not therefore *believe in Christ?* or must he therefore be without the Pale of Salvation? Is it possible that a Man can truly *believe in God* and be damned? But as he that *believes in Christ, believes in God,* so he that believes in God, believes in Christ: *For he that believes* on him, *that raised up Jesus from the Dead, his Faith shall be imputed to him for Righteousness,* and says Christ himself; *He that believeth my Word, and believeth on* him that sent me, *hath Everlasting Life:*[109] Has he that *believes in God* no Interest in this Expression? But more particular is that Place of the Apostle to the *Hebrews,* viz. *For he that cometh to God must believe that he is, and that he is a Diligent Rewarder of them that seek him.*[110] Now if those who so *believe* can come to God, the *Moral Man*'s Condition is not Dangerous even in the strictest Sense of the Word; not only such as have a *General Faith* of *Christianity,* and never adher'd to any particular Party, a Sense, we shall anon consider, but even those who never heard the History of Christ, nor had a distinct Knowledge of him, as we profess him.

For it seems a most unreasonable Thing, that *Faith in God* and keeping his Commandments should be no Part of the *Christian Religion:* But if a Part it be, as upon serious Reflection who dare deny it, then those before and since Christ's Time, who never had the External Law nor History, and have *done the Things contained in the Law, their Consciences not accusing nor Hearts Condemning, but excusing them before God,* are in some Degree concern'd in the Character of a true Christian. For Christ himself preach'd and kept his Father's Commandments, and came to fulfil and not to destroy the Law; and that not only in his own Person, but that *the Righteousness of the Law might be also fulfilled in us.*[111]

Let us but soberly consider *What Christ is,* and we shall the better know whether *Moral Men* are to be reckon'd Christians. What is Christ but *Meekness, Justice, Mercy, Patience, Charity* and *Virtue in Perfection?* Can we then deny a *meek Man* to be a Christian; a Just, a Merciful, a Patient, a Charitable and a Virtuous Man to be like Christ? *By me Kings Reign and Princes decree Justice,* saith Wisdom, yea, the *Wisdom that is from above;* so may I say here,

109. John 5:24; and Romans 4:22–24.
110. Hebrews 11:6.
111. Romans 8:4.

By Christ Men are *Meek, Just, Merciful, Patient, Charitable* and *Virtuous;*[112] and Christians ought to be distinguished by their Likeness to Christ and not their Notions of Christ; by his Holy Qualifications rather than their own Lofty Professions and Invented Formalities. What shall we say then of that Extravagancy which those Men are guilty of who upon hearing a sober Man commended, that is not of any great Visible Profession, will take upon them to cast him off with this Sentence; *Tush, he is but a* Moral Man; *he knows nothing of Saving Grace: he may be damn'd for all his Morality.* Nay, some have gone so far as to say and preach, if not print, *That there are Thousands of* Moral Men *in Hell.*

But 'tis worth our while to consider that he that sins *is not saved by Grace* in that State, and that the *Virtuous Man* is the *Gracious Man;* For 'tis the Nature and End of true Grace, to make Men so. Unanswerable is that Passage of the Apostle, to the *Romans, Therefore if the Uncircumcision keep the Righteousness of the Law, shall not his Uncircumcision be counted for Circumcision? and shall not Uncircumcision, which is by Nature, if it fulfil the Law, judge thee, who by the Letter and Circumcision dost transgress the Law? For he is not a Jew, who is one outwardly, neither is that Circumcision, which is outward in the Flesh; but he is a Jew, which is one inwardly, and Circumcision is that of the Heart, in the Spirit, and not in the Letter, whose Praise is not of Men, but of God.*[113] So that he who keeps the Law of God, and abstains from the Impurity of the World, is the *good Man,* the *Just Liver;* he is the Apostle's true *Jew* and *Circumcision.*

Wherefore it is not ill express'd by that extraordinary Man *J. Hales* of *Eaton: The Moral Man,* says he, *is a Christian by the surer Side:* As if he had said, *Speculations* may fail, Notions be mistaken, Forms wither, but Truth and Righteousness will stand the *Test;* and the Man that loves them will not be moved. He tells us, *That the Fathers had that Opinion of the Sincerity of the Life of some* Heathens, *that they believ'd God had in Store for such even his* Saving Grace, *and that he would make them Possessors of his Everlasting Kingdom.* And measuring your Satisfaction by the Pleasure I took in reading what the Author both quotes and comments upon this Subject, I will venture to transcribe him at large, whose Authority ought to go as far as his Reason, and he claims no

112. Proverbs 8:15; and James 3:17.
113. Romans 2:26–29.

more, nor indeed does any reasonable Man, since God himself seems to submit to that Method of overcoming us, to wit, Conviction, *viz.*[114]

† Let it not trouble you (saith he) that I entitle them to some Part of our *Christian Faith,* and therefore without Scruple to be receiv'd as Weak, and not to be cast forth as Dead. *Salvianus* disputing what Faith is; *Quid est igitur Credulitas vel Fides?* (saith he) *Opinor fideliter hominem Christo credere,* id est, *Fidelem Deo esse,* hoc est, *Fideliter Dei mandata servare,* What might this Faith be? (saith he) I suppose, it is nothing else, but *Faithfully to believe Christ;* and this is to be Faithful unto God; which is nothing else, but Faithfully to *keep the Commandments of God.*[115] Not therefore only a bare Belief, but the Fidelity and Trustiness of God's Servants, faithfully accomplishing the Will of our Master, is required as a Part of our *Christian Faith.*

Now, all those good Things which *Moral Men* by the *Light* of *Nature** do, are a Part of God's Will written in their Hearts: wherefore so far as they were Conscientious in performing them (if *Salvianus* his Reason be good;) so far have they Title and Interest in our Faith. And therefore *Regulus,* that Famous *Roman,* when he endured infinite Torments, rather than he would break his Oath, may thus far be counted a Martyr and Witness for the Truth.[116] For the Crown of Martyrdom sits not only on the Heads of those, who have lost their Lives, rather than they would cease to profess the *Name of Christ;* but on the Head of every one that

† *J. Hales* of *Eaton, Golden Remains,* Of dealing with Erring Christians, page 36, 37.

* Or the Light which comes with us into the World, and grows up with us, as we are of a Capacity to discern the Teachings of it. See *John* 1. 9. ch. 8. 12. *Rom:* 1. 19. *Ephes.* 5. 13. 1 *Job.* 1. 7. All agree in it, As to it's Universality. But the Beloved Disciple instructs us of it's Original, Nature and Use, in the first Chapter of his Evangelical History, deeply and clearly: They had it before Christ's coming, as may be seen in *Job* 18. 5, 6. ch. 21. 17. ch. 24. 13, 16. *Psalm* 27. 1. 36. 9.

114. The following extended quotation is taken from Hales's *Golden remains* (1673), pp. 36–37, Sermon on Galatians 6:7.

115. Salvian of Marseilles (ca. 400–480), *On the government of God,* republished in translation by Eva M. Sanford (New York, 1930), bk. 4, ch. 1.

116. Regulus, an imprisoned Roman commander, was sent by his Carthaginian captors to secure a prisoner exchange with Rome. He swore an oath to return if unsuccessful. Regulus himself argued against exchanging the prisoners, and—though urged not to by Romans—returned to Carthage as he had sworn, where he was tortured to death. See Augustine, *City of God,* bk. 1, ch. 15.

suffers for the Testimony of a *Good Conscience* and for Righteousness Sake. And here I cannot pass by one very General and Gross Mistake of our Age. For in our Discourses concerning the Notes of a *Christian Man,* by what Signs we may know a Man to be one of the *Visible Company of Christ,* we have so tied our selves to this outward Profession, that if we know no other Virtue in a Man, but that he hath con'd his Creed by Heart, let his Life be never so profane, we think it Argument enough for us to account him within the Pale and Circuit of the Church. On the contrary Side, let his Life be never so upright, if either he be little seen in, or peradventure quite ignorant of the Mystery of Christ, we esteem of him but as dead. And those, who conceive well of those Moral good Things, as of some Tokens giving Hope of Life, we account but as a Kind of *Manichees,* who thought the very Earth had Life in it. I must confess that I have not yet made that Proficiency in the Schools of our Age, as that I could see, why the Second Table and the Acts of it are not as properly the Parts of Religion and Christianity, as the Acts and Observations of the First? If I mistake, then it is St. *James* that hath abus'd me; for he describing Religion by its proper Acts, tells us, that *Pure Religion and undefiled before God and the Father, is, to visit the Fatherless and the Widows in their Affliction, and to keep himself unspotted of the World.*[117] So that the Thing which is an *especial refined Dialect* of the New *Christian Language* signifies nothing but *Morality* and *Civility,* that in the Language of the Holy Ghost imports *True Religion.* Thus far *J. Hales.*

He hath said so well on this Account, that there is little Need I should say any more; yet let me add thus much: Did Men mind the *Language* of the *Holy Ghost* more than their own Conceits, they would not stile those meer *Moral Men* in a Way of Disgrace, who are not of their *Perswasion;* it would suffice, that those that *Fear God and work Righteousness in all Nations are accepted of him;* That Christ himself hath said, *He that doth the Will of my Father which is in Heaven, shall enter into the Kingdom of Heaven;* and of them that work Iniquity, *Depart from me, I know you not.*[118]

My Friends, Let us not deceive our selves, *God will not be mocked; Such as we sow, we shall certainly reap.* The Tree is known by it's Fruits, and will be judg'd according to it's Fruits. *The Wages of Sin is Death:* Men will find it so;

117. James 1:27.
118. Acts 10:34–35; and Matthew 7.

and every Man shall receive his Reward suitable to his Work.[119] For People to talk of *Special Grace,* and yet be carried away by *Common Temptations:* To let Pride, Vanity, Covetousness, Revenge, *&c.* predominate, it is Provoking to God: But to conceit that the Righteous God will indulge his People in that Latitude, which he condemns in other Men, is abominable. 'Tis Sanctification, that makes the Saint; and Self-denial that constitutes the Christian; and not filling our Heads and elevating our Fancies by applying those Promises to our selves, which as yet we have no Interest in, though we may think they belong to no Body else: This *Spiritual Flattery* of our selves is most pernicious. I cannot but say, with the Apostle, *'Tis neither Circumcision nor Uncircumcision,* Jew *nor* Gentile (this not t'other Thing) *but the New Creature, created after Christ Jesus in Holiness: for without Holiness no Man shall ever see the Lord.*[120] And what is *Holiness,* but abstaining from Wickedness? And what's that but keeping the Law of God? *Great Peace have they that love thy Law,* said *David,* that had known the Trouble of breaking it: Therefore it is that *Grace and Truth are come by Jesus Christ,* to help us to *fulfil the Law,* not to excuse our *Disobedience to the Law:* And what before we were unable, this gives us Force to do.[121] So that *Christianity* is not an *Indulgence* of People under Weakness and Disobedience, but the Compleating and Perfection of that Righteousness which without him was but short and Imperfect, through the all-sufficient Grace and Power that came by Jesus Christ.

Give me Leave, I beseech you, for I have a Godly Jealousie upon me; I fear, lest the very *End of Christ's Coming is mistaken;* and of how dreadful a Consequence such a Mistake would be, you cannot possibly be ignorant, that believe there is *No Salvation in any other Name.* Let us hear the Testimony of Scripture: They are the Words of Christ himself, *I must preach the Kingdom of God for therefore am I sent.* Now, what is this Kingdom of God, but God's Government? And where is this Kingdom and Government to be set up, but in Man? So Christ tells us, *Behold the Kingdom of God is within you.* So that the Reason of his being sent, is, that the Kingdom and Government of the Devil may be destroyed, the strong Man that kept the House, the Heart, be dispossessed, and the Kingdom and Government of God in the Soul, erected and established. We are taught to pray for it, as little as we make of it. *Thy Kingdom*

119. Galatians 6:7; and Romans 6:23.
120. Romans 2:29; and Galatians 6:15.
121. Psalms 119:165; and John 1:16–17.

come, thy Will be done.[122] Would to God People would but consider what they Pray for! For they are scandaliz'd at the Thing they ask, and both neglect and revile the Substance of their own Prayers: *Thy Kingdom come, and thy Will be done;* but believe neither. It was the Office God designed his Son to. *The Thief* (says Christ) *does not come but to kill, to steal, and to destroy;* that is *to steal away the Heart from God, and to kill and destroy all good Desires and Inclinations in the Soul:* For the Devil is the Thief and Destroyer: *But I am come* (says Christ) *that ye might have Life, and that ye might have it more abundantly.*[123] Again, *O Death, I will be thy Death!* as if he had said, *I will kill that which kills the Soul: I will breath the Breath of Life into it again; and, by my Spirit and Grace, I will beget Holy Motions, and kindle Heavenly Desires in it after God, after the Kingdom of God, and the Righteousness thereof:* This is the *Newness of Life:*[124] And I will not only restore that Life the Soul has lost, but I will increase it: I will add to it, that it may have *Life more abundantly;* more Power and Strength to resist Evil, and embrace and delight in that which is Good.

Indeed he was Anointed of God for this Purpose; and is therefore called the *Restorer of Paths,* the *Repairer of Breaches,* and the *Builder up of Waste Places;* that is, he is ordained of God for the Recovery of Man from his *Fallen and Disobedient State,* This is the Reason of his Name: *Thou shalt call his Name* JESUS, said the Angel, *for he shall save his People from their Sins:*[125] Not from Wrath only, but from Sin, which is the Cause of Wrath. That is, of Bad Men, he will make them really Good Men; and of Sinful and Unholy, he will make them Holy and Righteous Men, such as truly believe in him. This is the Burden of *John*'s Testimony: *There is One,* says he, *that cometh after me, is mightier than I, He shall Baptize you with the Holy Ghost and with Fire; whose Fan is in his Hand, and he will throughly Purge his Floor.* And seeing *Jesus* coming to him, said, *Behold the Lamb of God, which taketh away the Sins of the World!*[126]

I know the Use that too many make of these Scriptures, as if they were an *Hebraism,* borrow'd from the *Old Sacrifices,* which may be said, *To take away Sin by taking away the Guilt, and not that the Natures of Men are Restored and Perfected.* And indeed, this is that Sense which I dread above all others, be-

122. This paragraph, respectively: Luke 4:43; Luke 17:21; and Luke 11:2.

123. John 10:10.

124. Hosea 13:14; and Romans 6:4.

125. Matthew 1:21.

126. Matthew 3:11–12; and John 1:29.

cause it perverts the *End of Christ's Coming,* and lodges Men in a Security pernicious to their own Souls. For though it is most true, that *Remission of Sin was, and is preached in his Name and Blood, and that Sin, in a Sense, may be said to be taken away, when the Guilt of the Sin is removed by Remission; yet this is only of Sin past, that upon Repentance is forgiven:*[127] But this is not the Whole, Full and Evangelical Sense, as Christ's own Words do plainly import. *For,* says he, *the Son of Man is come to save that which was Lost.* And upon another Occasion he expresseth himself to the same Purpose, and almost in the same Words, *For the Son of Man is come to seek and to save that which was Lost.*[128] Now, who is this that is Lost, but Man? And in what Sense can Man be said to be Lost, but by Sin and Disobedience? That it was which cast him out of the Presence and Garden of God, and put him in a Condition of Eternal Misery. If Christ then came to *Save Lost Man,* he must be understood to Save him from that which puts him into a Lost Condition, and that is Sin; for *The Wages of Sin is Death, and the Servant of Sin is a Son of Perdition.*[129]

Christ has determin'd this Point beyond all Exception, in his Discourse with the *Jews,* (*John* 8. 31, 32, 33, 34.) *Then said Jesus to those* Jews, *which believed on him, if ye continue in my Word, then are ye my Disciples indeed; and ye shall know the Truth, and the Truth shall make you Free.* What Freedom was this? Certainly from Sin; suitable to that Passage in his Prayer: *Sanctify them through thy Truth, thy Word is Truth.*[130] But some *Jews* present, proud of their Privileges, apprehended not the Liberty Christ spoke of, and therefore answer'd him thus: *We are* Abraham's *Seed, and were never in Bondage to any Man; how sayst thou, Ye shall be made Free?* Jesus answered them, *Verily, verily, I say unto you, whosoever committeth Sin, is the Servant of Sin.* In which Place it is very remarkable, that Men are only to be distinguished by their Works; that no Claims, Privileges, Successions, or Descents are available, *but he that commits Sin, is the Servant of Sin.*[131] So that Christ's *Free Man* is he that is freed from Sin: This is his Follower and Disciple. And as Christ oppos'd the Works of the *Jews,* who unjustly sought to kill him, to their Pretensions they made to be *Abraham's Seed;* so must we oppose the Actions of ill Men to their better

127. Acts 10:43; and Ephesians 1:7.
128. Matthew 18:10–14; and Luke 19:10.
129. Romans 6:23.
130. John 17:17.
131. John 8:34.

Professions: We must faithfully tell them, *He that commits Sin, is the Servant of Sin;* from which Servitude Christ came to *Save his People,* and is therefore rightly called, *The Saviour and the Redeemer.*

This Doctrine is closely followed by the Apostle *Paul* in his sixth Chapter to the *Romans. Therefore we are buried with him by Baptism into Death, that like as Christ was raised up from the Dead by the Glory of the Father, even so we also should walk in Newness of Life—Knowing this, that our Old Man is crucified with him, that the Body of Sin might be destroyed, that henceforth we should not serve Sin—Likewise reckon ye also your selves to be Dead indeed unto Sin, but alive unto God through Jesus Christ our Lord.* As if he had said, *The End of Christ's coming, is to turn People from their Sins; and that those who persist in their Disobedience, resist the Benefits that come by him.*

Let not Sin therefore reign in your Mortal Body, that ye should obey it in the Lusts thereof. Neither yield ye your Members as Instruments of Unrighteousness unto Sin; but yield your selves unto God, as those that are Alive from the Dead, and your Members as Instruments of Righteousness unto God—Know ye not, that to whom ye yield your selves Servants to obey, his Servants ye are to whom ye obey; whether of Sin unto Death, or of Obedience unto Righteousness?—For when ye were the Servants of Sin, ye were free from Righteousness. What Fruit had ye then in those Things, whereof ye are now ashamed? For the End of those Things is Death. But now being made Free from Sin, and become Servants to God, ye have your Fruit unto Holiness, and the End Everlasting Life. For the Wages of Sin is Death, but the Gift of God is Eternal Life, through Jesus Christ our Lord.

To conclude, nothing can be more apparent, than that Freedom from Actual Sinning, and giving Newness of Life to the Souls of Men, was the Great Reason of *Christ's Coming,* and the End for which he hath given us out of his Fulness of Grace and Truth, *Grace for Grace;* and that to be under *Grace,* and not under the Law, is not to have Liberty to do that now, which ought not to have been done before, or to be excused from former moral Obligations, as the *Ranters* interpret it;[132] but to be freed from the Condemnation of the Law, *First,* through Remission of the Sins that are past upon Faith and Repentance, and next, by freeing us of that Weakness by which we were disabled from

132. The Ranters were one of the many radical sects that appeared during the 1640s in England. Their views apparently extended to a denial of original sin and moral codes more generally, and they were accused of sexual licentiousness by their many opponents.

keeping God's Just Law, and fulfilling the Righteousness of it, in receiving and obeying the Light and Grace that comes by Jesus Christ.

Very pertinent is that Passage of the Apostle *Paul* to *Titus,* to our present Purpose, for it seems to comprehend the *End of Christ's Coming,* and the Faith and Duty of his People; which our Great *Selden,* after all his Painful Readings, and Curious Inquisitions, said, but a little before his Death, *Was the Most Weighty Passage of the whole Bible to him, as the Bible was the Best of Books in the World,* viz. *For the Grace of God, that bringeth Salvation, hath appeared to all Men, teaching us, that denying Ungodliness, and Worldly Lusts, we should live Soberly, Righteously, and Godly in this present World; looking for that Blessed Hope, and the Glorious Appearing of the Great God, and our Saviour Jesus Christ, who gave himself for us, that he might redeem us from all Iniquity, and purify unto himself a peculiar People, Zealous of Good Works.*[133]

In which comprehensive Passage, we find the *End of Christ's Coming* to be *Our Redemption from all Iniquity,* both to blot out our Sins that are past, and to purify our Hearts from the Sin that remains. We have the Means that works and brings this Salvation into our Souls, which is the Grace; and the Way, by which this Grace doth accomplish it, is by *Teaching us to deny Ungodliness and Worldly Lusts, and to live Soberly, Righteously, and Godly in this present World.* Which has this great Encouragement joyned to it, that those who so live, have only Right to look for that Blessed Hope and the Glorious Appearing of the Great God, and our Saviour *Jesus Christ.*

I will add the Testimony of his Beloved Disciple *John,* who has defined to us the *End of Christ's Coming,* thus: *Whosoever committeth Sin, Transgresseth also the Law; and ye know, that he was manifested to take away our Sins.* And to shew that this is understood, not only of the Guilt of Sins past, but of the Nature and present Power of Sin in Man, observe what follows; *Whosoever abideth in him* (Christ) *Sinneth not.* As if this Apostle had foreseen the present Mischief *Christianity* labours under both on the Side of Evil Men, and of but too many mistaken Professors. He adds, *Little Children, let no Man deceive you; he that doth Righteousness is Righteous, even as he is Righteous; he that committeth Sin is of the Devil, for the Devil sinneth from the Beginning.* (Now comes his most express Passage to the Matter in Hand) *For this Purpose the Son of God was manifested, that he might destroy the Works of the Devil:* Which is more than the Remission of Sins that are past; here is the Destruction of the

133. Titus 2:11–14.

Power and Kingdom of Satan. They that know not this, know not Christ as he should be known, not savingly. For as we, so our Lord is known by his Fruits, by the Works which he works in us: Therefore it is said, *That his own Works praise him.* And said Christ, *If I had not done among them the Works which no other Man did,* &c.[134] So that he referred to his Works to prove his Nature and Mission.

He therefore that lives in Sin denies *Christ,* by denying the End of his *Coming.* The Fool did not say with his Mouth, but *in his Heart, There is no God;*[135] yet but too many now a-days, plead with their Tongues and Pens for *Sin Term of Life,* by endeavouring to shew the Impossibility of over-coming Sin. But what saith this Apostle farther of the Business? *Whosoever is born of God, doth not commit Sin: In this the Children of God are manifest, and the Children of the Devil, whosoever doth not Righteousness, is not of God; neither he that loveth not his Brother. But if you walk in the Light, as God is in the Light, we have Fellowship one with another, and the Blood of Jesus Christ his Son, cleanseth us from all Sin. He that saith he abideth in Christ, ought himself also so to walk, even as Christ walked.* A little lower in the same Chapter he says, *I have written unto you, Young Men, because ye are strong, and the Word of God abideth in you, and ye have overcome the Wicked One.*[136]

I will add one Scripture-Testimony more in the present Case, and it is this: *Herein* (saith *John*) *is our Love made perfect, that we may have Boldness in the Day of Judgment, because as he is, so are we in this World.*[137]

Behold now the true *End of Christ's Coming!* viz. To *save from Sin* and to purge us from *all Iniquity;* that he might present us to God without Spot or Blemish.[138] Let us not then flatter our selves, for we shall be the Losers: Neither let us make that impossible through our Infidelity, which a Grain of Sincere Faith can make not only Possible but Easie. What has been, may be again; nay, in this Case must be. Did the First Christians *overcome the Wicked one?* so must the Last Christians too. Were those Ages led by the Holy Spirit, and taught by the *Grace of God* to *live God-like,* or like God in the World? so must we of these latter Ages too, if we will be blessed for ever; that, having *put off the old Man,* the Devil and his Works, we may *put on Christ* the new and heavenly

134. 1 John 3:4–10; and John 15:24.
135. Psalms 14:1; 53:1.
136. 1 John 3:9–10; 1:7; 2:6, 14.
137. 1 John 4:17.
138. Ephesians 5:27.

Man, the second *Adam,* with his Holy Life and Works; so shall *the Fruits of his Spirit* shine through us, which are *Love, Joy, Peace, Long-suffering, Patience, Gentleness, Faith, Meekness, Temperance; for they that are Christ's have Crucified the Flesh, with the Affections and Lusts:*[139] They hear his Voice that leads them out of the Concupiscences of this Vile World, and *they follow him, and he gives unto them Eternal Life, and a Stranger they will not follow.*[140] The World, the Flesh and the Devil make up this Stranger, and those that are carried away by this Stranger are in an Unreconciled State to God, and, so dying, must inevitably perish. Well, then will we be true Christians? Have we *Faith?* then let us take the Advice of that good Man *Peter; Let us add to our Faith Virtue, and to Virtue Knowledge, and to Knowledge Temperance, and to Temperance Patience, and to Patience Godliness, and to Godliness Brotherly-Kindness, and to Brotherly-Kindness Charity:* For says he, *if these Things be in you and abound, they make you, that ye shall neither be barren nor unfruitful in the Knowledge of our Lord Jesus Christ. But he that lacketh these Things is blind, and cannot see far off, and hath forgotten that he was purged from his old Sins. Wherefore the rather, Brethren, give Diligence, to make your Calling and Election sure; for if ye do these Things, ye shall never fall. For so an Entrance shall be ministred unto you abundantly into the Everlasting Kingdom of our Lord and Saviour Jesus Christ.*[141] Thus much, O ye *Protestants!* That profess a Reformation, and value your selves upon it, Of the true Reformed Doctrine of Godliness, a virtuous and good Life, without which your Profession will be the Aggravation of your Guilt. For know this once for all, that a true Reformation lies in the Spirit of Reformation, reforming the Minds and Manners of such as profess it. God Almighty open your Eyes and affect your Hearts with this great Truth.

Sect. 5. *The Fourth great Ecclesiastical Evil, is Preferring* Humane Authority *above* Reason *and* Truth.

THIS and the next Evil, which is the last now to be considered, to wit, *Propagation of Faith by Force, Religion by Arms,* are the Two Legs upon which the false Church hath in all Ages stood. Under this Degeneracy we find the *Jewish Church* at Christ's coming, and he complains of it, *Ye teach for*

139. Romans 13:14; and Galatians 5:22–24.
140. John 10:4–5.
141. 2 Peter 1:5, 7–11.

Doctrines the Traditions of Men, ye seek to kill me, a Man that has told you the Truth:[142] But I challenge the whole Account of Time, and Records of the World, which are come to the Hands of this Age, to tell me *When, Where,* and *by whom,* these Principles have been received, improved and used, in any Sort of Proportion or *Comparison,* with the Practice of that *Church,* which has long prided her self in the Name of *Catholick* and *Christian.* And yet I could wish nothing of these *Two Ill Principles* had found any Place amongst Us, that call our selves *Protestants;* though to the great Men of her *Communion,* in divers *Countries* of *Europe,* is chiefly owing most of that *Ignorance, Superstition, Idolatry, Persecution* and *Blood-shed* that have been among *Christians,* since the *Christian* Profession hath grown to any Power in the World. I shall consider them severally, respecting us, and in their due Order, with as much Brevity as well I can.

That *Humane Authority* hath been *preferred above Reason and Truth,* that is, That the *Apprehensions, Interpretations, Conclusions* and *Injunctions* of Men have been reputed the great Necessaries or Essentials to Salvation and Christian Communion, insomuch as a sober and reasonable Dissent hath been too often over-rul'd, not by Weight of Argument or Evidence of Truth, but by the Power and Numbers of Men in Ecclesiastical Office and Dignity, is, and speak Modestly, in a large Degree true among us. The First Church-Evil reprehended in this Discourse may begin the Proof, and give the first Witness upon this Part of the Charge, viz. *That Opinions have been made Articles of Faith; that is, The Constructions and Conclusions of Men from Sacred Writ, and not the Text it self, have been enjoyn'd and impos'd as Essential to Eternal Salvation, and External Christian Communion.* Insomuch as no *Reason, Scripture* or purest *Antiquity* hath been suffered to prevail against such Determinations, and too often not enough to excuse those that have pleaded for a Conscientious Dissent from them; the Authors of them either resting upon the Authority of their own Judgments, or conforming themselves to the Example of Ages less pure and clear.

I Conscientiously refuse to name Parties, because I am tender of giving the least Offence; but upon a Just Observance of those Revolutions of Protestancy that have been amongst us, we may see, with what Stiffness, not to say Obstinacy, several *Models of Religion* and *Draughts of Creeds* have been contended for. I would beseech every Party, in Christ's Name, to look into it self; for I

142. Matthew 15:9; Mark 7:7; and John 8:40.

don't, because such are best able (if they will be Impartial and put no Cheat upon themselves) to make the Application of what I say. However, I will name those Points, about which the Authority of Man, as it seems to me, has been so positive. Of *God,* as to his *Prescience* and *Predetermination:* Of *Christ,* as to his *Natures* and *Personality,* and the *Extent* of his Death and Intercession: Of *Free-Will* and *Grace:* Of *Faith* and *Works:* Of *Perseverance* and *Falling away:* Of the Nature and Power of the Church: And Lastly, of the *Dignity* and *Power* of the Clergy.

And if Men please but to lay their Hands upon their Hearts, and cast their Eyes upon the Scriptures; if they will but use the Light that God has afforded them, and bring such Debates and Results to the Test of that Light and the Sound Form of Words, the Holy Ghost hath used and preserv'd amongst us, I need not take the Employment upon me of pointing to Humane Authority among the several Parties of *Protestants,* as to these Points, since nothing will be clearer. For it is about the Meaning of this, and the Intention of that Place of Scripture, the Contest hath been and still is; and how to maintain and propagate those Conceits: So that the falling out is in the Wood of our own Opinions, and there the Contention is kindled, that consumes all about our Ears. A most unwarrantable Curiosity and Nicety, for the most Part, that hath more Influence upon our Passions, than our Practice, which is usually the worse in Point of Charity, and not the better for them in any Thing. O that we would but be impartial, and see our own Over-plus to the Scriptures, and retrench that redundancy, or keep it modestly! for 'tis an horrid Thing that we *Protestants* should assume a Power of ranging our human Apprehensions with the Sacred Text, and injoining our Imaginations for Indispensible Articles of *Faith* and *Christian Communion.*

But the next Proof of the Prevalency of *Humane Authority* amongst us *Protestants,* is *The great Power and Sway of the Clergy, and the People's Reliance upon them for the Knowledge of Religion, and the Way of Life and Salvation.* This is such plain Fact, that every Parish more or less proves it. Is not *Prophecy,* once the Church's, now engrost by them and wholly in their Hands? Who dare publickly *Preach* or *Pray,* that is not of that *Class* or *Order?* Have not they only the Keys in keeping? May any body else pretend to the Power of *Absolution* or *Excommunication?* Much less to constitute Ministers? Are not all Church Rites and Privileges in their Custody? Don't they make it their proper Inheritance? Nay, so much larger is their Empire than *Caesar*'s, that only they begin with Births and end with Burials: Men must pay them for *Coming* in and *Going* out of the World. *To pay for dying* is hard! Thus their Profits run from the Womb to the Grave, and that which is the Loss of others, is their Gain, and a Part of their Revenue. Both Lives and Deaths do bring Grist to their Mill, and Toll to their Exchequer, for they have an Estate in us for our Lives, and an Heriot at our Deaths.

'Tis of this great Order and Sept of Men only, that all *Synods* and *Convocations* are, of modern Ages, compounded; and what they determin, is called the *Canons* or *Decrees* of the *Church;* though, Alas! She is only to Obey, what they of the Gown Ordain; giving us thereby to understand, that they want the Authority of her Name, where they deny her to have a Part, or to be present.

But they have not only been the usual Starters of new Opinions, and the great *Creed-Makers* among *Christians,* but the Sway they have long had with the People, makes them so considerable an Interest in the Eyes of the *Civil Magistrate,* that he often finds it not for his Safety to disoblige them. Upon this it is, we see them so Successful in their Solicitations of Publick Authority to give its Sanction to their Opinions and Forms; and not only recommend them (which goes certainly a great Way with the People) but impose their Reception, and that on severe Penalties: Insomuch, that either Men must offer up their Understandings to their Fears, and dissemble Conviction to be safe, or else perish: There is no Medium. Something of this lies near us: God Almighty open our Eyes to see both the Truth and Mischief of this Thing.

But what shall I say of that implicit Reverence the People have for the Clergy, and Dependence upon them about *Religion* and *Salvation;* as if they were the only Trustees of Truth, and high Treasurers of Divine Knowledge to the Laity: And we daily see, that the blind Opinion they have of their Office (as that which is peculiar to that Order, and not common to Christians, be their Gifts as they will) disposes them to rely entirely upon their Performances. The Minister is Chooser and Taster and every Thing for them: They seem to have deliver'd up their Spiritual Selves, and made over the Business of Religion, the *Rights* of their *Souls* to their *Pastor;* and that scarcely with any Limitation of Truth too: And as if he were, or could be their *Guarantee,* in t'other World, they become very insolicitous of any further search here. So that if we would examine the respective Parishes of *Protestant* as well as *Popish* Countries, we shall find, and it is come to that sad pass, that very few have any other Religion than the Tradition of their Priest. They have given up their Judgment to him, and seem greatly at their Ease, that they have discharged themselves of the Trouble of *Working out their own Salvation and Proving all Things, that they might hold fast that which is good.*[143] And in the Room of that Care bequeath'd the Charge of those Affairs to a standing Pensioner for that Purpose.

Thus the Clergy are become a sort of Mediators betwixt Christ and us, that as we must go to God by Christ, so must we come to Christ by them: They must be, it seems, like the *High Priest* under the Law, who only enter'd into the *Holy of Holies;* whose *Lips preserved Knowledge;* and by them we must understand the *Divine Oracle.*[144] As if the Mysteries of Salvation were not to be intrusted with the Vulgar; or that it were a kind of Prophanation to expose them to their View, and the only way to make them cheap and contemptible to suffer *every Christian* to have the keeping of them; though they belong to *every Christian.* But this Language, thanks be to God, is that of Humane Authority that would magnify the Mysteries of Salvation by the Ignorance of those that should know them, as if the *Gospel-Dispensation* were not that of full Age, but Infancy or Minority.

'Tis true, the State of People under the Law and the *Levitical Priesthood* is called a State of *Bondage, Childhood* and *Minority,* and the Law therefore is term'd a *School-master* to bring us to Christ; but it is as true, that the State of Christianity is reputed the Age of *Grace, Freedom, Manhood* and *Inheritance* by the same Apostle:[145] And that we should have external Guardians of our Faith and Religion upon us after we are come to Years of Discretion, that might be very allowable under the feeble State of our Minority, is not to obtain greater Freedom, but to make our Case worse. For it is more tolerable to be used as Children when we are Children, and know nothing above that Condition, than when riper Years have brought us to the Understanding and Resentment of Men. But it is almost as unpardonable as it is unsufferable, to make that Infancy the Perfection of the *Christian-Religion,* as if there were nothing *beyond wearing a Bib and being fed, carried and govern'd as Nurses please;* that is, *as the Priest will.* It is a Knowing and Reasonable, and not a blind Obedience, that commends a Man: *Children* should be ruled, because they have not so ripe an Understanding or *Choice;* but because 'tis not so with Men, Reason ought to conduct them in their Duty, that the Service they perform to God, may be such as the Apostle calls a Reasonable one;[146] The

143. 1 Thessalonians 5:21.

144. On priests and the tabernacle, see Leviticus, *passim.*

145. Galatians 3:24–25.

146. Romans 12:1.

Will is no longer *Will* if not *Free,* nor *Conscience* to be reputed *Conscience,* where it is compelled. The Gospel is not the Time of Ceremonial Works, but of Faith, therefore not coercive, because out of our own Power; it is the Gift of God.

But though this be very unhappy, that so excellent a Reformation, founded upon the freest Principles of Inquiry, common to all that had Souls to save, should so miserably degenerate into *Formality* and *Ignorance, Implicit Faith* and *blind Obedience;* yet that Part of our History is most lamentable to me, where we find the *Noble Bereans,* the diligent Inquirers, People that desire to *prove all Things,* that they may *hold fast that which is good;*[147] such as would see with their own Eyes, and that dare not transfer the Right of Examination of Points that so nearly concern their Immortal Souls to any mortal Man; but who desire to make their Faith and Religion, the Faith and Religion of their *Conscience* and *Judgment,* that on which they dare depend and rest their Eternal Happiness in the Day of Judgment: That these, I say, should instead of being cherisht, be therefore *exposed to the Displeasure of the Clergy, the Scorn of the Rude Multitude, and the Prosecution of the* civil Magistrate, has some thing in it, I confess, is harsh and anxious to remember, and I only do it for this Purpose, that it may put us in mind of our great Declension from Primitive *Protestancy,* and how much Humane Authority has crept into the Affairs of Religion since that Time of the Day, when we made it a prime Article of our *Protestant Creed* to reject and renounce it.

And that you may yet see your selves short of your own Pretences, if not contrary to your express Principles, and how much you have narrow'd your selves from the use of your First Principle; let us suppose a *Turk* is convinced, that Christ is that, which he believed *Mahomet* to be, the *Greatest of all Prophets,* That *Mahomet* was an Impostor, That *Jesus* is the only Saviour and Mediator; but being Catechistically taught the Two Natures in one Person, the *Hypostatical Union,* in fine, the *Athanasian* Creed and other Articles of Faith, or Rites of your Church, not so clearly express'd in Scripture, nor easily apprehended or assented to, will not this poor Creature be looked upon either as *Infidel* or *Heretick,* and renounced all share in Christ and Christian Fellowship, because his Weakness or Understanding will not allow him to come up to the full Inventory of Articles believed and imposed by you? Certainly you must either be partial, and give him that Liberty you deny to Persons of equal

147. Acts 17:10–13; and 1 Thessalonians 5:21.

Tenderness, or else you must, after your present Streightness, conclude him *Infidel* or *Heretick,* tho' he believe one God, Christ to be the only Mediator, the Gift of the Spirit, the Necessity of Holiness, Communion and Charity. But I would beseech you that we may consider if this bears any Proportion with the Wisdom and Love of God, in sending Christ into the World to save you and me?

The Apostle *became all unto all, to win some;*[148] but this is *becoming all unto none, to force all:* he thereby recommends the *utmost Condescension* that can be lawful; but this Use of *Humane Authority* seems to make it unlawful to condescend: As if Faith *per Force* were better than *Love;* and *Conformity,* however it be come at, than *Christian Condescension:*

The blessed Apostle had his Eye to the *Good Intention* and *Sober Life* of the Weak; and used an holy Sort of Guile to catch them: He seems as if he dissembled the Knowledge of those *averse Opinions* which they held, or the Necessity of their embracing those Doctrines, which as yet they might not believe. He fell not to debate and canvass Points in Difference between them, which, instead of Union, would have enflam'd the Difference and rais'd Contention: No, no, *he became all unto all,* that is, he stooped to all *Capacities,* and humbled himself to those Degrees of Knowledge that Men had, and valued that which was good in all; and with this Sweetness he practised upon them to their farther Proficiency in the School of *Christ.* These Allurements were all his Injunctions? Nay, in this Case he makes it an Injunction to use no other: *Let us therefore (says he) as many as be perfect, be thus minded; and if in any Thing ye be* otherwise *minded, God shall reveal even this unto you.*[149] Which is to say, you shall not be imposed upon, stigmatiz'd or excommunicated for Want of full Satisfaction, or because you do not consent before Conviction; for *God shall reveal it to you;* you shall see and know what you do, and to God you shall owe your Knowledge and Conformity, and not to Human Authority and Imposition: Your Faith shall not be implicit, nor your Obedience blind, the Reason of your Hope shall be in you.

Pray let us compare this with the Language of our own Times, where because People cannot come up to the Prescriptions of Men, but plead the Liberty of Dissent, though with never so much Sobriety and true Tenderness of Conscience, they are upbraided after this Manner: *Are you wiser than your Su-*

148. 1 Corinthians 9:22.
149. Philippians 3:15.

periors? Were our Fore-fathers out of the Way? Did no body know the Truth 'till you came? Are you abler than all our Ministers *and* Bishops, *and your* Mother *the* Church? *Cannot it content you to* believe as she *believes? Is not this* Pride *and* Presumption *in you, a Design to make and head* Sects *and* Parties? with the like Entertainment.

Now this is that which you your selves, at least in the Persons of your Ancestors, have stiled *Popery;* yea, *Popery* in the Abstract; to wit, *Implicit Faith* and *Blind Obedience:* If so, then say I, let us also have a Case of *Popery* in *Protestant* Guise, for that *Popery* is likely to do us most Injury that is least suspected. I beg you, by the Love of God and Truth, and as you would lay a sure Foundation of Peace here, and eternal Comfort to your own Souls, that you would consider the Tendency of upbraiding and violently over-ruling the Dissent of Conscientious and Peaceable People: For if you will rob me once of the Liberty of my Choice, the Use of my Understanding, the Distinction of my Judgment, no Religion comes amiss; indeed it leads to no Religion. It was the Saying of the Old King to the then Prince of *Wales* and our present King; *Make the Religion of your Education the Religion of your Judgment:*[150] which to me is of the Nature of an Appeal from his Education to his Judgment about the Truth of his Religion that he was Educated in: And that Religion which is too tender to be examined is unsound: *Prove all Things, and hold fast that which is good,* lies as an Impeachment against Imposition, deliver'd upon Record by the Apostle *Paul* in the Name of the Holy Ghost. 'Twas the same Apostle that commended the *Bereans* of Old, for that *they diligently searched the Scriptures,* whether those Things, deliver'd by the Apostles concerning the *Messiah,* were true.[151]

Nay Christ himself, to whom all Power was given in Heaven and in Earth, submitted himself to the *Test:* He did not require them to believe him, because he would be believ'd; he refers them to the Witness that God bore to him: *If I bear Witness of my self, my Witness is not true.* He also sends them to the Scriptures; and pleads the Truth of his Authority from that of his *Doctrine and Miracles: If I had not done among them the Works which none other Man did.* And finally challenges them to convince him but of one Sin: *Which of you convinceth me of Sin? and if I say the Truth, why do ye not believe me?*[152]

150. Charles I, *Eikon Basilike* (London, 1649), ch. 27.

151. Acts 17:10–11.

152. John 5:31; 15:24; 8:46.

He offers to Reason the Matter, and submit himself to the Judgment of Truth, and well he might, who was Truth it self.

But an *Imposing Church* bears Witness of her self, and will be both Party and Judge: She requires Assent without Evidence, and Faith without Proof, therefore false: Christian Religion ought to be carried on only by that Way, by which it was introduced, which was *Perswasion; If any Man will be my Disciple, let him take up his Cross and follow me:*[153] And this is the Glory of it, that it does not destroy, but fairly conquer the Understanding.

I am not unacquainted with the Pretences of *Romanists* to *Abnegation,* to a Mortified and Self-denying Life, and I do freely acknowledge, that the Author of the *German Theology, Taulerus, Thomas a Kempis,* and other Mysticks in that Communion, have written Excellent Practical Things, but there is scarcely any Thing of this Violent *Popery* in those Tracts:[154] On the contrary, the very Nature and Tendency of them is Diametrically Opposite to the compulsory Spirit and Constitution of that Church, and all others that practise Imposition in Religion, whatever name they walk under.

And as it is one great Mark of the false Church to pervert the right End of True Doctrine, so hath she excelled in the Abuse of that Excellent Word *Self-denyal:* For she hath translated it from *Life* to *Understanding,* from Morals to Faith; *Subjugare intellectum in Obsequium fidei,* to subject the Understanding to the Obedience of Faith, is the perpetual Burden of their Song, and Conclusion of their Conferences. But what is this *Faith?* That which conquers the World and purifies the Heart? By no Means: But 'tis to believe that the Church of *Rome* is the *True Church,* and the *Pope* Christ's *Vicar,* and the *Visible Head* of that Church.

Thus that *Self-denyal* which relates to our *Wills* and *Affections* in a corrupt State, they apply to the Use of our Understanding about Religion, as if it were the same Thing to deny that which we understand and know to be the Will of God that we should deny, (which is the *Christian Self-denyal*) and to deny that very *Knowledge* and *Understanding* which is God's Gift and our Honour. Whereas *Religion* and *Reason* are so consistent, that *Religion* can neither be

153. Matthew 16:24; Mark 8:34; and Luke 9:23.

154. The *German Theology,* discovered and popularized by Martin Luther (perhaps written by Johannes of Frankfurt [ca. 1380–1440]), has been most recently published in English as *Theologia Germanica,* trans. Susanna Winkworth (London, 1937); Taulerus, or John Tauler (ca. 1300–1361), German Dominican, mystic, and preacher; and Thomas à Kempis (ca. 1379–1471), author of the *Imitation of Christ.*

understood nor maintain'd without *Reason:* For if this must be laid aside, I am so far from being infallibly assured of my Salvation, that I am not capable of any Measure or Distinction of Good from Evil, Truth from Falshood. Why? I have no Understanding, or at least, not the Use of any. All the Disadvantage the *Protestant* is under in this, is that of his greater Modesty, and that he submits his Belief to be tried, which the other refuses, under the Pretence of unaccountable Infallibility; to that Authority Reason Demurs; right Reason I mean; the Reason of the first Nine Verses of the First of *John.* For so *Tertullian,* and some other Ancients as well as Modern Criticks, gives us the Word *Logos;* and the Divine Reason is One in all; that Lamp of God which lights our Candle and enlightens our Darkness, and is the Measure and Test of our Knowledge.

So that whereas some People excuse their Embracing of that Religion by urging the Certainty that is in it, I do say, 'Tis but a *Presumption.* For a Man can never be certain of that, about which he has not the Liberty of Examining, Understanding or Judging: Confident (I confess) he may be; but that's quite another Thing than being certain.

Yet I must never deny, but that every Christian ought to believe as the Church believes, provided the Church be true; but the Question is, Which is that true Church? And when that is answer'd, as a Man may Unlawfully Execute a Lawful Sentence, so he may falsly believe as the True Church believes: For if I believe what she believes, only because she believes it, and not because I am convinced in my Understanding and Conscience of the Truth of what she believes, my Faith is false, though hers be true: I say, it is not true to me, I have no Evidence of it.

What is this *Church,* or *Congregation* rather (as worthy *Tindal* every where translates it)[155] *but a Company of People agreed together in the sincere Profession and Obedience of the Gospel of Christ.* Now look what Inducement they severally had to believe and embrace the Gospel and unite into Fellowship, that we must have to join with them: For as they made not one another an infallible Authority to one another, upon which they first embraced the Gospel, neither are we to ground our Belief thereof upon *their Authority jointly;* but as they had a Rule to believe and commune, so must we have the *same Rule* to embrace their Communion. So that the Church cannot properly be the Rule

155. William Tyndale (ca. 1492–1536), English biblical translator, religious reformer, and martyr. Tyndale's New Testament renders "ecclesia" as "congregation."

of my Faith, who have the same Faith, and Object for my Faith, that she has. I argue thus,

I must believe as the Church believes, that is, I must have the same Faith the Church has; then I must have the same Rule, because the Church can be no more the Rule of that Faith, than she can be that Faith of which some would make her the Rule. If then the Church has Faith, and that Faith have a Rule, and that she can no more be the Rule of her own Faith, than she can be that Faith it self, it follows she cannot be the Rule of the Faith of her Members, because those Members have the same Faith, and make up this Church. For that which is the Rule of the Congregation's Faith in general, must reasonably be the Rule of every Member's Faith that makes up that Congregation, and consequently of every Member that may hereafter adhere to it. So that to talk of believing as the Church believes, to flourish upon that Self-denyal and Humility, which takes all upon Trust, and revile those with the bitterest Invectives that are modestly scrupulous and act the *Bereans* for their Souls (who think that Easiness of Nature and Condescention may be better used, and in this Occasion is ill placed and dangerous) is to put the Knife to the Throat of Protestancy; and, what in them lies, to sacrifice it to implicit Faith and blind Obedience. For it cannot be denied but that the great Foundation of our Protestant Religion is *the Divine Authority of the Scriptures from without us, and the Testimony and Illumination of the Holy Spirit within us.* Upon this Foot the first Reformers stood, and made and maintain'd their *Separation* from *Rome,* and freely offered up their innocent Lives in Confirmation. With good Cause therefore it is the general Consent of all *sound* Protestant Writers, *That neither Traditions, Councils, nor Canons of any visible Church, much less the Edicts of any Civil Sessions or Jurisdiction, but the Scriptures only, interpreted by the Holy Spirit in us, give the final Determination in Matters of Religion, and that only in the Conscience of every Christian to himself.* Which Protestation made by the first publick *Reformers* against the Imperial Edicts of *Charles* the Fifth, imposing Church Traditions without Scripture Authority, gave first Beginning to the Name of *Protestant,* and with that Name hath ever been receiv'd this Doctrine, *which prefers the Divine Authority of the Scripture and Spirit to that of the Church and her Traditions.* And if the Church is not sufficient to be implicitly believed, as we hold it is not, what can there else be named of more Force with us, but the Divine Illumination in the Conscience, or Conscience in the best Sense of the Word; than which, God only is greater? But if any Man shall pretend that the Scripture judges, according to his Conceptions or Conscience, for other Men, and that they must take their Religious Measures by the Line of his Direction; such a Person makes himself greater than either Church, Scripture or Conscience. And, pray, let us consider if in any Thing the Pope is by our Protestant Divinity so justly resembled to Antichrist, as in assuming Infallibility over Conscience and Scripture, to determine as he thinks fit; and so in effect to give the Law to God, Scripture, Magistrates and Conscience. To this Protestants have, without Scruple, apply'd that to the *Thessalonians, Sitting in the Temple of God, exalting himself above all that is called God.*[156]

To check this Exorbitancy; the Apostle *Paul* demands, *Who art thou that judgest another's Servant? to his own Lord he stands or falls?*[157] Which showeth with great Evidence, that Christians of all Sizes, great and small, are but Brethren, and consequently, all Superiority, Lordship and Imposition are excluded: But if there be a Difference, 'tis in this, that, as Christ taught, *he that is greatest is to be Servant to the rest:*[158] But what is more opposite to a Servant than a Lord, and to Service than Injunction and Imposition, and that on Penalties too: Here it is that Christ is Lord and Lawgiver, who is only King of this inward Kingdom of the Soul. And it is to be noted that the Apostle did not write this to a private Brother; or in some special Case, but to the *Church,* as a General and standing Truth, and therefore now as *Authentick* and proper as then. And if this be true, I cannot see how any, or even the most Part of the *Church,* that are still but Brethren to the rest, of one voluntary *Communion* and *Profession,* can with any Shew of Reason impose upon them; and escape the Reproof of this Scripture: For all Societies are to govern themselves, according to their Institution, and first Principles of Union. Where there is Violence upon this Part, *Tyranny and not Order is introduced.* Now since *Perswasion* and *Conviction* began all true *Christian Societies,* they must uphold themselves upon the same free Bottom, *or they turn Antichristian.* I beseech you here, let us examine our selves faithfully, and I am perswaded that something of this will yet appear among some of us, who shew great Reverence to that free Name.

But to make good their unreasonable Conceit of *Church-Authority,* they object *Christ's* Words; *go tell the Church,*[159] that is, say they, *The Church is the Rule and Guide of Faith; whatever the Church agrees upon, and requireth your Assent to and Faith in, that you must necessarily believe and submit to.* But though, as

156. 2 Thessalonians 2:4.
157. Romans 14:4.
158. Matthew 23:11.
159. Matthew 18:15–18.

before, it is confest, in a Sense, we must believe as the true *Church* believes, yet not because she so believes; but for the same Reasons that she her self did and does so believe; in that none can truly believe as she believes; but must do so upon the same Principles and Motives, for which they believed, that first made up that *Christian Church.* To talk of being the *Rule* and *Guide* in Point of Faith, is to contradict Scripture, and justle Christ out of his Office, which is peculiar to him. He is given to his *Church* an *Head,* that is, a *Councellor,* a *Ruler,* a *Judge,* and is called a *Lawgiver,* and says the Apostle, *if any Man have not the Spirit of Christ, he is none of his;* and the *Children of God are led by the Spirit of God.*[160] *And he was Wisdom and Righteousness to the Church Apostolick,* and is so to his own *Church* all the World over. Besides 'tis absurd that the *Church* can be the Rule and Guide of Faith, for as such, *she must be her own Rule and Guide, the Faith of the Members being that of the Church,* which cannot be.

But what then can be the Meaning of Christ's Words, *Go tell the Church?* Very well. I answer, 'tis not about *Faith,* but *Injury,* that *Christ* speaks; and the Place explains it self, which is this: *Moreover, if thy Brother shall* trespass *against* thee, *go and tell him his Fault, between thee and him alone.* Here is *Wrong,* not *Religion; Injustice,* not *Faith or Conscience* concerned; as some would have it, to maintain their Church-Power. *If he shall hear thee, thou hast gained thy Brother, but if he will not hear thee, then take with thee one or two more, that in the Mouth of two or three Witnesses, every Word may be established; and if he shall neglect to hear them,* tell it unto the Church; *but if he neglect to hear the Church, let him be unto thee as an* Heathen Man *and a* Publican. *Verily I say unto you, whatsoever ye shall* bind *on* Earth, *shall be* bound in Heaven, *and whatsoever ye shall* loose *on Earth, shall be* loosed *in Heaven,* &c. The Matter and Manner of which Passage deliver'd by Christ, shews that he intended not to set up *Church Power about Faith and Worship,* unto which all must bow, even without, if not against Conviction. The Words *Trespass* and *Fault,* prove abundantly, that he meant private and personal Injuries, and that not only from the common and undeniable Signification and Use of the Words *Trespass* and *Fault,* but from the Way Christ directs and commands for Accommodation, *viz. That the Person wronged, speaks to him that commits an Injury alone,* if that will not do, *that he take one or two with him;* but no Man can think that if it related to *Faith* and *Worship,* I ought to receive the Judgment of one, or

160. Romans 8:9, 14.

two, or three, for a sufficient Rule. This has not been the Practice, at least not the Principle of the most degenerated *Church* since the primitive Times; for most, if not all, agree, *that nothing lower than the Church can determine about Matters of Faith* and even many with Reason cannot go so far; I mean as to Injunction and Imposition. Yet Christ seems to fix a Blame upon him, that complies not with the Person he has offended, and more if he refuse to give Satisfaction, after one or two have also entreated him; but therefore it cannot relate to Matters of Faith and Scruples of Conscience, but *Personal and Private Injuries.* Which is yet clearer from this Part of Christ's Saying, viz. *That in the Mouth of two or three Witnesses every Word may be established:* Which implies a *Tryal* and *Judicial* Proceeding, as is customary in civil Cases, about personal and private Trespasses; for it were not so proper to speak of Witnesses on any other Account. This is interpreted, beyond Exception, by the Apostle to the *Corinthians,* where he reproves and forbids them *to go to Law one with another before Unbelievers;* arguing thus, *Do you not know that the Saints shall judge the World; and if the World shall be judged by you, are ye unworthy to judge the smallest Matters?*[161] This shews the meaning of *Church* Authority in those Days, and is a natural Exposition upon *Christ's* Words, in Case of Trespass and Refractoriness, *tell the Church.* And 'tis yet the Practice of all Sober, just and quiet People, rather to refer their Controversies to approv'd Men, than to tear one another to Pieces at Law.

But it is worth our Notice, that as any Decision upon an *Arbitration,* obliges only the Parties to set down content with that award, be it loss or gain, which the Arbitrators think equal, as the next best Way to accomodate Differences, and not that such award should alter their first Thoughts and Opinions they had of their Right, or force them to declare they are of the Arbitrators Mind; so is it most unreasonable, where the *Church* is only an *Arbitrator* about personal *Trespasses,* or *Umpire* at most, from thence to imagine a Power to determine and impose Faith, and that upon severe Penalties, as well of this World unto which *Christ's Church* has no Relation, as of the other World. I say, this very Thing, well weighed, breaks all their Fallacies to Pieces, and decides the Business beyond all Contradiction, between those that stand upon the *Spirit within and the Scripture without,* on the one Hand, and such as meerly *rest upon the Traditions of Men and Authority of the Church,* on the other Hand. For, if in an Arbitration, I am not bound to be of the Arbitrators Mind, though

161. 1 Corinthians 6:1–2.

for Peace Sake I submit to their Award, and that the *Church Power,* in this Place controverted, relates only to external and personal Trespasses, Injuries or Injustices, as the Place it self plainly proves, there can be no Sense, Reason or Modesty in the Earth, on the Part of those High Church Men, from hence *to wring and extort the Power of defining, resolving and imposing upon all People, under temporal and eternal Punishment, Articles of Faith and Bonds of Christian Communion.*

I conclude this of the *Church,* with saying, that 'tis not *Identity of Opinion,* but *Justice,* not *Religious Uniformity,* but *Personal Satisfaction* that concerns the Text, and therefore Reason, sober Conscience and good Sense may at any Time lawfully insist upon their Claim, to be heard in all their Scruples or Exceptions, without Disrespect to that excellent Doctrine when rightly understood, *go tell the Church.*

To this, let me add something about this great Word *Church.* Some Men think they are sure enough, if they can but get within the *Pale of the Church,* that have not yet considered what it is. The Word *Church* signifies any Assembly, so the *Greeks* used it: And it is by worthy *Tindal* every where translated *Congregation.* It has a two fold Sense in Scripture. The first and most excellent Sense is that, in which she is called the *Body* and *Bride* of Christ. In this Respect she takes in all Generations, and is made up of the Regenerated, be they in Heaven or on Earth, thus *Ephes.* 1. 22, Ch. 5. 23. to 33. *Col.* 1: 16, 17, 18. *Heb.* 12. 22, 23. *Rev.* 21. 2. Chap. 22. 17. Here Christ only can be Head: This *Church* is washed from all Sin; not a *Spot* nor a *Wrinkle* left: Ill Men have nothing to do with this Church, within whose Pale is only Salvation; nor is this universal and truly *Catholick* Church capable of being convened to be told of Wrongs or Trespasses. The other Use of that Word in Scripture is always referred to particular Assemblies and Places, that is the *Church,* which by Christ's Doctrine, is to be told of Personal Injuries, and whose Determination, for Peace Sake, is to be adher'd and submitted to: They must of Necessity be the adjacent or most contiguous Company of Christian Believers, those to whom the Persons in Difference are by external Society and Communion related: And that such private and distinct Assemblies are called the Church, is apparent from the Acts and Writings of the Apostles: The Church of *Jerusalem, Antioch, Corinth, Ephesus, Smyrna, Pergamos, Thyatira, Sardis, Philadelphia, Laodicea, Rome, Galatia, Thessalonica, Crete,* &c. Peruse these Places, *Acts* 5. 11. and 9. 31. and 11. 22. 26. and 14. 23, 27. *Rom.* 15. 5. 1 *Cor.* 1. 2. and 4. 17. and 14. 4. *Rev.* 2. and 3 Chap. By which it plainly appears that the *universal and visible*

Church; so much bragg'd of, for the *Rule and Judge of Faith,* &c. is an upstart Thing, and like mean Families, or ill got Goods, it uses false Heraldry to give it a Title.

For the Apostolick Times, to which all others must vail, and by whom they must be tried, knew no such Conceit: And the Truth is, it was first started, when the Pride of one Man made him ambitious, and his Power able to bid for *Headship, Empire* and *Soveraignty:* It was then needful to his being *Universal Head,* that he should first have an *Universal Body.* But suppose such a Church there were, 'tis utterly impossible that such a Church could be called together in any one Place; or at any one Time, to be told, or to determine of any Thing: So that yielding the Thing by them desired, 'tis useless and impracticable to the Ends for which they desire it. But alas! who knows not, that loves not to be blind, that the Church among them is the *Priesthood?* The few cunning Men govern the Majority, and intitle their Conceits *the Canons of Christ's Church,* to give them Entrance and Acceptance: And then Humane Power and Force, the Policy and Weapons of this World, must be employed to back their Decrees. And all this comes from the *Ignorance* and *Idleness* of the People, that give the Pride and Industry of the Clergy an Opportunity to effect their Designs upon them. For so mean Spirited are the People, as to take all upon Trust for their Souls, that would not trust or take from an *Arch-Bishop* a brass Shilling or a slit Groat.

'Tis prodigious to think what *Veneration* the *Priesthood* have raised to themselves, by their usurpt Commission of *Apostleship,* their pretended Successions, and their *Clink Clank* of extraordinary Ordination. A *Priest, a God on Earth, a Man that has the Keys of Heaven and Hell; do as he says or be damn'd!* What Power like to this? The Ignorance of the People, of their Title and Pretences, hath prepared them to deliver up themselves into their Hands, like a crafty Usurer, that hedges in the Estate on which he has a Mortgage; and thus they make themselves *over in Fee* to the Clergy, and become their proper *Patrimony,* instead of being their Care, and they the true Ministers or Servants of the People: So that believing as the Church believes, is neither more nor less than rooking Men of their Understandings, or doing as ill Gamesters are wont to do, get by using false Dice. Come, come, it's believing as the *Priesthood* believes, which has made Way for the Offence, wise and good Men have taken against the Clergy in every Age. And did the People examine their Bottom, the Ground of their Religion and Faith, it would not be in the Power of their Leaders to cause them to err. An implicit Veneration to the Clergy begun the Misery. What, doubt my Minister, arraign his Doctrine, put him to the Proof! by no Means: But the Consequence of not doing it, has been the Introduction of much false Doctrine, Superstition and Formality, which gave just Occasion for Schism; for the Word has no Hurt in it's self, and implies only a Separation; which may as well be right as wrong.

But that I may not be taxed with Partiality, or upbraided with Singularity, there are two Men, whose Worth, Good Sense, and true Learning, I will at any Time engage against an entire Convocation of another Judgment, *viz. Jacobus Acontius* and *John Hales* of *Eaton,* that are of the same Mind, who, though they have not writ much, have writ well and much to the Purpose. I will begin with *Jacobus Acontius* at large, and do heartily beseech my Readers to be more than ordinarily intent in reading what I cite of him; their Care and Patience will be requited by his Christian and very acute Sense.[162]

> It remains that we speak of such Causes of the not perceiving that a Change of Doctrine is introduced, as consist in the Persons that are taught. Now they are chiefly two, *Carelesness* and *Ignorance. Carelesness* for the most Part ariseth hence, In that the People *trust too much* to their Pastors; and perswade themselves, that they will not slip into any Error, and that therefore they have small Need to have an Eye over them, but that they are bound rather to embrace whatsoever they shall hold forth, without any curious Examination. Hereunto may be added many other Businesses, whereunto Men addict themselves: For that Saying is of large Extent, *Where Men's Treasure is, there is their Heart,* and that other, *No Man can serve two Masters.*[163] Now, how it may come to pass that after a People hath once had a great Knowledge of Divine Truths, the said Knowledge may as it were vanish away, besides that Cause which hath been even now alledged, we shall in another Place make Discovery of some other Reasons. We shall for the present add only this one, that the People themselves are in a perpetual Kind of Mutation, some daily dying and departing, others succeeding and growing up in their Stead. Whence it comes to pass, That since the Change which is made in every Age is *small,* either the People cannot perceive it, or if they do observe it, yet they esteem it not of such Moment, as to think fit to move any

162. The following extended quotation is from Jacobus Acontius (ca. 1500–1567), *Satans Strategems* (London, 1648), bk. 4.

163. Matthew 6:21–24; Luke 12:34; and Luke 16:13.

Difference thereabout. This Thing also is of very great Force to keep the People from taking Notice of a Change in Doctrine, when Men shall perswade themselves, that they are not able to judge of Matters of Religion, as though *It is, It is not,* and other Words used in Scripture, do not signify the same which they do in common discourse; or as if nothing could be understood without some great Knowledge in the Tongues, and Arts or Sciences, and as if the Power of the Spirit were of no Efficacy without these Helps. Whereby it cometh to pass, that whilst they think they understand not even those Things which in some Sort they do understand, being expressed in most clear and evident Words, they do at length arrive to that Blockishness, that they cannot understand them indeed; so that, though they have before their Eyes a Sentence of Scripture so clear, that nothing can be more evident, yet if they to whose Authority they in all Things subject themselves, shall say any Thing Point blank opposite thereunto, they will give Credit unto them, and imagine themselves not to see that which they see as clear as the Light. And by these Means verily it comes to pass, that when the Doctrine of Religion is corrupted, the Mutation is not discover'd. Furthermore, when the Doctrine is once begun to be changed, it must needs be, that out of one Error another should spring and propagate infinitely; and God, for Just Reasons of his own, blinding them, Men bring upon themselves so great Darkness, and slip into such foul Errors, that if God of his Mercy open a Man's Eyes, and let him see those Errors he lives in, he can scarcely believe himself, or be perswaded that he was ever envelop'd with such blind Errors. Which thing is as true, and as well to be seen in Men of greatest Learning and Experience. If thou shalt thoroughly peruse the Writings of some of the School-men (as they call them) thou shalt in some Places meet with so much Acuteness, as will make thee admire: Thou shalt see them oftentimes cleave a fine Thread into many Parts, and accurately Anatomise a Flea, and a little after fall so foully, and avouch such Absurdities, that thou can'st not sufficiently stand amazed; wherefore we must obey that Advice of the Poet;

Principiis obsta, sero medicina paratur,
Cum mala per longas invaluere moras,

Resist betimes; that Med'cine stays too long,
Which comes when Age has made the Grief too strong.

Now there is Need of a double Caution, *viz.* That there be no Change made in the Doctrine, when it is pure: And if any Change be made, that there be notice taken of it. Now look what change is made in this Kind, all the Blame is laid upon those whose Office it is to instruct the People: For though themselves are the Authors of the Change, yet will the People impute it to the Ministers Sleepiness, and want of Care at least. It concerns therefore the Pastors and Teachers to be Eagle-eyed, and to be very well acquainted with those Causes whereby the Change of Doctrine becomes undiscover'd, and to have them at their Fingers Ends, and to be wary, that on no Hand they may miscarry. Now it will be an excellent Caution for the keeping of Doctrine pure, if they shall avoid all curious and vain Controversies: If they shall set before their Eyes the Scope and End of all Religious Doctrines, and likewise a Series or Catalogue of all such Things as make to the Attainment of that End (of which we formerly spake); if they shall affect, not only the Matter it self, but also, the Words and Phrases which the Holy Ghost in Scripture makes Use of, and exceedingly suspect all different Forms of Speaking. Not that I would have them speak nothing but *Hebraisms;* for so their Language would not be plain nor intelligible: but I wish that they would shun all such Expressions, as have been invented by overnice Disputants, beyond what was necessary to express the Sense of the *Hebrew* and *Greek,* and all those Tenets which Men by their own Wits do collect and infer from the Scriptures. Now of what Concernment this will be, we may gather by this Instance: The *Papists* think it one and the same Thing to say, *The Church cannot Err;* and to say in the Words of our Lord, *Wheresoever two or three shall be gathered together in my Name, there will I be in the midst of them.*[164] Yet is the Difference very great, which may thus appear, forasmuch as in Case any one shall conceive the Church to be the Pope, Cardinals, and Bishops anointed by the Pope; he hearing the aforesaid Sentence, will judge, that whatsoever they shall decree, ought to be of Force. But if he shall rather mind the Words of our Lord, and shall consider that those Kind of Men do regard nothing but their own Commodity, Wealth and Dominion; he will be so far from so understanding them, that peradventure not being able to allow the Deeds and Practices of these Men, he will come to hope from those

164. Matthew 18:20.

Words, That if himself, with some other good Men, loving God with their whole Heart, shall come together, and unanimously implore the Assistance of God, they shall be better able to determine what it is that ought to be believ'd and practised for the Attainment of Salvation, than if they should persist to put their Confidence in such Pastors. Now this Rule, that the Words of the Scripture ought to be used rather than any other, is then especially to be observ'd, when any Thing is delivered as a certain and tryed Truth, or as a Rule of Faith or Life, or out of which any other Thing is to be inferred. For in Expositions and Explanations, as there is need happily of greater Liberty, so is there less Danger if it be taken. For, when as the Word of God, and the Exposition thereof, are at one and the same Time both together in View as it were, there no Man can be ignorant, that the Exposition *is the Word of Man,* so that *he may reject it,* in case it seem impertinent. And look, by what Means a Man may hinder the Doctrine of Religion from being changed, by the selfsame he may find whether it be changed or no. Now every Man ought to compare the Doctrine of that Age wherein he lives, with no other Doctrine than that which was out of Question spotless, which is the Doctrine of the Apostles. Wherefore, notwithstanding that in our Age the Gospel is as it were revived, yet ought not any Man thus to think, that he ought to Examine whether the Gospel hath not lost any of that Purity whereunto it had at this Time arrived; he ought rather to look again and again, whether some Corruption do not yet remain, whether it be not in some Part as yet not sufficiently restored to its ancient Purity and Lustre; and confidently perswade himself, That he cannot be (that I may so speak) sufficiently superstitious in rejecting every Word which is not in the Scriptures. For as much as Man will ever be more wise and wary than the Holy Spirit, and can very hardly forbear to mingle somewhat from his own Head: So that whatever comes from Man, can never be sufficiently suspected. And because a Thing will be so much the better preserv'd, by how much the Greater is the Number of those that keep it; the People ought often to be put in Mind, that both the Reading of the Scriptures and the *Care of Religion belongs not to the Pastors of the Church only;* but that every one that would be sav'd ought to make diligent Search, whether any Corruption be already, or is for the future like to be introduc'd; and this to do no less carefully, than if he were perswaded that all beside himself were asleep: And whatsoever is wont to take the common People off from such Studies, Care must be taken that that Thing be wholly taken away. Concerning which Matter, we shall more conveniently discourse anon.

Now, Forasmuch as the Profit will be small, if some private Man shall observe that an Error is introduc'd, unless he discover the said Error, and lay it open: there must of Necessity be some Way how this may conveniently be done. Now there cannot be a more fitting Way, than that which the Apostle propounds to the *Corinthians. Let two or three Prophets speak, and let the rest judge; and if any thing be revealed to him that sits by, let the former be silent. For ye may all prophecy one by one, that all may learn, and all may be exhorted.*[165] If some one Person shall always speak in the Church, and no Man at any Time may contradict him, it will be a very strange Thing, if that one Man be not puffed up, if he do not fall into such a Conceit of himself, as to think that he is the only Man, that he only hath Understanding, he alone is wise: That all the rest are a Company of Brute Animals as it were, who ought to depend only upon him, and to do nothing but learn of him. And if any Man shall think, that himself likewise hath some Ability to teach, he will account that Man an heinous Offender. But what says the Apostle to this? *Did the Word of God come from you? or came it unto you only? If any seem to be a Prophet, or Spiritual; let him acknowledge what I write unto you to be the Commands of the Lord. But if any one be ignorant, let him be ignorant. Wherefore Brethren, labour that ye may Prophecy, and forbid not to speak with Tongues, let all Things be done decently and in order.*[166] It is exceedingly to be lamented, that this Custom, and the Practise of this Command of the Lord, is not again restored into the Churches, and brought into Use. But some Men may say, Such is the Rashness of this Age of ours, such the Boldness, such the Impudence, that if it were allowed to every one to speak in the Congregation, there will be no End of Brawls and Contention. Why so? Is a Man another Kind of Creature now, than what he was of Old? Thou wilt say, He is: For Mankind hath continually degenerated, grown worse and worse, and seems now to have attained the Top of Corruption. Is it so indeed? But, suppose it to be so; Thou that art the Teacher of the People, art not thou also thy self made of the

165. 1 Corinthians 14:29–31.
166. 1 Corinthians 14:36–39.

same Mold? Art not thou born in the same Age? Inasmuch as this Ordinance principally was intended to keep Pastors within the Bounds of Modesty that they may understand that they are not the Authors of the Word of God, that they have not alone received the Spirit: By how much the more Mankind hath degenerated, by so much the greater Need is there thereof; for that there is now more Rashness, Arrogance, Pride, than of Old; this is true, as well of the Pastors and Teachers, as of the rest of the People. Art thou a Prophet? Hast thou any Portion of the Spirit? If thou hast not, so unfitting it is, that thou alone should'st speak in the Congregation, that there will hardly be found any that deserves rather to be silenc'd, than thy self. But if thou art a Prophet, if thou hast the Spirit, mark what the Apostle says, *Acknowledge* (quoth he) *that those Things which I write, are the Commandments of the Lord.* Go to then, On the one Side we have the Judgment of our Lord, willing that Prophecy (for this is a Word that we are obliged to use) should be common to all, and that not for the Destruction, but the Salvation of the Church: On the other Side, we have thy Judgment, who fearest least that may breed Contention and Confusion; whose Judgment now ought we rather to stand to? If thou shalt conceive we must stand to thine, consider what thou assumest unto thy self, and what will become of thy Modesty. Our Lord, it should seem, understood not what a Kind of Creature Man was; he wanted thy Wisdom belike, to admonish him of the Danger; or haply he thought not upon that Corruption which should befal Mankind, whereby such a Liberty might prove unprofitable. But *Paul* answers thee, *That God is not the Author of Contention, but of Peace:*[167] Who well knowing what might move Contentions, what begat Peace, and not loving nor willing to have Contention, but Peace, willed that this Liberty of Prophecy should be in the Church. What can'st thou say to the contrary? What hast thou to object against God himself, wilt thou accuse him of Indiscretion? No Man hath so wicked a Tongue, as to dare to do it, Yet if thou shalt diligently search thine Heart, thou shalt find there a certain Disposition ready to contend even with God himself: Which Motion of thy Heart, must by no Means be hearken'd unto, but sharply repressed, and wholly subjected to the Spirit of God. It may seem peradventure an absurd Thing, that after some very learned Person hath

167. 1 Corinthians 14:33.

spoken, some contemptible Person shall be allow'd to contradict him. Can such a Person so do without great Rashness and Temerity? Were I to speak according to the Judgment of Man, verily I could not deny it. But if we be really perswaded, that the Knowledge of Matters Divine, ought not to be attributed to our *Watchings, Studies, Wits,* but to *God* and to his *Spirit,* wherewith he can in a Moment endue the simplest Person in the World, and that with no more Labour or Difficulty than if he were to give it to one that had spent *Nestor*'s Age in Study.[168] What Reason is there for me to judge that this Man does rashly and unadvisedly, if he shall arise and contradict? Is not the Spirit able to reveal somewhat to him, which he hath hidden from thee? Now, if the Spirit have revealed somewhat to him, and to that End revealed it that he might contradict, that by his Means the Thing may be revealed to the Church; shall I say that he hath done rashly in obeying the Holy Ghost? And if thou think otherwise, verily thou art not perswaded that the Spirit is the Author and Teacher of this Knowledge, but that all the Praise thereof is due to Studies, Watchings, and the Wits of Men. And if this be thy Judgment, I tell thee again, that thou art not only unworthy to be sole Speaker, but worthy rather to be the only Person not permitted to speak in the Congregation.

And that thou mayst the better understand, that the most unlearned ought to be allowed to speak, consider, God will have himself to be acknowledged the Author of his own Gifts: He will not have his Praise attributed unto our Studies or Wits, but unto himself. But if the Man that hath spent all his Life in Study, speak wisely, it is not attributed to God, but to Study: In Word, perhaps, it may be attributed to God, yet not without a vehement Reluctancy of our Judgment; and this is that which, I say, God will not abide. But if so be thou shalt hear a wise Word come out of the Mouth of some unlearned Person, thou must needs, whether thou wilt or no, acknowledge God to be the Author thereof. So, when God was minded to give unto *Israel* a Victory against the *Midianites,* under the Conduct of *Gideon;* and *Gideon* had gathered together Thirty Thousand Men, lest the *Israelites* should boast that they had gotten the Victory by their own Strength, and not by the Assistance of God, (which might have been conceived, if *Gideon* had fought with so numerous an

168. For Nestor, see Homer, *Iliad,* bk. 1.

Army) he would not suffer him to have above Three Hundred, that it might appear that he was the Cause of the Victory, and not the Number or Valour of those that fought.[169] Now, besides the Glory of God, hereby great Profit does accrue to the Church, For if the People shall see now one Man, now another, endued with the Spirit, beyond all Expectation; many will thereby be encouraged to hope for the same Gift, if they shall ask it: many will learn and profit; and it will thereby come to pass, that when Occasion shall be to choose a Minister, the Church shall not need to call strange and unknown Persons to that Office, but she may have of her own such as are fit to be chosen; Men whose Conversation and Manners are sufficiently known. And when the Number of such as are able to prophecy, shall be great, the Church will not be forced to use such Pastors as from their very Childhood have proposed to themselves such Office as the Reward of their Studies; and addicted themselves to the Study of Scripture and Religion, no otherwise then they would have done to some Trade, whereby they meant in Time to get their Living: So that a Man can expect but very few of them to prove other than Mercenary or Hireling Pastors.

Now, that it was the Custom of the *Jewish* Church, that all might thus Prophesie, we may hence conjecture, in that it is upon Record, *Luke* 4, how our Lord, *upon the Sabbath-day, according to the Custom, came into the Synagogue, took a Book and expounded a place of* Esay; and how, *being twelve Years of Age, he sate at* Jerusalem *in the Temple among the Doctors, and did Dispute.* For he could not so do by virtue of any ordinary Office, forasmuch as his Age was uncapable, neither did the Doctors know who he was. Yea rather, our Lord in so doing must needs make use of the Power which was granted to every one to speak. It remained in the *Christians* Congregations until the Times of *Constantine* at the least. Forasmuch as we have these Words of *Eusebius,* the Writer of Church Affairs, to that Effect: *If any Man inspired by the Grace of God, should speak unto the People, They all with great Silence, fixing their Eyes upon him, gave such Attention, as if he had brought them some Errand from Heaven.* So great was the Reverence of the Hearers, such order was seen among the Ministers. One after another, another after him. Neither were there only two or three that prophesied, according to what the

169. Judges 6–7.

Apostle said, but to all was given to speak; so that the Wish of *Moses* seems rather to have been fulfilled in them, when he said, *Would God all the People might Prophecy.*[170] There was no Spleen, no Envy, the Gifts of God were dispensed, every one according to his Ability, contributing his Assistance for the Confirmation of the Church: And all was done with Love, in such sort, That they strove mutually to honour each other, and every one to prefer another before himself. But to the End this common Prophecying may be profitable to the Church, we must diligently mark what the Apostle advises. For a sure Thing it is, that the Pride of Man is so great, that whatever hath once fallen from him, he will by any Means have it stand for a Truth; neither can he suffer that any Man should infringe the same. So that if he might be permitted to judge, that last spake, it will be a Miracle if a Man in his Life Time should see any one give way to him that contradicts him: What is *Paul*'s Advice therefore in this Case? *Let two or three Prophets speak, and let the rest judge.* He will not therefore have the same Persons to be Parties and Judges. And he adds a little after, *And the Spirit of the Prophets, is subject to the Prophets; for God is not the Author of Dissension, but of Peace.*[171] So that as soon as any Man hath spoken his own Mind, he ought to rest himself satisfied with the Judgment of the rest, and not obstinately to make no End of contending: If this be not done, a sure Thing it is; there will be no End of Strife. But what if any Man will not be content to submit to the Judgment of the rest: Verily I would avouch, that being sharply admonished, that he disturb not the Congregation, and that he go not against the Command of the Apostle, or rather of our Lord, commanding the Spirits of the Prophets to be subject to the Prophets, he ought to be cast out of the Society, though he should hold the prime Place in the Congregation. The People likewise must frequently be admonished, that Liberty for any one to speak in the Congregation, is not therefore granted by the Apostle, to the end every one should speak what comes to his Tongue's End, as if he were in a Market; but whereas he gives Liberty to him to speak to whom any Thing is revealed, he would have all Rashness and Impudence to be laid aside. He that reverences not the Church of God, let that Man know, he despiseth the Spirit of God, who

170. Numbers 11:26–29.

171. 1 Corinthians 14:29, 33.

> is President there; and shall be sure not to escape unpunished. Before a Man propounds any Thing to the Church, he ought to consider again and again, how sure a Manifestation he hath of that Thing, and whatever the Matter be, let him be sure not to forget a sober, modest, bashful Behaviour, without which Virtues, doubtless no good can be effected. But here we must attentively consider, both how far a Man ought to submit to the Judgment of the Congregation, and who may deservedly be accounted a Troubler of the Church. Verily, I conceive a Man ought so far to give way, as that after I have alledged what I had to say for my Opinion, if yet the rest shall not allow of my Judgment, I ought to give over defending of it, and cease to be troublesome to the Congregation concerning the same: But I ought not to be compelled to confess that I have erred, nor to deprecate any fault, while I do not yet understand that I have erred, for so I should sin against God. He therefore is a Troubler of the Church, that will not, so far as we have expressed, submit to the Judgment of the Church, but goeth on to be troublesome; but especially that Man who would exact of another that which he ought not to do; *viz.* to recant, being not perswaded that he is in an Error. But those Men are commonly reputed Troublers of the Church, who refuse to ratifie whatever shall any Ways fall out of the Pastors Mouths. Again, in this Place it may reasonably be demanded, whether, when that a Matter hath been once or twice debated, and some Man, knowing the Judgment of the Congregation, would again reduce it into Controversie, he ought to be heard, or enjoyned Silence, and take the Matter for determined: But of this we shall in another Place more conveniently dispute. That which remains therefore, is, that we wrestle with God, by daily Prayers, to grant that we may have the Use of this so soveraign and saving Liberty, so profitable to the Church, and that thereby we may reap Abundance of Fruit. And that he would, to that end, break and tame our Spirits with his Spirit, and render them mild and gentle: and not suffer, what he hath ordained for the Confirmation and Establishment of his Church, to be, by the Stubbornness and Perversness of our Wits and Minds, turned to the Mischief and Destruction thereof.

With much more to the same Purpose, too large to be here inserted.

What I have cited, makes an Apology, for doing so, needless; His whole Book is a most accurate Account of Satan's Stratagems, to cause and keep up

Divisions among *Christians;* deserving a first Place with the most Christian Writers since the Apostolical Times. He was an *Italian,* of excellent Natural and Supernatural Endowments, banisht about *Luther*'s Time for the Gospel.

Let us now inform our selves of the Judgment of that great Man of our own Country *J. Hales* of *Eaton* in his Treatise of the Power of the Keys.[172] Upon the Matter in hand, viz.

> To your second Query, *Whether the Keys were confined to the Apostles only?* The answer is in no case hard to give, it may perchance, in some case, be dangerous; *for there is a Generation of Men in the World, the* Clergy *they call them, who impropriate the Keys unto themselves, and would be very angry to understand, that others from themselves should claim a right unto them.* To your Question then, no doubt but originally none received the Keys from the Mouth of our Saviour, but the Apostles only; none did or ever could manage them with that Authority and Splendor, as the Apostles did, who were, above all most amply furnished with all Things fitting so great a Work. For whereas you seem to intimate, that the preaching Mission was communicated to others, as the seventy two Disciples, as well as the Apostles, you do but mistake your self, if you conceive that the Keys of the Gospel were any way committed to them: For concerning the Mystery of Jesus Christ, and him crucified for the Sins of the World (wherein, indeed, the opening the Kingdom of Heaven did consist) They received it not, they knew it not. To be the prime Reporters of this, was an Honour imparted only to the Apostles: Yet were they not so imparted, as that they should be confin'd to them. *Every one* that heard and received the Light of the saving Doctrine from them, *so far forth as he had understanding in the Ways of Life, had now the Keys of the Kingdom of Heaven committed to his Power, both for his own and others use. Every one, of what State or Condition soever, that hath any occasion offered him, to serve another in the Ways of Life,* Clergy, or Lay, Male or Female, *whatever he be, hath these Keys, not only for himself, but for the Benefit of others.* For if Natural Goodness teach every Man, *Lumen de Lumine, Erranti comiter monstrare viam,* &c.[173]

172. John Hales, *Treatise of the keys,* in his *Several Tracts, by the Ever Memorable Mr. John Hales of Eaton Coll.* (London, 1677), pp. 170–74.

173. Light from light, shows the way, like a companion, to one going astray.

> then how much more doth Christian Goodness require of every one, to his Ability, to be a Light to those who sit in Darkness, and direct their steps, who most dangerously mistake their Way? *To save a Soul, every Man is a Priest.* To whom I pray you, is that said in *Leviticus, Thou shalt not see thy Brother Sin, but shalt reprove, and save thy Brother?*[174] And if the Law binds a Man, when he saw his Enemies Cattel to stray, to put them in their Way; How much more doth it oblige him to do the like for the Man himself? See you not how the whole World conspires with me in the same Opinion? Doth not every Father teach his Son, every Master his Servant; every Man his Friend? How many of the Laity in this Age, and from time to time in all Ages, have by writing for the publick good, propagated the Gospel of Christ, as if some secret Instinct of Nature had put into Men's Minds thus to do, *&c.*

To this let me add his Sense of the Force of the Fathers Authority in the Decision of Controversies, and how far the Ancients, whether Fathers or Councils, ought to be interested in the Debates of these Times, which may not be improper to the present subject, because not a few build upon their Bottom, the Clergy to be sure, that pretend to direct the rest.[175]

> You shall find (says he) that all *Schisms* have crept into the Church by one of these three Ways; either upon Matter of Fact, or Matter of Opinion, or Point of Ambition. For the first; I call that Matter of Fact, when something is required to be done by us, which either we know or strongly suspect to be unlawful; so the first notable *Schism,* of which we read, in the Church, contained in it Matter of Fact; For it being, upon *Error,* taken for necessary that an *Easter* must be kept; and upon worse than Error, if I may so speak, (for it was no less than a Point of *Judaism,* forced upon the Church upon worse than Error, I say) thought further necessary, that the ground for the Time of our keeping that Feast, must be the Rule left by *Moses* to the *Jews;* there arose a stout Question, *Whether we were to Celebrate with the* Jews, *on the fourteenth Moon, or the* Sunday *following?* This Matter, though most unnecessary, most vain, yet caused as great a Combustion, as ever was in the Church, The

174. Leviticus 19:17.

175. The following quotation is taken from Hales, *Tract concerning schisme,* pp. 5–6.

West separating and refusing Communion with the East, for many Years together.[176] In this Fantastical Hurry, I cannot see, but all the World were Schismaticks: Neither can any Thing excuse them from that Imputation; excepting only this, that we charitably suppose that all Parties, out of Conscience, did what they did.

A Thing which befel them through the *Ignorance of their Guides, for I will not say their Malice, and that through the just Judgment of God, because through Sloth and Blind Obedience, Men examined not the Things which they were taught, but like Beasts of Burden, patiently couched down, and indifferently underwent whatsoever their Superiors laid upon them.* By the Way, by this you may plainly see the Danger of our Appeal unto Antiquity, for Resolution in Controverted Points of Faith, and how small Relief we are to expect from thence. *For if the Discretion of the chiefest Guides and Directors of the Church, did in a Point so trivial, so inconsiderable, so mainly fail them, as not to see the Truth in a Subject, wherein it is the greatest Marvel how they could avoid the Sight of it; can we, without Imputation of extream Grosness and Folly, think so Poor Spirited Persons, competent Judges of the Questions now on Foot, betwixt the Churches?* Pardon me! I know not what Temptation drew that Note from me.

How these Two worthy Men will come off, I can't tell: They have ventured fairly, and yet I think their Case not hazardous at all. You have them in three Points plain. First, *That relying upon the Clergy as Guardians of Truth to the People, and the People's not examining the Truth of Things from them, is not Apostolical, but Apostatical.* Secondly, *That no Councils or Fathers ought to be the Rule or Judge of our Faith.* Thirdly, *That to Save Souls, every Man is a Priest:* That is, the People are interested in the Christian Ministry, which is not tied to Times, Places, Persons and Orders, as under the Law; but free to all that have obtained Mercy and Grace from God. And therefore *Peter* calls the Believers, 1 *Pet.* ii. 5, 9. an Holy and Royal Priesthood. So that every Believer is a Priest to himself under the Gospel. But all this I have mentioned with design, if it be possible, to beat Men off that superstitious and dangerous Veneration they carry to the Names of *Church, Priesthood,* and *Fathers;* as if they were to be saved by them, and not by Christ, *who is the Only Head and Saviour*

176. On the Easter dispute, see ch. 5, p. 150, n. 23.

of the True Church, and God over all, Blessed for ever. And truly, when I consider the wide Dependence some People have upon the Church, whilst they know not what She is, *and make it a Principle not to enquire,* I am amaz'd, and often struck with Horror, to observe with what Confidence they expose their Souls. This Principle it is, and not *Enquiry,* that makes Men careless and unactive about their own Salvation. But let none deceive themselves, *as they Sow they shall Reap,* Gal. vi. 5. 7. *Every one must bear his own Burden.* 'Tis not to be saved to be within the Pale of any Visible Church in the World. That is putting an Eternal Cheat upon our selves. *Ill Things are ill Things, within or without the Pale:* That matters not; and as Sin can't be Christened, nor Impiety reconciled to Christianity by any Arts of Men, *So the Wages of Sin will be Death, Rom.* vi. 23. *Eternal Death.* To be therefore of the Church of which *Christ is Head, the Redeemed, Regenerated Church of Christ,* is quite another Thing, than to be of any Visible Society whatever; for in all such Communions there are, but too many, that have no True Title to Christianity. If then that *Immaculate Church, of which Christ is Head,* be made up only of *Holy and Regenerated Souls* throughout the Societies of *Christians,* this will administer but little Comfort to those, that presume upon their being within the Pale of the Visible Church, that are without the Pale of Virtue and Holiness.

But to proceed to those Scriptures that are irreconcileable to *implicit Faith and Blind Obedience: He that believeth, hath the Witness in himself,* 1 John v. 10. This General Rule respects no Persons: It is the Result of the *Holy Ghost* to all Believers. *Such have no Need to go to* Rome, *nor* Winifred's *Well,*[177] *to the Shrines of Saints, the Priests, nor the Church, for a Proof of their Faith.* They have an Evidence nearer Home: They have the Witness of their Faith, and the Reason of their Hope in themselves.

It is true, this is a Private Judge; but (as it happens) 'tis one of the *Holy Ghost's* setting up; of all Things, I confess, most destructive to *Papacy,* no Doubt; for there is a Judge in every Man, that sincerely believes, to whom he must stand and fall in this and the other World. *For* (saith the Apostle) *If our Heart condemn us, God is greater than our Heart, and knoweth all Things: Beloved, if our Heart condemn us not, then have we Confidence towards God.*

177. A place of pilgrimage to St. Winefride (ca. 600–660), the Welsh saint. A well purportedly sprang up on the site of her murder by Caradog (whose advances she had spurned), and the waters were said to have healing properties. (In another version of the tale, Winefride is raised to life and goes on to become a nun.)

1 John iii. 20, 21. That is, *the Witness in our selves discharges us. The Spirit beareth Witness with our Spirits, that we are the Children of God,* Rom. viii. 16. and Sons of the True Church: Not She that hath fatted her self with the Flesh of Saints, and died her Garments in the *Blood of Martyrs,* who hath Merchandized in the Souls of Men: But of that Church which is Crowned with Stars, and Cloathed with the Sun, and has the Moon under her Feet. A Church of Light and Knowledge, of Understanding and Truth, and not of implicit Faith and blind Obedience: One that tramples upon all Sublunary Glory, and not she that makes her Pretences to Religion a Decoy to catch the Empire of the World.

Of like Tendency is that Notable Passage of the Apostle *Paul* to the *Corinthians,* 2 Cor. xiii. v. *Examine your selves, whether ye be in the Faith; prove your own selves: Know ye not your own selves, how that* Jesus Christ *is in you, except ye be Reprobates?* Here is not a Word of the Pope, nor an External Judge; no Humane Inquisition or Authority. *Examine your selves, whether ye be in the Faith? Prove your own selves:* But which Way shall we do this? By Christ, who is the *Great Light,* that shines in our Hearts, to give us the Knowledge of God and our selves: *He that believes in him, has the Witness in himself; he is no Reprobate; his Heart condemns him not.*

To which I will add another Passage to the same Purpose, in his Epistle to the *Galatians,* Gal. vi. 4, 5. *But let every Man prove his own Work, then shall he have Rejoycing in himself alone, and not in another: For every Man shall bear his own Burden.* Here every Man is enjoyned to turn *Inquisitor* upon himself; and the Reason rendred shews the Justice of the Thing; *because my Rejoycing must be in my self alone, and not in another. I stand and fall to no Man; such as I Sow, I must Reap at the Hand of God,* if *Paul* say true. Men's Pardons are Vain, and their Indulgences Fictious; *For every Man shall bear his own Burden in that Great Day of the Lord.* It cannot therefore be Reasonably thought that another Man should have the keeping of my Understanding at my Eternal Cost and Charge, or that I must entirely depend upon the Judgment of a Man or Men, who erring, (and thereby causing me to err) cannot be Damned for me, but I must pay their Reckoning at the Hazard of my own Damnation.

I am not unacquainted with the great Objection that is made by *Roman Catholicks,* and some *Protestants* too, *High Church-Men* perhaps, *That Love the Treason, but hate the Traytor; That like this Part of Popery, but hate the Pope,* viz. *There are Doubts in Scripture, even about the most* important Points of Faith: *Some Body must guide the Weak; there must be some One Ultimate,*

External, and Visible Judge to appeal to, who must determine and conclude all Persons as to their Doubts and Apprehensions concerning the Interpretation of Scripture; *otherwise,* So many Men, so many Minds; *the* Church *would be filled with Controversie and Confusion.*

I Answer, That the Scriptures are made more doubtful than they are, by such as would fain preserve to themselves the Umpirage and Judgship of their Meaning. I deny it in Point of Fact, that Man's Duty is not most plainly exprest in all that concerns Eternal Salvation. But 'tis very strange, that when God intends nothing more by the Scriptures, than to reach the Capacities of Men, as to Things on which their Eternal Salvation depends, that no Book, if such Men say true, should be so obscure, or subject to so many various, nay, contradictory Constructions. Name me one Author, *Heathen, Jew,* or *Christian,* that ever wrote with that Obscurity and seeming Inconsistency, which some gladly pretend to find in the *Holy Scripture,* that they might have the use and keeping of them from the *Vulgar,* and make their own Ends by it. Is then every Body's Book to be understood but God's? Was that Writ not to be understood? In short, One of these Two Things must be True; *Either that God intended not to be understood, or to be understood, in what he commanded to be written.* If he resolved *Not to be understood,* it had been better there had been nothing writ; for then there had been no Doubts about the Meaning of it; but if it was his Purpose *To be understood of Men,* it must be supposed, that what he caused to be written, was plain enough for Men to understand, or he mist his own Aim and End, and writ it to no Purpose, which were too low and absurd a Thought of the Infinite Goodness and Wisdom.

If it should be told me, *That it is not denied but that the Scriptures may be understood by some Body, but not by every Body, for that the Great, Visible Judge must needs understand them, because it belongs to his Office to resolve those Doubts, and determine those Controversies that may arise about understanding them, but not every one that reads them.*

Answ. I must also say, that this is not True in Fact: For it is ridiculous to imagine, that *Luke* did not make *Theophilus* his own Judge in the reading of what he writ to him,[178] or that the Apostles in writing to the several Churches, as *Rome, Corinth, Ephesus,* &c. to whom they directed their Epistles, did not intend that they should understand what they writ, or that they erected any such Officer in the Church, as an Expounder of their Epistles to the Assem-

178. See Luke 1:3; and Acts 1:1.

bly to be necessarily believed. For we know in those Days, *the People made the Church,* they were the *χληρός* the *Clergy,* however it came about that it be now engrossed into fewer Hands, as you may see in the *Greek* of *Peter,* 1 Pet.v.4. *Μηδ' ὡς κατακυριεύοντες τῶν κλήρων,* which *κλήρων,* is Translated *Heritage* in all our Bibles. But this is as if the *Priests* only were the *Lord's Heritage;* which can't be, for a Reason obvious to all, namely, that they have long reign'd as Lords over God's Heritage, or Clergy, forbid expresly by *Peter,* therefore not the Heritage and Clergy over which they so Rule like Lords; by no Means. I will say no more but this, 'tis no Convincing Proof to me of their Humility. But to shut up this Argument about the Difficulty of Understanding the Scripture, and pretended Necessity of a Visible Judge; I say, *Whatsoever may be spoken, may be written;* or thus; *Whatsoever a Visible Judge can now say, the Holy Penmen by God's Direction might have written;* and what an Omniscient and Omnipotent God did know, and could do for Man's Salvation, an Omnibenevolent God, that tells us, *He delights not in the Death of one Soul, but rather that he should be saved,* would certainly have done for Man. And because God is as *Omnibenevolent,* as *Omniscient* and *Omnipotent,* we must conclude he has done it; and 'tis great Presumption, and a mean Shelter to Ignorance or Ambition, to raise a Credit to Human Devices, by beating down the True Value of the Scriptures.

They are dark; What follows? *They must not be read?* What follows then? *Why then such Teachers may do as they list with the People.* But did the *Pharisees,* with their broad Phylacteries, know God's Mind better than the Prophets?[179] Or could they deliver it clearer? No such Matter: It is by the same strange Figure, that the School-Men *know the Mind of Christ better than the Apostles, and that the Council of* Trent *can declare Faith more clearly than the Holy Ghost in the Scripture hath done; and yet this is the* English *of their Doctrine, that hold to us those* Lights *to read the Scripture by; and that would have us search their Canons and Decrees, to find out the Mind of the Holy Ghost in Scripture.*

The Confusions that are pretended to follow such an Enquiry, are but the wretched Arts of Selfish Men, as much as in them lies, to keep *Light and Truth out of the World.* When the Net was cast into the Sea, there came some Good, some Bad Fish; it was not the *Fisher's Fault they were no better.* Enquiry is not to be blamed for the ill Use weak, or worse Men, make of it. The *Bereans*

179. See Matthew 23:5.

might not all believe, though they might all search;[180] for Men don't enquire with equal Wisdom, Love, and good Desire: *Some seek and find not, some ask and receive not;* James iv.3. therefore must none ask or seek after that which is Good? Or because some ask or seek amiss, will it follow that the Thing it self is naught? If Superstition, Error, Idolatry, and Spiritual Tyranny be detected, and Truth discover'd, will it not more than make amends for all that Weakness and Folly some Men have brought forth by the Liberty of such an Enquiry? The Enemies of *Light* may be as Rhetorical as they please upon the Excess or Presumption of some, Bolder than Wise, and more Zealous than Knowing, but if they had nothing to lose by the Discovery, they would never be the Enemies of a *Christian Search.* It is to be fear'd, such get that Obedience and Subjection by a blind Devotion, which no Man could yield them upon better Information; And is it Reasonable that Men of that Stamp, should secure their Empire by the Ignorance of the People? Ignorance ought to be the Mother of Devotion with none but those that cannot be Devout upon better Terms: It is the Glory of a Man that he is Religious upon Reason, and that his Duty and (*Lev.* 22. 18, 29.) Sacrifice, are not Blind or forc'd, but Free and Reasonable. Truth upon Knowledge, though vext with Schism, Wise and Good Men will chuse before ignorant Religion, and all it's Superstitious Effects with Uniformity. Enough of this.

But this Notion *Of an Infallible Visible Judge, is as False in Reason as in Fact.* For first, it takes away the Use of every Man's Reason, and it is a *Contradiction to have any, unless he were such an Interpreter, and such a Judge, as would conclude us by Conviction, and not by Authority: That would be the most Welcome Person in the World.* But to over-rule my own Sight, to give the Lye to my own Understanding, say, *Black is White,* and that *Two and Three make Ten;* thus *Subjugare intellectum in Obsequium fidei;* to yield my Understanding to such an In-evident Way of Faith, nay, which is worse, to believe a Lye, for so it is to them, to whom the Thing to be believed, appears Untrue, is most Unreasonable.

If we must be *Led,* it had been easier for us to have been born Blind, we might then have better follow'd the *Dog and the Bell;* for we could not mend our selves; *but to See, and to be Led; and that in Ways we see to be foul or wrong, this is Anxious.* Here lies the Dispute: And truly here the Question might fairly end, *Either put out our Eyes, or let us use them:* But if we have Eyes for our

180. Acts 17:10–11.

Minds as well as for Bodies, I see no Reason why we should trust any Man, or Men, against the Eyes of our Understanding, any more than we ought to confide in them against the Sense and Certainty of the Eyes of our Bodies.

Where is the *poorest Mechanick* that would be paid his Labour in base Coin for Silver, by either *Pope or Bishop?* And can we be so Brutish, as to think our *Nobler Part* void of Distinction, about that *Treasure which is of Eternal Moment.* For though *Peter* was to feed the Sheep, yet the Sheep were not to follow *Peter,* but Christ.[181] *My Sheep hear my Voice,* says he, *and follow me, and a Stranger they will not follow,* John x. 14. Here is no Mediator betwixt Christ and his Sheep; nor does any Body else *hear his Voice for them; but they hear his Voice themselves.* And though the *Shepherd* may have many Servants, *yet He only is their Shepherd, and they are only the Sheep of his Fold.*

But there are three Places of Scripture, that come fresh into my Remembrance, that are very pertinent to the present Occasion. The first is this, Rom. i. 19. *That which may be known of God, is manifest in Men, for God hath shewed it unto them:* That is, *The Spirit of Man being the Candle of the Lord,* Prov. xx. 27. God hath enlightned it to manifest unto Man, what is necessary for him to know both of God and himself. Here is no Need of *Wax-Candles,* or *Tapers,* or a *Visible Guide and Church; for still, He that believes, has the Witness in himself.*

Another Passage is this: *Be ye Followers of me, even as I am also of Christ,* 1 Cor. xi. 1. In which the Apostle is so far from setting himself up a *Judge* over the Church of *Corinth,* that he makes his Appeal to them concerning his Doctrine and Conversation, regulating both by that of *His Lord Jesus Christ,* and making them Judges of the Truth of his Conformity to that Example. *Be ye Followers of me:* How? After what Manner? What! Absolutely, without Examination? Must we believe Thee without any Trial, and take what thou sayest for granted, without any more to do? No such Thing. *Be ye Followers of me, even as I also am of Christ:* I submit my self to be judg'd by you according to that Rule; and all Men and Churches are to be thus measur'd, that lay Claim to the Name of *Christian:* The Text will bear it.

The Third Passage is in his *Second Epistle* to the same Church of *Corinth;* 'tis this; 2 Cor. 4. 1, 2. *Therefore seeing we have this Ministry, as we have received Mercy, we faint not: but have renounced the hidden Things of Dishonesty, not walking in Craftiness, nor handling the Word of God deceitfully, but by Manifestation of the Truth, commending our selves to every Man's Conscience in the Sight*

181. John 21:15–17.

of God. Here is the utmost *Imposition* the Apostle makes Use of: He requires not Men to receive him without *Evidence,* and refers himself to that of their own *Consciences* in the *Sight of God.* This was the Way of making *Christians* then; it must be the Way of keeping and making Men Christians now.

Conscience, in the best Sense of the Word, has ever been allowed to be a *Bond* upon Men in all Religions: But that Religion, whoever holds it, which under Pretence of Authority, would supersede *Conscience,* and instead of making Men better, the End of Religion, make them worse, by confounding all Sense and Distinction betwixt *Good and Evil,* and resolving all into an *implicit Faith and blind Obedience* unto the Commands of a *visible Guide* and *Judge,* is false, it cannot be otherwise. For to admire what Men don't know, and to make it a Principle not to inquire, is the last Mark of *Folly* in the Believer, and of *Imposture* in the Imposer. To be short, a *Christian* implies a Man, and a Man implies *Conscience and Understanding;* but he that has no *Conscience* nor *Understanding,* as he has not, that has deliver'd them up to the Will of another Man, is no *Man,* and therefore no *Christian.*

I do beseech *you Protestants* of all Sorts, to consider of the Danger of this Principle, with Respect to *Religion. Of Old 'twas the Fool that said in his Heart, there is no God?*[182] But now, upon this Principle, Men must be made *Fools* in Order to *believe* there is one. Shall *Folly,* which is the *Shame,* if not the *Curse* of Man, be the Perfection of a *Christian?* Christ indeed has advised us to become as *little Children,*[183] but never to become such *Fools;* for as the Proverb is, this is *to be led by the Nose,* and not by our Wits. You know that God hates the *Sacrifices of Fools:* Eccle. 5. 1. *I will pray with the Spirit and with Understanding also,* saith the Apostle. 1 Cor. 14. Let us commend that Testimony, which we believe to be true, to the Consciences of Men, and let them have the Gospel Privilege of *Examination. Error* only loses upon Tryal: If this had been the Way to *Christianity,* with Reverence be it spoken, God had not made our Condition better, but worse; for this translates our Faith and Dependence upon God, to Man; and the Possibility, if not Probability of Mans erring, exposes us to a greater Insecurity than before: For *where I never trusted, I never could be deceived:* But if I must abandon my own Sense and Judgment, and yield my self up to the Faith and Authority of another (to say no more of the Blindness and Lameness of such Belief and Devotion) *what Security can I have, that the*

182. Psalms 14:1; 53:1.
183. Matthew 18:3; Mark 10:15; and Luke 18:17.

Man or Men whom I trust, may not err, and deceive me? And that Deceit is irreparable.

Again, since Man is a reasonable Creature, and that the more reasonable he is in his Religion, the nearer *to his own being he comes,* and to the Wisdom and Truth of his Creator, that did so make him: A Religion without Reason, imposed by an unaccountable Authority, against Reason, Sense and Conviction, cannot be the Religion of the God of Truth and Reason: For it is not to be thought that he requires any Thing that carries any Violence upon the Nature of his *Creature,* or that gives the Lye to that Reason or Sense with which he first endowed him. In short, either convince my Understanding by the Light of Truth and Power of Reason, or bear down my Infidelity with the Force of Miracles: For not to give me Understanding or Faith, and to press a *Submission* that requires both, is most unreasonable.

But if there were no other *Argument* than this, it goes a great Way with me, that as to such as have their *Understanding* at *Liberty,* if they are mistaken there may be Hopes of reclaiming them, by *informing them;* but where the *Understanding* and *Conscience* are enslaved to Authority, and where Men make it a Principal Doctrine, to suspect their own Sense, and Strive against their own Convictions; to move only by other Men's Breath and fall down to their Conclusions; *nothing seems to be left for the soundest Arguments, and clearest Truths, to work upon.* They had almost need to be *Re-Created* in Order to be converted; for who can reasonably endeavour to make him a *Christian,* that is not a Man; which he cannot be truly said to be, who has no Understanding, or resolves not to use it, but reject it, which is yet worse: For he that has no Understanding, has no Prejudice against it, but he that purposely denies and abuses it, is so much worse, as that he turns Enemy to him that has and uses his Understanding. He therefore can never be convinced of his Error, *who is prejudiced against the necessary Means of Conviction, which is the Use of his Understanding,* without which 'tis impossible he should ever be convinced.

To conclude, I have reserved, till last, one Argument, which is *ad Hominem,* unanswerable by us *Protestants,* and without yielding to which, we cannot be consistent with our selves, or be thought to do unto others, what we would have others do unto us, and that is this: *The Translation of the Scripture* was the painful Work of our *Ancestors;* and this I call *their most solemn Appeal to the People, against the Pope and Traditions of* Rome *in the Business of their Separation.* For when the Question arose of the divine Authority of this or the other Practice in the Doctrine or Worship of the *Roman Church,* presently they recurred to the Scriptures, and therefore made them speak *English,* that they might witness for them to the People. This *appeal* to the People in Defence of their Separation, by making them Judges of their Proceeding against the *Church,* according to the Testimony of the *Holy Scripture,* puts every Man in *Possession* of them. *Search the Scriptures,* say the first Protestants, *prove all Things; see if what we say against the Pope and Church of* Rome *be not true;* and in *Case* any Difficulty did arise, they exhorted all to wait upon God, for the divine Aid of his Spirit, to illuminate their Understandings, that one should not impose upon the other, but commend them to God: Be *Brotherly, Patient, Long-Suffering,* ready to help the *Weak, inform the Ignorant,* shew *Tenderness to* the *Mistaken,* and with *Reason* and *Moderation* to gain the Obstinate. In short, *Protestancy, is a restoring to every Man his just Right of Inquiry and Choice:* And to it's Honour be it ever spoken, there is a greater *Likelihood* of finding Truth, where all have Liberty to seek after it, than where it is denyed to all, but a few Grandees, and those too as short sighted as their *Neighbours.* But now let us *Protestants* examine, if we have not departed from this *Sobriety,* this *Christian Temperance?* How comes it that we who have been forgiven much, have our selves fallen upon *our Fellow-Servants,* who yet owe us nothing? Have not we refused them this reasonable *Choice?* Have we not *threatned, beaten* and *imprisoned them?* Pray consider, have you not *made Creeds,* framed Faiths, *formed* and *regulated a Worship;* and *strictly enjoyn'd* all Men's Obedience, by the Help of the Civil Power, upon Pain of great Sufferings, which have not been spared upon *Dissenters;* though they have been, in common, Renouncers and Protesters with you, against the *Pope* and *Church of Rome.* For this the Land mourns, Heaven is displeased, and all is out of due *Course.*

To give us the *Scriptures, and knock our Fingers for taking them:* To translate them that we may read them, *and punish us for endeavouring to understand and use them as well as we can,* both with respect to God and our Neighbour, is very unreasonable upon our *Protestant* Principles. I wish we could see the Mischief we draw upon our selves, and which is worse upon our Cause; for the *Papist,* in this Case, acts according to his Principle, but we against our Principle, which shews indeed that we profess the better Religion, but that we also are more condemnable. If we will consider it seriously, we shall find it not much more injurious to Scripture, Truth and good Conscience, that we believe as the Church believes, than that we believe as the Church says the Scripture would have us believe. For where is the Difference, since I am not allowed to use my Understanding about the Sense of Scripture any more than about the Faith or Worship from Scripture, but what is *handed* to me through the *Meanings* of the Church, or her Clergy, I see my self in as ill Terms, as if I had sat down with the old Doctrine *of believing as the Church believes.* And had the Controversy been only for the Word *Scripture,* without the Use and Application of it, for, at this Rate, that is all that is left us, truly the Enterprise of our Fathers had been weak and unadvised; but because nothing less was intended by them, and that the Translation of the Scripture was both the *Appeal* and *Legacy* of those *Protestant* Ancestors; for the Reasons before-mentioned, I must conclude we are much degenerated from the Simplicity of Primitive Protestancy, and need to be admonished of our Backslidings: And I heartily pray to Almighty God, that he would quicken us by his repeated Mercies and Providences to return to our first Love, to the Light and Spirit of his Son, that we may become Sons indeed, the Ground of true Christianity, and from whence the true Ministry hath it's Spring, which is open and free to those that are Proficients in that Holy School.

Let the Scriptures be free, Sober Opinion tolerated, Good Life cherish'd, Vice punish'd: Away with *Imposition, Nick-Names, Animosities,* for the Lord's Sake, and let the Scripture be our *Common Creed,* and *Pious Living* the *Test* of *Christianity,* that God may please to perfect his good Work of Grace he has begun, and deliver us from all our Enemies, both within and without.

Sect. 6. *Of the Propagation of Faith by Force.*

I AM now come to the last Point, and that is *Propagation of Faith by Force:* In which I shall, with the *Ecclesiastick,* consider the *Civil Magistrate's* Share herein: For tho' the Churchmen are principally guilty, who being profest Ministers of a Religion which renounces and condemns Force, excite the Civil Magistrate to use it, both to impose their own Belief, and suppress that of other Men's; yet the Civil Magistrate in running upon their Errands, and turning Executioner of their Cruelty upon such as dissent from them, involves himself in their Guilt.

That in this Protestant Country Laws have been made to prosecute Men for their Dissent from the National Worship, and that those Laws have been executed, I presume will not be deny'd: For not only our own Histories since the Reformation will furnish us with Instances unbecoming our Pretences, as the Case of *Barrow, Penrey, &c.* in Queen *Elizabeth*'s Time,[184] and others in the Reign of King *James* and *Charles* the First, but our own Age abounds with Proofs. *Thousands have been excommunicated and imprison'd; whole Families undone; not a Bed left in the House, not a Cow left in the Field, nor any Corn in the Barn: Widows and Orphans stript without Pity, no Regard being had to Age or Sex: And what for? only because of their Meeting to Worship God after another Manner than according to the Form of the Church of* England; *but yet in a very peaceable Way.*

Nor have they only suffered this by Laws intended against them, but, after an excessive Rate, by Laws known to have been never design'd against them, and *only intended against the Papists.* And in these Cases four Times the Value hath not served their Turn. We can prove Sixty Pounds taken for Thirteen, and not One Penny return'd, as we made appear before a *Committee* of the late Parliament, *which is the Penalty of four Offences for one;* to say nothing of the gross Abuses that have been committed against our Names and Persons, by Men of ill Fame and Life, that have taken the Advantage of our Tenderness, and the present Posture of the Law against us, to have their revengeful and covetous Ends upon us. And tho' we are yet unredrest, not a Session of Parliament has past these Seventeen Years, in which we have not humbly remonstrated our Suffering Condition: We have done our Part, which has been patiently to suffer and modestly to complain: It is yours now to hear our Groans, and, if ever you expect Mercy from God, to deliver us. The late Parliament, just before it's Dissolution, was preparing some Relief for us; if that Parliament could think of it, yea, begin it, we hope you will finish and secure it.

The better to remove all Scruples or Objections, that *Politically* or *Ecclesiastically,* on the Part of the State or the Church, may be advanced against us in this Request, I shall divide this Discourse into two Parts: First, *Caesar's Authority;* next, the *Church's Power in Things that relate to Faith and Conscience;* with my Considerations upon both.

* Our Blessed Lord and Saviour, Jesus Christ, did long since distinguish the *Things of* Caesar *from the Things of God,* in his plain and notable Answer unto that ensnaring Question of the *Jews, Is it lawful to pay Tribute to* Caesar *or not. Render* (says he) *unto* Caesar *the Things that are* Caesar's, *and to God the*

* *Note,* The greatest Part of what follows in this *Section,* was first printed by Way of *Appendix* to the *Continued Cry of the Oppressed for Justice, Anno* 1675.

184. John Penry and Henry Barrow, English Puritans hanged in 1593 for writing pamphlets critical of the established church.

Things that are God's: That is, *Divine Worship,* and all Things relating to it, belong unto God, *Civil Obedience to Caesar.*[185] God can only be the Author of right Acts of Worship in the Mind: This is granted by all; therefore it is not in the Power of any Man or Men in the World, to compel the Mind rightly to worship God. Where this is but attempted, God's Prerogative is invaded, and *Caesar,* by which Word I understand the *Civil Government, engrosseth All.* For he doth not only take his own things as much as he can, but the Things appertaining to God also; since if God hath not Conscience for his Share, he hath nothing. *My Kingdom,* says Christ, *is not of this World,*[186] nor is the Magistrate's Kingdom of the other World: Therefore he exceeds his Province and Commission when ever he meddles with the Rights of it. Let Christ have his Kingdom, he is sufficient for it; and let *Caesar* have his, 'tis his Due. *Give unto* Caesar *the Things that are* Caesar's, *and to God the Things that are God's.* Then there are Things that belong not to *Caesar,* and we are not to give those to him which belong not to him; and such are God's Things, Divine Things, Things of an Eternal Reference: But those that belong to *Caesar* and his Earthly Kingdom, must be, of Duty, rendred to him.

If any shall ask me, *What are the Things properly belonging to* Caesar? I answer in Scripture Language, *To love Justice, do Judgment, relieve the Oppressed, right the Fatherless, and in general be a Terror unto Evil-doers, and a Praise to them that do well;* for this is the Great End of Magistracy: And in these Things they are to be obey'd of Conscience as well as Interest.

But perhaps my Answer shall be reckoned too general and ambiguous, and a fresh Question started, *Who are the Evil-doers, to whom the Civil Authority ought to be Terrible?* But this ought in my Judgment to be no Question with Men that understand the Nature of Civil Authority; for those are the Evil-doers that violate those Laws which are necessary to the Preservation of Civil Society, as *Thieves, Murderers, Adulterers, Traytors, Plotters, Drunkards, Cheats, Vagabonds,* and the like mischievous and dissolute Persons: Men void of Virtue, Truth and Sincerity, the Foundation of all good Government, and only firm Bond of human Society. Whoever denies me this, must at the same Time say, *that Virtue is less necessary to Government than Opinion,* and that the most *Vitiated* Men, professing but *Caesar's Religion,* are the *best* Subjects to *Caesar's Authority,* consequently, that other Men, living never so honestly and

185. Matthew 22:17–21; Mark 12:14–17; and Luke 20:22–25.
186. John 18:36.

industriously, and having else as good a Claim to Civil Protection and Preferment, shall, meerly for their Dissent from that Religion, (a Thing they can't help; *for Faith is the Gift of God*)[187] be reputed the worst of Evil-doers; which is followed with exposing their Names to Obloquy, their Estates to Ruin, and their Persons to Goals, Exiles, and Abundance of other Cruelties. What is this, but to confound the *Things of Caesar* with the *Things of God,* Divine Worship with Civil Obedience, the Church with the State, and perplex human Societies with endless Debates about Religious Differences? Nay, is not this to erect new Measures to try the Members of Worldly Societies by, and give an Accession to another Power, than that which is necessary to the Constitution of Civil Government? But that which ought to deter wise Rulers from assuming and exercising such an Authority, is the Consideration of the pernicious Consequences of doing so.

For, *First,* It makes *Property,* which is the first and most fix'd Part of *English* Government floating and uncertain; for it seems, no Conformity to the Church, no Property in the State: And doubtless, the Insecurity of Property can be no Security to the Government: Pray think of that.

II. It makes me owe more to the Church than to the State; for in this Case, the Anchor I ride by, is not my Obedience to Laws relating to the Preservation of Civil Society, but Conformity to certain Things belonging to the Doctrine and Discipline of the Church: So that though I may be an honest, industrious *Englishman,* a great Lover of my Country, and an Admirer of the Government I live under, yet if I refuse to profess the Religion that either now is, or hereafter may be imposed, be it never so false, that is all one, I must neither enjoy the Liberty of my Person, nor the quiet Possession of my Estate.

III. This not only alters the Government, by sacrificing Men's Properties for that which cannot be called a Sin against Property, nor an Offence to the Nature of Civil Government, if any Transgression at all, but it narrows the Interest and Power of the Governours: For look what Number they cut off from their Protection, they cut off from themselves and the Government; not only rendring thereby a great Body of People useless, but provoking them to be Dangerous: To be sure it clogs the Civil Magistrate in his Administration of Government, making that necessary which is not at all necessary to him *as Caesar.*

187. Ephesians 2:8.

It is a Sort of *Duumvirateship* in Power, by which the Civil Monarchy is broken: For as that was a Plurality of Men, *so this is a Plurality of Powers.* And to speak freely, the Civil Power is made to act the Lackey, to run of all the unpleasant Errands the froward Zeal of the other sends it upon; and the best Preferment it receives for it's Pains, is to be *Informer, Constable,* or *Hangman* to some of the best Livers, and therefore the best Subjects in the Kingdom.

O! What greater Injustice to *Caesar* than to make his Government vary by such Modes of Religion, and oblige him to hold his Obedience from his People, not so much by their Conformity to him, as to the Church, a meer Relative of to'ther World.

IV. This is so far from resembling the Universal Goodness of God, who dispenses his Light, Air, Showers and comfortable Seasons to all, and whom *Caesar* ought always to imitate, and so remote from increasing the *Trade, Populacy* and *Wealth* of this Kingdom, as that it evidently tends to the utter Ruin of Thousands of *Traders, Artificers* and *Husbandmen,* and their Families; and by increasing the Charges, It must needs encrease the Poor of the Nation.

V. This must needs be a great Discouragement to Strangers from coming in, and setling themselves amongst us, when they have Reason to apprehend that they, and their Children after them, can be no longer secured in the Enjoyment of their *Properties,* than they shall be able to prevail with their Consciences to believe, *That* the Religion which our Laws do now, or shall at any Time hereafter approve and impose, is undoubtedly *True;* and that the Way of *Worshipping God,* which shall be at any Time by our Laws enjoyned, is, and shall be more agreeable to the Will of God, than any other Way in which God is Worshipped in the World.

VI. That *Way of Worship* we are Commanded Conformity to, doth not make *Better Livers,* that is a Demonstration, *Nor Better Artists,* for it cannot be thought that going to *Church,* hearing *Common-Prayer,* or believing in the present *Episcopacy,* learn Men *to Build Ships or Houses; to make Clothes, Shoes, Dials or Watches; Buy, Sell, Trade, or Commerce better, than any that are of another Perswasion.* And since these Things are *Useful,* if not *Requisite in Civil Society,* is not prohibiting, nay ruining, such Men, because they will not come to hear *Common-Prayer,* &c. destructive of *Civil Society?* Pray shew me better Subjects. If any object, *Dissenters have not always been so,* the Answer is ready, *Do not expose them, protect them in their Lives, Liberties and Estates; for in this present Posture they think they can call Nothing their own, and that all the Comforts they have in this World, are Hourly liable to Forfeiture for their Faith, Hope and Practice concerning the other World.* Is not this to destroy Nature and Civil Government, when People are ruined in their Natural and Civil Capacity, not for Things relating to either, but which are of a Supernatural Import?

VII. This deprives them of Protection, who protect the Government. *Dissenters* have a great Share in the Trade, which is the Greatness of this Kingdom; and they make a large Proportion of the *Taxes* that maintain the Government. And is it Reasonable, or can it be Christian, when they *Pay Tribute to Caesar,* to be preserved in an Undisturbed Possession of the *Rest,* that the *Rest* should be continually exposed for the Peaceable Exercise of their Consciences to God?

VIII. Neither is it a Conformity to True and Solid Religion, such as is Necessary to Eternal Salvation, wherein most Parties Verbally agree, but for a Modification of Religion; some peculiar Way of Worship and Discipline. *All confess One God, One Christ, One Holy Ghost, and that it is indispensably requisite to Live Soberly, Righteously, and Godly in this present Evil World,* 2 Tit. xi. 12. yet is one prosecuting the other for his Conscience, *Seizing Corn, Driving away Cattel, Breaking open Doors, taking away, and spoiling of Goods; in some Places not leaving a Cow to give poor Orphans Milk, nor a Bed to lie on; in other Places Houses have been swept so clean, that a Stool hath not been left to Sit on, nor so much as Working Tools to Labour for Bread. To say nothing of the Opprobrious Speeches, Bloody Blows, and Tedious Imprisonments, even to Death it self, through Nastiness of Dungeons, that many innocent People have suffered only for their Peaceable Conscience.*

IX. But this Way of proceeding for Maintenance of the National Religion, is of an ill Consequence upon this Account, that Heaven is barred as much as in Men lies, from all farther Illuminations. Let God send what *Light* he pleases into the World, it must not be received by *Caesar*'s People, without *Caesar*'s Licence; and if it happen that *Caesar* be not presently Convinced as well as I, that it is of God, I must either renounce my Convictions, and lose my Soul to please *Caesar,* or profess and persevere in my Perswasion, and so lose my Life, Liberty or Estate, to please God. This hath frequently occurr'd, and may again. Therefore I would entreat *Caesar* to consider the sad Consequence of Imposition, and remember both that God did never ask Man Leave to introduce Truth, or make farther Discoveries of his Mind to the World, and that it hath been a Woful Snare to those Governments that have been drawn to employ their Power against his Work and People.

X. This Way of Procedure endeavours to stifle, or else to punish Sincerity; for Fear or Hopes, Frowns or Favour, prevail only with base Minds; Souls degenerated from True Nobleness. Every Spark of Integrity must be extinguisht, where Conscience is sacrificed to Worldly Safety and Preferment. This Net holds no Temporizers: Honest Men are all the Fish it catches: But one would think they should make but an ill Treat to such as reckon themselves *Generous Men,* and what is more, *Christians* too. That which renders the Matter more unjustifiable, is the Temptation such Severity puts Men upon, not hardy enough to *Suffer for Conscience,* yet strongly perswaded they have *Truth* on their Side, to desert their Principles, and smother their Convictions, which in plain Terms, is to make of Sincere Men, Hypocrites: Whereas it is one Great End of Government, by all Laudable Means, to preserve Sincerity; for without it there can be no Faith or Truth in Civil Society. Nor is this all, for it's a Maxim worthy of *Caesar*'s Notice, *Never to think him True to* Caesar, *that is False to his own Conscience:* Besides, raped Consciences treasure up *Revenge,* and such Persons are not likely to be longer Friends to *Caesar,* than he hath Preferments to allure them, or Power to deter them from being his most implacable Enemies.

XI. There is not so ready a Way to *Atheism,* as this of extinguishing the *Sense of Conscience for Worldly Ends:* Destroy that *Internal Rule of Faith, Worship and Practice towards God,* and the Reason of my Religion will be Civil Injunctions, and not Divine Convictions; consequently, I am to be of as many Religions as the Civil Authority shall impose, however untrue or contradictory. *This Sacred Tye of Conscience, thus broken, farewel to all Heavenly Obligations in the Soul, Scripture-Authority, and Ancient Protestant Principles.* Christ may at this Rate become what the *Jews* would have had Him and His Apostles to be reputed, to wit, *Turners of the World up-side down,* as their Enemies represented them;[188] and the Godly Martyrs of all Ages, so many Self-Murtherers; for they might justly be esteem'd *Resisters of Worldly Authority,* so far as that Authority concerned it self with the Imposition of Religion, because they refused the Conformity commanded by it, even to Death.

And it may not be unworthy of *Caesar*'s Consideration, that from these Proceedings People are tempted to infer, there is nothing in Religion but *Worldly Aims and Ends,* because so much Worldly Power is abus'd, under the Name of Religion, to vex and destroy Men for being of another Religion; and that he hazards the best Hold and Obligation he hath to Obedience, which is Conscience: For where they are taught only to Obey for *Interest; Duty* and

188. Acts 17:6.

Conviction are out of Doors. By all Means let *Conscience* be Sacred, and *Virtue* and *Integrity* (though under Dissenting Principles) cherish'd: *Charity* is more powerful than *Severity,* and *Perswasion* than all the *Penal Laws* in the World.

Lastly, To the Reproach of this Course with wise Men, it hath never yet obtain'd the End desired, since instead of Compliance, the Difference is thereby widened, and the Sufferers are pitied by Spectators, which only helps to increase the Number of Dissenters, for whoever is in the Wrong, few think the Persecutor in the Right. This in all Ages, having been the Issue of severe Prosecution of Dissenters for Matters of Religion; what a Cruel, Troublesome, Thankless, Succesless Office is it for *Caesar* to be employ'd in? May he take better Measures of his Authority and Interest, and use his Power to the Encouragement of all the *Virtuous* and *Industrious,* and Just Punishment of the *Lazy* and *Vicious* in all Perswasions; so shall the Kingdom *Flourish,* and the Government *Prosper.*

Church Power supposeth a *Church* first. It will not be improper therefore to examine; *first,* What a Scripture New-Testament-Church is; and *next,* what is the Scripture-Power belonging to such a Church. A Scripture-Church as she may be called Visible, is *a Company or Society of People, believing, professing and practising according to the Doctrine and Example of Christ Jesus and his Apostles,* and not according to the *Scribes* and *Pharisees,* that *taught for Doctrine the Traditions of Men.* They are such as are Meek in Heart, Lowly in Spirit (*a*) Chast in Life, (*b*) Virtuous in all Conversation, (*c*) full of Self Denial, (*d*) Long-suffering and Patient, (*e*) not only forgiving, (*f*) but loving their very Enemies; which answers Christ's own Character of himself, Religion and Kingdom, which is the most apt Distinction that ever can be given of the Nature of his Church and her Authority, *viz. (g) My Kingdom is not of this World.* Which well connects with *Render unto* Caesar *the Things that are* Caesar's, *and unto God the Things that are God's.*[189]

It was an Answer to a very suspicious Question; for it was familiarly bruited *that he was a King, and came to possess his Kingdom, and was, by some, called the King of the* Jews.

The *Jews* being then subjected to the *Roman* Empire, it concerned *Pilate, Caesar's Deputy,* to understand his Pretensions, which upon better Informa-

189. (*a*) Titus 2:5–6; (*b*) 1 Peter 3:2; (*c*) Matthew 16:24, Mark 8:34, and Luke 9:23; (*d*) Colossians 1:11, and 2 Timothy 3:10; (*e*) Luke 6:37; (*f*) Luke 6:27, 6:35; and (*g*) John 18:36.

tion he found to center in this, *My Kingdom is not of this World, else would my Subjects fight for me.*[190] As if he had said, these Reports are a meer Perversion of my Peaceable and Self-denying Intentions; an Infamy invented by malicious *Scribes* and *Pharisees,* that they might the better prevail with *Caesar* to Sacrifice me to their hatred and revenge.

I am *Caesar*'s Friend, I seek none of his Kingdoms from him, nor will I sow Sedition, plot or conspire his Ruin; no, *Let all Men render unto* Caesar *the Things that are* Caesar's: That's my Doctrine; for I am come to erect a Kingdom of another Nature than that of this World, to wit, a *Spiritual Kingdom,* to be set up in the Heart; and Conscience is my Throne, upon that will I sit, and rule the Children of Men in Righteousness; and whoever *lives Soberly, Righteously and Godlily in this World,* shall be my good and loving Subjects. And they will certainly make no ill ones for *Caesar,* since such Virtue is the End of Government, and renders his Charge both more easie and safe than before. Had I any other Design than this, would I suffer my Self to be reproached, traduced and persecuted by a conquered People? Were it not more my Nature to suffer than revenge, would not their many Provocations have drawn from me some Instance of another kind than the Forbearance and Forgiveness I teach? certainly, were I animated by another Principle than the Perfection of Meekness and Divine Sweetness, I should not have forbidden *Peter* fighting, saying, *put up thy Sword,* or Instructed my Followers to bear Wrongs;[191] but have revenged all Affronts, and, by Plots and other Stratagems, have attempted Ruin to my Enemies, and the Acquisition of worldly Empire: And no doubt but they would have fought for me. Nay, I am not only patiently, and with Pity to Enemies, sensible of their cruel *Carriage* towards me for my Good Will to them, whose Eternal Happiness I only seek; but I foresee what they further intend against me: They design to crucifie me: And to do it, will rather free a Murderer than spare their Saviour. They will perform that *Cruelty* with all the Aggravation and Contempt they can; deriding me themselves, and exposing me to the Derision of others: They will mock my Divine Kingship with a *Crown* of *Thorns,* and in mine Agonies of Soul and Body, for a Cordial, give me *Gall* and *Vinegar* to drink. But notwithstanding all this, to satisfie the World that my Religion is above Wrath and Revenge, I can forgive them.

190. John 18:36.
191. Matthew 26:52; and John 18:11.

And to secure *Caesar* and his People from all Fears of Imposition, notwithstanding my Authority, and the many Legions of Angels I might command, both to my Deliverance, and the Enforcement of my Message upon Mankind; I resolve to promote neither with worldly Power; for it is not of the Nature of my Religion and Kingdom. And as I neither assume nor practice any such Thing my self, that am the great Author, Promoter and Example of this Holy Way; so have I not only never taught my Disciples to live or act otherwise, or given them a Power I refuse to use my self, but expresly forbad them, and warn'd them, in my Instructions, of exercising any the least Revenge, Imposition or Coercion towards any. This is evident in my Sermon preached upon the Mount, where I freely, publickly, and with much Plainness, not only *prohibited Revenge,* and *enjoyned Love to Enemies,* making it to be a great Token of true Discipleship to suffer Wrongs, and conquer Cruelty by Patience and Forgiveness;[192] which is certainly very far from Imposition or Compulsion upon other Men.

Furthermore, when I was strongly bent for *Jerusalem,* and sent Messengers before to prepare some Entertainment for me and my Company, in a Village belonging to the *Samaritans,* and the People refused because they apprehended I was going to *Jerusalem,* though some of my Disciples, particularly *James* and *John,* were provok'd to that Degree, that they asked me, if I were willing that they should command Fire from Heaven to destroy those *Samaritans,* as *Elias* in another Case had done; I turned about, and rebuked them, saying, *Ye know not what Manner of Spirit ye are of; for I am not come into the World to destroy Men's Lives, but,* by my peaceable Doctrine, Example and Life, to *save them.*[193]

At another Time, one of my Disciples relating to me some Passages of their Travails, told me of a certain Man they saw, that cast out Devils in my Name, and because he was not of their Company, nor followed them, said he, *we forbad him;* as if they thereby served and pleased me; but I presently testified my Dislike of the Ignorance and Narrowness of their Zeal, and, to inform them better, told them, they should not have forbid him; *for he that is not against us is for us.*[194]

My Drift is not Opinion, but Piety: They that cast out Devils, convert Sin-

192. Matthew 5:44–47.
193. Luke 9:51–56.
194. Luke 9:49–50.

ners, and turn Men to Righteousness, are not against me, nor the Nature and Religion of my Kingdom, and therefore ought to be cherisht rather than forbid. That I might sufficiently declare and inculcate my Mind in this Matter, I did at another Time, and upon a different Occasion, preach against all Coercion and Persecution for Matters of Faith and Practice towards God, in my Parable of the Sower, as my Words manifest, which were these; *The Kingdom of Heaven is likened unto a Man which sowed good Seed in his Field; but while Men slept, his Enemy came, and sowed Tares among the Wheat, and went his Way; but when the Blade sprung up, and brought forth Fruit, there appeared the Tares also; so the Servants of the Housholder came and said, didst thou not sow good Seed in thy Field? from whence then hath it Tares? he answered, an Enemy hath done this; the Servants said unto him, wilt thou then that we go and gather them up? but he said,* Nay, *lest while ye gather up the Tares, ye root up also the Wheat with them, let both grow together till the Harvest, and in the Time of Harvest I will say to the Reapers, gather ye together first the Tares, and bind them in Bundles to burn them, but gather the Wheat into my Barn.*

And that I might not leave so necessary a Truth mis-apprehended of my dear Followers, or liable to any Mis-constructions, my Disciples, when together, desiring an Explanation, I interpreted my Words thus:

He that soweth the good Seed is the Son of Man; the Field is the World; the good Seed are the Children of the Kingdom; but the Tares are the Children of the Wicked One; the Enemy that sowed them is the Devil; the Harvest is the End of the World; and the Reapers are the Angels.[195]

This Patience, this Long Suffering and great Forbearance belonging to my Kingdom and the Subjects of it; my Doctrine speaks it, and mine Example confirms it, and this can have no possible Agreement with Imposition and Persecution for Conscience. 'Tis true, I once whipt out the Profaners of my Father's Temple; but *I never whipt any in.* I call'd, I cry'd to every one that thirsted to come, and freely offer'd my Assistance to the Weary and heavy Laden; *but I never impos'd my Help, or forced any to receive me;* for I take not my Kingdom by Violence, but by Suffering. And that I might sufficiently deter my Followers from any such Thing, as I profess my self to be their Lord and Master, so have I commanded them to love one another in a more especial Manner.[196] But if instead thereof any shall grow proud, high-minded, and beat

195. Matthew 13:3–23; Mark 4:4–20; and Luke 8:5–15.
196. John 2:13–17; and John 15:12.

or abuse their Fellow-Servants in my Religious Family, when I come to take an Account of my Houshold, he shall be cut asunder, and appointed his Portion among the Unbelievers. Behold the Recompence I appoint to imposing Lordly Persons, such as count others Infidels, and to make them such Believers as themselves, will exercise Violence towards them, and if they prevail not, will call for *Fire from Heaven to devour them;* and if Heaven refuse to gratify their Rage, will fall a Beating and Killing, and think, it may be, they do God good Service too; but their Lot shall be with Unbelievers for ever.

Nay, I have so effectually provided against all Mastery, that I expresly charged them, *not to be many Masters; for one was their Master:* I told them, the greatest amongst them was to be Servant to the rest, not to impose upon the rest: Nay, that to be great in my Kingdom, they must become as gentle and harmless as *little Children,* and such cannot force and punish in Matters of Religion. In fine, I strictly commanded them *to love one another,* as I have loved them, who am ready to lay down my Life for the Ungodly, instead of taking away Godly Men's Lives for Opinions. And this is the great Maxim of my Holy Religion, *He that would be my Disciple, must* not Crucifie other Men, but *take up his Cross and follow me, who am meek and lowly,* and such as endure to the End, shall find Eternal Rest to their Souls; this is the Power I use, and this is the Power I give.[197]

How much this agrees with the Language, Doctrine and Example of Jesus Christ, the Son and Lamb of God, I shall leave them to consider that read and believe Scripture. But some affected to present Church-Power, and desiring their Ruin that conform not to her Worship and Discipline, will object, *That Christ did give his Church Power to bind and loose, and bid any Persons aggrieved tell the Church.*[198]

I grant it; but what binding was that? was it I Pray with outward Chains and Fetters, in nasty Holes and Dungeons? nothing less: Or, was it that his Church had that true Discerning in her, and Power with him, that what she bound, that is, condemned, or loosed, that is, remitted, should stand so in God's Sight and Christ's Account?

But tell the Church; and what then? Observe Christ's Extent in the Punish-

197. On masters and servants, Matthew 23:8–11; on little children, Matthew 18:3, 19:14, Mark 10:15, Luke 18:76; on loving one another, John 13:34–35, 15:12–17; on taking up the cross, Matthew 16:24, Mark 8:34, 10:21, and Luke 9:23.

198. Matthew 16:19; and 18:17–18.

ment of the Offender: *If the Offender will neither receive private Admonition, nor hear the Church, then* (says Christ) *let him be to thee as an* Heathen, *&c.* Here's not one Word of *Fines, Whips, Stocks, Pillories, Goals,* and the like Instruments of Cruelty, to punish the Heretick: For the Purport of his Words seems to be no more than this; If any Member of the Church refuse thy private Exhortation, and the Church's Admonition, look upon such a Person as obstinate and perverse, have no more to do with him; let him take his Course, thou hast done well, and the Church is clear of him.

Well, but say the *Church Fighters* of our Age, *Did not St.* Paul *wish them cut off that troubled the Church in his Time?* Yes: But with what Sword think you? Such as Christ bid *Peter* put up, or the *Sword of the Spirit, which is the Word of God?* Give him leave to explain his own Words; *For though we walk in the Flesh, We do not War after the Flesh; for the Weapons of our Warfare are not Carnal, but mighty through God, to the pulling down of strong Holds, casting down Imaginations, and every high Thing that exalteth it self against the Knowledge of God, and bringing every Thought into Obedience to Christ.*[199]

What think you of this? Here are Warfares, Weapons, Oppositions and Conformity, and not only no external Force about Matters of Religion used or countenanced, but the most express and pathetical Exclusion and disclaiming of any such Thing that can be given.

It was this great Apostle that askt that Question, *Who art thou that judgest the Servant of another? To his own Lord he standeth or falleth: but he shall stand; for God is able to make him stand.*[200] Can we think that Imposition or Persecution is able to Answer him this Question in the Day of Judgment? Do we with Reason deny it to the *Papacy?* With what Reason then can we assume it to our selves? Let us remember who said, *Not that we have Dominion over your Faith, but are Helpers of your Joy.*[201] *Helpers,* then not *Imposers* nor *Persecutors.* What Joy can there be in that to the Persecuted? But if *Paul* had no such Commission or Power over Conscience, I would fain know by what Authority more inferiour Ministers and Christians do claim and use it.

The Apostle *Peter* is of the same Mind; *Feed* says he, *the Flock of God, not*

199. On cutting off those who troubled the church, see Titus 3:10; on Christ bidding Peter to put up his sword, see Matthew 26:52; on the flesh and weapons of spiritual warfare, see 2 Corinthians 10:3–5.

200. Romans 14:4.

201. 2 Corinthians 1:24.

by Constraint, *&c. neither as being Lords over God's Heritage.* The Heritage of God is free, they have but one Lord in and of their Religion, *Christ Jesus,* and they are Brethren.[202]

The Apostle *Paul* says, *That where the Spirit of the Lord is there is Liberty,* but where *Coercion, Fines* and *Goals* are, there is no Liberty. Is it to be supposed that Men in these Days are instructed by the Spirit of the Lord to destroy People in this World for their Faith about the other World? That cannot possibly be; such mock at it. Again, says that Apostle to the Christians of his Time, *You are called to Liberty;*[203] from what I pray, *Sin and the Ceremonies of the Law?* And shall the End of that call be the enthralling Conscience to human Edicts in Religion, yea, about meer Ceremonies of Religion, under the Gospel? This would make our Case worse than the *Jews,* for their Worship stood on divine Authority; and if Christ came to make Men free from them, and that those very Ordinances are by the Apostle call'd beggarly Elements and a burdensom Yoak, Is it reasonable that we must be subject to the Injunctions of Men in the Worship of God, that are not of equal Authority with them?

The Apostle yet informs us, *for this End,* says he, *Christ both dyed and rose again, that he might be Lord both of the Dead and Living: But why dost thou judge thy Brother?*[204] Than which nothing can more expresly oppose the *Imposition, Excommunication,* and *Persecution* that are among us; 'Tis as if he had said, Christ is Lord of *Christians,* by what Authority dost thou pretend to judge his Servants? Thou also art but one of them: A Brother at most. Thou hast no Dominion over their Faith, nor hast thou Commission to be Lord over their Consciences; 'tis Christ's Right, his Purchase, he has paid for it: *For this End he both dyed and rose again, that he might be Lord of Dead and Living;* that he might rescue them, from the Jaws of Oppression; from those that usurp over their Consciences, and make a Prey of their Souls, *But why dost thou judge thy Brother?* If not *judge;* then not *Persecute, Plunder, Beat, Imprison* to Death our Brethren; that must needs follow. Come, let us *Protestants* look at Home, and view our Actions, if we are not the Men.

In short, *Let every Man be fully perswaded in his own Mind, and if any Thing be short, God will reveal it;*[205] let us but be patient. It was not *Flesh and Blood*

202. 1 Peter 5:2–3.
203. 2 Corinthians 3:17; and Galatians 5:13.
204. Romans 14:9–10.
205. Romans 14:5.

that revealed Christ to Peter, they are Christ's Words, therefore let us leave off the *Consultation, and Weapons of Flesh and Blood,* and trust Christ with his own Kingdom: He hath said, *that the Gates of Hell shall not prevail against it;*[206] and we cannot think that he would have us seek to *Hell's Gates* to maintain it: And if it is not of this World, then not to be maintain'd by *Force* and *Policy,* which are the Props of the Kingdoms of this World. *God,* the Apostle tells us, *has chosen the weak Things of this World, to confound the Mighty:*[207] Therefore he has not chosen the Strength and Power of this World, to suppress conscientious People, that as to humane Force, are justly accounted weakest and most destitute, in all Ages, of Defence.

I will here conclude my Scripture-Proofs with this Exhortation or Injunction rather of the Apostle. *Ye are bought with a Price, be not ye the Servants of Men.*[208] The Subject here is not *human,* wherein human Ordinances are to be obeyed; that is not the Question; but *Divine;* and those that for Fear or Favour of Men desert their Principles, and betray their Consciences, they renounce their Lord, deny him that bought them, and tread his Blood, the *Price* of their Souls, under their Feet: *Ye are bought with a Price,* Christ has purchas'd you, you are not your own, but his that bought you, therefore *be not the Servants of Men,* about God's Things or Christ's Kingdom; vail to no Man's Judgment, neither make Man's Determinations, your Rule of Faith and Worship. *Stand fast in the Liberty, wherewith he has made you free, and be not entangled again, into Bondage, for we are not come to that Mountain that we cannot touch, to* Sinai: We are not now to be kept under like *School-Boys* or *Minors:*[209] That Imposition might be useful then, which is a Bondage now. *Moses* was God's Servant and faithful, he saw, heard, and went up to the Mount for the People; *but Christians are come to Mount* Zion, *to* Jerusalem, *the Mother of Peace and Freedom.* Much then depended upon the Integrity of *Moses,* and yet God sent for the People near the Mount, that they might see his Glory; and wrought Wonders and Miracles to engage their Faith and vindicate the Integrity of *Moses* his Servant (as the 12, 13, 14, 15, and 16 Chapters of *Numbers* declares) and which none now can pretend to vouch the Exercise of their Authority: I say it pleased God then to appear by those Ways; *but now the Law is brought*

206. Matthew 16:18.
207. 1 Corinthians 1:27.
208. 1 Corinthians 7:23.
209. Galatians 5:1; and Hebrews 12:9–11.

Home to every Man's Heart, and every one shall know God for himself, from the least to the greatest, My Sheep, says Christ, *hear my Voice.*[210] And let us remember that there is no Possibility of Deception here, where there is no Necessity of trusting. In fine, *Ye are bought with a Price, be not ye the Servants of Men. One is Lord, even Christ, and ye are Brethren.*

But methinks I hear a stout Objection, and 'tis this: *At this Rate you will overthrow all Church-Discipline, all Censure of Errors, if no Man or Men can determine.* My Answer is ready and short, No Scripture Church-Discipline is hereby oppugned or weakned: *Let not the Sentence end in Violence upon the Conscience unconvinced:* Let who will *expound* or *determine,* so it be according to true Church-Discipline, which can be exercised on them only, who have willingly joyn'd themselves in that Covenant of Union, and which proceeds only to a Separation from the rest, a disavowing or disowning, and that only in Case of falling from Principles or Practices once received, or about known Trespasses: But never to any *Corporal or Pecuniary* Punishment; The *two Arms* of Anti-Christ, or rather of the great *Beast* which carries the *Whore.*

But let us observe what sort of Church-Government the Apostle recommends. *Avoid foolish Questions, and Genealogies, and Contentions, and Striving about the Law; for they are unprofitable and vain: A Man that is an Heretick, after the first and second Admonition, reject,* knowing that he that is such, is subverted, and sinneth, being *condemned of (or in) Himself;* or Self-condemned.[211]

It's very remarkable, *First,* That this great Apostle, instead of exhorting *Titus* to stand upon Niceties, and sacrifice Men's Natural Comforts and Enjoyments for Opinions of Religion, injoyns him to shun Disputes about them; leaving the People to their own Thoughts and Apprehensions in those Matters, as reputing the Loss of Peace, in striving, greater than the Gain that could arise from such an Unity and Conformity: Which exactly agrees with another Passage of his; *Let us therefore as many as be perfect, be thus minded; and if in any Thing ye be otherwise minded, God shall reveal even this unto you.*[212] He did not say you shall be *fined, pillaged, Excommunicated* and *flung* into Prison, if ye be not of our Mind.

2dly, That, in the Apostle's Definition, an *Heretick* is a *Self-condemned Per-*

210. Hebrews 8:10–11; and John 10:15–16.
211. 2 Timothy 2:23; and Titus 3:9–10.
212. Philippians 3:15.

son, one conscious to himself of Error and Obstinacy in it; but that are not conscientious Dissenters; for many ten Thousands in this Nation act as they believe, and dissent from the national Religion purely upon a Principle of Conscience to Almighty God; and would heartily conform if they could do it upon Conviction, or with any Satisfaction to their own Minds: And with Men of any Tenderness or common Sense, their continual great Sufferings in Person and Estate, and their Patience under them, are a Demonstration, or there can be none in the World, that Conscience and not Humour or Interest is at Bottom.

Nor can their Persecutors disprove them, unless they could search Hearts, and that is a little too far for a fallible Spirit to reach, and an infallible One they deny. So that the Apostle makes not the *Heretick* to lie upon the Side of Mis-believing, or not coming up to his Degree of Faith and Knowledge, but upon the Side of *Wilfully, Turbulently, Obstinately,* and *Self-condemnedly,* maintaining, Things inconsistent with the Faith, Peace and Prosperity of the Church.

Granting us then not to be Obstinate and Self-condemned Dissenters, and you cannot reasonably refuse it us, How do you prove us Erroneous in the other Part? All Parties plead Scripture, and that for the most opposite Principles. The Scripture, you say, cannot determine the Sense of it self; it must have an Interpreter: if so, he must either be *Fallible* or *Infallible:* If the first, we are worse than before; for Men are apt to be no less confident, and yet are still upon as uncertain Grounds: If the last, this must either be an *external* or an *internal* Judge: If an *external,* you know where you are without pointing; for there stands nothing between you and *Popery* in that Principle: If an *internal* Judge, either it is our selves or the Spirit of Christ dwelling in us: Not our selves, for then the Rule would be the Thing ruled, which cannot be; and if it be the Spirit of Christ Jesus, and the Apostle tells us, *Rom.* 8. *That unless we have the Spirit we are none of Christ's,* then is the Neck of Imposition broken; and what hast thou to do to judge me? Let me stand or fall to my own Master: And upon this Foot when *Luther, Zuinglius, Calvin, Melancthon, Beza, Bullinger, Zanchius* Abroad, and *Tindal, Barns, Cranmer, Ridley, Hooper, Jewel, Bradford, Philpot, Sanders, Rogers, &c.* at Home; and as good Men, and constant Martyrs, in Ages before them.

But suppose Conscientious Dissenters as ill Men as the Apostle describes an *Heretick* to be; what is the Punishment? This is close to the Point: Stand it.

3*dly. A Man that is an Heretick after the first and second Admonition, re-*

ject;[213] that is, deny his Communion, declare he is none of you, condemn his Proceedings by a publick Censure from among your selves. What more can be strained, by the fiercest Prosecutors of Men for Religion, out of these Words?

But will we be governed by the Rules of Holy Writ? Have we any true Veneration for the Exhortations and Injunctions therein? Then let us soberly consider, what the Apostle *Paul* advises and recommends to his beloved *Timothy* upon the present Occasion, and I dare promise an End to *Contest* and Persecution for Religion. *Flee youthful Lusts; but follow Righteousness, Faith, Charity, Peace, with them that call on the Lord out of a pure Heart; but foolish and unlearned Questions avoid, knowing that they do gender Strifes. And the Servant of the Lord must not strive, but be gentle unto all Men, apt to teach, patient, in Meekness instructing those that oppose themselves, if God peradventure will give them Repentance to the acknowledging of the Truth.* 2 Tim. 2. 22, 23, 24, 25.

There is such a Depth of Wisdom lodged in this one Passage, that I find Difficulty to express my self upon it, and yet I shall with Pleasure endeavour it. Here is both *Faith* and *Government, Religion* and *Duty,* all that becomes us towards God, our Brethren, our Neighbour, our Selves, yea, our Opposers and Enemies.

Flee youthful Lusts: that is, avoid Sin, turn away from every Appearance of Evil, flee the Temptation as soon as thou seest it, lest it ensnare thee; but follow Righteousness, Charity and Peace; seek and love Holiness and there will be Charity and Peace to thy self, and in thee, to all Men. Rom. 14. 17. 1 Cor. 4. 20. For the *Kingdom of God stands in Righteousness and Peace and Joy in the Holy Ghost;* not in Contest about Words, nor in maintaining foolish and unlearned Questions, *which reach not the Soul,* nor carry any Force upon our Affections, nor learn Men to be better, to have more *Piety, Virtue, Goodness;* but are meer Notions and Speculations, that have no Influence upon Holy Living, or Tendency to the Regiment of our Passions: Such Questions as the Curiosity or Wantonness of Men's Wit or restless Fancy are apt to start under Pretence of Divine Truth, and Sublime Mysteries: These Niceties, Conceits and Imaginations of Men, (not bottomed on the Revelation of the Eternal Spirit, but Human Apprehension and Tradition) *such Questions avoid, meddle not with them;* but, next to Youthful Lusts, flee them by all Means; for they draw to *Strife,* to *Heats, Animosities, Envy, Hatred* and *Persecution,* which unbecome the Man of God; for says this Apostle, *He must not strive, but be gentle unto*

213. Titus 3:10.

all Men, apt to teach, patient: Let his Rank, Notion, Opinion or Faith be what it will, he must not be Fierce, nor Censorious, much less should he persecute or excite *Caesar* to do it for him; no such Matter: *He must be apt to teach* and inform the Ignorant; and in Case it succeed not, he ought not to be Outrageous, or go about to whip or club it into him: He must be *patient,* that is, he must not think to force and bend things to his own Will or Time, but commit his Honest Endeavours to God's Blessing, *that can raise, of the Stones of the Streets, Children unto* Abraham.[214] This Sort of Man will serve God *against his Will,* instead of submitting his Will to God's: There is no Evil he will stick at to serve God his Way, he will plunder and kill for God's Sake, and meritoriously send all his Passions upon the Errands of his ignorant Zeal; and the Trophies that it loves, are the Spoils and Havock it makes upon Mankind; the most unnatural and dangerous Temper in the World. Our Blessed Lord, that knew what was in Man, has left us his Remark upon it, *Luke* 9. 55. The Want of this Patience has been the Undoing of all.

But some will object, *O! but it is not Ignorance! 'tis Obstinacy and Opposition:* Hardly judged, my Friend; but admit it were so, here's a Receipt for the Malady, and that of the Apostle's prescribing. Observe the following Words: *In Meekness instructing those that oppose themselves, if God peradventure will give them Repentance, to the acknowledging of the Truth.*[215] Then not *Fining, Plundering, Beating, Stocking, Imprisoning, Banishing* and *Killing,* even Opposers themselves, for Religion; unless there be a Way of doing these Things with Gentleness, Patience and Meekness; which I confess I think no Body ever heard of.

But as the Apostle gives *Timothy* another Method than is now used by the Sons of Violence for reclaiming Opposers, so the Reason of the Counsel makes all other Ways unlawful, *viz. If God peradventure will give them Repentance to the Acknowledgment of the Truth.* I would hereupon enter the List with a Persecutor: Is Repentance in my own Power, or is it in thine to give me? The Apostle says neither: 'Tis God's Gift alone; *If God peradventure will give them Repentance, &c.* Since Repentance then is in the Case, and that God alone can give it, of what Use are Violent Courses, which never beget Repentance? On the contrary, they have rarely fail'd to raise Prejudice and beget Hardness in the Sufferer, and Pity in the Beholder.

214. Matthew 3:9; and Luke 3:8.
215. 2 Timothy 2:24–25.

But was this the Evangelical Rule and Practice! Yes, that it was. O then! whence comes *Imposition, Force, Cruelty, Spoil of Goods, Imprisonments, Knockings, Beatings, Bruisings, Stockings, Whippings, and Spilling of Blood for Religion?* What Church is that whose Officers are so far from clothing the Naked that they strip the Clothed; from feeding the Hungry, that they take their Bread from them; and those, some of them, poor Widows and helpless Orphans? And so remote are they from visiting the Sick and Imprison'd, that they drag away their Beds from under them, and cast their Persons into Prison for Conscience Sake. Nay, some have been so unnatural that they haled away an Honest Man from a Meeting to Goal at *Reading,* a while since, not permitting him to take Leave of his poor Wife, newly delivered, and in a Dying Condition, though she much desired it, and liv'd but just by the Meeting, from whence they took him; with an Hundred more Things, that I forbear being particular in, because I would not be thought to provoke when I aim only at Christian Reproof and Amendment. In fine, What are they that for no other Cause pass such *Dreadful Excommunications,* as render the Excommunicants little better than *Outlawed Persons,* subjecting their Civil and Natural Rights to their Pride, Passion, Interest or Revenge, unless they will purchase their Enjoyment at the dear Rate of giving their own Consciences the Lye? For what else can be the Consequence of conforming to that I do not believe? Is not this to destroy sincere Men, and make and save Hypocrites? When it is but too palpable that Vice reigns without Controul, and few of these busy Men, these *Conscientious-Hunters,* give themselves the thought of correcting Manners, defending Virtue, or suppressing Vice.

O, that such as are concerned would soberly consider if any Thing be so Scandalous to True Religion as Force! Who can think that Evidence Good that is extorted? And what a Church is that which is made up of such Proselytes, or that employs such Means to make them? It is *base Coyn* that needs Imposition to make it current, but true Metal passeth for it's own intrinsick Value. O where is that Christian Meekness, Patience and Forbearance! How many have been ruined, that were never exhorted, and excommunicated before they were once admonished? This is not to serve God, but worldly Interest: It's quite contrary to Christ's Counsel and his Followers and Practice. He came to save, and not to destroy Nature, to magnify his Grace. You pretend most of you, to dislike *J. Calvin*'s unconditional Reprobation, yet practise it: If you say, no, *Conformity* is your Condition, I answer, It is as unreasonable to require an Impossibility, as cruel to damn Men for not doing it: For, as you say, *his Doctrine makes God to command them to repent, that cannot repent; and yet damn them if they repent not:* So *you enjoin Men to relinquish their present Faith and Worship, and conform to yours, which is not in their Power to do, yet damn them in a temporal Respect if they refuse it:* For you make such an unavoidable Dissent punishable with the Destruction of Men's Liberties and Estates. You had better leave off valuing your selves upon the Mercy and Well-natur'dness of that Tenet of the Universal Love of God to Mankind 'till you love more than your selves, and abominate that the Church of *England* should be the Elect to the Civil Government and all others as Reprobates, since you pretend to detest the like Injustice in *John Calvin*'s Notion of Election and Reprobation.[216]

And the Truth of it is, this helps on *Atheism* as much as any Enormity in the Land; when witty Men are not willing to take Pains to examine after the Truth and Excellency in Religion, so that People that call themselves Christ's Ministers and the Apostles Successors and Followers, affect and seek Government, and yet twice deny it, when they go to receive it: That some others grow Lordly, live Voluptuously, and watch after the biggest Preferments, not being excited by most Service for God, but earthly Power and Wealth for themselves; and that, at the same Time, they persecute Men of more Self-denyal, for Matters of Opinion about Faith and Worship towards God; so that *Non-Conformity* to the Church, *No Protection* from the State. Which, among *Protestants,* is so much the more unreasonable; *First,* Because they, by these Courses, implicitly own and assume the highest Infallibility and Perfection, and yet deny any such Thing. For it supposes that nothing is Truer, nothing Perfecter; or else they both persecute Men to embrace a Fallible and Imperfect Religion, and with cruel Penalties provide against any thing more true or Infallible; which is the greatest Injury to the World that can be, in as much as it is a plain Endeavour to frustrate all those excellent Prophecies and gracious Promises God hath given, and the Holy Scriptures declare of the latter Days. But *Secondly,* It exposes *Protestants* to the Lash and Scorn of the *Papist* unavoidably; for, at this Rate, you that, with Reason, think it Ignorance and Irreligion in the *Papist* to imagine himself discharged in God's Account, by believing only as the Church believes, conceive your selves, at the same Time, justify'd by believing only as a *few of your own Doctors,* or else as the State believes. But if the Church cannot use Force in Religion, because she cannot in-

216. On Calvin, see ch. 2, p. 57, n. 36.

fallibly determine to the Conscience without Convincement, much less ought a few *Doctors* or the Civil Authority to use Force where they can much less judge. Unless you would make them the Civil Executioners of your Displeasure who have no Civil Power to give them such Commission; and to be sure no Ecclesiastical Authority to Exercise any Force or Violence about Religion. For the Papist, judging by his Principles, punishes them that believe not as the Church believes, *though against Scripture;* but the *Protestant,* who teaches every one to believe the Scripture, *though against Church-Authority,* persecutes, against his own Principles, even them that in any Particular so believe as he, in general, teaches them to believe. This is hard, but true upon the *Protestant;* for what is plainer than that he afflicts those, that, according to his own Doctrine, believe and honour Holy Scripture, but, against it, will receive no Human Interpretation. *Them,* I say, who interpret Scripture to themselves, *which, by his Position, none but they to themselves can interpret; Them,* that use the Scripture no otherwise, by his own Doctrine, to their Edification, than He himself uses it to their Punishing; and so whom his Doctrine acknowledges true Believers, his Discipline persecutes as Hereticks.

To sum up all at this Time, If we must believe as *Caesar* appoints, why not then as the Church believes? But if not as either, *without Convincement,* pray how can Force be lawful? Let me recommend one Book to you, that of Right claims a Place with you, and that is *Bishop* Taylor'*s of Liberty of Prophecy;*[217] never answer'd, that I have heard of, and I have Reason to believe, never will be attempted; for indeed it is unanswerable. That was the Judgment of a Doctor under Persecution, I could be glad if it might be the Practice of Bishops in their Power: I may say the same of *J. Tillotson*'s sober and seasonable Discourse before the Commons on the Fifth of *November.*[218] And, the Truth is, I am the more earnest with you at this Time, because I find that God daily shews us he has great *good Will* to poor *England.* O why should we drive him from us by our Disobedience to him, and our Severities to one another! He has lately put a Price into our Hands, and continues to pour his Favours upon us: All depends upon a sincere Reformation and our Perseverance therein.

To give Testimony of this, *let us with our whole Hearts turn to God, and*

217. Jeremy Taylor, *Theologike eklektike; or A discourse on the liberty of prophesying* (London, 1647).

218. John Tillotson, *A sermon preached November 5, 1678, at St. Margarets, Westminster* (London, 1678).

keep his Holy Law; and let us but be jealous of his Glory, *by punishing Vice, and cherishing Virtue,* and we may assure our selves he will interest himself in our Safety. Of this we cannot doubt; for he who has begun to do it under our Disobedience, will not desert us in our sincere Repentance. And as this is our Duty to God, without which we vainly hope for Deliverance, so is there a Duty we owe to one another, that is the next requisite to our Preservation.

Let, therefore, all *Asperities* be avoided, *Nick-Names* forbidden, and the *Oppressed Protestant* delivered. Revive the noble Principle of *Liberty of Conscience,* on which the Reformation rose: *For in Vain do we hope to be deliver'd from* Papists, *'till we deliver our selves from* Popery. This *Coercion* upon *Conscience* and *Persecution* for *Religion* are that Part of *Popery* which is most justly hated and feared: And if we either fear or hate *Popery* for it's Cruelty, *shall we practise the* Cruelty *we fear or hate it for?* God forbid! No, not on those that have used it to us. This were the Way to be deserted of God, and left to their Cruelty. The same Sins will ever fix the same Odium, and find the same Punishment where-ever they are; yea greater, by how much Protestants pretend to better Things: If they burnt your Ancestors, don't you *strip* and *starve* your Brethren: Remember the many Thousands now persecuted in this Kingdom for the Sake of their tender and very peaceable Consciences; *Husbands are unlawfully separated from their Wives, and Parents from their Children, their Corn, Cattle and Houshold-stuff swept away, perhaps at the Instigation of some lewd and indigent Informer, or to please the Malice of an ill-dispos'd Neighbour.* In the mean Time many, once sufficient, are expos'd to Charity, the Fruits of their honest Labour and Bread of their poor helpless Children being now made the Forfeiture of their Conscience.

Friends and Country Men, there is a deep Doctrine in this Providence; examine it well, that you may reap the Benefit of it: And among the rest, let me tell you, this is not the least Part of it, that *God is* shewing you Mercy, that *you may shew Mercy,* and has awaken'd you at the Brink of the Pit, *that you may help your Brethren out of it,* ay, your Enemies. Be wise and considerate; It will be much your own Fault if you are not happy. And truly I have no Manner of Scruple, but God will preserve us, if we will not cast away our selves. For our own *Sins* and *Folly* can only direct the Hand that seeks to hit and hurt us; and shall we make it successful to our own Ruin? *Let us therefore turn away from all Impiety; let the Magistracy discourage and punish it; and let us forbear and love one another.* If we begin with God, we shall end with God, and that is with *Success:* Else, be assured, we shall only inherit the Wind of our own Invention, and be deserted of him then, when we shall most want him.

In short, reverence the present Providence; and though your Lives have not deserv'd it, let them now be grateful and not abuse it. Pursue your Advantages throughly, but wisely; be as temperate as zealous, and to your Enemies as generous as just. Insult not over ill Men for the Sake of their ill Principles, but pity their Unhappiness, whilst you abhor the Cause of it: Let them see that you had rather inform than destroy them, and that you take more Pleasure in their Conversion than your own Revenge. This will be the greatest Confutation upon them, that they be taught the Goodness of your Religion by the Mildness of it; and by it's Mercy the Cruelty of their own. The Indian *Atabaliba* rejected the *Romish Baptism* because of the *Spanish Tyranny;* whence it was usual with those Poor *Americans* to desire they might not go to *Heaven* if the *Spaniards* went thither. I know there be little Arts used to prevent *Protestant Union,* and that in a *Protestant Guise?* and 'tis a *Trick,* not of Yesterday, to put one Party of *Protestants* upon devouring four or five, that both the *Protestant* Church may have the Odium of *Eating* or *Devouring* her own *Children, and that another Interest, behind the Hangings,* may find the more easy and creditable Accession to the Chair: It is the Men of this Strain, though under Disguise, that now seek to distract you; and to effect it the better, old Stories must be had up, *Acts of Oblivion violated, the Dead disturb'd, their Tombs rifled, and they haled out of their Graves to receive a new Sentence:* That condemning the *Living* of that Interest by the *Dead,* they might be deserted of those, that, to say True, cannot be long safe without them.

If any Thing Sober and Judicious be propos'd for allaying Asperities, accomodating Differences, and securing to Prince and People a just and legal Union of Interest, as our Government requires, we must presently be told of 41, and 42, as if there were a sort of *Necromancy* in the Numbers, or that the naming of those Figures (long since made Cyphers by an *Act of Oblivion*) had Power enough to lay the active and generous Spirits of our Times:[219] But they find themselves mistaken in their *black* Art, *and that Things as well as Times*

219. "41, and 42" refer to 1641 and 1642; opponents of toleration frequently associated religious dissenters with the instigators of the Civil Wars and the execution of Charles I. The 1660 Act of Oblivion (12 Car. II, c. 2) pardoned most of those who had opposed the royal cause during the Civil Wars.

are changed; The Mask is off, and he that runs may read, *Res Nolunt malè Administrari.*[220]

Men in their Pleas and Endeavours for Truth, Justice and Sincere Religion will not be overborn or staggered by such stale and trifling Reflections, rarely used, of late, but to palliate wretched Designs, or discredit good ones with Men of weak Judgment, though perhaps of loyal Principles.

I beseech you let us not be unskilful in these Tricks, that we may not be mistaken or abused by them: I cannot tell a Time in which the Minds of all Sorts of *Protestants* have been more powerfully and unanimously engag'd to endeavour a good Understanding between the King and People. And as I am sure it was never more needed, so, let me say, no Age hath put a richer Price into the Hands of Men, or yielded a fairer Occasion to fix an happy and lasting Union upon: In order to which let me prevail with you that we may study to improve this great Principle as the necessary Means to it, viz. *That God's Providence and our own Constitution have made the Interest of Prince and People* One; *and that their Peace and Greatness lie in a most industrious and impartial Prosecution of it.*

Those that teach other Doctrine, as *that the Prince hath an Interest apart from the Good and Safety of the People,* are the sole Men that get by it, and therefore find themselves oblig'd to study their Misunderstanding; because they only are disappointed and insecured by their Union.

Experience truly tells us that such Persons have another Interest than that which leads to a common Good, and are often but too artificial in interesting Princes in the Success of it: But prudent and generous Princes have ever seen that it is neither safe nor just; and that no Kingdom can be govern'd with true Glory and Success but there *where the Interest of the Governour is one with that of the Governed,* and where there is the strictest Care to steer all Transactions of State, *by the Fundamentals, or the first and great Principles of their own Constitution:* Especially, since swerving from them hath always made Way for Confusion and Misery in Government. Our own Stories are almost every where vext by this Neglect; and those of our Neighbours must submit to the same Truth.

To conclude and sum up the whole Discourse; If you will both cure present and prevent future Grievances, it will greatly behove you to take a most deliberate and unbyass'd View of the present State of Things, with their proper

220. The matter refuses to be badly managed.

Causes and Tendencies. Let us confront our *Ecclesiastical* Matters with the plain *Text* and *Letter* of Holy *Scripture;* this is *Protestant.* And let us compare our *Civil* Transactions with the *Ancient Laws and Statutes* of the Realm; this is *English.* And I do humbly and heartily beseech Almighty God, that he would so dispose the Hearts of Prince and People, as that firm Foundations may be now laid for a Just and Lasting Tranquility to these Nations: And believe me if you please, unless they are Just and Equal they cannot last. Time will prove it, because it always has, and that God is unchangeable in the Order and Justice of his Providence. And, since Righteousness exalts a Nation, and that Sin is the Shame of any People:[221] therefore will I close with *David*'s Prayer, Psal. 7. 9. *O let the Wickedness of the Wicked come to an End, but Establish the Just: For the Righteous God tryeth the Hearts and the Reins.*

An APPENDIX of the CAUSES and CURE of *Persecution.*

I IMPUTE all Persecution for Religion to these Seven ensuing Causes, tho properly speaking, there is but one Original Cause of this Evil, and that is the Devil, as there is but one Original Cause of Good, and that is God.

I. The first Cause of Persecution is this, *That the Authors and Users of it have little or no Religion at Heart;* They are not subject to the Ground and first Cause of true Religion in their own Souls; for it is the Part of true Religion to *humble* the Mind, *break* the Heart, and *soften* the Affection; It was God himself that said, *Unto this Man will I look, even to him that is poor and of a contrite Spirit, and trembles at my Word;*[222] not one that breaks Pates, and plunders Goods for Religion. *Blessed are they that mourn, said Christ, they shall be comforted;*[223] but not Those that sell *Joseph* and make Merry. *Blessed are the poor in Spirit, for theirs is the Kingdom of God;* Those that are low in their own Eyes; not such as devour and damn all but themselves. *Blessed are the Meek, for they shall inherit the Earth;* such as are gentle and ready to help, and not Tyrannize over Neighbours. *Blessed are the Merciful, for they shall obtain Mercy;* what then shall become of those that are Cruel, under Pretence of

221. Proverbs 14:34.

222. Isaiah 66:2.

223. Here and in the following sentences Penn refers to the Beatitudes, Matthew 5; for the reference to selling Joseph and making merry, see Genesis 37:28.

doing it for God's Sake? *Blessed are the Peace-makers, for they shall be called the Children of God;* then Disturbers and Destroyers of their peaceable Neighbours shall not be called so. *Blessed are they that hunger and thirst after Righteousness, for they shall be filled;* but not those that hunger and thirst after our Corn and Cattel, Houses and Land for Conscience sake. *And Blessed are you,* says Christ, *when Men shall Revile and Persecute you, &c.* Then not those that Revile and Persecute others that are Sober and Harmless: Not one Blessing to his Conscience-hunting Doctrine and Practice, that devour the Widow and Orphans for Religion. Were Men inwardly and truly Religious, they would have so low an Opinion of themselves, so tender a Regard to Mankind, so great an awe of Almighty God, as that none of these froward Passions would have any Sway with them. But, the Mischief is, *unmortified Passions pretend to Religion;* a proud, impatient, arrogant Mind would promote it; than which, nothing of Man is more remote from it; mistaking the very Nature and End of Christ's peaceable Religion, *Which* if the Apostle *James* say true, *is to visit the Fatherless and Widow, and keep our selves unspotted of the World.*[224] But, on the contrary, They turn Widow and Fatherless out of House and Home, and spot themselves with the Cruelty and Injustice of usurping their poor Patrimony, the Bread of their Lives, and Sustenance of their Natures: Such Men as these are void of natural Affection; their Religion has no Bowels, or they are without Mercy in the Profession of it; which is the *Reverse* of true Religion, that *makes us love Enemies, do good to them that hate us, and pray for them that despitefully use us:*[225] And so much stronger, in Souls truly Religious, is the Power of Love to Mankind than any self revenging Passion, that from an humble and serious Reflection upon the Mercies and Goodness of God to them, they do not only suppress any rising of Heart against their Persecutors (much more against peaceable Dissenters) but with much softness and Charity, commiserate their Ignorance and Anger: Offering to inform them, and praying that they may be forgiven. This is to be Religious, and therefore those that Persecute for Religion any ways are *Irreligious.*

II. The next Cause of Persecution is the gross but general mistake which People are under concerning the Nature of the Church and Kingdom of Christ: For the lamentable Worldliness of Mens Minds hath put them upon those Carnal Constructions which have made Way for all the external Coercion and

224. James 1:27.
225. Matthew 5:44.

Violence, used by bad and suffer'd by good Men, on the Score of Religion, from the Beginning. And no wonder if ordinary Persons tumble upon this Construction, when the Disciples of Jesus shew'd themselves so ill read in the Mysteries of his Kingdom, that after all the Intimacy they had had with him, they refrain'd not to ask, *When shall the Kingdom be restored to* Israel.[226] They look't abroad, had a Worldly *Idea* in their Minds; *Jews* like, they waited for external Deliverance from the Power of the *Romans,* rather than an Internal Salvation from the Dominion of *Satan;* and interpreted those Words to Worldly Loss and Freedom, which did relate to the Loss and Redemption of the Soul: But Jesus taught them better Things; yet so, as not to deny or flatly discourage and rebuke them; for that, though true, might have been more at that Time, than they could have born; therefore he winds off with them upon the Time and the Season of the Thing, knowing that the Time was at Hand, that they should be better taught and satisfied of the Nature of his Kingdom, unto which he referred them. *When the Spirit of Truth comes, it shall lead you into all Truth, &c:*[227]

That the Kingdom of Christ is not of this World, has been before observed, and the Reason is so great that all Men of Common Sense must allow it, upon Christ's Principle and Argument; for says he, *then would my Servants fight for me;*[228] truly implying, because the Kingdoms of this World are evidently set up and maintained by worldly Force, and that he will have no worldly Force used in the Business of his Kingdom, that therefore it is not of this World. Consequently, those that attempt to set up his Kingdom by worldly Force, or make that their Pretence to use it, are none of his Servants: They are truly but Men of this World; such as seek an Earthly, and not an Heavenly Crown and Kingdom: Themselves, and not Christ Jesus. Where, by the way, let me observe, that though the *Jews,* to engage *Pilate* the more easily to their side, impeach't *Christ* of being an Enemy to *Caesar,* they were Enemies, and *He* appeared a *Friend* to *Caesar;* for he came to reform the Lives of Men, to make them better Subjects; to obey *Caesar,* not for Fear, but for *Conscience-sake:* A way to make *Caesar*'s Province, both easie and safe. But the *Jews* would have had him *Caesar*'s Enemy; one that should have forceably rescu'd them from *Caesar* Power; That was what they waited for; *a Captain General* to head the

226. Acts 1:6.
227. John 16:13.
228. John 18:36.

Revolt, and with an High Hand to overbear and captive *Caesar,* as he had done them: And, 'tis more than probable, that this Appearance being after quite another Manner and to another End than they expected; They therefore rejected him; their Hearts being set upon the Desire of Worldly Empire:

But to return; Christ told his Disciples, *that he had chosen them out of the World;*[229] how pray? Not to converse or live bodily in it? No such Matter: But he had chosen or *singled them from the Nature, Spirit, Glory, Policy and Pomp of this World.* How Persons, so qualified, can make a Worldly Church or Kingdom, unless they desert Christ's Doctrine, is past my Skill to tell. So that the Capacity that Christians stand in to Christ is Spiritual, and not Worldly or Carnal; and for that Reason not Carnal or Worldly, but Spiritual Methods and Weapons only are to be used to inform or reclaim such as are Ignorant or Disobedient. And if we will give Ancient Story credit, we shall find that Worldly Weapons were never employed by the Christian Church till she became Worldly, and so ceast to be truly Christian.

But why should I say the *Church?* the most abused Word in the World; It is her Leaders have taught her to err; and that of *believing as the Church believes,* is so far from being true in Point of Fact as well as Reason, that the Church her self has long believed as the Clergy, that is, the Priest, believed, ever since that Sort of Men have practised a Distinction from, and Superiority upon, the Laity. He that will peruse the Ecclesiastical Story delivered us by *Eusebius Pamphilus, Socrates Scholasticus, Evagrius, Ruffinus, Sozomen,* and more especially the Councils, B. *Usher,* ay, and *Baronius himself,* will find but too many and sad Instances of the Truth of this.[230]

In short, People apprehending the Church and Kingdom of Christ to be Visible and Worldly, like other Societies and Governments, have thought it not only to be Lawful, but Necessary to use the Arts and Force of this World to support his Church and Kingdom; especially since the Interest of Religion hath been incorporated with that of the *Civil Magistrate:* For from that Time he hath been made *Custos utriusque Tabulae,*[231] and such as offend, though

229. John 15:19.

230. See the ecclesiastical histories of Eusebius Pamphilus, Socrates Scholasticus, Evagrius (ca. 536–94), Rufinus of Aquileia (345–410), Salminius Hermias Sozomen (d. 447 or 448), Bishop James Usher (1581–1656), and Venerable Cesare Baronius (1538–1607).

231. Guardian of both tables: i.e., the First Table of the Ten Commandments outlined human duties toward God; the Second, duties toward fellow human beings.

about Church Matters, have been reputed Transgressors against the State, and consequently the State interested in punishing the Offence. Whereas had *Christians* remain'd in their primitive Simplicity and Purity, in the Self-denying, Patient and Suffering Doctrine of *Christ;* Christianity had stood in Holy Living and not in Worldly Regiment; and it's Compulsion would have been Love, it's Arms Reasons and Truth, and it's utmost Rigour, even to obstinate Enemies or Apostates, but Renouncing of their Communion, and that not till much Forbearance and many Christian Endeavours had been used to reclaim them.

To sum up all; The Kingdoms of this World, stand in outward, Bodily and Civil Matters, and here the Laws and Power of Men reach and are effectual. But the Kingdom and Church of Christ, that is chosen out of the World, stands not in *Bodily Exercise* (which the Apostle says profits little) nor in Times nor Places, but in Faith, and that Worship which Christ tells us is in *Spirit and in Truth:*[232] To this no worldly Compulsion can bring or force Men; 'tis only the Power of that King of Righteousness whose Kingdom is in the Minds and Souls of the Just, and he rules by the Law of his own free Spirit, which, like the Wind, *Bloweth where it listeth:*[233] And as without this Spirit of Regeneration no Man can be made a Member of Christ's Church or Kingdom, and less a Minister, so neither is it in the Power of Man to command or give it, and consequently all worldly Force employ'd to make Men Members of Christ's Church and Kingdom is as ineffectual as unnatural. I could be very large upon this Point, for it is very fruitful, and so much the Cause of Persecution, that if there were never another to be assign'd, this were enough; and upon due Consideration it must needs meet with every Man's Judgment and Experience, I will here add the Sense of Memorable *Hales* of *Eaton* upon this Subject.[234]

> When our Saviour, in the *Acts,* after his Resurrection, was discoursing to his Disciples concerning the Kingdom of God, they presently brake forth into this Question, *Wilt thou now restore the Kingdom unto* Israel?[235] Certainly this Question betrays their Ignorance: Their Thoughts still ran upon a Kingdom, *like unto the Kingdoms of the World,* notwithstanding they had so long and so often heard our Saviour to the

232. 1 Timothy 4:8; and John 4:23–24.
233. John 3:8.
234. Hales, "Sermon on John 18:36," in *Golden remains,* pp. 153–55.
235. Acts 1:6.

contrary: Our Saviour therefore shortly takes them up, *Non est vestrum,* your Question is nothing to the Purpose; the Kingdom that I have spoken of is *another Manner of* Kingdom than you conceive. Sixteen hundred Years, *& quod excurrit,*[236] hath the Gospel been preached unto the World, and is this Stain spunged out yet? I doubt it. Whence arise those novel and late Disputes, *de Notis Ecclesiae,* of the Notes and *Visibility* of the Church? Is it not from hence, they of *Rome* take the World and the Church to be like *Mercury* and *Sosia* in *Plautus* his Comedies, so like one another, that one of them must wear a *Toy* in his Cap, that so the Spectators might distinguish them;[237] whence comes it, that they stand so much upon *State* and *Ceremony* in the Church? Is it not from hence, that they think the Church must come in like *Agrippa* and *Bernice* in the *Acts μετὰ πολλῆς φαντασίας,* as St. *Luke* speaks, with a great deal of *Pomp,* and *Train,* and *Shew,* and *Vanity?*[238] And that the Service of God, doth necessarily require this Noise and Tumult of outward State and Ceremony? Whence comes it, that we are at our Wits End, when we see Persecution, and Sword, and Fire, to range against the true Professors of the Gospel? Is it not because, as these bring Ruin and Desolation upon the Kingdoms of the World, so we suppose they work no other Effect in the Kingdom of Christ? All these Conceits, and many more of the like Nature, spring out of no other Fountain than that *old inveterate Error,* which is so hardly wiped out of our Hearts, That the *State* of the *Church* and Kingdom of Christ, doth hold some *Proportion,* some *likeness* with the State *and managing of temporal Kingdoms:* Wherefore to pluck out of our Hearts, *Opinionem tam insitam, tam vetustam,* a Conceit so ancient, so deeply *rooted* in us, our Saviour spake most excellently, most pertinently, and most fully, when he tells us that his *Church,* that his *Kingdom is not of this World.*[239]

In which Words of his, there is contained the true Art of discovering and knowing the true Nature and Essence of the *Church.* For as they which make *Statues,* cut and pare away all Superfluities of the Matter

236. And more have passed.

237. In Plautus's (ca. 255–184 B.C.E.) *Amphitryon,* Mercury assumes the form of the slave Sosia. To distinguish Mercury from the actual Sosia (upon the latter's return), the god wears a plume in his hat, ostensibly visible only to the audience.

238. The account of Paul before Agrippa and Bernice is found in Acts 25–26.

239. John 18:36.

upon which they work; so our Saviour, to shew us the true Proportion and Feature of the *Church,* prunes away the *World,* and all Superfluous excrescencies, and sends her to be seen, at he did our first Parents in Paradise, *stark naked:* As those *Elders* in the *Apocryphal* Story of *Susanna,* when they would see her Beauty, commanded to take off her Mask;[240] so he that longs to see the Beauty of the *Church,* must pull off that *Mask* of the *World,* and outward shew. For as *Juda* in the *Book* of *Genesis,* when *Thamar* sat vail'd by the Way Side, knew not his Daughter from an Whore;[241] so whilst the *Church,* the Daughter and Spouse of Christ, *sits vail'd with the World,* and *Pomp* and *Shew,* it will be an hard Matter to discern her from an *Harlot.* But yet further, to make the Difference betwixt these Kingdoms the more plainly to appear, and so better to fix in your Memories, I will briefly touch some of those Heads, in which they are most notoriously differenced.

The first Head wherein the Difference is seen, are the Persons and Subjects of this Kingdom: For as the *Kingdom* of *Christ is not of this World,* so the *Subjects* of this *Kingdom* are *Men* of *another World,* and not of this. Every one of us bears a double Person, and accordingly is the Subject of a double Kingdom: The *Holy Ghost,* by the *Psalmist,* divides Heaven and Earth betwixt God and Man, and tells us, as for God, *He is in Heaven, but the Earth has he given to the Children of Men:* So hath the same Spirit, by the Apostle St. *Paul,* divided every one of our Persons into Heaven and Earth, into an outward and earthly Man, and into an inward and Heavenly Man:[242] This *Earth,* that is, this *Body* of Clay hath he given to the *Sons of Men,* to the *Princes* under whose Government we live; but *Heaven,* that is, the *inward* and *spiritual Man,* hath he reserved unto *himself:* They can restrain the *outward Man,* and moderate our *outward Actions* by *Edicts* and *Laws;* they can tye our Hands and our Tongues;—*Illâ se jactet in aula AEolus:*[243] Thus far they can go, and when they are gone thus far, they can go no farther: But to rule the *inward Man* in our *Hearts* and *Souls,* to set up an Impartial Throne in our *Understandings,* and *Wills,* this Part of our Government belongs to

240. Book of Susanna, Apocrypha.

241. Genesis 38:12–16.

242. Psalms 115:16; and 2 Corinthians 4:16.

243. Virgil *Aeneid* 1.140–41: "Let Aeolus rule in the locked prison of the winds."

> *God* and to *Christ:* These are the Subjects, this the Government of his Kingdom: Men may be Kings of Earth and Bodies, but Christ alone is the King of Spirits and Souls. Yet this *inward Government* hath Influence upon our *outward Actions:* For the Authority of Kings over our outward Man is not so absolute, but that it suffers a great Restraint; it must stretch no farther than the Prince of our inward Man pleases: For if secular Princes stretch out the Skirts of their Authority to command ought by which our Souls are prejudic'd, the King of Souls hath in this Case given us a greater Command, *That we rather obey God than Men.*[244]

III. A Third Great Cause of Persecution for Religion is this, *that Men make too many Things necessary to be believed to Salvation and Communion. Persecution* entred with *Creed-making;* for it so falls out, that those who distinguish the Tree in the Bulk, cannot with the like Ease discern every Branch or Leaf that grows upon it; and to run out the necessary Articles of Faith to every good or true Thing that the Wit of Man may deduce from the Text, and so too, as that I ought to have a distinct *Idea* or *Apprehension* of every one of them, and must run them over in my Mind as a Child would conn a Lesson by Heart, of which I must not miss a Tittle upon my Salvation; this I think to be a Temptation upon Men to fall into Dispute and Division, and then we are taught, by long Experience, that he that has most Power will oppress his Opinion that is weaker; whence comes Persecution: This certainly puts Unity and Peace too much upon the Hazard. *Mary*'s Choice therefore was not of many Things, *but the one Thing necessary,* as Christ, the Lord of the true Divinity Terms it. *Luke* 10. 42. And pray what was this one needful Thing, *but Christ Jesus himself, and her Faith, Love and Obedience in and to him?* Here is no perplex'd Creed to subscribe, no *System* of *Divinity* to charge the Head with; This *One needful Thing* was *Mary*'s Choice and Blessing: May it be ours, and, I should hope a quick End to Controversies, and consequently to Persecutions.

IV. Another Cause of Persecution, is *The Prejudice of Education, and that Byass Tradition gives to those Men, who have not made their Religion the Religion of their Judgment:* For such will forbid all the Inquiry which might question the Weakness or Falshood of their Religion, and had rather be deceiv'd in an honourable Descent, than be so uncivil to the Memory of their Ancestors as to seek the Truth, which found, must reprove the Ignorance of their Ages;

244. Acts 5:29.

of this, the vainest of all Honours, they are extream careful; and at the very Mention of any Thing, to them new, tho' as old as Truth, and older than this World, are easily urg'd into a Tempest, and are not appeased but by a *Sacrifice.* This Ignorance and Want of Inquiry helps on Persecution.

V. Another Reason, and that no small one, is *Self-Love* and *Impatience of Men under Contradiction,* be it of Ignorance, that they are angry with what they cannot refute, or out of private Interest, it matters not: Their Opinion must reign alone, they are tenacious of their own Sense and can't indure to have it questioned, be there never so much Reason for it. Men of their Passions are yet to learn that they are ignorant of Religion, by the want they have of Mortification; such Persons can easily let go their Hold on Charity, to lay violent Hands upon their Opposers: If they have Power, they rarely fail to use it so; not remembring, that when they absolv'd themselves from the Tye of Love, Meekness and Patience, they abandoned true Religion, and contended not for the Faith, once deliver'd to the Saints,[245] which stood therein, but for meer Words.

It is here that proud Flesh, and a capricious Head disputes for Religion, and not an humble Heart and a Divine Frame of Spirit. *Men that are angry for God, Passionate for Christ, that can call Names for Religion, and fling Stones for Faith,* may tell us they are *Christians* if they will, but no Body would know them to be such by their Fruits; to be sure they are no *Christians* of Christ's making.

I would to God that the Disputants of our Time did but calmly weigh the Irreligiousness of their own Heats for Religion, and see if what they contend for will quit the Cost, will countervail the Charge of departing from Charity, and making a Sacrifice of Peace to gain their Point. Upon so seasonable a Reflection I am confident they would find that they rather show their Love to Opinion than Truth, and seek Victory more than Concord.

Could Men be contented, as he whom they call their Lord was, *to declare their Message, and not strive for Proselytes, nor vex for Conquest,* they would recommend all to the Conscience, and if it must be so, patiently endure Contradiction too, and so lay their Religion, as he did his, not in Violence but Suffering: But I must freely profess, and in Duty and Conscience I do it, that I cannot call that Religion, which is introduced against the Laws of Love, Meekness and Friendship: Superstition, Interest or Faction, I may.

245. Jude 3.

There is a Zeal without Knowledge, that is Superstition; there is a Zeal against Knowledge, that is *Interest* or *Faction,* the true *Heresie;* there is a Zeal with Knowledge, that is *Religion;* therefore blind Obedience may be Superstition, it can't be Religion; And if you will view the Countries of Cruelty, you shall find them superstitious rather than Religious. *Religion* is *gentle,* it makes Men *better,* more friendly, loving and patient then before. And the Success, which followed *Christianity,* whilst the ancient Professors of it *betook* themselves to no other Defence, plainly proves both the Force of those passive Arguments above all corporal Punishments, and that we must never hope for the same Prosperity, *till we fall into the same Methods.* Gal. 5. 22. James 3. 17. Are Men impatient of having their Conceits own'd? they are then most to be suspected. Error and Superstition, like crackt Titles, *only fear to be searcht, and run and cry for Authority and Number.* Truth is plain and stedfast, without Arts or Tricks; will you receive her, well; if not, there is no Compulsion. But, pray tell me, what is that desired Uniformity that has not Unity, and that Unity, which has not Love, Meekness and Patience in it? I beseech you hear me, for those Men depart from the Spirit of *Christianity* that seek with Anger and Frowardness to promote it. Let us not put so miserable a Cheat upon our selves, nor such an Affront upon *Christianity* as to think *that a most gentle and patient Religion can be advanced by most ungentle and impatient Ways.* I should sooner submit to an humble Opposition, than to the greatest Zealot in the World, and rather deliver up my self to him that would modestly drop a controverted Truth, than to such as seek tempestuously to carry it; for even Error, bashfully and patiently defended, endangers Truth, in the Management of imprudent and hasty Zeal; and gives to it that Lustre, which only *good Eyes* can see from Gold. Alas! it is for want of considering that Men don't see, that to disorder the Mind in Controversie is a greater Mischief, than to carry the Point can be a Benefit; inasmuch as it is not to be Religious to apprehend rightly, but to do well: The latter can scarcely be without the former, but the former often is without the latter, which brings me to my sixth Cause of Persecution.

VI. Another, and that no small Cause of *Persecution, is a Misapprehension of the Word* Religion. For when once the Ignorance or Prejudice of Men, has perswaded them to lay more weight upon their own *Opinion,* or *Dissent* of their Neighbours, than in Truth the Thing will bear, to excuse their Zeal or justifie their Spleen or Credit, they presently heighten the Difference to a *new Religion;* whence we so frequently hear of such Reflections as these, *new Gospels* and *Faiths, upstart Religions and Lights,* and with the like *Scare-Crows,* amuse the Vulgar, and render their own Design of ruining honest Men the more practicable. But I would obviate this Mischief; for a *new Religion* has a *new Foundation,* and consequently where there is the *same Foundation,* there cannot be a *new Religion.* Now the *Foundation* of the Christian Religion is Christ, and that only is another *Religion* than the Christian which professes another *Foundation,* or corruptly adds to that *Foundation;* by adding of other Mediators, and introducing a new Way of Remission of Sin: Which at least cannot be said of the several sorts of *Protestants?* For *Protestants* therefore to reproach each other with *new Religions and Gospels;* and by their indecent and unchristian Behaviour, to enflame their own Reckoning, and draw into more Discord, is a Sin against God, an Injury to the common Cause of *Protestancy,* and to the Security of the civil Interest of that Country, where the Inhabitants are of that Religion, as well as a real Injustice to one another: For *Protestants* don't only agree in the *same Fundamentals of Christianity,* but of *Protestancy* too, that is, in the Reasons of Separation from *Rome,* which was also *Christian.* Let not every circumstantial Difference or Variety of *Cult* be *Nicknam'd a new Religion,* neither suffer so ill an Use to be made of such Dissents as to carry them beyond their true Bounds; for the Meaning of those Arts of ill Men, is to set the People farther off from one another than they really are, and to aggravate Differences in Judgment to Contrariety in Affection: And when they have once inflam'd them to Variance and Strife, nothing can hinder Persecution but Want of Power; which being never wanted by the strongest Side, the Weakest, though truest, is opprest, not by Argument but Worldly Weapons.

VII. The *seventh* and *last* Cause I shall now assign for Persecution is this, *That Holy Living is become no Test among us, unless against the Liver.* The Tree was once known by it's Fruits: It is not so now: The better Liver, the more dangerous, *is not a Conformist,* and so the more in Danger, and this has made Way for Persecution. There was a Time, when Virtue was Venerable and good Men admired; but that is too much derided, and Opinion carries it.

He that can perswade his Conscience to comply with the Times, *be he Vicious, Knavish, Cowardly, any Thing,* he is protected, perhaps preferred. A Man of Wisdom, Sobriety and Ability to serve his King and Country, *if a Dissenter,* must be blown upon for a *Phanatick,* a Man of *Faction,* of *disloyal* Principles, and what not?

Rewards and Punishments are the Magistrates Duty and the Government's *Interest and Support.* Rewards are due to Virtue, Punishments to Vice. Let us not mistake nor mis-call Things; let Virtue be what it always was in Government; *good Manners, sober and just Living;* and Vice, *ill Manners and dishonest Living.* Reduce all to this; Let *such good Men have the Smiles and Rewards, and such ill Men the Frowns and Punishments of the Government:* This ends Persecution, and lays Opinion to Sleep. Ill Men will make no more Advantages by such Conformity, nor good Men no more suffer for Want of it.

In short: As that Religious Society deserves not the Protection of the Civil Government which is inconsistent with the Safety of it; so those Societies of Christians that are not only not Destructive of the Civil Government, but Lovers of it, ought, by the Civil Government, to be secured from Ruin.

God Almighty open our Understandings and Hearts, and pour out the *Spirit of thorough Reformation* upon us; for it is in the *Spirit,* and not in the Words of Reformation, that the Life and Prosperity of Reformation stands; that so we may be all conscientiously dispos'd to seek and pursue those things which make for Love, Peace and Godliness, that it may be well with us and ours, both here and for ever.

> *For yet a little while and the* Wicked shall not be; *yea, thou shalt diligently consider his Place, and it shall not be; but the Meek shall inherit the Earth, and shall delight themselves in Abundance of Peace. The Wicked Plotteth against the Just, and gnasheth upon him with his Teeth; the Lord shall laugh at him; for he seeth that his Day is coming.* Psal. 37. 10, 11, 12, 13.

The Judgment of King JAMES and King CHARLES the First about Persecution for Religion.

WE FIND it asserted by King *James* in his Speech to the Parliament in the Year 1609. *That it is a pure Rule in Divinity, That God never loves to plant his Church with* Violence *and* Blood: And he furthermore said, *It was usually the Condition of* Christians *to be* Persecuted, *but not to* Persecute.[246]

And we find the same Things in Substance asserted again by his Son, King *Charles* the First, in his Book known by the Name of ΕΙΚΩΝ ΒΑΞΙΛΙΚΗ, printed for *R. Royston,* as followeth.

246. James I, "Speech to Parliament, 21 March 1609/1610," in *King James VI and I: Political Writings,* ed. Johann P. Sommerville (Cambridge, 1994), p. 199.

Page 67. In his Prayer to God, he said, *Thou seest how much* Cruelty, *amongst* Christians, *is acted under the Colour of Religion; as if we could not be* Christians, *unless we Crucify one another.*

Page 28. *Make them at length seriously to consider, that nothing* Violent *and* Injurious, *can be Religion.*

Page 70. *Nor is it so proper to hew out Religious Reformations by the* Sword, *as to polish them by* fair *and* equal Disputations, *among those that are most concern'd in the Differences, whom not Force but Reason ought to convince.*

Sure, in Matters of Religion, those Truths gain most upon Men's Judgments and Consciences, which are least urged with Secular Violence, *which weakens Truth with Prejudices.*

Page 115. *It being an Office not only of Humanity, rather to use* Reason *than* Force, *but also of* Christianity *to seek Peace and ensue it.*

Some Words of Advice from King CHARLES the First to the then Prince of *Wales,* now King of *England, &c.*

Page 165. M*Y COUNSEL and Charge to you is, That you seriously consider the former Real or Objected Miscarriages, which might Occasion my Troubles, that you may avoid them,* &c.

Beware of Exasperating any Faction, by the Crosness and Asperity of some Men's Passions, Humours and private Opinions, employ'd by you, grounded only upon Differences in lesser Matters, which are but the Skirts and Suburbs of Religion, wherein a Charitable Connivance and Christian Toleration, often dissipates their Strength, when rougher Opposition fortifies, and puts the Despised and Oppressed Party into such Combinations, as may most enable them to get a full Revenge on those they count their Persecutors.

Page 166. *Take Heed that Outward Circumstances and Formalities of Religion devour not all.*

A BRIEF
EXAMINATION
AND
STATE of Liberty Spiritual,
BOTH
With Respect to Persons in their Private *Capacity*, and in their *Church Society* and *Communion* (1681)

Written for the Establishment of the Faithful, Information of the Simple-Hearted, and Reproof of the Arrogant and High-minded, by a Lover of True Liberty, as it is in Jesus.
William Penn.

To go amongst the People of the Lord, called *Quakers.*

If the Son *shall make you* Free, *ye shall be Free* indeed. John 8. 36.
If we walk in the Light as he is in the Light, we have Fellowship *one with another, and the Blood of Jesus Christ his Son cleanseth us from all Sin,* 1 John 1. 7.

To the People of the Lord, called *QUAKERS.*

Dear Friends and Brethren,

I*T HATH of long Time rested with some pressure upon my Spirit, for* Zion's *Sake, and the Peace of* Jerusalem, *to write something of the* Nature of True Spiritual Liberty; Liberty, *one of the most Glorious Words and Things in the World, but little understood, and frequently abused by many. I beseech Almighty God to preserve you, his People, in the right Knowledge and Use of that Liberty, which Jesus Christ, the Captain of our Salvation, hath purchased for us, and is redeeming us into, who hath* led Captivity captive, *and is* giving Gifts to them that truly believe in his Name.[1] *Christ's Liberty is obtain'd through Christ's Cross; they that would be his Free-men, must be his Bonds-men, and wear his blessed Yoke.*[2] *His Liberty is* from Sin, not to Sin; *to do his Will, and not our*

1. Ephesians 4:8.
2. Matthew 11:29–30.

own; no, not to speak an Idle Word. 'Tis not I that live (*saith the Apostle*) but Christ that liveth in me, *who had* set him Free from the Power of Sin, and brought Immortality to Light *in him; whence he learned thus to triumph,* O Death, where is thy Sting! O Grave, where is thy Victory![3] *This is the Personal Freedom that comes by* Jesus Christ, *to as many as receive him in the Way, and for the End for which God hath given him, to wit,* to be a Saviour and a Leader, to save us from our Corruptions, and guide us in the Narrow Way of his Holy Cross, and through the strait Gate of Self-denyal, *which leads to Eternal Life. And as many as have enter'd at this Door, are come to have* Unity with God, and one with another; To love him above all, and their Neighbours as themselves;[4] *yea, to prefer each other before themselves. Such will not violate the great Law of their Lord and Master;* Love one another;[5] *the* New, *and yet the* Old Commandment: *These dwell in* Love, *and so they dwell in* God; for God is Love. *'Twas the beloved Disciple's Testimony, and it comes up to what another Man of God hath said, namely,* The Church that dwells in God, if she dwells in God, then in Love; consequently her Members are in Union, of one Mind in Church Matters, since she has but one Head to Rule her.[6]

Peruse this brief Discourse in this Love, and it may be to Edification. My Aim is to assert the Truth, detect Error, and point in true Brotherly Kindness at those Shoals and Sands some by Mistake, or Overboldness, have and may run upon. O Friends! *I greatly desire, that the Spirit of* Love, Wisdom, and a sound Understanding, of Meekness, Judgment and Mercy, *may ever rest upon you, that blamelesly you may be kept, an Holy Family, at Unity with it self, to the Lord God your Redeemer, that he over all may in you, through you, and by you, be Exalted, Honoured and Praised, who is worthy and blessed for ever.*

A Brief EXAMINATION, *&c.*

Quest. W*HAT is Spiritual Liberty?*

Answ. It is twofold; there is a true and a false Liberty, as a true and false Spirit, the right discerning of which concerns every one's Eternal Well-being.

3. Galatians 2:20; and 1 Corinthians 15:55.
4. Matthew 22:36–40.
5. John 13:34–35.
6. See 1 John 4:16; and 1 John 3:11; see also Colossians 1:8; and Ephesians 1:22.

Qu. *What is true Spiritual Liberty?*

Answ. Deliverance from Sin by the Perfect Law in the Heart, *The Perfect Law of Liberty* James 2. otherwise called, *The Law of the Spirit of Life in Christ Jesus, that makes free from the Law of Sin and Death;* else-where stiled, *The Law of Truth writ in the Heart,* which makes Free indeed, as saith Christ, *If the Son shall make you Free, ye shall be Free indeed.*[7] So that the Liberty of Gods People stands *in the Truth, and their Communion in it,* and in the Perfect Spiritual Law of Christ Jesus, which delivers and preserves them from every Evil Thing that doth or would embondage. In this blessed Liberty, it is not the Will nor Wisdom of Man, neither the vain Affections and Lusts that rule, or give Law to the Soul; for the Minds of all such as are made Free by the Truth, are by the Truth conducted in doing and suffering through their Earthly Pilgrimage.

Qu. *What is False Liberty?*

Answ. A Departing from this blessed Spirit of Truth, and *a Rebelling against this Perfect Law of Liberty in the Heart,*[8] and being at Liberty to do our own Wills; upon which cometh Reproof and Judgment.

Qu. *But are there not some Things wherein we ought to be left to our own Freedom?*

Answ. We are not our own, for we are bought with a Price; and in all Things ought we to glorify God with our Bodies, Souls and Spirits, which are the Lord's.[9]

Qu. *But must we have a Motion or Command from the Spirit of Truth for all Things that we do?*[10]

Answ. That may be according to the Truth, which may not be by the immediate Motion or Command of the Truth; for that is according to the Truth, that is not against the Mind of the Truth, either particularly or generally exprest. The Truth commands me to *do all to the Praise and Glory of God;*[11] but not that I should wait for a Motion to do every particular Thing. For *Example:* The variety of Actions in Trading, Commerce and Husbandry, the Variety of Flesh, Fish and Fowl for Food, with more of the same Nature, in all which

7. Romans 8:2; and John 8:31–32, 36.

8. For the "spirit of truth," see 1 John 4:6; for the "perfect law of liberty," see James 1:25.

9. 1 Corinthians 6:20; 7:23.

10. "Motion" refers to an inward source of outward action; see Romans 7:5.

11. 1 Corinthians 6:20.

there is a Choice and Liberty, but still according to the Truth, and within the Holy Bounds and Limits of it.

Qu. *Then it seems there are some Things left to our Freedom.*

Answ. Yes; but it must still be according to the Mind of God's Truth: There are Things enjoyned, such as relate to our Duty to God, to our Superiors, to the Houshold of Faith and to all Men and Creatures, these are *Indispensible.* There are also Things that may be done or left undone, which may be called *Indifferent;*[12] as what sort of Meat I will eat to day, whether I will eat Flesh, Fish or Herbs, or what Hours I will eat my Meals at, with many such outward Things of Life and Converse; yet even in such Cases I ought to act according to the Truth, in the Temperance and Wisdom of it.

Qu. *But doth not Freedom extend farther than this; for since God hath given me a Manifestation of his Spirit to profit withal, and that I have the Gift of God in my self, should I not be lest to act according as I am free and perswaded in my own Mind, in the Things that relate to God, left looking upon my self as obliged by what is revealed unto another, though it be not revealed unto me, I should be led out of my own Measure, and act upon another's Motion, and so offer a blind Sacrifice to God?*

Answ. This is true in a Sense, that is, if thou art such an one that canst do nothing against the Truth, but for the Truth, then mayst thou safely be left to thy Freedom in the Things of God, and the Reason is plain; because thy Freedom stands in the Perfect Law of Liberty, in the Law of the Spirit of Life in Christ Jesus, and in the Truth, which is Christ Jesus, which makes thee Free indeed, that is, perfectly Free from all that is Bad, and perfectly Free to all that is *Holy, Just, Lovely, Honest, Comely, and of good Report;*[13] but if thou pleadest thy Freedom against such Things, yea, obstructest and slightest such *Good,*

12. The category of "indifferent" things, or *adiaphora,* played a central role in early modern toleration debates, often used by tolerationists to argue against compulsion on matters not central to Christian doctrine. Initially, the term referred to rituals that do not appear in the New Testament; later it was broadened to demarcate fundamental articles of faith from matters that do not reach to the essence of salvation. The concept of *adiaphora* was elaborated by Erasmus and further developed by Melanchthon (see especially his *Loci Communes* [1555], chs. 34, 35). The best recent discussion of indifferent matters, especially in their elaboration by Erasmus, is Gary Remer, *Humanism and the Rise of Toleration* (University Park, Pa., 1996), pp. 50–101.

13. James 1:25; John 8:32; and Philippians 4:8.

Wholesome and *Requisit* Things, thy Freedom is Naught, Dark, Perverse, out of the Truth, and against the perfect Law of Love and Liberty.

Qu. *But must I conform to Things whether I can receive them or no? Ought I not to be left to the Grace and Spirit of God in my own Heart?*

Answ. To the first Part of the Question, Nay; to the last, Yea. But now let us consider what is the Reason thou canst not receive them: Is the Fault in the Things themselves? Are they inconsistent with Truth, or will not the Truth own or assent unto them, or is the Fault in thee? that is to say, Is it thy Weakness, or thy Carelesness; If thy *Weakness,* it is to be born with, and to be informed; if thy *Carelesness,* thou ought'st to be admonished; for it is a dangerous Principle, and pernicious to true Religion, and which is worse, it is the *Root of Ranterism* to assert, *That nothing is a Duty incumbent upon thee, but what thou art perswaded is thy Duty;*[14] for the Seared Conscience pleads his Liberty against all Duty, the *Dark* Conscience is here unconcerned, the *Dead* Conscience is here uncondemned, unless this Distinction be allowed of, that there may be an Ignorance or an Insensibility from *Inability* or *Incapacity,* or a Dark *Education;* and an Ignorance and Insensibility, from *Carelesness, Disobedience, Prejudice,* &c. So that though thou art not to conform to a Thing ignorantly, yet thou art seriously to consider, why thou art ignorant, and what the Cause of such Ignorance may be; certainly it can't be in God, nor in his Gift to thee; it must then needs be in thy self, who hast not yet received a Sense for or against the Matter, about which thou art in doubt. To the second Part of the Question; *Ought I not to be left to the Grace of God in my own Heart? Ans.* That is of all Things most desirable, since they are well left that are there left; for there is no Fear of want of Unity, where all are left with the one Spirit of Truth; they must be of one Mind, they can't be otherwise. So that to plead this against Unity, is to abuse the very Plea, and to commit the greatest Contradiction to that very Doctrine of Scripture, viz. *That all should be guided by the Grace and Spirit of God in themselves;*[15] for the End of that Doctrine is certainty. *They shall all know me, saith the Lord, from the least to the greatest. And I will give them one Heart, and one Way, that they may fear me for ever, for the Good of them, and of their Children after them,* Jer. 32. 39. *And I will give them one Heart, and I will put a new Spirit within you; and I will take the Stony Heart out of their Flesh, and will give them an Heart of Flesh,* Ezekiel 11. 19. *And the Multitude of them*

14. For the Ranters, see ch. 5, p. 193, n. 132.
15. John 6:31.

that believed were of one Heart, and of one Soul, Acts 4. 32. Is not this Unity too? *I will restore unto you a pure Language; they shall be of one Heart and of one Mind, and great shall be their Peace.*[16] Therefore I must say to thee, Friend, What if thou wilt not be left with the Grace and Spirit of God in thy self, nor wait for it's Mind, nor be watchful to it's Revelations, nor humble and quiet till thou hast received such necessary Manifestations, but pleadest against the Counsel of the Spirit of the Lord in other faithful Persons, under the Pretence of being left to his Spirit in thy self; by which Means thou opposest the Spirit to the Spirit, and pleadest for Dis-unity, under the Name of *Liberty;* I ask thee, May not I exhort thee to the Practice of that I am moved to press thee to the Practice of? If not, thou art the Imposer, by restraining me from my *Christian Liberty;* and not only so, but away goeth Preaching, and with it the Scriptures, that are both appointed of God for *Exhortation, Reproof* and *Instruction.*[17]

Quest. *But are there not various Measures, diversities of Gifts, and several Offices in the Body?*[18]

Answ. True; but therefore are not the Members of one Mind, one Will, and one Judgment in common and universal Matters, especially relating to the Family and Church of God; And indeed there can't be a falser Reasoning than to conclude *Discord* from *Diversity, Contrariety* from *Variety.* Is there Contrariety of *Bloods, Lifes, Feelings, Seeings, Hearings, Tastings, Smellings,* in one and the same Body, at one and the same Time? No such Matter: Experience is a Demonstration against all such Insinuations. So that though it be granted, that there is Diversity of Gifts, yet there is no Disagreement in Sense; and though Variety of Offices, yet no Contrariety in Judgment concerning those Offices. Well, say the Holy Scriptures of Truth, *there is but one God; the Lord our God is but one Lord; there is but one God and Father of all Things; (that are good) and there is but one Lord, one Faith, and One Baptism;*[19] and his Light, Life and Spirit is at Unity with it self in all; what comes from the Light, Life or Spirit in one, it is the same in Truth and Unity to the rest, as if it did rise in themselves: This is seen in our Assemblies every Day, and will be throughout all Generations in the Church of God, among those that live in the lowly Truth, in which the pure Sense and sound Judgment stands; *God is not the God of*

16. Zephaniah 3:9.
17. 2 Timothy 3:16–17.
18. Romans 12:3–8; 1 Corinthians 12; and Hebrews 2:4.
19. Deuteronomy 6:4; Ephesians 4:4–6.

Confusion, but Order:[20] Every one in his Order is satisfied, hath Unity and true Fellowship with whatever comes from the Life of God in another; for this precious Life reacheth throughout the Heritage of God, and is the common Life that giveth the common Feeling and Sense to the Heritage of God. Degree or Measure in the same Life can never contradict or obstruct that which is from the same Life for the common Benefit of the Family of God. *The Lord is the Unmeasurable and Incomprehensible Glorious Being of Life,* yet have we Unity with him in all his Works, who are come to his Divine Measure of Light and Truth in our own Hearts, and live therein; and shall we not have Unity with that which proceeds from a Fellow Creature? In short, the Saints Way is in the Light, wherein there is neither Doubt nor Discord; yea, they are Children of the Light, and called *Light,* and *The Lights of the World;*[21] and can it be supposed that such should disagree and contradict each other in their exterior Order and Practice in the Church before the World; O the blessed seamless Garment of Jesus! where that is known, these Things can never rise. But yet again, *The Just Man's Path* is not only a Light, *but a shining Light,* Brightness it self: Certainly there can be no Stumbling. It is also said, *That Light is sown for the Righteous;*[22] then the Righteous shall never want Light upon any Occasion: And saith that beloved Evangelist and Apostle of our Lord Jesus Christ, *They that walk in the Light, have Fellowship one with another,* 1 John 1. Whence it is easy to conclude, they that go out of the Fellowship, go out of the Light; but if they that walk in the Light, have Fellowship one with another, what shall we say of those that plead being left to the Light to justify their not having Fellowship one with another? and, which is yet worse, who suppose People may conscientiously and Justifiably Dissent within themselves, and that by Reason of the Variety of the Degrees of the Spirit and Grace that are given of God unto them; as if the lesser Degree may dissent from the greater, because of it's not being able to comprehend it. And to make this Principle more Authentick, such tell us, *This is the Ancient Principle of Truth;* and object, *How will you else be able to maintain the* Quakers *Principles?* The Fallacy of all which, lieth (as I said before) in not rightly distinguishing between Diversity and Disagreement, Variety and Contrariety; for this Diversity hath Concord, and this Variety hath Unity? And it is a Blindness that hath too much of late hap-

20. 1 Corinthians 14:33.
21. Matthew 5:14.
22. Proverbs 4:18; and Psalms 97:11.

pened to some, by going from the one Life and Spirit of our Lord Jesus Christ, first to fall into Disagreements, and then plead for it, under the Notion of *Diversity of Measures.* I would ask all such Persons, who arrogate to themselves such a peculiar Knowledge of the Ancient Principles of Truth, or the *Quakers* first Principles; 1st, *Whether they believe there be a Christian Body?* 2dly, *Whether this Body hath an Head?* 3dly, *Whether Christ be not this Head?* 4thly, *Whether this Head be without Eyes, Ears, Smell and Taste, and this Body without Sense and Feeling?* If not, *Whether this Head Seeth, Heareth, Smelleth, Tasteth* DIFFERINGLY *and* CONTRARILY *to it self? And whether this Body hath a contrary Feeling at the same Time about the same Thing?* And if it be true, that the Church of Christ, redeemed by his most precious Blood to live to him, see with the same Eye, hear with the same Ear, speak with the same Mouth, live by the same Breath, and are led by the same Spirit, where is this *Disagreement, Contrariety* or *Dissent* about the Things of his *Church?*

Quest. *But the Members of Christ's Church in the Primitive Times had* different Apprehensions; *as the Apostles, and the People gathered by them.*

Answ. Pray let me know who they were, and in what Cases?

Quest. *The Persons were* PAUL *and* PETER, *and those* Christians *that differed about Meats; and the Scripture is plain in the Case.*[23]

Answ. The *Difference* between *Peter* and *Paul* (in the *Acts*) testifies the Weakness of *Peter,* and the Place justifies *Paul*'s Reproof of his too great Compliance with the *Jews* in some of their *Rites;* which makes against *Liberty of various Practices,* in the Church of Christ, and not for indulging them. That Instance about the Difference of *Christians* as to *Meats,* &c. has nothing in it to the End for which it is alledged; for this related not to *Church-Order* or *Communion,* but *Private* and *Personal Freedoms,* what each might do with Respect to themselves; that is, they might make Laws to themselves, in Things that only concern'd private Persons, and it centred there; Here, *What I will eat, When I will eat,* Things to my self, and for my self, as a Man having Power over my own Appetite: The *Liberty* in Things Private, Personal, and Indifferent, makes nothing for *Dissenting about Church Matters in Things of Communion and Society,* and that also are not indifferent, as to *eat Fish,* or *eat Flesh,* or

23. The contention between the apostles is related in Acts 11:2–3 and 15:5. For the differences between Peter and Paul, see Galatians 2:11–14. The issue of meats refers to whether Christians ought to refrain from eating meats sacrificed to idols (see Romans 14:13–23 and 1 Corinthians 8).

eat Herbs, plainly is: But necessary; As to be careful and orderly about the External Business of the Church: These are no *Jewish Rites,* nor *Shadowy Ceremonies,* no *Meats* nor *Drinks* that are Private and Personal, where Weakness is apt to mistake (That were an Unnecessary and an *Unchristian Yoke to bear*) but Things comely, orderly, and of good Report, that tend to Purity, Peace and Diligence in Things acceptable to God, and requisite among his People in their Temporal Christian Capacity. And herein the Apostle *Paul* exercised his Godly *Authority;* and we find that not only those that opposed themselves to it, as thinking, *he took too much upon him, (demanded a Mark of Christ's speaking in him)* are in Scripture branded with Contention. But the true Believers, that had in themselves a *Mark of Christ's speaking in him,* were of *One Mind, and avoided such as were given to Contention;* for it was not the Custom of the Churches of Christ. Thus were Christ's People of *One Heart,* in Things relating to their Communion. Yet a little farther; They that have the Mind of Christ, are of one Mind; for Christ is not divided:[24] They that have Christ for their Head, have One Counsellor and Prophet, One Seer and Bishop, they disagree not in their Judgments in Things relating to him, and the Good of his Church; they have one and the same Guide; *For the one Spirit, into which they have all drank, and by it are baptized into one Body, leads them all.*[25] Now to every Member is *a Measure of the same Spirit given to profit with;* and though every Member is not an *Eye,* nor an *Ear,* nor a *Mouth,* yet every Member hath Unity with the *Eye,* with the *Ear,* with the *Mouth,* in their proper and respective Acts, and they one with the other: The *Eye* sees for the *Mouth,* the *Mouth* speaks for the *Eye,* and the *Ear* hears for *both;* this Variety hath no Discord, but in this Diversity of Gifts and Offices, each Member is sensible of the other, and moves and Acts by one and the same Life, Spirit and Guidance, which is Omnipresent, proportionable to every Member in it's distinct Office. It must be granted, that there are Helps in the Church, as well as that there is a Church at all; and the Holy Ghost has compared those Helps (as is before-mentioned) to several Members and Senses of Man's Body, as an *Eye,* an *Hand,* a *Foot, Hearing, Smelling, &c.* All then cannot be the Eye, neither can all be the Hand, for then they would confound their Office, and act disagreeably to the Ordination of the great Orderer of his Church. And if I will not comply with him that God hath made an *Eye,* because I am not that Eye, or an Hand, because

24. 1 Corinthians 1:13.

25. The following discussion draws on 1 Corinthians 12.

I am not that Member my self, nor a Party to the Action, or Performance of that Member, I resist the Lord, though under Pretence of resisting Man for the Lord's Sake. And truly, this is the Rock that some of our own Time, as well as Persons of former Ages, have split upon, they have not been contented with their own Station in the Body, they have not kept to their own Gift, nor been taken up with the Duty of their own Place in the Church. If he that is a Foot would be an Hand, and the Hand covets to be an Eye, envying others their allotted Station, through Height of Mind, and walking loose from the Holy Cross, there can be no such Thing as Concord and Fellowship in the Church of Christ.

Farthermore, since the Spirit of the Lord is one in all, it ought to be obey'd through another, as well as in one's self; and this I affirm to you, That the same lowly Frame of Mind that receives and answers the Mind of the Spirit of the Lord in a Man's self, will receive and have Unity with the Mind of the same Spirit through another, and the Reason is plain; Because the same Self-evidencing Power and Virtue that ariseth from the Measure of the Spirit of Truth in one's self, and that convinceth a Man in his own Heart, doth also attend the Discovery of the Mind of the same Spirit, when delivered by another; for the Words of the *Second Adam, the quickning Spirit,*[26] through another, are Spirit and Life, as well as in thy own Particular; this is discern'd by the Spiritual Man that judgeth all Things, although the Carnal Man pleadeth, *Being left to his Freedom;* and it may be talks of *being left to the Spirit in himself too;* the better to escape the Sense and Judgment of the Spiritual Man:[27] It is my earnest Desire, that all that have any Knowledge of the Lord, would have a tender Care how they use that Plea against their faithful Brethren, that God put into their Mouths against the persecuting Priests and Hirelings of the World, namely, *I must mind the Spirit of God in my self;* for though it be a great Truth that all are to be left thereunto, yet it is as true, that he whose Soul is left with the Spirit of Truth in himself, differs not from his Brethren that are in the same Spirit; and as true it is, that those who err from the Spirit of Truth, may plead, *being left to the Spirit in themselves,* against the Motion and Command of the Spirit through another, when it pleaseth not his or her High Mind and perverse Will; for a Saying may be true or false, according to the subject Matter it is spoken upon, or applied to; We own the Assertion, we deny the Application: There

26. 1 Corinthians 15:45, 47; and John 5:21.

27. Romans 8:5–9; 1 Corinthians 3:3–4; and 2 Corinthians 10:4.

lies the Snare. 'Tis true, the People of God ought to be left to the Guidings of the Spirit of God in themselves; but for this to be so applied, as to disregard the Preachings or Writings of Christ's enlightned Servants, because by them applied properly to the Preaching or Writing of false Prophets and Seducers, will by no Means follow. I say the Doctrine is true, but not exclusively of all external Counsel or Direction; therefore false in Application, where Men are allowed to have had the Fear of God, and the Mind of his Spirit, and are not prov'd to have acted in their own Wills and Wisdom, or without the Guidance of the Spirit of God, about the Things of his Church and Kingdom.

Quest. *But though this be True, which hath been alledged for Heavenly Concord, yet what if I do not presently see that Service in a Thing, that the Rest of my Brethren agree in; In this Case, what is my Duty and theirs?*

Answ. It is thy Duty to wait upon God in Silence and Patience, out of all Fleshly Consultations; and as thou abidest in the *Simplicity of the TRUTH,* thou wilt receive an Understanding with the Rest of thy Brethren, about the Thing doubted. And it is their Duty, whilst thou behavest thy self in Meekness and Humility, to bear with thee, and carry themselves tenderly and loving towards thee; but if on the contrary, thou disturbest their Godly Care and Practice, and growest Contentious, and exaltest thy Judgment against them, they have Power from God to Exhort, Admonish, and Reprove thee; and (if thou perseverest therein) in His Name to refuse any farther Fellowship with thee, till thou repentest of thy Evil.[28]

Quest. *But lest I should mistake, when thou speakest of True Liberty, that it stands in being made Free by the Truth, from all Unrighteousness,* dost thou mean, That *no other Persons ought to have the Liberty of Exercising their Dissenting Consciences, but that Force may be Lawful to reduce such as are reputed Erroneously Conscientious?*[29]

Answ. By no Means: It were a great Wickedness against God, who is Lord of the Souls and Spirits of Men, and ought to preside in all Consciences, who,

28. 2 Timothy 4:2; Ephesians 5:11; 2 Thessalonians 3:15; and Titus 3:10.

29. The notion of an erroneous conscience implies that one can be objectively mistaken about a sincerely held belief, and it was a long-standing element of orthodox Christian theology. The distinction goes back to St. Jerome and is fully elaborated in Thomas Aquinas's *Disputed Questions about Truth* (q. 16–17). For a concise overview, see Timothy C. Potts, "Conscience," in *The Cambridge History of Later Medieval Philosophy,* ed. Norman Kretzmann, Anthony Kenny, and Jan Pinborg (Cambridge, 1982), pp. 687–704.

as the Apostle saith, *Is the Only Potentate, and hath Immortality.*[30] For though I give the True Liberty of Soul and Conscience to those only that are set Free by the Power of Christ, from the Bondage of Sin, and Captivity of Death, yet do I not intend, that any Person or Persons should be in the least harm'd for the External Exercise of their Dissenting Consciences in Worship to God, though Erroneous; for though their Consciences be blind, yet they are not to be forced; such Compulsion giveth no Sight, neither do Corporal Punishments produce Conviction: This we above all People, in our Day, have withstood, in Speaking, Writing and Suffering, and, blessed be God, continue so to do with Faithfulness. For *Faith* is the Gift of God,[31] and forced Sacrifices are not pleasing to the Lord.

Quest. *But according to thy Argument, it may be my Fault, that I have not the Gift of Faith; and upon this Presumption, it may be, thou wilt inflict some Temporal Penalties upon me.*

Answ. No such Matter; for such Kind of Faults are not to be punished with Temporal or Worldly Penalties; for whether the Errors be through Weakness or Wilfulness, not relating to Moral Practice, all External Coercion and Corporal Punishment is excluded. *For the Weapons of our Warfare are not Carnal, but Spiritual.*[32]

Quest. *But what then is the Extent of the Power of the Church of Christ, in Case of Schism or Heresy?*

Answ. The Power that Christ gave to his Church was this, *That Offenders, after the first and second Admonition,* (not Repenting) *should be Rejected:*[33] Not Imprisoned, Plundered, Banished, or put to Death; this belongs to the Whore and false Prophet: O! all these Things have come to pass for Want of Humility, for Want of the ancient Fear, and keeping in the quiet Habitation of the Just:[34] The Truth in you all shall answer me. And this I affirm, from the Understanding I have received of God, not only that the Enemy is at work to scatter the Minds of Friends, by that loose Plea, *What hast thou to do with me? Leave me to my Freedom and to the Grace of God in my self,* and the like; but this Proposition and Expression, as now understood and alledged, is a Deviation from, and a Perversion of the Ancient Principle of Truth; for this is the

30. 1 Timothy 6:15.
31. Ephesians 2:8.
32. 2 Corinthians 10:4.
33. Titus 3:10.
34. Proverbs 3:33.

plain Consequence of this Plea, if any one (especially if they are but lately convinced) shall say, *I see no Evil in paying Tythes to Hireling Priests, in that they are not claimed by Divine Right, but by the Civil Laws of the Land. I see no Evil in Marrying by the Priest, for he is but a Witness.* Furthermore, *I see no Evil in Declining a Publick Testimony in Suffering Times, or hiding in Times of Persecution, for I have* Christ's *and* Paul's *Examples.*[35] *I see no Evil in Worshipping and Respecting the Persons of Men; for whatever others do, I intend a sincere Notice that I take of those I know, and have a good Esteem for.* Lastly, *I see no Evil in keeping my Shop shut upon the World's* Holidays *and* Massdays, (as they call them) *though they are rather Lewdly and Superstitiously than Religiously kept; for I would not willingly give any Offence to my Neighbours.*[36] And since your Testimony is against Imposition, and for leaving every one to the Measure of the Grace which God hath given him, not only, *No Man hath Power to reprove or judge me, but I may be as good a Friend as any of you, according to my Measure.* And now, here is *Measure set up against Measure,* which is Confusion it self—*Babel* indeed: This is that very Rock both Professors and Prophane would long since have run us upon, namely, *That a Way is hereby opened to all the World's Libertines, to plead the Light within for their Excesses;* Which indeed grieves the Spirit of God, and was severely judged by our Friends in the Beginning, and is still reproved by them that keep their Habitation, though some are become as wandring Stars through their own Pride,[37] and the Prevalency of the Hour of Temptation that hath overtaken them; whereas had they kept in the Channel of Love and Life, in the Orb and Order of the Celestial Power, they had shined as fixed Stars in the Firmament of God for ever. And from the deep Sense that I have of the Working of the Enemy of *Zion*'s Peace, to rend and divide the Heritage of God, who under the Pretence of crying down *Man, Forms* and *Prescriptions,* is crying down the *Heavenly Man Christ*

35. Tithes were a long-standing issue for religious dissenters in England. See Margaret James, "The Political Implications of the Tithes Controversy in the English Revolution, 1640–1660," *History* 26 (1941): 1–18. On Jesus and Paul hiding, see John 8:59; John 12:36; Mark 7:24; and Acts 9:25.

36. Here Penn refers to the issue of closing one's shop for "worldly" holidays. Devout and pious Christians ought not, in his view, refrain from labor on such "lewd" or "superstitious" occasions. Not wanting to offend one's neighbors by staying open for business on such days, Penn suggests, represents a failure of nerve unworthy of a true Christian.

37. Jude 13.

Jesus, his blessed Order and Government, which he hath brought forth by his own Revelation and Power through his faithful Witnesses. This I farther testify, *First,* That the Enemy, by these fair Pretences, strikes at the Godly Care and Travail that dwells upon the Spirits of many faithful Brethren, that all Things might be preserved Sweet, Comely, Virtuous, and of good Report in the Church of God.[38] *Secondly,* That there never was greater Necessity of this Godly Care than at this Day, since we were a People, wherein the Cross, by too many, is not so closely kept to as in Days past, and in which there is not only a great Convincement, but a young Generation descended of Friends, who though they retain the Form their Education hath led them into, yet many of them adorn not the Gospel with that sensible, weighty, and heavenly Conversation as becomes the Children of the Undefiled Religion, and the Seed of that precious Faith which works by the Love that overcomes the World.[39] And the Lord God of Heaven and Earth, that hath sent his Son Christ Jesus a Light into our Hearts and Consciences, to whose Search and Judgment all ought to (and must) bring their Deeds, and render up their Account, beareth Holy Record, that for this End hath he moved upon the Spirits of his Servants, and for this good End only have his Servants given forth, recommended, and put in Practice, those Things that are now in Godly Use among his People, whether in this or other Nations, relating to *Men's* and *Women's Meetings,* and their divers and weighty Services. And farther; in the Fear of the Almighty God, I shall add, That Heavenly Peace and Prosperity dwell with those who are found in an holy and zealous Practice of them; wherefore I warn all, that they take Heed of a slighting and obstinate Mind, and that they have a Care how they give Way to the Outcry of some, falsly, entituled, *Liberty of Conscience against Imposition,* &c. for the End thereof is to lead back again, and give Ease to the Carnal Mind, which, at last, will bring Death again upon the Soul to God, and the living Society of his Children. And indeed, it is a great Shame that any who have ever known the Truth of God in the inward Parts,[40] and the sweet Society of Brethren, especially those who were early in the Work of this blessed Day and heavenly Dispensation, should so far depart from the Fear and Awe of the Lord, as to use such Unsavoury, as well as Untrue Expressions; this is very far from that meek Spirit of Jesus, and the first Love, which they

38. Philippians 4:8.
39. John 16:33.
40. Luke 11:39.

pretend to have so singularly kept in, which beareth all Things, suffereth all Things, and endureth all Things, and teacheth to keep the Word of Patience in the Hour of Tribulation;[41] Nay, but this is judging of Spiritual Things with a Carnal and Prejudiced Mind, stumbling at the Matter, for the Sake of the Persons through whom it comes, not eying nor weighing the Spirit the Thing arises from, but the Person by whom it is spoken, which darkens the Eye of the Understanding, and blinds, by Prejudice, the Mind that should discern, taste and judge; from whence many Mischiefs have sprung to the Church of Christ in divers Ages: Nor is it the least Evil this Spirit of Strife is guilty of, even at this Day, that it useth the Words, *Liberty of Conscience* and *Imposition,* against the Brethren, in the same Manner as our suffering Friends have been always accustomed to intend them against the persecuting Priests and Powers of the Earth, as if it were the same Thing to admonish and reprove Conceited, High-minded, Loose or Contentious Persons in the Church, as to compel Conformity in Matters of Faith and Worship, by Worldly Violence, upon the Persons and Estates of Conscientious Dissenters: O such Iniquity God will not leave unreproved!

This, *Dear Friends,* I send amongst you, as a Token of my true Love, in the Revelation of the free Spirit of our God and Father, who have ever been a Friend to true Liberty, as in the State according to Law, so in the Church according to Scripture, and as it standeth in the Truth of Jesus, that makes them who love it free indeed.[42] Let us all keep low, and remember the Rock from whence we were hewn,[43] and dwell in a tender and reverent Sense of the daily Mercies and Providences of the Lord, looking well to our own Growth and Prosperity in his heavenly Way and Work, then shall the Desire of our Hearts be more and more after him, and the Remembrance of his Name; and with our Love to God, will our Love increase one towards another, helping and aiding one another: And I no ways doubt, but God that has brought us out of the Land of *AEgypt,* and out of the House of *Bondage,* and delivered us from the *Mouth* of the *Lyon* and the *Paw* of the *Bear,*[44] will preserve his People from this Uncircumcised Spirit that is not in Covenant with God, nor under the Yoke

41. 1 Corinthians 13:7; and Romans 5:3, 12:12.
42. John 8:36.
43. Isaiah 51:1.
44. 1 Samuel 17:37.

of his Holy Royal Law of *True Spiritual Liberty;* for they that keep and walk in the Light of Jesus, are fenced from the Power of this Crooked Serpent,[45] that seeks whom he may betray; nor are any stung by him but the Unwatchful, the Listeners and Harkners after his jealous Whispers, and detracting Insinuations: They are such as make their Dwelling in the Earth, where his Region is, and where he creeps and twists, who is Earthly, Sensual and Devilish, and so is all the Wisdom that comes from him.[46]

My Dear Friends: Keep, I pray you, in the Simplicity of the *Truth, and Cross of JESUS,* and wait for your Daily Bread, and to be Daily Renewed from the Lord; look to your Increase about Eternal Riches, *and be sure to lay up Treasure in Heaven that fadeth not away,*[47] that your Faith and Hope may have Eternal Foundations, which the cross Occurrences of Time, and Fears of Mortality cannot move: And beware of that Loose and Irreverent Spirit, which has not those in high Esteem among you, that are *Faithful in the Lord's Work, and that labour in His Blessed Word and Doctrine.* I plainly see a Coldness and Shortness on this Hand; and be the Pretence as it will, it is not pleasing to the Lord. They that love Christ, his Servants are dear to them, and they bear a tender Regard to their Trials, Travails, Spendings and Sufferings, who seek not yours, but you, that you may all be *Presented Blameless at the Coming of the Great God, and our Saviour Jesus Christ;*[48] that so the Gospel-Ministry and Testimony may be held up with Holy Fervent Love, and Godly Esteem, to the keeping under every raw and exalted Mind, and whatever may slight and turn against it, lest God that has Richly Visited us with His Fatherly Visitations, and Day springing from on High,[49] should remove His Blessing from amongst us, and place *His Candlestick* among other People.[50] Be Wise therefore, *O Friends!* For behold He is at the Door that must have an Account of your Stewardship:

45. Job 26:13; and Isaiah 27:1.

46. James 3:15.

47. Luke 12:33–34.

48. 1 Corinthians 1:8; and 1 Thessalonians 5:23.

49. See the prophecy of Zacharias, in Luke 1:78–79.

50. The candlestick was part of the Tabernacle (commanded by God in Exodus 25) and a sign of God's continuing presence with the Israelites. Revelation 2:5 cautions thus: "Remember therefore from whence thou art fallen, and repent, and do the first works; or else I will come unto thee quickly, and will remove thy candlestick out of his place, except thou repent."

Be watchful, keep to your First Love and Works, that so you may endure to the End, and be Saved. And having Overcome, you may have Right to Eat of the Tree of Life, which is in the Midst of the Paradise of God.[51]

> *The God of Peace, who hath brought* Our Dear Lord Jesus *from the Dead, and us with Him, more abundantly enrich you all with Wisdom and Knowledge, in the Revelation of Himself, through Faith in His Son, by whom in these Last Days He hath spoken to us, who is the Blessed and Only Potentate, King of Kings, and Lord of Lords, who only hath Immortality;*[52] *to whom be Honour and Power Everlasting.* Amen.

Your Friend and Brother, in the Tribulation and Salvation of the Enduring Kingdom of our God,

William Penn.

Worminghurst in *Sussex*,
the 20th of the 9th
Month, 1681.

51. Revelation 22:14.
52. 1 Timothy 6:15.

A PERSWASIVE to Moderation to *Church-Dissenters,* in Prudence and Conscience: *Humbly submitted to the KING and His Great Council* (1686)

The EPISTLE.

HAVING of late Time observ'd the *Heat, Aversion* and *Scorn* with which some Men have treated all Thoughts of Ease to *Church Dissenters,* I confess I had a more than ordinary Curiosity to examine the Grounds those Gentlemen went upon: For I could not tell how to think Moderation should be a Vice, where Christianity was a Virtue, when the Great Doctor of that Religion commands, that *Our Moderation be known unto all Men;* and why? *For the Lord is at Hand:*[1] And what to do? but to judge our *Rancor,* and retaliate and punish our *Bitterness* of Spirit. And, to say true, 'tis a severe Reflection we draw upon our selves, that though *Pagan Emperors* could endure the *Addresses* of *Primitive Christians,* and *Christian Caesars* receive the *Apologies* of *Infidels,* for Indulgence, yet it should be thought, of some Men, an Offence to seek it, or have it of a Christian Prince, whose Interest I dare say it is, and who himself so lately wanted it: But the Consideration of the Reason of this Offence, will increase our Admiration; for they tell us, *'tis dangerous to the Prince to suffer it,* while the Prince is himself a *Dissenter:* This Difficulty is beyond all Skill to remove, that it should be against the Interest of a *Dissenting* Prince to indulge *Dissent.* For though it will be granted there are Dissenters on differing Principles from those of the Prince, yet they are still Dissenters, and *Dissent* being the Prince's Interest, it will naturally follow, that those Dissenters are in the Interest of the Prince, whether they think on it or no.

Interest will not lye: Men embark'd in the same Vessel, seek the Safety of the *Whole* in their *Own,* whatever other Differences they may have. And *Self-Safety* is the highest worldly Security a Prince can have; for though all Parties would rejoyce their own Principles prevailed, yet every one is more solicitous

1. Philippians 4:5.

about it's own Safety, than the other's Verity. Wherefore it cannot be unwise, by the Security of All, to make it the Interest as well as Duty of All, to advance that of the Publick.

Angry Things, then, set aside, As Matters now are, *What is best to be done?* This I take to be the Wise Man's Question, as to consider and answer it, will be his Business. *Moderation* is a Christian Duty, and it has ever been the Prudent Man's Practice. For those *Governments* that have used it in their Conduct, have succeeded best in all Ages.

I remember it is made in *Livy* the Wisdom of the *Romans,* that they relaxed their Hand to the *Privernates,* and thereby made them most faithful to their Interest. And it prevailed so much with the *Petilians,* that they would endure any Extremity from *Hannibal,* rather than desert their Friendship, even then, when the *Romans* discharged their Fidelity, and sent them the Despair of knowing they could not relieve them.[2] So did one Act of *Humanity* overcome the *Falisci* above Arms: Which confirms that noble Saying of *Seneca, Mitius imperanti Melius paretur,* the mildest Conduct is best obeyed.[3] A Truth Celebrated by *Grotius* and *Campanella:*[4] Practised, doubtless, by the bravest Princes: For CYRUS exceeded, when he built the Jews a Temple, and himself no Jew: ALEXANDER astonished the Princes of his Train with the profound Veneration he paid the High Priest of that People: And AUGUSTUS was so far from suppressing the *Jewish Worship,* that he sent *Hecatombs* to *Jerusalem* to increase their Devotion.[5] *Moderation* fill'd the Reigns of the most Renowned *Caesars:* And Story says, they were *Neros* and *Caligulas* that loved Cruelty.

But others tell us that Dissenters are mostly *Antimonarchical,* and so not to be indulged, and that the Agreement of the Church of *England* and *Rome* in *Monarchy* and *Hierarchy,* with their Nearness in other Things should oblige her to grant the *Roman* Catholicks a special Ease, exclusive of the other Dissenters. But with the Leave of those Worthy Gentlemen, I would say, no Body is against that which is for him: And that the Aversion apprehended to be in some against the *Monarchy,* rather comes from Interest than Principle: For Governments were never destroy'd by the Interests they preserve.

2. Livy, *History of Rome,* bk. 8, ch. 21 (Petilians); bk. 23, ch. 20 (Privernates).

3. Niccolò Machiavelli, *Discourses,* bk. 3, ch. 20; Seneca, in Sir Edward Coke, *Third part of the Institutes* (London, 1644), ch. 2.

4. Hugo Grotius, *Politick maxims and observations* (London, 1654).

5. On Cyrus, see the book of Ezra; on Alexander, see Josephus, *Antiquities of the Jews,* bk. 11, ch. 8; Augustus (62 B.C.E.–14 C.E.) was the first Roman emperor.

In the next Place, it is as plain, that there is a *Fundamental* Difference between those Churches in Religion and Interest. In *Religion,* it appears by a Comparison of the *Thirty Nine Articles* with the Doctrine of the *Council* of *Trent.*[6] In *Interest,* they differ; Fundamentally, because our Church is in the Actual Possession of the Churches and Livings that the other Church claims. What better Mixture then can these two Churches make than that of *Iron* and *Clay?* Nor do I think it well judged, or wise, in any that pretend to be Sons of the Church of *England,* to seek an Accommodation from the Topick of *Affinity,* since 'tis that some of her Dissenters have always objected, and she as constantly deny'd to be true.

I say, this Way of Reconciling or Indulging *Roman Catholicks* stumbles far greater Numbers of People of nearer Creeds, and gives the Church of *England* the Lye. But suppose the Trick took, and they only of all Dissenters had Indulgence, yet Their *Paucity* considered, I am sure, a Pair of Sir *Kenelm Digby*'s Breeches would set with as good a Grace upon the late Lord *Rochester*'s Dwarf. Upon the whole Matter, Let Men have *Ease,* and they will keep it; For those that might plot to get it, would *not plot to lose it.* Men love the Bridge they need and pass: And that Prince who has his People fast by Interest, holds them by the strongest human Tye; for other Courses have failed as often as they have been tried. Let us then once try a True Liberty: Never did the Circumstances of any Kingdom lye more open and fair to so blessed an Accommodation than we do at this Time.

But we are told, *The King has promised to maintain the Church of England:* I grant it: But if the *Church of England* claims the *King's Promise of Protection,* her *Dissenters* cannot forget *That* of his *Clemency:* And as they were both great, and admirably distinguished, so by no Means are they inconsistent or impracticable.

Will not his Justice let him be wanting in the *One?* And can his Greatness of Mind let him leave the *Other* behind him in the Storm, *unpity'd* and *unhelp'd?* Pardon me, we have not to do with an insensible Prince, but one that has been *Touch'd with our Infirmities:*[7] More than any Body fit to judge our Cause, by the Share he once had in it. Who should give *Ease like the Prince that has wanted it?* To suffer for his own Conscience, looked Great; but to deliver other

6. The Thirty-Nine Articles form the doctrinal basis of the Anglican Church; for the Council of Trent, see ch. 3, p. 101, n. 17.

7. Hebrews 4:15; and Matthew 8:17.

Men's, were Glorious. It is a Sort of paying the Vows of his Adversity, and it cannot therefore be done by any one else, with so much *Justice* and *Example.*

Far be it from me to solicite any Thing in Diminution of the Just Rights of the *Church of England:* Let her rest protected where she is. But I hope, none will be thought to intend her Wrong, for refusing to understand the *King's Promise* to her, in a *Ruinous Sense* to all Others; and I am sure she would understand her own Interest better, if she were of the same Mind. For it is morally impossible that a *Conscientious Prince* can be thought to have ty'd himself to compel others to a Communion, that himself cannot tell how to be of; or that any thing can oblige him to shake the Firmness of those he has confirmed by his own *Royal Example.*

Having then so Illustrious an Instance of *Integrity,* as the Hazard of the Loss of *Three Crowns* for *Conscience.* Let it at least excuse Dissenters *Constancy,* and provoke the Friends of the *Succession* to *Moderation,* that no Man may lose his *Birth-Right* for his *Perswasion,* and us to live *Dutifully,* and so *Peaceably* under our own Vine, and under our own Fig-Tree, with *Glory to God on High,* to the *King Honour,* and *Good-will to all Men.*

A Perswasive to *Moderation,* &c.

MODERATION, the Subject of this Discourse, is in plainer *English, Liberty of Conscience to* Church *Dissenters:* A Cause I have, with all Humility, undertaken to plead, against the Prejudices of the Times.

That there is such a Thing as *Conscience,* and the *Liberty* of it, in Reference to *Faith* and *Worship* towards God, must not be denied, even by those, that are most scandal'd at the *Ill* Use some seem to have made of such Pretences. But to settle the Terms: By *Conscience,* I understand *the Apprehension and Perswasion a Man has of his Duty to God:* By *Liberty of Conscience,* I mean, *A Free and Open Profession and Exercise of that Duty;* especially in *Worship:* But I always premise this *Conscience* to keep within the Bounds of *Morality,* and that it be neither *Frantick* nor *Mischievous,* but a *Good Subject,* a *Good Child,* a *Good Servant,* in all the Affairs of Life: As exact to yield to *Caesar* the Things that are *Caesar*'s, as jealous of withholding from *God* the Thing that is *God*'s.

In brief, he that acknowledges the civil *Government* under which he lives, and that maintains no Principle hurtful to his Neighbour in his Civil Property.

For he that in any Thing violates his Duty to these Relations, cannot be said to observe it to God, who ought to have his Tribute out of it. Such do not reject their *Prince, Parent, Master* or *Neighbour,* but God who enjoyns that Duty to them. Those Pathetick Words of Christ will naturally enough reach the Case, *In that ye did it not to them, ye did it not to me;*[8] for Duty to such Relations hath a Divine Stamp: And Divine Right runs through more Things of the World, and Acts of our Lives, than we are aware of: And Sacrilege may be committed against more than the Church. Nor will a Dedication to God, of the Robbery from Man, expiate the Guilt of Disobedience: For though Zeal could turn *Gossip* to Theft, his Altars would renounce the Sacrifice.

The *Conscience* then that I state, and the *Liberty* I pray, carrying so great a *Salvo* and Deference to publick and private Relations, no ill Design can, with any Justice, be fix'd upon the Author, or Reflection upon the Subject, which by this Time, I think, I may venture to call a *Toleration.*

But to this so much craved, as well as needed, *Toleration,* I meet with two Objections of weight, the solving of which will make Way for it in this Kingdom. And the first is a Disbelief of the Possibility of the Thing. *Toleration of Dissenting Worships from that establish'd, is not practicable* (say some) *without Danger to the State, with which it is interwoven.* This is Political. The other Objection is, *That admitting Dissenters to be in the Wrong, (which is always premised by the National Church) such Latitude were the Way to keep up the Dis-union, and instead of compelling them into a better Way, leave them in the Possession and Pursuit of their old Errors,* This is *Religious.* I think I have given the Objections fairly, 'twill be my next Business to answer them as fully.

The Strength of the first Objection against this Liberty, is the *Danger* suggested to the *State;* the Reason is, the National Form being *interwoven* with the Frame of the Government. But this seems to me only said, and not only (with Submission) not prov'd, but not true: For the Establish'd Religion and Worship are no other Ways interwoven with the Government, than that the Government makes Profession of them, and by divers Laws has made them the *Currant Religion,* and required all the Members of the State to conform to it.

This is nothing but what may as well be done by the Government, for any other Perswasion, as that. 'Tis true, 'tis not easy to change an Established

8. Matthew 25:40, 45.

Religion, nor is that the Question we are upon; but *State Religions* have been chang'd without the Change of the *States.* We see this in the Governments of *Germany* and *Denmark* upon the *Reformation:* But more clearly and near our selves, in the Case of *Henry the Eighth, Edward the Sixth, Queen Mary* and *Elizabeth;* for the Monarchy *stood,* the Family *remained* and *succeeded* under all the Revolutions of State-Religion, which could not have been, had the Proposition been generally true.

The Change of Religion then, does not *necessarily* change the Government, or alter the State; and if so, *a fortiori,* Indulgence of Church-Dissenters, does not *necessarily* hazard a Change of the State, where the present State-Religion or Church remains the same; for That I premise.

Some may say, *That it were more facile to change from one National Religion to another, than to maintain the Monarchy and Church, against the Ambition and Faction of divers Dissenting Parties.* But this is improbable at least. For it were to say, That it is an easier Thing to change a whole Kingdom, than with the Sovereign Power, followed with *Armies, Navies, Judges, Clergy,* and all the *Conformists* of the Kingdom, to secure the Government from the Ambition and Faction of *Dissenters,* as differing in their Interests within themselves, as in their Perswasions; and were they united, have neither Power to awe, nor Rewards to allure to their Party. They can only be formidable, when headed by the Sovereign. They may stop a *Gap,* or make, by his *Accession,* a Ballance: Otherwise, 'till 'tis harder to fight broken and divided Troops, than an entire Body of an Army, it will be always *easier* to maintain the Government under a Toleration of Dissenters, than in a total Change of Religion, and even then it self has not fail'd to have been preserved. But whether it be more or less easy, is not our Point; if they are many, the Danger is of Exasperating, not of making them easy; for the Force of our Question is, Whether such Indulgence be safe to the State? And here we have the first and last, the best and greatest Evidence for us, which is *Fact* and *Experience,* the Journal and Resolves of Time, and Treasure of the Sage.

For, *First,* The *Jews,* that had most to say for their Religion, and whose Religion was *Twin* to their State, (both being joined, and sent with Wonders from Heaven) *Indulged* Strangers in their Religious Dissents. They required but the Belief of the *Noachical* Principles, which were common to the World: No *Idolater,* and but a *Moral Man,* and he had his *Liberty,* ay, and some *Privileges* too, for he had an Apartment in the Temple, and this without Danger to the Government. Thus *Maimonides,* and others of their own Rabbies, and *Grotius* out of them.[9]

The *Wisdom* of the *Gentiles* was very admirable in this, that though they had many Sects of Philosophers among them, each dissenting from the other in their Principles, as well as Discipline, and that not only in Physical Things, but Points *Metaphysical,* in which some of the Fathers were not *free,* the School-men *deeply engaged,* and our present Academies but too much *perplexed;* yet they *indulged* them and the best Livers with singular Kindness: The greatest Statesmen and Captains often becoming *Patrons* of the Sects they best affected, honouring their *Readings* with their Presence and Applause. So far were those Ages, which we have made as the Original of Wisdom and Politeness, from thinking *Toleration* an Error of State, or dangerous to the Government. Thus *Plutarch, Strabo, Laertius,* and others.[10]

To these Instances I may add the Latitude of Old *Rome,* that had almost as many Deities as Houses: For *Varro* tells us of no less than *Thirty Thousand* several *Sacra,* or Religious Rites among her People, and yet without a Quarrel:[11] Unhappy Fate of *Christianity!* the best of Religions, and yet her Professors maintain less Charity than Idolaters, while it should be peculiar to them. I fear, it shews us to have but little of it at Heart.

But nearer Home, and in our own Time, we see the Effects of a discreet *Indulgence,* even to Emulation. *Holland,* that *Bog* of the world, neither Sea nor dry Land, now the *Rival* of tallest Monarchs; not by *Conquests, Marriages,* or Accession of *Royal Blood,* the usual Ways to Empire, but by her own superlative *Clemency* and *Industry;* for the one was the Effect of the other: She cherished her People, whatsoever were their *Opinions,* as the reasonable Stock of the Country, the Heads and Hands of her Trade and Wealth; and making them easy in the main Point, their *Conscience,* she became Great by them; This made her fill with *People,* and they filled her with *Riches* and *Strength.*

And if it should be said, *She is upon her Declension for all that.* I answer, All States must know it, nothing is here *Immortal.* Where are the *Babylonian,*

9. Moses Maimonides (1135–1204), Jewish philosopher and exegete; and Hugo Grotius (1583–1645), Dutch jurist and humanist.

10. Plutarch (ca. 45–120), *Lives of the Noble Greeks and Romans;* Strabo (ca. 64 B.C.E.–23 C.E.), *Geography;* Diogenes Laertius (fl. 3d century C.E.), *Lives and Opinions of Eminent Philosophers.*

11. On Varro, see ch. 3, p. 105, n. 19.

Persian, and *Grecian* Empires? And are not *Lacedaemon, Athens, Rome* and *Carthage* gone before her? Kingdoms and Commonwealths have their *Births* and *Growths,* their *Declensions* and *Deaths,* as well as private Families and Persons. But 'tis owing neither to the *Armies* of *France,* nor *Navies* of *England,* but her own *Domestick* Troubles.

Seventy Two sticks in her Bones yet: The growing Power of the Prince of *Orange,* must, in some Degree, be an *Ebb* to that State's Strength; for they are not so unanimous and vigorous in their Interest as formerly: But were they secure against the Danger of their own Ambition and Jealousy, any Body might insure their Glory at *five per Cent.* But some of their greatest Men apprehending they are in their *Climacterical Juncture,* give up the Ghost, and care not, if they must fall, by what Hand it is.

Others chuse a *Stranger,* and think one afar off will give the best Terms, and least annoy them: Whilst a considerable Party have chosen a *Domestick* Prince, *Kin* to their early Successes by the *Fore-father's Side* (the Gallantry of his Ancestors) And that his own Greatness and Security are wrapt up in theirs, and therefore modestly hope to find their Account in his Prosperity. But this is a Kind of Digression, only before I leave it, I dare venture to add, that if the Prince of *Orange* changes not the Policies of that State, he will not change her Fortune, and he will mightily add to his own.

But perhaps I shall be told, *That no Body doubts that* Toleration *is an* agreeable *Thing to a Commonwealth, where every one thinks he has a Share in the Government; ay, that the one is the Consequence of the other, and therefore most carefully to be avoided by all Monarchical States.* This indeed were shrewdly to the Purpose, in *England,* if it were but true. But I don't see how there can be one true Reason advanc'd in Favour of this Objection: *Monarchies,* as well as *Commonwealths,* subsisting by the Preservation of the People under them.

But, *First,* if this were true, it would follow, by the *Rule of Contraries,* that a *Republick* could not subsist with *Unity* and *Hierarchy,* which is *Monarchy* in the Church; but it must, from such *Monarchy* in *Church,* come to *Monarchy* in *State* too. But *Venice, Genoa, Lucca,* seven of the *Cantons* of *Switzerland,* (and *Rome* her self, for she is an *Aristocracy*) all under the loftiest *Hierarchy* in Church, and where is no *Toleration,* shew in Fact, that the contrary is true.

But, *Secondly,* This Objection makes a Commonwealth the better Government of the Two, and so overthrows the Thing it would establish. This is effectually done, if I know any thing, since a Commonwealth is hereby rendred a more copious, powerful and beneficial Government to Mankind, and is made better to answer Contingencies and Emergencies of State, because this subsists *either* Way, but *Monarchy* not, if the Objection be true. The one prospers by *Union* in Worship and Discipline, and by *Toleration* of Dissenting Churches from the National. The other only by an *Universal Conformity* to a National Church. I say, this makes *Monarchy* (in it self, doubtless, an admirable Government) *less Powerful, less Extended, less Propitious,* and finally *less Safe* to the People under it, than a *Commonwealth;* In that *no Security* is left to *Monarchy* under Diversity of Worships, which yet no Man can defend or forbid, but may often arrive, as it hath in *England,* more than five Times, in the Two Last Ages. And truly 'tis natural for Men to chuse to settle where they may be safest from the *Power* and *Mischief* of such Accidents of State.

Upon the whole Matter, it is to reflect the *last Mischief* upon *Monarchy,* the worst Enemies it has could hope to disgrace, or endanger it by; since it is to tell the People under it, that they must either *conform,* or be *destroy'd,* or to save themselves, turn *Hypocrites,* or *change* the Frame of the Government they live under. A Perplexity both to *Monarch* and *People,* that nothing can be greater, but the Comfort of knowing the Objection is *False.* And that which ought to make every reasonable Man of this Opinion, is the Cloud of Witnesses that almost every Age of *Monarchy* affords us.

I will begin with that of *Israel,* the most exact and sacred Pattern of *Monarchy,* begun by a valiant Man, translated to the best, and improv'd by the wisest of Kings, whose Ministers were neither *Fools,* nor *Fanaticks:* Here we shall find Provision for Dissenters: Their *Proselyti Domicilii* were so far from being compelled to their National Rites, that they were expresly forbid to observe them. Such were the *Egyptians* that came with them out of *Egypt,* the *Gibeonites* and *Canaanites,* a great People, that after their several Forms, worshipt in an *Apartment* of the same Temple. The *Jews* with a Liturgy, they without one: The *Jews* had *Priests,* but these none: The *Jews* had Variety of Oblations, these People burnt Offerings only. All that was required of them was the natural Religion of *Noah,* in which the Acknowledgment and Worship of the true God, was, and it still ought to be, the main Point; nay, so far were they from Coercive Conformity, that they did not so much as oblige them to observe their *Sabbath,* though one of the Ten Commandments: *Grotius* and *Selden* say more. Certainly this was great Indulgence, since so unsuitable an Usage lookt like *prophaning* their Devotion, and a common *Nusance* to their National Religion. One would think by this, that their Care lay on the Side of preserving their Cult from the *Touch* or *Accession* of Dissenters, and not of *forcing* them, by *undoing* Penalties, to conform. This must needs be evident: For if God's *Religion* and *Monarchy* (for so we are taught to believe it) did not, and would not, at a Time when Religion lay *less* in the Mind, and *more* in Ceremony, compel Conformity from Dissenters, we hope we have got the best Presidents on our side.

But if this Instance be of most Authority, we have another very exemplary, and to our Point Pertinent; for it shews what *Monarchy* may do: It is yielded us from the famous Story of *Mordecai.*[12] He, with his *Jews,* were in a bad plight with the King *Ahasuerus,* by the ill Offices *Haman* did them: The Arguments he used were drawn from the common Topicks of *Faction* and *Sedition, That they were an odd and dangerous People, under differing Laws of their own, and refused Obedience to his;* So denying his *Supremacy.* Dissenters with a witness: Things most tender to any Government.

The King thus incensed, commands the Laws to be put in Execution, and decrees the Ruin of *Mordecai* with all the *Jews:* But the King is timely intreated, his Heart softens, the Decree is revok'd, and *Mordecai* and his Friends saved. The Consequence was, as extream Joy to the *Jews,* so Peace and Blessings to the King. And that which heightens the Example, is the *Greatness* and *Infidelity* of the Prince: Had the Instance been in a *Jew,* it might have been placed to his *greater Light,* or *Piety:* In a petty Prince, to the *Paucity* or *Intireness* of his Territories: But that an *Heathen,* and King of One Hundred and seven and twenty Provinces, should *throughout* his vast Dominions not fear, but *practise Toleration* with good Success, has something admirable in it.

If we please to remember the Tranquility, and Success of those Heathen *Roman* Emperours, that allowed *Indulgence;* that *Augustus* sent *Hecatombs* to *Jerusalem,* and the wisest honoured the *Jews,* and at least spared the divers Sects of *Christians,* it will certainly oblige us to think, that Princes, whose Religions are *nearer of kin,* to those of the Dissenters of our Times, may not unreasonably hope for quiet from a discreet Toleration, especially when there is nothing peculiar in *Christianity* to render Princes unsafe in such an *Indulgence.* The admirable Prudence of the Emperour *Jovianus,* in a quite contrary Method to those of the Reigns of his Predecessors, settled the most *Imbroiled* Time of the Christian World, *almost to a Miracle;* for though he found the Heats of the *Arrians* and *Orthodox* carried to a barbarous Height, (to say nothing of the *Novatians,* and other dissenting Interests) the Emperour esteeming

12. On Mordechai, see Esther, esp. ch. 3.

those Calamities the Effect of Coercing Conformity to the Prince's or State's Religion, and that this Course did not only waste *Christians,* but expose *Christians* to the Scorn of *Heathens,* and so scandal those whom they should convert, he resolutely declared, *That he would have none* molested *for the different Exercise of their Religious Worship;* which (and that in a trice (for he reigned but seven Months) calm'd the impetuous Storms of Dissention, and reduced the Empire, before agitated with the most uncharitable Contests) to a wonderful *Security* and *Peace;* Thus a *kindly Amity* brought a *Civil Unity* to the *State;* which endeavours for a forc'd Unity never did to the Church, but had formerly filled the Government with incomparable *Miseries,* as well as the Church with Incharity: And which is sad, I must needs say, that those *Leaders* of the *Church* that should have been the *Teachers* and *Examples* of Peace, in so singular a Juncture of the *Churches* ferment, did, more than any, *blow the Trumpet, and kindle the Fire of Division.* So dangerous is it to *Super-fine* upon the Text, and then *Impose* it upon Penalty, for Faith.

Valentinian the Emperour (we are told by *Socrates Scholasticus*) *was a great Honourer of those that favoured his own Faith; but so, as he molested not the* Arrians *at all.* And *Marcellinus* farther adds in his Honour, *That he was much Renown'd for his Moderate Carriage during his Reign; insomuch, that amongst sundry Sects of Religion, he troubled no Man for his Conscience, imposing neither This nor That to be observed; much less, with menacing Edicts and Injunctions, did he* compel *others, his Subjects, to bow the Neck, or* conform *to that which himself Worshipped, but left such Points as clear and untoucht as he found them.*[13]

Gratianus, and *Theodosius* the Great, *Indulg'd* divers Sorts of *Christians;* but the *Novatians* of all the Dissenters were prefer'd: Which was so far from *Insecuring,* that it preserv'd the *Tranquility* of the *Empire.* Nor till the Time of *Celestine* Bishop of *Rome,* were the *Novatians* disturbed; And the *Persecution* of them, and the Assumption of the *secular Power,* began much at the same Time. But the *Novatians* at *Constantinople* were not dealt withal; for the *Greek* Bishops continued to permit them the quiet Enjoyment of their dissenting Assemblies; as *Socrates* tells us in his fifth and seventh Books of Ecclesiastical Story.

I shall descend nearer our own Times; for notwithstanding no Age has been more furiously moved, than that which *Jovianus* found, and therefore the Ex-

13. Socrates Scholasticus, *Ecclesiastical History,* bk. 5, ch. 1; Ammianus Marcellinus (ca. 330–94 C.E.), *History,* bk. 30, ch. 9, sec. 5.

periment of Indulgence *was never better made,* yet to speak more in View of this Time of Day, we find our Contemporaries, of remoter Judgments in Religion, under no manner of Difficulty in this Point. The *Grand Seignior, Great Mogul, Czars* of *Muscovia, King* of *Persia;* the Great *Monarchs* of the *East* have *long allow'd and prosper'd with a Toleration:* And who does not know that this gave Great *Tamerlane* his mighty Victories? In these Western Countries we see the same Thing.

Cardinal d'Ossat in his 92d Letter to *Villeroy,* Secretary to *Henry* the Fourth of *France,* gives us Doctrine and Example for the Subject in hand;[14]

> Besides (says he) that Necessity has no Law, be it in what Case it will; our *Lord Jesus Christ* instructs us by his Gospel, *To let the Tares alone, lest removing them may endanger the Wheat.* That other *Catholick* Princes have allow'd it without *Rebuke.* That particularly the Duke of *Savoy,* who (as great a Zealot as he would be thought for the Catholick Religion) Tolerates the Hereticks in three of his Provinces, namely, *Angroyne, Lucerne* and *Perone.* That the King of *Poland* does as much, not only in *Sweedland,* but in *Poland* it self. That all the Princes of the *Austrian* Family, that are celebrated as Pillars of the *Catholick Church,* do the like, not only in the Towns of the Empire, but in their proper Territories, as in *Austria* it self, from whence they take the Name of their Honour. In *Hungary, Bohemia, Moravia, Lusatia, Stirria, Camiolia* and *Croatia* the like. That *Charles* the Fifth, Father of the King of *Spain,* was the Person that taught the King of *France,* and other *Princes,* how to yield to such Emergencies. That his Son, the present King of *Spain,* who is esteemed *Arch Catholick,* and that is, as the *Atlas* of the *Catholick Church, Tolerates* notwithstanding at this Day, in his Kingdoms of *Valentia* and *Granada,* the *Moors* themselves in their *Mahometism,* and has offered to those of *Zealand, Holland,* and other *Hereticks* of the Low Countries, the *free Exercise* of their pretended Religion, so that they will but *acknowledge* and *Obey* him in *Civil Matters.*

It was of those Letters of this extraordinary Man, for so he was (whether we regard him in his Ecclesiastical Dignity, or his greater Christian and Civil Pru-

14. Cardinal Arnaud d'Ossat (1536–1604). A number of versions of d'Ossat's letters would have been available to Penn in French editions, including *Lettres d'illustrissime et reverendissime Cardinal d'Ossat,* 2 vols. (Paris, 1624).

dence) that the great Lord *Fulkland* said, *A Minister of State should no more be without* Cardinal d'Ossat's *Letters, than a Parson without his Bible.* And indeed, if we look into *France,* we shall find the Indulgence of those Protestants, hath been a flourishing to that Kingdom, as their *Arms* a Succour to their King. 'Tis true, that since they helpt the Ministers of his Greatness to Success, that haughty Monarch has chang'd his Measures, and resolves their Conformity to his own Religion, or their Ruin; but no Man can give another Reason for it, than that he thinks it for his Turn to please that Part of his own Church, which are the present necessary and unwearied Instruments of his absolute Glory. But let us see the End of this Conduct, it will require more Time to approve the Experiment.

As it was the Royal Saying of *Stephen, King* of *Poland,* That he was a *King of* Men, *and not of* Conscience; *a Commander of* Bodies, *and not of* Souls. So we see a *Toleration* has been practised in that Country of a long Time, with no ill Success to the State; the Cities of *Cracovia, Racovia,* and many other Towns of *Note,* almost wholly dissenting from the common *Religion of the Kingdom,* which is *Roman Catholick,* as the others are *Socinian* and *Calvinist,* mighty opposite to that, as well as to themselves.

The King of *Denmark,* in his large Town of *Altona,* but about a Mile from *Hamburgh,* and therefore called so, that is, *All-to-near,* is a pregnant Proof to our Point. For though his Seat be so remote from that Place, another strong and insinuating State so near, yet under his *Indulgence* of divers Perswasions, they enjoy their *Peace,* and he that *Security,* that he is not upon better Terms in any of his more *immediate* and *Uniform* Dominions. I leave it to the thinking Reader, if it be not much owing to this *Freedom,* and if a contrary Course were not the Way for him to furnish his Neighbours with Means to Depopulate that Place, or make it uneasie and chargeable to him to keep?

If we look into other Parts of *Germany,* where we find a Stout and Warlike People, fierce for the Thing they opine, or believe, we shall find, the Prince *Palatine* of the *Rhine* has been safe, and more potent by his *Indulgence,* witness his *Improvements* at *Manheim:* And as (believe me) he acted the Prince to his People in other Things, so in this to the Empire; for he made bold with the Constitution of it in the Latitude he gave his Subjects in this Affair.

The *Elector* of *Brandenburg* is himself a *Calvinist,* his People mostly *Lutheran,* yet in Part of his *Dominions,* the *Roman Catholicks* enjoy their Churches quietly.

The Duke of *Newburg,* and a *strict Roman Catholick,* Brother in Law to the present Emperor, in his Province of *Juliers,* has, not only at *Dewsburg, Mulheim,* and other Places, but in *Duseldorp* it self, where the Court resides, *Lutheran,* and *Calvinist,* as well as *Roman Catholick,* Assemblies.

The Elector of *Saxony,* by Religion a *Lutheran,* in his City of *Budissin,* has both *Lutherans* and *Roman Catholicks* in the same Church, parted only by a Grate.

In *Ausburg,* they have two chief Magistrates, as their *Duumvirat,* one must always be a *Roman Catholick,* and the other a *Lutheran.*

The Bishop of *Osnabrug* is himself a *Lutheran,* and in the Town of his Title, the *Roman Catholicks,* as well as *Lutherans,* have their Churches: And which is more, the next Bishop must be a *Catholick* too: For like the Buckets in the Well, they take turns: One way to be sure, so that one be but in the Right.

From hence we will go to *Sultzbach,* a small Territory, but has a great Prince, I mean, in his own *extraordinary* Qualities; for, among other Things, we shall find him act the Moderator among his People. By Profession he is a *Roman Catholick,* but has *Simultaneum Religionis Exercitium,*[15] not only *Lutherans* and *Roman Catholicks* enjoy their different Worships, but *alternatively* in one and the same Place, the same Day; so ballancing his Affection by his Wisdom, that there appears neither Partiality in him, nor Envy in them, though of such opposite Perswasions.

I will end these Foreign Instances with a Prince and Bishop, all in one, and he a *Roman Catholick* too, and that is the Bishop of *Mentz;* who admits, with a very peaceable Success such *Lutherans,* with his *Catholicks,* to enjoy their Churches, as live in his Town of *Erford.* Thus doth Practice tell us, that neither *Monarchy* nor *Hierarchy* are in danger from a Toleration. On the contrary, the Laws of the Empire, which are the Acts of the *Emperour,* and the *Soveraign Princes* of it, have Tolerated these three Religious Perswasions, *viz.* The *Roman Catholick, Lutheran* and *Calvinist,* and they may as well tolerate three more, for the same Reasons, and with the same Success. For it is not their *greater Nearness* or consistency in Doctrine, or in Worship; on the contrary, they differ much, and by that, and other Circumstances, are sometimes engaged in great Controversies, yet is a Toleration practicable, and the Way of Peace with them.

And which is closest to our Point, at home it self, we see that a *Toleration* of the *Jews, French* and *Dutch* in *England,* all *Dissenters* from the *National Way:*

15. The simultaneous exercise of religion.

And the Connivance that has been in *Ireland:* and the down-right *Toleration* in most of the Kings *Plantations* abroad, prove the Assertion, *That Toleration is not dangerous to Monarchy.* For Experience tells us, where it is in any Degree admitted, the King's Affairs prosper most; *People, Wealth* and *Strength* being sure to follow such *Indulgence.*

But after all that I have said in Reason and Fact, why *Toleration* is safe to *Monarchy,* Story tells us that worse Things have befallen Princes in Countries under *Ecclesiastical Union,* than in Places under divided Forms of Worship; and so Tolerating Countries stand to the Prince, upon more than equal Terms with *Conforming ones.* And where Princes have been exposed to hardship in tolerating Countries, they have as often come from the Conforming, as Non-conforming Party; and so the *Dissenter* is upon equal Terms, to the Prince or State, with the *Conformist.*

The first is evident in the *Jews,* under the Conduct of *Moses;* their Dissention came from the Men of their own Tribes, such as *Corah, Dathan* and *Abiram,* with their Partakers.[16] To say nothing of the *Gentiles.*

The Miseries and Slaughters of *Mauritius* the Emperor, prove my Point, who by the greatest *Church-men* of his Time was withstood, and his Servant that perpetrated the *Wickedness, by them,* substituted in his Room, because more officious to their Grandure. What Power but that of the *Church,* dethroned *Childerick,* King of *France,* and set *Pepin* in his Place? The Miseries of the Emperours, *Henry* the fourth and fifth, Father and Son, from their rebellious Subjects, raised and animated by the Power of *Conformists,* dethroning both, as much as they could, are notorious. 'Tis alledg'd, that *Sigismund* King of *Sweedland,* was rejected by that *Lutheran* Country, because he was a *Roman Catholick.*

If we come nearer home, which is most suitable to the Reasons of the *Discourse,* we find the *Church-men* take part with *William Rufus,* and *Henry* the first, against *Robert* their elder Brother; and after that, we see some of the greatest of them *made Head* against their King, namely *Anselm* Arch-Bishop of *Canterbury,* and his Party, as did his Successor *Thomas* of *Becket* to the second *Henry. Stephen* usurp'd the Crown when there was a *Church Union:* And King *John* lived *miserable* for all that, and at last died *by one of his own Religion too.* The Dissentions that agitated the Reign of his Son *Henry* the third, and the *Barons* War, with Bishop *Grosteeds* Blessing to *Mumford* their General: The

16. Numbers 16.

Deposition and *Murther* of the second *Edward,* and *Richard,* and sixth *Henry,* and his Son the Prince. The Usurpation of *Richard* the Third, and the Murther of the Sons of *Edward* the fourth, in the Tower of *London.* The *civil War* that followed between him and the Earl of *Richmond,* afterwards our Wise *Henry* the seventh, were all perpetrated in a Country of *one Religion,* and by the Hands of *Conformists.* In short, if we will but look upon the civil War that so long raged in this Kingdom, between the Houses of *York* and *Lancaster,* and consider that they professed but one and the same Religion, and both back't with Numbers of Church-men too (to say nothing of the Miserable end of many of our Kings princely Ancestors in *Scotland,* especially the first and third *James*) we shall find Cause to say, *That Church-Uniformity is not a Security for Princes to depend upon.*

If we will look next into Countries where *Dissenters* from the National Church are *Tolerated,* we shall find the *Conformist* not less Culpable than the *Dissenter.*

The Disorders among the *Jews,* after they were settled in the Land that God had given them, came not from those they tolerated, but themselves. They *cast off Samuel,* and the Government of the *Judges.* 'Twas the Children of the *National* Church, that fell in with the Ambition of *Absolom,* and animated the Rebellion against their Father *David.* They were the same that revolted from *Solomon*'s Son, and cryed in behalf of *Jeroboam, To your Tents, O Israel!*[17]

Not two Ages ago, the Church of *France,* too generally fell in with the Family of *Guise,* against their lawful Soveraign, *Henry* the Fourth: Nor were they without Countenance of the greatest of their Belief, who stiled it an *Holy War:* At that Time, fearing (not without Cause) the *Defection* of that Kingdom from the *Roman* See. In this Conjuncture, the *Dissenters* made up the best Part of that King's Armies, and by their *Loyalty* and *Blood,* preserv'd the *Blood Royal* of *France,* and set the Crown on the Head of that Prince. That King was twice Assassinated, and the last Time Murdered, as was *Henry* the third, his Predecessor; but they fell, one by the Hand of a *Churchman,* the other, at least by a *Conformist.*

'Tis true, that the next civil War was between the *Catholicks* and the *Huguenots,* under the Conduct of *Cardinal Richlieu,* and the *Duke of Rohan:* But as I will not justifie the Action, so their *Liberties* and *Cautions* so solemnly settled

17. On casting off Samuel's government, see 1 Samuel 7:15–8:22; on Absalom, 2 Samuel 15–18; and on Jeroboam's rebellion against Rehoboam, 1 Kings 12.

by *Henry* the Fourth, as the Reward of their singular Merit, being by the Ministry of that *Cardinal* invaded, they say, they did but defend their Security, and that rather against the *Cardinal,* than the *King,* whose Softness suffered him to become a Property to the great *Wit* and *Ambition* of that Person: And there is this Reason to believe them, that if it had been otherwise, we are sure that King *Charles* the First would not in the least have countenanced the Quarrel.

However, the *Cardinal,* like himself, wisely knew when to stop. For though he thought it the Interest of the Crown, to moderate their Greatness, and check their Growth, yet having fresh in Memory the Story of the foregoing Age, he saw, *'Twas Wise to have a Ballance upon Occasion.* But this was more than recompenc'd in their fixt Adhesion to the Crown of *France,* under the Ministry and Direction of the succeeding *Cardinal,* when their Perswasion had not only Number, and many good Officers to value it self upon, but yielded their *King* the ablest Captain of the Age, namely, *Turene:* It was an *Huguenot* then, at the Head of almost an *Huguenot* Army, that fell in with a *Cardinal* himself (see the Union Interest makes) to maintain the Imperial Crown of *France,* and that on a *Roman-Catholick's Head:* And together *with their own Indulgence, that Religion, as National too,* against the Pretences of a *Roman-Catholick Army,* headed by a Prince Brave and Learned of the same Religion.

I mention not this, to prefer one Party to another; for contrary Instances may be given else-where, as Interests have varied. In *Sweedland* a Prince was rejected by *Protestants;* And in *England* and *Holland,* and many of the *Principalities of Germany, Roman-Catholicks* have approv'd themselves Loyal to their *Kings, Princes and States.* But this suffices to us that we gain the Point; for it is evident in Countries where *Dissenters* are Tolerated, the *Insecurity of the Prince and Government may as well come from the Conforming, as Dissenting Party,* and that it comes not from Dissenters, *because such.*

But how Happy and Admirable was this Civil Union between the *Cardinal* and *Turene?* Two most opposite Religions, both follow'd by People of their own Perswasion: One says his *Mass,* t'other his *Directory:* Both invoke *One Deity,* by several Ways, for *One Success,* and it followed with Glory, and a Peace to this Day. O why should it be otherwise now! What has been may be: Methinks Wisdom and Charity are on that Side still.

It will doubtless be objected, *That the Dissenting Party of* England, *fell in with the State-Dissenter in our late Civil, but Unnatural War:* And this seems to be against us, yet *Three Things* must be confessed: *First,* That the War rather made the *Dissenters,* than the *Dissenters* made the War. *Secondly,* That those that were then in being, were not Tolerated, as in *France,* but prosecuted. And, *Lastly,* That they did not lead, but follow great Numbers of *Church-Goers,* of all Qualities, in that unhappy Controversie; and which began upon other Topicks than Liberty for *Church-Dissenters.* And though they were herein blameable, Reason is Reason, in all Climates and Latitudes. This does not affect the Question: Such Calamities are no *necessary Consequences of Church-Dissent,* because they would then follow in all Places where *Dissenters* are *Tolerated,* which we see they do not: But these may sometimes indeed be the Effects of a violent Endeavour of *Uniformity, and that under all Forms of Government,* as I fear they were partly here under our Monarchy. But then, this teaches us to conclude, that a *Toleration* of those, that a contrary Course makes uneasie and desperate, may prevent or cure *Intestine Troubles;* as *Anno Forty Eight;* it ended the Strife, and settled the Peace of *Germany.*[18] For 'tis not now the Question, *How far Men may be provoked, or ought to resent it;* but, *Whether Government is Safe in a Toleration, especially Monarchy:* And to this Issue we come in Fact, *That 'tis Safe, and that Conformists* (generally speaking) *have, for their Interests, as rarely known their Duty to their Prince, as Dissenters for their Consciences.* So that the Danger seems to lye on this Side, of *forcing Uniformity* against Faith, upon severe Penalties, rather than of a discreet *Toleration.*

In the next Place, I shall endeavour to shew the *Prudence* and *Reasonableness* of a *Toleration,* by the great Benefits that follow it.

Toleration, which is an Admission of *Dissenting Worships, with Impunity to the Dissenters, secures Property,* which is *Civil Right,* and *That Eminently the Line and Power of the Monarchy:* For if no Man suffer in his *Civil Right* for the Sake of such *Dissent,* the Point of *Succession* is settled without *a Civil War, or a Recantation;* since it were an absurd Thing to imagine, that a Man born to *Five Pounds a Year,* should not be liable to forfeit his Inheritance for *Non-Conformity,* and yet a *Prince of the Blood, and an Heir to the Imperial Crown, should be made incapable of Inheritance for his Church-Dissent.*

The Security then of *Property, or Civil Right,* from being forfeitable for Religious Dissent, becomes a Security to the *Royal Family,* against the Difficulties lately labour'd under in the Business of the *Succession.*[19] And though I have no Commission for it, besides the great Reason and Equity of the Thing it self, I dare say, there can hardly be a *Dissenter* at this Time of Day so void of Sense

18. The Peace of Westphalia (1648) ended the Thirty Years' War.
19. That is, the Exclusion Crisis (see the introduction).

and Justice, as well as Duty and Loyalty, as not to be of the same Mind. Else it were to deny that to the *Prince,* which he needs, and prays for from him. Let us not forget the Story of *Sigismund* of *Sweedland,* of *Henry the Fourth* of *France,* and especially of our *Own Queen Mary.* Had *Property* been fix't, the Line of those Royal Families could not have met with any Let or Interruption. 'Twas this Consideration that prevail'd with Judge *Hales,* though a strong *Protestant,* after King *Edward*'s Death, to give his Opinion for *Queen Mary*'s Succession, against that of all the Rest of the Judges to the contrary: Which Noble President, was recompenc'd in the Loyalty of *Archbishop* Heath, *a Roman Catholick,* in favour of the Succession of *Queen Elizabeth:* And the same Thing would be done again, in the like Case, by Men of the same Integrity.

I know it may be said, *That there is little Reason now for the Prince to regard this Argument in Favour of Dissenters, when it was so little heeded in the Case of the* Presumptive Heir *to the Crown.* But as this was the Act and Heat of Conforming Men within Doors, so if it were, in Counsel or Desire, the Folly and Injustice of any Dissenters without Doors, shall many entire Parties pay the Reckoning of the few busie Offenders? They would humbly hope, that the singular Mildness and Clemency, which make up so great a Part of the King's publick Assurances, will not leave him in his Reflection here.

'Tis the Mercies of Princes, that above all their Works, give them the nearest Resemblance to Divinity in their Administration. Besides, it is their Glory to measure their Actions by the Reason and Consequence of Things, and not by the Passions that possess and animate private Breasts: For it were fatal to the Interest of a Prince, *that the Folly or Undutifulness of any of his Subjects,* should put him out of the Way, or tempt him *to be unsteady to his Principle and Interest:* And yet, with Submission, I must say, it would be the Consequence of Coercion: For, by exposing *Property for Opinion,* the Prince exposes the Consciences and Property of his own Family, and plainly *Disarms* them of all Defence, *upon any Alteration of Judgment.* Let us remember, *That several of the same Gentlemen, who at first Sacrificed Civil Rights for Non-Conformity in common Dissenters, fell at last to make the Succession of the Crown the Price of Dissent in the next Heir of the Royal Blood.* So dangerous a Thing it is to hazard Property to serve a Turn for any Party, or suffer such Examples in the Case of the meanest Person in a Kingdom.

Nor is this all the Benefit that attends the Crown by the Preservation of Civil Rights; for the Power of the Monarchy is kept more Entire by it. The King has the Benefit of his whole People, and the Reason of their Safety is owing to their Civil, and not Ecclesiastical Obedience: *Their Loyalty to* Caesar, *and not Conformity to the Church.* Whereas the other Opinion would have it, *That no Conformity to the Church, No Property in the State:* Which is to clog and narrow the Civil Power, for at this Rate, *No Church-Man, No English-Man;* and, *No Conformist, No Subject.* A Way to *alien* the King's People, and practise an *Exclusion* upon him, from, it may be, a Fourth Part of his Dominions. Thus it may happen, that the ablest Statesman, the bravest Captain, and the best Citizen may be disabled, and the Prince forbid their Employment to his Service.

Some Instances of this we have had since the late King's Restoration: For upon the first *Dutch-War,* Sir *William Penn* being commanded to give in a List of the ablest Sea-Officers in the Kingdom, to serve in that Expedition, I do very well remember he presented our present King with a Catalogue of the knowingest and bravest Officers the Age had bred, with this Subscrib'd, *These Men, if his Majesty will please to admit of their Perswasions, I will answer for their Skill, Courage and Integrity.* He pickt them by their Ability, not their Opinions; and he was in the Right; for that was the best Way of doing the King's Business. And of my own Knowledge, *Conformity robb'd the King at that Time of Ten Men, whose greater Knowledge and Valour, than any One Ten of that Fleet, had in their Room, been able to have saved a Battel, or perfected a Victory.* I will Name Three of them: The *First* was Old Vice Admiral *Goodson,* than whom, No-body was more Stout, or a Seaman. The *Second,* Captain *Hill,* that in the *Saphire,* beat Admiral *Everson* Hand to Hand, that came to the Relief of *Old Trump.* The *Third,* was Captain *Potter,* that in the *Constant Warwick,* took Captain *Beach,* after Eight Hours smart *Dispute.* And as evident it is, *That if a War had proceeded between this Kingdom and* France *Seven Years ago, the Business of* Conformity *had deprived the King of many Land-Officers, whose Share in the late Wars of* Europe, *had made knowing and able.*

But which is worst of all, such are not Safe, with their *Dissent,* under their own Extraordinary Prince. For, *though a Man were a Great Honourer of his* King, *a Lover of his* Country, *an Admirer of the* Government: *In the Course of his Life, Sober, Wise, Industrious and Useful, if a* Dissenter *from the Establisht Form of Worship, in that Condition there is no* Liberty *for his Person, nor* Security *to his Estate:* As *Useless* to the Publick, so *Ruin'd* in himself. For this *Net catches the Best.* Men True to their Conscience, and who indulged, are most like to be so to their Prince; whilst the rest are left to *cozen* him by their Change; for that is the *Unhappy End of Forc'd Conformity in the Poor Spir-*

ited Compliers. And this must always be the Consequence of *necessitating the Prince to put more and other Tests upon his People, than are requisite to secure him of their Loyalty.*

And when we shall be so Happy in our Measures, as to consider this Mischief to the *Monarchy,* it is to be hop'd, it will be thought expedient to disintangle *Property from Opinion,* and cut the untoward Knot some Men have tyed, that hath so long hamper'd and gaul'd the Prince as well as People. It will be then, when Civil Punishments shall no more follow Church Faults, that the *Civil Tenure* will be recover'd to the Government, and the *Natures* of Acts, Rewards and Punishments, so distinguish'd, as *Loyalty* shall be the Safety of *Dissent,* and the whole People made useful to the Government.

It will, perhaps, be objected, *That Dissenters can hardly be obliged to be True to the Crown, and so the Crown unsafe in their very Services; for they may easily turn the Power given them to serve it, against it, to Greaten themselves.* I am willing to obviate every Thing, that may with any Pretence be offerr'd against our intreated Indulgence. I say *No,* and appeal to the *King* himself (against whom the Prejudices of our late Times ran highest, and who therefore has most Reason to Resent) If ever He was better Lov'd or Serv'd, than by the *Old Round-headed Seamen,* the Earl of *Sandwich,* Sir *William Penn,* Sir *J. Lawson,* Sir *G. Ascue,* Sir *R. Stanier,* Sir *J. Smith,* Sir *J. Jordan,* Sir *J. Harmon,* Sir *Christopher Minns,* Captain *Sansum, Curtins, Clark, Robinson, Molton, Wager, Tern, Parker, Haward, Hubbard, Fen, Langhorn, Daws, Earl, White;* to say nothing of many yet Living, of Real Merit, and many Inferior Officers, Expert and Brave. And to do our *Prince* Justice, He *deserv'*d it from them, by his Humility, Plainness and Courage, and the Care and Affection that he always shew'd them.

If any say, *That most of these Men were Conformists,* I presume to tell them, I know as well as any Man, they Serv'd the King never the Better for that: On the contrary, 'twas all the Strife that some of them had in themselves, in the doing that Service, that they must not serve the King without it; and if in that they could have been Indulged, they had perform'd it with the greatest Alacrity. *Interest* will not lye. Where People find their Reckoning, they are sure to be *True.* For 'tis Want of Wit that makes any Man false to himself. 'Twas he that knew all Men's Hearts, that said, *Where the Treasure is, there will the Heart be also.*[20] Let Men be easie, safe, and upon their Preferment with the Prince, and they will be Dutiful, Loyal, and most Affectionate.

20. Matthew 6:21; and Luke 12:34.

Mankind by Nature fears Power, and melts at Goodness. Pardon my Zeal, I would not be thought to plead for *Dissenters Preferment;* 'tis enough they keep what they have, and may live at their own Charges. Only I am for having the *Prince have Room for his Choice,* and not be crampt and stinted by Opinion; but imploy those who are best able to serve him: And, *I think out of Six Parties, 'tis better picking, than out of One,* and therefore the Prince's Interest is to be Head of all of them, which a *Toleration effects in a Moment,* since those *Six* (divided Interests, within themselves) having but *One Civil Head,* become one intire *Civil Body to the Prince.* And I am sure, I have *Monarchy* on my Side, if *Solomon* and his Wisdom may stand for it, who tells us, *That the Glory of a King is in the Multitude of his People.*[21]

Nor is this all, *for the Consequences of such an Universal Content, would be of infinite Moment to the Security of the Monarchy, both at Home and Abroad. At Home, for it would Behead the Factions without Blood, and Banish the Ringleaders without going abroad.* When the *Great Bodies of Dissenters* see the Care of the *Government for their Safety,* they have no Need of their Captains, nor these any Ground for their Pretences: For as they us'd the People to value themselves, and raise their Fortunes with the *Prince,* so the People follow'd their Leaders to get that Ease, they see their Heads promised, but could not, and the *Government* can, and does give them.

Multitudes cannot Plot, they are too many, and have not Conduct for it, they move by another Spring. *Safety is the Pretence of their Leaders:* If once they see they enjoy it, they have yet Wit enough not to hazard it for any Body: For the Endeavours of Busie Men are then discernable; but a State of Severity gives them a Pretence, by which the Multitude is easily taken. Men may indiscreetly Plot to get what they would never Plot to lose. *So that Ease is not only their Content, but the Prince's Security.*

This I say, upon a Supposition, *That the Dissenters could agree against the Government;* which is a begging of the Question: For it is improbable (if not impossible without *Conformists*) since, *besides the Distance they are at in their Perswasions and Affections, they dare not hope for so Good Terms from one another, as the Government gives:* And that Fear, with Emulation, would draw them into that Duty, that they must all fall into a Natural Dependence, which I call, *Holding of the Prince, as the Great Head of the State.*

From Abroad, we are as Safe as from within our selves: For if *Leading Men*

21. Proverbs 14:28.

at Home are thus disappointed of their Interest in the People, *Foreigners will find here no Interpreters of their* dividing Language, *nor Matter* (*if they could*) *to work upon.* For the Point is gain'd, the People they would deal in, are at their Ease, and cannot be bribed; and those that would, can't deserve it.

It is this that makes *Princes* live *Independent* of their Neighbours: And, to be loved at Home, is be feared Abroad: One follows necessarily the other. Where Princes are driven to seek a foreign Assistance, the Issue either must be the *Ruin* of the *Prince,* or the absolute *Subjection* of the *People;* not without the Hazard of becoming a Province to the Power of that Neighbour that turns the Scale. These *Consequences* have on either Hand an *ill Look,* and should rebate Extremes.

The *Greatness* of *France* carries those *Threats* to all her Neighbours, that, politically speaking, 'tis the *Melancholiest* Prospect *England* has had to make since *Eighty Eight:*[22] The *Spaniard* at that Time, being shorter in all Things but his *Pride* and *Hope,* than the *French* King is now, of the same *Universal Monarchy.* This Greatness, begun with the *Eleventh Lewis,* some will have it, has not been so much advanced by the Wisdom of *Richlieu,* and Craft of *Mazarene,* no, nor the *Arms* of the present *Monarch,* as by the *Assistance* or *Connivance* of *England,* that has most to lose by him.

O. Cromwell began, and gave him the Scale against the *Spaniard.* The Reason of State he went upon, was the Support of Usurp'd Dominion: And he was not out in it; for the *Exile* of the *Royal Family* was a great Part of the Price of that Aid: In which we see, how much *Interest* prevails above *Nature.* It was not *Royal Kindred* could shelter a King against the Solicitations of an *Usurper* with the *Son* of his *Mother's Brother.*

But it will be told us by some People, *We have not degenerated,* but exactly followed the same Steps ever since, which has given such an Increase to those Beginnings, that the *French Monarchy* is almost above our Reach. But suppose it were true, What's the Cause of it? It has not been old Friendship, or nearness of Blood, or Neighbourhood. Nor could it be from an Inclination in our Ministers, to bring Things here to a like Issue, as some have suggested; for then we should have clogged his Successes, instead of helping them in any Kind, lest in so doing, we should have put it into his Power to hinder our own.

But perhaps our *Cross* Accidents of State may sometimes have compelled

22. That is, the Spanish Armada.

us into his Friendship, and his Councils have carefully improved the one, and husbanded the other to great Advantages, and that this was more than made for our *English* Interest: And yet 'tis but too true, that the *extreme Heats* of some Men, that most inveighed against it, went too far to strengthen that Understanding, by not taking what would have been granted, and creating an Interest at Home, that might naturally have dissolv'd that Correspondence Abroad.

I love not to revive Things that are uneasily remembred, but in Points most tender to the late King, he thought himself sometimes too closely pressed, and hardly held; and we are all wise enough now to say, a milder Conduct had succeeded better: For if reasonable Things may be reasonably prest, and with such private Intentions, as induce a Denial, Heats about Things doubtful, unwise or unjust, must needs harden and prejudice.

Let us then create an Interest for the Prince at *Home,* and *Foreign Friendships* (at best, uncertain and dangerous) will fall of Course; for if it be allowed to *Private Men,* shall it be forbid to *Princes* only, to know and to be true to their own Support?

It is no more than what every Age makes us to see in all Parties of Men. The Parliaments of *England, since the Reformation, giving no Quarter to Roman Catholicks,* have forc'd them to the *Crown for Shelter.* And to induce the *Monarchy to yield them the Protection they have needed,* they have with mighty Address and Skill, recommended themselves as the *Great Friends of the Prerogative,* and so successfully too, that it were not below the Wisdom of that Constitution, to reflect what they have lost by that Costiveness of theirs to *Catholicks.* On the other Hand, the *Crown* having treated the *Protestant Dissenters* with the Severity of the Laws that affected them, suffering the Sharpest of them to fall upon their Persons and Estates, they have been driven successively to *Parliaments for Succour,* whose Priviledges, with equal Skill and Zeal, they have abetted: And our late Unhappy Wars are too plain a Proof, how much their Accession gave the Scale against the Power and Courage of both *Conformists and Catholicks,* that adhered to the *Crown.*

Nor must this *Contrary Adhesion be imputed to Love or Hatred,* but *Necessary Interest:* Refusal in one Place, makes Way for Address in another. If the Scene be changed, the Parts must follow; for as well before, as after *Cromwell's Usurpation,* the *Roman Catholicks* did not only promise, *The most ready Obedience to that Government, in their Printed Apologies for Liberty of Conscience; but actually treated by some of their Greatest Men, with the Ministers of those*

Times, for Indulgence, *upon the Assurances they offer'd to give of their* Good Behaviour *to the Government, as then Establish'd.*

On the other Hand, we see the *Presbyterians,* That in *Scotland* began the War, and in *England* promoted and upheld it to *Forty Seven,* when ready to be supplanted by the *Independents,* wheel to the King. In *Scotland* they Crown him, and come into *England* with an Army to restore him, where their Brethren joyn them; but being defeated, *They Help, by Private Collections,* to support him Abroad; and after the Overthrow of Sir *George Booth*'s Attempt, to almost a Miracle, restore him. And which is more, a Great Part of that Army too, whose *Victories* came from the *Ruin* of the Prince they restored.

But to give the last Proofs our Age has of the Power of *Interest,* against the Notion oppos'd by this Discourse. *First,* the *Independents* themselves, held the *Greatest Republicans* of all Parties, were the most Lavish and Superstitious Adorers of Monarchy in *Oliver Cromwell,* because of the Regard he had to them; allowing him, and his Son after him, to be *Custos Utriusque Tabulae,* over all Causes, as well Ecclesiastical as Civil, *Supreme Governour.* And next, the *Conformists* in Parliament, reputed the most *Loyal and Monarchical Men,* did more than any Body question and oppose the late King's *Declaration of Indulgence;* even They themselves would not allow so much Prerogative to the Crown, but pleaded and opposed his Political Capacity.

This proves the *Power of Interest,* and that *All Perswasions center with it:* And when they see the *Government* engaging them with a *Fix'd Liberty of Conscience,* they must for their own Sakes seek the Support of it, by which it is maintained. This *Union,* directed under the Prince's Conduct, would Awe the Greatness of our Neighbours, and soon restore *Europe* to its Ancient Ballance, and that into his Hand too: So that *He may be the Great Arbiter of the Christian World.* But if the Policy of the Government, places the Security of it's Interest in the *Destruction of the Civil Interest of the Dissenters,* it is not to be wondred at, if they are less found in the Praises of it's Conduct, than others, to whom they are offered up a Sacrifice by it.

I know it will be insinuated, *That there is Danger in Building upon the Union of divers Interests;* and this will be aggravated to the *Prince,* by such as would engross *His Bounty,* and intercept *His Grace* from a great Part of his People. But I will only oppose to that meer Suggestion, Three Examples to the contrary, with this Challenge, That if after Rummaging the Records of all Time, they find one Instance to contradict me, I shall submit the Question to their Authority.

The *First,* is given by those *Christian Emperors,* who admitted all Sorts of *Dissenters into their Armies, Courts and Senates.* This, the Ecclesiastical Story of those Times, assures us, and particularly *Socrates, Evagrius,* and *Onuphrius.*

The next Instance, is that of *Prince* William *of* Orange, who by a timely *Indulgence,* united the scattered Strength of *Holland,* and, all animated by the *Clemency,* as well as *Valour* of their Captain, crown'd his Attempts with an extraordinary Glory; and, what makes, continues Great.

The *last;* is given us by *Livy,* in his Account of *Hannibal's Army;* "That they consisted of divers *Nations, Languages, Customs* and *Religions:* That under all their Successes of War and Peace, for *Thirteen Years together,* they never mutiny'd against their General, nor fell out among themselves."[23] What *Livy* relates for a Wonder, the Marquis *Virgilio Malvetzy* gives the Reason of, to wit, their *Variety* and Difference, *well managed by their General;* for, said he, "It was impossible for so many *Nations, Customs* and *Religions* to combine, especially when the General's equal Hand gave him more Reverence with them, than they had of Affection for one another. This (says he) some would wholly impute to *Hannibal;* but however great he was, I attribute it to the Variety of People in the Army: For (adds he) *Rome*'s Army was ever less given to Mutiny, when ballanced with Auxiliary Legions, than when intirely *Roman.*" Thus much in his Discourse upon *Cornelius Tacitus.*[24]

And they are neither few, nor of the weakest Sort of Men, that have thought the *Concord* of *Discords* a firm Basis for Government to be built upon. The Business is to *Tune* them well, and that must be the Skill of the *Musician.*

In Nature we see all Heat *consumes,* all Cold *kills:* That three Degrees of Cold to two of Heat, allays the Heat, but introduces the contrary Quality, and over-cools by a Degree; but *two Degrees* of *Cold* to *two* of *Heat,* makes a *Poize* in Elements, and a *Ballance* in Nature. And in those Families where the evenest Hand is carried, the Work is best done, and the Master is most reverenced.

This brings me to another Benefit, which accrues to the *Monarchy* by a *Toleration,* and that is a *Ballance at Home:* For though it be improbable, it may so happen, that either the Conforming or Non-conforming Party may be undutiful; the one is then a Ballance of the other. *This might have prevented much Mischief to our second and third* Henry, *King* John, *the second* Edward,

23. Livy, *History of Rome,* bk. 28, ch. 12.

24. Virgilio Malvezzi, *Discourses upon Cornelius Tacitus,* trans. Sir Richard Baker (London, 1642), discourse 59, pp. 475–77.

and Richard, *and unhappy* Henry *the Sixth, as it undeniably saved the* Royal Family *of* France, *and secured* Holland, *and kept it from Truckling under the* Spanish Monarchy. While all hold of the Government, 'tis that which gives the Scale to the most Dutiful; but still, no farther than to shew it's Power, and awe the Disorderly into Obedience, not to destroy the *Ballance,* lest it should afterwards want the Means of *Over-poizing Faction.*

That this is more than Fancy, plain it is, that the *Dissenter* must firmly adhere to the Government for his *Being,* while the *Church-man* is provided for. The one subsists by it's *Mercy,* the other by it's *Bounty.* This is tied by *Plenty,* but that by *Necessity,* which being the last of Tyes, and strongest Obligation, the Security is greatest from him, that it is fancy'd most unsafe to *Tolerate.*

But besides this, the *Tranquility* which it gives at Home, will both oblige those that are upon the Wing for *Foreign Parts,* to *pitch here again;* and at a Time when our Neighbouring Monarch is wasting his People, excite those Sufferers into the King's Dominions, whose Number will encrease that of his Subjects, and their Labour and Consumption, the Trade and Wealth of his Territories.[25]

For what are all *Conquests,* but of People? And if the Government may by *Indulgence* add the Inhabitants of Ten Cities to those of it's own, it obtains a *Victory* without Charge. The Ancient Persecution of *France* and the *Low Countries,* has furnish'd us with an invincible Instance; for of those that came hither on that Account, we were instructed in most useful *Manufactures,* as by Courses of the like Nature, we lost a great Part of our *Woollen Trade.* And as Men, in Times of Danger, draw in their Stock, and either transmit it to other Banks, or bury their Talent at Home for Security (that being out of Sight, it may be, out of Reach too, and either is fatal to a Kingdom) so this Mildness obtained, setting every Man's Heart at rest, every Man will be at Work, and the Stock of the Kingdom employ'd: which, like the Blood, that hath it's due Passage, will give Life and Vigour to every Member in the publick Body.

And here give me Leave to mention the Experiment made at Home by the late King, in his *Declaration of Indulgence.* No Matter how well or ill built that Act of State was, 'tis no Part of the Business in Hand, but what Effect the *Liberty of it* had upon the *Peace* and *Wealth* of the Kingdom, may have Instruction

25. In 1685, Louis XIV revoked the Edict of Nantes, which had guaranteed French Protestants the right to worship since its promulgation by Henry IV in 1598.

in it to our present Condition. 'Twas evident, that all Men laboured cheerfully, and traded boldly, when they had the *Royal Word* to keep what they got, and the *King* himself became the *Universal Insurer* of Dissenters Estates. *Whitehall,* then, and St. *James*'s, were as much visited and courted by their respective Agents, as if they had been of the *Family:* For that which eclipsed the *Royal Goodness,* being by his *own Hand* thus remov'd, his benign Influences drew the Returns of Sweetness and Duty from that Part of his Subjects, that the Want of those Influences had made barren before. Then it was that we look'd like the Members of one Family, and Children of one Parent. Nor did we envy our eldest Brother, *Episcopacy,* his Inheritance, so that we had but a Child's Portion: For not only *Discontents vanish'd,* but no Matter was left for ill Spirits, foreign or domestick, to *brood* upon, or hatch to Mischief. Which was a plain Proof, that it is the *Union* of *Interests,* and not of *Opinions,* that gives Peace to Kingdoms.

And with all Deference to Authority, I would speak it, the *Liberty* of the Declaration seems to be our *English Amomum* at last: The *Sovereign Remedy* to our *English* Constitution. And, to say true, we shifted Luck (as they call it) as soon as we had lost it; *like those that lose their Royal* Gold, *their* Evil *Returns.* For all Dissenters seemed then united in their Affection to the *Government,* and followed their Affairs without Fear or Distraction. *Projects,* then, were stale and unmerchantable, and no Body cared for them, because no Body wanted any: That gentle *Opiate,* at the Prince's Hand, laid the most Busy and Turbulent to Sleep: But when the Loss of that *Indulgence* made them uncertain, and that uneasy; Their Persons and Estates being again exposed to pay the Reckoning of their *Dissent,* no doubt but every Party shifted then as they could: Most grew selfish, at least, jealous, fearing one should make Bargains apart, or exclusive of the other. This was the fatal Part *Dissenters* acted to their common Ruin: And I take this Partiality to have had too great a Share in our late Animosities; which, by fresh Accidents falling in, have swelled to a mighty Deluge, such an one as hath over-whelmed our former civil Concord and Serenity. And pardon me, if I say, I cannot see that those *Waters* are like to *asswage,* 'till this *Olive-Branch* of *Indulgence* be some Way or other restored: The *Waves* will still cover our Earth, and a Spot of Ground will hardly be found in this glorious Isle, for a great Number of useful People to set a quiet Foot upon. And, to pursue the Allegory, What was the *Ark* it self, *but the most apt and lively* Emblem *of* Toleration? A Kind of *Natural Temple of Indul-*

gence. In which we find *two of every* living Creature dwelling together, of *both* Sexes too, that they might *propagate;* and that as well of the *unclean* as *clean* Kind: So that the *baser* and less useful Sort were saved.[26] Creatures never like to change their Nature, and so far from being whipt and punish'd to the Altar, that they were expresly forbid. *These were Saved, these were Fed and Restored to their Ancient Pastures.* Shall we be so mannerly as to complement the *Conformists* with the Stile of *Clean,* and so humble as to take the *Unclean* Kind, to our selves, who are the less Noble, and more Clownish Sort of People? I think verily we may do it, if we may but be saved too by the *Commander* of our *English Ark.* And this the *Peaceable* and *Virtuous Dissenter* has the less Reason to fear, since *Sacred Text* tells us, *'Twas Vice,* and *Not Opinion,* that brought the Deluge upon the rest. And here (to drop our Allegory) I must take Leave to hope, that though the Declaration be gone, if the Reason of it remain, I mean the *Interest of the Monarchy,* the *King* and His *Great Council* will graciously please to think a *Toleration,* no Dangerous nor Obsolete Thing.

But as it has many *Arguments* for it, that are drawn from the Advantages that have and would come to the Publick by it, so there are divers *Mischiefs* that must unavoidably follow the *Persecution* of *Dissenters,* that may reasonably disswade from such Severity. For they must either be *ruined, fly,* or *conform;* and perhaps the last is not the *Safest.* If they are *Ruin'd* in their Estates, and their Persons *Imprisoned,* modestly computing, a *Fourth* of the *Trade* and *Manufactury* of the Kingdom *sinks;* and those that have helped to maintain the Poor, must come upon the *Poor's Book* for *Maintenance.* This seems to be an *Impoverishing* of the Publick. But if to avoid this, they transport themselves, with their *Estates,* into other Governments; nay, though it were to any of the King's Plantations, the Number were far too great to be spared from Home. So much principal Stock wanting to turn the yearly Traffick, and so many People too, to consume our yearly Growth, must issue *fatally* to the *Trade* one Way, and to the *Lands* and *Rents* of the Kingdom the other Way.

And lastly, If they should resolve, neither to *suffer* nor *fly,* but *conform* to prevent both. It is to be enquired, if this *Cure* of *Church-Division* be *safe* to the State; or not rather, a raking up *Coals under Ashes,* for a future Mischief? He whom Fear or Policy hath made *Treacherous* to his own Conscience, ought not to be held *True* to any thing but his own *Safety* and *Revenge.* His Conformity gives him the first, and his Resentment of the Force that compels it,

26. Genesis 6–9.

will on no Occasion let him want the last. So that *Conformity cozens* no Body but the Government: For the *State Fanatick* (which is the *unsafe* Thing to the State) being *christen'd* by *Conformity,* he is eligible every where, with Persons the most devoted to the Prince: And all Men will hold themselves *protected* in their Votes by it.

A Receipt to make *Faction keep, and preserve Disloyalty against all Weathers.* For whereas the Nature of *Tests* is to *discover,* this is the Way to *conceal* the Inclinations of Men from the Government. *Plain Dissent* is the *Prince with a Candle in his Hand:* He sees the *Where* and *What* of Persons and Things: He discriminates, and makes that a Rule of Conduct: But forc'd *Conformity* is the *Prince in the Dark:* It blows out his Candle, and leaves him without Distinction. Such Subjects are like *Figures in Sand,* when Water is flapt upon them, they run together, and are indiscernible: Or *written Tradition,* made *illegible* by writing the *Oaths* and *Canons* upon it: *The safest Way of blotting out Danger.*

I know not how to forbear saying, that this *necessary Conformity* makes the Church *dangerous* to the State: For even the *Hypocrisy* that follows, makes the Church both *conceal* and *protect* the *Hypocrites,* which, together with their *Liberality* to the *Parson, Charity to the Poor, and Hospitality to their Neighbours,* recommends them to the first Favour they have to bestow. That *Fort* is *unsafe,* where a Party of the *Garrison* consists of *disguised Enemies;* for when they take their Turns at the *Watch,* the *Danger* is hardly evitable. It would then certainly be for the *Safety* of the *Fort,* that such Friends in *Masquerade* were industriously *kept out,* instead of being *whipt in.*

And it was something of this, I remember, that was made an Argument for the *Declaration of Indulgence,* in the Preamble, to wit, *the greater Safety of the Government, from* Open *and* Publick, *than Private, dissenting Meetings of Worship;* as indeed the rest bear the same Resemblance. For these were the Topicks, *Quieting* the People, *Encouraging* Strangers to come and live among us, and *Trade* by it; and lastly, *Preventing* the Danger that might arise to the *Government* by *Private Meetings:*[27] Of greater Reason then from *Private Men,* not less discontented, but more concealed and secure by the Great *Brake* of Church Conformity. It is this will make a *Comprehension* of the next Dissenters to the Church *dangerous,* tho' it were practicable, of which Side soever it be. For in

27. Preamble to 1672 Declaration of Indulgence, in J. P. Kenyon, *Stuart Constitution* 2d ed. (Cambridge, 1986), 382.

an Age, the *present Frame of Government* shall feel the Art and Industry of the Comprehended. So that a *Toleration* is in Reason of State to be prefer'd. And if the Reasons of the *Declaration* were ever good, they are so still, because the Emergencies of State that made them so, remain; and our Neighbours are not less powerful to improve them to our Detriment.

But it will be now said, *Though the Government should find it's Account in what has been last alledged, this were the Way to overthrow the Church, and encourage Dissenters to continue in their Errors.* Which is that second main Objection I proposed at first, to answer in it's proper Place, and that I think is this:

I humbly say, if it prove the Interest of the three considerable *Church-Interests* in this Kingdom, a *Relaxation,* at least, can hardly fail us. The three *Church Interests* are, That of the *Church of England;* That of the *Roman Catholick Dissenter;* and, That of the *Protestant Dissenter.*

That the *Church of England* ought *in Conscience and Prudence* to consent to the Ease desired.

I pray, first, that it be considered, how great a Reflection it will be upon her Honour, that from a *Persecuted,* she should be accounted a *Persecuting Church:* An Overthrow none of her *Enemies* have been able to give to her many *excellent Apologies.* Nor will it be excused, by her saying, *She is in the Right,* which her Persecutors were not; since this is a Confidence not wanting in any of them, or her *Dissenters:* And the Truth is, it is but the Begging of a Question, that will by no Means be granted.

No body ought to know more than *Churchmen,* that *Conscience cannot be forced.* That Offerings against *Conscience,* are as *odious* to God, as *uneasie* to them that make them. That God loves a *free Sacrifice.* That Christ *forbad Fire,* though from Heaven (it self) to punish *Dissenters;* and commanded that the *Tares should grow with the Wheat till the Harvest.* In fine, that we should *love Enemies* themselves: And to exclude worldly Strife for Religion; *That his Kingdom is not of this World.* This was the Doctrine of the *Blessed Saviour* of the *World.*[28]

28. Psalms 54:6. On Christ refusing to call down fire, see Luke 9:51–56; on the tares and wheat, see Matthew 13:24–30; on loving enemies, see Matthew 5:44, Luke 6:27, 35; and on the otherworldliness of Christ's kingdom, see John 18:36.

Saint *Paul* pursues the same Course: Is glad Christ is Preached, be it of *Envy;* the worst Ground for *Dissent* that can be. It was he that ask't that hard, but just Question, *Who art thou that judgest another Man's Servant? To his own Lord he standeth or falleth.* He allows the Church a Warfare, and Weapons to perform it, but they are not *Carnal,* but *Spiritual.* Therefore it was so advised, that every Man in Matters of Religion, should be *fully perswaded in his own Mind,* and if any were short or mistaken, God would, in his Time, Inform them better.

He tells us of *Schismaticks* and *Hereticks* too, and their Punishment, which is to the Point in Hand: He directs to a *first* and *second Admonition,* and if that prevail not, *reject them:* That is, *refuse* them Church Fellowship, *disown* their Relation, and *deny them Communion.* But in all this there is not a Word of *Fines* or *Imprisonments,* nor is it an excuse to any Church, that the *Civil Magistrate* executes the Severity, while they are *Members of her Communion, that make or execute the Laws.*[29]

But if the Church could gain her Point, I mean *Conformity,* unless she could gain *Consent* too, 'twere but *Constraint* at last. A Rape upon the Mind, which may encrease her Number, *not her Devotion.* On the contrary, the rest of her Sons are in danger by their Hypocrisie. The most close, but watchful and Revengeful Thing in the World. Besides, the Scandal can hardly be removed: To *over value Coin,* and *Rate Brass to Silver,* Beggars any Country; and to own them for *Sons* she *never begat,* debases and destroys any Church. 'Twere better to *indulge* foreign Coin of *intrinsick Value,* and let it pass for it's Weight. 'Tis not Number, but *Quality:* Two or three sincere Christians, that *form* an Evangelical Church: And though the Church were *less, more Charity* on the one Hand, and *Piety* on the other, with exact Church-Censure, and less *civil Coercion,* would give her Credit with Conscience in all Sects; without which, their Accession it self would be no Benefit, but disgrace, and hazard to her Constitution.

And to speak prudently in this Affair, 'tis the *Interest* of the *Church of England,* not to suffer the Extinction of *Dissenters,* that she may have a *Counter-Ballance* to the *Roman Catholicks,* who, though few in Number, are great in *Quality,* and greater in their foreign Friendships and Assistance. On the other

29. On envy, see Philippians 1:15; on judging, see Romans 2:1–2; on spiritual weapons, see 2 Corinthians 10:4; on persuasion, see Romans 14:5; and on admonitions, see Titus 3:10–11.

Hand, it is her Interest to Indulge the *Roman Catholick,* that by his Accession, she may at all Times have the *Ballance* in her own Hand, against the *Protestant Dissenter,* leaning to either, as she finds her *Doctrine* undermined by the one, or her *Discipline* by the other; or lastly, her *Civil Interest* endangered from either of them.

And it is certainly the *Interest* of both those *Extremes* of *Dissent,* that *She,* rather than either of them should hold the *Scale.* For as the *Protestant Dissenter* cannot hope for any Tenderness, exclusive of *Roman Catholicks,* but almost the *same Reasons* may be advanced against him. So on the other Hand, it would look imprudent, as well as unjust, in the *Roman Catholicks,* to solicite any Indulgence *exclusive* of *Protestant Dissenters.* For besides that, it keeps up the Animosity, which it is their Interest to bury; the Consequence will be, to take the Advantage of Time, to snatch it from one another, when an united *Request* for *Liberty,* once granted, will oblige both Parties, in all Times, for Example-sake, to have it Equally preserved. Thus are all Church Interests of *Conformists* and *Dissenters* rendered consistent and safe in their Civil Interest one with the other.

But it will last of all, doubtless, be objected, *That tho' a Toleration were never so desirable in it self, and in it's Consequence beneficial to the Publick, yet the Government cannot allow it, without Ruin to the Church of* England, *which it is obliged to maintain.*

But I think this will not affect the Question at all, unless by maintaining the *Church of England,* it is understood that he should force whole Parties to be of her Communion, or knock them on the Head: Let us call to mind, that the Religion that is true, allows no Man to do Wrong, that Right may come of it. And that nothing has lessen'd the Credit of any Religion more, than declining to support it self by it's *own Charity* and *Piety,* and taking Sanctuary in the Arms, *rather than the Understandings of Men. Violences* are ill Pillars for Truth to rest upon. The *Church of England* must be maintain'd: Right, but can't that be done without the *Dissenter* be destroyed? In vain then did Christ command *Peter* to put up his Sword, with this Rebuke, *They that take the Sword, shall perish with the Sword,* if his Followers are to draw it again. He makes killing for *Religion,* Murder, and deserving Death: Was he then in the Right, Not to call Legions to his Assistance?[30] And are not his Followers of these Times in the Wrong, to seek to uphold their Religion by any Methods

30. Matthew 26:52–54.

of Force. The *Church of England* must be maintain'd, therefore the *Dissenters,* that hold almost the same Doctrine, must be Ruin'd. A Consequence most unnatural, as it is almost impossible. For besides that, the *Drudgery* would unbecome the civil Magistrate, who is the Image of divine Justice and Clemency, and that it would fasten the Character of a *False* Church, upon one that desires to be esteemed a *True One;* she puts the Government upon a Task that is hard to be performed. *Kings can no more make Brick without Straw, than Slaves:*[31] The Condition of our Affairs is much chang'd, and the Circumstances our Government are under, differ mightily from those of our Ancestors. They had not the same Dissents to deal with, nor those Dissents the like Bodies of People to render them formidable, and their Prosecution mischievous to the State. Nor did this come of the *Prince's* Neglect or Indulgence: There are other Reasons to be assigned, of which, the Opportunities Domestick Troubles gave to their Increase and Power, and the Severities used to suppress them, may go for none of the least. So that it was as *involuntary* in the *Prince,* as to the *Church* Anxious. And under this Necessity to tye the Magistrate to old Measures, is to be regardless of Time, whose *fresh* Circumstances give *Aim* to the Conduct of Wise Men in their present Actions. Governments, as well as Courts, *change* their Fashions: The *same Clothes* will not always serve: And Politicks made *Obsolete* by new Accidents, are as *unsafe* to follow, as antiquated Dresses are ridiculous to wear.

Thus *Sea-men* know, and teach us in their daily Practice: They *humour the Winds,* though they will *lie* as near as they can, and *trim* their Sails by their Compass: And by Patience under these constrained and uneven Courses, they gain their Port at last. This justifies the Government's change of Measures from the change of Things; for *res nolunt malè Administrari.*[32]

And to be free, it looks more than Partial, to Elect and Reprobate too. That the *Church of England* is prefer'd, and has the *Fat of the Earth, the Authority of the Magistrate, and the Power of the Sword in her Sons Hands, which comprehend all the Honours, Places, Profits, and Powers of the Kingdom,* must not be repined at: Let her have it, and keep it all, and let none dare seek or accept an Office that is not of her. But to ruin *Dissenters* to compleat her Happiness, (pardon the Allusion) is *Calvinism* in the worst Sense; for this is that *Horren-*

31. The reference is to Exodus 5.

32. The affair refuses to be badly managed.

dum Decretum reduc'd to Practice: And to pursue that ill-natur'd Principle, *Men are civilly Damn'd for that they cannot help,* since Faith is not in Man's Power, though it sometimes exposes one to it.[33]

It is a severe Dilemma, that a Man must either renounce *That* of which he makes Conscience in the Sight of God, or be *Civilly* and *Ecclesiastically Reprobated:* There was a Time, when the *Church of England* her self stood in need of Indulgence, and made up a great Part of the *Non-Conformists* of this Kingdom, and what she then wanted, she pleaded for, I mean a *Toleration,* and that in a general Style, as divers of the Writings of her Doctors tell us: Of which let it be enough but to mention that excellent Discourse of Dr. *Taylor, Bishop of Down,* entituled, *Liberty of Prophecy.*[34]

And that which makes *Severity* look the worse in the Members of the *Church of England,* is the Modesty she professes about the Truth of the Things she believes: For though perhaps it were indefensible in any Church to compel a Man to that which she were infallibly assured to be true, unless she superseded his Ignorance by *Conviction, rather than Authority,* it must, doubtless, look rude, to punish Men into Conformity to that, of the Truth of which, the Church her self pretends no Certainty.

Not that I would less believe a Church so cautious, than one more confident; but I know not how to help thinking Persecution harsh, *when they Ruin People for not believing that, which they have not in themselves the Power of believing,* and which she *cannot give them,* and of which her self is *not infallibly assured.* The Drift of this is *Moderation,* which well becomes us poor Mortals, *That for every Idle Word we speak, must give an Account at the Day of Judgment,* if our Saviour's Doctrine have any credit with us.[35]

It would much mitigate the Severity, if the Dissent were *Sullen, or in Contempt:* But if Men can't help or hinder their Belief, they are rather *Unhappy* than *Guilty,* and more to be *pitied* than *blamed.* However they are of the reasonable Stock of the Country, and tho' they were unworthy of *Favour,* they may not be unfit to live. 'Tis Capital, at Law, to destroy *Bastards,* and *By-blows* are laid to the Parish to keep: They must maintain them at last: And shall not these natural Sons, at least, be laid at the Door of the Kingdom? Unhappy

33. On Calvin's *horrendum decretum,* see ch. 2, p. 57, n. 36.
34. Jeremy Taylor, *Theologike eklektike* (London, 1647).
35. Matthew 12:36.

Fate of *Dissenters!* to be less heeded, and more destitute than any Body. If this should ever happen to be the Effect of their own Folly, with Submission, it can never be the Consequence of the *Government's Engagements.*

Election does not necessarily imply a *Reprobation* of the rest. If God hath elected some to Salvation, it will not follow of course, that he hath absolutely rejected all the rest. For tho' he was God of the *Jews,* he was God of the *Gentiles* too, and they were his People, tho' the *Jews* were his peculiar People. *God respects not Persons,* says St. *Peter,* the good of all Nations are accepted. The Difference at last, will not be of *Opinion,* but *Works: Sheep* or *Goats,* All, of all Judgments will be found: And *Come, Well done;* or *Go ye Workers of Iniquity,* will conclude, their Eternal State: Let us be careful therefore of an *Opinion-Reprobation* of one another.[36]

We see the God of Nature hath taught us softer Doctrine in his great Book of the World: His *Sun shines,* and his *Rain falls upon all.* All the Productions of Nature are by *Love,* and shall it be proper to *Religion* only to propagate by *Force?* The poor *Hen* instructs us in Humanity, who, to defend her feeble Young, refuses no Danger. All the *Seeds* and *Plants* that grow for the use of Man, are produced by the kind and warm Influences of the Sun. 'Tis *Kindness* that upholds Humane Race. People don't *Multiply in Spight:* And if it be by *gentle* and *friendly* Ways, that Nature produces and matures the Creatures of the World, certainly *Religion* should teach us to be *Mild* and *Bearing.*

Let your Moderation be known to all Men, was the saying of a great Doctor of the Christian Faith, and his Reason for that Command *Cogent, For the Lord is at Hand.*[37] As if he had said, Have a care what you do, be not *bitter* nor *violent,* for the *Judge is at the Door:* Do as you would be done to, lest what you deny to others, God should *refuse to you.*

And after all this, shall the *Church of England* be less tender of Men's *Consciences,* than our *common Law* is of their *Lives,* which had rather a *Thousand Criminals* should escape, than that *One Innocent* should perish? Give me leave to say, that there are many *Innocents* (Conscience excepted) now exposed, Men honest, peaceable and useful; free of ill Designs; that pray for *Caesar,* and pay their Tribute to *Caesar.*

If any tell us, *They have, or may, ill use their Toleration.* I say, this must be

36. For the citation to Peter, see Acts 10:34; on sheep and goats, see Matthew 25:31–46.
37. Philippians 4:5.

look't to, and not Liberty therefore refused; for the *English Church* cannot so much forget her own Maxim to Dissenters, That *Propter abusum non est Tollendus usus.*[38] It suffices to our *Argument,* 'tis no *necessary* Consequence, and that *Fact* and *Time* are for us. And if any misuse such Freedom, and entitle *Conscience* to *Misbehaviour,* we have other Laws enough to catch and punish the Offenders, without *treating* One Party *with the Spoils of* Six. And when Religion becomes no Man's Interest, it will hardly ever be any Man's Hypocrisy. Men will chuse by Conscience, which at least preserves Integrity, though it were mistaken: And if not in the wrong, Truth recompences Inquiry, and Light makes amends for Dissent.

And since a plain Method offers it self, from the Circumstances of our ease, I take the Freedom to present it for the *Model* of the *intreated Toleration.*

Much has been desired, said and prest, in Reference to the late King's being *Head* of a *Protestant League,* which takes in but a Part of the Christian World; the *Roman* and *Grecian* Christians being excluded. But I most humbly offer, that our Wise Men would please to think of another Title for our *King,* and that is *Head* of a *Christian League,* and give the Experiment here at Home in his own Dominions.

The *Christian Religion is admired of All in the Text,* and by *All* acknowledged in the *Apostle*'s *Creed.* Here every Party of *Christians* meet, and center as in a General. The several *Species of Christians,* that this *Genus* divideth it self into, are those divers Perswasions we have within this Kingdom; The *Church of England, Roman-Catholicks, Grecians, Lutherans, Presbyterians, Independents, Anabaptists, Quakers, Socinians:* These I call so many Orders of Christians, that unite in the Text, and differ only in the *Comment;* All owning *One Deity, Saviour and Judge, Good Works, Rewards and Punishments:* Which Bodies once Regulated, and holding of the Prince as *Head of the Government, Maintaining Charity, and Pressing Piety, will be an Honour to Christianity, a Strength to the Prince, and a Benefit to the Publick:* For in Lieu of an unattainable, (at best an unsincere) *Uniformity,* we shall have in *Civils Unity, and Amity in Faith.*

The *Jews* before, and in the Time of *Herod,* were divided into divers Sects. There were *Pharisees, Sadducees, Herodians,* and *Essenes.* They maintain'd their Dissent without Ruin to the Government: And the Magistrates fell under no Censure from Christ for that *Toleration.*

38. Use (or a practice) must not be destroyed on account of its being abused.

The *Gentiles,* as already has been observed, had their *Divers Orders of Philosophers,* as Disagreeing as ever Christians were, and that without Danger to the Peace of the State.

The *Turks* themselves show us, that both other Religions, and divers Sects of their own, are very Tolerable, with Security to their Government.

The *Roman Church* is a considerable Instance to our Point; for She is made up of divers *Orders* of both Sexes, of very differing Principles, fomented sometimes to great Feuds and Controversies; as between *Franciscans, Dominicans, Jesuits,* and *Sorbonists;* yet without Danger to the Political State of the Church. On the contrary, She therefore cast her self into that Method, *That She might safely give Vent to Opinion and Zeal, and suffer both without Danger of Schism.* And these Regulars are, by the Pope's Grants, priviledg'd with an Exemption from Episcopal Visitation and Jurisdiction.

GOD Almighty inspire the King's *Heart, and the Hearts of His Great Council, to be the Glorious Instruments of this Blessing to the Kingdom.*

I shall conclude this PERSWASIVE, with the Judgment of some *Pious Fathers,* and *Renowned Princes.*

Q*UADRATUS* and *Aristides* wrote *Two Apologies* to *Adrian,* for the Christian Faith, and against the Persecution of it.[39]

Justin Martyr, an Excellent Philosopher and Christian, writ Two Learned *Disswasives* against Persecution, which he Dedicated (as I take it) to *Antoninus Pius,* and *Marcus Aurelius Antoninus.*[40]

Melito, Bishop of *Sardis,* a Good and Learned Man, writ a smart Defence for the *Christian Religion,* and a *Toleration,* Dedicated to *Verus.*[41]

Tertullian, in his most sharp and excellent Apology for the Christians, fastens Persecution upon the *Gentiles,* as an inseparable Mark of *Superstition* and *Error,* as he makes the *Christian Patience a Sign of Truth.* In his Discourse to *Scapula,* he says, *'Tis not the Property of Religion to Persecute for Religion; She should be received for Her self, not Force.*[42]

39. Quadratus presented his apology (which survives only in fragments) to Hadrian ca. 125; Aristides, an Athenian Christian, ca. 140.

40. Justin Martyr, *First Apology* and *Second Apology.*

41. Melito, bishop of Sardis, wrote during the 170s.

42. Tertullian, *Apology;* and *Ad Scapulam,* ch. 2.

Hilary, an early and learned Father, against *Auxentius,* saith, *The Christian Church does not persecute, but is persecuted.*[43]

Atticus, Bishop of *Constantinople,* would by no Means have the Minister of *Nice* to respect any Opinion or Sect whatsoever, in the Distribution of the Money sent by him for the Relief of Christians; and by no Means to prejudice those that practise a contrary Doctrine and Faith to theirs: That he should be sure to relieve those that Hunger and Thirst, and have not wherewith to help themselves, and make that the Rule of his Consideration. In short, he made the *Hereticks* to have his Wisdom in Admiration, in that he would by no Means trouble or molest them.[44]

Proclus (another Bishop of *Constantinople*) was of this Opinion, *That it was far easier by fair Means to allure unto the Church, than by Force to compel:* He determined to vex no Sect whatever, but restored to the Church the Renowned Virtue of *Meekness,* required in Christian Ministers.[45]

If we will next hear the *Historian*'s own Judgment upon a Toleration, *I am of Opinion* (says he) *that he is a Persecutor, that in any Kind of Way, molesteth such Men as lead a Quiet and Peaceable Life:* Thus *Socrates* in his Third Book: In his Seventh he tells us, *That the Bishop of* Sinada, *indeed, did banish the Hereticks, but neither did he this* (says he) *according to the Rule of the* Catholick Church, *which is not accustomed to persecute,* lib. 7.[46]

Lactantius tells the angry Men of his Time, thus, *If you will with Blood, Evil and Torments, defend your Worship, it shall not thereby be defended, but polluted.*[47]

Chrysostom saith expresly, *That it is not the Manner of the Children of God, to persecute about their Religion, but an evident Token of Antichrist.*

Thus the *Fathers* and *Doctors* of the first Ages. That *Emperors* and *Princes* have thus believed, let us hear some of Greatest Note, and most pressing to us.

Jerom, a Good and Learned Father, saith, *That Heresie must be Cut off with the Sword of the Spirit.*[48]

Constantius, the Father of *Constantine the Great,* laid this down for a Prin-

43. Hilary of Poitiers, *Contra Auxentium Arrianum.*

44. Atticus, Patriarch of Constantinople, 406–25.

45. Proclus, Patriarch of Constantinople (d. 446 or 447).

46. Socrates Scholasticus, *Ecclesiastical History,* bk. 3, ch. 12; bk. 7, ch. 3.

47. Lactantius, *Divine Institutes,* bk. 5, ch. 20.

48. Jerome (ca. 340–420); possibly a reference to "To Pammachius against John of Jerusalem," sec. 3, which refers to the Arians as "pierced by the sword of the Spirit."

ciple, *That those that were Disloyal to God, would never be Trusty to their Prince.* And which is more, he liv'd thus, and so dy'd, as his Great Speech to his Great Son, on his Death-Bed, amply evidences.

Constantine the Great, in his Speech to the *Roman Senate,* tells them, *There is this Difference between Humane and Divine Homage and Service, that the one is compell'd, and the other ought to be free.*

Eusebius Pamphilus, in the Life of *Constantine,* tells us, that in his Prayer to God, he said, *Let thy People, I beseech thee, desire and maintain Peace, Living free from Sedition to the common Good and Benefit of all the world; and those that are led away with Error, let them desire to live in Peace and Tranquility with the Faithful: For Friendly Humane Society and Commerce with them, will very much avail to bring them to the Right Way. Let no Man molest another, but let every one follow the Perswasion of their own Conscience: But let those that have a True Opinion concerning God, be perswaded, that such as regulate their Lives by God's Holy Laws, do lead an Holy and Upright Life: But those that will not conform thereunto,* may have Liberty to erect and set up Altars. *But we will* Maintain *the Church and True Religion, which thou hast committed to our Defence. Moreover, we desire that they may Joyfully receive and welcome this General Offer of Peace and Concord.*[49]

This was the Judgment of the Most Celebrated Emperor that ever professed the *Christian Faith.* I have cited other Emperors in the Body of this Discourse; but because the Worst are to be commended when they do well, *Valens* himself, charm'd with the Sweetness and Strength of the Philosopher *Themistius,* in his Elegant Oration, grew Moderate towards the Orthodox, whom a little before he had severely treated: Of which these were the Heads; *That he Persecuted without Reason People of Good Lives: That it was no Crime to think or believe otherwise than the Prince believed: That he ought not to be troubled at the Diversity of Opinions: That the* Gentiles *were much more divided in their Judgment than the* Christians: *That it sufficeth, that every Sect aimed at the Truth, and lived virtuously.*[50] We have had Modern Royal Examples too.

Stephen, King of *Poland,* declared his Mind in the Point controverted, thus, *I am King of Men, and not of Conscience; a Commander of Bodies, and not of Souls.*

49. Eusebius, *Life of Constantine,* bk. 2, ch. 56.
50. Themistius, Oration 5.

The King of *Bohemia* was of Opinion, *That Mens Consciences ought in no Sort to be violated, urged, or constrained.*

And *Lastly,* let me add (as what is, or should be of more Force) the Sense of King *James* and King *Charles* the First, Men, as of Supreme Dignity, so famed for their Great Natural Abilities and acquired Learning; *It is a sure Rule in Divinity* (said King *James*) *that God never loves to Plant his Church by Violence and Bloodshed.* And in his Exposition on the Twentieth of the *Revelations,* he saith, *That Persecution is the Note of a False Church.*[51]

And in the Advice of King *Charles* the First, to the late King, he says, *Take Heed of abetting any Factions; your* Partial *adhering to any one Side, gains you not so great Advantages in some Men's Hearts, (who are* Prone *to be of their King's Religion) as it loseth you in others, who think themselves, and their Profession, first despised, then persecuted by you.*

Again, *Beware of Exasperating any Factions, by the Crosness and Asperity of some Men's Passions, Humours, or Private Opinions, imployed by you, grounded only upon their Difference, in lesser Matters, which are but the Skirts and Suburbs of Religion; wherein a* Charitable Connivence *and* Christian Toleration, *often dissipates their Strength, whom rougher Opposition fortifies, and puts the despised and oppressed Party into such* Combinations, *as may most enable them to get a full Revenge on those they count their* Persecutors, *who are commonly assisted by that* Vulgar Commiseration *that attends all that are said to suffer under the Notion of* Religion.

Always keep up Solid Piety, *and those* Fundamental Truths *(which mend both Hearts and Lives of Men) with* impartial Favour and Justice. *Your Prerogative is best shown and exercised in* Remitting, *rather than* Exacting *the Rigour of Laws; there being nothing worse than* Legal Tyranny.[52]

51. James I, "Speech to Parliament 21 March 1609/10," in *King James VI and I: Political Writings,* ed. Johann P. Sommerville (Cambridge, 1994), p. 199; James I, *Ane fruitfull meditatioun* (Edinburgh, 1588).

52. Charles I, *Eikon Basilike* (London, 1649), ch. 27.

Good ADVICE to the *Church of England, Roman-Catholick,* and *Protestant Dissenter:* In which it is endeavoured to be made appear, that it is their Duty, Principle, and Interest, to abolish the Penal LAWS and TESTS (1687)

Beati Pacifici[1]

To the READER.

Reader,

N*O MATTER* Who, *but* What; *and yet if thou wouldst know the Author, he is an* English-Man, *and therefore obliged to this Country, and the Laws that made him Free.*

That Single Consideration were enough to command this Undertaking; for 'tis to perswade his Country-Men to be delivered of the greatest Yoak a Nation can well suffer under; Penal Laws for Religion, *I mean.*

And now thou hast both the Who, *and* What: *If thou art* Wise *and* Good, *Thou art above my* Epithets, *and more my Flatteries; If not, I am in the Right to let 'em alone.* Read, Think, *and* Judge. Liberty, English *and* Christian, *is all that is sought in the ensuing Discourse.*

Adieu.

GOOD ADVICE, *&c.*

PART I.

I MUST own, it is my Aversion at this Time, to meddle with *Publick Matters,* and yet my Duty to the *Publick* will not let me be Silent. They that move by Principles, must not regard Times nor Factions, *but what is Just, and what is Honourable;* and *That* no Man ought to scruple, nor no Time or Interest to Contest.

The Single Question I go upon, and which does immediately concern and

1. Blessed are the peacemakers (Matthew 5:9).

exercise the Minds of the Thinking, as well as Talking Men of this Kingdom, is, *Whether it be fit to Repeal the Penal Laws and Tests, in Matters of Religion, or not?* I take the Affirmative of the Question, and humbly submit my Reasons to every Reasonable Conscience. I say Reasonable, because *That* which knows not it's own Duty, Principle and Interest, is not so, and *That which is not willing to do to others as it would be done by,* less deserves to be thought so.

Now there are Three Sorts of People that will find themselves concerned in this Question, *The Church of England, the Roman Catholick,* and *the Protestant Dissenter,* and these make up the whole Body of the Kingdom; If it appear to be their Duty, Principle and Interest, the Question is gain'd, and no Body is left to complain; and if I am mistaken, it is with so great an Inclination to serve them all, that their Good Nature cannot but plead my Excuse, especially when they consider I am neither mov'd by Hopes nor Fears. Private Loss or Gain being farther from my Thought, than I hope they are from a Good Understanding.

I say, *First,* then it is the Duty of all of them, because they all profess that Religion which makes it their common Duty to do it; *Christianity* I mean: For no Christian ought to deprive any Man of his Native Right for Matters of Faith and Worship towards God, in the Way that he thinks most agreeable to the Will of God; because it is necessary to a Christian to believe, *That Faith is the Gift of God alone,*[2] *and that He only is Lord of Conscience, and is able truly to Enlighten, Perswade, and Establish it;* and consequently that prejudicing Men in their Persons or Estates, or depriving them of any Station in the Government, they might otherwise, in their Turn, be capable to serve the Publick in, is contrary to the *Tenderness and Equity of that Religion;* which will yet farther appear, if we consider that Christianity is the *Sole Religion of the World, that is Built on the Principles of Love; which brought with it the greatest Evidences of Truth: Equally convincing our Understandings with* it's Light, *and bearing down our Senses with* it's Miracles: *Which silenc'd the Oracles of the Heathens by the Divine Power present with it; and vanquisht their Hearts, that had left nothing else to conquer, leading Kings and Emperors with their Courts and Armies in Triumph, after the* Despised Cross of Him, *who was the Holy and Blessed Author of it.*

It was He that laid not his Religion in Worldly Empire, nor used the Methods of Worldly Princes to Propagate it; as it came from Heaven, so *That* only

2. Ephesians 2:8.

should have the Honour of protecting and promoting it. His whole Business to Mankind, from first to last, was *Love.* 'Twas first Love in his Father to send Him (as Saint *John* teaches) *God so loved the World, that He sent His Son,* &c. It was Love in Jesus Christ to come on that Errand; that He, *who thought it no Robbery to be Equal with God, should take the Form of a Servant to adopt us Children, and make himself of no Reputation with the World, that he might make us of Reputation with God His Father.*[3]

And he did not only come in much Love, but preach'd it and prest it both to Friends and Foes; *Love one another; Love Enemies; Do Good to them that Hate you; Forgive them that Trespass against you; What you would that other Men should do unto you, do that unto them: By these Things shall all Men know you are my Disciples; for I came not to destroy Men's Lives,* no, not for Religion it self; *for my Kingdom, Power, Force, Weapons, and Victory, are not of this World.* In all this, *Love* prevails: It was His Great, His New, His Last Commandment; of all his Disciples, the most pursued by *His Beloved One,* that in his Bosom had learn'd His Heart, as his Divine Doctrine of Love in his Epistles tells us.

As He Liv'd in Love, so He Died in Love, with us, and for us, *and that while we were Rebellious too;* ay, *He Pray'd and Dy'd for them who put Him to Death, shewing us* (says St. *Peter) an Example that we should follow His Steps.* And what are they? Doubtless the Steps of Love, the Path he trod: *To do Good to Mankind, Enemies as well as Friends, that we may be like our Heavenly Father, that causes His Sun to shine, and His Rain to fall upon the Just and Unjust.* This must be the Apostle's Meaning, for the Rest of His Passion was inimitable.[4]

Now if this be *the Doctrine of Christ, the Nature of Christianity, the Practice of the Primitive Church,* that like *Adam,* was *Created in full Strength, Beauty and Wisdom,* and so an Example to succeeding Ages of Religion, and to which we so often refer as our Original; with what Pretence to a Christian Conscience, can any one stickle to keep *Imprisoning, Banishing, Impoverishing, Hanging and Quartering Laws on Foot for Religion Sake,* but especially against such as are by Creed Professors of Christianity as well as themselves.

I know the Case is put hard by those that have the Laws on their Side, *We do this to save our selves;* but an harder Case than Christ's can never be put, whose Answer in his, ought to resolve theirs fully.

Christ is sent by his Father for the Salvation of the World: He introduces

3. John 3:16; and Philippians 2:8.
4. 1 Peter 2:21; and Matthew 5:45.

and proves his Mission by Miracles, and the Great Authority of his Word and Doctrine: His Followers fully satisfied who He was, whence He came, what He taught, and how eminently confirm'd, grew impatient at Contradiction; they could not bear the least Dissent; for when some of the *Samaritans* refused to entertain their Lord, because they thought he was going for *Jerusalem,* the Place of their greatest Aversion, these Disciples were for having but the Word from his Mouth, and they would, in Imitation of *Elijah, have called for Fire from Heaven to have destroy'd them.* But He turned and rebuked them, and said, *Ye know not what Manner of Spirit ye are of, for the Son of Man is not come to Destroy Men's Lives, but to Save them.*[5] This Answer is to Purpose, and for all Times, to be sure Christian Ones; and the higher the Pretensions of any Party are to Christianity, the more inexcusable if they practice the contrary. Would not Christ then hurt them that refused him, and can we hurt our Neighbours for not receiving us? He condemned that *Spirit* in *His Disciples,* and shall we uphold the *same Spirit,* and that by Law too, which He condemned by his Gospel? *This is Killing for God's Sake, expresly charg'd by Christ with Impiety. They shall think,* says he to his Disciples, *they do God good Service to kill you;* Who should think so? *Why the Christian Persecutors.* Is it their Property to do so? Yes; What shall one think then of those Christians that profess it.

The *Jews* were grievously punished of God, for that Abomination of Sacrificing their Children to *Moloch,*[6] but these Laws, though they change the Object, they have not lessen'd the Sin; *for they offer up Man, Woman and Child,* and tho' they say, *'Tis to God,* no Matter for that, since it makes their Case worse, for 'tis to imagine that so Good, so Just, so Sensible, so merciful a Being, can take Pleasure in so much Cruelty. Well, *But if we must not knock Folks on the Head, what must we do with them?* Take an Answer at the Mouth of Truth and Wisdom: *Let the Tares and Wheat grow together till the Harvest;* What's that? He tells you, *'Tis the End of the World;*[7] so that whatever the Church of *England* is, 'tis certain Christ is for a Toleration, and His Doctrine is always in Fashion: What He was, He is, and will be; He went not by Reasons of State, or Customs of Countries; His Judgment was better Built, who came to give Law, and not to receive it, and 'tis *A Light and Rule to all Times. And He that Loves Father, or Mother, or Wife, or Children, or House, or Land, better than HIM,*

5. Luke 9:51–56.
6. Amos 5:26–27; and Acts 7:42–43.
7. Matthew 13:24–30.

that is, *His Doctrine* (of which this is so great a Part) *is not worthy of Him;*[8] and I fear no other Reason induces the Church of *England* to decline it.

To confirm what has been said, tho' I design Brevity, let me not lose another Passage very pregnant to our Purpose; when His Disciples had accomplish'd their First Mission, at their Return they gave Him the *History of their Travels:* Among the rest, they tell Him of One they met with, *That in His Name Cast out Devils,* but because He would not follow with them, *They forbad Him:* Here is at least a *Dissenting Christian,* tho' *a Believer,* yet it seems not One of that closer Congregation; we also see their Zeal and Sentence. But what says the Master yet alive, and with them, *the Infallible Doctor, in whose Mouth was no Guile, who had not the Spirit by Measure, and was the Great Wisdom of God to His People,* Was He of the same Mind, or did He leave them without Rule in the Point? His Answer is this: *And JESUS said to them,* Forbid Him not, *for he that is not against us is for us.*[9] The Prohibition is taken off, and their Judgment revers'd; and from His, to be sure, there lies no Appeal. For tho' a Power of Decision were allow'd to some One or more on Earth, in Matters obscure and undetermin'd, *Yet in Cases already adjudged by the Son of God Himself, who had the Chair, and could not Err,* there can be no Room for another Judge.

Now to apply it, I must first say, I find no such Disciples among those that are of the Side of keeping up the Penal Laws; God knows, the Disparity is but too unequal. But next, if they were all *Twelve in Westminster-Abby,* and should be of the Side of upholding the *Penal Laws* (which is the wrong Side they were of before) I should beg their Pardon, if I were of their Master's Mind, and objected his Wisdom to their Zeal, and his Gentle Rule to their harsh and narrow Judgment. And I beseech the *Church of England* to consider, that no Pretence can excuse Her Dissent, and less Her cross Practice to the Judgment of Her Saviour: *A Judgment that seems given and settled for the Conduct of the Church on the like Occasions, in succeeding Times: And 'tis pity any Worldly Thing should have Place with Her to divert Her Obedience.* Did *Christ then come to Save Men's Lives, and not to Destroy them?* And should She (She I say that pretends to be a Reformed Church) uphold those Laws that do destroy them? HE, Alas! went to another Village instead of Burning them, or theirs, for refusing Him. And She forbids any, that belongs to any other, to lodge in Her's, upon Pain of losing Life or Estate: *This may make Her a* Samaritan In-

8. Matthew 10:37.

9. Mark 9:38–40; and Luke 9:49–50.

deed, *but* Not the Good One, *whose Example would have taught Her, instead of these sharp and ruder Remedies, to have poured the Oil of Peace and Gladness into those Chops and Wounds, that Time, and Heats of all Hands, had made in every Religious Party of Men.* Nor does She lose any Thing by Repealing those Laws, but the Power of Persecuting, and a Good Church would never have the Temptation. Come, Some-Body must begin to Forgive, let Her not leave that Honour to another, nor draw upon Her self the Guilt and Mischief of refusing it. She pretends to fear the *Strokes of the Romanists,* but I would fain know of Her, if following their Example will Convert them, or Secure Her? Does She hope to keep them out by the Weapons that have fail'd in their Hands, or can She Honourably censure Persecution in them, and yet use it Her self?

But she is extremely scandal'd and scared *at the Severity upon Protestants in France.*[10] 'Tis certainly very ill; but do not the Laws she is so fond of point at the same Work, *Conformity,* or *Ruin.* And don't we know, that in some Places, and upon some Parties, her Magistrates have plow'd as deep Furrows, especially within these six and Twenty Years. *Husbands separated from their Wives, Parents from their Children, the Widow's Bed and the Orphans Milk made a Prize for Religion, Houses stript, Barns and Fields swept clean, Prisons crowded without Regard to Sex or Age, and some of both Sorts dungeon'd to Death, and all for Religion.* If she says they were *peevish Men, Bigots,* or mov'd by *private Interest,* she still made the Laws, and says no more for her self than the *French* say for their King, which yet she refuses to take for an Answer. Perhaps I could parallel some of the severest Passages in that Kingdom out of the Actions of some Members of the Church of *England* in *cool Blood,* that are even yet for continuing the *Penal Laws* upon their plundered Neighbours; so that this Reflection of hers upon *France,* is more popular than just from her. But I beseech her to look upon a Country four Times bigger than *France, Germany* I mean, and she will there see both Religions practis'd with great Ease and Amity, yet of this we must not hear one Word: I hope it is not for Fear of imitating it. However, 'tis disingenuous to object the Mischiefs of Popery to a general Ease, when we see it is the Way to prevent them. This is but in the Name of Popery *to keep all to her self,* as well from Protestant Dissenters as Roman Catholicks. How Christian, how equal, how Safe, that narrow Method is, becomes her well to consider, and methinks she ought not to be long about it.

I know she flatters her self, and others too believe, she is a *Bulwark* against

10. That is, revocation of the Edict of Nantes.

Popery; and with that, without any farther Security to other Protestants, wipes her Mouth of all old Scores, and makes her present Court for Assistance. But when that Word *Bulwark* is examin'd, I fear it appears to mean no more than this, *That she would keep out Popery for that Reason, for which she apprehends Popery would turn her out,* viz. *Temporal Interest.* But may I without Offence ask her, when she kept Persecution out? Or if she keeps out Popery for any Body's Sake but her own? Nay, if it be not to hold the Power she has in her Hands, that she would frighten other Parties (now she has done her Worst) with what Mischief Popery would do them when it has Power. But to speak freely, can she be a Bulwark in the Case, that has been bringing the worst Part of Popery in these six and twenty Years, if *Persecution be* so as she says it is. This would be called *Canting* to the World in others. But I hear *she begins to see her Fault, is heartily sorry for it, and promises to do so no more:* And why may not Popery be as wise, that has also burnt her Fingers with the same Work? Their praying for Ease by *Law,* looks as if they chose That, rather than Power, for Security; and if so, Why may not the Papists Live as well as she Reign? I am none of their Advocate, I am no Papist, but I would be just and merciful too. However, I must tell her, that keeping the Laws on Foot, by which she did the Mischief, is none of the plainest Evidences of her Repentance: They that can believe it, have little Reason to quarrel at the Unaccountableness of Transubstantiation. It is unjust in Popery to invade her Privileges, and can it be just in her to provoke it, by denying a Christian Liberty? Or can she expect what she will not give? Or not do as she would be done by, because she fears others will not observe the same Rule to her? Is not this *doing Evil that Good may come of it,* and that uncertain too, against an express Command as well as common Charity?[11] But to speak freely, whether we regard the Circumstances of the King, the Religion of his Children, the Inequality of the Number and Strength of those of each of their Communions, we must conclude, that the Aversion of the Church of *England* to this intreated Liberty, cannot reasonably be thought to come from the Fear she has of the Prevalency of Popery, but the Loss of that Power the Law gives her to domineer over all Dissenters. And is not this a *Rare Motive* for a Christian Church to continue Penal Laws for Religion? If her Piety be not able to maintain her upon equal Terms, methinks her having so much the whip Hand and Start of all others, should satisfy her Ambition, and quiet her Fears; for 'tis possible

11. Romans 3:8.

for her to keep the Churches if the Laws were abolished; all the Difference is, she could not Force: She might perswade and convince what she could: And pray, Is not that enough for a true Church, without *Goals, Whips, Halters* and *Gibbets?* O what Corruption is this that has prevail'd over Men of such Pretensions to Light and Conscience? that they do not, or will not, see nor feel their own Principles one Remove from themselves; but sacrifice the noblest Part of the Reformation to Ambition, and compel Men to truckle their tender Consciences to the Grandure and Dominion of their Doctors.

But because the Sons of the Church of *England* keep, at this Time, such a Stir in her Favour, and fix her Excellency in her Opposition to Popery, it is worth while to consider a little farther, if really the most feared and disagreeable Part of Popery, in her own Opinion, does not belong to her, and if it does, should we not be in a fine Condition, to be in Love with our Fetters, and to Court our Misery?

That Part of *Popery* which the Church of *England* with most Success objects against, is her *Violence.* This is that only she can pretend to fear: Her Doctrines she partly professes, or thinks she can easily refute. No Body counts her Doctors *Conjurers* for their *Transubstantiation,* or *dangerous* to the State for their *Beads,* or their *Purgatory. But forcing others to their Faith, or ruining them for refusing it, is the terrible Thing we are taught by her to apprehend.* Now granting this to be the Case, in Reference to the Roman Religion, where it is in the Chair. I ask, if the Church of *England,* with her better Doctrines, has not been guilty of this Impiety, and for that Cause more blameable than the Church she opposes so much? If we look into her Acts of State, we find them many, and bitter, against all Sorts of Dissenters. There is nigh twenty Laws made, and yet in Force, to constrain Conformity, and they have been executed too, as far and as often as she thought it fit for her Interest to let them. *Some have been Hang'd, many Banish'd, more Imprison'd, and some to Death; and abundance Impoverish'd;* and all this merely for Religion: Though, by a base and barbarous Use of Words, it has been call'd *Treason, Sedition, Routs and Riots;* the worst of Aggravations, since they are not contented to make People unhappy for their Dissent, but rob them of all they had left, *their Innocency.* This has been her State Act, to coin Guilt, and make Men dangerous, to have her Ends upon them. But that Way of Palliating Persecution, by rendering a Thing that it is not, and punishing Men for Crimes they never committed, shews but little Conscience in the Projectors. The Church of *England* cries out against Transubstantiation, because of the Invisibility of the Change. She don't see Christ there, and therefore he is not there, and yet her Sons do the same Thing. For though all the Tokens of a Riot are as invisible in a Dissenter's Meeting, as that in the Transubstantiation, yet it must be a Riot without any more to do; the English of which is, 'tis a Riot to pray to God in the humblest and peaceablest Manner in a Conventicle.

I know it is said, *The Blood-shed in the foregoing Reign, and the Plots of the Papists against Queen* Elizabeth, *drew those Laws from the Church of* England. But this was no Reason why she should do ill because they had done so: Besides, it may be answered, that that Religion having so long intermixt it self with worldly Power, it gave Way to take the Revenges of it. And certainly the Great Men of the Church of *England* endeavouring *to intercept Queen* Mary, *by proclaiming the Lady* Jane Gray, *and the Apprehension the Papists had of the better Title of* Mary *Queen of* Scots, *together with a long Possession,* were scurvy Temptations to kindle ill Designs against that extraordinary Queen. But tho' nothing can excuse and less justify those cruel Proceedings, yet if there were any Reason for the Laws, it is plainly remov'd, for the Interests are joined, and have been since King *James* the first came to the Crown. However, 'tis certain there were Laws enough, or they might have had them, to punish all civil Enormities, without the Necessity of making any against them as Papists. And so the civil Government had stood upon it's own Legs, and Vices only against it had been punishable by it. In short, it was the falsest Step that was made in all that great Queen's Reign, and the most dishonourable to the Principles of the first Reformers, and therefore I know no better Reason why it should be continued, than that which made the *Cardinal* in the History of the *Council of Trent* oppose the Reformation at *Rome.* That tho' it was true that they were in the Wrong, yet the admitting of it *approv'd the Judgment of their Enemies, and so good-night to Infallibility.*[12] Let not this be the Practice of the Church of *England,* and the rather, because she does not pretend to it: But let her reflect, that she has lost her King from her Religion, and they that have got him, naturally hope for Ease for theirs by him, that 'tis the End they laboured, and the great Use they have for him, and I would fain wonder that she never saw it before; but whether she did or no, why should she begrudge it, at least refuse it now? since 'tis plain, that there is nothing we esteem dangerous in Popery that other Laws are not sufficient to secure us from: Have we not enough of them? let Her think of more, and do the best she can to *dis-*

12. Paolo Sarpi, *The history of the Council of Trent* (London, 1676).

cover Plotters, punish Traytors, suppress the Seditious, and keep the Peace better than those we have can enable us to do. But, for God's Sake, let us never direct Laws against Men for the Cause of Religion, or punish them before they have otherwise done amiss. Let Men's Works, not their Opinions, turn the Edge of the Magistrate's Sword against them, else 'tis beheading them before they are born.

By the Common Law of this Kingdom there must be some *real and proper Overt-act* that proves Treason; some *Malice* that proves Sedition; and some *violent Action* that proves a Rout or Riot. If so, to call *any Sort of Religious Orders,* the one, or *praying to God in any Way out of Fashion,* the other, is preposterous, and punishing People for it, down right *Murder* or *Breach of the Peace,* according to the true Use of Words and the old Law of *England.*

If the Church of *England* fears the Growth of Popery, let her be truer to the Religion she owns, and betake her self to *Faith,* rather than *Force,* by a *Pious, Humble,* and a *Good Example:* To *convince* and *perswade,* which is the highest Honour to any Church, and the greatest Victory over Men. I am for a National Church as well as she, so it be by *Consent,* and not by *Constraint.* But coercive Churches have the *same Principle,* though not the same *Interest.* A Church, *by Law Establish'd,* is a State Church, and that is no Argument of Verity, unless the State that makes her so be infallible; and because that will not be asserted, the other can never oblige the Conscience, and consequently the Compulsion she uses, is unreasonable. This very Principle *justifies the King of* France, *and the Inquisition.* For Laws being equally of Force in all Countries where they are made, it must be as much a Fault in the Church of *England*'s Judgment to be *a Protestant at* Rome, *or a Calvinist at* Paris, as to be a *Papist at* London: Then where is Truth or Conscience but in the Laws of Countries! which renders her an *Hobbist,* notwithstanding her long and loud Clamours against the *Leviathan.*[13]

I beg her, for the Love of Christ, that she would think of these Things, and not esteem me her Enemy for performing the Part of so good a Friend. Plain-dealing becomes that Character; no Matter whether the Way be agreeable, so it be right: We are all to do our Duty, and leave the rest to God: He can best answer for our Obedience, that Commands it; and our Dependence upon his Word will be our Security in our Conduct. What Weight is it to a Church, that

13. In *Leviathan* (London, 1652), ch. 42, Thomas Hobbes united civil and ecclesiastical supremacy in a single absolute sovereign.

she is *the Church by Law Establish'd,* when no human Law can make a true Church? A True Church is of *Christ's making,* and is by Gospel Establish'd. 'Tis a Reflection to a Church that would be thought true, to *stoop* to human Laws for her Establishment. I have been often scandal'd at that Expression from the Sons of the Church of *England,* especially those of the Robe, *what do you talk for? our Religion is by Law Establish'd,* as if that determined the Question of it's Truth against all other Perswasions.

The *Jews* had this to say against our Saviour, *We have a Law, and by our Law he ought to Dye.*[14] The Primitive Christians, and some of our first Reformers, died *as by Law Established,* if that would mend the Matter; but does that make it lawful to a Christian Conscience? we must ever demur to this Plea. No greater Argument of a Church's Defection from Christianity than turning Persecutor. 'Tis true, the Scripture says, *The Earth shall help the Woman,* but that was to save her self, *not to destroy others:* For 'tis the Token that is given by the Holy Ghost of a false Church; *That none must Buy or Sell in her Dominions that will not receive her Mark in their Forehead, or Right Hand.*[15] That is, by going to Church against Conscience, or bribing lustily to stay at Home.

Things don't change tho' Men do. Persecution is still the same, let the Hand alter never so often; But the Sin may not: For doubtless it is greatest in those that make the highest Claim to Reformation. For while they plead their own Light for doing so, they hereby endeavour to *extinguish* another's Light that can't concur. What a Man can't do, *it is not his Fault he don't do, nor should he be compelled to do it, and least of all punish'd for not doing it. No Church can give Faith, and therefore can't force it; for what is Constrain'd is not Believ'd; since Faith is in that Sense free, and Constraint gives no Time to assent; I say, what I don't will is not I, and what I don't chuse is none of mine, and another's Faith can't save me tho' it should save him.* So that this Method never obtains the End designed, since it saves no body, because it converts no body; it may breed *Hypocrisy,* but that is quite another Thing than *Salvation.*

What then is the Use of Penal Laws? only to shew the Sincerity of them that Suffer, *and Cruelty of those that make and execute them.* And all Time tells us they have ever fail'd those that have leaned upon them; They have always been Losers at last; Besides, it is a most unaccountable Obstinacy in the Church of *England* to stickle to uphold them, for after having made it a Matter of Reli-

14. John 19:7.
15. Revelation 12:16; 13:17.

gion and Conscience to address the late King in Behalf of This, to think he should leave Conscience behind him in *Flanders,* or when they waited on him to the Crown, that he should send it thither upon a Pilgrimage, is want of Wit at best, pardon the Censure. Could they Conscientiously oppose his Exclusion for his Religion, and now his Religion because he will not leave it? Or can they reasonably maintain those *Tests* that excluded him when *Duke of York,* while they endured none to *hinder him from the Crown?* I heartily beg the Church of *England*'s Excuse, if I say I can't apprehend her: Perhaps the Fault is mine, but sure I am she is extremely dark. How could she hope for this King without his Conscience? or conceive that his Honour or Conscience would let him leave the Members of his Communion under the Lash of so many Destroying Laws? Would she be so serv'd by a Prince of her own Religion, and she in the like Circumstances? She would not, let her talk 'till *Doom's-day.*

To object the King's Promise, when he came to the Crown, against the Repeal of the Penal Laws, shews not his Insincerity, but her Uncharitableness, or that really she has a very weak Place: For it is plain the King *first declared his own Religion,* and then *promised to maintain her's;* but was that to be without, or together with his own? His Words shews he intended that his own should *Live,* tho' t'other might *Reign.* I say again, it is not credible that a Prince of any Sincerity can refuse a Being to his own Religion, when he continues another in it's well-being. This were to act upon *State* not *Conscience,* and to make more Conscience to uphold a Religion he cannot be of, *than of giving Ease to one his Conscience obliges him to be of.* I cannot imagine how *this Thought* could enter into any Head that had Brains, or Heart that had Honesty. And, to say true, they must be a Sort of State Consciences, *Consciences as by Law Established,* that can follow the Law against their Convictions.

But this is not all I have to observe from that Objection: It implies too evidently, first, that she thinks her self *shaken,* if the Penal Laws be repealed; then by Law Establish'd she must mean, *Established by those Penal Laws.* Secondly, That the King having promised to maintain her, as by Law Established, *he ought not to endeavour their Repeal by which she is established.* I confess this is very close arguing, but then she must not take it ill, if all Men think her ill founded; for any thing must be so, that is established by destroying Laws? Laws, that *Time* and *Practice* have declared Enemies to *Property* and *Conscience.* O let her not hold by that Charter, nor point thither for her Establishment and Defence, if she would be thought a Christian Church.

Plutarch had rather one should think there never was such a Man in the

World, than that *Plutarch* was an ill Man. Shall the Church of *England,* that glories in a greater Light, *be more concerned for her Power than her Credit?* To be, than to be that which she should be? I would say, far be it from her, for her own Sake, and which is of much more Moment, for the Sake of the general Cause of Religion.

Let us see therefore if there be not another Way of understanding those Words more decent to the King, and more honourable for her, *viz.* that she is in the *National Chair, has the Churches and Revenues, and is Mother of those that do not adhere to any separate Communion, and that the King has promised to maintain her in this Post from the Invasions of any other Perswasion that would wrest these Privileges out of her Hands:* This he promised formerly; this he has very particularly repeated in his gracious Declaration: But to ruin Men that would not conform, while himself was so great a Dissenter, and came such, to her Knowledge, to the Crown, can be no Part of his Promises in the Opinion of Common Sense and Charity. Is there no Difference to be observed between not turning her out, and Destroying all others not of her Communion: He will not turn her out, there's his Promise, and he has not done it; There's his Performance: Nor will he do it, I am confident, if she pleases. But there's no Manner of Necessity from this Engagement that all Parties else are to be confounded. Tho' if it were so, 'tis ill Divinity to press such Promises upon a Prince's Conscience, that can't be performed with a good One by Any Body.

Let us remember how often she has upbraided her Dissenters with this, *Render to Caesar the Things that are Caesar's,* whilst they have returned upon her t'other half of the Text, *and render unto God the Things that are God's.*[16] It happens now that *God* and *Caesar* are both of a Mind, which perhaps does not always fall out, at least about the Point in Hand. Will she dissent from both now? Her Case, believe me, will be doubtful then. I beg her to be Considerate. 'Tis the greatest Time of Trial she has met with since she was a Church. To acquit her self like a Member of Christ's Universal One, let her keep nothing that voids her Pretensions. The *Babylonish* Garment will undo her. Practices inconsistent with her Reformation will ruin her. The *Martyr*'s Blood won the Day, and her Severity has almost lost it. They suffered by Law, she makes Laws *for Suffering.* Is this an Imitation of their Practice, *to uphold the Weapons of their Destruction?* I must tell her, 'tis being a *Martyr* for Persecution, and not by it. Another Path than that the Holy Ancients, and our humble Ancestors

16. Matthew 22:21; Mark 12:17; and Luke 20:25.

trod, and which will lead her to be deserted and contemned of every Body that counts it safer to follow the blessed Rule and practice of Christ and his inspired Messengers, than her narrow and worldly Policies. But that which heightens the Reproach, is the Offer of the Romanists themselves to make a perpetual Civil Peace with her, and that she refuses. Would the Martyrs have done this? surely no. Let her remember the first Argument honest old *Fox* advances against that Church, is the Church of *England*'s present Darling, *viz.* Penal Laws for Religion; as she may see at the Beginning of his first Volume: Doubtless he was much in the Right, which makes her extremely in the Wrong. Nothing, says the Prophet, must harm in God's Holy Mountain, and that's the Church, says *Fox,* and therefore he says, Christ's Church never Persecutes.[17] Leave then God with his own Work, and Christ with his own Kingdom. As it is not of the World, let not the World touch it; no, *not to uphold it,* though they that bear it should trip by the Way. Remember *Uzzah,* he would needs support the Ark *when the Oxen* Stumbled; *but was struck Dead for his Pains.*[18] The Presumption is more than parallel. Christ promised *to be present with his Church to the End of the World.* He bids them *fear not,* and told them, *that sufficient was the Day for the Evil thereof.*[19] How? with Penal Laws? no such Matter; but his Divine Presence. Therefore it was, He called not for *Legions* to fight for him, because his Work needed it not. They that want them have another Sort of Work to do: And 'tis too plain, that *Empire,* and not Religion, has been too much the Business. But, O let it not be so any more! To be a *True* Church is better than to be a *National* One; especially as so upheld. *Press Virtue, Punish Vice, Dispense with Opinion; Perswade,* but don't *Impose.* Are there *Tares* in Opinion? let them alone; you heard *they are to grow with the Wheat 'till Harvest,* that is, *the End of the World. Should they not be plucked up before?* No; and 'tis *Angels* Work at last too. Christ, that knew all Men, saw no Hand on Earth fit for that Business. Let us not then usurp their Office. Besides, *we are to love Enemies;* this is the Great Law of our Religion;[20] *by what Law then are we to Persecute them?* and if not Enemies, not Friends and Neighbours certainly.

The Apostle rejoyced *that Christ was Preached out of Envy,*[21] If so, I am sure we ought not to envy Christians the Enjoyment of the Liberty of their Con-

17. Isaiah 11:9; John Foxe, *Actes and Monuments.*

18. 2 Samuel 6:3–7.

19. Matthew 28:20; 6:34.

20. Matthew 13:24–30; Matthew 5:44–46; and Luke 6:27–32.

21. Philippians 1:15.

sciences. Christianity should be propagated by the Spirit of Christianity, and not by Violence or Persecution, for that's the Spirit of Antichristianity. Nor for Fear of it, should we, of Christians, become Antichristians. Where is Faith in God? Where is Trust in Providence? Let us do our Duty, and leave the rest with Him; *and not do Evil that Good may come of it;*[22] for that shews a Distrust in God, and a Confidence in our own Inventions for Security. No Reason of State can excuse our Disobedience to his *Rule;* and we desert the Principles of our Heavenly Master when we decline it. The Question is about Conscience, about this we can none of us be too tender, nor exemplary. 'Tis in right doing that Christians can hope for Success; and for true Victory only through Faith and Patience. But if to avoid what we fear, we contradict our Principles, we may justly apprehend *that God will desert us in an unlawful Way of maintaining them.* Perhaps this may be God's Time of trying all Parties, what we will do; whether we will rely upon him or our own feeble Provisions; whether we will allow what we our selves, in our Turn, *have all of us desired;* if not, may we not expect to suffer the Thing we would inflict? for our Penal Laws cannot secure us from the Turns of Providence, and less support us under them. Let us consider the true Ground of the Difficulty that is made, if it be not partial and light in God's Scale; for to that Tryal all Things must come, and his Judgment is inevitable as well as infallible. Besides, if we have not tried all other Methods, we are inexcusable in being so tenacious for this. I do therefore, in all Humility, beseech all Sorts of Professors of Christianity in these Kingdoms, to abstract themselves from those Jealousies which worldly Motives are apt to kindle in their Minds, and with an even and undisturbed Soul pursue their Christian Duty in this great Conjuncture: Considering *the Race is not to the Swift, nor the Battle to the Strong,* and that for all our Watchmen, *'tis God alone* (at last) *that keeps the City.*[23] Not that I would decline a fitting, but an unchristian Provision: For though the Foundation were never so true, yet if our Superstructure be *Hay* and *Stubble,* (our own narrow Devices) the Fire will consume it, and our Labour will be worse than in vain.[24] Let us not therefore *Sow what we would not Reap, because we must Reap what we Sow:* And remember who told us, *what we measure to others shall be measured to us*

22. Romans 3:8.
23. Ecclesiastes 9:11; and Psalms 127:1.
24. 1 Corinthians 3:12–13.

again.[25] Let us therefore do unto all Parties of Men, *as we would be done unto by them in their Turn of Power:* Lest our Fear of their Undutifulness, *should tempt us out of our Duty,* and so draw upon our selves the Mischiefs we are afraid of. Sacred Writ is full of this, in the Doctrine of both Testaments; and, as we profess to believe it, we are inexcusable if we do not practise it. Let the Spirit then of Christian Religion prevail: Let our Policies give Way to our Duty, and our Fears will be overcome of our Hopes, which will not make us ashamed at the last and great Judgment: where, O God! let us all appear with Comfort.

I could yet enlarge upon this Subject; for nothing can be more fruitful. I could say, that a Church that *Denies* Infallibility, cannot *force,* because she cannot be *certain,* and so *Penal Laws* (tho' it were possible that they could be lawful in others) in her, *would be Unjust.* That Scripture leaves Men to *Conviction* and *Perswasion.* That the true Church-Weapons are *Light* and *Grace;* and her Punishments, *Censure* and *Excommunication.* That *Goals* and *Gibbets* are Inadequate Methods for Conversion, and that they never succeeded. That this forbids all farther Light to come into the World, and so limits the Holy One, which in Scripture is made a great Sin. And, lastly, That such ensnare their own Posterity that may be of another Mind, and forfeit by it the Estates they have so carefully transmitted to them. Thus far against Imposition. And against Compliance, I could say, that it's to betray God's Sovereignty over Conscience; To defy Men; Gratify Presumption; Soil and Extinguish Truth in the Mind; Obey Blindfold; make over the Soul without Security; turn Hypocrite, and abundance more; each of which Heads might well merit an whole Chapter. But this having been well and seasonably considered elsewhere, I shall now proceed to the second Part of this Discourse, in which I will be as brief, and yet as full as I can.

PART II. *That 'tis the Principle of Men of Note of all Parties.*

BUT what Need Is there of this, may some say, when all Parties profess to be of the same Judgment, *That Conscience ought not to be forced, nor Religion imposed upon Men at their Civil Peril?* I own they are all of that Mind, at one Time or other, and therefore, that I may purge my self of any Animosity to

25. Matthew 7:1–2; and Luke 6:37–38.

the Doctrine of the Church of *England,* I will ingenuously confess the severe Conduct I have argued against is not to be imputed to her Principles; but then her Evil will be the greater, that in Fact has so notoriously contradicted them. I know some of her Defenders will hardly allow that too; tho' the more candid give us their Silence or Confession: For they tell us, *'tis not the Church that has done it;* which, unless they mean, the Laws were not made at Church, must needs be false, since those that made and executed them were of her own Communion, and are that great Body of Members that constitute her a Church; but, by her shifting them off, 'tis but reasonable to conclude that she tacitly condemns what she publickly disowns. One would think then it should not be so hard to perswade her to quit them, in the Way she made them, or to enjoyn her Sons to do it, if that Language be too harsh for her. This she must hear of some Way, and I pray God she may endeavour to do her Duty in it. She is not alone; for every Party in Power has too evidently lapsed into this Evil; tho' under the Prevalency and Persecution of another Interest they have ever writ against Club-Law for Religion. And to the End that I may do the *Reformation* Right, and the Principles of the Church of *England* Justice, I must say, that hardly one Person of any note, died in the Time of Queen *Mary,* that did not pass Sentence upon Persecution as Antichristian, particularly *Latimer, Philpot, Bradford, Rogers,* very Eminent Reformers. The Apologies that were writ in those Times, are of the same Strain, as may be seen in *Jewel, Haddon, Reynolds, &c.* and the Papists were with reason thought much in the wrong by those Primitive Protestants, for the Persecution that they raised against them, for Matters of pure Religion. But what need we go so far back? Is it not recent in Memory, that Bishop *Usher* was Employ'd to *O. Cromwell* by some of the Clergy of the Church of *England* for Liberty of Conscience? Dr. *Parr,* in the Life of Dr. *Usher* Primate of *Armagh,* fol. 75. has that Passage thus.[26]

> *Cromwell* forbidding the Clergy, under great Penalties, to teach Schools, or to perform any Part of their ministerial Function; some of the most considerable Episcopal Clergy in and about *London,* desired my Lord *Primate* that he would use his Interest with *Cromwell,* (since they heard he pretended a great Respect for him) that as he granted Liberty of Conscience to almost all Sorts of Religions, so the Episcopal

26. Richard Parr, *The life of the most reverend Father in God, James Usher* (London, 1686), p. 75.

> Divines might have the same Freedom of serving God in their private Congregations (since they were not permitted the publick Churches) according to the Liturgy of the Church of *England;* and that neither the Ministers, nor those that frequented that Service, might be any more hindered, or disturbed by his Soldiers: So according to their Desire, he went and used his utmost Endeavours with *Cromwell,* for the taking off this Restraint, which was at last promised (though with some Difficulty) and that they should not be molested, provided they meddled not with any Matters relating to his Government.

Certainly those Gentlemen were of my Mind, And to give Dr. *Hammond* his due, who I understand was one of them, he left it to the Witnesses of his End, as his dying Counsel to the Church of *England,* That they displaced no Man out of the University or present Church, but that by Love, and an Holy Life they should prevail upon those in Possession to come into their Church. But this lookt so little like the Policy and Ambition of the Living, that they resolved it should be Buried with him. This I had from an eminent Hand in *Oxford,* a Year or two after his Death. An older Man out liv'd him, and one of the most Learned and Pious of that Communion, Bishop *Sanderson* I mean: They were the two great Men of their Sort that was of the Party. Let us see what this Reverend Man says to our Point.

> The Word of God doth expresly forbid us to subject our Consciences to the Judgment of any other, or to usurp a Dominion over the Consciences of any One. *Several Cases of Conscience discussed in Ten Lectures in the Divinity School at* Oxford, 3 Lect. 30 Sect. pag. 103. printed 1660.
>
> He is not worthy to be Christ's Disciple, who is not the Disciple of Christ *alone.* The Simplicity and Sincerity of the Christian Faith, hath suffered a great Prejudice since we have been divided into Parties, neither is there any Hope that Religion should be restored to her former Original and Purity, until the Wounds that were made wider by our daily Quarrels and Dissentions, being anointed with the *Oyl of Brotherly Love,* as with a Balsam, shall begin to close again, and to grow entire into the same Unity of Faith and Charity, *ibid. Sect. 29.*
>
> The Obligation of Conscience doth not signify any Compulsion, for, to speak properly, the Conscience can no more be compelled than the Free-will. *ibid.* 4. *Lecture Sect.* 5. pag. 109.
>
> The express Commandment of God doth oblige the Conscience

properly by it self and by it's own Force; and this Obligation is absolute, because it doth directly and always oblige, and because it obligeth all Persons, and the Obligation of it is never to be cancelled. *None but God alone* hath Power to impose a Law upon the Conscience of any Man, to which it ought to be subjected, as obliging by it self,—This Conclusion is prov'd by the Words of the Apostle, *There is but one Law-giver, who can both save and destroy.*[27] In which Words two Arguments do offer themselves to our Observation; In the first place they assert there is but one Legislator; not one picked out amongst many; not one above many; but one exclusively, that is to say, One, and but one only. The Apostle otherwise had made use of a very ineffectual Argument, to prove what he had propounded; for he rebuketh those who unadvisedly did pass their Judgment either on the Persons, or the Deeds of other Men, as the Invaders of their Rights. *Who art Thou* (saith he) *who dost judge another?*[28] As if he should have said, dost thou know thy self, what thou art, and what thou dost? It doth not belong to Thee to thrust thy sawcy Sickle into the harvest of another Man, *much less boldly to fling thy self into the Throne of Almighty God.* If already Thou art Ignorant of it, then know, that it belongeth to him *alone* to judge of the Consciences of Men, *to whom alone it doth belong to impose Laws upon the Consciences of Men,* which none can do but God alone. *ibid pag.* 111, 112, 113.

The Condition and Natural Estate of the Conscience itself is so placed as it were in the middle *betwixt* God and the will of Man, as that which is usually and truly spoken of Kings and Emperours, may as truly be verified of the Conscience of every Man, *Solo Deo minores esse, nec aliquem in Terris superiorem agnoscere; They are less than God only, and on Earth do acknowledge no Superior.* That Speech of the Emperour *Maximilian* the first is very memorable, *Conscientiis Dominari velle, est Arcem Caeli invadere; To exercise a Domination over Consciences, is to invade the Tower of Heaven.* He is a Plunderer of the Glory of God, and a *nefarious Invader* of the Power that is due unto him, whosoever he is that shall claim a right to the Consciences of Men, or practice an Usurpation over them. *ibid. Sect.* 11. *pag.* 115.

27. James 4:12.
28. Ibid.

And yet this is the sad Consequence of imposing Religion upon Conscience, and punishing Non-conformity with worldly Penalties.

Let us now hear what the late *Bishop* of *Down* says in his *Lib. of Prophesy* to our Point,[29]

> I am very much displeased that so many Opinions and new Doctrines are commenced amongst us, but more troubled, that every Man that hath an Opinion thinks his own and other Men's Salvation is concerned in it's maintenance, but most of all, that Men should be Persecuted and Afflicted for disagreeing in such Opinions, which they cannot with sufficient Grounds obtrude upon others necessarily, because they cannot propound them Infallibly, and because they have no Warrant from Scripture so to do; for if I shall tye other Men to believe my Opinion, because I think I have a Place of Scripture which seems to warrant it to my Understanding; why may he not serve up another Dish to me in the same Dress, and exact the same Task of me to believe the contradictory? *Liberty of Prophesy,* Epist. Dedicat. p. 8, 9.
>
> The Experience which Christendom hath had in this last Age is Argument enough that *Toleration of differing Opinions* is so far from disturbing the Publick Peace, or destroying the Interest of Princes and Common-wealths, that it does advantage to the Publick, it secures Peace, because there is not so much as the *Pretence of Religion* left to such Persons to contend for, it being already indulged to them. *ibid.* pag. 21.
>
> It is a proverbial saying, *Quod nimia familiaritas servorum est conspiratio adversus Dominum,*[30] and they who for their Security run into Grots and Cellars, and Retirements, think that they being upon the defensive, those Princes and those Laws that drive them to it are their Enemies, and therefore they cannot be secure, unless the Power of the one, and the Obligation of the other be lessened and rescinded; and then the being restrained, and made miserable, endears the discontented Persons mutually, and makes more hearty and dangerous Confederations, *ibid.* Page 23.
>
> No Man speaks more unreasonably, than he that *denies to Men the Use of their Reason in Choice of their Religion.* ibid. pag. 169.

29. Jeremy Taylor, *Theologike eklektike* (London, 1647).

30. Excessive familiarity among slaves constitutes a conspiracy against the master.

> *No Christian is to be put to Death, Dismembred, or otherwise directly Persecuted for his Opinion, which does not teach Impiety or Blasphemy,* ibid. pag. 190.
>
> There is a popular Pity that follows all Persons in Misery, and that Compassion breeds likeness of Affections, and that very often produces Likeness of Perswasion; and so much the rather, because there arises a Jealousie and pregnant Suspicion that they who Persecute an Opinion are destitute of sufficient Arguments to confute it, and that the Hangman is the best Disputant. *ibid. Page* 197, 198.
>
> If a Man cannot change his Opinion when he lists, nor ever does heartily or resolutely, but when he cannot do otherwise, then to use Force, may make him an Hypocrite, but never to be a right Believer, and so instead of erecting a Trophy to God and true Religion, *we build a Monument for the Devil.* ibid. p. 200.
>
> The Trick of giving Persons differing in Opinion over to the secular Power, at the best is no better than *Hypocrisy,* removing Envy from themselves, and laying it upon others, a refusing to do that in external Act, *which they do in Counsel and Approbation.* ibid. pag. 209.

Thus far *Bishop Taylor,* and one of the most Learned Men of the Church of *England* in his Time.

Let me add another Bishop, held Learned by all, and in great Reputation with the Men of his Communion, and among them *the Lords Spiritual and Temporal in Parliament assembled,* who have sufficiently declared against this persecuting Spirit on the Account of Religion, by their full Approbation of, and *Thanks returned to the Bishop of* S. Asaph *for his Sermon Preached before them* November *the* 5*th,* 1680. *and their Desire that he would Print and Publish that Sermon.*[31] The Bishop says, that, "They who are most given to Hate and to Destroy others, especially those others who differ from them in Religion, they are not the *Church of God,* or at least they are so far corrupt in that particular." *pag.* 8.

Again he says,

> That, of Societies of Men, Christians, of all others, are most averse from Ways of Violence and Blood; especially from using any such Ways upon

31. William Lloyd, *A sermon preached before the House of Lords, on November 5, 1680* (London, 1680).

the Account of Religion: And among Christian Churches, where they differ among themselves, if either of them use those Ways upon the Account of Religion, they give a strong Presumption against themselves that they are not truly Christians. *ibid. pag.* 9.

There is reason for this, because, we know that Christ gave Love for the Character by which his Disciples were to be known. *John* 13. 35. *By this shall all Men know that you are my Disciples, if you have love to one another.* And lest Men should unchristen others first, that they may Hate them, and Destroy them afterwards, Christ enlarged his Precept of Love, and extended it even to Enemies, and not only to ours, but to the Enemies of our Religion, *Matt.* 5. 43, 44. *ibid. Pag. 9.*

As our Holy Religion excells all others in this admirable temper, so by this we may usually judge who they are that excel among Christian Churches, when there happens any Difference between them, whether touching the Faith, or the Terms of Communion. They that were the more Fierce, they generally had the worst Cause. *ibid. pag.* 12, 13.

The Council of *Nice* suppressed the *Arrians* by no other Force, but putting *Arrians* out of their Bishopricks; they could not think Hereticks fit to be trusted with cure of Souls; but otherwise, as to *Temporal Things,* I do not find that they inflicted any kind of Punishments; but when the *Arrians* came to have the *Power* in their Hands, when theirs was come to be the *Imperial Religion,* then Depriving was nothing, Banishment was the least that they inflicted. *ibid. pag.* 14.

Neither our Religion, nor our Church, is of a *persecuting* Spirit. I know not how it may be in particular Persons; but I say again, it is not in the *Genius* of our Church: She hath no Doctrine that *teacheth Persecution. ibid.* p. 20.

I would have no Man punished for his Religion, no not them that destroy Men for Religion. *ibid. pag.* 37.

Dr. *Stillingfleet* comes short of none of them on this Subject.*

Our Saviour, says he, never *pressed* Followers as Men do *Soldiers,* but said, *If any Man will come after me, let him take up his Cross* (not his

* *Irenicum,* a Weapon-Salve for the Churches Wounds, by *E. Stillingfleet* Rector of *Sutton* in *Bedfordshire,* in Preface to the Reader.

Sword) *and follow me.* His was ἥμερος καὶ φιλάνθρωπος νομοθεσία,[32] his very Commands shewed his Meekness; his Laws were sweet and gentle Laws; not like *Draco*'s that were writ in Blood,[33] unless it were his own that gave them. His Design was to ease Men of their former Burdens, and not lay on more; the Duties he required were no other but such as were necessary, and withal very just and reasonable. He that came to take away the insupportable Yoke of Jewish Ceremonies, certainly did never intend to gall the Necks of his Disciples with another instead of it. And it would be strange the Church should require more than Christ himself did; and make other Conditions of her Communion, *than our Saviour did of Discipleship.* What possible reason can be assigned or given why such Things should not be sufficient for Communion with a Church, *which are sufficient for Eternal Salvation?* And certainly those Things are sufficient for that, which are laid down as necessary Duties of Christianity by our Lord and Saviour in his Word. *What Ground can there be why Christians should not stand upon the same Terms now which they did in the Time of Christ and his Apostles?* Was not Religion sufficiently guarded and fenced in them? Was there ever more true and cordial Reverence in the Worship of God? What *Charter* hath Christ given the Church to *bind Men up to more than himself hath done?* or to exclude those from her Society who may be admitted into Heaven? Will Christ ever thank Men at the great Day for keeping such out from Communion with his Church, when he will vouchsafe not only Crowns of Glory to them, but it may be *Aureolae* too, if there be any such Things there? The Grand Commission the Apostles were sent out with, was only to *teach what Christ had commanded them.*[34] Not the least Intimation of any Power given them to impose or require any Thing beyond what himself had spoken to them, or they were directed to by the Immediate Guidance of the Spirit of God.

Without all Controversy, the main Inlet of all the Distractions, Confusions and Divisions of the Christian World, hath been by adding other Conditions of Church Communion than Christ hath done.

There is nothing the *Primitive Church* deserves greater Imitation by

32. Gentle and benevolent law-giving.

33. Draco promulgated his severe code of laws in Athens ca. 621 B.C.E.

34. Matthew 28:19.

us in, than in that admirable Temper, Moderation and Condescension which was used in it towards all the Members of it.

This admirable Temper in the Primitive Church might be largely cleared from that Liberty they allowed freely to Dissenters from them in Matters of Practice and Opinion; as might be cleared from *Cyprian, Austin, Jerome,* and others. — Leaving the Men to be won by observing the true decency and order of Churches, whereby those who act upon a true Principle of Christian Ingenuity may be sooner drawn to a Compliance in all lawful Things, than by Force and rigorous Impositions, which make Men suspect the Weight of the Thing it self, when such Force is used to make it enter. *In the Preface.*

The same is in effect declared by the *House of Commons,* when they returned their Thanks to Dr. *Tillotson, Dean of Canterbury,* for his Sermon Preached before them *November* the 5th, 1678.[35] *desiring him to Print that Sermon,* where he says, upon our Saviour's Words,

Ye know not what Manner of Spirit ye are of, Ye own your selves to be my Disciples, but do you consider what Spirit now Acts and Governs you? not that surely which my Doctrine designs to mould and fashion you into, which is not a *Furious and Persecuting,* and *Destructive Spirit,* but Mild and Gentle, and Saving; tender of the Lives and Interests of Men, even of those who are our greatest Enemies *pag.* 6, 7.

No Difference of Religion, no Pretence of Zeal for God and Christ can warrant and justifie this Passionate and Fierce, this Vindictive and Exterminating Spirit. *ibid. pag.* 7.

He (*i.e.* Christ) came to introduce a Religion, which consults not only the Eternal Salvation of Men's Souls, but their Temporal Peace and Security, their Comfort and Happiness in this World. *ibid. pag.* 8.

It seemed good to the Author of this Institution to compel no Man to it by Temporal Punishment. *ibid. pag.* 13.

To *separate* Goodness and Mercy From God, Compassion and Charity from Religion, is to make the two best Things in the World, God and Religion, good for nothing. *ibid. pag.* 9.

True Christianity is not only the best, but the best natured Institution

35. John Tillotson, *A sermon preached November 5, 1678 at St. Margarets, Westminster* (London, 1678).

> in the World; and so far as any Church is departed from good Nature, and become Cruel and Barbarous, so far it is degenerated from Christianity. *ibid. pag.* 30.

Thus far Dr. *Tillotson,* who, to be sure, deserves not to be thought the least Eminent in the present Church of *England.* Let us hear what Dr. *Burnet* says to it.

"Men are not Masters of their own Perswasions, and cannot change their Thoughts as they please; he that believes any Thing concerning Religion, *cannot turn as the Prince commands him, or accommodate himself to the Law, or his present Interests,* unless he arrive at that *Pitch of Atheism,* as to look on Religion only as a Matter of Policy, and an Engine for Civil Government": *Dr.* Burnet's *History of the Rights of Princes,* &c. in his Preface, pag. 49.[36]

'Tis to this Doctor's Pains, She owes the very *History of Her Reformation;* and, as by it he has perpetuated his Name with Her's, certainly he must have Credit with Her, or She can deserve none with any Body else; for no Man could well go farther to oblige Her.

Let me here bring in a Lay Member of the *Church of England,* Sir *Robert Pointz,* in *His Vindication of Monarchy,*[37] who yields us an excellent Testimony to the Matter in Hand:

> The Sword *availeth little* with the Souls of Men, unless to *destroy* them together with their Bodies, and to make Men *Desperate,* or *Dissemblers in Religion,* and when they find Opportunity, to fall into *Rebellion,* as there are many Examples, *pag.* 27.
>
> In the Ancient Times of Christianity, such Means were not used as might *make Hereticks and Schismaticks more obstinate than docible, through the preposterous Proceedings of the Magistrates and Ministers of Justice, in the Execution of Penal Laws,* used rather as *Snares* for Gaining of Money, and Pecuniary Mulcts impos'd, rather as *Prices* set upon Offences, than as Punishments for the Reformation of Manners, *ibid. pag.* 28.
>
> The *Ancient Christians* were forbidden by the *Imperial Law,* as also

36. Gilbert Burnet, *The history of the rights of princes in the disposing of ecclesiastical benefices and church-lands* (London, 1682).

37. Sir Robert Poyntz, *A vindication of monarchy and the government long established in the Church and Kingdome of England* (London, 1661).

> by the Laws of other Christian Nations, under a great Penalty, *To meddle with the Goods of* Jews, *or* Pagans, living Peaceably, *ibid. pag.* 29.
>
> For, the Goods of the *Jews,* although Enemies to the Christian Religion, *cannot for the Cause of Religion come by Escheat unto Christian Princes,* under whom they live. *Ibid. pag.* 29.
>
> It is truly said, that *Peace,* a Messenger whereof an *Angel* hath been chosen to be, *is scarce Established by the Sword;* and the *Gospel,* the *Blessed Peace,* cannot be published by the *Sound of Cannon,* neither the *Sacred Word* be convey'd unto us, by the *Impious Hands of Soldiers;* neither *Tranquillity* be brought to the Persons and Consciences of Men, *by that which bringeth Ruin unto Nations,* ibid. pag. 70.

He has said Much in a Little; the Talent and Honour of Men truly Great. I give this still to the *Church of England's Principles,* which yet makes it harder for Her, to Justifie Her Practice in Her Use of Power. But let us hear a King speak, and One the *Church of England* is bound to hear by many Obligations.

King *Charles* the First, out of his *Tender and Princely Sense of the sad and bleeding Condition of the Kingdom,* and his unwearied Desires to apply such Remedies, as by the Blessing of Almighty God, might settle it in Peace, by the Advice of his Lords and Commons of Parliament, Assembled at *Oxford,* propounded and desired, *That all the Members of Both Houses might securely Meet in a Full and Free Convention of Parliament, there to Treat, Consult, and Agree upon such Things, as may conduce to the Maintenance and Defence of the* Reformed Protestant Religion, *with due Consideration to all Just and Reasonable Ease to Tender Consciences.* The King's Message of a Treaty, *March* 3. 1643. from *Oxford,* Superscribed to the Lords and Commons of Parliament Assembled at *Westminster.*

In the King's Twentieth Message for Peace, *January* 29, 1645, he has these Words, *That by the Liberty offered in his Message of the 15th present, for the* Ease of their Consciences who will not Communicate in the Service already Established by Act of Parliament in this Kingdom, *He intends that all other Protestants, behaving themselves Peaceable in, and towards the Civil Government, shall have the* Free Exercise *of their* Religion, *according to their own Way.*

In the Thirty Third Message for Peace, *November* 14, 1647, there are these Words, *His Majesty considering the great present Distempers concerning* Church-Discipline *and that the* Presbyterian Government *is now in Practice, His Majesty to eschew* Confusion, *as much as may be, and for the Satisfaction of His Two Houses, is content that the said Government be Legally permitted to stand in the same Condition it now is, for Three Years; Provided, that His Majesty, and those of his Judgment (or any other who cannot in* Conscience *submit thereunto) be not obliged to comply with the* Presbyterial Government, *but have* Free Practice of their own Profession, *without receiving any Prejudice thereby.* From the Isle of *Wight.*

In his Declaration to all his People, *January* 18, 1645, from *Carisbrook* Castle, after the Votes of no Address, He says, *I have Sacrificed to My Two Houses of Parliament, for the Peace of the Kingdom, All but what is much more dear to me than my Life, my* Conscience *and my* Honour.

In his Letter to the Lords, Gentlemen and Committee of the *Scotch* Parliament, together with the Officers of the Army, *July* 3, 1648, from *Carisbrook* Castle—*As the Best Foundation of Loyalty is Christianity, so True Christianity is Perfect Loyalty.*

ΕΙΚΩΝ ΒΑΞΙΛΙΚΗ. Ch. 6. Upon His Majesty's Retirement from *Westminster.—Sure it ceases to be Counsel, when not* Reason *is used, as to Men to* Perswade, *but* Force and Terror, *as to Beasts, to drive and compel Men to whatever Tumultuary Patrons shall Project. He deserves to be a* Slave *without Pity or Redemption, that is content to have* his Rational Sovereignty of his Soul, *and Liberty of his* Will and Words *so captivated.*—Again, Ibid. *Sure that Man cannot be blameable to God or Man, who seriously endeavours to* See the Best Reason of Things, *and faithfully follows what he takes for* Reason; *the* Uprightness *of his Intentions will excuse the possible Failing of his* Understanding.—Again, Ibid. *I know no Resolutions more worthy a* Christian King, *than to prefer his* Conscience *before his Kingdoms.*

Chap. 12. Upon the Rebellion and Troubles in *Ireland.—Some Kind of Zeal counts* All Merciful Moderation, Lukewarmness, *and had rather be* Cruel, *than accounted* Cold, *and is not seldom more greedy to Kill the Bear for his Skin, than for any Harm he hath done.*—Ib. O my GOD, Thou seest how much Cruelty among Christians is acted under the Colour of Religion, as if we could not be Christians, unless we Crucify one another.

Chap. 13. Upon the calling the *Scots,* and their coming—*Sure, in Matters of* Religion, *those* Truths *gain most on* Men's Judgments and Consciences, *which are least urged with* Secular Violence, *which weakens* Truth *with Prejudices; and is unreasonable to be used, till such Means of Rational Conviction hath been applied, as leaving no Excuse for Ignorance, condemns Men's Obstinacy to de-*

serv'd Penalties.—Violent Motions are neither Manly, Christian, *nor* Loyal.—The proper Engine of Faction is Force; *the Arbitrator of Beasts, not of* Reasonable Men, *much less of* Humble Christians *and* Loyal Subjects, *in Matters of Religion.*

Chap. 14. Upon the Covenant.—*Religion requires* Charity *and* Candor *to others of different Opinions—Nothing Violent and Injurious can be Religious.*

Chap. 15. Upon the many Jealousies raised, and Scandals cast upon the King, to stir up the People against him.—*In Point of True Conscientious Tenderness (attended with Humility and Meekness, not with proud or arrogant Activity, which seeks to hatch every Egg of indifferent Opinion to Faction or Schism) I have oft declared how little I desire* My Laws and Scepter *should intrench over God's Soveraignty,* who is the Only King of Men's Consciences.

Chap. 27. To the Prince of *Wales.—Take Heed of abetting to any Factions; your* Partial *adhering to any One Side, gains you not so great Advantages in some Men's Hearts, (who are* Prone *to be of their King's Religion) as it loseth you in others, who think themselves, and their Profession, first despised, then persecuted by you.—My Counsel and Charge to you is, That you seriously consider the former Real or Objected Miscarriages, which might occasion my Troubles, that you may avoid them.—A* Charitable Connivence, *and* Christian Toleration, *often dissipates their Strength, whom* Rougher Opposition *fortifies.—Always keep up* Sound Piety, *and those* Fundamental Truths (*which mend both Hearts and Lives of Men*) *with Impartial Favour and Justice.—Your Prerogative is best shewed and exercised in* Remitting, *rather than exacting the Rigour of the Law, there being nothing worse than Legal Tyranny:*

And as this was the Sense and Judgment of a King, that Time, and the greatest Troubles had inform'd with a Superiour Judgment, (and which to be sure highly justifies the Measures that are now taken) So Dr. *Hudson,* His *Plain Dealing Chaplain,* must not be forgotten by us on this Occasion, who took the Freedom to tell His Royal Master, *That he look'd upon the Calamities he labour'd under, to be the Hand of GOD upon Him, for not having given GOD His Due over Conscience.*

One can easily imagine this to be *Reformation Language,* and then it is not hard to think, how low that Church must be fallen, that from so Free and Excellent a Principle, is come to make, execute, and uphold *Penal Laws for Religion, against Her Conscientious Neighbours;* but it is to be hoped, *That like* Nebuchadnezzar's Image, *whose Feet was a Mixture of* Iron and Clay, *and therefore could not stand for ever,*[38] Persecution *will not be able to mix so with the Seed of Men, but that* Humanity *will overcome it, and Mankind One Day be delivered from that Iron, Hard, and Fierce Nature.*

I have done with my *Church of England's Evidences against Persecution:* And for the *Judgment of all Sorts of Dissenters in That Point,* let their Practice have been what it will, nothing is clearer, *than that they disallow of Persecution,* of which their Daily Addresses of Thanks to the KING, for His General Ease, by His Excellent Declaration, are an undoubted Proof.

Thus then we see, it is evident, that it is not only the *Duty of all Parties, as they would be thought Christians, to Repeal Penal Laws for Religion,* but upon a Fair Enquiry, *We see it is the avowed Principle of every Party, at one Time or other, that* Conscience *ought not to be compell'd, nor* Religion *impos'd upon Worldly Penalties.* And so I come to the Third and Last Part of this Discourse.

PART III. *It is the Interest of all Parties, and especially the Church of* ENGLAND.

As I take all Men to be unwillingly separated from their Interests, and consequently ought only to be sought and discours'd in them, so it must be granted me on all Hands, *That Interests change as well as Times, and 'tis the Wisdom of a Man to observe the Courses, and humour the Motions of his Interest, as the Best Way to preserve it.* And lest any ill-natur'd, or mistaken Person, should call it *Temporizing,* I make this early Provision; *That I mean, no immoral, or corrupt Compliance: A Temporizing,* deservedly base with Men of Vertue, and which in all Times, my Practice, as well as Judgment, hath shown the last Aversion to. For upon the Principle I now go, and which I lay down, as common and granted in Reason and Fact, with all Parties concern'd in this Discourse, that Man does not change, that *Morally* follows his Interest under all it's Revolutions, because to be True to his Interest, is his First Civil Principle. I premise this, to introduce what I have to offer, with Respect to the Interests to be now treated upon.

And first, I say, *I take it to be the Interest of the Church of* England, *to abolish the Penal Laws, because it never was Her Interest to make them.* My Reasons for that Opinion are these, *First,* They have been an Argument to invalidate

38. Daniel 2:31–35.

the Sufferings of the *Reformers,* because if it be unlawful to disobey Government about Matters of Religion, they were in the wrong. And if they say, *O but they were in Error that punish'd their Non-Conformity;* I answer, *How can She prove that She is Infallibly in the Right?* And if this cannot be done, She compels to an Uncertainty upon the same Terms. *Secondly,* She has overthrown the Principles upon which She separated from *Rome:* For if it be Unlawful to plead Scripture and Conscience, to vindicate Dissent from Her Communion, it was Unlawful for Her upon the same Plea, *To Dissent from the Church of Rome;* unless She will say again, *That She was in the Right, but the other in the Wrong;* and She knows this is no Answer, but a begging of the Question; *For they that Separate from Her, think themselves as Serious, Devout, and as much in the Right as She could do.* If then *Conscience and Scripture,* interpreted with the *Best Light* She had, were the Ground of Her Reformation, She must allow the Liberty She takes, *Or She Eats Her Words, and Subverts Her Foundation;* than which nothing can be more Destructive to the Interest of any Being, Civil or Ecclesiastical. *Thirdly,* The *Penal Laws* have been the *Great Make-Bate* in the Kingdom from the Beginning: For if I should grant that She had been once truly the *Church of England,* I mean, consisting of all the *People of England,* (which She was not, for there were divers Parties Dissenting from the First of Her Establishment) yet since it afterwards appear'd She was but One Party, tho' the biggest, She ought not to have made Her Power more National than Her Faith, nor Her Faith so by the Force of Temporal Authority. 'Tis true, She got the Magistrate of Her Side, but She engaged him too far: For She knew, *Christ did not leave Caesar Executor to His Last Will and Testament,* and, that *That* should be the Reason why She did so, was none of the *Best Ornaments to Her Reformation.* That She was but a Party, tho' the biggest, by the Advantages that Temporal Power brought Her, I shall easily prove, but I will introduce it with a short Account of our State-Reformation here in *England.*

Henry the Eighth, was a Kind of *Hermaphrodite* in Religion, or in the Language of the Times, a *Trimmer;* being a *Medly of Papist and Protestant,* and that Part he acted to the Life, or to the Death rather; Sacrificing on the same Day Men of Both Religions, because one was not *Protestant enough,* and t'other *Papist enough for him.* In this Time were some *Anabaptists,* for the Distinction of *Church of England,* and *Calvinist,* was not then known.

Edward the Sixth succeeded, a Prince that promised Virtues, that might more than ballance the Excesses of his Father, and yet by Archbishop *Cranmer,* was compell'd to Sign a Warrant to Burn *Poor Joan of Kent,* a Famous Woman, but counted an *Enthusiast:* But to prove what I said of him, 'twas not without frequent Denials and Tears, and the Bishop taking upon him to answer for it at God's Judgment, of which I hope his Soul was discharg'd, tho' his Body, by the same Law, suffer'd the same Punishment in the succeeding Reign. Thus even the *Protestants began with Blood for Meer Religion,* and taught the *Romanists,* in succeeding Times, how to deal with them.

At this Time the Controversie grew warm between the *Church of England* and the *Calvinists,* that were the Abler Preachers and the Better Livers. The Bishops being mostly Men of State, and some of them looking rather backward than forward, Witness the Difficulty the King had to get *Hooper* Consecrated Bishop, without Conformity to the Reserved Ceremonies.

Queen Mary came in, and ended the Quarrel at the Stake. Now *Ridley* and *Hooper* hug, and are the Dearest Brethren, and Best Friends in the World. *Hooper* keeps his Ground, and *Ridley* stoops with his Ceremonies to t'others farther Reformation. But this Light and Union *flow'd* from their Persecution: For those abroad at *Frankfort,* and other Places, were not upon so good Terms: Their Feuds grew so great, that the one refused Communion with the other; many Endeavours were used to quench the Fire, but they were ineffectual; at best it lay under the *Ashes of their Affliction for another Time;* for no sooner was *Queen Elizabeth* upon Her Throne, than they returned, and their Difference with them. They managed it civilly for a While, but Ambition in some, and Covetousness in others on the one Hand, and Discretion giving Way to Resentment on the other, they first ply the *Queen* and *Her Ministers,* and when that ended in *Favour of the Men of Ceremony,* the others arraign'd them before the First Reformers abroad, at *Geneva, Basil, Zurich,* &c. The Leading Prelates by their Letters, as Dr. *Burnet* lately tells us, in his Printed Relation of his Travels, clear themselves to those first Doctors of any such Imputation, and lay all upon the *Queen,* who, for Reasons of State, would not be brought to so Inceremonious a Way of Worship, as that of the *Calvinists.*[39]

At this Time there were *Papists, Protestants, Evangelists, Praecisians, Ubiquitists, Familists,* or *Enthusiasts,* and *Anabaptists* in *England;* when the very First Year of Her Reign, *A Law for Uniformity in Worship and Discipline was En-*

39. Gilbert Burnet, *Dr. Burnet's travels; or, Letters containing an account of what seemed most remarkable in Switzerland, Italy, France, and Germany, &c* (Amsterdam, 1687).

acted, and more followed of the severest Nature, and sometimes executed.[40] Thus then we see that there never was such a Thing as a *Church of England* since the Days of *Popery,* that is, *A Church or Communion, containing all the People of the Kingdom,* and so cannot be said to be so much as a *Twin of the Reformation;* nevertheless, She got the Blessing of the Civil Magistrate: She made Him Great, to be Great by Him: If She might be the *Church,* He should be the *Head.* Much Good may the *Bargain* do her. Now is the Time for Her to stand to Her Principle. I never knew any Body exceed their Bounds, *that were not met with at last.* If we could escape Men, God we cannot, *His Providence* will overtake us, and find us out.

By all this then it appearing, that the *Church of England* was not the Nation, the Case is plain, *That the Penal Laws were a Make-Bate,* for they Sacrificed every Sort of People whose Consciences differed from the *Church of England;* which first put the *Romanists* upon flattering Prerogative, and courting it's Shelter from the Wrath of those Laws. The Address could not be unpleasant to Princes; and we see it was not; for *King James,* that came in with Invectives against *Popery,* entring the *Lists with the Learned of that Church,* and charging Her with all the Marks the *Revelation* gives to that of *Antichrist,* grew at last so tame and easie towards the *Romanists,* that our own Story tells us of the Fears of the Increase of *Popery* in the latter Parliament of his Reign.

In *King Charles* the First's Time, no Body can doubt of the Complaint, because that was in great Measure the Drift of every Parliament, and at last One Reason of the War. On the other Hand, *the Severity of the Bishops,* against Men of their own Principles, and in the Main, of their own Communion, either because they were more Zealous in Preaching, more follow'd of the People, or could not wear some odd Garment, and less, lead the Dance on a *Lord's Day* at a Maypole, (the Relick of *Flora,* the *Roman Strumpet*)[41] or perhaps for Rubbing upon the Ambition, Covetousness, and Laziness of the Dignified, and Ignorance and Looseness of the *Ordinary Clergy of the Church,* (of which I could produce Five Hundred Gross Instances) I say these Things bred bad Blood, and in Part, gave Beginning to those Animosities, that at last broke

40. The 1559 Act of Uniformity (1 Elizabeth I, c. 2) is reprinted in *The Tudor Constitution: Documents and Commentary,* ed. G. R. Elton (Cambridge, 1960), pp. 401–4.

41. Flora, the Roman goddess of spring; such festivities as the circling of the Maypole on May Day occasioned long-standing Puritan grievances against "worldly" holidays in early modern England. See also ch. 6, p. 284, n. 36.

forth, with some other Pretences, into all those National Troubles that agitated this poor Kingdom for Ten Years together, in which the *Church of* England *became the Greatest Loser, Her Clergy turn'd out, Her Nobility and Gentry Sequester'd, Decimated, Imprisoned,* &c. And whatever She is pleas'd to think, nothing is Truer, *than that Her Penal Laws, and Conduct in the Star-Chamber, and High Commission Court in Matters of Religion,* was Her Overthrow.

'Tis as evident, the same Humour, *since the Restoration of the late King,* has had almost the same Effect. For nothing was grown so little and contemptible, as the *Church of England* in this Kingdom, She now intitles Her self *The Church of:* Witness the Elections of the Last Three Parliaments before this. I know it may be said, *The Persons Chosen were Church-Goers;* I confess it, for the Law would have them so. But no Body were more averse to the Politicks of the Clergy; insomuch that the Parson and the Parish almost every where divided upon the Question of their Election. In Truth, it has been the *Favour and Countenance of the Crown,* and not Her intrinsick Interest or Value, that has kept Her up to this Day; else *Her Penal Laws,* the *Bulwark of the Church of England,* by the same Figure, that She is One *against Popery,* had sunk her long since.

I hope I may, by this Time, conclude, without Offence, that the *Penal-Laws* have been a *Make-Bate* in the Great Family of the Kingdom, setting the Father against his Children, and Brethren against Brethren; not only giving the Empire to one, but endeavouring to extinguish the rest, and that for this, the *Church of England* has once paid a severe Reckoning. I apply it thus: Is it not Her Interest to be careful She does it not a second Time? She has a fair Opportunity to prevent it, and keep Her self where She is; that is, *The Publick Religion of the Country, with the Real Maintenance of it;* which is a plain Preference to all the rest.

Violence and Tyranny are no Natural Consequences of *Popery,* for then they would follow every where, and in all Places and Times alike. But we see in Twenty Governments in *Germany,* there is none for Religion, nor was for an Age in *France;* and in *Poland,* the Popish Cantons of *Switzerland, Venice, Lucca, Colonia,* &c. where that Religion is Dominant, the People enjoy their Ancient and Civil Rights, a little more steadily then they have of late Times done in some *Protestant Countries nearer Home,* almost ever since the Reformation. *Is this against Protestancy? No; but very much against Protestants.* For had they been True to their Principles, we had been upon better Terms. So that the *Reformation was not the Fault,* but not keeping to it better than some have done; For whereas they were *Papists* that both obtain'd the *Great Charter,* and *Charter of Forests,* and in the successive Reigns of the Kings of their Religion, industriously labour'd the Confirmation of them, as the *Great Text of their Liberties and Properties,* by above Thirty other Laws; we find almost an equal Number to destroy them, and but One made in their Favour since the *Reformation,* and that shrewdly against the *Will of the High Church-Men too;* I mean, *The Petition of Right,* in the Third Year of *Charles* the First.[42] In short, They desire a Legal Security with us, and we are afraid of it, lest it should Insecure us; when nothing can do it so certainly as their Insecurity; *For Safety makes no Man Desperate.* And he that seeks Ease by Law, therefore does it, because he would not attempt it by Force. Are we afraid of their Power, and yet provoke it? If this Jealousie and Aversion prevail, it may drive Her to a Bargain with the Kingdom for such General Redemption of Property, as may *Dissolve our Great Corporation of Conscience,* and then She will think, *That Half a Loaf had been Better than No Bread;* and that it had been more advisable to have *parted with Penal Laws,* that only serv'd to Dress Her in Satyr, than have lost *All* for keeping them; especially when it was but parting with *Spurs, Claws and Bills, that made Her look more like a* Vultur *than a* Dove, *and a* Lion *than a* Lamb.

But I proceed to my next Reason, why it is Her Interest to Repeal those Penal Laws, (tho' a greater cannot be advanc'd to Men than Self-Preservation) and That is, *That She else breaks with a King heartily inclin'd to preserve Her by any Way that is not Persecuting, and whose Interest She once pursu'd at all Adventures, when more than She sees was suggested to Her by the Men of the Interest She opposed, in Favour of His Claim.* What then has befallen Her, that She changes the Course She took with such Resolutions of Perseverance? For bringing Him to the Crown with this Religion, could not be more Her Duty to His Title, or Her Interest to support Her own, than it is still, *To be fair with Him.* If She ow'd the One to Him, and to Christianity, She is not less indebted to Her self the other. Does He seek to impose His own Religion upon Her? By no Means. There is no Body would abhor the Attempt, or, at all Adventures, condemn it more than my self. What then is the Matter? *Why, He desires Ease for His Religion;* She does not think fit to consider Him in this, (No, not the King She brought with this Objection to the Crown) Certainly She is much in the Wrong, and shows Her self an *Ill Courtier,* (tho' it was become

42. For the Petition of Right, see ch. 2, p. 45, n. 26.

Her Calling) first, *To give Him Roast-Meat, then beat Him with the Spit.* Is not this to quit those High Principles of Loyalty and Christianity She valu'd Her self once upon, and what She can, provoke the Mischiefs She fears? Certainly this is dividing in Judgment from Him, that She has acknowledged to be *Her Ecclesiastical Head.*

My *Fifth Reason* is, That as the *Making* and *Executing* the *Penal Laws* for *Religion* affects all the several Parties of *Protestant Dissenters* as well as the *Papists* (the Judges in *Vaughan*'s Time, and he at the Head of them, giving it as their Opinion, they were equally exposed to those Laws) and that they are thereby naturally driven into an Interest with them; so it is at this Time greatly the Prudence of the *Church of England* to repeal them, for by so doing She divides that *Interest* that *Self-preservation* allows all Men to pursue, that are united by Danger: And since She is assured the *Papists* shall not have the less Ease, in this King's Time than if the Laws were Repealed, and that her Fears are not of the succeeding Reigns, how is their Repeal a greater Insecurity, especially, when by that, she draws into her Interest all the *Protestant Dissenters,* that are abundantly more considerable than the *Papists,* and that are as unwilling that *Popery* should be *National* as her self. For if this be not granted, see what Reputation follows to the *Church of England.* She tells the King she does not desire his Friends should be Persecuted, yet the Forbearance must not be by *Declaration,* to save the *Government,* nor by *Law,* to save her: and without one of these Warrants, every Civil Magistrate and Officer in *England* is Perjur'd that suffers them in that *Liberty against Law.* How can she be sincerely willing that should be done, that she is not willing should be done *Legally?*

But, *Sixthly,* the *Church of England* does not know but they or some other Party may at one Time or other prevail. It seems to me her *Interest* to set a good Example, and so to bespeak easy Terms for her self. I know of none intended, and believe no Body but her self can place her so low, yet if it were her Unhappiness, I think to have *Civil Property* secured out of the Question of Religion, and *Constraint* upon *Conscience* prevented by a Glorious *Magna Charta for the Liberty of it,* were not a Thing of ill *Consequence* to her *Interest.*[43]

43. To allay suspicions of James's motivations, some proposed a "new Magna Charta" to secure the civil rights of all regardless of their religious beliefs. For a critique, see Thomas Comber, *Three considerations proposed to Mr. William Penn, concerning . . . his new Magna Charta for liberty of conscience* (London, 1688).

Let us but consider what other Princes did for their own *Religion,* within the last *Seven Reigns,* when they came to the Crown, and we cannot think so soft and equal a Thing as an *Impartial Liberty of Conscience,* after all that has been said of a *Popish Successor,* an ordinary *Character* of a *Prince,* or a mean *Assurance* to us: This ought not to slip her Reflection. Besides, there is some Care due to Posterity: Tho' the present Members of her *Communion* may escape the *Temptation,* their Children may not: They may *change* the Religion of their Education, and Conscientiously chuse some other *Communion.* Would they submit the *Fortunes* they leave them to the *Rape* of Hungry *Courtiers, Bigots and indigent Informers,* or have their Posterity *Impoverish'd, Banish'd* or *Executed* for Sober and Religious *Dissent?* God knows into whose Hands these Laws at last may fall, what Mischief they may do, and to whom. Believe me, a King of the Humour of Sir *J. K.* of the *West,* or Sir *W. A.* of *Reading,* or Sir *R. B.* or Sir *S. S.* of *London,* would, with such *Vouchers,* quickly make a *Golgotha* of the *Kingdom.* If She thinks her self considerable in *Number* or *Estate,* She will have the more to lose. Let her not therefore Establish that in the Prejudice of others, that may in the Hands of others turn to her Prejudice.

Lastly, I would not have her miss the Advantage that is designed her by those that perhaps she thinks worst of. I dare say no body would willingly see the *Presbyterian* in her *Chair,* and yet that may happen to be the Consequence of her Tenaciousness in a little Time. For if the Aversion her Sons promote by wholesale against *Popery* should prevail, the Remains of it in her self are not like to escape that Reformation. I mean, her *Episcopal Government,* and the *Ceremonies* of her Worship, for which she has vex'd the most Conscientious People of this Kingdom above an Age past. And the *Presbyterian* being a Rich, Industrious and Numerous Party, as well among the Nobility and Gentry, as Trading and Country People, I cannot see but the next Motion, naturally speaking, is like to tend that Way; for other Parties, however well esteemed, may seem too great a Step of Reformation at once, and methinks she has tasted enough of that *Regiment,* to be once wise, and keep the *Ballance* in her own Hands. And certain it is, that nothing will so effectually do this, as the entreated Liberty of Conscience; for then there will be four Parties of Dissenters besides her self, to *Ballance* against any Designs that may *warp* or *byass* Things to their *Advancement.* And that which ought to induce the Church of *England* not a little to hasten as well as do the Thing, is this; She is now a Sort of National Church by *Power,* she will then be the Publick Church by Concurrence of all Parties. Instead of Enemies to invade or undermine her, they that should do it are made the Friends of her Safety by the Happiness they enjoy through her *Complacency:* And if any should be so unnatural or ungrateful to her, the Interest of the rest will oblige them to be her *Spies* and *Security* against the Ambition of any such *Party.* I do heartily pray to *God* that he would *enlighten the Eyes of her Leaders,* and give them good Hearts too, that *Faction may not prevail against Charity,* in the Name of Religion: And, above all, that she would not be proud of her Numbers, or stand off upon that Reflection; for that alone will quickly lessen them in a Nation loving Freedom as much as this we live in: And what appears in the Town is an ill Glass to take a Prospect of the Country by: There are Parishes that have Fifteen Thousand Souls in them, and if two come to Church it is Matter of Brag, tho' half the rest be sown among the several *Dissenting Congregations* of their Judgment. I would not have her mistaken, though *Popery* be an unpopular Thing, 'tis as certain she of a long Time has not been Popular, and on that Principle never can be: And if she should Plow with that Heifer now, and gain a little by the Aversion to Popery; when it is discerned that Popery does return to the civil Interest of the Kingdom they will quickly be Friends. For besides that, we are the easiest and best-natur'd People in the World to be appeased: There are those Charms in Liberty and Property to *English Nature,* that no Endeavours can resist or disappoint. And can we reasonably think the *Romanists* will be wanting in that, when they see it is their own (and perhaps their only) Interest to do so? These are the Arguments which, I confess, have prevailed with me to importune the *Church of England* to yield to the *Repeal of all the Penal Statutes,* and I should be glad to see them either well *refuted* or *submitted to.*

I shall now address my self to those of the *Roman Church,* and hope to make it appear it is their *Interest* to sit down thankfully with the *Liberty of Conscience* herein desired, and that a *Toleration and no more,* is that which all *Romanists* ought to be satisfied with. My *Reasons* are these: *First,* The *Opposition* that *Popery* every where finds: For in *Nothing* is the Kingdom so much of a Mind as in this *Aversion:* 'Tis no News, and so may be the better said and taken. I say then this *Unity,* this *Universality,* and this *Visibility* against *Popery,* make the *Attempt,* for more than *Liberty of Conscience,* too great and dangerous. I believe there may be some poor *silly Bigots* that hope bigger, and talk farther, but who can help that? there are weak People of all Sides, and they will be making a *Pudder:* But what's the *Language of their true Interest,* the Infallible Guide of the wiser Men? *Safety* certainly; and that in succeeding Reigns to chuse: And if so, their Steps must be modest, for they are *Watch'd* and *Number'd.* And tho' their Prudence should submit to their Zeal, both must yield to *Necessity,* whether they like it or no, What they convert upon the Square, *Perswasion* I mean, is their own, and much Good may it do them. But the Fear is not of this, and for compelling the averse *Genius* of the Kingdom, *they have not the Means,* whatever they would do if they had them: Which is my *Second Reason.* I say *they have not the Power,* and that is what we apprehend most. There are three Things that prove this in my *Opinion.* First, *their Want of Hands,* next, *Want of Time,* and lastly, *their Intestine Division;* which, whatever we think, is not Inconsiderable. They are *few,* we must all agree, to the Kingdom, upon the best Computation that could be made: Out of *Eighty Millions of People,* they are not *Thirty Thousand,* and those but thinly sown up and down the Nation; by which it appears that the Disproportion of the *Natural Strength* is not less than *Two Hundred and Seventy Persons to One.* So that *Popery* in *England* is like a *Spirit without a Body,* or, *a General without an Army.* It can hurt *no more, than Bullets without Powder,* or, *a Sword and no Hand to use it.* I dare say, there is not of that Communion, enough at once, to make all the Coal-Fires in *London,* and yet we are apprehensive they are able to consume *the whole Kingdom.* I am still more *afraid of her Fears* than of them; for tho' they seem high, she thinks their *Religion* in no Reign has appeared much lower.

O, but they have the King of their Side, and he has the Executive Power in his Hands! True, and this I call the *Artificial Strength of the Kingdom.* But I say, first we have his Word to bind him. And tho' some may think our Kings cannot be tyed by their People, certainly they may be tyed by themselves. What if I don't look upon the Act of both Houses to oblige the King, *his own Concession must;* and that may be given in an *Act of State.* I take the King to be as well obliged in *Honour and Conscience* to what he promises his People in another Method, as if it had been by his *Royal Assent in Parliament;* for an honest Man's Word is good every where, and why a King's should not I can't tell. 'Tis true, the Place differs, and the Voice comes with greater Solemnity, but why it should with greater Truth I know not. And if the *Church of* England will but be advised to give him the Opportunity of keeping his repeated Word with her, and not deprive her self of that Advantage by *Jealousies* and *Distances* that make her suspected, and may force him into another Conduct, I cannot help believing that the King will to a Tittle let her feel the Assurance and Benefit of his *Promises.*

But next, *we have his Age for our Security,* which is the *Second Proof, of the Second Reason,* why the *Papists* should look no farther than a *Toleration.* This is the Want of Time I mentioned. They have but *one Life in the Lease,* and 'tis out of their Power *to Renew;* and this Life has lived fast too, and is got within *Seven of Threescore;* A greater Age than most of his Ancestors ever attained. *Well, but he has an Army, and many Officers of his own Religion.* And if it be so, *What can it do?* It may suppress an *Insurrection,* but upon the Attempts we foolishly fear, they were hardly a Breakfast to the Quarters they live in. For if they were together, all the Confines or remote Parts of the Nation would rise like Grass upon them; and, if dispersed, to be sure they have not Strength for such an Attempt.

But if they are not sufficient, there is a Potent Prince not far off can help the Design, who is not angry with Protestancy at Home only. Suppose this, Is there not as potent *Naval Powers* to assist the *Constitution* of the *Kingdom* from such *Invasions?* Yes, *and Land One's too.* And as the *Protestant Governments* have more Ships than the other, so an equal *Land Force,* when by such Attempts to make *Popery* Universal, they are awakened to the Use of them: But certainly we must be very Silly to think the King should suffer so great a Shock to his own Interest, as admitting an Army of Foreigners to enter his Kingdom on any Pretence, must necessarily occasion. These *Bull Beggars,* and *Raw-heads and Bloody-Bones,* are the Malice of some and Weakness of others. But Time, that informs Children, will tell the *World the Meaning of the Fright.*

The *Third Proof* of my *Second Reason,* is, *The Intestine Division among themselves.* That *Division,* weakens a great *Body,* and renders a small one *harmless,* all will agree. Now, that there is such a Thing as *Division* among them is Town-talk. The *Seculars* and *Regulars* have ever been two *Interests* all the *Roman Church over,* and they are not only so here, but the *Regulars* differ among themselves. There is not a *Coffee-House* in Town that does not freely tell us that the *Jesuits* and *Benedictines* are at Variance, that Count *Da,* the Pope's Nuncio, and Bishop *Lyborn,* Dissent mightily from the *Politicks* of the first; Nay, t'other Day the Story was, *that they had prevailed entirely over them.* The *Lords* and *Gentlemen* of her *Communion* have as warmly contested about the *Lengths* they ought to go, *Moderation* seems to be the *Conclusion.* Together they are *little,* and can do little; and, divided, they are *Contemptible* instead of Terrible.

Lastly, The *Roman Church* ought to be *Discreet,* and think of nothing farther than the entreated general Ease, because it would be an Extreme that must beget another in the succeeding Reign. For, as I can never think her so weak as well as base, that after all her Arguments for the *Jus Divinum* of Succession, she should, in the Face of the World, attempt to violate it in the Wrong of One of another *Perswasion,* (for that were an Eternal Loss of her with Mankind.) So, if she does not, and yet is Extravagant, she only rises higher to fall lower than all others in another Reign. This were provoking their own Ruin. And, to say true, either Way would, as the *Second Letter has it, Discredit her for ever, and make true Prophets of those they had taken such Pains to prove false Witnesses.* And supposing her to reckon upon the Just Succession, nothing can recommend her, or continue her Happiness in a Reign of another Judgment, but this *Liberty equally maintained,* that other Perswasions, more numerous, for that Reason as well as for their own Sakes, are obliged to insure her. Here the Foundation is broad and strong, and what is built upon it has the Looks of *long Life.* The *Indenture* will at least be *quinque-partite,* and Parties are not so mortal as Men. And as this joyns, so it preserves Interest entire, which amounts to a *Religious Amity* and a *Civil Unity* at the worst.

Upon the whole Matter, I advise the Members of the *Roman Communion* in this Kingdom, to be moderate, 'tis their Duty, and it belongs to all Men to see it and feel it from them, and it behoves them mightily they should; for the first Part of this *Discourse* belongs to their *Hopes,* as well as to the *Church of England's Fears, viz. The Duty and Spirit of Christianity.* Next, Let them do *good Offices* between the King and his Excellent Children, for as that will be well taken by so affectionate a Father, so it gives the Lye to their Enemies Suggestions, and recommends them to the Grace and Favour of the Successors. And having said this, I have said all that belongs to them in particular. There is left only my Address to the *Protestant Dissenters,* and a General *Conclusion* to finish this *Discourse.*

Your Case, that are called *Protestant Dissenters,* differs mightily from that of the *Church of England and Rome.* For the first hath the *Laws* for her, the last the *Prince.* Those Laws are *against* you, and she is not willing they should be Repealed: The *Prince* offers to be kind to you if you please; Your *Interest,* in this *Conjuncture,* is the *Question.* I think none ought to be made, that it is the *Liberty of Conscience* desired, because you have much more Need of it, having neither *Laws* nor *Prince* of your Side, nor a Successor of any of your *Perswasions.* The *Fears* of *Popery* I know reach you; but it is to be remembred also, that if the Laws are not Repealed, there wants no *New Ones* to Destroy you, of the *Papists* making; so that every Fear you are taught to have of their Repeal, is against your selves. Suppose your *Apprehensions well grounded,* you can but be Destroy'd; Which is most comfortable for you to suffer, by *Law* or *without it?* The *Church of England, by her Penal Laws, and the Doctrine of Headship,* has Armed that *Religion* (as it falls out) to Destroy you. Nay, has made it a Duty in the King to do it, from which (he says) nothing but *an Act of Parliament* can absolve him, and that she is not willing to allow. And is it not as reasonable that you should seek their Repeal, that if you suffer from the *Papists,* it may be without *Human Law,* as well as against *Christ's Law,* as for the *Church of England* to keep them in Force, because if she suffers, it shall be against the *Laws* made to uphold her? For not repealing them, brings you an inevitable Mischief, and her, at most, but an uncertain Safety; tho' 'tis certain, she at the same Time will sacrifice you to it. And yet if I were in her Case, it would please me better to remove *Laws* that might reproach me, and stop my Mouth when turn'd against me, and be content; that if I suffer for my *Religion,* it is against the *Law of God, Christianity,* and the *Fundamentals* of the Old and True *Civil Government of my Country,* before such Laws helpt to spoil it. In short, you must either *go to Church,* or *Meet,* or *let fall your Worshipping of God* in the Way you believe. If the first, you are *Hypocrites,* and give away the Cause, and reproach your dead Brethren's Sincerity, and gratify the old Accusation of *Schism, Ambition,* &c. and finally lose the Hope and Reward of all your Sufferings. If the second, *viz.* that you *meet against Law,* you run into the Mouth of the *Government,* whose Teeth are to meet in you and Destroy you, *as by Law Established.* If the last, you deny your *Faith, overthrow your own Arguments, fall away from the Apostolical Doctrine of assembling together, and so must fall into the Hands of God, and under the Troubles of your own Consciences and Woundings of his Spirit, of which 'tis said,* who can bear them. So that nothing is plainer than that *Protestant Dissenters* are not oblig'd to govern themselves after such *Church of England Measures,* supposing her *Fears* and *Jealousies* better Bottom'd than they are: For they are neither in this King's Time in the same Condition, with her, if the *Penal Laws* remain in Force, nor like to be so, if she can help it, in the next Reign, if they are not repealed in this; so that they are to be certainly Persecuted now, in Hopes of an *uncertain Liberty* then. Uncertain both whether it will be in her *Power,* and whether she will do it if it be. The *Language* of *Fear* and *Assurance* are two Things, *Affliction* promises what *Prosperity* rarely performs. Of this the Promises made to induce the late King's *Restoration,* and the Cancelling of the former *Declaration,* and what followed upon both are a plain Proof. And tho' the last *Westminster Parliament* inclin'd to it; no Body so much opposed it as the *Clergy,* and the most *Zealous Sons of that Church:* And if they could or would not then see it to be reasonable, I can't see why one should trust to People so selfish and short-sighted. But if she will stoop to all those *Dissenting Interests* that are *Protestant,* it must either be by a *Comprehension,* and then she must part with her *Bishops,* her *Common-Prayer,* her *Ceremonies,* and this it self is but *Presbyterian;* (and she must go lower yet, if she will comprehend the rest) or, if not, she must *Persecute,* or give this *Liberty of Conscience* at last; which, that she will ever yield to uncompel'd, and at a Time too, when there is none to do it, while she refuses it under her present pressing Circumstances, I confess I cannot apprehend. But there is yet one Argument that can never fail to oblige your Compliance with the General Ease intreated, *viz. That the Penal Laws are against our Great Law of Property, and so void in themselves.* This has been the *Language* of every *Apology,* and that which, to say true, is not to be answered: How then can you decline to help their Repeal, that in *Conscience, Reason* and *Law,* you think void in their own Nature?

Lastly, There is nothing that can put you in a Condition to help your selves, or the *Church of England,* against the *Domination* of *Popery,* but that which she weakly thinks the Way to hurt you both, *viz. The Repeal of the Penal Laws.* For, as you are, you are *tyed* Hand and Foot, you are not your own Men, you can neither serve her nor your selves, you are fast in the Stocks of her Laws, and the Course she would have you take, is to turn *Martyrs* under them to support them: If you like the *Bargain* you are the best natur'd People in the World, and something more. And since *Begging* is in Fashion, I should desire no other *Boon;* for upon so plain a Loss of your Wits, your Estates will of Course fall a Stray to the Government, so that without the Help of a *Penal Law,* you make an admirable Prize.

I have no Mind to end so pleasantly with you, I have a sincere and Christian Regard to you and yours. *Be not Cozened, nor Captious, at this Juncture.* I know some of you are told, if you lose this Liberty, *you Introduce Idolatry,* and for *Conscience Sake* you cannot do it. But that's a pure Mistake, and improved, I fear, by those that know it so, which makes us the worse; for it is not *Introducing Idolatry, (taking for granted that Popery is so)* but saving the People from being Destroy'd that profess that *Religion.* If *Christ* and his *Apostles* had taken this Course with the World, they must have *Killed* them instead of *Converting* them. 'Tis your Mistake to think the *Jewish* rigorous *Constitution* is adequate to the *Christian Dispensation;* by no Means: That one Conceit of *Judaising Christianity* in our Politicks, has filled the World with *Misery,* of which this poor Kingdom has had it's Share. *Idolaters* are to be *Enlightned* and

Perswaded, as St. *Paul* did the *Athenians* and *Romans,*[44] and not *knocked on the Head,* which mends no Body. And, to say a *Christian Magistrate* is to do that, that a *Christian* can't do, is ridiculous; unless, like the *Bishop of Munster,* who goes like a Bishop one Part of the Day, and a Soldier the other, he is to be *a Christian in the Morning, and a Magistrate in the Afternoon.* Besides, 'tis one Thing to enact a *Religion National,* and *Compel Obedience to it,* (which would make this Case abominable indeed) and another Thing to take off *Christian Penalties* for the Sake of such Mistakes, since that is to give them Power to hurt others, and this only to save you from being hurt for *meer Religion.*

To conclude my Address to you, of all People, it would look the most disingenuous in you, and give you an Air, the least Sensible, Charitable and Christian, not to endeavour such an Ease, that have so much wanted it, and so often and so earnestly pressed it, even to Clamour. But that you should do it for their Sakes who have used you so, and that the Instruments of their Cruelty, the Penal Laws, *should from a Common Grievance become a Darling to any among you, will be such a Reproach to your Understandings and Consciences, that no Time or Argument can wipe off, and which I beseech God and you to prevent.*

The CONCLUSION.

I SHALL conclude with one Argument, that equally concerns you all, and that is this; You claim the *Character* of *Englishmen.* Now, to be an *Englishman,* in the Sense of the Government, is to be a *Freeman,* whether *Lord* or *Commoner,* to hold his Liberty and Possessions *by Laws of his own consenting unto,* and not to forfeit them upon Facts made Faults, by Humour, Faction, or Partial Interest prevailing in the Governing Part against the Constitution of the Kingdom; but for Faults only, that are such in the Nature of Civil Government; to wit, *Breaches of those Laws that are made by the whole, in Pursuance of common Right, for the Good of the Whole.*

This Regard must at no Time be neglected, or violated towards any one Interest; for the Moment we concede to such a Breach upon our *General Liberty,* be it from an Aversion we carry to the Principles of those we expose, or some little sinister and temporary Benefit of our own, we Sacrifice our selves in the Prejudices we draw upon others, or suffer them to fall under; for our

44. For Paul at Rome, see Acts 28:16–30; at Athens, Acts 17:15–34.

Interest in this Respect is common. If then as *Englishmen,* we are as mutually interested in the inviolable Conservation of each other's Civil Rights, as Men embark'd in the same Vessel are to save the Ship they are in for their own Sakes, we ought to Watch, Serve and Secure the Interest of one another, because it is our own to do so; and not by any Means endure that to be done to please some narrow Regard of any one Party, *which may be drawn in Example at some other Turn of Power to our own utter Ruin.*

Had this Honest, Just, Wise and English Consideration prevail'd with our Ancestors of all Opinions from the Days of *Richard* the Second, there had been less *Blood, Imprisonment, Plunder, and Beggary* for the *Government of this Kingdom* to answer for. Shall I speak within our own Knowledge, and that without Offence, there has been Ruin'd, since the late King's Restoration, above *Fifteen Thousand Families,* and more than *Five Thousand Persons* Dead under Bonds for Matters of *meer Conscience* to God: But who hath laid it to Heart? It is high Time now we should, especially when our King, with so much Grace and Goodness leads us the Way.

I beseech you all, if you have any Reverence towards God, and Value for the Excellent Constitution of this Kingdom, any Tenderness for your Posterity, any Love for your Selves, you would embrace this happy Conjuncture, and pursue a common Expedient; That since we cannot agree to meet in one *Profession of Religion,* we may entirely do it in this common civil Interest where we are all equally engaged; and therefore we ought for our own Sakes to seek one another's Security, that if we cannot be the Better, we may not be the worse for our Perswasions, in Things, that bear no relation to them, and in which, it is impossible we should Suffer, and the Government escape, that is so much concern'd in the civil Support and Prosperity of every Party and Person that belongs to it.

Let us not therefore uphold *Penal Laws* against any of our Religious Perswasions, nor make *Tests* out of each others Faiths, to exclude one another our civil Rights; for by the same Reason that denying *Transubstantiation* is made One to exclude a *Papist,* to own it, may be made one to exclude a *Church of England Man,* a *Presbyterian,* an *Independent,* a *Quaker,* and *Anabaptist:* For the Question is not who is in the right in Opinion, but whether he is not in Practice *in the wrong,* that for such an Opinion deprives his Neighbour of his common Right? Now 'tis certain there is not one of any Party, that would willingly have a Test made out of his Belief, to abridge him of his native Priviledge; and therefore neither the Opinion of *Transubstantiation* in the Papists, *Episco-*

pacy in the Church of *England* Man, *Free-will* in the Arminian, *Predestination* in the Presbyterian, *Particular Churches* in the Independent, *Dipping of adult People* in the Anabaptist, nor *not swearing* in the Quaker, ought to be made a *Test* of, to deprive him of the Comforts of his Life, or render him incapable of the Service of his Country, to which by a natural Obligation he is indebted, and from which, no Opinion can discharge him, and for that Reason, much less should any other Party think it fit, or in their Power to exclude him.

And indeed it were ridiculous to talk of giving Liberty of Conscience (which yet few have now the fore-head to oppose) and at the same Time imagine those *Tests* that do exclude Men that Service and Reward, ought to be continued: For though it does not immediately concern me, being neither *Officer* nor *Papist,* yet the Consequence is general, and every party, even the Church of *England,* will find her self concern'd upon Reflection; For she cannot assure her self it may not come to be her turn.

But, Is it not an odd Thing, that by leaving them on foot, every Body shall have Liberty of Conscience *but the Government?* For while a Man is out of Office, he is *Test*-free, but the Hour he is chosen to any Station, be it in the *Legislation* or *Administration,* he must *wiredraw* his Conscience to hold it, or be excluded with the Brand of Dissent: And can this be equal or wise? Is this the Way to employ Men for the good of the Publick, where *Opinion prevails above Virtue,* and *Abilities are submitted to the Humour of a Party;* surely none can think this a *Cure* for Division, or that Animosities are like to be prevented by the only Ways in the World that beget and heighten them. Nor is it possible that the ease that should be granted can continue long, when the *Party* in whose Favour they are not repeal'd, may thereby be enabled to turn the Point of the Sword again upon Dissenters.

I know *Holland* is given in Objection to this Extent of Freedom, where only *one Perswasion has the Government,* though the rest their Liberty: But they don't consider, first, *how much more* Holland *is under the Power of Necessity than we are.* Next, *That our Constitutions differ greatly.* For the first, 'tis plain, in the little compass they live in; the Uncertainty and Precariousness of the Means of their Subsistence: That as they are in more Danger of Drowning, so nearer ruin by any Commotion in the State, than other Countries are. *Trading* is their Support, *This,* keeps them busy, *That,* makes them Rich; and *Wealth,* naturally gives them *Caution* of the Disorders that may spoil them of it. This makes the governing Party wary how they use their Power, and the other Interests tender how they resist it; for upon it, they have Reason to fear a *Publick Desolation;* since *Holland* has not a natural and *Domestick Fund* to rely upon, or return to, from such National Disorders.

The next Consideration is as clear and cogent; our *Constitutions differ mightily:* For though they have the Name of a *Republick,* yet in their Choice, in order to the Legislature, they are much less free then we are: And since the *Freeholders* of all the Parties in *England* may Elect, which in *Holland* they can no more do than they can be chosen, there is good reason why all may be elected to serve their King and Country here, that in *Holland* cannot be chosen or serve. And if our Power to chuse be larger than theirs in *Holland,* we are certainly then a freer People, and so ought not to be confin'd, as they are, about what Person it is that must be chosen: Methinks it bears no Proportion, and therefore the Instance and Objection are improper to our Purpose.

But it is said by some, *That there cannot be two predominant Religions, and if the* Church of England *be not that,* Popery *by the King's Favour is like to be so.* It is certain that *two predominant Religions,* would be two Uppermosts at once, which is nonsense every where: But as I cannot see what need there is for the Church of *England* to lose her Churches or Revenues, so while she has them, Believe me, she is *Predominant* in the Thing of the World that lies nearest her Guides. But if I were to speak my Inclination, I cannot apprehend the Necessity of any *Predominant* Religion, understanding the Word with *Penal Laws* in the tail of it: The Mischief of it, in a Country of so many powerful Interests as this, I can easily understand, having had the Opportunity of seeing and feeling it too: And because nothing can keep up the Ball of Vengeance like such a *Predominant Religion,* and that *Penal Laws* and *Tests* are the Means of the Domination, I, for that Reason, think them fit to be Repeal'd, and let English Mankind say, *Amen.*

I do not love Quibling, but 'tis true, to a Lamentation, that there is little of the *Power of Religion* seen where there is such a predominant one, unless among those it Domineers over.

I conclude, they that are so *Predominant,* and they that seek to be so (be they who they will) move by the same Spirit and Principle, and however differing their Pretensions and Ends may be, the odds are very little to me, by which it is I must certainly be Opprest.

Dare we then *do* (for once) *as we would be done by,* and show the World, we are not Religious *without Justice,* nor Christians *without Charity:* That *False self* shall not govern us against *True self;* nor *Opportunity* make us Thieves to our Neighbours, for Gods Sake? The End of *Testing* and *Persecuting* under every Revolution of Government. If this we can find in our Hearts to do, and yet as Men, and as Christians, as English Men, we do but do our Duty, let the *Penal Laws* and *Tests* be Repeal'd; and in order to it, *Let us now take those Measures of Men and Things,* that may give our Wishes and Endeavours the best Success for the publick Good, that our *Posterity* may have more Reason to bless our Memories for their *Freedom* and *Security,* than for their *Nature* and *Inheritance.*

{ PART III }

General Principles and Specific Events

THE
Proposed Comprehension Soberly, and Not Unseasonably, Consider'd (1672)

ALTHOUGH the Benefits wherewith Almighty God has universally bless'd the whole Creation, are a sufficient Check to the Narrowness of their Spirits, who would unreasonably confine all Comforts of Life within the streight Compass of their own Party (as if to recede from their Apprehensions, whereof themselves deny any Infallible Assurance, were Reason good enough to deprive other Dissenters of Nature's Inheritance, and which is more peculiar, *England's Freedoms.*) Yet since it fares so meanly with those Excellent Examples, that many vainly think themselves then best to answer the End of their being born into the World, when by a *Severity,* which least of all resembles the *God of Love,* they rigorously prosecute the Extirpation of their Brethren: Let it not seem Unreasonable, or Ill-timed, that we offer to your more serious Thoughts, the great Partiality and Injustice, that seem to be the Companions of a *Comprehension,* since you only can be concerned at this Time, to prevent it, by a more Large and Generous Freedom.[1]

First, then, *Liberty of Conscience* (by which we commonly understand the free Exercise of any Dissenting Perswasion) is but what has been generally pleaded for, even by the *Warmest Sticklers* for a *Comprehension,* and without which it would be utterly impossible they should be comprehended: The Question then will be this, *What Ground can there be, why Some, and not All, should be Tolerated?* It must either respect *Conscience* or *Government:* If it be upon Matter of mere *Religion,* What Reason is there that one Party should be Tolerated, and another Restrained; since all those Reasons, that may be urged by that Party, which is *Comprehended,* are every whit as proper to the Party *Excluded?* For if the Former say, *They are Orthodox,* so say the Latter too; If the one urge, *It is impossible they should believe without a Conviction; that the Understanding cannot be Forced; that Mildness gains most; that the True Reli-*

1. Toleration referred to liberty of worship outside the Anglican church, whereas comprehension denoted the movement to enlarge the parameters of acceptable Anglican belief and practice to encompass orthodox Protestants.

gion never Persecuted; that Severity is most Unworthy of her; that Sound Reason is the only Weapon which can Disarm the Understanding; that Coercion doth rather Obdurate than Soften; and that they therefore chuse to be sincere Dissenters, rather than Hypocritical Conformists: The other Party says the same. *In fine,* There can be nothing said for Liberty of Conscience, upon Pure Conscientious Grounds, by any one Party in *England,* that every one may not be interested in, unless *Any* will undertake to judge that of *Five Sorts of Dissenters,* Two are really such on Convictions, and Three upon meer Design. But if such Sentence would be lookt upon as most Arrogant and Unjust, how can it be Reasonable, that those whom some endeavour to exclude, should be thus prejudg'd, and such as are comprehended, be therefore so only from a strong Opinion of their Reality: We may conclude then, that since Liberty of Conscience is what in it self *Comprehenders* plead, and that it is evident, to affirm this, or that, or the other Party *Orthodox,* is but a meer Begging of the Question. What may be urged for one, is forceable for any other: *Conscience* (not moveable but upon Conviction) being what all pretend themselves alike concerned in.

But they say, that such as are like to be comprehended, are Persons, *not Essentially* Differing; that it were pity to exclude them whose *Difference* is rather in Minute Matters, than any Thing Substantial, whereas you err in Fundamentals. But how Paradoxal soever such may please to think it, that we should therefore plead the Justice of taking those in, Some unkindly would have left out, we know not; however, we believe it most reasonable to do so; For certainly the Reason for Liberty or Toleration, should hold Proportion with the weighty Cause of Dissent, and the Stress Conscience puts upon it. Where Matters are Trivial, they are more blameable that make them a Ground for Dissent, than those who perhaps (were that all the Difference) would never esteem them worth contending for, much less that they should rend from that Church, they otherwise confess to be a True One: So that whoever are Condemnable, certainly those who have been Authors and Promoters of Separation upon meer Toys and Niceties, are not most of all others to be justified. Had they conscientiously offer'd some Fundamental Discontent, and pleaded the Impossibility of reconciling some Doctrines with their Reason or Conscience, yet promising quiet Living, and all Due Subjection to Government, they might have been thus far more excusable, that People would have had Reason to have said; Certainly small Matters could not have induc'd these Men to this Disgraceful Separation, nor any thing of this Life have tempted them to this so Great and Troublesome Alteration: *But to take Pet at a Ceremony, then Rend from the Church, set up a New Name and Model, gather People, raise Animosity, and only make fit for Blows,* by a Furious Zeal kindled in their Heads, against a few *Ineptiae,* meer Trifles; and being utterly vanquish'd from these Proceedings, to become most earnest Solicitors for a *Comprehension;* though at the same Time of hot Pursuit after this Privilege, to seek nothing more than to prevent others of Injoying the same Favour, under the Pretence of more *Fundamental Difference;* Certainly this shews, that had such Persons Power, they would as well Disallow of a *Comprehension* to those who are the Assertors of those Ceremonies they recede from, as that for meer Ceremonies they did at first Zealously Dissent, and ever since remain more Unjustifiably Fierce for such *Separation.* And truly, If there were no more in it than this, it would be enough for us to say, That some in *England* never Rent themselves from the Church at all, much less for little Matters: that they never endeavour'd her Exile, but she found them upon her Return, which they opposed not, nor yet since have any Ways sought to install themselves in her Dignities, or enrich themselves by her Preferments. We appeal then to all Sober Men, if what is generally called the *Episcopal* Party of *England,* can with Good Conscience, and True Honour disinherit those of their Native Rights, Peace, and Protection, and leave them as Orphans to the wide World, indeed a Naked Prey to the Devourer, who from first to last have never been concerned, either to endeavour their Ruin, or any Ways withstand their Return, whilst it may be some of those, who have been the most Vigorous in both, and that for *Circumstantial,* and not *Essential Differences,* may be reputed more deserving of a *Comprehension,* than we are of a *Toleration.*

But it will be yet said, *You are Inconsistent with Government, They are not, therefore You are Excluded, not out of Partiality, but Necessity.* What Government besides their own they are consistent with, we leave on the Side of Story to tell, which can better speak their Mind than we are either able or willing to do: But this give us Leave to say in General, If any apprehend us to be such as merit not the Care of our *Superiors,* because supposed to be *Destructive* of the *Government,* let us be call'd forth by Name, and hear our Charge; and if we are not able to answer the Unbyast Reason of Mankind, in Reference to our Consistency with the Peace, Quiet, Trade, and Tribute of these Kingdoms, then, and not before, deny us all Protection. But that Men should be concluded before heard, and so sentenced for what they really are not, *is like beheading them before they are Born.* We do aver, and can make it appear, that there is no one Party more Quiet, Subject, Industrious, and in the Bottom of their very Souls, greater Lovers of the Good Old *English* Government and Prosperity of these Kingdoms among the *Comprehended,* than, for ought we yet see, may be found among those who are like to be unkindly *Excluded;* However, if such we were in any one Point, *Cure rather than Kill us;* and seek the Publick Good *some cheaper way than by our Destruction;* Is there no *Expedient* to prevent Ruin? Let *Reason qualify Zeal,* and *Conscience Opinion.*

To Conclude, If the Publick may be secured, and Conscience freely exercised by all, for the same Reasons, it may by some (and since Liberty of Conscience, is Liberty of Conscience, and the Reasons for it, equivalent) We see not in the whole World, why any should be depriv'd of That, which others for no better Reasons are like to enjoy.

Let it not then be unworthy of such to remember, that God affords his refreshing *Sun to all;* The Dung-hill is no more excepted than the most delightful Plain, and his *Rain falls alike* both upon the Just and Unjust:[2] He strips not Mankind of what suits their Creaturely Preservation; *Christians* themselves have no more peculiar Privilege in the Natural Benefits of Heaven, than *Turks* or *Indians.* Would it not then be strange, that *Infidels* themselves, much less any Sort of *Christians,* should be deprived of Natural Privileges for meer *Opinion,* by those who pretend to be the *Best Servants of* that *God,* who shews them quite another Example, by the Universality of his Goodness as Creator; And *Believers in that Christ,* who himself preacht the *Perfection of Love, both to Friends and Enemies,* and laid down his Life to confirm it when he had done. If Men should love their Enemies, doubtless they ought at least to forbear their Friends: And though some Differences in Judgment about *Religion* be a sufficient Reason to excommunicate a Man the Air Ecclesiastical, yet nothing certainly of that Sort ought to Dis-privilege Men of their Air Natural and Civil to breath freely in: And let that *Good* our Superiors have observed to be the *Fruit of our Toleration,* not be weakned or blasted by an Untimely *Comprehension* of some, to the *Exclusion* of the rest; since the Reason holds the same for the less formidable Separatists, that may not be however any whit less Conscientious.

We will omit to mention, how much more Suitable it were to *State-Matters,* that all Parties should be kept upon an equal Poize, a Thing most true in it self,

2. Matthew 5:45.

and most secure to the *Publick Magistrate;* and will conclude at this Time, That though we no Ways design a *Mis-representing* of any, much less their *Exception,* and least of all their *Persecution;* yet, a *Comprehension* either respecting the *Persons* and their *Qualifications,* or their *Separation,* and the Grounds and Reasons of it, We seriously believe, can never be consistent with that *Conscience, Honor, Wisdom,* and *Safety,* that ought to be the *Mark,* those who are concerned in it, should take their Aim by. But if a *Comprehension* should at last be compass'd, it is not doubted by many wise Men, but it will be found as Impracticable as other *Acts* more seemingly *Severe* have been, and at last will necessitate to that well-order'd universal Toleration of all, who both profess and practise *Peace, Obedience, Industry,* and *Good Life,* which will best please Almighty God, and rejoyce the Hearts of all Good Men.

From Real Friends to KING *and* COUNTRY.

ENGLAND's *Great Interest, in the* CHOICE *of this* NEW PARLIAMENT *Dedicated to All Her* Free-Holders *and* Electors (1679)

SINCE it hath pleased *God* and the *King,* to begin to revive and restore to us our *Ancient Right of Frequent Parliaments,* it will greatly concern us, as to our present Interest, and therein the *Future Happiness of our Posterity,* to act at this Time with all the *Wisdom, Caution and Integrity we can.* For besides, that 'tis our own Business, and that if by a Neglect of this Singular Opportunity, we desert our Selves, and forsake our own Mercies, *We must expect to be Left of God, and Good Men too.* It may be there has never happened, not only in the Memory of the Living, but in the Records of the Dead, *so odd and so strange a Conjuncture as this we are under.* It is made up of so many unusual and important Circumstances (all affecting us to the very Heart) that whether we regard the Long Sitting of the *Late Parliament,* or it's abrupt and most unexpected *Dissolution,* or the *Prorogation* of the last, and it's surprising *Dissolution,* or the strong *Jealousies* of the People, and that *Universal Agitation* that is now upon the *Spirit of the Nation,* and the Reasons and Motives thereof (so far as we can reach them) *there seems never to have been a Time, wherein this Kingdom ought to show it self more Serious and Diligent in the Business of it's own Safety.*

To be plain with you, *All is at Stake:* And therefore I must tell you, That the Work of this Parliament is,

First, To pursue the Discovery and Punishment of the *Plot:* For that has been the *Old Snake in the Grass,* the *Trojan Horse,* with an Army in the Belly of it.[1]

Secondly, To remove, and bring to Justice, those *Evil Counsellors, and Corrupt and Arbitrary Ministers of State,* that have been so Industrious to give the King Wrong Measures, to turn Things out of their Ancient and Legal Channel of Administration, and Alienate his Affections from his People.

Thirdly, To Detect and Punish the *Pensioners* of the former *Parliament,* in

1. For the controversy surrounding the Popish Plot and the Exclusion Crisis of 1678–81, see the introduction.

the Face of the Kingdom: This Breach of Trust, being Treason against the Fundamental Constitution of our Government.

Fourthly, To secure to us the Execution of our *Ancient Laws by New Ones,* and, among the rest, such as relate to *Frequent Parliaments,* the only True Check upon *Arbitrary Ministers,* and therefore feared, hated, and opposed by them.

Fifthly, That we be secur'd from Popery and Slavery, and that *Protestant-Dissenters* be eased.

Sixthly, That in Case this be done, the King be released from his *Burdensome Debts* to the Nation, and eas'd in the Business of his Revenue. And let me be free with you, if you intend to save *Poor England,* You must take this General Measure, viz. *To guide and fix your Choice upon Men, that you have Reason to believe are Well-Affected, Able and Bold, To Serve the Country in these Respects.*

The Words of the *Writ,* (at least, the *Import* of them) are, *To Chuse Wise Men, Fearing God, and Hating Covetousness:* And what to do? says the same Writ, *To Advise the King of the Weighty Matters of the Kingdom.* Let us not then play the Fools or Knaves, to *Neglect or Betray the Common Interest of our Country by a base Election: Let neither Fear, Flattery, nor Gain Biass us.* We must not make our Publick Choice, the Recompence of *Private Favours* from our Neighbours; they must excuse us for that: The Weight of the Matter will very well bear it. This is our Inheritance, *All* depends upon it: Men don't use to lend their Wives, or give their Children to satisfie *Personal Kindnesses;* nor must we make a *Swop of our Birth-Right,* (and that of our Posterity too) *for a Mess of Pottage,*[2] *a Feast, or a Drinking-Bout;* there can be no Proportion here: And therefore none must take it ill, that we use our Freedom about that, which in it's Constitution, is the *Great Bulwark of all our Ancient English Liberties.* Truly, our not considering what it is to *Chuse a Parliament,* and how much *All* is upon the Hazard in it, may, at last, *Lose us Fatally by our own Choice.* For I must needs tell you, if we miscarry, it will be our *Own Fault;* we have no Body else to blame: For such is the Happiness of our Constitution, *That we cannot well be destroy'd, but by our selves: And what Man in his Wits, would Sacrifice his Throat to his own Hands?*

We, the *Commons of England,* are a great Part of the Fundamental Government of it; and *Three Rights* are so peculiar and inherent to us, that if we

2. See Genesis 25:29–34.

will not throw them away for *Fear* or *Favour,* for *Meat and Drink,* or those other little present Profits, *that Ill Men offer to tempt us with,* they cannot be altered or abrogated. And this I was willing to give you a brief Hint of, that you may know, *What Sort of Creatures you are, and what your Power is,* lest through Ignorance of your own Strength and Authority, you turn Slaves to the Humours of those, that properly and truly are but your Servants, and ought to be used so.

The *First of these Three Fundamentals is Property,* that is, *Right and Title to your own Lives, Liberties and Estates:* In this, every Man is a Sort of *Little Soveraign* to himself: No Man has Power over his *Person,* to Imprison or hurt it, or over his Estate to Invade or Usurp it: Only your own Transgression of the Laws, (and those of your own making too) lays you open to Loss; *which is but the Punishment due to your Offences,* and this but in Proportion to the Fault committed. So that the *Power of England* is a *Legal Power,* which truly merits the *Name of Government.* That which is not Legal, *is a Tyranny,* and not properly a *Government.* Now the Law is Umpire between *King, Lords and Commons,* and the *Right and Property is One in Kind through all Degrees and Qualities in the Kingdom:* Mark that.

The *Second Fundamental,* that is, *your Birthright and Inheritance,* is *Legislation,* or the Power of making Laws; *No Law can be made or abrogated in* England *without you.* Before *Henry* the Third's Time, your *Ancestors,* the *Freemen of England,* met in their own Persons, but their Numbers much increasing, the Vastness of them, and the Confusion that must needs attend them, making such Assemblies not practicable for Business, this Way of *Representatives* was first pitch'd upon as an Expedient, both to Maintain the *Common Right,* and to avoid the Confusion of those mighty Numbers. So that now, as well as then, *No Law can be made, no Money Levied, nor a Penny Legally Demanded* (even to defray the Charges of the Government) *without your own Consent:* Than which, tell me, what can be Freer, or what more Secure to any People?

Your *Third Great Fundamental Right and Priviledge is Executive,* and holds Proportion with the other Two, in Order to compleat both your *Freedom and Security,* and that is, *Your Share in the Judicatory Power, in the Execution and Application of those Laws, that you agree to be made.* Insomuch as *No Man, according to the Ancient Laws of this Realm, can be adjudg'd in Matter of* Life, Liberty, *or* Estate, *but it must be by the Judgment of* His Peers, *that is, Twelve Men of the Neighbourhood, commonly called a* JURY; though this hath been infringed by *Two Acts,* made in the late *Long Parliament,* One against the *Quakers* in Particular, and the Other against *Dissenters* in General, called, *An Act against Seditious Conventicles,* where Persons are adjudged Offenders, and Punishable without a *Jury;* which, 'tis hoped, this ensuing Parliament will think fit in their Wisdom to Repeal, though with less Severity, than one of the same Nature (*as to punishing Men without Juries*) was by *Henry* the Eighth, who, for Executing of it, Hang'd *Empson* and *Dudley.*

Consider with your selves, that there is nothing more your Interest, than for you to understand your *Right in the Government,* and to be constantly Jealous over it; for your *Well-Being* depends upon it's Preservation.

In all Ages there have been *Ill Men,* and we, to be sure, are not without them now, such as being conscious to themselves of ill Things, and dare not stand a *Parliament,* would put a *Final Dissolution* upon the very Constitution it self, to be safe, that so we might never see another.

But this being a Task too hard to compass, their next Expedient is, *To make them for their Turn,* by *Directing and Governing the Elections;* and herein they are very Artificial, and too often Successful: Which indeed is worse for us than if we had none. For thus the Constitution of *Parliaments* may be destroy'd by *Parliaments,* and we, who by Law are *Free,* may hereby come to be made *Slaves* by Law. If then you are *Free, and resolve to be so,* if you have any Regard to GOD's Providence, in giving you a *Claim to so Excellent a Constitution,* if you would not void *Your own Rights,* nor lay a *Foundation of Vassallage to your Unborn Followers, the Poor Posterity of your Loins,* for whom God and Nature, and the *Constitution of the Government,* have made you *Trustees,* then seriously weigh these following PARTICULARS.

I. In your present Election, *Receive no Man's Gift, or Bribe, to Chuse him;* but be assured, *That he will be False to you, that basely Tempts you to be False to your Country, your self, and your Children.* How can you hope to see GOD with Peace, *That turn Mercenaries in a Matter, on which depends the Well-Being of an Whole Kingdom, for present and future Times?* Since at a Pinch, *One Good Man Gains a Vote, and Saves a Kingdom;* And what does any *County,* or *Burgess-Town* in *England* know, but all may depend upon their making a *Good Choice?* But then to Sell the Providence of GOD, and the Dear-bought Purchase of your Painful Ancestors for a *Little Money,* (that after you have got it, *you know not how little a While you may be suffered to keep it*) is the *Mark of a Wretched Mind.* Truly, such ought not to have the Power of a *Freeman,* that would so abuse his own, and hazard other Men's Freedom by it: He deserves to be cast over Board, that would *Sink the Vessel,* and thereby drown the Company embark't with him.

Honest Gentlemen will think they give enough for the Choice, that pay their *Electors* in a constant, painful, and chargeable Attendance; But *Such as give Money to be Chosen, would get Money by being Chosen; they design not to serve you, but themselves of you; and then fare you well.* As you will answer it to Almighty GOD, I intreat you to shew your Abhorrence of this infamous Practice: It renders the very Constitution contemptible, that any should say, *I can be Chosen, if I will spend Money, or give them Drink enough:* And this is said not without Reason, *Elections,* that ought to be Serious Things, and Gravely and Reasonably perform'd, being generally made the Occasions of more Rudeness and Drunkenness, than any of the *Wild May-Games* in Use among us.

Thus by making *Men Law-Breakers,* they are it seems, made fit to *Chuse Law-Makers,* their *Choice being the Purchase of Excess.* But must we always owe our *Parliaments to Rioting and Drunkenness?* And must Men be made Uncapable of all *Choice,* before they chuse their *Legislators?* I would know of any of you all, if in a Difference about a Private Property, *an Horse or a Cow,* or any other Thing, you would be as easie, indifferent, and careless in chusing your *Arbitrators?* Certainly you would not: With what Reason then can you be unconcern'd in the Qualifications of Men, upon *whose Fitness and Integrity* depends all, you, and your Posterity may enjoy? Which leads me to the other PARTICULARS.

II. Chuse no Man that has been a *Reputed Pensioner;* 'tis not only against your *Interest,* but it is disgraceful to you, and the *Parliament* you chuse. The *Representative* of a Nation ought to consist of the Most Wise, Sober, and Valiant of the People; not Men of mean Spirits, or *Sordid Passions,* that would Sell the Interest of the People that chuse them, to advance their own, or be at the Beck of some Great Man, in Hopes of a *Lift to a Good Employ:* Pray beware of these. You need not be streightned, the Country is Wide, and the Gentry Numerous.

III. By no Means chuse a Man that is an *Officer at Court,* or whose Employment is *Durante bene placito,* that is, *At Will and Pleasure;* nor is this any Reflection upon the King, who being One Part of the Government, should leave the other Free, and without the least Awe or Influence, to bar, or hinder it's Proceedings. Besides, an *Officer* is under a Temptation to be *Byast,* and to say True, *An Office in a Parliament-Man,* is but a softer and safer Word for a *Pension:* The Pretence it has above the other, is the Danger of it.

IV. In the next Place, Chuse no *Indigent Person,* for those may be under a Temptation of abusing their Trust, to gain their own Ends: For such do not *Prefer* you, which should be the End of their *Choice,* but *Raise themselves by you.*

V. Have a Care of *Ambitious Men* and *Non-Residents,* such as live about Town, and not with their Estates, who seek Honours and Preferments *Above,* and little, or never, embetter the *Country* with their *Expences or Hospitality,* for they intend *themselves,* and not the Advantage of the *Country.*

VI. Chuse *No Prodigal or Voluptuous Persons,* for besides that they are not Regular enough to be *Law-Makers,* they are commonly *Idle;* and though they may wish well to *your Interest,* yet they will lose it, rather than their Pleasures; they will scarcely give their *Attendance,* they must not be relied on. So that such Persons are only to be preferred before those, *That are Sober to do Mischief:* Whose *Debauchery is of the Mind: Men of Unjust, Mercenary, and Sinister Principles; who, the Soberer they be to themselves, the Worse they are to you.*

VII. Review *the Members of the Last Parliaments, and their Inclinations and Votes, as near as you can learn them,* and the Conversation of the Gentlemen of your own Country, that were not Members, and take your Measures by both, by that which is your *True and Just Interest,* at this Critical Time of the Day, and you need not be divided or distracted in your Choice.

VIII. Rather take a *Stranger,* if recommended by an *Unquestionable Hand,* than a Neighbour *Ill Affected to your Interest.* 'Tis not pleasing a Neighbour, because Rich and Powerful, but *Saving England,* that you are to Eye: Neither Pay, or Return Private Obligations at the Cost of the Nation; let not such Engagements put you upon *Dangerous Elections,* as you love your Country.

IX. Be sure to have your Eye upon *Men of Industry and Improvement.* For those that are Ingenious, and Laborious to Propagate the *Growth of the Country,* will be very tender of weakning or impoverishing it: *You may trust such.*

X. Let not your Choice be flung upon *Men of Fearful Dispositions,* that will let *Good Sense, Truth,* and your *Real Interest* in any Point sink, rather than displease some one or other Great Man. If you are but Sensible of your *Own Real Great Power,* you will wisely chuse those, that will, by all Just and Legal Ways, firmly keep, and zealously promote it.

XI. Pray see, that you chuse *Sincere Protestants;* Men that don't play the *Protestant in Design,* and are indeed *Disguis'd Papists,* ready to pull off their Mask, when Time serves: You will know such by their *Laughing at the Plot, Disgracing the Evidence, Admiring the Traytor's Constancy,* that were forc'd to it, or their Religion and Party were gone beyond an *Excuse or an Equivocation.* The contrary, are Men that thank God for this Discovery, and in their Conversation Zealously direct themselves in an Opposition to the *Papal Interest,* which indeed is a Combination against *Good Sense, Reason and Conscience,* and to introduce a blind Obedience without (if not against) Conviction. And that Principle which introduces Implicit Faith and Blind Obedience in Religion, will also introduce Implicit Faith and Blind Obedience in *Government.* So that it is no more the Law in the one than in the other, but *the Will and Power of the Superior, that shall be the Rule and Bond of our Subjection.* This is that *Fatal Mischief Popery brings with it to Civil Society,* and for which such Societies ought to beware of it, and all those that are Friends to it.

XII. *Lastly,* Among these, be sure to find out, and cast your *Favour, upon Men of Large Principles,* such as will not Sacrifice *their Neighbour's Property* to the Frowardness of their own Party in Religion: *Pick out such Men, as will Inviolably Maintain Civil Rights, for all that will Live Soberly and Civily under the Government.*

Christ *did not Revile those that Reviled Him, much less did He Persecute those that did not Revile Him.* He rebuk'd His Disciples, that would have destroyed those that did not follow, and conform to them, saying, *Ye know not what Spirit ye are of; I came not to Destroy Men's Lives, but to Save them.* Which made the Apostle to say, *That the Weapons of their Warfare were not Carnal, but Spiritual.*[3] This was the *Ancient Protestant Principle,* and where *Protestants* Persecute for Religion, *they are False to their own Profession, and Turn* Papists *even in the worst Sense,* against whom their Ancestors did so stoutly exclaim. Read the *Book of Martyrs* of all Countries in *Europe,* and you will find I say True: *Therefore beware also of that Popery.* Consider, that such Partial Men don't love *England,* but a *Sect;* and prefer *Imposed Uniformity, before Virtuous and Neighbourly Unity.* This is that Disturber of Kingdoms and States, and until the *Good Man,* and not the *Opinionative Man,* be the Christian in the Eye of the Government, to be sure, while Force is used to propagate or destroy *Faith,* and *the outward Comforts of the Widow and Fatherless, are made a Forfeit for the Peaceable Exercise of their Consciences to God,* He that Sits in Heaven, and Judgeth Righteously, whose Eye pities the Oppressed and Poor of the Earth, will with-hold His Blessings from us.

O lay to Heart, the *Grievous Spoils and Ruins* that have been made upon

3. Luke 9:56–57; and 2 Corinthians 10:4.

your harmless Neighbours, for near these Twenty Years, who have only desired to enjoy their Consciences to God, according to the Best of their Understandings, and to Eat the Bread of Honest Labour, and to have but a *Penny for a Penny's-Worth* among you: *Whose Ox or Ass have they taken? Whom have they wronged? Or when did any of them offer you Violence? Yet Sixty Pounds have been distrained for Twelve, Two Hundred Pounds for Sixty Pounds. The Flocks been taken out of the Fold, the Herd from the Stall; not a Cow left to give Milk to the Orphan, nor a Bed for the Widow to lie on; whole Barns of Corn swept away, and not a Penny return'd;* and thus bitterly prosecuted even by Laws made against *Papists.* And what is all this for? *Unless their Worshipping of God according to their Conscience; for they injure no Man, nor have they offered the least Molestation to the Government.*

Truly, I must take Liberty to tell you, If you will not endeavour to redress these Evils in your Choice, I fear God will suffer you to fall into great Calamity by those you hate. You are afraid of *Popery,* and yet many of you practice it; For why do you fear it, but for it's *Compulsion* and *Persecution?* And will you *compel* or *persecute* your selves, or chuse such as do? If you will, pray let me say, *You hate the Papists, but not Popery.* But God defend you from so doing, and direct you to do, as you would be done by; that chusing such as love *England,* her *People,* and their *Civil Rights,* Foundations may be laid for that Security and Tranquillity, which the Children unborn may have Cause to rise up and bless your *Names* and *Memories* for. Take it in good Part, I mean nothing but *Justice* and *Peace* to all; and so conclude my self,

Your Honest Monitor and Old England's *True Friend,*

PHILANGLUS.

A Letter from a Gentleman in the Country, to His Friends in London, upon the Subject of the Penal Laws and Tests (1687)

Quod tibi non vis fieri, alteri non feceris[1]

Printed in the Year 1687.

Gentlemen,

I WONDER mightily at the News you send me, that so many of the Town are averse to the *Repeal* of the Penal Statutes; surely you mean the Clergy of the present Church, and those that are Zealous for their Dignity and Power: For what part of the Kingdom has felt the Smart of them more, and at all times, and on all occasions represented their mischief to the Trade, Peace, Plenty and Wealth of the Kingdom, so freely as the Town has always done? But you unfold the Riddle to me, when you tell me, *'tis for fear of Popery,* tho I own to you, I cannot comprehend it, any more then you do Transubstantiation: For that we should be afraid of Popery for the sake of Liberty, and then afraid of it because of Persecution, seems to me absurd, as it is, that Liberty should be thought the high way to Persecution. But because they are upon their fears, pray let me tell you mine, and take them among the rest in good part.

If the *Romanists* seek ease by Law, 'tis an Argument to me they desire to turn good Countrymen, and take the Law for their Security, with the rest of their Neighbours; and a greater Complement they cannot put upon our English Constitution, nor give a better pledge of their desires to be at peace with us. But if we are so Tenacious as we will keep on foot the greatest blemish of our Reformation, viz. our *Hanging, Quartering, Plunder Banishing Laws;* Is it not turning them out of this quiet course, and telling them if they will have ease, they must get it as they can, for we will never conceed it? And pray tell me if this be not thrusting them upon the methods we fear they will take, at the same time that we give that, for the reason why we do so.

If Law can secure us, which is the plea that is made, we may doubtless find an expedient in that which may repeal these, if the danger be not of Liberty it self, but of our loosing it by them at last; for there is no mischief the wit

1. Do not do to others what you would not want done to you.

of man can invent, that the wit of man cannot avoid. But that which I confess makes me melancholy, is that methinks we never made more haste to be confined; no not in the business of the *Declaration of Indulgence*, when in the name of Property that was actually damn'd, which at least reprieved it; and the price the Church of *England* gave for it, *viz.* her promise of a legal ease, actually failed us: For instead of saving our selves from Popery, we are by these partialities provoking it every day, and methinks foolishly for our own safety; because there can be no other end in doing so, then securing that Party which calls it self the *Church of England,* that is in her Constitution none of the best Friends to Property; for mens Liberties and Estates are by her Laws made forfeitable for Non-conformity to Her: And I Challenge the Records of all time since Popery got the Chair in *England,* to produce an eight part of the Laws, to ruin men or Conscience, that have been made since the other has been the national Religion, which is, I say, a scandal to the Reformation.

She says, she is afraid of Popery, because of its Violence, and yet uses Force to compel it; *Is not this resisting Popery with Popery?* which we shall call loving the Treason but hating the Traytor: She would have Power to Force or Destroy others, but they should not have Power to Force or Destroy her, no not to save themselves: Shift the hand never so often, this *Weapon* is still the same. 'Twere happy therefore that all Parties were disarm'd of this Sword, and that it were put where it ought only to be, in the Civil Magistrates hand, to terifie Evil Doers, and cherish those that do well, remembering S *Peter's* saying (in *Cornelius*'s case) for an Example, *I perceive now of a truth that God is no respecter of Persons, but those that fear him, and work Righteousness in all Nations shall be accepted:*[2] Else what security does the Church of *England* give to the great body of her Dissenters that she will not do what she fears from Popery, when she has a Prince of her own Religion upon the Throne, that has made so fair a Progress these last six and twenty Years in ruining families, for nonconformity under Princes of an other Perswasion. Come, Interest will not lye, she fears Liberty, as much as Popery: Since those that want, and plead for the one, are an hundred times more in number than the Friends of the other, and all of her side, that Popery should not mount the Chair: So that she would get more then she would lose by the Repeal, if an equal desire to subject both Popish and Protestant Dissenters to her Power and Government be not the Principle she walks by in her present Aversion.

2. Acts 10:34–35.

And to shew you that this is the case, and that her aversion to Popery is a sham to the Liberty desired, the Dissenters are of no use to her, while the penal Laws are on foot; for by them they are put in the power of a Prince of the Religion of the Church she fears; but the moment they are repealed, so far as concerns the preventing Popery to be national, the Dissenters are equally interested with the Church of *England* against it. But then here is the mischief; This Liberty takes the Rod out of her hand; she can no more *whip people into her Churches,* and she perhaps may modestly suspect her own vertue and ability to preach them thither.

In short, if she were in earnest against Popery, more then in love with her own Power and Grandure; that is, if the World were not in the way, she would rejoyce to deliver Men of her own Religion, that are so much more numerous then the Papists, that they might ballance against her fears of their prevailing: But to cry she is for Liberty to Protestant Dissenters, and make the demonstration of it, her *keeping up the Laws that ruin them,* and then say it is for fear of the Religion the Prince owns, and yet force them into his hands by doing so, is, I must confess, something incomprehensible.

Besides, properly and naturally speaking, the Church of *England* is the People of *England,* and when its apply'd to a Party, 'tis a Faction to the whole; and that Title has no more Truth in it, then 'tis sence to say the Roman Catholick Church, which in English, is a particular Universal Church: And pray is there no room left to consider this hard case of the Kingdom? I hope the civil Magistrate will, who is the supream Pastor of this civil Church on Earth. Is she then no more then a Party? no certainly. And how great a one, a true Liberty of Conscience would best tell us, and that is the true reason, and not Popery, that she is tender in the point.

I conclude then, that whilst those of that Religion only desire to be upon the Level with others; I mean upon *Native Rights,* the *Great Charter,* what we all of us call, our *Birth-right,* let us not refuse it, lest God suffer them to prevail to curb our partiallity. There are Laws enough to punish Offenders against the State, if these were repealed, and not condemn People by *Anticipation. That Law which catches a Protestant will catch a Papish Traytor, Riotor or Seditious Person.* Again, let us reflect, that we have a Prince of Age, and more honour; the prospect of three excellent Princes of the Protestant Religion, the paucity of the Papists, the number of the Enemies of their Communion, their unity in that aversion: what greater security can we have in the World? *Policy, Honour, Religion, Number, Unity, ay, Necessity too,* conspire to make us safe: for all these are concerned in the means of our preservation; unless our fears and our follies should prevail: which I confess I apprehend most; for they will be deserted of God, that forsake him and themselves too; *who dare do a certain evil that a supposed good may come of it,*[3] *contradict their own Principles, deny what they expect, sow what they would not reap, do to others what they would not that others should do to them:* But there is a God in Heaven, and he is just: He will meet to us what we measure to one another, and his Judgment is inevitable. I therefore advise the Church of *England* to be as ready in her Christian complyances as is possible: *First,* because it is impious to keep up distroying Laws for Religion, when her Saviour tells her upon this very Question, *That he came not to destroy mens lives but to save them.*[4] *Secondly,* Because by this she will wipe off the Reproach she throws by continuing them, upon her own Apologies for Liberty of Conscience, when under the wheel of Power. *Thirdly,* Because Liberty to the Papists by Law, is bringing them into the legal interest of the Kingdom, and will prevent the force, they may else be driven to, by being made and left desperate: For its not to be thought they will willingly pay the reckoning in another Reign, if by any means they can prevent it; and keeping up the penal Laws can be no security to the Church of *England* from such attempts, though they may provoke them upon her. *Fourthly,* She hereby saves her dissenters; and if it be really her inclination to do so, she has no other way, and this unites them to her in affection and interest, if not in Worship. But if on the contrary she persists obstinately to refuse this national paciffick; the dissenters, I hope, will consider their honest Interest, *Conscience and Property,* and to imbrace those oppertunities to secure them, that God in his all-wise providence is pleased to yield them in this conjuncture. Thus Gentlemen, you have my thoughts upon your News, pray communicate them to our acquaintance, and believe that I am, Yours, &c.

POST-SCRIPT.

For the *Tests* that *are* so much discoursed of, I shall only say, that 'tis, an other mystery of the Times to me, how the Church of *England,* that was against the *Exclusion,* can be for them that were design'd for a *Preamble* to it; since in

3. Romans 3:8.
4. Luke 9:56–57.

so doing, she is for that which was contrived to introduce the *Exclusion* she was so Zealously against.[5] I confess I never understood her very well, and she grows more and more unintelligible; but this I know, that she must either be sorry for what she has done, or she did not know what she did. The first reflects upon her Loyalty, the last upon her understanding; and because I think that the least, and likeliest evil, I conclude she is no infallible Guide upon the Question.

Another thing you tell me, that gives great offence is, his Majesties turning out Protestants, and putting in People of his Religion. This I conceive a fault, that the Church of *England* is only answerable for. Other Princes have been so unhappy as to Suffer *Tests* and *Marks* of distinction that have broken and disorder'd their Kingdoms, by depriving those of their Temporal comforts, that would not receive them; and this People, esteemed a mighty grievance; and were frequent and elegant in their complaints about it. We have a King now, that would remove these *Marks* of distinction, and secure all men upon their native Right and Bottom, That all Parties might sit safely under their own Vine, and under their own Fig-tree;[6] so that now, *who is for Liberty?* becomes the *Test.* Are they then fit to be trusted that are out of his Interest, and against the Liberty he is for, and the Nation wants and craves? Or is it good-sense, that he (who is mortal as well as other men) should leave the Power in those hands, that to his face show their aversion to the Friends of his Communion tho he offers to maintain her still? She had the offer to keep them, upon that Principle that must heal and save the Kingdom, *Liberty of Conscience:* which shows the King was willing to be served by her sons to chuse, if upon the same general Principle with himself: wherefore 'tis the Gentlemen of the Church of *England* that turn themselves out of power, rather than endure Liberty of Conscience to others; and shall this Vice be their Vertue. They must be heartily in love with persecution that can sacrifice their Places to the upholding of penal Laws for Religion, because they would not let others, not only, not come in, but not live at their own Charges: A fine thing to suffer for, Their Ancestors were Martyers by penal Laws, but these for them. The cause is chang'd whatever they think, and I am afraid they are chang'd too for want of thinking. I Profess, I pity them with all my Heart, and wish them more

5. On the Test Act and Exclusion Crisis, see the introduction.

6. 1 Kings 4:25.

Wit, and better Consciences next time against next time, if ever they have it; for these, if they will believe me, will hardly ever make so good a Bargin for them, as they have lost by them. More of this, if you like it, next time, and till then, Adieu.

FINIS.

{ PART IV }

An Expanding Vision for the Future

An ESSAY towards the *Present* and *Future* Peace of *Europe* by the Establishment of an *European* DYET, PARLIAMENT, or ESTATES (1693)

Beati Pacifici. Cedant Arma Togae[1]

To the READER.

Reader,

I *HAVE undertaken a Subject that I am very sensible requires one of more sufficiency than I am Master of to treat it, as, in Truth, it deserves, and the groaning State of* Europe calls for; *but since Bunglers may stumble upon the Game, as well as Masters, though it belongs to the Skilful to hunt and catch it, I hope this Essay will not be charged upon me for a Fault, if it appear to be neither Chimerical nor Injurious, and may provoke abler Pens to improve and perform the Design with better Judgment and Success. I will say no more in Excuse of my self, for this Undertaking, but that it is the Fruit of my solicitous Thoughts, for the Peace of* Europe, *and they must want Charity as much as the World needs Quiet, to be offended with me for so* Pacifick *a Proposal. Let them censure my Management so they prosecute the Advantage of the Design; for 'till the* Millenary *Doctrine be accomplished, there is nothing appears to me so beneficial an Expedient to the Peace and Happiness of this Quarter of the World.*

1. Blessed are the peacemakers (Matthew 5:9); Let arms yield to the toga (refers to the Roman custom of generals laying down their swords and taking up the toga upon entering Rome, as a symbol of setting aside their military command and entering into their civic role).

An ESSAY *towards the Present and Future* PEACE of EUROPE, *&c.*

Sect. I. *Of PEACE, and it's Advantages.*

HE MUST not be a Man, but a Statue of Brass or Stone, whose Bowels do not melt when he beholds the bloody *Tragedies* of this War, in *Hungary, Germany, Flanders, Ireland,* and at Sea. The Mortality of sickly and languishing Camps and Navies, and the mighty Prey the Devouring Winds and Waves have made upon Ships and Men since 88.[2] And as this with Reason ought to affect human Nature, and deeply Kindred, so there is something very moving that becomes prudent Men to consider, and that is the vast Charge that has accompanied that Blood, and which makes no mean Part of these *Tragedies;* Especially if they deliberate upon the uncertainty of the War, that they know not how or when it will end, and that the Expence cannot be less, and the Hazard is as great as before. So that in the Contraries of Peace we see the Beauties and Benefits of it; which under it, such is the Unhappiness of Mankind, we are too apt to nauseate, as the full Stomach loaths the Honey-Comb; and like that unfortunate Gentleman, that having a fine and a good Woman to his Wife, and searching his Pleasure in forbidden and less agreeable Company, said, when reproach'd with his Neglect of better Enjoyments, *That he could love his Wife of all Women, if she were not his Wife,* tho' that increased his Obligation to prefer her. It is a great Mark of the Corruption of our Natures, and what ought to humble us extremely, and excite the Exercise of our Reason to a nobler and juster Sense, that we cannot see the Use and Pleasure of our Comforts but by the Want of them. As if we could not taste the Benefit of Health, but by the Help of Sickness; nor understand the Satisfaction of Fulness without the Instruction of Want; nor, finally, know the Comfort of Peace but by the Smart and Penance of the Vices of War: And without Dispute that is not the least Reason that God is pleased to Chastise us so frequently with it. What can we desire better than *Peace,* but the *Grace* to use it? *Peace* preserves our Possessions; We are in no Danger of Invasions: Our Trade is free and safe, and

2. England under William III was at war almost constantly in opposing James II's attempts to retake the throne and in heading a Grand Alliance against France.

we rise and lye down without Anxiety. The Rich bring out their Hoards, and employ the poor Manufacturers: Buildings and divers Projections, for Profit and Pleasure, go on: It excites Industry, which brings Wealth, as that gives the Means of Charity and Hospitality, not the lowest Ornaments of a Kingdom or Commonwealth. But War, like the Frost of 83, seizes all these Comforts at once, and stops the civil Channel of Society. The Rich draw in their Stock, the Poor turn Soldiers, or Thieves, or Starve: No Industry, no Building, no Manufactury, little Hospitality or Charity; but what the Peace gave, the War devours. I need say no more upon this Head, when the Advantages of Peace, and Mischiefs of War are so many and sensible to every Capacity under all Governments, as either of them prevails. I shall proceed to the next Point. *What is the best Means of Peace,* which will conduce much to open my Way to what I have to propose.

Sect. II. *Of the Means of Peace, which is* Justice *rather than War.*

AS *JUSTICE* is a Preserver, so it is a better Procurer of *Peace* than War. Tho' *Pax quaeritur bello,* be an usual Saying, *Peace is the End of War,* and as such it was taken up by *O. C.* for his Motto:[3] Yet the Use generally made of that expression shews us, that properly and truly speaking, Men seek their Wills by *War* rather than Peace, and that as they will violate it to obtain them, so they will hardly be brought to think of Peace, unless their Appetites be some Way gratified. If we look over the Stories of all Times, we shall find the Aggressors generally moved by Ambition; the Pride of Conquest and Greatness of Dominion more than Right. But as those *Leviathans* appear rarely in the World, so I shall anon endeavour to make it evident they had never been able to devour the Peace of the World, and ingross whole Countries as they have done, if the *Proposal* I have to make for the Benefit of our present Age had been then in Practice. The Advantage that Justice has upon War is seen by the Success of *Embassies,* that so often prevent War by hearing the *Pleas* and *Memorials* of *Justice* in the Hands and Mouths of the *Wronged Party.* Perhaps

3. Oliver Cromwell.

it may be in a good Degree owing to *Reputation* or *Poverty,* or some particular *Interest* or *Conveniency* of *Princes* and *States,* as much as *Justice;* but it is certain, that as War cannot in any Sense be justified, but upon Wrongs received, and Right, upon Complaint, refused; so the Generality of Wars have their Rise from some such Pretension. This is better seen and understood at Home; for that which prevents a Civil War in a Nation, is that which may prevent it Abroad, *viz. Justice;* and we see where that is notably obstructed, War is Kindled between the *Magistrates* and *People* in particular Kingdoms and States; which, however it may be unlawful on the Side of the *People,* we see never fails to follow, and ought to give the same Caution to *Princes* as if it were the Right of the People to do it: Tho' I must needs say, *the Remedy is almost ever worse than the Disease:* The Aggressors seldom getting what they seek, or performing, if they prevail, what they promised. And the *Blood and Poverty* that usually attend the Enterprize, weigh more on Earth, as well as in Heaven, than what they lost or suffered, or what they get by endeavouring to mend their *Condition,* comes to: Which *Disappointment* seems to be the Voice of Heaven, and Judgment of God against those violent Attempts. But to return, I say, *Justice is the Means of Peace,* betwixt the *Government* and the *People,* and one *Man* and *Company* and another. It prevents *Strife,* and at last ends it: For besides *Shame* or *Fear,* to contend longer, he or they being under *Government,* are constrained to bound their *Desires* and *Resentment* with the *Satisfaction* the Law gives. Thus *Peace* is maintain'd by *Justice,* which is a Fruit of *Government,* as *Government,* is from *Society,* and *Society* from *Consent.*

Sect. III. *GOVERNMENT, it's Rise and End under all Models.*

G*OVERNMENT* is an Expedient against *Confusion;* a Restraint upon all *Disorder;* Just Weights and an even Ballance: That one may not injure another, nor himself, by *Intemperance.*

This was at first without *Controversie, Patrimonial,* and upon the Death of the Father or Head of the Family, the eldest Son, or Male of Kin succeeded. But Time breaking in upon this Way of Governing, as the World multiply'd, it fell under other *Claims* and *Forms;* and is as hard to trace to it's Original, as are the Copies we have of the first Writings of *Sacred* or *Civil* Matters. It is certain the most Natural and Human is that of *Consent,* for that binds freely (as I may say) when Men hold their *Liberty* by true *Obedience* to Rules of their own making. No Man is Judge in his own Cause, which ends the *Confusion* and *Blood* of so many *Judges* and *Executioners.* For out of *Society* every Man is his own *King,* does what he lists, at his own Peril: But when he comes to incorporate himself, he submits that *Royalty* to the *Conveniency* of the *Whole,* from whom he receives the Returns of *Protection.* So that he is not now his own Judge nor Avenger, neither is his *Antagonist,* but the *Law,* in indifferent Hands between both. And if he be Servant to others that before was free, he is also served of others that formerly owed him no *Obligation.* Thus while we are not our own, every Body is ours, and we get more than we lose, the Safety of the *Society* being the Safety of the *Particulars* that constitute it. So that while we seem to submit to, and hold all we have from *Society,* it is by *Society* that we keep what we have.

Government then is the *Prevention* or *Cure* of *Disorder,* and the Means of *Justice,* as that is of *Peace:* For this Cause they have *Sessions, Terms, Assizes* and *Parliaments,* to over-rule Men's *Passions* and *Resentments,* that they may not be *Judges* in their own *Cause,* nor *Punishers* of their own *Wrongs,* which as it is very incident to Men in their *Corrupt State,* so, for that Reason, they would observe no Measure; nor on the other Hand would any be easily reduced to their Duty. Not that Men know not what is right, their Excesses, and wherein they are to blame: by no Means; nothing is plainer to them: But so depraved is Human Nature, that without Compulsion, some Way or other, too many would not readily be brought to do what they know is right and fit, or avoid what they are satisfy'd they should not do: Which brings me near to the Point I have undertaken; and for the better Understanding of which, I have thus briefly treated of *Peace, Justice* and *Government,* as a necessary *Introduction,* because the Ways and Methods by which *Peace* is preserved in particular *Governments,* will help those *Readers,* most concerned in my Proposal, to conceive with what Ease as well as Advantage the Peace of *Europe* might be procured and kept; which is the End designed by me, with all Submission to those Interested in this little *Treatise.*

Sect. IV. *Of a General Peace, or the Peace of* Europe, *and the Means of it.*

IN MY first Section, I shewed the *Desirableness of Peace;* in my next, the Truest Means of it; to wit, *Justice, Not War.* And in my last, that this Justice was the Fruit of *Government,* as Government it self was the Result of *Society;* which first came from a Reasonable Design in Men of Peace. Now if the *Soveraign Princes of Europe,* who represent that Society, or Independent State of Men that was previous to the Obligations of Society, would, for the same Reason that engaged Men first into Society, *viz. Love of Peace and Order,* agree to meet by their Stated Deputies in a *General Dyet, Estates,* or *Parliament,* and there Establish Rules of Justice for Soveraign Princes to observe one to another; and thus to meet Yearly, or once in Two or Three Years at farthest, or as they shall see Cause, and to be Stiled, *The Soveraign or Imperial Dyet, Parliament, or State of Europe;* before which Soveraign Assembly, should be brought all Differences depending between one Soveraign and another, that cannot be made up by private Embassies, before the Sessions begins; and that if any of the Soveraignties that Constitute these Imperial States, shall refuse to submit their Claim or Pretensions to them, or to abide and perform the Judgment thereof, and seek their Remedy by Arms, or delay their Compliance beyond the Time prefixt in their Resolutions, all the other Soveraignties, United as One Strength, shall compel the Submission and Performance of the Sentence, with Damages to the Suffering Party, and Charges to the Soveraignties that obliged their Submission: To be sure *Europe* would quietly obtain the so much desired and needed Peace, to *Her harrassed Inhabitants;* no Soveraignty in *Europe,* having the Power, and therefore cannot show the Will to dispute the Conclusion; and, consequently, *Peace* would be procured, and continued in *Europe.*

Sect. V. *Of the Causes of Difference, and Motives to Violate Peace.*

THERE appears to me but Three Things upon which Peace is broken, viz. To *Keep,* to *Recover,* or to *Add. First,* To Keep what is One's Right, from the Invasion of an Enemy; in which I am purely *Defensive. Secondly,* To Recover, when I think my self Strong enough, that which by Violence, I, or my Ancestors have lost, by the Arms of a Stronger Power; in which I am Offensive: Or, *Lastly,* To increase my Dominion by the Acquisition of my Neighbour's Countries, as I find them Weak, and my self Strong. To gratify which Passion, there will never want some Accident or other for a Pretence: And knowing my own Strength, I will be my own *Judge and Carver.* This *Last* will find no Room in the *Imperial States:* They are an unpassable Limit to that Ambition. But the other *Two* may come as soon as they please, and find the Justice of that Soveraign Court. And considering how few there are of those *Sons of Prey,* and how early they show themselves, it may be not once in an Age or Two, this Expedition being Established, the Ballance cannot well be broken.

Sect. VI. *Of Titles, upon which those Differences may arise.*

BUT I easily foresee a Question that may be answered in our Way, and that is this; *What is Right? Or else we can never know what is Wrong: It is very fit that this should be Established.* But that is fitter for the Soveraign States to resolve than me. And yet that I may lead a Way to the Matter, I say that Title is either by a long and *undoubted Succession,* as the Crowns of *Spain, France* and *England;* or by *Election,* as the Crown of *Poland,* and the *Empire;* or by *Marriage,* as the Family of the *Stewarts* came by *England;* the *Elector of Brandenburgh,* to the Dutchy of *Cleve;* and we, in Ancient Time, to divers Places abroad; or by *Purchase,* as hath been frequently done in *Italy* and *Germany;* or by Conquest, as the *Turk* in *Christendom,* the *Spaniards* in *Flanders,* formerly mostly in the *French* Hands; and the *French* in *Burgundy, Normandy, Lorrain, French-County,* &c. This last, Title is, Morally Speaking, only Questionable. It has indeed obtained a Place among the Rolls of Titles, but it was engross'd and recorded by the Point of the Sword, and in Bloody Characters. What cannot be controuled or resisted, must be submitted to; but all the World knows the Date of the length of such Empires, and that they expire with the Power of the Possessor to defend them. And yet there is a little allowed to Conquest to, when it has the Sanction of Articles of Peace to confirm it: Tho' that hath not always extinguished the Fire, but it lies, like Embers under Ashes, ready to kindle so soon as there is a fit Matter prepared for it. Nevertheless, when Conquest has been confirmed by a Treaty, and Conclusion of

Peace, I must confess it is an Adopted Title; and if not so Genuine and Natural, yet being engrafted, it is fed by that which is the Security of *Better Titles, Consent.* There is but one Thing more to be mentioned in this Section, and that is from what Time Titles shall take their Beginning, or how far back we may look to confirm or dispute them. It would be very bold and inexcusable in me, to determine so tender a Point, but be it more or less Time, as to the last General Peace at *Nimeguen,*[4] or to the commencing of this War, or to the Time of the Beginning of the Treaty of Peace, I must submit it to the Great Pretenders and Masters in that Affair. But something every Body must be willing to give or quit, that he may keep the rest, and by this Establishment, be for ever freed of the Necessity of losing more.

Sect. VII. *Of the Composition of these Imperial States.*

THE Composition and Proportion of this *Soveraign Part,* or *Imperial State,* does, at the first Look, seem to carry with it no small Difficulty what Votes to allow for the Inequality of the Princes and States. But with Submission to better Judgments, I cannot think it invincible: For if it be possible to have an Estimate of the Yearly Value of the several Soveraign Countries, whose Delegates are to make up this August Assembly, the Determination of the Number of Persons or Votes in the States for every Soveraignty, will not be impracticable. Now that *England, France, Spain,* the *Empire,* &c. may be pretty exactly estimated, is so plain a Case, by considering the Revenue of Lands, the Exports and Entries at the Custom-Houses, the Books of Rates, and Surveys that are in all Governments, to proportion Taxes for the Support of them, that the least Inclination to the *Peace of Europe,* will not stand or halt at this Objection. I will, with Pardon on all Sides, give an Instance far from Exact; nor do I pretend to it, or offer it for an Estimate; for I do it at Random: Only this, as wide as it is from the Just Proportion, will give some Aim to my *Judicious Reader,* what I would be at: Remembring, I design not by any Computation, an Estimate from the Revenue of the Prince, but the Value of the Territory, the Whole being concerned as well as the Prince. And a Juster Measure it is to

4. The Treaty of Nimeguen terminated the continental war in 1679.

go by, since one Prince may have more Revenue than another, who has much a Richer Country: Tho' in the Instance I am now about to make, the Caution is not so Necessary, because, as I said before, I pretend to no Manner of Exactness, but go wholly by Guess, being but for Example's Sake. I suppose the *Empire of Germany* to send Twelve; *France,* Ten; *Spain,* Ten; *Italy,* which comes to *France,* Eight; *England,* Six; *Portugal,* Three; *Sweedland,* Four; *Denmark,* Three; *Poland,* Four; *Venice,* Three; the *Seven Provinces,* Four; *The Thirteen Cantons,* and little *Neighbouring Soveraignties,* Two; Dukedoms of *Holstein* and *Courland,* One: And if the *Turks* and *Muscovites* are taken in, as seems but fit and just, they will make *Ten a Piece more.* The *Whole makes Ninety.* A great Presence when they represent the *Fourth; and now the Best and Wealthiest Part of the Known World; where Religion and Learning, Civility and Arts have their Seat and Empire.* But it is not absolutely necessary there should be always so many Persons, to represent the larger Soveraignties; for the Votes may be given by one Man of any Soveraignty, as well as by Ten or Twelve: Tho' the fuller the Assembly of States is, the more Solemn, Effectual, and Free the Debates will be, and the Resolutions must needs come with greater Authority. The Place of their First Session should be Central, as much as is possible, afterwards as they agree.

Sect. VIII. *Of the Regulation of the Imperial States in Session.*

TO AVOID Quarrel for Precedency, the Room may be Round, and have divers Doors to come in and go out at, to prevent Exceptions. If the whole Number be cast into Tens, each chusing One, they may preside by Turns, to whom all Speeches should be addressed, and who should collect the Sense of the Debates, and state the Question for a Vote, which, in my Opinion, should be by the *Ballot,* after the Prudent and Commendable Method of the *Venetians:*[5] Which in a great Degree, prevents the ill Effects of Corruption; because if any of the Delegates of that High and Mighty Estates could be so Vile, False, and Dishonourable, as to be influenced by Money, they have the Advantage

5. The Venetian balloting system, designed to make corruption impossible, consisted of a series of votes involving drawn lots and colored balls. See George B. McClellan, *The Oligarchy of Venice* (Boston, 1904), pp. 159–60.

of taking their Money that will give it them, and of Voting undiscovered to the Interest of their Principals, and their own Inclinations; as they that do understand the *Balloting Box* do very well know. A Shrewd Stratagem, and an Experimental Remedy against *Corruption,* at least Corrupting: For who will give their Money where they may so easily be Cozened, and where it is Two to One they will be so; for they that will take Money in such Cases, will not stick to Lye heartily to them that give it, rather than wrong their Country, when they know their Lye cannot be detected.

It seems to me, that nothing in this *Imperial Parliament* should pass, but by Three Quarters of the Whole, at least Seven above the Ballance. I am sure it helps to prevent Treachery, because if Money could ever be a Temptation in such a Court, it would cost a great Deal of Money to weigh down the wrong Scale. All Complaints should be delivered in Writing, in the Nature of *Memorials;* and *Journals* kept by a proper Person, in a *Trunk or Chest,* which should have as many differing Locks, *as there are Tens in the States.* And if there were a *Clerk for each Ten,* and a *Pew or Table for those Clerks in the Assembly;* and at the End of every Session, *One out of each Ten,* were appointed to Examine and Compare the *Journal of those Clerks,* and then lock them up as I have before expressed, it would be clear and Satisfactory. And each Soveraignty if they please, as is but very fit, may have an *Exemplification,* or *Copy of the said Memorials,* and the *Journals of Proceedings upon them.* The *Liberty and Rules of Speech,* to be sure, they cannot fail in, who will be the *Wisest* and *Noblest* of each Soveraignty, for it's own Honour and Safety. If any Difference can arise between those that come from the same Soveraignty, that then One of the Major Number do give the Balls of that Soveraignty. I should think it extreamly necessary, that every Soveraignty should be present under great Penalties, and that none leave the Session without Leave, till *All* be finished; and that Neutralities in Debates should by no Means be endured: For any such Latitude will quickly open a Way to unfair Proceedings, and be followed by a Train, both of seen, and unseen Inconveniencies. I will say little of the *Language* in which the *Session of the Soveraign Estates should be held,* but to be sure it must be in *Latin* or *French;* The first would be very well for *Civilians,* but the last most easie for Men of Quality.

Sect. IX. *Of the Objections that may be advanced against the Design.*

I WILL first give an Answer to the Objections that may be offered against my *Proposal:* And in my next and last Section, I shall endeavour to shew some of the manifold Conveniences that would follow this *European League,* or *Confederacy.*

The first of them is this, *That the strongest and Richest Soveraignty will never agree to it, and if it should, there would be Danger of Corruption more than of Force one Time or other.* I answer to the first Part, he is not stronger than all the rest, and for that Reason you should promote this, and compel him into it; especially before he be so, for then, it will be too late to deal with such an one. To the last Part of the Objection, I say the Way is as open now as then; and it may be the Number fewer, and as easily come at. However, if Men of Sense and Honour, and Substance, are chosen, they will either scorn the Baseness, or have wherewith to pay for the Knavery: At least they may be watch't so, that one may be a check upon the other, and all prudently limited by the Soveraignty they Represent. In all great Points, especially before a final Resolve, they may be obliged to transmit to their Principals, the Merits of such important Cases depending, and receive their last Instructions: which may be done in four and Twenty Days at the most, as the Place of their Session may be appointed.

The Second is, *That it will endanger an Effeminacy by such a Disuse of the Trade of Soldiery: That if there should be any Need for it, upon any Occasion, we should be at a Loss as they were in* Holland in 72.

There can be no Danger of Effeminacy, because each Soveraignty may introduce as temperate or Severe a Discipline in the Education of Youth, as they please, by low Living, and due Labour. Instruct them in Mechanical Knowledge, and in natural Philosophy, by Operation, which is the Honour of the *German* Nobility: This would make them Men: Niether *Women* nor *Lyons:* For *Soldiers* are t'other Extream to Effeminacy. But the Knowledge of Nature, and the useful as well as agreeable Operations of Art, give Men an Understanding of themselves, of the World they are born into, how to be useful and serviceable, both to themselves and others; and how to save and help, not injure or destroy. The Knowledge of Government in General; the particular Constitutions of *Europe;* and above all, of his own Country, are very recommending Accomplishments. This fits him for the *Parliament,* and *Council at Home,* and the *Courts of Princes and Services* in the *Imperial States abroad.* At least, he is a good Common-Wealths-Man, and can be useful to the Publick, or retire, as there may be Occasion.

To the other Part of the Objection, *Of being at a loss for Soldiery as they were in* Holland *in* 72. The Proposal answers for it self. One has War no more than the other; and will be as much to seek upon Occasion. Nor is it to be thought that any one will keep up such an Army after such an *Empire* is on Foot, which may hazard the Safety of the rest. However, if it be seen requisit, the Question may be askt, by Order of the Soveraign States, why such an one either raises or keeps up a formidable Body of Troops, and he obliged forthwith to reform or Reduce them; lest any one, by keeping up a great Body of Troops, should surprize a Neighbour. But a small Force in every other Soveraignty, as it is capable or accustomed to maintain, will certainly prevent that Danger and Vanquish any such Fear.

The Third Objection is, *That there will be great Want of Employment for younger Brothers of Families; and that the Poor must either turn Soldiers or Thieves.* I have answer'd that in my Return to the Second Objection. We shall have the more *Merchants and Husbandmen,* or *Ingenious Naturalists,* if the Government be but any Thing Solicitous of the *Education of their Youth:* Which, next to the present and immediate Happiness of any Country, ought of all Things, to be the *Care* and *Skill* of the Government. For such as the Youth of any Country is bred, such is the next Generation, and the Government in good or bad Hands.

I am come now to the last Objection, *That Soveraign Princes and States will hereby become not Soveraign; a Thing they will never endure.* But this also, under Correction, is a Mistake, for they remain as Soveraign at Home as ever they were. Neither their Power over their People, nor the usual Revenue they pay them, is diminished: It may be the War Establishment may be reduced, which will indeed of Course follow, or be better employed to the Advantage of the Publick. So that the *Soveraignties* are as they were, for none of them have now any Soveraignty over one another: And if this be called a lessening of their Power, it must be only because the great Fish can no longer eat up the little ones, and that each Soveraignty is *equally defended* from Injuries, and disabled from committing them: *Cedant Arma Togae* is a Glorious Sentence; the *Voice of the Dove; the Olive Branch of Peace.* A Blessing so great, that when it pleases God to chastise us severely for our Sins, it is with the *Rod of*

War, that, for the most Part, he whips us: And Experience tells us none leaves deeper Marks behind it.

Sect. X. *Of the real Benefits that flow from this Proposal about Peace.*

I AM come to my last Section, in which I shall enumerate some of those many *real Benefits* that flow from this Proposal, for the Present and Future *Peace* of *Europe.*

Let it not, I pray, be the least, that it prevents the Spilling of so much *Humane and Christian Blood:* For a Thing so offensive to God, and terrible and afflicting to Men, as that has ever been, must recommend our Expedient beyond all Objections. For what can a Man give in Exchange for his Life, as well as Soul? And tho' the chiefest in Government are seldom personally exposed, yet it is a Duty incumbent upon them to be tender of the Lives of their People; since without all Doubt, they are accountable to God for the Blood that is spilt in their Service. So that besides the Loss of so many Lives, of importance to any Government, both for Labour and Propagation, the Cries of so many Widows, Parents and Fatherless are prevented, that cannot be very pleasant in the Ears of any Government, and is the *Natural Consequence* of *War in all Government.*

There is another *manifest Benefit* which redounds to *Christendom,* by this *Peaceable* Expedient, *The Reputation of Christianity will in some Degree be recovered in the Sight of Infidels;* which, by the many Bloody and unjust *Wars* of *Christians,* not only with them, but *one* with *another,* hath been greatly impaired. For, to the Scandal of that Holy Profession, *Christians,* that glory in their *Saviour's Name,* have long devoted the Credit and Dignity of it, to their worldly Passions, as often as they have been excited by the Impulses of Ambition or Revenge. They have not always been in the Right: Nor has Right been the Reason of *War:* And not only *Christians* against *Christians,* but the same Sort of *Christians* have embrewed *their Hands in one another's Blood:* Invoking and Interesting, all they could, the *Good* and *Merciful God to prosper their Arms to their Brethren's Destruction:* Yet their *Saviour* has told them, *that he came to save, and not to destroy the Lives of Men:* To give and plant *Peace* among Men: And if in any Sense he may be said to send *War,* it is the *Holy War* indeed; for it is against the *Devil,* and not the *Persons of Men.* Of all his Titles this seems the most Glorious as well as comfortable for us, that he is the *Prince of Peace.* It is his *Nature,* his *Office,* his *Work* and the *End* and excellent Blessing of his Coming, who is both the Maker and Preserver of our *Peace* with God. And it is very remarkable, that in all the *New Testament* he is but once called *Lyon,* but frequently the *Lamb of God;* to denote to us his *Gentle, Meek and Harmless Nature;* and that those, who desire to be the *Disciples* of his *Cross and Kingdom,* for they are *inseparable,* must be like him, as St. *Paul,* St. *Peter* and St. *John* tell us.[6] Nor is it said the *Lamb* shall lye down with the *Lyon,* but the *Lyon* shall lye down with the *Lamb.* That is, *War* shall yield to *Peace,* and the Soldier turn Hermite. To be sure, *Christians* should not be apt to strive, nor *swift* to Anger against any Body, and less with one another, and least of all for the uncertain and fading Enjoyments of this lower World: And no Quality is exempted from this Doctrine. Here is a wide Field for the Reverend Clergy of *Europe* to act their Part in, who have so much the Possession of Princes and People too. May they recommend and labour this pacifick Means I offer, which will end Blood, if not Strife; and then *Reason,* upon free Debate, will be *Judge,* and not the *Sword.* So that both *Right* and *Peace,* which are the Desire and Fruit of wise Governments, and the choice Blessings of any Country, seem to succeed the Establishment of this Proposal.

The third Benefit is, that it saves *Money,* both to the Prince and People; and thereby prevents those Grudgings and Misunderstandings between them that are wont to follow the devouring Expences of *War;* and enables both to perform Publick Acts for *Learning, Charity, Manufacturies,* &c. The Virtues of Government and Ornaments of Countries. Nor is this all the *Advantage* that follows to *Soveraignties,* upon this *Head* of Money and good *Husbandry,* to whose Service and Happiness this short Discourse is dedicated; for it saves the great Expence that frequent and splendid Embassies require, and all their Appendages of *Spies and Intelligence,* which in the most prudent Governments, have devoured mighty Sums of Money; and that not without some *immoral Practices also:* Such as *Corrupting* of *Servants* to betray their *Masters,* by revealing their Secrets; not to be defended by *Christian* or *Old Roman Virtue.* But here, where there is nothing to fear, there is little to know, and therefore the *Purchase* is either *cheap,* or may be wholly *spared.* I might mention *Pen-*

6. For Jesus as the lion of Judah, see Revelation 5:5; as lamb, see John 1:29, 36; Acts 8:32; and 1 Peter 1:19.

sions to the *Widows* and *Orphans* of such as dye in *Wars,* and of those that have been *disabled* in them; which rise high in the Revenue of some Countries.

Our fourth Advantage is, that the *Towns, Cities and Countries, that might be laid waste by the Rage of War, are thereby preserved:* A Blessing that would be very well understood in *Flanders* and *Hungary,* and indeed upon all the *Borders* of *Soveraignties,* which are almost ever the *Stages* of Spoil and Misery; of which the Stories of *England and Scotland* do sufficiently inform us without looking over the *Water.*

The fifth Benefit of this Peace, is the *Ease and Security of Travel and Traffick:* An Happiness never understood since the *Roman Empire* has been broken into so many *Soveraignties.* But we may easily conceive the Comfort and *Advantage* of travelling through the Governments of *Europe,* by a *Pass* from any of the *Soveraignties* of it, which this League and State of *Peace* will *naturally make Authentick:* They that have travel'd *Germany,* where is so great a Number of *Soveraignties,* know the Want and Value of this Priviledge, by the many *Stops and Examinations* they meet with by the Way: But especially such as have made the *great Tour of Europe.* This leads to the Benefit of an *Universal Monarchy,* without the Inconveniencies that attend it: For when the whole was one *Empire,* tho' these Advantages were enjoyed, yet the several Provinces, that now make the *Kingdoms and States of Europe,* were under some Hardship from the great Sums of *Money* remitted to the Imperial Seat, and the Ambition and Avarice of their several Pro*consuls* and *Governours,* and the great *Taxes* they paid to the *Numerous Legions of Soldiers,* that they maintained for their own Subjection, who were not wont to entertain that Concern for them (being uncertainly there, and having their Fortunes to make) which their respective and proper *Soveraigns* have always shown for them. So that to be *Ruled by Native Princes or States,* with the Advantage of that Peace and Security that can only render an *Universal Monarchy desirable,* is peculiar to our Proposal, and for that Reason it is to be preferred.

Another Advantage is, *The Great Security it will be to* Christians *against the Inroads of the* Turk, *in their most Prosperous Fortune.* For it had been impossible for the *Port,* to have prevailed so often, and so far upon *Christendom,* but by the Carelessness, or Wilful Connivence, if not Aid, of some *Christian Princes.* And for the same Reason, why no *Christian Monarch* will adventure to oppose, or break such an Union, the *Grand Seignior* will find himself obliged to concur, for the Security of what he holds in *Europe:* Where, with all his Strength, he would feel it an Over-Match for him. *The Prayers, Tears, Treason,*

Blood and Devastation, that War has cost in Christendom, *for these Two last Ages especially, must add to the Credit of our Proposal, and the Blessing of the* Peace *thereby humbly recommended.*

The Seventh Advantage, of an *European, Imperial Dyet, Parliament,* or *Estates,* is, *That it will beget and increase Personal Friendship between Princes and States,* which tends to the Rooting up of Wars, and Planting Peace in a Deep and Fruitful Soil. For Princes have the Curiosity of seeing the Courts and Cities of other Countries, as well as Private Men, if they could as securely and familiarly gratify their Inclinations. It were a great Motive to the Tranquility of the World, *That they could freely Converse Face to Face, and Personally and Reciprocally Give and Receive Marks of Civility and Kindness.* An *Hospitality* that leaves these Impressions behind it, will hardly let Ordinary Matters prevail, to Mistake or Quarrel one another. Their *Emulation would be in the Instances of Goodness, Laws, Customs, Learning, Arts, Buildings;* and in particular those that relate to *Charity,* the True Glory of some Governments, where Beggars are as much a Rarity, as in other Places it would be to see none.

Nor is this all the Benefit that would come by this *Freedom* and *Interview of Princes:* For *Natural Affection* would hereby be preserved, which we see little better than lost, *from the Time their Children,* or *Sisters, are Married into other Courts.* For the present State and Insincerity of Princes forbid them the Enjoyment of that Natural Comfort which is possest by Private Families: Insomuch, that from the Time a Daughter, or Sister, is Married to another Crown, Nature is submitted to Interest, and that, for the most Part, grounded not upon Solid or Commendable Foundations, but *Ambition,* or *Unjust Avarice.* I say, this Freedom, that is the Effect of our Pacifick Proposal, restores *Nature* to Her Just Right and Dignity in the Families of Princes, and them to the Comfort She brings, wherever She is preserved in Her proper Station. Here *Daughters* may Personally intreat their *Parents,* and *Sisters* their *Brothers,* for a Good Understanding between them and their *Husbands,* where Nature, not crush'd by Absence, and Sinister Interests, but acting by the Sight and Lively Entreaties of such near Relations, is almost sure to prevail. They cannot easily resist the most affectionate Addresses of such powerful Solicitors, *as their Children, and Grand-Children,* and their *Sisters, Nephews,* and *Neices:* And so backward from *Children to Parents,* and *Sisters to Brothers,* to keep up and preserve their own Families, by a good Understanding between their Husbands and them.

To conclude this Section, there is yet another Manifest Privilege that follows this *Intercourse* and Good Understanding, which methinks should be very moving with Princes, *viz. That hereby they may chuse Wives for themselves,* such as they Love, and not by *Proxy,* meerly to gratify Interest; an ignoble Motive; and that rarely begets, or continues that *Kindness* which ought to be between Men and their Wives. A Satisfaction very few Princes ever knew, and to which all other Pleasures ought to resign. Which has often obliged me to think, *That the Advantage of Private Men upon Princes, by Family Comforts, is a sufficient Ballance against their Greater Power and Glory: The One being more in* Imagination, *than* Real; *and often* Unlawful; *but the other,* Natural, Solid, *and* Commendable. Besides, it is certain, Parents Loving Well before they are Married, which very rarely happens to Princes, *has Kind and Generous Influences upon their Offspring: Which, with their Example, makes them better Husbands, and Wives, in their Turn.* This, in great Measure, prevents Unlawful Love, and the Mischiefs of those Intriegues that are wont to follow them: What *Hatred, Feuds, Wars, and Desolations have, in divers Ages, flown from Unkindness between Princes and their Wives?* What *Unnatural Divisions among their Children, and Ruin to their Families, if not Loss of their Countries by it?* Behold an Expedient to prevent it, a Natural and Efficacious One: Happy to Princes, and Happy to their People also. For Nature being renewed and strengthened by these Mutual Pledges and Endearments, I have mentioned, will leave those soft and kind Impressions behind in the Minds of Princes, that *Court and Country* will very easily discern and feel the Good Effects of: Especially if they have the Wisdom to show that they Interest themselves in the Prosperity of the Children and Relations of their Princes. For it does not only incline them to be Good, but engage those Relations to become Powerful Suitors to their Princes for them, if any Misunderstanding should unhappily arise between them and their *Soveraigns:* Thus ends this *Section.* It now rests to conclude the Discourse, in which, if I have not pleased my *Reader,* or answered his Expectation, it is some Comfort to me I meant well, and have cost him but little Money and Time; and Brevity is an Excuse, if not a Virtue, where the Subject is not agreeable, or is but ill prosecuted.

The CONCLUSION.

I WILL conclude this *My Proposal of an European, Soveraign,* or *Imperial Dyet, Parliament,* or *Estates,* with that which I have touch'd upon before, and which falls under the Notice of every One concerned, by coming Home to their Particular and Respective Experience within their own *Soveraignties.* That by the same *Rules of Justice and Prudence,* by which Parents and Masters Govern their Families, and Magistrates their Cities, and Estates their Republicks, and Princes and Kings their Principalities and Kingdoms, *Europe* may Obtain and Preserve *Peace among Her Soveraignties.* For Wars are the *Duels of Princes;* and as Government in Kingdoms and States, *Prevents Men being Judges and Executioners for themselves,* over-rules Private Passions as to Injuries or Revenge, and subjects the Great as well as the Small to the *Rule of Justice,* that Power might not vanquish or oppress Right, nor one Neighbour act an *Independency and Soveraignty upon another,* while they have resigned that Original Claim to the Benefit and Comfort of Society; so this being soberly weighed in the Whole, and Parts of it, it will not be hard to conceive or frame, nor yet to execute the Design I have here proposed.

And for the better understanding and perfecting of the *Idea,* I here present to the *Soveraign Princes and Estates of Europe,* for the Safety and Tranquility of it, I must recommend to their Perusals, Sir *William Temple*'s *Account of the United Provinces;*[7] which is an Instance and Answer, upon *Practice,* to all the Objections that can be advanced against the Practicability of my Proposal: Nay, it is an Experiment that not only comes to our Case, but exceeds the Difficulties that can render it's Accomplishment disputable. For there we shall find *Three Degrees of Soveraignties to make up every Soveraignty in the General States.* I will reckon them backwards: First, *The States General themselves;* Then the *Immediate Soveraignties* that Constitute them, which are those of the *Provinces,* answerable to the *Soveraignties of Europe,* that by their *Deputies* are to compose the *European Dyet, Parliament,* or *Estates,* in our Proposal: And then there are the several Cities of each *Province,* that are so many *Independent* or *Distinct Soveraignties,* which compose those of the *Provinces,* as those of the *Provinces* do compose the *States General* at the *Hague.*

But I confess I have the Passion to wish heartily, that the Honour of Proposing and Effecting so Great and Good a Design, might be owing to *England,* of all the Countries in *Europe,* as something of the Nature of our Expedient was, in Design and Preparation, to the Wisdom, Justice, and Valour, *Of Henry the Fourth of France,* whose Superior Qualities raising His Character above those of His Ancestors, or Contemporaries, deservedly gave Him the Stile of

7. Sir William Temple, *Observations upon the United Provinces of the Netherlands* (London, 1676).

Henry the Great. For *He was upon obliging the Princes and Estates of* Europe *to a Politick Ballance,* when the *Spanish Faction,* for that Reason, contrived, and accomplished *His Murder,* by the Hands of *Ravilliac.* I will not then fear to be censured, for proposing an *Expedient* for the Present and Future *Peace of Europe,* when it was not only the *Design, but Glory of One of the Greatest Princes that ever Reigned in it;* and is found Practicable in the Constitution of One of the Wisest and Powerfullest States of it. So that to conclude, I have very Little to answer for in all this Affair; because, if it succeed, I have so Little to deserve: For this *Great King's Example tells us it is fit to be done;* and Sir *William Temple*'s *History* shews us, by a Surpassing Instance, *That it may be done;* and *Europe,* by Her incomparable Miseries, makes it now *Necessary to be done:* That my Share is only thinking of it at this Juncture, and putting it into the Common Light for the Peace and Prosperity of *Europe.*

INDEX

This book is set in Minion, a typeface designed by Robert Slimbach specifically for digital typesetting. Released by Adobe in 1989, Minion is a versatile neohumanist face that shows the influence of Slimbach's own calligraphy.

Printed on paper that is acid-free and meets the requirements of the American National Standard for Permanence of Paper for Printed Library Materials, z39.48-1992. ♾

Book design by Richard Hendel,
Chapel Hill, North Carolina
Typography by Tseng Information Systems, Inc.,
Durham, North Carolina
Printed and bound by Edwards Brothers, Inc.,
Ann Arbor, Michigan